T0355394

HANDBOOK ON

the Gospels

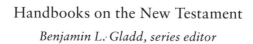

Handbooks on the New Testament

Benjamin L. Gladd, series editor

ALSO IN THIS SERIES:

Handbook on Acts and Paul's Letters
by Thomas R. Schreiner

Handbook on Hebrews through Revelation
by Andreas J. Köstenberger

HANDBOOK ON

the Gospels

Benjamin L. Gladd

B

Baker Academic

a division of Baker Publishing Group

Grand Rapids, Michigan

© 2021 by Benjamin L. Gladd

Published by Baker Academic
a division of Baker Publishing Group
PO Box 6287, Grand Rapids, MI 49516-6287
www.bakeracademic.com

Printed in the United States of America

All rights reserved. No part of this publication may be reproduced, stored
in a retrieval system, or transmitted in any form or by any means—for
example, electronic, photocopy, recording—without the prior written
permission of the publisher. The only exception is brief quotations in
printed reviews.

Library of Congress Cataloging-in-Publication Data
Names: Gladd, Benjamin L., author.
Title: Handbook on the Gospels / Benjamin L. Gladd.
Description: Grand Rapids, Michigan : Baker Academic, a division
    of Baker Publishing Group, [2021] | Series: Handbooks on the New
    Testament | Includes bibliographical references and index.
Identifiers: LCCN 2020049528 | ISBN 9781540960160 (cloth)
Subjects: LCSH: Bible. Gospels—Introductions.
Classification: LCC BS2555.52 .G53 2021 | DDC 226/.061—dc23
LC record available at https://lccn.loc.gov/2020049528

This book draws on ideas found in chapters 4–7 of *The Story Retold* by
G. K. Beale and Benjamin L. Gladd. Copyright © 2020 by Gregory K. Beale
and Benjamin L. Gladd. Used by permission of InterVarsity Press, P.O.
Box 1400, Downers Grove, IL 60515, USA. www.ivpress.com

Unless otherwise indicated, Scripture quotations are from THE HOLY
BIBLE, NEW INTERNATIONAL VERSION®, NIV® Copyright © 1973,
1978, 1984, 2011 by Biblica, Inc.® Used by permission. All rights reserved
worldwide.

Scripture quotations labeled AT are the author's own translation.

Scripture quotations labeled HCSB are from the Holman Christian Standard Bible®, copyright © 1999, 2000, 2002, 2003, 2009 by Holman Bible
Publishers. Used by permission. Holman Christian Standard Bible®, Holman CSB®, and HCSB® are federally registered trademarks of Holman
Bible Publishers.

Scripture quotations labeled NASB are from the New American Standard Bible® (NASB), copyright © 1960, 1962, 1963, 1968, 1971, 1972, 1973,
1975, 1977, 1995 by The Lockman Foundation. Used by permission. www
.Lockman.org.

Scripture quotations labeled NETS are from *A New English Translation of
the Septuagint*, © 2007 by the International Organization for Septuagint
and Cognate Studies, Inc. Used by permission of Oxford University Press.
All rights reserved.

In keeping with biblical principles of
creation stewardship, Baker Publishing Group advocates the responsible
use of our natural resources. As a
member of the Green Press Initia-
tive, our company uses recycled
paper when possible. The text paper
of this book is composed in part of
post-consumer waste.

21 22 23 24 25 26 27   7 6 5 4 3 2 1

For my parents,
Kevin and Sue

Contents

Series Preface

The Handbooks on the New Testament are the counterpart to the well-received, four-volume set Handbooks on the Old Testament by Baker Academic. With a myriad of New Testament commentaries and introductions, why pen yet another series? The handbooks stand unique in that they are neither introductions nor commentaries. Most New Testament commentaries work in the trenches with verse-by-verse expositions, whereas introductions fly at forty thousand feet above the biblical text. This series lies between these two approaches. Each volume takes a snapshot of each New Testament passage without getting bogged down in detailed exegesis. The intent is for the reader to be able to turn to a particular New Testament passage in the handbook and quickly grasp the sense of the passage without having to read a considerable amount of the preceding and following discussion. This series is committed to summarizing the content of each major section of the New Testament. Introductory issues are not ignored (authorship, dating, audience, etc.), but they are not the focus. Footnotes, too, are used sparingly to keep the readers attuned to the passage. At the end of each chapter, the author includes a brief, up-to-date bibliography for further investigation.

Since the handbook focuses on the final form of the text, authors pay special attention to Old Testament allusions and quotations. The New Testament writers quote the Old Testament some 350 times and allude to it well over a thousand. Each author in this series notes how a good portion of those Old Testament allusions and quotations shape the passage under discussion. The primary audience of the handbook series is laypeople, students, pastors, and professors of theology and biblical studies. We intend these volumes to find a home in the classroom and in personal study. To make the series more accessible, technical jargon is avoided. Each volume is theologically and pastorally informed. The authors apply their observations to contemporary issues within the church and to the Christian life. Above all, our prayer and our desire are that this series would stimulate more study and serious reflection on God's Word, resulting in godly living and the expansion of the kingdom.

Benjamin L. Gladd

Author's Preface

I should have written this volume years ago. Penning this project on the Gospels afforded me the opportunity to sit down and pensively work through all four narratives. It's been a delight. Tracing the flow of thought, charting the characters, and returning again and again to the OT increased my personal faith in and devotion to Christ.

The impetus for this project, and the Baker handbooks at large, stems from the lack of accessible and robustly evangelical resources for students, pastors, and teachers. When working on an unfamiliar text, I often turn to a commentary, only to be bogged down in the morass of word-by-word exegesis. Detailed and technical commentaries are necessary for the steady growth of the church. I wanted, though, to produce a volume on the Gospels that retains a close reading of the text while maintaining clarity and accessibility.

In quoting from the NIV (2011) and generally relying upon its outlines and parallels of the Gospels, I've attempted to add yet another layer of accessibility for the readers. Brevity and directness characterize the three-volume Baker handbook series on the NT. Tom Schreiner's volume spans Acts and all thirteen of Paul's letters, while Andreas Köstenberger distills Hebrews through Revelation. This volume on the Gospels covers only four books, so I decided early on to delve a bit deeper into the text than the other two handbooks do.

A few introductory remarks are in order. Commentators have pursued every imaginable angle on how the Gospels function in a wider Greco-Roman context and in the various strands of Judaism. There's little doubt that the four evangelists share points of contact with these environments. My *primary* aim, though, is to read the narratives with care and situate the Gospels within the history of redemption by recognizing and exploring OT concepts, allusions, and quotations. I *secondarily* draw attention to Jewish and Greco-Roman culture and life. The three Baker New Testament handbooks are sensitive to a biblical-theological reading of the text, and this project reflects this emphasis. I often point readers back to critical OT passages and events that prophetically anticipate Jesus's ministry, and I do not hesitate to point forward to other NT passages that address the same theme or event.

While the study of every imaginable aspect of the Gospels continues unabated, I also make little attempt to engage the avalanche of secondary literature. It's dizzying how much has been written in the last twenty years. At times, I give the reader the various options for differing interpretations and try to point the reader in the right direction. At the end of each chapter, I include a handful of sources to give readers a starting point for further investigation.

Critical scholars drove a wedge between the historical Jesus and the Gospels many years ago. While I do believe that the four evangelists accurately (and theologically!) narrate the career of Jesus, my primary focus in this project is to study the individual narratives—four unique books that retell Jesus's life, death, and resurrection. It's the same Jesus, the same gospel. These accounts present four distinct yet complementary accounts of what transpired nearly two thousand years ago.

Scholars don't often agree when it comes to issues related to the Gospels, but one area where the stars have aligned is the priority of Mark's Gospel. The vast majority of commentators presuppose that Mark was written first, and then Matthew and Luke borrowed his material in composing their Gospels. My project assumes the direction of this textual relationship. Where things get fuzzier is the possibility of another source, often designated "Q" (German *Quelle* for "source"). For many reasons, scholars in recent decades have begun to cast doubt on this written source. While I still hold to the "two-source" theory—Matthew and Luke borrowed from Mark and Q—I'm unsure if Q is exclusively a written document. It may very well be composed of oral and written material. Further, Austin Farrer's hypothesis (Matthew borrows from Mark, and Luke borrows from Matthew and Mark), having gained significant ground in the last ten or so years, remains an attractive alternative.

There's a reason why one cannot easily find a one-volume project on the four Gospels written by the same author: the amount of overlapping material between the Synoptics is significant. I've marked the general parallels between the Gospels using the two slashes (//); and instead of repeating myself throughout the project, I refer the reader to where I've discussed the passage in some detail elsewhere (indicated with an arrow: →). Since Mark is likely the first Gospel published, I encourage readers to begin there.

I'm thankful to Reformed Theological Seminary for graciously granting me a sabbatical, during which I wrote the majority of the manuscript. I'm also thankful for Brandon Crowe's and Dennis Johnson's comments and critiques of portions of this manuscript. I'm indebted to Bryan Dyer and Eric Salo at Baker for guiding this project and the other two handbooks. My hope is that students, pastors, and teachers would again take up the Gospels and be refreshed in the salvation they so cherish in the Son of Man.

Abbreviations

General and Bibliographic

//	parallels
→	indicates a cross-reference to within this commentary
AT	author's translation
Brenton (Theo.)	Sir Lancelot Brenton's translation of Theodotion's Septuagint
ET	English translation
frag.	fragment
Gk.	Greek
Heb.	Hebrew
LXX	Septuagint
MT	Masoretic Text
OG	Old Greek (Septuagint)
par.	parallel text(s)
Theo.	Theodotion's Septuagint

English Bible Versions

ESV	English Standard Version
HCSB	Holman Christian Standard Bible
KJV	King James Version
NASB	New American Standard Bible
NET	New English Translation
NETS	New English Translation of the Septuagint
NIV	New International Version
NIV 1984	New International Version, 1984 edition
NLT	New Living Translation
NRSV	New Revised Standard Version

Old Testament

Gen.	Genesis
Exod.	Exodus
Lev.	Leviticus
Num.	Numbers
Deut.	Deuteronomy
Josh.	Joshua
Judg.	Judges
Ruth	Ruth
1–2 Sam.	1–2 Samuel
1–2 Kings	1–2 Kings
1–2 Chron.	1–2 Chronicles
Ezra	Ezra
Neh.	Nehemiah
Esther	Esther
Job	Job
Ps. (Pss.)	Psalm (Psalms)
Prov.	Proverbs
Eccles.	Ecclesiastes
Song of Sol.	Song of Solomon
Isa.	Isaiah
Jer.	Jeremiah
Lam.	Lamentations
Ezek.	Ezekiel
Dan.	Daniel
Hosea	Hosea
Joel	Joel

Amos	Amos
Obad.	Obadiah
Jon.	Jonah
Mic.	Micah
Nah.	Nahum
Hab.	Habakkuk
Zeph.	Zephaniah
Hag.	Haggai
Zech.	Zechariah
Mal.	Malachi

New Testament

Matt.	Matthew
Mark	Mark
Luke	Luke
John	John
Acts	Acts
Rom.	Romans
1–2 Cor.	1–2 Corinthians
Gal.	Galatians
Eph.	Ephesians
Phil.	Philippians
Col.	Colossians
1–2 Thess.	1–2 Thessalonians
1–2 Tim.	1–2 Timothy
Titus	Titus
Philem.	Philemon
Heb.	Hebrews
James	James
1–2 Pet.	1–2 Peter
1–3 John	1–3 John
Jude	Jude
Rev.	Revelation

Other Primary Texts

Apostolic Fathers

1 Clem.	1 Clement
Barn.	Epistle of Barnabas

Bede

Hist. eccl.	*Historia Ecclesiastica (Church History)*

Clement of Alexandria

Paed.	*Paedagogus*

Dead Sea Scrolls

CDa	*Damascus Document*

Eusebius

Hist. eccl.	*Historia ecclesiastica*

Irenaeus

Haer.	*Adversus Haereses (Against Heresies)*

Josephus

Ag. Ap.	*Against Apion*
Ant.	*Jewish Antiquities*
J.W.	*Jewish War*

Old Testament Apocrypha

1 Esd.	1 Esdras
Jdt.	Judith
1 Macc.	1 Maccabees
2 Macc.	2 Maccabees
Sir.	Sirach
Sus.	Susanna
Tob.	Tobit
Wis.	Wisdom of Solomon

Old Testament Pseudepigrapha

2 Bar.	2 Baruch
1 En.	1 Enoch
2 En.	2 Enoch
Jub.	Jubilees
Let. Aris.	Letter of Aristeas
Pss. Sol.	Psalms of Solomon
Sib. Or.	Sibylline Oracles
T. 12 Patr.	Testaments of the Twelve Patriarchs
T. Adam	Testament of Adam
T. Jud.	Testament of Judah
T. Mos.	Testament of Moses
T. Sol.	Testament of Solomon

Philo

Flacc.	*In Flaccum (Against Flaccus)*
Ios.	*De Iosepho (On the Life of Joseph)*
Praem.	*De praemiis et poenis (On Rewards and Punishments)*
Prov.	*De providentia (On Providence)*
Vit. Mos.	*De vita Mosis (On the Life of Moses)*

Rabbinic Works

b.	tractate of the Babylonian Talmud
Shabb.	Shabbat

m.	tractate of the Mishnah
Git.	Gittin
Hag.	Hagigah
Miqw.	Mikwa'ot
Ned.	Nedarim
Nid.	Niddah
Pesah.	Pesahim
Sanh.	Sanhedrin
Sheqal	Sheqalim
Sukkah	Sukkah
Tehar.	Teharot
Yoma	Yoma

Secondary Sources

AB	Anchor Bible
AcBib	Academia Biblica
AGJU	Arbeiten zur Geschichte des antiken Judentums und des Urchristentums
AnBib	Analecta Biblica
ANRW	*Aufstieg und Niedergang der römischen Welt*
AOTC	Apollos Old Testament Commentary
BBR	*Bulletin for Biblical Research*
BDAG	Frederick W. Danker, Walter Bauer, William F. Arndt, and F. Wilbur Gingrich. *Greek-English Lexicon of the New Testament and Other Early Christian Literature.* 3rd ed. Chicago: University of Chicago Press, 2000
BECNT	Baker Exegetical Commentary on the New Testament
BETL	Bibliotheca Ephemeridum Theologicarum Lovaniensium
Bib	*Biblica*
BIS	Biblical Interpretation Series
BNTC	Black's New Testament Commentaries
BSac	*Bibliotheca Sacra*
BST	Bible Speaks Today
BTCB	Brazos Theological Commentary on the Bible
BTNT	Biblical Theology of the New Testament
BZNW	Beihefte zur Zeitschrift für die neutestamentliche Wissenschaft
CBQ	*Catholic Biblical Quarterly*
CBQMS	Catholic Biblical Quarterly Monograph Series
CC	Concordia Commentaries
DJG	*Dictionary of Jesus and the Gospels.* 2nd ed. Edited by Joel B. Green, Jeannine K. Brown, and Nicholas Perrin. Downers Grove, IL: InterVarsity, 2013
DRev	*Downside Review*
ECC	Eerdmans Critical Commentary

ECIL	Early Christianity and Its Literature
ESBT	Essential Studies in Biblical Theology
ExpTim	*Expository Times*
ICC	International Critical Commentary
ITS	International Theological Studies
IVPNTC	InterVarsity Press New Testament Commentary
JBL	*Journal of Biblical Literature*
JETS	*Journal of the Evangelical Theological Society*
JPTSup	Journal of Pentecostal Theology Supplement Series
JSNT	*Journal for the Study of the New Testament*
JSNTSup	Journal for the Study of the New Testament Supplement Series
JTS	*Journal of Theological Studies*
LHBOTS	Library of Hebrew Bible/Old Testament Studies
LNTS	Library of New Testament Studies
NAC	New American Commentary
NCBC	New Century Bible Commentary
NIBC	New International Biblical Commentary
NICNT	New International Commentary on the New Testament
NICOT	New International Commentary on the Old Testament
NIGTC	New International Greek Testament Commentary
NIVAC	NIV Application Commentary
NovT	*Novum Testamentum*
NovTSup	Supplements to Novum Testamentum
NSBT	New Studies in Biblical Theology
NTL	New Testament Library
NTS	*New Testament Studies*
PNTC	Pillar New Testament Commentary
RB	*Revue Biblique*
RBS	Resources for Biblical Study
SBL	Society of Biblical Literature
SBLDS	Society of Biblical Literature Dissertation Series
SBLMS	Society of Biblical Literature Monograph Series
SBLSP	*Society of Biblical Literature Seminar Papers*
SBLSymS	Society of Biblical Literature Symposium Series
SBT	Studies in Biblical Theology
SCM	Student Christian Movement
SHBC	Smyth & Helwys Bible Commentary
SNTSMS	Society for New Testament Studies Monograph Series
SP	Sacra Pagina
TJ	*Trinity Journal*
TNTC	Tyndale New Testament Commentaries
WBC	Word Biblical Commentary
WUNT	Wissenschaftliche Untersuchungen zum Neuen Testament
ZECNT	Zondervan Exegetical Commentary on the New Testament

CHAPTER ONE

The Gospel of Matthew

Introduction

Authorship and Date

While contemporary scholars often deny that Matthew wrote the First Gospel, a great deal of evidence exists for attributing the authorship of the First Gospel to him. One line of argumentation is the title itself. The extant manuscripts of all four Gospels include the titles. For example, the title of the First Gospel reads, "According to Matthew" (*kata Maththaion*), and the title of the Second Gospel reads, "According to Mark" (*kata Markon*). Luke's and John's Gospels follow suit. Many commentators supposed that the early church tagged the four Gospels after their publication to differentiate them from one another. But recently, a handful of scholars have argued that these titles are original. If the titles were present upon publication, then they go a long way in determining authorship. Matthew, also known as Levi (Mark 2:14 // Luke 5:27–28), was a Jewish tax collector and one of the Twelve (Matt. 9:9; 10:3; Mark 3:18; Luke 6:15; Acts 1:13). This explains why within the First Gospel an emphasis on taxation is discernable (see 9:9; 10:3; 17:24–27). The early church, too, assumes that Matthew wrote this Gospel (e.g., Irenaeus, *Haer.* 1.26.2, 3.1.1; Eusebius, *Hist. eccl.* 1.7.10, 3.24.5, 3.39.16).

The dating of the First Gospel turns on its relationship to Mark's and Luke's Gospels and on the predictive nature of the Olivet Discourse (24:1–25:46). Since it appears that Matthew depends on Mark, a Gospel likely published in the early to mid-60s, and many of the events outlined in the Olivet

Discourse were initially fulfilled in AD 70, Matthew's Gospel was likely published in the mid to late 60s.

Purpose

Matthew, possibly writing from Antioch of Syria, writes to a largely Jewish audience and to some gentile Christians. Jesus of Nazareth, the First Gospel argues, is the centerpiece of the history of redemption. All of Israel's institutions, events, and individuals as chronicled throughout the Old Testament anticipate Jesus as the long-awaited Davidic King and true Israel. Jesus is also "Immanuel"—God has drawn near to humanity (Matt. 1:23). Mark highlights the *preparation* and mysterious *arrival* of the kingdom, Luke underscores its *scope*, and Matthew puts his finger on the *growth* of the kingdom.

Outline

Matthew, Mark, and Luke generally trace Jesus's ministry along geographic lines, moving from Jesus's baptism in Judea to his public ministry in Galilee and then to Jerusalem. Matthew, though, intersperses five blocks of teaching that outline a particular dimension of the eternal kingdom (5:1–7:29; 10:1–11:1; 13:1–53; 18:1–19:1; 23:1–26:1). Jesus's teaching also explains and reinforces his actions.

Prologue (1:1–3:17)
The Genealogy (1:1–17)
The Birth of Jesus (1:18–25)
Flight to Egypt (2:1–18)
Home in Nazareth (2:19–23)
John the Baptist (3:1–17)
Baptism of a Remnant of Israelites (3:1–12)
Baptism of Jesus as True Israel (3:13–17)

Stage 1: Jesus in Galilee (4:1–18:35)

The Wilderness Temptation and the Beginning of Jesus's Public Ministry (4:1–25)
Success in the Judean Wilderness (4:1–11)
Announcing the Kingdom in Galilee (4:12–17)
Calling the First Disciples and Healing the Sick (4:18–25)

The End-Time Restoration of the Gentiles (15:1–39)
Eating with Unwashed Hands (15:1–20)
The Faith of a Canaanite Woman (15:21–28)
The Feeding of the Four Thousand (15:29–39)
The Heresy of the Jewish Leaders and the Truthful Confession of Peter (16:1–28)
Jewish Leaders Test Jesus (16:1–4)
The False Teaching of the Jewish Leaders (16:5–12)
Peter's Confession and Jesus's Prediction of Death (16:13–28)
Jesus as the Enthroned Son of Man and Faithful Israel (17:1–27)
The Transfiguration (17:1–20)
The Suffering Son of Man and the Temple Tax (17:22–27)
Relating to One Another within the Kingdom (18:1–35)
A Kingdom Outlook (18:1–5)
Persevering in the Kingdom (18:6–9)
Promoting the Worth of Kingdom Citizens and Preserving the End-Time Temple (18:10–35)

Stage 2: The Journey to Jerusalem (19:1–20:34)

On the Road to Jerusalem (19:1–30)
Disputation with the Jewish Leaders on Divorce (19:1–12)
Entry into the Kingdom (19:13–30)
A Suffering Son of David (20:1–34)
Parable of the Vineyard Workers (20:1–16)
Third Passion Prediction and a Request for Honor (20:17–28)
Healing Two Blind Men (20:29–34)

Stage 3: Jesus in Jerusalem (21:1–28:20)

The Arrival of Israel's King and Its Implications (21:1–22:46)
Triumphal Entry (21:1–11)
Judging Israel's Temple and the Cursing of the Fig Tree (21:12–22)
Parables of the Two Sons and the Wicked Tenants (21:23–46)
Parable of the Banquet (22:1–14)
War of Words (22:15–46)

Prologue (1:1–3:17)

The Genealogy (1:1–17)

Two of the four Gospels include a genealogy. Luke squeezes his between John's imprisonment and the wilderness temptation (Luke 3:21–37), but the First Gospel is the only one that leads with it (1:1–17). Matthew not only opens his Gospel with a genealogy; he introduces the genealogy (and the prologue) with a critical phrase: "*the genealogy [biblos geneseōs] of Jesus Christ.*" The wording alludes to two salient texts from the Genesis narrative: "*this is the account [hē biblos geneseōs] of the heavens and the earth*" (2:4) and "*this is the written account [hē biblos geneseōs] of Adam's family line*" (5:1). The connection is intentional, setting the whole of Jesus's ministry on a redemptive-historical trajectory. Jesus, the last Adam, has come to reverse the effects of the first Adam's transgression and establish the new age—the age of righteousness and obedience. The first creation was marked with a genealogy, and now the new creation will follow suit. By opening the genealogy with an allusion to Genesis 2:4 and 5:1, Matthew indicates that *all* of the First Gospel, at some level, should be read as an account of Jesus bringing life to a fallen world.

Matthew explicitly describes Jesus as "the Messiah the son of David, the son of Abraham" (1:1). By ordering David's name before Abraham's even though Abraham came first, the evangelist draws attention to Jesus's royal pedigree. Above all, the genealogy impresses upon Matthew's readers that Jesus is the long-awaited Son of David. He's cut from the same royal cloth. The structure of the genealogy, too, reflects an emphasis on Jesus's messiahship. Matthew's arrangement contains three chronological sections: premonarchical period (1:2–6a), monarchical period until the exile (1:6b–11), and the deportation until the long-awaited Messiah (1:12–16).

In addition to the genealogy's Davidic focus, one can discern God's sovereign hand in the unfolding of Israel's history. As we read about the people of God in the OT, we may wonder why biblical authors included so many odd stories with seemingly incidental details. But if we take a step back, as Matthew does, and look at the history of redemption from God's perspective, we discover that there are no random events. God plans all of it, from beginning to end, so that a redeemer would arrive and bring his glory to the ends of the earth.

Why does Matthew include the patriarch Abraham in a genealogy so focused on David? Matthew does so for at least three cardinal reasons: God assured Abraham that he would be the father of a "great nation," the nation would occupy the promised land (Gen. 12:1–9; 15:4–20, etc.), and Israel would bless the nations (Gen. 12:3). Jesus is not simply a descendant of Abraham—he is *the* descendant, and as such he fulfills God's promises to Israel's patriarchs. Jesus is true Israel who, on account of his obedience, inherits the true land of promise (i.e., the new creation) and "blesses" the gentiles. All three dimensions of the Abrahamic covenant—innumerable descendants, desirable land, and worldwide blessing—are truly and initially fulfilled in Jesus. Of course, there's a sense in which the Abrahamic covenant was partially fulfilled in the OT, but such fulfillment often fell short of God's extensive promises. Jesus fulfills the Abrahamic covenant in a more complete and qualitative manner. The commands that God holds Abraham, the patriarchs, and Israel to obey (e.g., Gen. 12:1–3; 17:1–9) are fully met in the person of Jesus.

The connection to Abraham's role as the "father of many nations" (Gen. 17:5) may explain why Matthew includes four women in his genealogy: Tamar, Rahab, Ruth, and Bathsheba. At least three of them are gentile, and we are unsure of Bathsheba's ancestry (2 Sam. 11:3). In listing these women, Matthew anticipates the conversion of the nations through Jesus's ministry. The time has arrived for God to turn his attention to the gentiles and bring them into the fold of Israel en masse. Scandal colors the stories of all four women as well, paving the way for the social scandal of the virgin birth (1:19).

At the end of the genealogy, Matthew informs the reader that there are "fourteen generations in all from Abraham to David, fourteen from David to the exile to Babylon, and fourteen from the exile to the Messiah" (1:17). The number fourteen is an issue; the first and second groups contain fourteen names, but the third lists only thirteen. Scholars try to explain this oddity by repeating names (i.e., Jeconiah), but it's unclear if Matthew intends the reader to do so. At the very least, Matthew encourages his audience to ponder the symbolic value of fourteen. Scholars have agonized over this issue for decades. One attractive and popular solution is the Jewish technique of counting called *gematria*. Each letter of the Hebrew alphabet corresponds to a numerical value. The name "David" in Hebrew is composed of three consonants totaling fourteen: D (4), W (6), D (4). Notice also that there are *three* letters, resembling *three* units of fourteen generations. While such a practice may seem odd to us, *gematria* was practiced somewhat regularly in Judaism (e.g., Sib. Or. 1:137–46) and in the early church (e.g., Barn. 9:7).

The Birth of Jesus (1:18–25)

After establishing Jesus as king and true Israel in the genealogy (1:1–17), Matthew moves on to the birth narrative (1:18–2:25). We learn that Mary becomes pregnant through the miraculous work of the Spirit (1:18), but when Joseph learns of the pregnancy, he naturally assumes it is the result of infidelity. Not wanting to make a public spectacle of the matter, he thinks it best to "divorce her quietly" (1:19; cf. Deut. 22:20–24; 24:1).

The "angel of the Lord" then intervenes and reveals to Joseph the true nature of Mary's pregnancy. This is the first of four appearances of the "angel of the Lord" in the First Gospel (1:20; 2:13, 19; 28:2). Often in the OT and especially within apocalyptic literature, angels feature prominently, divulging various revelations in dreams or visions (e.g., Gen. 31:11; Dan. 7:16; 8:15–19; Zech. 4:1). Before Jesus is born, an angel tells Joseph to name the child "Jesus, because he will save his people from their sins" (1:21). This verse is particularly revealing in that the angel unveils the ultimate reason why Jesus, the end-time king and true Israel, has come—to save people from sin.

Jesus's name (in Hebrew, literally "Joshua") means "the Lord saves," a title embodying God's delivering character and plan of redemption. One of the most concrete examples of God saving his people is his deliverance of the

Israelites from Egyptian bondage. For example, Exodus 14:30 states, "That day the LORD *saved* [*yosha*] Israel from the hands of the Egyptians, and Israel saw the Egyptians lying dead on the shore" (cf. Exod. 18:8; Ps. 106:21; Hosea 13:4). Again, Deuteronomy 33:29 reads,

> Blessed are you, Israel!
>> Who is like you,
>> a people *saved* [*nosha*] by the LORD?
> He is your shield and helper
>> and your glorious sword.
> Your enemies will cower before you,
>> and you will tread on their heights.

But God not only saved his people in the first exodus; he promises to save them once more and with great finality in the second exodus (Isa. 25:9; 43:12; 45:17; Ezek. 37:23; Hosea 1:7; Zech. 9:9). There is a coming consummate salvation. Jesus's Hebrew name, "Joshua," also alludes to Moses's successor, the one who led Israel into the promised land (Josh. 1:1–5:12) and vanquished the majority of the Canaanites (Josh. 5:13–12:24). Joshua's entrance into the promised land and his victory over the Canaanites there prophetically foreshadows Jesus's entrance into the new promised land and victory over the spiritual Canaanites. In bearing the name "Jesus"/"Joshua," Jesus of Nazareth will exterminate Israel's longtime foe and bring about an unparalleled act of redemption: the salvation of individuals from the bondage of sin. As a result of the fall of Adam and Eve, humanity's greatest problem is estrangement from God. Sin drove a wedge between God and those made in his image. So God sent his Son to come into the world to solve humanity's sin problem by bearing the Father's wrath and reconciling us with him.

After the angel instructs Joseph to name his son Jesus, the narrator comments, "All this took place *to fulfill* what the Lord had said through the prophet: 'The virgin will conceive and give birth to a son, and they will call him Immanuel' (which means 'God with us')" (1:23; cf. Isa. 7:14). Here we stumble upon the first of ten "fulfillment formula" quotations, where Matthew explicitly connects the person of Jesus to large swaths of the Old Testament (1:22; 2:15, 17, 23; 4:14; 8:17; 12:17; 13:35; 21:4; 27:9). The word for "fulfill" (*plēroō*) occurs sixteen times in Matthew, and nearly all occurrences are tied to the OT. In contrast, Mark uses the term only twice and Luke nine times. The point is that Matthew keeps his audience focused on Israel's Scriptures and how Jesus, at every point in his ministry, fulfills every word.

In the immediate context of Isaiah 7, the prophet predicts that a "young woman" (or "virgin") will give birth to a child named "Immanuel" (7:13–14). The birth of Isaiah's son shortly but incompletely fulfills this prediction (Isa. 8:3–4; cf. 8:8, 10, 18). Yet, a few chapters later, Isaiah 9:1–7 prophesies that the Davidic heir will also be called "Mighty God, Everlasting Father, Prince of Peace." Matthew reads Isaiah 7 and 9 together, asserting that Jesus fulfills the prophecies of Isaiah from long ago. Jesus is both Immanuel (1:23) and the long-awaited Davidic heir (1:1, 17). Some doubt the miracle of the virgin birth, but Matthew and the other NT writers firmly rest many doctrines on its historicity. Without the virgin birth, we lose the incarnation, substitutionary atonement, and believers' justification, to name a few.

The scandal that befell Joseph because of his soon-to-be bride's pregnancy (1:18–19) was providential in the eyes of Matthew, for he points out that "all this took place to fulfill what the Lord had said" (1:22). Matthew also translates the second title, "Immanuel," for his audience. It means "God with us" (1:23). Richard Hays observes that the phrase "God with us" is a structural marker, occurring at the beginning, middle, and end of the First Gospel (1:23; 18:20; 28:20),[1] and that "these [three] references frame and support everything in between."[2]

One could also argue that the expression "God with us" captures not only a great deal of the First Gospel but the entire trajectory of redemption. God designed the entire cosmos to be his sanctuary. God promises Adam and Eve that if they completely obey his commands, heaven will descend and he will dwell fully with them and their descendants. They disobey. So God promises Israel, a corporate Adam, that if they completely obey his laws, he will dwell with them intimately (Exod. 4:22; 19:6). They disobey too. So now God has taken it upon himself to bring his presence to humanity in the person of Jesus.

The presence of God in Jesus suggests that the physical temple in Jerusalem is now defunct. How can there be two rival temples? One, a person, and the other, a human-made composition of earthly materials. From the beginning, God has intended to dwell with people, not in buildings. In the words of Stephen, "the Most High does not live in houses made by human hands" (Acts 7:48; cf. 1 Kings 8:27; 2 Chron. 2:6). Matthew's quotation of Isaiah 7:14 in 1:22–23 is highly significant to the First Gospel and Jesus's ministry at large. God's glory has descended in the person of Jesus, and if God's glory

---

1. Richard B. Hays, *Reading Backwards: Figural Christology and the Fourfold Gospel Witness* (Waco: Baylor University Press, 2014), 38.

2. Hays, *Reading Backwards*, 38.

has now taken up residence in Jesus, then the physical temple has come to an end. As the narrative moves forward, we should expect to see this theme snowball, culminating in Jesus's death and resurrection. Spoiler alert: Matthew doesn't disappoint.

We should also consider Matthew's pairing of two names—Jesus and Immanuel. In the first instance the angel explains the significance, and in the second instance the narrator unpacks the meaning of the name:

> She will give birth to a son, and you are to give him the name *Jesus*, because he will *save his people from their sins*. (1:21)

> The virgin will conceive and give birth to a son, and they will call him *Immanuel* (*which means "God with us"*). (1:23)

The name "Jesus" means, as we mentioned above, the "*Lord* saves," whereas the name "Immanuel" means "God with us." By bringing the two names together, Matthew wants his readers to understand each title in light of the other. *Jesus in Matthew's Gospel should be primarily understood as the Lord incarnate who has come to save humanity and dwell with them.* God's presence on earth is a presence for deliverance. Every time we come across the name "Jesus" in the First Gospel, we must not lose sight of Matthew's rich and comforting presentation.

Chapter 1 closes with Joseph heeding the angelic commanded in 1:20 by following through with their marriage. Since Joseph was "faithful to the law" (1:19), he did not "consummate their marriage until she had given birth" (1:25). Once the baby is born, Joseph names him Jesus. Chapter 1 begins with the genealogy of Jesus and ends with his birth. The reader has much to digest from chapter 1: Jesus is *the* descendant of Abraham and David who will rule over Israel and the nations, dwell with humanity, and, most importantly, save people from sin.

Flight to Egypt (2:1–18)

Chapter 2 fleshes out Jesus's role as king and true Israel on many levels. Once Jesus, the "sign child" (1:22–23, quoting Isa. 7:14), is born, magi come to Jerusalem to worship him (2:2). Identifying the magi has preoccupied a host of commentators. While magi are found in a wide variety of literature,[3] we need only to draw our attention to the use of "magi" (*magoi*) in the LXX.

---

3. Raymond E. Brown, *The Birth of the Messiah: A Commentary on the Infancy Narratives in the Gospels of Matthew and Luke* (Garden City, NY: Image Books, 1977), 167–77.

This term, found only in one of the Greek translations of the book of Daniel (Theo.), refers to Babylonian wise men who were responsible for interpreting dreams and visions and failed to recount to Nebuchadnezzar his dream and its interpretation (Dan. 1:20; 2:2, 10, 27; 4:7; 5:7, 11, 15). In Daniel 2, 4, and 5, Daniel succeeds where these "wise men" fail. The tables are turned here in Matthew's narrative—they outwit Herod. They succeed where he fails. Further, the magi pay homage to Jesus, whose wisdom far outstrips the prophet Daniel and confounds the "wise men" of Jerusalem.

The magi recognize the significance of the child, for they ask, "Where is the one who has been born *king of the Jews*?" (2:2). Such an admission stands in stark contrast to Herod, who is labeled "king" in 2:1 and 2:3. Moreover, the magi claim that they saw "his star when it rose" (2:2). Numbers 24:17, most likely a messianic prophecy, reads, "I see him, but not now; I behold him, but not near. *A star will come out of Jacob*; a scepter will rise out of Israel." In the book of Revelation, Jesus calls even himself "the bright Morning Star" (Rev. 22:16). The point is that there is a biblical tradition associating the coming Messiah with a "star." Further, this same title, "king of the Jews" (2:2), is found at the end of Matthew's narrative when Pilate labels Jesus the "king of the Jews" (27:11, 29, 37). Matthew's references to Jesus's royalty at the moments of his greatest humility—his birth and death—indicate that this king was born to die.

From the beginning, enemies surround Jesus. Herod the Great, the Roman-appointed ruler of Israel at this time,[4] discovers that a rival king (Jesus) has been born, and his fear of competition leads to genocide. Herod the Great was no stranger to murder, as he killed two wives and three sons. He was a ruler willing to hold on to the throne at any cost. Matthew goes on to mention yet another party: "When King Herod heard this he was *disturbed* [*etarachthē*], and all Jerusalem with him" (2:3). Herod is not the only offended party—all Jerusalem was likewise "disturbed." The word "disturbed" here is often found in the LXX in the context of military operations when an inferior army stands in terror in the presence of a superior one (e.g., Deut. 2:25; 1 Chron. 29:11; Isa. 19:3; Jdt. 7:4; 14:19 LXX). Such a usage makes good sense here, as Herod and Israel stand in defiance to King Jesus and tremble in fear of an unparalleled ruler. Even before Jesus begins his public ministry, Matthew highlights the hostility between Jesus and Israel—a hostility that will culminate in the nation killing its long-awaited Messiah.

Herod orders the experts in the Law, the OT scholars of the day, to inform him where the Messiah was to be born (2:4). The Jewish leaders put their

---

4. Herod died in 4 BC, explaining why many scholars peg Jesus's birth at around 5 BC.

finger on Micah 5:2–4, a passage that predicts the birth of the Messiah in the inauspicious town of Bethlehem. Why Bethlehem? It was the hometown of King David (1 Sam. 16:1; 17:12), so it is hardly surprising that the Messiah, the true descendant of David (1:1), would also be from there. Herod summons the magi to lead him to Jesus, but, despite his best-laid plans, the magi take "another route" home because they were "warned in a dream not to go back to Herod" (2:12).

When the magi finally locate Jesus, they offer "gold, frankincense and myrrh" (2:11). The book of Micah may still be uppermost in Matthew's mind here, since Micah 4:13 predicts the "wealth" of the "many nations" coming to Zion as a result of God's victory over Israel's enemies at the very end of history (cf. Josh. 6:24; Isa. 60:5–7; Hag. 2:6–7). When the magi bow down and worship Jesus, they symbolize the nations paying obeisance to God's Anointed One. We cannot miss the irony here: Israel is marshaled against the Messiah, whereas the nations willfully submit to him.

In the first exodus, Pharaoh fails to murder all the male Israelite newborns, and Moses survives; in the second exodus, Herod fails to kill Jesus, a greater Moses. Chapter 2 is rife with the typological parallels between Moses and Jesus:

Jesus	Moses
Lives in Egypt (2:13)	Lives in Egypt (Exod. 1:1)
Archenemy is Herod (2:3)	Archenemy is Pharaoh (Exod. 1:8)
Herod perceives Jesus to be a threat (2:3)	Pharaoh perceives the Israelites to be a threat (Exod. 1:9–10)
Herod attempts to kill Jewish boys two years old and younger in Bethlehem (2:16)	Pharaoh attempts to kill all male Hebrew babies in Egypt (Exod. 1:16)
Herod attempts to manipulate the magi (2:8)	Pharaoh attempts to manipulate the Hebrew midwives (Exod. 1:15–16)
Herod is "outwitted" by the magi (2:16)	Pharaoh is outwitted by the Hebrew midwives (Exod. 1:19)
God protects Jesus (2:13)	God protects the male Israelite babies (Exod. 1:20)

Jesus's ministry never strays from this Mosaic trajectory: Jesus will, in the shadow of Moses, lead his people out of bondage (sin), ensure their arrival to a new mountain sanctuary (Jesus), and mediate a new covenant (Sermon on the Mount).

An angel warns Joseph in a dream that Herod is on the prowl, looking to devour Jesus. So Joseph and Mary escape to Egypt for refuge (2:13). The movement to Egypt prompts Matthew to explain its redemptive-historical significance: "So he got up, took the child and his mother during the night and left for Egypt, where he stayed until the death of Herod. And so was fulfilled what the Lord had said through the prophet: '*Out of Egypt I called my son*'" (2:15). Matthew claims that Hosea 11:1 was "fulfilled" in Jesus's journey to Egypt, even as a baby.

Matthew quotes the OT over fifty times in his Gospel, and his quotation of Hosea 11:1 is one of his most perplexing citations. According to Hosea 11:1, Yahweh recalls his *past* dealings with Israel in the exodus using the metaphor of sonship. But Matthew reads this passage as a *prophecy* concerning Jesus's flight to Egypt. More than a handful of scholars argue that Matthew contravenes the meaning of Hosea 11:1 in asserting that Jesus "fulfilled" it. How could Matthew view Hosea 11:1 as a prophecy of an individual since the immediate context of Hosea 11 refers to the first exodus of Israel as a nation?

We could examine a host of cogent and viable options that uphold the integrity of Matthew's use of the OT here, but we will focus on two.[5] (1) Hosea 11:1–4 certainly underscores God's past faithfulness in delivering his people from Egypt despite Israel's faithlessness. Verse 2 states, "The more they [the Israelites] were called, the more they went away from me [Yahweh]." But the prophet Hosea is not only concerned about God's past dealings with Israel; he looks toward the future, when God will reaffirm his covenantal commitment to them. Hosea's expectation is based upon the Pentateuch's expectation of a second exodus, for the Pentateuch itself contains this reality. Deuteronomy 28:68 states, for example, "*The Lord will send you back in ships to Egypt* on a journey I said you should never make again." Then, a few chapters later, we read, "Even if you have been banished to the most distant land under the heavens, from there the Lᴏʀᴅ your *God will gather you and bring you back*. He will bring you to the land that belonged to your ancestors" (Deut. 30:4–5).

Not only does Hosea anticipate a second exodus; he hints at how the second exodus will come about. At the beginning of the book, Hosea predicts that Israel will "appoint one leader" who will play a critical, representative role leading the people out of "the land" once more (Hosea 1:11). The prophet anticipates God sending Israel into exile once more to "Egypt" (or Assyria) on account of her idolatry. Then God will redeem the nation from exile and bring it to the promised land (see 7:11, 16; 8:13; 9:3; 11:5). The second exodus is typologically patterned after the first exodus.

(2) The OT displays a strong bond between the one and the many. We label this phenomenon "corporate solidarity." The behavior of a single

---

5. My line of argumentation is indebted to G. K. Beale, "The Use of Hosea 11:1 in Matthew 2:15: One More Time," *JETS* 55 (2012): 697–715.

individual affects the entire community. Kings represent nations, fathers represent families, and so on (see, e.g., 2 Sam. 21:1; 1 Chron. 21:1–17). The book of Hosea exemplifies this movement between the one and the many. The most memorable portions of Hosea heavily lean on corporate solidarity. God commands Hosea to "marry a promiscuous woman," symbolizing Yahweh's relationship with his idolatrous people (Hosea 1:2). Hosea's wife, a single person, represents an entire nation. The same can be said for Hosea's children, "Jezreel," "Lo-Ruhamah," and "Lo-Ammi" (Hosea 1:3–9). By the time Hosea's readers come to 11:1, they are quite aware of Hosea's penchant for corporate solidarity and sensitive to the prophet's expectations for a second exodus. Yes, Hosea 11:1 squarely recalls the first exodus, but behind this retrospection lies the assumption that God will appoint a representative head who will play a critical role in leading his people out of bondage once more.

Matthew's use of Hosea 11:1, then, comports with Hosea's use of the Pentateuch: God's past actions anticipate future actions. It is possible, even likely, that Matthew (and the other NT writers) read and reread the OT prophets, discovering how to interpret the OT. The OT prophets interpret earlier parts of Scripture (e.g., the Pentateuch) and apply them to their own historical circumstances and even integrate them into their prophetic oracles. Further, Jesus himself probably instructed Matthew and the other disciples how to interpret the OT during the course of his ministry. Even in Matthew's genealogy, we can discern a great deal of how he reads the OT. Matthew is not simply rattling off a list of names in the genealogy; he perceives a strong typological connection between the lives of named Israelites and the life of Jesus. God's past dealings with Israel anticipate his future dealings with Jesus. So the First Evangelist's use of Hosea 11:1 falls very much in line with what we discover in Hosea and Matthew itself. Using a blend of typology and verbal prophecy, Matthew paints Jesus as God's true "son," who repeats Israel's career. But instead of disobedience and rebellion, faithfulness and submission mark Jesus's relationship with his Father.

Home in Nazareth (2:19–23)

Matthew devotes the last portion of chapter 2 to Jesus's family migrating to Nazareth. While intending to return home to Judea, Joseph learns that Archelaus, a son of Herod, is now ruling over the territory. Archelaus was known for his abusive tactics (e.g., Josephus, *Ant.* 17.339–55), so an angel commands Joseph to head north to the "district of Galilee," where he will safely provide for his family (2:22). They end up in a rural, agricultural town in

Lower Galilee with a small population around five hundred[6] called Nazareth, thus fulfilling the OT promise "that he would be called a Nazarene" (2:23). Perhaps the OT passage in mind is Isaiah 11:1: "A shoot will come up from the stump of Jesse; from his roots *a Branch* [Heb. *netser*] will bear fruit." According to Isaiah 11, the Messiah will be a descendant of Jesse and David who will rule with justice and restore the people of God (11:3–4, 10–11). As many scholars point out, the word for "Branch" (*netser*) is close to the name "Nazareth" (Gk. *Nazōraios*).

In chapters 1–2, Matthew attaches the word "fulfill" (*plēroō*) to four events in the birth narrative, and each of these OT prophecies is, at some level, fulfilled in an unexpected manner.

OT Prophecy "Fulfilled"	Unexpected Turn of Events
Isaiah 7:14	Scandal of Mary's pregnancy (1:18–21)
Hosea 11:1	Mary and Joseph's flight to Egypt (2:13–15)
Jeremiah 31:15	Slaughter of Jewish boys two years old and younger (2:17)
Isaiah 11:1	Home in Nazareth (2:21–23)

These fulfillments remind the reader that the early years of Jesus, as dramatic and perilous as they may be, are still in keeping with OT expectations. If the beginning of Jesus's Scripture-fulfilling life is fraught with difficulty, how much more will his public ministry be?

John the Baptist (3:1–17)

BAPTISM OF A REMNANT OF ISRAELITES (3:1–12)

Chapter 3 opens with a loose transitional phrase, "in those days" (3:1), and Matthew's audience encounters John the Baptist preaching the nearness of the "kingdom of heaven" (3:2). Because the kingdom is "near" and the second exodus is at hand (3:2; cf. Isa. 40:3), Israel must respond accordingly and repent of her sins (// Mark 1:3–8 // Luke 3:2–17). If the Israelites are unwilling to respond favorably to John's message, they will be on the receiving end of divine wrath (→Mark 1:3). John's baptism of "repentance" (3:11) challenges the nation's institutions; a purifying river baptism in the Jordan and Israel's temple-based sacrificial system in Jerusalem are mutually exclusive.

John's odd appearance and peculiar diet call to mind the great prophet Elijah, symbolizing Israel's rebellious condition (2 Kings 1:8). Verses 5–6 indicate

---

6. Richard A. Freund and Daniel M. Gurtner, "Nazareth," in *T&T Clark Encyclopedia of Second Temple Judaism*, ed. Daniel M. Gurtner and Loren T. Stuckenbruck (London: Bloomsbury T&T Clark, 2020), 2:539.

that a considerable crowd responded favorably to John's message: "All Judea and the whole region of the Jordan . . . were baptized." The positive response of the crowd stands in chisel-sharp relief to the Jewish leaders' rejection of John. One unique feature of the First Gospel is the conflict between Jesus and the Jewish leaders. All four Gospels highlight this acrimonious theme in their narratives, but Matthew's presentation of this conflict is exceptional. At every turning point, the Jewish authorities display a great deal of hostility toward Jesus (e.g., 7:15–23; 12:22–45; 23:1–39; 24:4–5, 10–12, 23–24). Since Israel's leaders stand against Jesus, it's unsurprising that they are allied against John the Baptist.

When John lays eyes on the approaching leaders, he announces, "You brood of vipers! Who warned you to flee from *the coming wrath*?" (3:7; cf. 12:34; Rom. 1:18). After announcing their doom, John goes right to the nub of the issue: "Do not think you can say to yourselves, 'We have Abraham as our father.' I tell you that out of these stones God can raise up children for Abraham" (3:9). The Pharisees and Sadducees are resting in their identity as physical children of Abraham; but they are not his spiritual descendants. Ultimately, only two lines exist in the story of redemption: godly and ungodly. The godly line lays claim to the promises of God by faith, whereas the ungodly remain hostile to God and his people (see Gen. 3:15). So John the Baptist claims that "out of these stones God can raise up children for Abraham" (3:9). The restored covenant community—the true Israel and genuine children of Abraham—will now find their ultimate identity around King Jesus, *the* son of Abraham.

John continues his tirade against the hostile Jewish leaders in 3:11–12, where he predicts that one who comes after him will be "more powerful." In contrast to John's baptism of water, the coming one will "baptize . . . with the Holy Spirit and fire." The arrival of God's Spirit is highly eschatological, as the OT prophets expected the Spirit to descend upon God's people at the very end of history (e.g., Joel 2:28–32). According to Matthew and Luke, the end-time arrival of the Spirit is associated with "fire" and inextricably tethered to the ministry of the coming one (3:11 // Luke 3:16). That is, when the figure following John's baptism arrives, it will be a day of judgment for those who reject John's message (3:12; cf. Isa. 4:4; 5:24; 29:6; 30:24; Amos 7:4; Mal. 4:1).

BAPTISM OF JESUS AS TRUE ISRAEL (3:13–17)

Whereas Israel's authorities shun John's baptism, Jesus welcomes it (3:13–17 // Mark 1:9–11 // Luke 3:21–22 // John 1:31–34). Jesus's baptism may strike the reader as odd: if Jesus was born without sin (1:18), then why would he need to identify with John's summons to "repent" of sin (3:2)? John picks up on this problem when he attempts to "deter" Jesus from being baptized: "I [John] need to be baptized by you, and do you come to me?" (3:14). Jesus's response to this theological dilemma is clear: "It is proper for us to do this [baptism] to *fulfill all righteousness*" (3:15). Matthew is the only evangelist to isolate this problem explicitly and record the exchange between John and Jesus. Recall Matthew's emphasis on "fulfillment" in his Gospel and how he is at pains to demonstrate that Jesus's ministry falls in line with OT expectations. So, when Jesus says that his baptism is necessary "to fulfill all righteousness," the OT must be in view here. The tricky term "righteousness" refers to actions that fall in line with God's holy and just character (cf. Gen. 15:6; 18:19; Exod. 34:7; Lev. 19:15; Ps. 10:7 LXX [11:7 ET]). Therefore, Jesus's baptism functions on two levels: he fulfills OT expectations *and* he sets right what Israel got wrong.

In the previous passage, Jesus, even as a baby, identifies with corporate Israel in his flight to Egypt (2:13–15). As *the* descendant of Abraham and the true Israel (1:1), Jesus retraces the nation's steps. Where they went, he goes. By being baptized in the Jordan, Jesus here formally identifies with Israel. He, like Israel passing through the Red Sea at the exodus, passes through the chaotic waters and emerges victorious. But, unlike Israel, he remains faithful to the covenant, preserving God's law and eradicating the enemy from the promised land (4:1–11). There's a bit of tension here that will ultimately be resolved at the cross. Righteous Jesus identifies with unrighteous Israelites so that he might "save" them (1:21). At the cross, the Righteous One will become unrighteous, so that the unrighteous might be declared righteous (cf. 2 Cor. 5:21).

When Jesus emerges from the water, the Spirit "descends like a dove." The presence of a dove at Jesus's baptism also symbolizes the end-time Spirit, who ushers in a new stage of God's plan of redemption, the dawn of the new creation (e.g., Gen. 8:8–12; Isa. 32:15–16; Ezek. 36:26–30). As the heavens open, the Father declares, "This is my Son, whom I love; with him I am well pleased" (3:17). Matthew names all three persons of the Trinity, recalling the end of Matthew's narrative, when the disciples are commissioned to baptize "in the name of the Father and of the Son and of the Holy Spirit" (28:19). All three work together at the beginning of the narrative and at the end in ushering in the new creation, much like all three participate in the first creation (Gen. 1:2, 26; John 1:1–3; Col. 1:15–16).

Why does the Father announce that Jesus is his "Son" at the baptism? Was Jesus not God's Son before this event? Though a few argue that Jesus *became* God's Son at the baptism, Matthew is presenting Jesus's sonship along redemptive-historical lines. Throughout Matthew's narrative, Jesus is viewed as Yahweh incarnate and his preexistence is implied (e.g., 8:27; 14:27–28; 17:2;

22:44). So Matthew must be primarily (but not exclusively) thinking in terms of Jesus as true Israel and the royal son of David *in his humanity*. This would explain why the Father's brief announcement, "This is my Son, whom I love; with him I am well pleased," alludes to 2 Samuel 7:14 and Psalm 2:7, two passages that predict the arrival of Israel's Messiah. The point of Jesus's baptism is, then, that God declares his Son to be the long-awaited Messiah, who has come to right humanity's wrongs.

Stage 1: Jesus in Galilee (4:1-18:35)

The Wilderness Temptation and the Beginning of Jesus's Public Ministry (4:1-25)

Success in the Judean Wilderness (4:1-11)

Now that Jesus is anointed by the Spirit and equipped to rule, he will head to battle. All three Synoptics include the wilderness temptation (Matt. 4:1-11 // Mark 1:12-13 // Luke 4:1-13), but only Matthew and Luke disclose what transpired. Mark puts his finger on Jesus's identity as the last Adam and true Israel, and Matthew and Luke tease out this twofold emphasis throughout their narratives. Matthew has already stated that Jesus is the "son of Abraham" (1:1) and true Israel, God's "son" (2:15, quoting Hosea 11:1). In 2:15 baby Jesus retraces Israel's steps in fleeing to Egypt, where he symbolically experiences a small-scale Egyptian exile on behalf of Israel. Righteousness must prevail. At his baptism, Jesus once again identifies with Israel in that he, like the nation, passes through the waters of chaos (3:13-17). He identifies with Israel's forty-year wilderness wanderings in his forty-day wilderness temptation (4:1-11; →Luke 4:1-13). Jesus begins to eradicate the devil from the cosmos in stark contrast to the failure of the second generation of Israelites to purge the pagan nations from Canaan (Josh. 23:12-16). Putting all four events together, we perceive a nice chronological progression that roughly falls in line with Israel's history:

Jesus	Nation of Israel
Flees to Egypt with Joseph and Mary as God's "son" (2:15, quoting Hosea 11:1)	Migrates to Egypt as God's "firstborn son" (Exod. 4:22)
Baptized in the Jordan (3:13-17)	Crosses the Red Sea (or "Sea of Reeds"; Exod. 14:19-31)
Tempted for forty days in the wilderness (4:1-11)	Wanders in the wilderness for forty years (Num. 32:13)
Succeeds in the wilderness and begins to expel Satan from the cosmos (4:11)	Fails in the wilderness and fails to expel the inhabitants of Canaan (Joshua)

We must also keep in mind that the nation of Israel is understood to be a corporate Adam throughout the Pentateuch. Just as God created Adam and Eve and installed them in Eden, so too he creates Israel and installs them in the promised land. At Sinai, God offers Israel eternal life in the new creation if they succeed (Lev. 18:5; Deut. 4:1; Ezek. 18:9; 20:11; Matt. 19:17; Rom. 10:5; Gal. 3:12). But like Adam and Eve, Israel breaks God's law and forfeits the promise of life. They, like all of humanity, are affected by Adam and Eve's fall. The Israelites cannot obey the law perfectly. But, embedded within Israel's law and persisting throughout the Pentateuch, hope remains for a future individual to fill Adam's and Israel's shoes and obey where they fail (e.g., Gen. 3:15). Matthew carefully crafts his narrative to present Jesus as the fulfillment of these OT expectations. As the true and faithful Israel, he establishes the end-time kingdom and spearheads the new creation. The wilderness climax of the comparison indicates that Jesus, through his successful resistance of the devil's temptations, has begun to expunge Satan's presence from the cosmos.

Announcing the Kingdom in Galilee (4:12–17)

John the Baptist's arrest in Judea forms the catalyst for Jesus's return to Galilee (4:12). Though growing up in Nazareth for nearly thirty years (Luke 3:23), Jesus tactically decides to make Capernaum the base of his operations (4:13). Matthew once again invokes the OT to explain why Jesus moves to Capernaum; it is "to fulfill" Isaiah 9:1–2:

> Land of Zebulun and land of Naphtali,
>> the Way of the Sea, beyond the Jordan,
>> Galilee of the Gentiles—
> the people living in darkness
>> have seen a great light;
> on those living in the land of the shadow of death
>> a light has dawned. (Matt. 4:15–16)

Isaiah 9 predicts that God will redeem some Northern Israelites who live in "Galilee of the Gentiles" (9:1). This geographic section of Israel was the first to succumb to the Assyrian invasion in 733 BC,[7] but Isaiah anticipates a future restoration of the Northern tribes. Their reestablishment will take place through the promised Messiah, who will "reign on David's throne and over his kingdom" (Isa. 9:7).

---

7. John Oswalt, *The Book of Isaiah, Chapters 1–39*, NICOT (Grand Rapids: Eerdmans, 1986), 239.

Matthew's use of Isaiah 9:1–2 as Jesus transitions to Capernaum makes good sense for four reasons: (1) Jesus, as true Israel, has gone into Egypt, passed through the chaotic waters, and successfully defeated the devil, so he can now spark the return of the Israelites from spiritual captivity; (2) Jesus provokes the restoration of *all* the tribes of Israel; (3) he fulfills Isaiah's prophecy that the Messiah "will reign on David's throne" (see 4:17); (4) by including the phrase "Galilee of the *Gentiles*," Matthew lays the foundation for the inclusion of the gentiles in Jesus's Galilean ministry.

Calling the First Disciples and Healing the Sick (4:18–25)

Having proclaimed the saving message of the kingdom, Jesus calls his first four disciples (// Mark 1:16–20 // Luke 5:2–11). Like Mark's narrative, Matthew's describes the calling of Peter (Simon) and Andrew and then the calling of James and John. Three of these disciples—Peter, James, and John—will constitute Jesus's inner circle; though this group is not as prominent as they are in Mark, they are the only disciples who will witness the transfiguration (17:1; cf. 26:37).

All four disciples are fishermen by trade, but Jesus demands that they now "follow" him (4:19, 21). They are confronted with a difficult decision: Will they continue in the safety of their profession, or will they step out in faith and follow Jesus? Both groups respond positively and follow Jesus. James and John even "left the boat and their father," cutting ties with their profession and family (4:22; cf. 8:21–22; 10:35–37; 19:29). Matthew's audience must likewise make the same decision. Is Jesus worth following even if it entails financial and familial hardships? The answer, as Matthew makes clear, is yes.

Chapter 4 climaxes with Jesus healing a throng of people with an extensive list of maladies from all over. These micro-level healings illustrate Jesus's macro-level ministry of "saving" humanity from their plight (1:21). The fall plunged the created order into chaos and rebellion. Here, though, Jesus turns the tide on account of his success in the wilderness temptation. With Satan's grip on creation now broken, Jesus has the power and authority to reverse the curses.

Matthew goes to great lengths to highlight the universal scope of Jesus's restoration. Matthew's extensive list of the crowd's ailments in 4:23–24 outstrips Mark's and Luke's accounts (// Mark 3:7–10 // Luke 6:17–18):

"every disease"
"sickness"

"all who were ill with various diseases"
"those suffering severe pain"
"the demon-possessed"
"those having seizures"
"the paralyzed"

In listing these various conditions, Matthew wants his readers to grasp the totality of the salvation Jesus offers. The new creation has arrived in the ministry of Jesus of Nazareth. There is no malady that is beyond his reach. Further, Matthew divulges where the crowd is from: "Galilee, the Decapolis, Jerusalem, Judea, and the region across the Jordan" (4:25). With the exception of Samaria, as many commentators point out (see 10:5), much of Palestine is in mind here. Thus, Jesus has come to save *all* the tribes of Israel. In 4:1–11 he rids the territory of the devil, and here in 4:23–25 he begins to populate it with God-fearing followers (4:25). God's glory is filling the promised land.

The Sermon on the Mount (5:1–7:29)

The Nine Blessings or "Beatitudes" (5:1–12)

With the "whole of Israel"[8] being represented in the massive crowds in 4:25, the stage is now set for the famous "Sermon on the Mount" (cf. Luke 6:20–49). Verse 1 states that "when he [Jesus] saw the crowds, he went up on a mountainside and sat down." But then the narrative zooms in on the disciples: "His *disciples* came to him and he began to teach *them*" (5:1–2). Is Jesus ignoring the crowds at the base of the mountain? The end of the discourse divulges the answer: "When Jesus had finished saying these things [the Sermon on the Mount], *the crowds* were amazed at his teaching" (7:28). Matthew wants his audience to pick up on Jesus's two-tiered audience—the disciples gather at the top of the mountain, whereas the crowds gather at its base. Such a presentation is significant because it informs us of Jesus's identity. Not coincidentally, according to Exodus 19, the nation of Israel gathers at the base of Sinai as their leader meets with God (Exod. 19:2–24). Farther up the mountain, only Aaron, Nadab, Abihu, and the seventy elders of Israel gathered (Exod. 24:1), leaving the highest point of Sinai for Moses (Exod. 24:2). Could it be that Matthew's presentation of the disciples and the crowds follows this pattern? Given the overwhelming connections between Matthew's Gospel (especially the Sermon on the Mount) and the book of Exodus, I think it is likely.

8. Donald A. Hagner, *Matthew 1–13*, WBC 33A (Grand Rapids: Zondervan, 1993), 81.

If the crowds in 4:25 and 7:28 correspond to the nation of Israel and the disciples correspond to the leaders of Israel, then Matthew presents Jesus as Yahweh incarnate *and* a new Moses:

Book of Exodus	Matthew 4:25–7:28
Nation of Israel (base of Sinai)	Crowds (base of mountain)
Leaders of Israel (farther up Sinai)	Disciples (top of mountain)
Moses (top of Sinai)	Jesus as new Moses (top of mountain)
Yahweh (top of Sinai)	Jesus as Yahweh incarnate (top of mountain)

In Matthew's version of the Sermon on the Mount, an account that is modeled after Sinai, God the Father is not mentioned. God himself speaks only two times in all of Matthew: at Jesus's baptism and at the transfiguration (3:17; 17:5). So the two separate parties that are present at Sinai (Yahweh and Moses) are now joined together in one person. This observation frames the Sermon on the Mount in that we must generally understand the discourse as, first, originating from Jesus as Yahweh incarnate and a new Moses. Thus, the discourse is deemed to be a *divine* mandate. There is no intermediary figure. Second, Matthew frames the sermon in this manner so that his readers see that the law is given to true Israel, the restored people of God.

Matthew's placement of several key events on mountains uniquely sets his Gospel apart from the other three Gospels (4:8; 5:1; 8:1; 14:23; 15:29; 17:1, 9; 24:3; 26:30; 28:16). Often in the Old Testament, God's presence is associated with mountains. The garden of Eden is the first mountain where God dwells and manifests his glorious presence to Adam and Eve (Gen. 2:8–14; Ezek. 28:13–14). Israel's encounter with God at Sinai is the standard by which all subsequent encounters with God are measured.[9] Sinai itself is also portrayed as a grand temple (Exod. 3:5; 19–24). At the very end of history, Isaiah predicts that Israel and the nations will trek to the "mountain of the LORD's temple" in the "last days" (Isa. 2:2; cf. Mic. 4:7). Mountains, therefore, are a rich symbol of God's covenantal presence.

Jesus's communion with the disciples on the mountain here in Matthew 5–7 should be understood against this rich OT backdrop. In Exodus 33:18 Moses pleads with the Lord to "show" his "glory" atop Sinai. But the Lord does not permit it; instead, he only reveals "his back" to Moses because "no one may see [God] and live" (Exod. 33:20, 23). Fundamentally, a holy God cannot dwell among sinners. Matthew understands, though, that Jesus as Yahweh incarnate

---

9. Jeffrey J. Niehaus, *God at Sinai: Covenant and Theophany in the Bible and the Ancient Near East* (Grand Rapids: Zondervan, 1995).

is the embodiment of God's glory. John's Gospel states it like this: "The Word became flesh and made his dwelling among us. *We have seen his glory*, the glory of the One and Only" (John 1:14). At the Sermon on the Mount, then, the disciples are experiencing the glory of God. Moses longed for this day!

In Exodus 19–23 Moses instructs the Israelites how they are to remain ritually clean in the midst of a pagan environment. If the nation responds to the covenant with perfect obedience, God promises to vanquish their enemies and give them life—an existence that is fit for the new heavens and earth (Deut. 6:2; 30:15). But, like Adam and Eve, the Israelites fail to obey, succumbing to pride and idolatry. In the Sermon on the Mount, Jesus rehearses the well-known story but with a twist: instead of failure, Israel is marked by obedience to the covenant. Participants of the true Israel will obey these commands, because their representative, Jesus, obeyed in the wilderness.

The Sermon on the Mount (5:1–7:29) is the first of five teaching blocks in Matthew's narrative, perhaps modeled after the five books of the Pentateuch (10:1–11:1; 13:1–53; 18:1–19:1; 23:1–26:1), with each discourse ending with the same wording:[10]

Discourse 1	"When Jesus had finished saying these things" (7:28)
Discourse 2	"After Jesus had finished instructing his twelve disciples" (11:1)
Discourse 3	"When Jesus had finished these parables" (13:53)
Discourse 4	"When Jesus had finished saying these things" (19:1)
Discourse 5	"When Jesus had finished saying all these things" (26:1)

The first section of the sermon contains nine "beatitudes" (5:3–11), and the entire discourse of 5:2–7:29 is likely tied to these beatitudes. The sermon broadly falls into a threefold outline: nine blessings (5:3–12), the body of the sermon (5:13–7:12), and three curses (7:13–17). We can then break down the body into three dominant themes: Jesus and the law (5:17–48), participation in the new temple (6:1–18), and the social implications of living in the overlap of the ages (6:19–7:12).[11]

Each beatitude begins with the word "blessed" (*makarios*), a term that is found a total of thirteen times in the First Gospel. In the LXX, the word *makarios* is found in key passages such as Psalm 1:1 ("*Blessed* [*makarios*] is the one"), often in the context of divine favor or blessing (see, e.g., Ps. 32:1–2; 33:9 [ET 33:8]; 39:5 [ET 39:4]). When we consider its meaning here in Matthew

10. Craig S. Keener, *The Gospel of Matthew: A Socio-Rhetorical Commentary* (Grand Rapids: Eerdmans, 2009), 37.
11. This outline is generally indebted to Dale C. Allison Jr., "The Structure of the Sermon on the Mount," *JBL* 106 (1987): 423–45.

5:3–11, we must not lose sight of the immediate context. In 4:17 Jesus is proclaiming the arrival of the "kingdom of heaven," and in 4:23–25 he heals a large crowd, an event that demonstrates the in-breaking of the new creation. So when Jesus declares that this crowd and the disciples are "blessed," he most likely refers to *eschatological* favor (cf. Dan. 12:12 LXX). God has poured out his "blessing" upon the hearers because of the arrival of the new age *through* the ministry of Jesus. The Sermon on the Mount, then, is a summons to live wisely in the overlap of the ages.

The first eight beatitudes state the reality of end-time blessing followed by the basis for that blessing. For example, "Blessed are those who mourn, *for* [*hoti*] they will be comforted" (5:4). The subject of each blessing—the "poor in spirit," "those who mourn," the "meek," "those who hunger and thirst for righteousness," the "merciful," the "pure in heart," the "peacemakers," and "those who are persecuted because of righteousness"—resonates with OT examples of God dispensing favor upon his people (e.g., Ps. 24:4; 37:11; Isa. 57:15; 61:2).

The first and eighth beatitudes are accompanied by the *present* eschatological benefit of participating in the "kingdom of heaven," whereas the second through seventh beatitudes are cast as *future* promises:

Blessed are the poor in spirit, for **theirs is the kingdom of heaven.** (5:3)

Blessed are those who mourn, for they *will be comforted.* (5:4)

Blessed are the meek, for they *will inherit* the earth. (5:5)

Blessed are those who hunger and thirst for righteousness, for they *will be filled.* (5:6)

Blessed are the merciful, for they *will be shown mercy.* (5:7)

Blessed are the pure in heart, for they *will see* God. (5:8)

Blessed are the peacemakers, for they *will be called* children of God. (5:9)

Blessed are those who are persecuted because of righteousness, for **theirs is the kingdom of heaven.** (5:10)

In framing these beatitudes with the present reality of the end-time kingdom (5:3, 10), Jesus assures the audience of their participation in it. The remaining beatitudes give the audience further insight into what their future holds in the end-time kingdom. The kingdom is not marked by physical power and prominence but by inward holiness and adherence to God's will. In this vein, the ninth and final beatitude sets the stage for what will become of all those who follow Jesus: "Blessed are you *when* people insult you, persecute you and falsely say all kinds of evil against you because of me . . . for in the same way they persecuted the prophets who were before you" (5:11–12). What does life look like for those belong to the kingdom? Kingdom citizens are confident of God's eschatological approval while they endure the world's disapproval.

Jesus and the Law (5:13–48)

After exhorting his audience to be "salt" and "light" to the world around them (5:13–16), Jesus explains the relationship between his teaching and the Mosaic law: "Do not think that I have come to abolish the Law or the Prophets; I have not come to abolish them but *to fulfill them*" (5:17). A great deal of debate surrounds the precise meaning of this passage, and we cannot enter into it here. Suffice it to say that the "law" that Jesus prescribes in the Sermon on the Mount is not *antithetical* to the law that Moses issued; rather, it *fulfills* Moses's instruction. Jesus even says that he did not "come to abolish" the Mosaic commandments but to "fulfill them" (5:17). Jesus is essentially claiming that the Sermon on the Mount fulfills OT patterns and expectations. The Mosaic covenant anticipated Jesus's person, actions, and teaching.

With the arrival of the new age, God calls members of true Israel to live in light of their identity. But he doesn't leave them to do so under their own power. He fills them with his Spirit so that they may fulfill the eternal new covenant. These new-covenant ethics are not antithetical to the Mosaic administration; they largely stand in continuity with it (Deut. 6:4; Jer. 31:31–34; Ezek. 36:25–27). While the Mosaic covenant certainly had an internal dimension (see Exod. 20:17; Ps. 119), *the old covenant was largely temporal and external in nature, and it physically separated Israel from her neighbors.* These end-time kingdom ethics do not assume Israel's status as a theocratic nation living in the "old age." Instead, they are intended for a community of saints, a people who have been reconstituted around King Jesus in the eschatological "new age."

The remaining section of chapter 5 relates to this internal dimension of the new covenant in contrast to the external dimension of the old. Most of these verses include four elements: (1) the phrase "you have heard that it was said"; (2) a reference to Israel under the old covenant, "the people long ago"; (3) Jesus's contrasting message introduced by "but I tell you"; and (4) the new ethic for true Israel under the new covenant ("you [all]").

Matthew 5:21-22: *"You have heard that it was said to the people long ago*, 'You shall not murder, and anyone who murders will be subject to judgment.' *But I tell you . . ."*	Exodus 20:13 // Deuteronomy 5:17
Matthew 5:27-28: *"You have heard that it was said,* 'You shall not commit adultery.' *But I tell you . . ."*	Exodus 20:14 // Deuteronomy 5:18
Matthew 5:31-32: *"It has been said,* 'Anyone who divorces his wife must give her a certificate of divorce.' *But I tell you . . ."*	Deuteronomy 24:1-4
Matthew 5:33-34: "Again, *you have heard that it was said to the people long ago*, 'Do not break your oath, but fulfill to the Lord the vows you have made.' *But I tell you . . ."*	Leviticus 19:12; Numbers 30:2; Deuteronomy 23:21
Matthew 5:38-39: *"You have heard that it was said,* 'Eye for eye, and tooth for tooth.' *But I tell you . . . "*	Exodus 21:24; Leviticus 24:20; Deuteronomy 19:21
Matthew 5:43-44: *"You have heard that it was said,* 'Love your neighbor and hate your enemy.' *But I tell you . . ."*	Leviticus 19:18

All these examples set the standard for how the people of God relate to one another within the covenant community in the new age. Radical devotion characterizes the people of the new age. If believers walk according to Jesus's ethics, then the world will observe their "good deeds" and, in turn, "praise" their "Father in heaven" (5:16). This is precisely God's intention, as he outlined in Exodus 19:6: "You [Israel] will be for me a kingdom of priests and a holy nation." True followers of Jesus will indeed bless creation, multiply in it, and mediate God's presence (see Gen. 1:28).

Participation in the New Temple (6:1–18)

One tangible expression of life in the kingdom is, as we have already seen, a concern for one's neighbor (5:21–47). But the Sermon on the Mount never loses sight of the ultimate aim—pleasing God and not currying favor from individuals. What is also striking about the Sermon on the Mount is the personal devotion that believers enjoy with God as the end-time temple. While the OT certainly indicates that a remnant of Israelites were devoted to the Lord on an individual and personal level (e.g., Ps. 119), the intimacy that we discover here in the Sermon on the Mount is nearly without precedent. For example, the phrase "your Father" (with singular and plural words for "your") occurs fifteen times in the sermon! The rich themes of almsgiving, prayer, forgiveness, and fasting that are taken up here are bound up with the believers' identity as the eschatological dwelling place of God.

In his conversation about oaths in 5:34–35, Jesus draws his audience's attention to the cosmic reality of God's presence: "Do not swear an oath at all: either by *heaven, for it is God's throne*; or by the *earth, for it is his footstool*; or by Jerusalem, for it is the city of the Great King." A careful reading of Genesis 1–2 reveals God creating a vast cosmic temple, wherein God sovereignly rules and dwells. Parallels between the creation account in Genesis 1–2 and the construction of the temple in the book of Exodus are many, and several scholars contend that God is indeed fashioning a cosmic temple in Genesis 1–2.

Just as the earthly temple was divided into three parts, so also is the cosmos divided into three parts. The outer courtyard of the temple contained the washbasin and the altar, symbolizing the land and sea (1 Kings 7:23–25; Ezek. 43:14–16). Indeed, Isaiah 66:1 even states that the "earth" is God's "footstool." Moving a step closer to God's presence, the second section of the temple (or the Holy Place) symbolized the visible heavens and was lined with gold, containing the altar of incense (1 Kings 6:20), the "bread of the Presence" resting on a table (1 Kings 7:48), and ten lampstands fashioned out of gold (1 Kings 7:49). The final and most sacred section of the temple is the Holy of Holies, which symbolized the invisible heavens, where God dwells. This section, separated by an embroidered curtain, was also lined with gold and housed the ark of the covenant. Above the ark, two cherubim faced each other, symbolizing the throne of God in heaven, which is also surrounded by cherubim (Ps. 80:1; 99:1; Isa. 6). Jesus is reminding the disciples of ancient Israelite cosmology in order to direct their attention to the significance of their conduct. In this new era, the disciples are *part* of God's cosmic temple, wherein he rules and reigns as sovereign King. Where they go, God's empowering presence goes with them. They must recognize that their ultimate allegiance must always be to him and not to "the others" (6:2).

In his discussion of giving to the poor, Jesus unpacks this theme of allegiance to the indwelling God by pitting two attitudes against one another. On the one hand, the "hypocrites" seek to be "honored by others" in that they "announce it [their giving] with trumpets." The result is that "they have received their reward in full" (6:2). That is, hypocrites are ultimately bent on pleasing individuals, so when they garner the praise of others, they receive precisely what they have desired—humankind's approval. Their "reward," then, is fleeting and inconsequential. But citizens of the kingdom have a radically different outlook on life, and the way they relate to their neighbors differs from the world's standards. Believers wholly serve their "Father in heaven" (6:1). This is the third occurrence of the phrase "Father in heaven" (*ton patera hymōn ton en tois ouranois*). This phrase, occurring seven times in the Sermon of the Mount, is incredibly important to Matthew's narrative here and the summons to live in the overlap of the ages.

Prayer to the cosmic King also stands in stark contrast to the practice of the "hypocrites" (6:5). Authentic prayer should entail sweet communion with the God and must not be used as an opportunity to be "seen by others" (6:5). The Lord's Prayer (6:9–13), one of the most well-known passages in the Bible, contains a host of rich themes that echo throughout Matthew's narrative. A full analysis of the prayer is outside the scope of this project (→Luke 11:2–4), so we will restrict ourselves to four observations: (1) Prayer is rooted in God's identity as sovereign King over the cosmos (6:9). Prayer is predicated upon God's absolute sovereignty over the created order. Why pray if he cannot control the course of history and govern every aspect of our lives? (2) God's name is to be "hallowed" or "set aside" (*hagiasthētō*; 6:9). The verb *hagiazō* is often tied to God's holy presence in the temple (e.g., Exod. 28:37; 29:1; Lev. 16:4, 19 LXX). But, as we have seen since 1:23 (quoting Isa. 7:14), God's presence is taken up in the person of Jesus, for he is Yahweh incarnate *on earth*. In a word, heaven has come down—just as the OT promised so long ago (e.g., Isa. 64:1). To "set aside" God's "name," then, means to promote this glorious presence to the ends of the earth (see, e.g., Exod. 9:16; Ps. 8:1, 9). (3) If God's presence extends through the ministry of his followers, then the advancement of the kingdom naturally follows. This is probably the meaning of the line "your *kingdom* come, your will be done, on *earth* as it is in *heaven*" (6:10). Temple and kingdom go hand in hand: God fills his domain (kingdom) with his presence (temple). (4) The result of the inauguration of God's kingdom on earth is the ability to overcome "the evil one" (6:13). Jesus's success in the wilderness (4:1–11) benefits his followers in that they now participate in his victory.

Social Implications of Living in the Overlap of the Ages (6:19–7:12)

The last block of chapter 6 continues the theme of authentic worship in the kingdom (// Luke 11:34–36; 12:22–31). Believers must "store up . . . treasures in heaven" and not "on earth" (6:20). While it is true that heaven has begun to descend in the person of Jesus (1:23), believers still live in the already-not-yet of the new creation. They live now in the overlap of the ages, when heaven and earth remain distinct. When Jesus returns a second time, at the very end of history, then heaven and earth will be joined wholly together (Rev. 21–22). Until then, these two realities remain separate. It follows that believers must pursue their new creational inheritance, an inheritance that God will grant them in the future. Why should believers be consumed with material possessions when these things will pass away upon the full realization of God's plan for creation?

A related dimension to the believers' conduct in the end-time kingdom is their radical dependence upon the Father's sovereign rule (6:25–34). Unbelievers are consumed with questions such as "'What shall we eat?' or 'What shall we drink?' or 'What shall we wear?'" (6:31) because they attempt to govern their own affairs independently of the Father. Kingdom citizens, however, live at all times in the presence of their Master and humbly submit to his will. A life saturated in humility and steadfast in God's grace will naturally avoid unwarranted judgment upon others (7:1–5 // Luke 6:41–42). Why pass judgment when we ourselves are most deserving of death and estrangement from God?

The section ends with a fitting summary of how Jesus desires his disciples to live in the overlap of the ages: "So in everything, do to others what you would have them do to you, for this sums up the Law and the Prophets" (7:12 // Luke 6:31). This "Golden Rule" is a summary of God's will along the same lines as the two great commandments Matthew presents later: love God and love others (22:37–40). In so loving one another, believers fulfill the righteous requirements of God's law—both the Mosaic law and the law in the new age.

Three Warnings (7:13–29)

Life in the new age is not all roses; great suffering and rejection are always at hand. Indeed, as Jesus maintains, godly living will require relentless pursuit of him and his message. Jesus provides three warning signs along this treacherous kingdom journey. Resembling the famous "two ways" of Deuteronomy 30:15–20, the first warning is the briefest yet most difficult. Believers are to "enter through the narrow gate," an entryway that "leads to life" (7:13–14). The gate most likely refers to the person of Jesus, the life-giving One. If Jesus is the narrow gate, then what is the "broad . . . road that leads to destruction" (7:13)? This wide road is everything outside of Jesus that contends for the allegiance of God's people. In the immediate context, Matthew pairs it with false teaching (7:15–23). Jesus sets unshakable demands upon his audience. If they are to "work out" their "salvation" (Phil. 2:12), then they must continue to persevere in following him in holy living and sound doctrine.

The second warning explains the first warning in more detail (7:15–23). Here Jesus warns his disciples about "false prophets" donning "sheep's clothing," apparel that belies their true identity as "ferocious wolves" (7:15; cf. 10:16). Old Testament prophets expect the advent of false teachers in the "latter days" (e.g., Dan. 11:32), but Jesus's teaching remains difficult to grasp because of the presence of false teaching within the establishment of the kingdom.

29

False teaching was expected to occur *before* the establishment of the kingdom, whereas Jesus explains that false teaching and the kingdom now coexist and run parallel to one another. The false teachers have the appearance of legitimate members of the covenant community. That is, they appear to be "sheep" within the flock, but they are actually ravenous wolves, always on the prowl to devour God's people. What separates true and false teachers is their conduct—"by their fruit you will recognize them" (7:20). Keep in mind that false teachers are self-deceived (7:21–23)!

The third and final warning is a bit curious (7:24–27). Jesus transitions from false teachers in 7:15–23 to building houses (// Luke 6:47–49). The "wise man" builds a "house on the rock," whereas the "foolish man" builds a "house on sand" (7:24, 26). There may be more to this oft-repeated saying than meets the eye. The First Evangelist uses verb "to build" (*oikodomeō*) eight times in his narrative, and he connects many of them with the temple (see, e.g., 21:42; 26:61; 27:40). The closest parallel to this saying is 16:18, where Jesus declares Peter (*Petros*) to be a "rock" (*tē petra*) on which he "will build" (*oikodomēsō*) his "church." A few commentators relate the saying in 16:18 to the inauguration of the end-time temple.[12] What if the third warning in 7:24–27 is likewise a command to establish the eschatological temple on the foundation of Jesus's kingdom ethics? Like the beginning of the Sermon on the Mount, where believers are identified as "salt" and "light" (5:13–16), this is a radical call to missions. "Wise" temple building, therefore, entails a commitment to promote God's glory based upon Jesus's kingdom teaching (the "rock"), whereas "unwise" temple building is an attempt to promote the kingdom based upon human plotting and false teaching (the "sand").

Faith That Heals and Perseveres (8:1–34)

Cleansing the Leper, the Centurion, and a Multitude (8:1–17)

Chapters 5–7 disclose *what* is required of those living within the kingdom, whereas chapter 8 reveals *who* is admitted to the kingdom. After Jesus came down from the mountain, "large crowds followed him" (8:1). We can safely assume that this is the same group of individuals who had gathered at the base of the mountain during the Sermon on the Mount (5:1; 7:28–29). As the crowd watches, a leper emerges from the crowd and pleads with Jesus: "Lord, if you are willing, you can make me *clean*" (8:2 // Mark 1:40–45 // Luke 5:12–15). This man, despite being ritually impure and in close proximity to the crowd,

12. R. T. France, *The Gospel of Matthew*, NICNT (Grand Rapids: Eerdmans, 2007), 623.

pleads with Jesus to make him clean so that he can reunite with his family and community. Jesus touches the man, an act that would normally make one ritually impure, and he cleanses the man of his leprosy (8:3). Through Jesus, an outsider is now granted access to the new covenant community.

This theme continues in the following episode, where the narrator focuses on Capernaum, where a centurion, apparently a God-fearing gentile who built the local synagogue (Luke 7:5), asks Jesus to heal one of his servants (// Luke 7:1–10). He appeals, "Lord, . . . my servant lies at home paralyzed, suffering terribly" (8:6). What makes this healing different from the previous one is the incredible faith of the centurion. In contrast to Jesus touching the leper in 8:3, the centurion is confident that Jesus need only "say the word" and his "servant will be healed" (8:8). Jesus stands "amazed" at the centurion's reply—the only time in Matthew's narrative where Jesus is "amazed" (cf. 8:27; 9:33; 15:31; 21:20; 22:22; 27:14). He goes on to make a staggering affirmation: "I have not found anyone in Israel with such great faith" (8:10). Though the centurion practices Judaism to a large degree, he is still an outsider to Israel. But his faith in Jesus's ability to heal is so strong that he is admitted into the true Israel of God. Indeed, his faith is greater than that of most within the nation (8:12; cf. 3:7–12; 13:14–15)! In fulfillment of OT expectations, gentiles are participating fully in true Israel (e.g., Isa. 2:2; 25:6). But this passage makes clear that gentiles enjoy their citizenship *through faith* in Jesus and not in adherence to the law of Moses.

The section ends with the healing of Peter's mother-in-law and many who were demon possessed (8:14–17 // Mark 1:29–34 // Luke 4:38–41). This brief section nicely sets up Jesus's exorcism of the two demoniacs in 8:28–34, an episode that is symbolically represented by the stilling of chaotic waters (8:23–27). Matthew 8:14–17 also sheds light on the redemptive-historical significance of Jesus's healings. Unlike Mark's and Luke's accounts of the event, Matthew's account cites Isaiah 53:4: "This was to *fulfill* what was spoken through the prophet Isaiah: 'He took up our infirmities and bore our diseases'" (8:17). He makes explicit what Mark and Luke imply. This OT quotation brings Jesus's physical miracles in line with the OT in that he is clearly identified with Isaiah's suffering servant (Isa. 52:13–53:12). But this quotation also looks forward to a spiritual dimension of Jesus's ministry—his work on the cross. We have seen and will see Jesus heal a great deal of physical "diseases" and "sicknesses" (4:23–24; 9:35), but on the cross he will heal God's people of the worst kind of disease—sin. This forward-looking expectation explains why Matthew cites Isaiah 53:4, a passage that speaks of the substitutionary nature of the servant's work ("he took up *our* infirmities and bore *our* diseases").

Following the Lord of Creation (8:18–34)

The theme of true discipleship runs throughout Matthew's narrative. Notice Matthew's emphasis on this theme in chapter 8:

Large crowds *followed* him. (8:1)
Jesus . . . said to those *following* him. (8:10)
I will *follow* you wherever you go. (8:19)
Jesus told him, "*Follow* me." (8:22)
His disciples *followed* him. (8:23)

When the disciples make their way across to the "other side of the lake"—the first boat crossing—two individuals approach Jesus, desiring to become one of his followers (8:18–22 // Luke 9:57–60). Rather than accepting them on the basis of their willingness, Jesus urges them to first consider what they are signing up for. Whereas Mark and Luke include the calling of the Twelve earlier in their narratives (Mark 3:16–19 // Luke 6:14–16), Matthew strategically delays this calling account so that he can first spell out in detail what Jesus demands of his followers (10:1–4).

Becoming a true disciple means that one must believe Jesus's self-disclosure, even if Jesus exceeds that person's expectations. In the stilling of the storm, Jesus reveals himself to be not just one who *heals* but one who *governs* all of creation (// Mark 4:36–41 // Luke 8:22–25). Sandwiched between two exorcism accounts (8:16–17; 8:28–34) lies one of the most significant demonstrations of Jesus's identity and call to discipleship in all of Matthew. While there is much here to unpack (→Mark 4:35–41), we will restrict ourselves to two dimensions of the miracle.

First, the storm upon the Sea of Galilee symbolizes demonic opposition to Jesus and his followers. According to the OT, chaotic waters figuratively refer to God's enemies. For example, Psalm 74:13–14 reads, "It was you [the Lord] who split open the sea by your power; you broke *the heads of the monster in the waters*. It was you who crushed the heads of Leviathan and gave him as food to the creatures of the desert" (cf. Ezek. 32:2; Dan. 7:2, etc.). This explains why Matthew strongly ties the stilling of the storm to demonic activity in the immediate context.

Second, Jesus identifies himself with Yahweh in that he has come to judge the inimical forces of evil. Only the God of Israel possesses such an ability (e.g., Ps. 89:8–10). But this is not a general judgment; it is an eschatological one. His judgment upon Satan and his spiritual allies fulfills the prophetic expectation that the Lord would redeem Israel and vanquish her enemies in the "latter days" (e.g., Isa. 11:13; 29:5). All three Synoptics stress the storm's ferocity, but Matthew oddly describes the storm as a "quaking" or "shaking": "And behold, there arose a great *shaking* [*seismos*] on the sea" (8:24 AT). The term "shaking" occurs fourteen times in the NT for events such as the crucifixion (27:54), the resurrection (28:2), and Paul and Silas's jail break (Acts 16:26). The book of Revelation associates "shaking" with judgment (Rev. 6:12; 11:13; 16:18), perhaps explaining why Matthew employs the word: divine judgment is near. Notice *how* Jesus judges the onslaught of evil: "[He] rebuked the winds and the waves" (8:26). This is precisely how he exorcised the demons in the previous context: "He drove out the spirits *with a word*" (8:16).

The reaction of the disciples is rather predictable: "Lord, save us!" (8:25). This is the fifth use of the title "Lord" (*kyrios*) in chapter 8, a term that the Greek translations use to render Yahweh or Lord in the OT. What is stunning here is their plea for Jesus to "save" them. Matthew has already disclosed the primary aim of Jesus's ministry—to "save his people from their sins" (1:21). In judging the demons, Jesus does precisely that, yet the disciples sadly remain oblivious to it. He reclaims the created order from the curse of sin but in a profoundly more robust way than what the disciples expect.

The faithlessness of the disciples in 8:23–27 is starkly juxtaposed with the faithfulness of the centurion in 8:5–13. Like the disciples, the centurion acknowledges that Jesus is "Lord" (8:6, 8), but he, unlike the disciples, unswervingly trusts him (8:8–9). Jesus even states that he has "not found anyone in Israel with such great faith" (8:10). The disciples, though, are deemed men "of little faith" (8:26).

Chapter 8 finishes with the exorcism of two demoniacs in the "region of the Gadarenes," an area to the east and southeast that is associated with gentiles (// Mark 5:1–17 // Luke 8:26–37). Mark's and Luke's narratives focus on a single demoniac, whereas Matthew states that there were "two demon-possessed men" (8:28). Matthew's Gospel has a tendency to include pairs. Here we find two demoniacs, and later we will encounter two sets of two blind men (9:27; 20:30) and two donkeys (21:2). Why Matthew decides to include these pairs is unclear. Perhaps it entails the OT principle of two witnesses (Deut. 17:6–7; 19:15, 19).

Matthew compresses this event that occupies twenty verses in Mark into seven verses, focusing not so much on the perilous condition of the demoniac(s) as on Jesus's judgment upon his enemies (→Mark 5:1). Matthew uniquely adds that the demoniacs had prevented others from passing through that territory (8:28). Perhaps Matthew includes this phrase because it strikes at the heart of Jesus's purpose—the expansion of God's end-time presence on earth. According to 5:35, the earth is God's "footstool," where he intends to dwell and reign. Before Jesus's arrival, these demons inhibited the spread of God's glory.

The disciples' question at the end of the stilling of the storm—"What kind of man is this?" (8:27)—is ironically answered by the demons in 8:29: "What do you want with us, *Son of God*?" (cf. 14:33). Matthew applies the title "Son of God" to Jesus in 2:15 with reference to Jesus being God's true "son" in his flight to Egypt. Where Israel failed as God's "son" (Exod. 4:22), Jesus is deemed true Israel because he is God's faithful "son" (3:17). In the wilderness temptation, the title "Son of God" is twice found on the lips of the devil (4:3, 6). Jesus again retraces Israel's wilderness wanderings and expels God's enemies from the earth, just as Israel was to purge the idolatrous inhabitants of Canaan. Here in the exorcism, though, Matthew wants his readers to consider not just Jesus's faithful sonship but also his deity. Jesus is God's *unique* Son. This is why he is able to still the raging sea and expel the demons from the created order.

As in the earlier account of Jesus driving "out the spirits *with a word*" (8:16) and in his verbal rebuke of the storm (8:26), here Jesus simply commands the demons to "Go!" (8:32) into the pigs, where they flee into the sea and perish in the water (8:32). The effect of the exorcism becomes clear: the two men are restored, and the "whole town" now has access to that territory (8:34). God's kingdom is exploding, even among the gentiles.

Following King Jesus as the Life-Giving Son of God (9:1–34)

The Healing of the Paralytic and the Calling of Matthew (9:1–13)

The movement from Jesus's identity as the divine "Son of God" in 8:29 to the healing of the paralytic in 9:1–8 flows naturally (// Mark 2:3–12 // Luke 5:18–26). In both instances, Jesus performs what only God can do. Crossing the lake once more and heading northwest, Jesus returns to "his own town"—that is, Capernaum (see Mark 2:1). Soon word gets out that Jesus is back home, so a crowd gathers at a house and several men bring Jesus a paralytic. Whereas Mark and Luke disclose several details about the crowded home, Matthew gets right to the point: Jesus issues forgiveness of sins and then proceeds to heal the paralytic (9:2, 6).

When Jesus pronounces the forgiveness of sins, the Jewish leaders become enraged because Jesus is undercutting the temple cult and, more importantly, he is functioning as God himself. Only God possesses the authority to forgive sins (→Mark 2:6–7). According to 1:21, an angel tells Joseph that his son will bear the name "Jesus, because he will save his people from their sins." By healing the paralytic and announcing the forgiveness of the man's sins, he continues to fulfill this prophecy. But the account of the paralytic also looks forward to Jesus's work on the cross in that he forgives sins on the basis of his forthcoming atoning sacrifice. Matthew is the only evangelist to add that the crowd "praised God [the Father], who had given such authority [to forgive sins] to [Jesus]" (9:8). Though the statement is only one line, its wording highlights the complex and unique relationship that Jesus enjoys with his Father as the "sent" one (see 11:27; John 5).

Jesus appoints four individuals to be his disciples in 4:18–22, and now he adds a fifth: Matthew, the tax collector (// Mark 2:14–17 // Luke 5:27–32). Whereas Mark and Luke call the individual "Levi," the First Gospel uses the name "Matthew" (9:9). Jews often had two names (e.g., Simon and Peter [4:18]), so we ought to identify Matthew, the author of the First Gospel, with Levi. Tax collectors in the first century were not well liked, as they represented Rome's authority and were often unscrupulous in their dealings (→Luke 5:27–39).

What's significant about this account is Jesus's association with "many tax collectors and sinners" who dined with him at Matthew's house (9:10). Intimate fellowship with these unpopular and ritually unclean individuals provokes the Jewish leaders to ask the disciples, "Why does your teacher eat with tax collectors and sinners?" (9:11). Not even giving his disciples a chance to answer, Jesus responds with a direct assault against the leaders: "It is not the healthy [the Jewish leaders] who need a doctor, but the sick [the tax collectors and sinners]" (9:12). Climactically, Jesus then commands them to "learn what this means: 'I desire mercy, not sacrifice'" (9:13). Partially quoting Hosea 6:6, he strikes at the heart of the law: God is more concerned with inward, heartfelt obedience than external, legalistic rituals (cf. Mic. 6:6–8; 1 Sam. 15:22). What was true in the OT remains true in the NT. Further, now that Jesus is the true temple, and forgiveness is only available in him (1:21; 6:12; 9:2, 6), the Jewish leaders must repent and imitate the newly minted disciple, Matthew, by trusting in Jesus. The question remains: Will Matthew's audience imitate him and follow Jesus at all costs, or will they be content with vain religious externals?

New Wineskins and the In-Breaking of the New Age (9:14–26)

According to the OT, forgiveness of sin is a badge of the new age (e.g., Jer. 31:31–34), so Matthew's dual emphasis on forgiveness and the in-breaking of the new creation in 9:14–34 makes good sense. Jesus informs John's disciples that his disciples refrain from fasting because of the presence of the "bridegroom" and the arrival of "new wine" (9:15–17 // Mark 2:18–22 // Luke 5:33–39). Old Testament prophets list wine on the menu when metaphorically describing the great banquet at the end of history when God dwells with his people in the eternal new cosmos. Isaiah 25:6 states, for example, "On this mountain the LORD Almighty will prepare a feast of rich food for all peoples, a banquet of aged wine—the best of meats and the finest of wines" (cf. Jer. 31:12–14; Hosea 14:7; Joel 3:18; Amos 9:13–14). Jesus claims, then, that his ministry marks the new age of redemption.

The next several events in Matthew's narrative flow from this governing principle. The first passage zooms in on the synagogue leader's daughter and the woman with the issue of blood (9:18–26 // Mark 5:22–43 // Luke 8:41–56). All three evangelists sandwich the raising of the daughter of a leader (Mark and Luke identify him as "Jairus") around the healing of a ritually unclean woman, forcing the reader to interpret them together (→Mark 5:21–43). The main idea is that Jesus, the agent of the new creation and the ultimate purifying sacrifice, gives life to all who trust in him. He makes clean what is unclean: the dead girl (Num. 19:11) and the woman with the issue of blood (Lev. 15:19).

An Unexpected Messiah and the Hardening of the Jewish Leaders (9:27–34)

For all the extensive healings that we have come across in Matthew's narrative (4:23–25; 8:1–17; 9:1–8, 18–25), Matthew has omitted one thus far: the healing of the blind. All four Gospels mention Jesus healing the blind, but Matthew's and Mark's presentations of the blind contain additional layers of symbolism flowing through the main arteries of their narratives. Like Mark, Matthew delays to include the blind because of the symbolic significance of their healing (see Mark 8:22–26 for the first mention of the blind).

Here in 9:27–31, Jesus heals two blind men who clearly identify him as the Messiah ("Son of David" [cf. 1:1]), and immediately forbids them to disclose the matter to anyone. Why would Jesus command them to keep quiet? Does he not want others to spread the good news of the kingdom? Does not Jesus send out the disciples in the following section to do this very thing (9:35–10:42)? The answer lies in the *nature* of Jesus's messiahship. Indeed, he is the end-time Messiah and the "Son of David," but his ministry differs from the expectations of the two blind men (→Mark 4:1–41). Nestled in this narrative is the healing of a demon-possessed man, an action that irritates the Jewish leaders. They, too, cannot square Jesus's identity with their own expectations of the coming Messiah. These leaders suffer from their own kind of blindness. But, unlike the blind men, they do not seek "mercy," since they wrongly attribute Jesus's power to Satan (→12:22–37).

Appointing the Twelve Disciples (9:35–10:42)

The Need for a Faithful Shepherd (9:35–38)

Jesus's ministry in Galilee frames the appointment of the twelve disciples. Notice Jesus's extensive traveling and healing: "Jesus went through *all the towns and villages*, teaching in their synagogues, proclaiming the good news of the kingdom and healing *every disease and sickness*" (9:35). Matthew wants to convey the scope of Jesus's ministry. The next verse then indicates the result: "When he saw the crowds, he had compassion on them, because they were *harassed* [*eskylmenoi*] and *helpless* [*errimmenoi*], *like sheep without a shepherd*" (9:36). The voice of the two terms "harassed" and "helpless" (lit. "to throw down") is passive, and a careful reader is left with the question, *Who* is harassing and making them helpless? It may not be a coincidence that immediately preceding and following this event are references to demonic activity (9:34; 10:1). So the idea may be that the devil's minions have been "harassing" and "throwing down" God's people, and Jesus intends to restore and protect them.

The next line, "like sheep without a shepherd," alludes to Numbers 27, where Moses, after seeing the land of Canaan (27:12), pleads with God to "appoint someone over this community to go out and come in before them . . . so the Lord's people will not be like *sheep without a shepherd*" (27:16–17). Moses asks for another mediator, one who will faithfully rule on behalf of God and ensure the survival of the community. Joshua initially fulfills this expectation (27:18), but as the OT unfolds, we learn that all of Israel's leaders eventually fail. Only the coming Messiah would ultimately serve as God's faithful shepherd (2 Sam. 5:2; 1 Kings 22:17; Ezek. 34).

As the true and faithful Moses, Jesus fulfills these expectations by protecting the covenant community from the onslaught of demons, who have afflicted God's people since the fall. Like Moses, Jesus also recognizes the need for additional leadership: "The harvest is plentiful but the workers are few. Ask the Lord of the harvest, therefore, to send out workers into his harvest field" (9:37–38). These "workers" will become mini Moses figures and fulfill the OT prophecies by ensuring the safety and protection of the "field," or true Israel (cf. 10:6).

The Twelve Disciples as Faithful Shepherds (10:1–42)

We are more than a third through Matthew's narrative and we finally encounter the appointment of the Twelve, the second of five teaching blocks (cf. 5:1–7:29; 13:1–53; 18:1–35; 24:1–25:46). Matthew has delayed his account of the appointment of the Twelve in comparison to Mark's and Luke's narratives

(// Mark 3:13–19 // Luke 6:14–16). Why? Matthew's readers are probably to assume that the Twelve have been following much of Jesus's ministry up to this point. The appointment follows the Sermon on the Mount (chs. 5–7) and several episodes that demonstrate Jesus's unique identity as the Lord incarnate. Jesus breaks the mold of his followers' tightly held expectations; concerned about genuine discipleship, Matthew postpones this account so that the disciples have some sense of what they are signing up for when Jesus commissions them.

The twelve disciples, symbolizing the restored twelve tribes of Israel, are first and foremost appointed "to drive out impure spirits and to heal every disease and sickness" (10:1). This directive is precisely what Jesus accomplished in 9:32–36 where he expelled demons and healed "every disease and sickness." Since Jesus is the divine Son of God (1:1) and true and faithful Israel who has begun to vanquish the devil and redeem all of creation, he has "authority" to pass on to his disciples. The success of the disciples is inseparably fused with the success of Jesus. His victory is their victory. The appointment of the Twelve here in chapter 10 is reminiscent of the famous Great Commission in 28:18 but with a critical difference: "Jesus came to [the disciples] and said, '*All authority in heaven and on earth* has been given to me. Therefore, go and make disciples of all nations.'" In 28:18 we discern an *escalated* authority. Why the difference? Jesus has been enthroned at the Father's right hand as the Son of Man who has vanquished evil in his death and begun to rule over the cosmos in his resurrection. The authority that Jesus dispenses to the disciples in 10:1 is a foretaste of the authority that he will soon enjoy and confer upon his disciples in the Great Commission.

Jesus first tells the disciples where they are *not* to go: "Do not go among the Gentiles or enter any town of the Samaritans" (10:5). The point here is not that the gentiles or Samaritans are excluded from the kingdom but that ethnic Jews receive priority. This resonates quite well with the strong NT conviction that the apostles first proclaim the gospel to the Jews and then to the gentiles (e.g., Acts 1:8; Rom. 1:16; 2:9–10; 15:8–9). The disciples are to target initially the "lost sheep of Israel" (10:5–15) and *then* expand their mission to the surrounding nations (10:17–42). Israel's failure to fulfill this mission in the OT anticipates the success of true Israel in the NT.

In Matthew's account, the commissioning of the twelve disciples is accompanied with sobering expectations: "Be on your guard; you will be handed over to the local councils and be flogged in the synagogues. On my account you will be brought before governors and kings as witnesses to them and to the Gentiles. But when they arrest you, do not worry about what to say or how to say it. At that time you will be given what to say, for it will not be you speaking, but the Spirit of your Father speaking through you" (10:17–20

// Mark 13:9). Jesus assures the disciples that they will follow in his footsteps and eventually be rejected by their own people. Such rejection is deserving of God's end-time wrath—a fate even more terrible than the annihilation of Sodom and Gomorrah (10:15).

The disciples must gain comfort from knowing that the Spirit will give them insight and the right words to say to their captors (10:20; cf. John 15:26–27). The disciples will function as the mouthpiece of God to the world and, especially, to their adversaries. The disciples of Jesus will succeed in reaching the nations, yet their success comes with a steep price tag: rejection by their own Jewish community and the Roman Empire.

At the end of the commission, Jesus promises the disciples that they represent him in their ministry efforts, just as he represents the Father (10:40). The words of the disciples are the very words of Jesus, and the words of Jesus are the words of God. Verse 41 then discloses the operating principle: "Whoever welcomes a prophet as a prophet will receive a prophet's reward." Here the disciples are viewed as standing in the tradition of the OT prophets who herald God's message to the people (cf. 5:12). If their audience believes the message of the disciples, the audience "will receive . . . a reward" and inherit eternal life.

Galilee's Rejection of John and Jesus (11:1–30)

John the Baptist (11:1–19)

Jesus has finished informing the Twelve that they should expect nothing less than rejection—within and beyond the borders of Israel (10:14–20). Chapter 11 then transitions to John's imprisonment, the result of his faithful proclamation of God's prophetic message to Israel (// Luke 7:18–35). If John suffers because of his faithful ministry (4:12), how much more will the followers of Jesus suffer on account of their faithfulness to the message of the kingdom?

At the beginning of chapter 11, John dispatches his followers to Jesus to confirm that he is indeed "the one who is to come" (11:3). Jesus exceeds expectations, and even John is beginning to have his doubts. Jesus responds to the inquiry with language reminiscent of the prophet Isaiah: "The blind receive sight, the lame walk, those who have leprosy are cleansed, the deaf hear, the dead are raised, and the good news is proclaimed to the poor" (11:5). Jesus alludes to several passages in Isaiah: 26:19; 29:18–19; 35:5–6; 42:7, 18; and 61:1. The gist of these texts is that God will restore "blind" Israel so that she may grasp God's redemptive acts and experience his glory in the new creation, all of which will be accomplished through an end-time servant figure. Jesus claims that his ministry indeed fulfills Isaiah's promises.

The new creation has dawned, but John finds it hard to grasp that the new creation arrives *alongside* the end-time tribulation. The OT expected that the tribulation would first arrive, and *then* the new creation. Mysteriously, the kingdom and the tribulation now overlap (→13:11–52). Jesus unflinchingly demonstrates that he is Israel's Messiah, all the while insisting that suffering defines his ministry.

The narrative then shifts from Jesus informing John's disciples about his messiahship to Jesus addressing the crowd about his relationship to John (11:7). John the Baptist's identity comes into focus here in 11:7–19, where Matthew confronts his audience with two key principles of Jesus's ministry:

1. "Among those born of women there has not risen anyone greater than John the Baptist." (11:11a)
2. "Whoever is least in the kingdom of heaven is greater than he." (11:11b)

The first statement describes John's unparalleled career in announcing the coming Messiah. As great as Moses, Elijah, Elisha, Isaiah, Jeremiah, Zechariah, and other prophets were, they never prefaced the arrival of Israel's Messiah and the divine Son of God (11:10, quoting Mal. 3:1; →Mark 1:2). John stands at the precipice of a new stage in the history of redemption. He is depicted as a transitional figure of sorts, caught between the end of the old age and the beginning of the new. So as "great" as John is, he is never a full-blown citizen of the new age. This explains why the second statement claims that any participant in the end-time kingdom is "greater" than John the Baptist. Such teaching is difficult to grasp, explaining why Jesus punctuates it with the saying, "Whoever has ears, let them hear" (11:15; cf. 13:9, 43). Only those *within* the kingdom can comprehend it.

Matthew's narrative then explores the reason why so many within Israel, especially her leaders, remain calloused toward John and ultimately Jesus's ministry. Jesus compares "this generation" to a child's outdoor game: "We [John and Jesus] played the pipe for you [this generation], and you did not dance; we sang a dirge, and you did not mourn" (11:17; cf. 12:39–45; 16:4; 17:17; 23:36; 24:34). The point is that the Jewish leaders and unbelievers within Israel did not respond favorably to John and Jesus's kingdom message.

Judgment upon Unbelieving Cities (11:20–24)

The following section unpacks in more detail what Jesus means by "this generation" in 11:16 and why they will be judged (// Luke 10:13–15). *Because* Israel has by and large rejected John and Jesus (11:20), God will rain down his judgment upon her. Jesus identifies three cities in which "most of his miracles had been performed": Chorazin, Bethsaida, and Capernaum (11:21–23). Bethsaida and Capernaum are located on the northwest shore of the Sea of Galilee, whereas Chorazin is about two miles north of Capernaum. Up to this point in Matthew's narrative, Jesus's ministry has generally been confined to this broad region (cf. 8:28–34).

Jesus issues a series of "woes" against the three cities. Woe oracles in the OT are associated with assured judgment (e.g., Isa. 3:9, 11; Jer. 48:1; Ezek. 16:23). There's no escape (→23:13–38). These cities are privy to the miracles and sermons in which Jesus demonstrates his identity as the long-awaited Son of David and God incarnate. Instead of embracing him, "this generation" rejects him. Jesus goes on to compare these three cities with two notoriously wicked ones in the OT. Tyre, often paired with Sidon (15:21; Mark 3:8; 7:31; Luke 6:17), is the focus of several judgment oracles (Isa. 23; Jer. 25:21–38; Ezek. 27:1–28:26). Sodom hardly requires introduction as it is famously understood, even in our modern culture, as the epicenter of sexual perversion and wickedness (Gen. 18–19). Astoundingly, Jesus claims that Tyre, Sidon, and Sodom are better off than Chorazin, Bethsaida, and Capernaum, for they would have responded favorably to Jesus's ministry. Matthew's audience is left wondering about the future of Jesus's ministry. If Galilee has rejected Jesus, how will the capital city of Jerusalem respond to him? Will the nation as a whole reject her Messiah?

The Hidden Wisdom of God (11:25–30)

The last section of chapter 11 is a further explanation of *why* "this generation" has rejected Jesus (11:25–27). In a moving soliloquy, the spotlight shines on Jesus praising his Father for revealing the mystery of Jesus's identity and the nature of his kingdom to a privileged few (// Luke 10:21–22). The praise begins with Jesus identifying God as "Father, Lord of heaven and earth" (11:25). "Heaven" and "earth" are often paired in Matthew's Gospel, far surpassing Mark's and Luke's use of the two terms (5:18; 6:10; 16:19; 18:18–19; 24:30, 35; 28:18). We noted in 5:34–35 that God sovereignly rules from his invisible throne in "heaven," a rule that extends all the way to the "earth." Moreover, we argued that Matthew's language hints at God's larger program of expanding his heavenly rule on the earth through his Son so that the earth can ultimately be filled with the glory of God. Therefore, in describing his Father as the "Lord of heaven and earth," Jesus has in mind the establishment of the end-time kingdom. He is essentially claiming that the in-breaking of the eschatological kingdom differs from expectations, having been "hidden" from the "wise and learned" (i.e., the Jewish leaders and, by implication, the nation as a whole). Instead, the kingdom is "revealed" to "little children" (i.e., those who trust and follow Jesus). Though only a few verses, this paragraph brings some resolution to a difficult question: Why does Israel reject the very person she's waiting for? The audience must wait for the answer until chapter 13, where Matthew will take up this knotty issue once more.

After describing his unique, revelatory relationship with his Father (11:25–27), Jesus shifts his attention from the Father to those gathered around him: "Come to me, all you who are weary and burdened, and I will give you rest" (11:28). In a saying unique to Matthew's account, here we have one of the most poignant statements in the First Gospel. "Rest" in the OT and Second Temple Judaism is complex, ultimately bound up with Israel's land and God's presence among his people. If Israel obeys the law and functions as a light to the surrounding nations, then God promises to take up residence with them. He will be their God and they will be his people. Over time, Israel's call to Sabbath "rest" becomes a burden because of the sheer weight of legalism. When Jesus claims that he can give "rest," he makes at least two astounding claims: (1) according to the OT, only God is able to offer true "rest" to Israel (e.g., Lev. 25:2; 2 Sam. 7:11; 1 Kings 8:56), so Jesus is explicitly claiming to be God incarnate; and (2) Jesus is offering eschatological rest, a rest that was never achieved in the OT on account of Israel's disobedience (Ps. 95; Heb. 3:7–4:11). Jesus's rest entails intimate communion with God in the new creation. Since Jesus is "Immanuel" or "God with us" (1:23), he is able to give end-time rest to all those who trust in him.

Growing Conflict with the Jewish Leaders (12:1–50)

Jesus as Lord of the Sabbath (12:1–14)

With Jesus being identified as the true Sabbath "rest," the one offering that rest to all who follow him (11:28–30), the transition to him being the "Lord of the Sabbath" in the first section of chapter 12 is quite natural (// Mark 2:23–28 // Luke 6:1–5). The beginning of 12:1 forges a tight connection with the previous section—"*At that time* Jesus went through the grainfields on the Sabbath"—and Matthew is the only evangelist to make that connection (// Mark 2:23 // Luke 6:1). The Pharisees object to what they perceive to be a violation of the Sabbath: "His disciples were hungry and began to pick some heads of grain and eat them" (12:1). Hostility between Jesus and the Jewish leaders has been brewing (9:3, 11, 34), and it's just a matter of time before it spills over. Israel's leaders are proactively looking for concrete evidence to bring charges against Jesus (12:10).

Jesus responds to the accusation with the OT precedent of King David partaking of the showbread in the temple (→Mark 2:23–28). This OT precedent is prefaced with a not-so-subtle rebuke of the Jewish leaders by Jesus: "Haven't you read . . . ?" Of course they have! Variations of the clause "haven't you read" are found six times in Matthew's Gospel, underscoring the OT anticipation of the various dimensions of Jesus's ministry and the responsibility of the Jewish leaders to have grasped it (12:3, 5; 19:4; 21:16, 42; 22:31).

Jesus appeals to 1 Samuel 21:1–6, where the high priest grants King David access to the showbread because of David's status as a priest-king (→Luke 6:1–11). Jesus connects his ministry to David's in that he, too, should have authority over the Sabbath because he's *the* ultimate priest-king—Immanuel (1:23) and the descendant of David (1:1). As God in the flesh, Jesus is the true substance of Israel's physical temple. He has, to use John's language, "made his dwelling among us" (John 1:14), thus rendering the earthly temple obsolete. Matthew alone includes the critical line: "I [Jesus] tell you that something greater than the temple is here" (12:6). The Jewish leaders have failed to see Jesus as the true and ultimate temple of God who grants end-time Sabbath rest to his followers.

If Jesus presents himself as the "Lord of the Sabbath" (12:8) and the temple of God, then his audience must perceive him as the true source of holiness. Animal sacrifices are ultimately ineffective at purifying God's people, so Jesus will lay down his life as an atoning sacrifice to cleanse and redeem those who are unclean. This is precisely what we discover in the following account of Jesus healing the man with the shriveled hand (12:9–14). The miracle takes place in the synagogue, a public place of worship, on the Sabbath (12:9–10). According to Jewish oral tradition, breaking the Sabbath is permitted for life-threatening circumstances. For example, one often-cited passage from the Mishnah states, "And any matter of doubt as to danger to life overrides the prohibitions of the Sabbath" (m. Yoma 8.6). This man with the withered hand is not suffering from a life-threatening issue, but that is not the point in Jesus's eyes—he is still unwhole. So Jesus, as the Lord of the Sabbath and the true temple of God, restores his body. As expected, the Jewish leaders fail to see the true spiritual significance of Jesus's actions and soon plot "how they might kill" him (12:14).

Jesus as Isaiah's Suffering Servant (12:15–21)

While the narrator has dropped hints along the way that Jesus is destined to die (5:10–12; 10:24, 38–39), Jesus's death will now begin to take center stage.

Immediately following the Jewish leaders' decision to kill Jesus, Matthew cites several lines from Isaiah 42 in 12:18–21. According to Isaiah, an individual or "servant" will successfully and faithfully obey God and bear the guilt of Israel (Isa. 42:1–9; 49:1–13; 50:4–11; 52:13–53:12). Though Matthew only cites Isaiah 42:1–4, he most likely has *all* of the servant passages in mind, if not the entire section of Isaiah 40–66. Matthew's readers are to take comfort in knowing that Jesus's ministry is falling very much in line with the OT's expectations—even if he subverts the expectations of the religious leaders. Indeed, he is "fulfilling what was spoken through the prophet Isaiah" (12:17). Jesus will fulfill Isaiah's prophecies by dying on behalf of the "many" (Isa. 53:11–12) and becoming the catalyst of the new creation. His atoning death will lead to the restoration of God's people, including Jews and gentiles (Isa. 49:6). The Jewish leaders are convinced that they are protecting God's people from harm by killing Jesus. In their eyes, their zealous defense of God's law is righteous. In reality, though, they are scheming against Jesus, the truly righteous One.

Continued Blindness (12:22–50)

Ignorance toward Jesus's identity and mission persists throughout the remaining section of chapter 12. The first part focuses on the failure of the Jewish leaders (12:22–45 // Mark 3:23–27 // Luke 11:17–32), whereas the second part concerns the failure of Jesus's family (12:46–50 // Mark 3:31–35 // Luke 8:19–21). Both parties are guilty of not grasping Jesus's ministry in light of the OT, especially the book of Isaiah.

Jesus heals a blind and mute "demon-possessed man," prompting the crowd to respond, "Could this be the Son of David?" (12:22–23; cf. 1:1). While there may not be an obvious connection between healing, exorcisms, and the arrival of the Messiah, Isaiah 42:6–7 reads, "I will keep you [God's servant] . . . to open eyes that are *blind*, to free captives from *prison*, and to release from the *dungeon* those who sit in *darkness*." This promise, though figurative, is not a far cry from what we find here in 12:22. The healing of the blind and mute demoniac symbolizes Jesus's identity as Isaiah's servant figure, who restores those in spiritual exile and brings them to the promised land of the new creation. The point is inescapable: the Jewish leaders refuse to admit that Jesus is God's anointed Son (3:16–17; 12:18). In their eyes, Jesus is the "prince of demons" because of his unparalleled authority over the spiritual realm (12:24–25; cf. 9:34).

Jesus responds with a captivating illustration of a divided kingdom: "Every kingdom divided against itself will be ruined, and every city or household divided against itself will not stand" (12:25). Why would Jesus, if he is the "prince of demons," vanquish one of his own soldiers? Instead, Jesus expels demons "by the Spirit of God" because the "kingdom of God" has arrived (12:28). The proof is in the eschatological pudding. The end-time kingdom *must* be inaugurated because of Jesus's power over the demonic realm. Therefore, since Jesus is obviously the long-awaited Messiah, such cold rejection by the Jewish leaders ultimately stems from their wicked hearts (12:30–37).

The Jewish leaders' plea for a "sign" in the following section (12:38) is somewhat disingenuous because they have already concluded that Jesus is a fraud (12:24). They want a confirming or validating miracle that will remove all doubt as to Jesus's identity. The Jewish leaders "seek a heaven-sent spectacle (cf. 16:1, 'sign from heaven'), like the exodus 'signs' that forced the Hebrews to believe."[13] Jesus responds harshly by labeling them "a wicked and adulterous generation" (12:39). They are typologically like the first generation of Israelites, filled with idolatry (Deut. 32:20–21; Num. 14:27), and no sign will convince them to embrace God's redemption in his Son. Jesus will not give in to these demands for a sign since he, like Jonah, will be validated by emerging from the "heart of the earth" on the third day (12:40). Unlike the "men of Nineveh" who responded positively to God's messenger (Jon. 3:5), these Jewish leaders (and the majority of the Israelites) will remain calloused toward Jesus when he performs the consummate "sign of Jonah"—the resurrection (12:40; 16:4). Jesus also offers the "Queen of the South" as an example of receptivity to God's revelation because she responded positively to Solomon's unrivaled wisdom (1 Kings 10:1; 2 Chron. 9:1). She, too, will judge "this generation" (12:42).

In a single chapter, Matthew underscores Jesus's fulfillment of and superiority over one OT institution and two OT figures:

I tell you that something *greater than the temple* is here. (12:6)

And now something *greater than Jonah* is here. (12:41)

And now something *greater than Solomon* is here. (12:42)

If Jesus genuinely fulfills these OT types, then why do the Jewish leaders and his own family reject him? That looming question takes center stage in chapter 13.

---

13. Grant R. Osborne, *Matthew*, ZECNT (Grand Rapids: Zondervan, 2010), 485.

Parables of the Kingdom (13:1–52)

The Parable of the Sower and the Mysteries of the Kingdom (13:1–50)

Matthew's readers have been waiting some time for this third teaching section. The exposition of the nature of the kingdom in 13:1–52 is perhaps the most insightful explication of the kingdom and the nature of Jesus's messiahship in all of the NT (// Mark 4:1–20, 30–32 // Luke 8:4–15; 13:18–21).

5:1–7:29	Discourse 1: Living in the Kingdom (Sermon on the Mount)
10:5–11:1	Discourse 2: The Proclamation of the Kingdom
13:1–53	**Discourse 3: The Nature of the Kingdom**
18:1–19:1	Discourse 4: Relating to One Another within the Kingdom
24:1–25:46	Discourse 5: The Overthrow of the Physical Temple and the Emergence of the New Temple (Olivet Discourse)

Chapter 13 opens with a strong connection to the preceding material: "*That same day* Jesus went out of the house and sat by the lake" (13:1). Matthew ties the unbelief of Jesus's family (12:46–50) to the section on the kingdom of God so that the reader can understand *why* so many are rejecting the very one for whom they are waiting. Three of the teaching discourses are prefaced with Jesus first sitting and then teaching (5:1; 13:1; 24:3)—a unique element to Matthew's Gospel. Perhaps this literary feature highlights Jesus as an end-time Moses figure whose teaching represents a climactic form of revelation (cf. 23:2).

The first parable, the parable of the sower (or the parable of the seeds), is given in 13:3–9 and then interpreted in 13:18–23. Sandwiched between the parable and its interpretation is an explanation of parables in general. The disciples want to know why so much of Jesus's teaching (and action) is filled with parables (13:10). The reason lies in the condition of the human heart, for parables have a softening/hardening effect upon the hearer. Parables simultaneously reveal and conceal. God will, in fulfillment of Isaiah's prophecy, further harden those who remain recalcitrant to divine revelation on account of their idolatry (13:13–15), whereas he will soften those who accept Jesus's message. The prophet Isaiah predicted hundreds of years earlier that the nation of Israel would be hardened toward God's redemption because of their wicked idolatry. Instead of clinging to the one true God, they worship and adore their idols—images that are blind, deaf, and dumb (Isa. 1:29–30; 6:9–10). In turn, God promises to transform the idolatrous nation into the very idols she worships! Israel will become blind, deaf, and dumb (→Mark 4:12). While Mark says that the parables are given "so that" unbelievers will be *further* hardened (Mark 4:12), Matthew states that Jesus uses parables because some within Israel are *presently* hardened (13:13). These

46

two perspectives are not incompatible with one another; Matthew is simply underscoring the *present* state of affairs. In any case, Matthew explicitly claims that Jesus's parables fulfill the "prophecy of Isaiah" (13:14).

What is implicit in Mark is made explicit in Matthew. Isaiah's prophecy continues to be fulfilled along the lines of typology and verbal fulfillment (→Mark 4:12). All those who stand in opposition to Jesus, especially the Jewish leaders, remain in continuity with their wicked ancestors who lived during Isaiah's prophetic ministry. Instead of trusting in God's message of salvation, Israel has rejected Jesus by and large. They have clung to human tradition rather than God himself. This is the general point of the parable of the sower in 13:3–9. Only those who persevere in their faith will be granted access into the kingdom.

After Jesus outlines the parable of the sower (13:1–10), he informs his disciples that God graciously revealed the "mysteries of the kingdom" to them (13:11 AT). The phrase "mysteries of the kingdom" captures the First Evangelist's description of the kingdom in his Gospel and the descriptions found in the Synoptics at large (Matt. 13:11 // Mark 4:11 // Luke 8:10). The term "mystery" (*mystērion*) finds its point of origin in the book of Daniel, particularly chapters 2 and 4. There, mystery constitutes an eschatological revelation that God previously hid but later revealed. God divulges this revelation in two stages—an initial revelation and then a subsequent interpretive revelation. According to Daniel, the content of the mystery entails God's end-time judgment upon the rebellious nations and the establishment of the eternal kingdom (Dan. 2:29–47; cf. 7:1–27). New Testament writers employ the term to refer to revelation that contains new and surprising elements (e.g., Rom. 11:25; 16:25; 1 Cor. 2:7; 15:51; Eph. 3:3–4). God largely hid certain doctrines from his covenant community in the OT, but he has now revealed them in the NT. When Jesus asserts, then, that God has revealed to the disciples the "mysteries of the kingdom," he means that they stand at a critical point in the history of redemption. They are about to learn certain aspects of the eternal kingdom that God did not fully disclose in the OT.

Chapter 13 includes seven parables, each underscoring a unique dimension of the in-breaking of the nature of the kingdom. Notice how the last six parables all begin with the key phrase "the kingdom of heaven is *like*" (13:24, 31, 33, 44, 45, 47). Further, the material contained here in chapter 13 is more comprehensive than the parallel accounts in Mark 4 and Luke 8:

Parable	Meaning
Parable of the sower (13:3–9, 18–23)	The nature of genuine faith
Parable of the weeds (13:24–30, 37–43)	The mysterious nature of the overlap of the ages

Parable	Meaning
Parable of the mustard seed (13:31-32)	The slow growth of the inaugurated kingdom yet its eventual domination
Parable of the yeast (13:33)	The slow growth of the inaugurated kingdom
Parable of hidden treasure (13:44)	The genuine fulfillment of OT prophecies related to the kingdom
Parable of the pearl (13:45-46)	The genuine fulfillment of OT prophecies related to the kingdom
Parable of the net (13:47-50)	The mysterious nature of the overlap of the ages

The first parable, the parable of the seeds (13:3–9), and the second parable, the parable of the weeds (13:24–30), are the only two parables in Matthew's Gospel that are explicitly interpreted (13:18–23, 37–43). In mediating and interpreting end-time revelation, Jesus may be consciously in step with the prophet Daniel, who also received and interpreted eschatological revelations or "mysteries" (Dan. 2, 4, 7, 8, 10–12). In addition, both parables are interrupted by intervening material. Matthew probably wants his audience to pay close attention to these two parables, as they are critical for a right understanding of the kingdom.

These seven parables communicate three salient principles: (1) The kingdom Jesus inaugurates generally differs from OT expectations. A critical tenet of the prophesied latter-day kingdom is the ultimate destruction of unrighteousness and foreign oppression immediately preceding the kingdom's establishment (e.g., Dan. 2:44; Pss. Sol. 17:24). But, paradoxically, Jesus teaches that two groups of people coexist simultaneously: those who belong to the kingdom and those who do not. The people of the old age and the citizens of the new age *overlap*. (2) The fulfillment of the end-time kingdom is *slow* but steady. While the OT generally predicts that the kingdom would arrive suddenly and all at once, Jesus claims that the kingdom comes gradually. The kingdom has been inaugurated and will continue to grow, but it remains to be consummately fulfilled. (3) The arrival of the kingdom, though different from expectations, remains a *genuine* fulfillment of OT prophecy.

At the end of the chapter, we get a fitting appraisal of Jesus's teaching: "Therefore every teacher of the law who has become a disciple in the kingdom of heaven is like the owner of a house who brings out of his storeroom *new treasures as well as old*" (13:52). Here the kingdom is likened unto a "teacher of the law" or a scribe who furnishes "new treasures as well as old." Jesus's teaching concerning the kingdom involves both "new" and "old" insights. His teaching stands in both continuity and discontinuity with the OT. The continuity of Jesus's teaching is that the unexpected, already-not-yet kingdom truly fulfills OT prophecies concerning the kingdom (Gen. 49; Num. 24; Dan. 2; Matt. 5:17). The kingdom has arrived! Yet, on the other hand, the fullness of the kingdom remains a future reality.

Comprehension of the Mysteries of the Kingdom (13:51–52)

One of Matthew's contributions to our understanding of the disciples is his insistence that the disciples have, at least on some level, grasped Jesus's identity and his teaching on the kingdom. Mark's Jesus, though, remains quite enigmatic at times, which explains why the disciples are often perplexed. At the end of the discourse, Jesus asks the disciples, "*Have you understood [synēkate]* all these things? . . . 'Yes,' they replied" (13:51). The wording here is quite similar to what we find in Daniel 11 and 12 concerning the "wise ones" who grasp end-time revelation concerning the establishment of God's eternal kingdom (Dan. 11:35 [LXX-OG]; 12:3 [LXX-OG]; 12:10 [LXX-Theo.]). Though the word group for "understanding" (*syniēmi*) is relatively common in the NT, in Matthew this word takes on special meaning in several key verses, especially 13:13–15, 19, 23, 51, and 15:10. Jesus's disciples—the true scribes—are beginning to have "insight" into the end-time events predicted by Daniel that are beginning to be fulfilled in their midst. Such a positive statement stands in stark contrast to Matthew's evaluation of Israel's "teachers of the law," who have rejected God's revelation in Jesus and "failed to rightly interpret the eschatological fulfillment of Scripture and recognize Jesus's messianic identity and authority" (see 23:1–39).[14]

Rejection and Revelation (13:53–14:36)

Rejection at Home (13:53–58)

Matthew is the only evangelist to place Jesus's rejection in his hometown immediately following the parables of the kingdom (13:53–58 // Mark 6:1–6 // Luke 4:14–30). In doing so, he sets the disciples in sharp relief to Jesus's longtime friends, who ultimately fail to understand his teaching. Whereas the disciples are beginning to grasp the nature of the kingdom (13:51), the Nazarenes don't "because of their lack of faith" (13:58). They, too, are fulfilling Isaiah's prophecy of "hearing but never understanding" (13:14, quoting Isa. 6:9). Jesus's friends from Nazareth, while they do perceive his unique teaching and "miraculous powers," never truly follow him.

Those in Nazareth are "offended" or scandalized as a result of Jesus's display of miracles (13:57; cf. 11:6). That is, miracles had a hardening effect

14. G. Thellman, "Scribes," *DJG*, 844.

upon the town of Nazareth. Like his parables, Jesus's miracles are laced with symbolism, either softening or hardening hearts. We have seen several examples of miracles in Matthew's Gospel where the audience is receptive to Jesus's identity (e.g., 4:23–25; 9:8), but there are other examples of those who reject him despite witnessing his divine power (e.g., 11:20–23). What separates the two groups? Faith in Jesus. God's grace warms the hearts of individuals to perceive Jesus's true identity and to trust in him (e.g., 8:10; 9:2, 22, 28, 29; 15:28).

The list of those who have rejected Jesus is growing: Herod the Great (2:3), the Pharisees (3:7; 9:34; 12:24, 38), the Sadducees (3:7), "teachers of the law" or the scribes (9:3), the cities of Chorazin, Bethsaida, and Capernaum (11:21–23), Jesus's family (12:46–50), and, finally, Nazareth (13:53–58). Such rejection, as devastating as it may be, is not entirely unexpected: "A prophet is not without honor except in his own town and in his own home" (13:57). The OT, as Jesus explains in Luke's version of this event, is filled with a long line of prophets who are rejected by their own (cf. Luke 4:25–27).

Herod's Rejection of John the Baptist (14:1–12)

The walls are closing in and Jewish hostility toward the righteous is growing. Matthew is the only evangelist to wed Jesus's rejection at Nazareth (13:53–58) with John the Baptist's martyrdom at the hands of Herod (14:1–12 // Mark 6:14–29 // Luke 9:7–9). The narrator wants his audience to align these characters so that Jesus's death will, like John's, be ignominious and at the hands of the Jewish authorities. Jesus's own friends reject him, and the political authorities reject John. Both figures are considered "prophets" (13:57; 14:5) who have "miraculous powers" (13:54; 14:2; →Mark 6:14–29).

Matthew refers to Herod using his official name, "Herod the tetrarch" (14:1). He, also known as Herod Antipas, is the son of Herod the Great. Rome divided Herod the Great's territory between his three sons, Herod Antipas, Archelaus, and Philip. Herod Antipas reigned for nearly forty years and managed to accomplish a great deal politically. He divorced his wife so that he could marry his half-brother's wife, Herodias. John the Baptist had objected to this illicit marriage, provoking Herod to imprison him, leading eventually to his death (14:3–12).

The Feeding of the Five Thousand (14:13–21)

Upon hearing the news about John the Baptist, Jesus immediately "withdraws" to a "solitary place" by boat (14:13). Is Jesus withdrawing out of fear of

Herod? Is he afraid for his life? The word here for "withdraw" (*anechōrēsen*) is found fourteen times in the NT, ten of which occur in Matthew. The word is associated with Jesus fleeing to Egypt with his parents (2:12–14), the death of John the Baptist (4:12), and the Jewish leaders' plot to kill Jesus (12:15). Perhaps the word carries symbolic overtones, too, in that it is the opposite of the paradigmatic 1:23, where the angel tells Joseph that Jesus will be "Immanuel" because he is "God with us." If Jesus's presence is associated with God's glory, then perhaps the lack of Jesus's presence is an expression of divine judgment, much like the glory of the Lord departing from the temple in Jerusalem in the days of Eli. He is now Ichabod (see 1 Sam. 4:21) because he "withdraws" his glory from Nazareth. But if Nazareth is a ghost town of glory, then the five thousand assembled are the temple.

The feeding of the five thousand, the only miracle repeated in all four Gospels (Matt. 14:13–21 // Mark 6:33–44 // Luke 9:10–17 // John 6:5–13), is fraught with redemptive-historical significance. When we read this event in light of Israel's wilderness wandering on their journey to Sinai and God's gracious provision of manna (Exod. 16), we discover that Jesus is the Lord incarnate who gives his presence as true and ultimate nourishment to those who follow him (→Mark 6:32–44). Matthew depicts Jesus as the Davidic King who has "compassion" upon his flock and (re)gathers them as the true end-time people of God (14:14; cf. 1:1; 9:36; 2 Sam. 5:2; 1 Kings 22:17; Ezek. 34). The meal itself anticipates the Passover meal in 26:26, where Jesus will also give thanks and break bread with his disciples, an act that prefigures his death as an atoning sacrifice. The Lord incarnate who dwells with true Israel in the feeding of the five thousand will ultimately lay down his life for them as a sacrifice. He is the Lord of Israel, her shepherd, *and* the sacrificial lamb.

Walking on the Water (14:22–36)

Following the feeding of the five thousand, Jesus instructs his disciples to head toward "the other side" of the Sea of Galilee (14:22), likely a reference to the eastern side of the lake, in what constitutes a third lake crossing (cf. 8:18; 9:1). In one of the most theologically pregnant passages in all of Matthew, chapter 14 ends with Jesus walking on the water to save the disciples (// Mark 6:45–56 // John 6:16–21). In taking inventory of the OT allusions, we find that Matthew again presents Jesus as Yahweh in the flesh (14:25, cf. Job 9:8; Matt. 14:27, cf. Exod. 3:13–14; →Mark 6:45–52). For example, Peter's use of "Lord" (*kyrios*) in 14:28 and 30 is noteworthy, evoking the eminent title "Lord" in the OT (cf. 4:7, 10; 7:21–22; 8:2, 6, 8; 9:28; 12:8).

Not found in Mark's narrative, a remarkable exchange between Peter and Jesus appears in Matthew's episode, wherein Peter attempts to walk on the water (14:28–31; cf. John 6:16–24). Though Peter has been named three times prior in the narrative (4:18; 8:14; 10:2), this is the first time we see him in action. Matthew invites his audience to read the stilling of the storm with this account of Jesus walking on the water, as the parallels between the two are striking:

Stilling of the Storm (8:23-27)	Jesus Walking on the Water (14:22-33)
Takes place on the Sea of Galilee (8:23)	Takes place on the Sea of Galilee (14:22)
A storm or "quaking" occurs on the water (8:24)	The disciples' boat was "buffeted by the waves because the wind was against it" (14:24)
The disciples are called "you of little faith" (8:26)	Peter is called "you of little faith" (14:31)
Jesus asks the disciples why they are "afraid" (8:26)	Jesus commands Peter to not be "afraid" (14:27)
The disciples respond to the miracle with a question: "What kind of man is this?" (8:27)	The disciples recognize who Jesus is by worshiping him and confessing that he is the "Son of God" (14:33)

Two observations are in order: (1) Peter's failure provokes Jesus to "save" him from the chaotic waters—that is, the demonic forces (→8:24). A thoughtful reader will immediately recollect the angel's promise that Jesus will "save his people from their sins" (1:21). In delivering Peter from the forces of evil, Jesus tangibly demonstrates that he has indeed come to rescue humanity from their plight. (2) The effect of this deliverance is recognition of who Jesus truly is. The stilling of the storm ends with a question, "What kind of man is this?" (8:27), whereas this event ends with the disciples answering their original question: "Truly you are the Son of God" (14:33; cf. 8:29). The disciples bow down before Jesus and worship him, an act that unequivocally demonstrates Jesus's divinity (cf. 4:10; 28:9, 17). We find traces of the same pattern at the end of Matthew's Gospel, where the disciples doubt yet worship (28:17).

Chapter 14 ends on a high note as they arrive in Gennesaret, an area to the south of Capernaum. Though they intended to arrive on the eastern side of the lake (14:22), the raging storm apparently blew them back to the northwest side. At the end of chapter, Jesus manifests his miraculous power by healing a great number of people (14:34–36). The God who delivers Peter from the clutches of the evil one is the same God who heals "the sick."

The End-Time Restoration of the Gentiles (15:1–39)

Eating with Unwashed Hands (15:1–20)

The Jewish leaders are not finished with Jesus (// Mark 7:1–23). They pursue him "from Jerusalem" (15:1). As the narrative progresses, the term "Jerusalem" becomes all the more ominous. The word is found five more times, and each occurs in the context of suffering and death (16:21; 20:17–18; 21:1, 10). The city that should embrace her Messiah will be the city that horrifically crucifies him. Because the disciples "don't wash their hands before they eat," the leaders ask Jesus, "Why do your disciples *break* the tradition of the elders?" (15:2). Fundamental to the oral tradition of first-century Judaism is ritual purity. To eat without first washing one's hands was to defile oneself.[15] So the Jewish leaders fault Jesus's disciples for not maintaining the oral "tradition of the elders."

Jesus responds with a question of his own, raising the stakes: "Why do you *break* the command of God for the sake of tradition?" (15:3). He then quotes the OT twice: Exodus 20:12 (// Deut. 5:16) and Exodus 21:17 (// Lev. 20:9). These OT passages command the Israelites to maintain fidelity to their parents, but within Jewish oral tradition there existed a legal loophole that could be exploited in favor of the children. Instead of the children using their possessions to take care of their parents, they could declare such items "devoted to God" (15:5). They could swear an oath that these possessions belong to God and him alone, thereby removing the items from the class of possessions that ought to be used in honoring one's parents.[16] Jesus pits the OT *against* the tradition of first-century Judaism. The OT is deemed the "word of God," whereas the Jewish leaders are embracing human "tradition" (15:6).

The Jewish leaders are "hypocrites" in that their devotion to God is only external. They have, as Jesus points out, fulfilled the words of Isaiah 29:13: "These people honor me with their lips, but their hearts are far from me. They worship me in vain; their teachings are merely human rules" (15:8–9). Jesus links, perhaps typologically, the idolatrous Israelites in Isaiah's day with the Jewish leaders in Jesus's day. Human religiosity is at the expense of hostility and rejection of God's plan of redemption. As a result, God promises to confound the "wisdom" of Israel's leaders in the eighth century: "Once more I will astound these people with wonder upon wonder; the wisdom of the

---

15. See D. A. Carson, "Matthew," in *Matthew–Mark*, vol. 9 of *Expositor's Bible Commentary*, rev. ed., ed. Tremper Longman III and David E. Garland (Grand Rapids: Zondervan, 2010), 397.

16. For example, the tractate Nedarim in the Mishnah contains a thorough discussion of acceptable and unacceptable oaths.

wise will perish, the intelligence of the intelligent will vanish" (Isa. 29:14; cf. 1 Cor. 1:19). Matthew implicitly claims that God has done so in the person of Jesus. So when Jesus interacts with and debates the Jewish leaders throughout his ministry and especially in the remaining portion of the narrative (16:1–4; 19:3–12; 21:23–46; 23:1–39), Matthew wants his readers to view these interactions through the lens of God's utter defeat of hubris and false pretense.

The discussion ends with Jesus explaining what *genuine* defilement looks like. In contrast to the Jewish leaders, who regarded unclean hands as ritual defilement, Jesus argues that true defilement stems from an unclean heart. Jesus's teaching on the matter is difficult for his audience to grasp, and we can observe three distinct parties in this passage: the Jewish leaders (15:1–9), the "crowd" (15:10–11), and the disciples (15:12–20). Each comprehends the teaching in varying degrees. Jesus makes no attempt to instruct the Jewish leaders on the nature of true defilement, but he does so with the crowd and the disciples. He tells the crowd that true defilement originates from the heart and not from food (15:10–11). The disciples receive the most explanation (cf. 13:16–51). The Jewish leaders argue for ritual uncleanness on the basis of externals, whereas Jesus states that true uncleanness originates from within. With the coming of Jesus, we learn the true depths of sin and our inability to cleanse ourselves. Such an act of purification can only be found on the cross.

The Faith of a Canaanite Woman (15:21–28)

Matthew narrates how Jesus left "that place" (i.e., Gennesaret; 14:34) to go to the "region of Tyre and Sidon" (15:21). Again, Jesus "withdrew" from the presence of the Jewish leaders, removing his restorative presence from their midst (→14:13) and headed toward Tyre and Sidon, a largely gentile territory. The discussion of ritual purity in the context (15:1–20) and this episode with the Canaanite woman both turn on Jesus's identity as the true temple (// Mark 7:24–30). With his coming, he determines who is clean and unclean. Since food does not cause ritual impurity in the new age, a key Israelite plank of ethnic distinction has now been removed, paving the way for gentiles to become full-blown participants in the covenant community.

Matthew labels the individual a "Canaanite woman" (15:22). This is the only occurrence of the term "Canaanite" (*Chananaios*) in the entire NT, likely carrying symbolic weight. Matthew's emphasis on Jesus as an end-time Joshua figure who eradicates the land of everything unclean fits well with what we discover in this episode (e.g., 1:21; 4:1–11). Here we have a foreigner in the land, a Canaanite (!) whom we expect to be expelled. But Jesus, the messianic "Son of David" (15:22), expels the true foreigner: the demon (15:28).

In contrast to the earlier account of the disciples, who have "little faith" (8:26; 14:31), this woman possesses "great faith" (15:28; cf. 8:10). In addition, this *Canaanite* stands in stark contrast to the *Jewish* leaders who pride themselves on their Jewish identity and inheritance of the land. Jesus reverses the status of both parties: the Canaanite woman inherits the new creation, and the Jewish leaders have been banned from it. One's allegiance to Jesus is the only determining factor.

The Feeding of the Four Thousand (15:29–39)

The status of gentiles remains uppermost in Matthew's narrative as he recounts the feeding of the four thousand in the following section (15:29–39). In Mark's account, Jesus and the disciples travel from Tyre and Sidon to the Decapolis, where he heals a deaf and mute man and then feeds the four thousand (Mark 7:31–8:10). Matthew's account probably should be understood along the same lines, meaning the feeding of the four thousand likely took place in a gentile region.

Matthew first draws the readers' attention to Jesus once again ascending a "mountainside," where he will heal and feed the "great crowds" (15:29–30). By reporting that Jesus positioned himself on a mountain, the evangelist depicts Jesus as Yahweh incarnate dwelling with his people (→ 5:1). Here we have gentiles assembled at a mountain, seeking the Lord's favor in healing. Several prominent passages from Isaiah may be in mind on a conceptual level. Isaiah predicts, for example, that in the "last days" the nations will stream to the "mountain of the LORD's temple," where they will inherit salvation and learn the law of God (Isa. 2:2–5 // Mic. 4:1–4). At the end of Isaiah, too, the prophet predicts that the nations will, at the very end of history, bring their "wealth" and "riches" to Israel (Isa. 60:5). Could it be that Matthew wants his readers to see these passages as initially fulfilled in the feeding of the four thousand? Instead of bringing their "wealth," these gentiles present the sick by laying "them at his [Jesus's] feet" (15:30; cf. 2:11).

When Jesus heals them, the crowd responds with effusive "praise" to the "God of Israel" (15:31; cf. Isa. 29:23). Earlier, Jesus healed a paralytic, resulting in a Jewish crowd "praising God" (9:8). But here, the gentiles confess that God is the Lord of "Israel," demonstrating that they now recognize their status as end-time, spiritual Israelites. The feeding of the four thousand (15:32–39) stands very much in line with the feeding of the five thousand (14:13–21; →Mark 8:1–10). The key difference lies in the audience. In the feeding of the five thousand, Jesus demonstrated his identity as Israel's God, who nourishes the Jewish people with his presence; here, his life-giving presence dwells with gentiles. Immanuel has come to the nations!

The Heresy of the Jewish Leaders and the Truthful Confession of Peter (16:1–28)

Jewish Leaders Test Jesus (16:1–4)

In the previous section, Jesus and the disciples venture to Magadan, a location unknown to us (15:39), and Matthew may want us to locate our present passage there. In any case, what sets this interaction in 16:1–4 (// Luke 12:54–56) apart from Jesus's previous interactions with the Jewish leaders is his insistence that they, despite being experts in the OT, "cannot interpret the signs of the times" (16:3). That is, they are unable to grasp Jesus's identity as the end-time Messiah and the Son of David (1:1). The Pharisees and Sadducees approach Jesus in order to "test" (*peirazontes*) him (16:1). Matthew deploys this term in the wilderness temptation (4:1, 3), so he may want his audience to view this event as an extension of the devil's trickery. Though he has lost the cosmic battle and D-Day is over, the devil still inspires the false teachers to lure people to destruction (cf. 19:3; 22:18, 35; 2 Thess. 2:7; 1 John 2:18).

The Jewish leaders ask Jesus to validate his identity, but Jesus peels away the veneer of religiosity. He states that the Jewish leaders, though able to forecast the weather, are unable to "interpret the signs of the times" (16:3). In some sense, this is a wonderful summary of Jesus's entire public ministry. When he performs "signs"—namely, speaking in parables and performing miracles—those who are spiritually attuned (e.g., the Canaanite woman) see Jesus for who he truly is, whereas those who are hardened as a result of their spiritual idolatry (e.g., the Jewish leaders) are unable to do so. The phrase "a wicked and adulterous generation" resonates with a few OT texts that depict Israel in a state of idolatry, suggesting that the Pharisees and Sadducees are, perhaps typologically, following suit (16:4; Num. 32:13; Hosea 3:1).

The False Teaching of the Jewish Leaders (16:5–12)

Leaving Magadan, they head "across the lake" (16:5), the fourth crossing thus far (cf. 8:18; 9:1; 14:22). Matthew's odd note that the disciples "forgot to take bread" sets up the entire discussion about the harmful influence of the Jewish leaders. He frames the account of 16:5–12 around the "yeast of the Pharisees and Sadducees" (16:6, 12), so we must understand the entire discussion in 16:5–12 in light of the false teaching of the Jewish leaders.

Jesus warns his disciples, "Be careful" and "Be on your guard" (16:6). The latter term, "be on your guard" (*prosechete*), is often found in the context of false teaching throughout the NT (e.g., Acts 20:28; 1 Tim. 1:4; 4:1; Titus 1:14; Heb. 2:1). The term was even used in 7:15 when Jesus warns his disciples to "*watch out* for false prophets." At the end of our passage, Matthew adds, "He [Jesus] was not telling them to guard against the yeast used in bread, but against *the teaching* of the Pharisees and Sadducees" (16:12). What sort of false teaching is Jesus referring to? In the immediate context, Jesus accuses the disciples of misunderstanding the redemptive-historical significance of the feeding of the five thousand and four thousand (14:13–21; 15:29–39). In both accounts, Jesus is the true "bread," who nourishes his people with his life-giving presence. He is the one who will bring about the final Passover celebration, wherein God will decisively redeem his people through Jesus (→Mark 6:30–44). The Jewish leaders have consistently resisted identifying Jesus as the divine Son of God and the legitimate heir of David's throne (1:1), so Jesus commands the disciples to resist all forms of deception (note the three imperatives in 16:6, 11).

Peter's Confession and Jesus's Prediction of Death (16:13–28)

After arriving at Caesarea Philippi, Jesus pointedly asks the disciples, "Who do people say the Son of Man is?" (16:13 // Mark 8:27–29 // Luke 9:18–20). We are a little more than halfway through Matthew's narrative, and the disciples have experienced an incredible amount of Jesus's ministry. The disciples quickly reply, "Some say John the Baptist; others say Elijah, and still others, Jeremiah or one of the prophets" (16:14). In some sense, these suggestions are not altogether incorrect—Jesus is certainly aligned with OT prophets (11:9, 14; 12:39; 13:57; 14:2; 21:11). But Jesus is more than a prophet, as Matthew's narrative has borne out. Remember, according to 1:1, Matthew is presenting Jesus of Nazareth as *the* "son of David" (i.e., the Messiah) and *the* "son of Abraham" (i.e., true Israel). More than a human, Jesus is also identified with Israel's eternal Lord.

Jesus will not leave the matter alone, pressing further: "But what about you [disciples]? . . . Who do you say I am?" (16:15). Jesus wants to know if his *disciples* are grasping the significance of his ministry, not the crowds. Peter pipes up and confesses, "You are the Messiah, the Son of the living God" (16:16). Peter is quite right in acknowledging that Jesus is the long-awaited Messiah (→Mark 8:29). In Mark's account, Peter states, "You are the Messiah" (Mark 8:29), and in Luke's account we read, "God's Messiah" (Luke 9:20); but here in 16:16, the confession also includes a second statement: "Son of the living God."

The title "Son of God" occurs at several critical junctures in Matthew on the lips of a wide variety of speakers:

Devil	"If you are the Son of God" (4:3, 6)
Two demoniacs	"What do you want with us, Son of God?" (8:29)
Disciples	"Truly you are the Son of God" (14:33)
Peter	"You are . . . the Son of the living God" (16:16)
High priest	"Tell us if you are the Messiah, the Son of God" (26:63)
Thieves/rebels on the cross	"Come down from the cross, if you are the Son of God" (27:40)
Jewish leaders	"Let God rescue him . . . for he said, 'I am the Son of God'" (27:43)
Centurion	"Surely he was the Son of God!" (27:54)

Certainly, the OT viewed the coming Messiah as God's "son" (2 Sam. 7:14; Ps. 2), but the question is whether or not that is all Peter has in mind. Since the phrase "Son of God" is pregnant with meaning, possessing overtones of divine identity (4:3, 6; 14:33; 27:43, 54), it seems that Peter is beginning to comprehend that Jesus is the Messiah *and* the divine Son of God. The disciples have been privy to several exceptional events that demonstrated his claim to be God in the flesh (e.g., the stilling of the storm [8:23–27]; the exorcism of the two demoniacs [8:28–34]; Jesus walking on water [14:22–33]), so it makes sense for Peter to affirm it here. Though he probably doesn't understand what the title entails fully at this point in the narrative, he will after Jesus's death and resurrection.

The next verse explains the basis for the confession: it was revealed "by my [Jesus's] Father in heaven" (16:17). In other words, God ultimately grants Peter the proper insight into Jesus's identity. Indeed, he "revealed" it (cf. 10:26; 11:25). Peter did not and cannot figure it out on his own. This is a startling comment, because Matthew has been at pains to demonstrate that Jesus is the fulfillment of the OT; it should have been evident that Jesus is the Messiah and the divine Son of God from a careful reading of Israel's Scriptures. But a true grasp of Jesus's identity is ultimately a divine revelation. God's revelation to Peter is not at odds with the OT; rather, it fulfills it! Just as the nature of the kingdom is a revealed mystery (13:11), so also is Jesus's identity. In other words, one can grasp Jesus's true identity only by God's gracious and special revelation, an unveiling that is derived from the Scriptures (→Luke 24:13–35).

As a result of Peter's confession, Jesus promises that he is "blessed" (see 5:3–12) and that "on this rock [Peter]" Jesus will "build" his "church" (16:18). The amount of scholarly debate on this critical text is staggering, but we will limit ourselves to one dimension of the passage. Matthew once more displays a concern for the cosmos and the establishment of God's end-time kingdom and temple on earth. Consider the three dimensions of the cosmos listed here: "heaven" (16:17, 19), "earth" (16:19), and "Hades" or the underworld (16:18). We argued in 5:34–35 that the language of "heaven," "earth," "footstool," and "Jerusalem" betrays a central theme in the First Gospel—the disciples are part of the in-breaking of God's cosmic temple, wherein he rules and reigns as sovereign King. Whereas Mark is generally concerned for the *purification* of the created order so that God's kingdom and temple can take up residence, Matthew is largely concerned for the mysterious *growth* of the kingdom within the created order. So when Jesus promises that he will "build" God's people upon "Peter" (Gk. *Petros*, meaning "rock"), he means that the expansion of the end-time kingdom and new temple will flow through Peter and the disciples.[17] The growth of temple and kingdom cannot be stopped, since Satan and his minions have already been bound (see 12:29). (Note the strong connection between 16:18–19 and Rev. 1:18; 20:1, 2.)

The last part of chapter 16 and the previous context (16:5–12) provide more information on *how* Peter and the disciples will participate in the explosion of the kingdom and temple on earth (16:21–28 // Mark 8:31–9:1 // Luke 9:22–27). They will carry out their mission through sound doctrine (16:5–12) and rigorously following the crucified Lord (16:21–28; →Mark 8:31–38).

Jesus as the Enthroned Son of Man and Faithful Israel (17:1-27)

The Transfiguration (17:1–20)

The transfiguration takes place, according to Matthew, "after six days" (17:1). This time stamp is unusual given that Matthew typically uses the expression "that same day" (13:1) or "in those days" (3:1) or a reference to Jesus's resurrection on the "third day" (16:21; 17:23). At the very least, the expression "after six days" ties the previous context (16:21–28) with the transfiguration in 17:1–13. Somehow the "coming of the Son of Man" (16:27–28) relates to our passage (see below). There may be another interpretive layer: according to Exodus 24:15–16, Moses waited at Sinai for six days until he was summoned on the seventh day.

Matthew often casts Jesus as a second and greater Moses figure, so strong parallels between the transfiguration and the giving of the law at Sinai are hardly surprising.

17. G. K. Beale, *The Temple and the Church's Mission: A Biblical Theology of the Dwelling Place of God*, NSBT 17 (Downers Grove, IL: InterVarsity, 2004), 187.

Transfiguration	Giving of the Law at Sinai
Takes place on a "high mountain" (17:1)	Takes place on Mount Sinai/Horeb (Exod. 19:2)
God appears to Moses, Elijah, Jesus, and the disciples in a "bright cloud" (17:5)	God appears to Moses and Israel in a "thick cloud" (Exod. 19:16)
Jesus talks to Moses and Elijah (17:3)	God talks to Moses (Exod. 20:1–31:18)
The disciples were "terrified" at the presence of God (17:6)	Israel "trembled" at the presence of God (Exod. 19:16)
God declares Jesus to be his "Son" (17:5)	God commands Israel to be a "kingdom of priests" and a "holy nation" (19:6)
Jesus and the disciples "were coming down the mountain" (17:9)	Moses "came down from" the mountain (Exod. 34:29)

The transfiguration is found in all three Synoptics (Matt. 17:1–13 // Mark 9:2–13 // Luke 9:28–36), so we need not repeat in detail what we will discuss elsewhere (→Mark 9:2–13). Our purpose here is to consider how this event functions in the immediate and broad context of the narrative. Above all, Matthew desires his readers to view this event primarily through two lenses. The transfiguration demonstrates (1) that Jesus is the enthroned Son of Man who has begun to reign over the cosmos and (2) that he is true Israel who is succeeding in obeying the will of his Father. We will briefly discuss each in turn.

First, Matthew's description of Jesus—"his face shone like the sun and his clothes became white as the light" (17:2)—is close to the description of the Ancient of Days in Daniel 7:9 and the angel in Daniel 10:5–6 (cf. Judg. 5:31). The enigmatic figure of the son of man in Dan. 7 is probably in Matthew's mind too, as he alludes to Daniel 7:13 in 16:28 ("the Son of Man coming in his kingdom"). Strengthening the connection to Daniel 7 and 10 is the apostle John's awareness of Daniel 7 and 10 in his portrayal of Jesus as the son of man in Revelation 1:13–16, where John likewise uses nearly identical language to depict Christ, whose "face was like the sun shining." The reaction of terror by the disciples (17:6) and Jesus's command "Don't be afraid" (17:7), only found in Matthew's account, are close to what we find in Daniel 10:7, 11, 12, and 19. The upshot is that Matthew, following Mark, presents Jesus as the end-time Son of Man figure who has begun to inherit the cosmic rule because of his faithfulness in the wilderness temptation. The fourth beast is not ultimately Rome but Satan.

Second, in light of the parallels between the giving of the law at Sinai and the transfiguration, Matthew identifies Jesus with Yahweh while also distinguishing him from the Father. There's a plurality within the Godhead. At the same time, the evangelist affirms Jesus's humanity in that the Father announces to the disciples that Jesus is his faithful "Son" (17:5). "Son" here probably captures Jesus's unique divine relationship to his Father *and* his role as true Israel (see 3:13–4:11). The Father is "pleased" with Jesus because of his faithfulness. Recall that at Sinai God commanded Israel to be faithful in their adherence to the law and in their commission to be a light to the nations (Exod. 19:5–6). In contrast to the failure of Israel, Jesus has obeyed God's law perfectly and begun to bring gentiles into the people of God. Whereas the Israelites committed idolatry immediately after receiving the law (Exod. 32), Jesus descends from the mountain and faithfully relies upon his Father in exorcising the demon from the child (17:18). The disciples were unable to cast out the demon because they were embodying the idolatrous attitudes of the first generation of Israelites at Sinai, who attempted to take things into their own hands (17:20). They should know by now that the growth of the kingdom and temple—that is, "this mountain"—can occur only through faith in God (17:20).

The Suffering Son of Man and the Temple Tax (17:22–27)

After the transfiguration, Matthew includes the second of three passion predictions (16:21; 17:22–23; 20:17–19). Jesus issues his first prediction before the transfiguration in Caesarea Philippi (16:21) and then discloses the second one right after the transfiguration in Galilee (17:22–23). When Jesus predicts his death the first time, Peter responds with utter disbelief and anger (16:22). After the second passion prediction, though, the disciples are "filled with grief" (17:23). Jesus's death is becoming a reality, and his followers are slowly coming to grips with it. In sandwiching the transfiguration between these two predictions, the narrative forces the readers to bring together Jesus's impending death and resurrection with his enthronement as the Son of Man. Jesus will rule over the cosmos as the exalted Son of Man *through* his death and resurrection (→Mark 8:34–9:1).

The discussion of the temple tax (17:24–27), an episode unique to Matthew, appears odd and even out at place at first blush. Many Jews, such as the Pharisees, believed that all adult males were required to pay a temple tax annually (Exod. 30:13) to secure funds for the upcoming Passover celebration in Jerusalem.[18] So two "collectors" ask Peter if Jesus will follow through with his obligation. Note that the community at Qumran believed that one should pay the tax only once (4Q159 1 II, 6–7).[19] Jesus then tells Peter that "kings of the earth collect duty and taxes" but not "from their own children" (17:25).

---

18. Osborne, *Matthew*, 663.
19. Eckhard J. Schnabel, *Jesus in Jerusalem: The Last Days* (Grand Rapids: Eerdmans, 2018), 176.

That is, kings tax their citizens but not their own flesh and blood. Jesus claims that his disciples, though they are "children" of the true king (i.e., Jesus, as the royal Son of Man) and belong to the end-time temple, still must pay the temple tax. The miraculous provision of the coin in the fish's mouth (17:27) demonstrates that while Jesus indeed fulfills the old covenant, his disciples are still responsible to obey their authorities "so that" they "may not cause offense" (17:27). The disciples must remain winsome to their Jewish brothers and sisters so that they may effectively share the gospel with them. R. T. France is right to conclude, "The story is thus an illustration of Jesus' willingness to comply with the conventions of the society to which he belonged rather than cause unnecessary offence."[20]

Relating to One Another within the Kingdom (18:1–35)

A Kingdom Outlook (18:1–5)

We now come to the fourth teaching discourse in the First Gospel (// Mark 9:33–37 // Luke 9:46–48). Much of what is found in chapter 18 is a concrete application of Jesus's original teaching in the Sermon on the Mount (5:1–7:29). The first discourse unpacks how believers *live* within the kingdom (5:1–7:29), the second concerns how believers *expand* the kingdom (10:5–11:1), the third develops the *nature* of the kingdom (13:1–53), and the fourth unpacks how kingdom citizens *relate* to one another (18:1–19:1).

The chapter opens with the disciples approaching Jesus "at that time" and asking him, "Who, then, is the greatest in the kingdom?" (18:1). The temporal phrase "at that time" and the conjunction "then" inform the reader that the previous context is somehow connected to the disciples' question in 18:1 (→18:10–35). The disciples are still struggling with a fundamental misconception about their status within the kingdom. Throughout the narrative, Jesus affirms the disciples' participation in the kingdom and their status as the restored people of God. We can even see traces of this salient theme in the immediate context, where Jesus reminds them that they are the Son of Man's "children" or true heirs (17:26). Moreover, we suggested above that Daniel 7 is a constitutive part of the OT background of the transfiguration. If that is the case, then Matthew may want his readers to ponder Daniel 7 once more in 18:1.

According to Daniel 7, the "holy people" benefit in the Son of Man's victory. They "will receive the kingdom and will possess it forever" (Dan. 7:18) and will inherit "the sovereignty, power and greatness of all the kingdoms

20. R. T. France, *The Gospel according to Matthew*, rev. ed., TNTC (Grand Rapids: Eerdmans, 1985), 272.

under heaven" (Dan. 7:27). Could it be that the disciples developed this passage and other eschatological texts in the wrong direction? Perhaps they are applying a worldly desire for power and prestige in their understanding of the kingdom. Whatever the case, the Twelve have clearly misconstrued their status within the kingdom, so Jesus outlines four themes that flow from the original line of questioning: proper outlook (18:1–5), persevering faith (18:6–9), promotion of a believer's worth (18:10–14), and preservation of the end-time people of God (18:15–35).

Jesus disabuses the disciples of their prideful outlook by tangibly illustrating a proper disposition: "Whoever takes the lowly position of this child is the greatest in the kingdom of heaven" (18:4). In the ancient world, children lacked considerable rights and privileges, so Jesus commands his followers to embody the same humble attitude. Pride has no place among God's people.

Persevering in the Kingdom (18:6–9)

The second section is an admonition to forsake sin to secure citizenship within the kingdom. Jesus warns the disciples not to become a cause of stumbling to others (18:6) or to themselves (18:8–9). Here the "world" (*kosmos*) is depicted as the source of the problem, and therefore Jesus issues a "woe" judgment against it (→23:13–39). Note the NLT's rendering: "What sorrow awaits the world, because it tempts people to sin" (18:7a). In 16:23 Jesus calls Peter "Satan" and says that he is a "stumbling block" to him. Jesus then goes on to say that although "such things [stumbling blocks] must come . . . woe to the person through whom they come" (18:7b). A second "woe" is aimed at the intermediary. Though the passage is somewhat difficult, the main point is clear: kingdom citizens must pursue righteousness because God will one day judge the world, Satan, and all who cause others to "stumble."

Promoting the Worth of Kingdom Citizens and Preserving the End-Time Temple (18:10–35)

The parable of the lost sheep, one of the most well-known parables, admirably illustrates the incalculable worth of each person in the kingdom. Just as a shepherd goes to great lengths to preserve just one of his sheep, so the Father will save each member of his flock. The final section is an exhortation to preserve the holiness of God's people in light of their identity as the end-time temple.

In 18:15–35 the focus is on the strong connection between God's glorious presence in heaven and his people on earth. Verse 20 undergirds much of the material here: "Where two or three gather in my name, there I am with them." "Immanuel" occurs at the beginning (1:23), here in the middle (18:29), and at the end of Matthew's narrative (28:20). When viewed through this lens, Jesus's concern for holiness (18:15–20) and forgiveness (18:21–35) makes good sense. With the incarnation, we have reached the long-awaited stage of redemptive history in which God takes up residence among his people. He promises to do so at the beginning of creation, and he is now making good on his promises. The transfiguration (17:1–13) tangibly reminds the disciples of Jesus's identity as Yahweh incarnate, and now he commands them to live in light of that reality. In a word, God's people must root out all forms of sin and disharmony because his glory dwells in their midst.

▪ Stage 2: The Journey to Jerusalem (19:1–20:34)

On the Road to Jerusalem (19:1–30)

Disputation with the Jewish Leaders on Divorce (19:1–12)

After the conclusion of the fourth teaching discourse, Jesus heads south toward Jerusalem. Jesus's ministry has been hitherto confined to the north, in Galilee (4:12–18:35); but the narrative shifts here, taking a dramatic turn. Instead of heading directly south to Jerusalem, Jesus travels southeast "to the other side of the Jordan" (19:1) and then approaches Jerusalem from Jericho (20:29). It is not completely clear why he does so, but several scholars argue that Jesus purposely avoids Samaria (→10:5).

Jesus is not alone as he departs Galilee: "Large crowds followed him, and he healed them" (19:2). Jesus's success as the Son of God is thus evident once more. The narrative swiftly transitions into another interrogation between Jesus and the Pharisees in 19:3. The "test" here is consonant with the testing found in 4:3 and 16:1:

Agent(s) of Testing	Purpose of Testing
The devil	"The tempter [ho peirazōn] came [proselthōn] to him and said, 'If you are the Son of God, tell these stones to become bread.'" (4:3)
Pharisees and Sadducees	"The Pharisees and Sadducees came [proselthontes] to Jesus and tested [peirazontes] him by asking him to show them a sign from heaven." (16:1)
Pharisees	"Some Pharisees came [proselthon] to him to test [peirazontes] him. They asked, 'Is it lawful for a man to divorce his wife for any and every reason?'" (19:3)

The same formula of "coming" and "testing" is found in three places in the narrative. The first two are tied to Jesus's identity, whereas the third one concerns a particular legal issue. Perhaps the point is to set the tone for the last portion of Jesus's ministry. If the Jewish leaders (and, by implication, the nation of Israel) were hostile toward Jesus's ministry in Galilee, how much more will they be in Jerusalem?

The debate here in 19:3–12 (// Mark 10:1–12) is an example of a "conflict story," a designation given to a group of sayings in the Gospels that presents a striking debate between Jesus and the Jewish leaders, who pride themselves in their knowledge of Israel's Scriptures and in their role as guardians of oral tradition. In Matthew's narrative, we have encountered this phenomenon five times, with each debate gaining intensity (9:1–12; 12:1–14, 22–45; 15:1–20; 16:1–4). The debate on marriage in our passage is not unrelated to the fourth discourse in chapter 18.

Taking a step back, we note that one of Matthew's contributions is his presentation of Jesus as an unrivaled teacher. His wisdom is unparalleled because he is God on earth. While he is certainly a prophet, he is more than a prophet. He simultaneously mediates truth and is the source of truth. The Jewish leaders challenge Jesus's claims in a war of words, but all attempts to deceive or outwit Jesus prove futile.

The OT background may add color to these wisdom disputations or polemics, as we see similar encounters in the narratives of Joseph, Esther, and Daniel. The most relevant background figure is Daniel, since Matthew's narrative displays a host of connections to that book. Daniel's narrative includes a series of "court narratives" that demonstrate the superiority of apocalyptic wisdom over against the wisdom of the elite. In chapters 2, 4, and 5, W. Lee Humphreys discerns what he calls "tales of court contest" in the book of Daniel.[21] These "contests" highlight the superiority of God's wisdom over against the wisdom of the Babylonian "wise" men. The Babylonians are portrayed in the book of Daniel as incompetent and idolatrous; they turn out to be unwise and foolish in each case. Daniel, though, is genuinely wise because his wisdom is derived from the one true God.[22] Read in this light, the confrontations between Jesus and the Jewish leaders, especially as his death looms, are sharpened. No friendly dialogue here; this is a battle.

---

21. W. Lee Humphreys, "A Life-Style for Diaspora: A Study of the Tales of Esther and Daniel," *JBL* 92 (1973): 211–23.

22. See Benjamin L. Gladd, *Revealing the* Mysterion: *The Use of Mystery in Daniel and Second Temple Judaism with Its Bearing on First Corinthians*, BZNW 160 (Berlin: de Gruyter, 2008), 43–49.

The weapons that the Jewish leaders brandish in our passage are oral tradition and Scripture. In 19:3 the Pharisees ask, "Is it lawful for a man to divorce his wife for any and every reason?" Here they broach a well-known debate between two schools within Pharisaism—Hillel and Shammai (see m. Git. 9.9–10). The school of Hillel argued that grounds for divorce were twofold: adultery or "indecency" (see Deut. 24:1) *and* "any and every reason" (19:3). On the other hand, the school of Shammai narrowed the grounds for divorce and only permitted it in the case of "indecency" or adultery. By the first century AD, the Hillelite interpretation became widespread and eventually won the day.[23] So the Pharisees are asking Jesus to comment on this debate (note Matthew's addition of "any and every reason" compared to Mark 10:2).

Jesus responds by quoting Genesis 1:27 and 2:24: "Haven't you read . . . that at the beginning the Creator 'made them male and female,' and said, 'For this reason a man will leave his father and mother and be united to his wife, and the two will become one flesh'?" (19:4). God designed marriage to be a permanent institution, a covenant relationship that mirrors God's covenant with his people (→Mark 10:1–12). In response, the Pharisees attempt to take Jesus off guard by then citing Deuteronomy 24:1 in 19:7 and pitting Scripture (Gen. 1–2) against Scripture (Deut. 24). In doing so, they resemble the devil, who likewise "tested" Jesus in citing Psalm 91:11–12 during the wilderness temptation (4:6). Climactically, Jesus wins the argument by interpreting Deuteronomy 24:1 through the lens of Genesis 1–2, contextualizing Scripture along a redemptive-historical plane. The Torah permits divorce because the Spirit has yet to arrive and "circumcise" the hearts of the Israelites (Deut. 30:5–6). Genesis 2:24 has always been (Deut. 31:16–17; Mal. 2:15) and continues to be (1 Cor. 6:16; Eph. 5:31) the model for marriage.

Entry into the Kingdom (19:13–30)

In stark contrast to the arrogant Jewish leaders in 19:3–12, Jesus teaches that admittance into the kingdom can only be obtained through humility and complete dependence upon him (19:13–15 // Mark 10:13–16 // Luke 18:15–17). Only those willing to embody the "lowly position" of a child are fit (18:4). Children know instinctively that they are radically dependent upon the provision of their parents and those in authority. They are unable to provide for themselves. Likewise, all who desire to inherit the end-time kingdom must do so in complete submission to Jesus. This principle is wonderfully illustrated in the following section, where an individual, though claiming to be utterly

---

23. D. Instone-Brewer, "Divorce," *DJG*, 213.

devoted to God, is ultimately unwilling to give up the one thing he loves the most—his exceeding wealth (19:16–22 // Mark 10:17–30 // Luke 18:18–30; →Mark 10:17–22).

Chapter 19 ends with Jesus's incredible promise to reward those who unreservedly follow him. The question Peter poses to Jesus in 19:27 is unique to Matthew: "We have left everything to follow you! *What then will there be for us?*" Jesus's answer, also unique to Matthew, is riveting: "Truly I tell you, at the renewal of all things, when the Son of Man sits on his glorious throne, you who have followed me will also sit on twelve thrones, judging the twelve tribes of Israel" (19:28). Much can be said here, but we will limit ourselves to three brief points.

(1) "When the Son of Man sits on his glorious throne" appears to conflate Daniel 7:9 (a reference to the Ancient of Days) and 7:13 (a reference to the enthronement of the son of man after defeating the fourth beast). If these two texts are in mind, then Jesus is claiming that he will share in ruling the cosmos with his Father, the Ancient of Days. (2) Since Jesus will inherit the right to rule because of his end-time victory, he will extend his rule through his followers, whom he represents as the "Son of Man" (see Rev. 3:21). (3) The seeds of Daniel 7 have already been sown in the transfiguration (17:1–8), so Matthew probably has that previous event in mind. The transfiguration demonstrates that Jesus has begun to rule over the cosmos through his defeat of the devil in the wilderness temptation, whereas our present passage emphasizes his consummate rule at the very end of history and his prerogative to extend his rule through the disciples (see Rev. 21:14). God's people can be confident that they, too, will enjoy the new creation and "inherit the earth" (5:5) because of their union with the Son of Man.

A Suffering Son of David (20:1-34)

Parable of the Vineyard Workers (20:1–16)

The parable of the vineyard workers (20:1–16), only found here in the First Gospel, is bracketed by the same line: "But many who are first will be last, and many who are last will be first" (19:30); "So the last will be first, and the first will be last" (20:16). Somehow the parable illustrates this principle. The parable opens in the following manner: "The kingdom of heaven is like" (20:1). This expression occurs only here and in chapter 13 (13:31, 33, 44, 45, 47, 52). The mysterious inauguration of the kingdom (13:11) probably lies in the background of this parable. In the previous saying, Jesus announces that only persevering disciples will "sit on twelve thrones, judging the twelve tribes of Israel" (19:28). It would be natural for the disciples to become consumed by their apparent self-worth. But *all* citizens of the kingdom receive equal treatment. Admission into the kingdom firmly depends upon God's grace.

Matthew's Gospel contains two parables about vineyards (20:1–16; 21:33–46), whereas Mark and Luke include only one (Mark 12:1–12; Luke 20:9–19). The present parable underscores the owner's right to pay as he sees fit, whereas the parable of the wicked tenants highlights abuse within the vineyard. What is common to both, though, is that God is the "landowner" (20:1; 21:33; see Isa. 5:1–7). In this parable the vineyard is equated with the kingdom (20:1), whereas in the later parable the vineyard is Israel (21:43–45). Lastly, the workers here are righteous citizens of the kingdom, but the "tenants" in 21:33–46 are unrighteous.

The general meaning of the parable is not too difficult to unpack: the owner of the vineyard has every right to pay his workers equally, regardless of how much time they earn on the clock. The measure of the reward is not commensurate with the amount of energy expended. In the same way, God's people possess an equal inheritance of the new creation, a right that does not ultimately depend upon how much we have quantifiably sacrificed. What is required is complete abandonment (19:29), an act that will vary from person to person owing to differing circumstances.

Third Passion Prediction and a Request for Honor (20:17–28)

The third and final passion prediction (20:17–19 // Mark 10:32–34 // Luke 18:31–33), sandwiched between two passages concerning the inverted status of kingdom citizens, provides the most detail concerning Jesus's death. The first two are more general, predicting Jesus's death at the hands of the Jewish leaders and his eventual resurrection "on the third day" (16:21; 17:22), but this third prediction states that he will be "handed over to the Gentiles" and then "mocked and flogged and crucified." Recall that Jesus is the "son of Abraham" (1:1) who will, in fulfillment of God's promises to Abraham (e.g., Gen. 17:1–16), become a "blessing" to the nations and be the catalyst of their conversion (12:18–21, quoting Isa. 42:1–4). Ironically, though the nations nail him to the cross, some of the gentiles are converted and "blessed" by God through his death (27:54)! This is also the first reference to Jesus being "crucified." Earlier in Matthew's narrative, Jesus told his disciples that they must "take up their cross" and that they must be willing to suffer (10:38; 16:24), but this is the first time Jesus explicitly claims that he will die *on a cross*.

Suffering and humiliation continue to be a topic of conversation in the following section (20:20–28). Matthew's version of the request of James and John, the two sons of Zebedee (4:21; 10:2; 26:37), differs from Mark's presentation in that here the mother of the two disciples does the asking (Mark 10:35–41). We are unsure why Matthew shines the spotlight on her, but it may be related to her presence later in the narrative, when she observes Jesus's death "from a distance" (27:55–56). Whatever the case, we can be confident that James, John, and their mother are on the same page. Jesus corrects the misunderstanding of James and John about their status in the new creation. The focus of the text is on the *future* aspect of the kingdom's arrival.[24] God's people will reign in the new creation (Rev. 22:5), but the "sons of thunder" (Mark 3:17) desire glory and honor *without* suffering and death. Apparently, James and John have yet to grasp the mysteries of the kingdom (13:11–50)—that is, the paradoxical overlap of the two ages. Jesus promises that they will eventually "drink" from his "cup" (cf. Ezek. 23:31–32; Zech. 12:2), a reference to Jesus's and their own suffering and death (Acts 12:2; cf. Rev. 1:9). A few chapters later, the mother of the two disciples will behold with her own eyes the macabre death of Jesus. Perhaps she recalled this conversation in that moment of horror. How could she not?

The discussion ends with Jesus claiming to be the ultimate servant, one who "did not come to be served, but to serve, and *to give his life as a ransom for many*" (20:28). Jesus's wording is drawn from Isaiah 53:10–12: "Yet it was the LORD's will to crush him and cause him to suffer, and though the LORD makes his life an offering for sin . . . My righteous servant *will justify many*, and he will bear their iniquities. . . . *He poured out his life unto death*, and was numbered with the transgressors. For *he bore the sin of many*." The servant vicariously bears Israel's curse so that God's people might receive covenant blessings. He dies in place of "many," triggering the new exodus of Israel (→Mark 10:45).

Healing Two Blind Men (20:29–34)

As Jesus and the disciples venture to Jerusalem to celebrate Passover, they pass through Jericho, a key city on the journey. The trek from Jericho to Jerusalem can be made in a single day,[25] and all three Synoptics place this event before Jesus enters into Jerusalem for passion week (Matt. 20:29–34 // Mark 10:46–52 // Luke 18:35–43). While Mark and Luke mention only one blind person, Matthew includes two (20:30). One unique feature of Matthew's narrative is his proclivity to include pairs (8:28; 9:27; 21:7; 27:51).

---

24. Carson, "Matthew," 487.

25. A. D. Riddle, "The Passover Pilgrimage from Jericho to Jerusalem," in *Lexham Geographic Commentary on the Gospels*, ed. B. J. Beitzel and K. A. Lyle (Bellingham, WA: Lexham, 2016), 398.

The thrust of the narrative is the acknowledgment that Jesus is the "Lord, Son of David" (20:30, 31). Matthew has insisted from the beginning that Jesus is the long-awaited heir to David's throne (1:1, 17; 9:27; 12:3, 23; 15:22; 20:30). But as the narrative has unfolded, the reader has learned that Jesus's kingship is not marked by political might but by suffering and defeat. Ironically, the two blind men here in 20:29–34 can see more clearly than James and John in the previous passage (20:20–28; cf. 13:14–17)! The blind men may not see physically, but they do perceive spiritually—an act of faith that results in them receiving their physical sight (20:34).

Stage 3: Jesus in Jerusalem (21:1–28:20)

The Arrival of Israel's King and Its Implications (21:1–22:46)

Triumphal Entry (21:1–11)

Approaching Jerusalem, Jesus commands two of his disciples to enter Bethphage and procure a donkey and a colt (21:1–2) for the triumphal entry (// Mark 11:1–10 // Luke 19:29–38 // John 12:12–15). In all likelihood, Jesus had prearranged the procurement of the animals ahead of time in order to avoid unwanted attention during the festival. Riding on a donkey into Jerusalem is infused with symbolic significance, so all those attached to the triumphal entry, especially the owner of the animals, are at risk with the Jewish leaders.[26] Whereas Mark and Luke include only a "colt," Matthew includes a donkey and "her colt." It's unclear why he lists two animals, but it may be simply practical: unridden colts would most likely need their mother present to remain calm.[27] Matthew points out that Jesus's instructions "took place to fulfill what was spoken through the prophet" (21:4). This is the ninth of ten fulfillment formulas (1:22; 2:15, 17, 23; 4:14; 8:17; 12:17; 13:35; 21:4; 27:9), and the last formula was eight chapters ago.

According to the quotation of Zechariah 9:9 in 21:5, Jesus's actions fulfill Zechariah's prophecy that Israel's king would arrive on a donkey *after* vanquishing her enemies (Zech. 9:1–8). In contrast to a king riding a war horse, the donkey connotes peace throughout the kingdom. The war has already been won (→Mark 11:1–11). The symbolism of the donkey brings also to mind Solomon riding on King David's "own mule" so that Zadok and Nathan might "anoint him king over Israel" (1 Kings 1:33–34). Matthew has already

---

26. Schnabel, *Jesus in Jerusalem*, 156.
27. Craig L. Blomberg, "Matthew," in *Commentary on the New Testament Use of the Old Testament*, ed. G. K. Beale and D. A. Carson (Grand Rapids: Baker Academic, 2007), 64.

identified Jesus as someone "greater than Solomon" (12:42), so both characters are probably aligned here typologically. But Jesus's reign exceeds the reign of David and Solomon. Though they reigned during a high point in Israel's history, internal turmoil marked their rule; Jesus's rule is unsullied and marked by uncompromising faithfulness.

The pilgrims or the "very large crowd" appear to have witnessed the healing of the two blind men (20:29; 21:8) and now, after seeing Jesus riding on a donkey, perceive the significance of the symbolic gesture and cry out, "Hosanna to *the Son of David*! Blessed is he who comes in the name of the *Lord*!" (21:9). The title "Lord" is often joined with "Son of David" in Matthew's narrative (15:22; 20:30–31; 21:9; 22:43, 45). The most recent occurrence is in the previous passage, where the two blind men declare Jesus to be the "Lord, Son of David" (20:30–31). The pilgrims' declaration is fascinating because Jesus is *both* figures—he is simultaneously the true descendant of David and Yahweh incarnate. While the pilgrims are probably thinking along political lines (note the quotation of Ps. 118:25–26 in 21:9), Matthew's readers have discovered throughout the narrative that Jesus is Israel's "Lord" *and* Messiah (e.g., 14:33). Jesus's actions ring throughout Jerusalem as the "whole city" is "stirred" (21:10; cf. Mark 15:11; Luke 23:5), so it's only a matter of time until he clashes with the Jewish and Roman authorities.

Judging Israel's Temple and the Cursing of the Fig Tree (21:12–22)

Jesus's public demonstration as Israel's Messiah is the basis for his judgment upon the temple in 21:12–17 (// Mark 11:15–18 // Luke 19:45–47 // John 2:13–25), for often in the OT, kings exercise authority over the temple (e.g., 1 Sam. 21:6; Ps. 110:4). Originally, Adam was a king-priest in the garden (Gen. 1:28; 2:15). As the consummate king-priest and last Adam, Jesus marches to the area of the temple where the Israelites exchange currency in order to purchase the appropriate sacrifices. Overturning "the tables of the money changers," he brings the entire sacrificial system to a halt (21:12). Jesus then quotes Isaiah 56:7 and Jeremiah 7:11 (→Mark 11:15–18), demonstrating that the reason for his judgment upon the temple is twofold: (1) the Israelites prevented the nations from worshiping the one true God (Isa. 56:7), and (2) the Israelites boasted in the presence of the temple (Jer. 7:11).

Only Matthew narrates the effect of Jesus's actions among the crowd: "The blind and the lame came to him at the temple, and he healed them" (21:14). Healing the "blind" and the "lame" explicitly demonstrates Jesus's identity as the long-awaited Messiah who ushers in the new age (see 11:5; Isa.

35:5; 61:1). Jesus is unabashedly claiming to be the source of the new creation and Israel's King.

Predictably, the authorities are outraged at Jesus's behavior (21:15), seeking an explanation from him. But Jesus fuels the fire and quotes Psalm 8:2, where "children" and "infants" establish "a stronghold against [God's] enemies" because they recognize God's unmatched power to rule the cosmos. In quoting Psalm 8:2, Jesus claims that the nearby children have more insight into Jesus's authority than the Jewish leaders! He may also claim to fulfill the expectation of Psalm 8 that a ruler would arrive and vanquish all expressions of evil, in contrast to the first Adam, who failed to rule over God's enemies (Ps. 8:3–8; cf. Heb. 2:6–8).

After spending the night in Bethany, probably at the home of Lazarus (21:17; cf. John 12:1), Jesus and the Twelve return to Jerusalem and stumble upon a fig tree (21:19). The cursing of the fig tree in 21:18–22 (// Mark 11:12–14, 20–24), an action that parallels the judgment upon the temple (→Mark 11:12–21), symbolizes Jesus's judgment upon the nation for not bearing fruit (21:19). The nation should respond well to John the Baptist's and Jesus's ministry, but they refuse.

Parables of the Two Sons and the Wicked Tenants (21:23–46)

Matthew devotes the next portion of the narrative to Jesus's public interaction with the Jewish leaders in the "temple courts" (21:23 // Mark 11:27–33 // Luke 20:1–8). Riding on a donkey into Jerusalem and overturning the tables of the money changers will certainly raise some political eyebrows. His actions are clear enough—Jesus of Nazareth is a threat to the Jewish way of life. Jesus follows up the first exchange concerning his "authority" (→Mark 11:27–33) with a parable about two sons that is unique to Matthew (21:28–32). The short parable cuts to the heart of the matter. The two sons represent two parties: the first son represents the "tax collectors and the prostitutes," whereas the second son embodies the Jewish authorities or "you" (21:31). The worst of the worst—that is, the tax collectors and the prostitutes—respond positively to God's call, but the religious leaders remain calloused toward Jesus's ministry. One's destiny is ultimately bound up with allegiance to Jesus and not to Israel's customs and traditions.

Jesus then delivers a knockout punch—the parable of the wicked tenants (21:33–46 // Mark 12:1–12 // Luke 20:9–19). We need not cover the parable in detail (→Mark 12:1–12), so we will only isolate a few unique details. The gist of the parable is Israel's continued rejection of the prophets, despite God's forbearance. Against the backdrop of Isaiah 5, God is the "landowner," the vineyard is Israel, the tenants are the Jewish leaders/nation, the servants are the prophets, the "son" is Jesus, and the "other tenants" are mostly gentiles. When the tenants reject the son, God's patience has worn out. Something must be done. So God decides to "rent the vineyard to other tenants" who will faithfully carry out his will (21:41). Capping off the parable, Jesus quotes Psalm 118:22–23: "The stone the builders rejected has become the cornerstone; the Lord has done this, and it is marvelous in our eyes" (21:42). Psalm 118 features prominently three times during passion week:

21:9, quoting Ps. 118:26 (Ps. 117:26 LXX)	"'Hosanna to the Son of David!' *'Blessed is he who comes in the name of the Lord!'* 'Hosanna in the highest heaven!'"
21:42, quoting Ps. 118:22–23 (Ps. 117:22–23 LXX)	"Have you never read in the Scriptures: *'The stone the builders rejected has become the cornerstone; the Lord has done this, and it is marvelous in our eyes'?*"
23:39, quoting Ps. 118:26 (Ps. 117:26 LXX)	"For I tell you, you will not see me again until you say, *'Blessed is he who comes in the name of the Lord.'*"

Psalm 118:26 frames the section, with the first quotation appearing on the lips of the pilgrims entering Jerusalem a few days prior (21:9) and the final quotation anticipating Israel submitting to the reign of Jesus at his second coming (cf. Phil. 2:10–11). Sandwiched in the middle is the way in which Jesus will execute his reign as the Promised One—he will rule, ironically, as a result of being rejected by Jewish authorities. Their rejection leads to his exaltation.

Participation in the "kingdom" is now transferred "from you [the leaders] and *given to a people* who will produce its fruit" (21:43). The wording here closely matches Daniel 7:27, where "the sovereignty, power and greatness of *all the kingdoms* under heaven *will be handed over to the holy people of the Most High*." According to the immediate context of Daniel 7, the victory of the "son of man" (Dan. 7:13–14) is applied to the "people of the Most High" because they identify with him. His victory is their victory. Instead of trusting in Jesus as the Son of Man, the Jewish leadership rally against him. If the context of Daniel 7 is in mind, then the Jewish authorities are identified with the fourth beast (cf. 24:29–31). Further still, Jesus alludes to the book of Daniel again in the following verse:

Matt. 21:44 (// Luke 20:18)	Daniel 2:34–35
"Anyone who falls on *this stone will be broken to pieces*; anyone on whom it falls *will be crushed*."	"*A rock* was cut out, but not by human hands. It struck the statue on its feet of iron and clay and *smashed them*. Then the iron, the clay, the bronze, the silver and the gold were *all broken to pieces*. . . . But the *rock* that struck the statue became a huge mountain and filled the whole earth."

Here in Daniel 2 the rock, identified as either the Messiah or the eternal kingdom, crushes the fourth and final earthly kingdom, resulting in the establishment of God's worldwide temple that "fills the whole earth" (cf. Dan. 2:44–45). Again, if the religious authorities do not submit to the authority of Jesus and his identity as the "rock" and "cornerstone" of the end-time temple (see 7:24–25; 16:18), they will be obliterated in judgment. The reaction of the "chief priest" and the Pharisees is hardly surprising, since Jesus has found them culpable for the nation's dire situation (21:45).

Parable of the Banquet (22:1–14)

The parable of the wedding banquet teases out the themes already set forth in the two previous parables (21:28–44 // Luke 14:16–24). A king throws a banquet for his son's wedding and invites a host of guests to attend. The initial guests, though, refuse the offer, as they are more concerned about their own personal agendas than the king's. Some of the guests even murder the king's messengers. Angered, the king arms his troops and wages war against them. Not to be deterred, the king then sends out his servants to the "streets," where they "gathered all the people they could find, the bad as well as the good." The table is set, the royal family is present, and the "wedding hall" is finally "filled with guests" (22:10). But there is more to the story. As the king moves throughout the crowd, he is taken aback by a man not decked in the proper attire. So the king issues a command to his servants that the man be bound and tossed outside, "where there will be weeping and gnashing of teeth" (22:13). The final verse of the section divulges the overall point: "Many are invited, but few are chosen" (22:14).

Probably in line with the two previous parables, the "king" is God and his "son" is Jesus (22:2). The parable of the banquet may recall Isaiah 25:6–12, where God holds a meal with "all peoples" in the new creation. According to Isaiah 25, the source of provision is not primarily physical sustenance but God's glorious presence. His all-encompassing glory nourishes Israel and the nations. The first set of guests in the parable appear to be the Jewish people, who, on account of their devotion to their own livelihood and their opposition to King Jesus, are either passed over or destroyed (22:4–7; see 21:39–41). The second set of guests are likely gentiles who embrace Jesus (22:8–10). They constitute "all peoples" of Isaiah 25:6. The description of the man not wearing wedding attire, though odd at first, fits quite well with Matthew's narrative. Allegiance to Jesus of Nazareth is not simply a one-time decision but a lifelong commitment. Like the seed falling upon rocky soil and eventually withering (13:20–21), this individual responded initially to the invitation of the banquet but failed to come prepared. Jesus offers the message of the kingdom to all, but only a few will enter it, and fewer still will persevere.

War of Words (22:15–46)

The triumphal entry and Jesus's judgment upon Israel's temple drew the attention of Israel's leadership (21:1–17). The parable of the tenants leaves little doubt in the minds of the Jewish leaders that Jesus's identity and mission stand at odds with their cherished traditions (21:33–44). Something must be done. They look to "arrest" Jesus soon, but they are unsure *how* to do so (21:46). How can they publicly arrest such a popular figure at the Passover festival in the "temple courts" (21:23)? Wouldn't his many followers prevent it? Apparently, the leaders decide to "trap" him with a three-pronged assault: taxation (22:15–22), the doctrine of the resurrection (22:23–33), and the greatest commandment (22:34–40 // Mark 12:13–37 // Luke 20:20–44 →Mark 12:13–37). If Jesus incriminates himself, that will go a long way in assuaging the populace, which is largely on his side.

Matthew uniquely states that the line of questioning from the Jewish leaders flows from an "evil intent" (22:18). The word here for "evil" (*ponēria*) reminds the readers of several earlier passages that speak of the devil as the "evil one" (*ponēros*; 5:37; 6:13), who influences people to imitate him and likewise be "evil" (5:39; 7:11; 9:4; 12:34). The idea, then, is that these Jewish leaders are ultimately doing the bidding of their "evil" father, the devil, who inspires them to trap Jesus in his words. But Jesus never falters. The Pharisees and the Herodians ask Jesus to weigh in on the issue of Rome's authority over Israel, perhaps hoping that he will align himself against Rome and give the empire a reason to arrest him (22:17). Jesus instead argues that believers should respect the authority of Rome *and* God, since God is ultimately sovereign over all the nations (22:21; cf. Rom. 13:1–7).

The next round of interrogation moves to the topic of resurrection; the instigators are the Sadducees, who famously deny the possibility of resurrection (22:23–33). Jesus counters the Sadducees' grandiose hypothetical discussion with a passage from the Pentateuch, the only part of the OT that the Sadducees accept as canonical. He argues that since Yahweh is *still* the God of Israel's patriarchs, he will raise them from the dead (22:31–32).

The last round of questioning is over "the greatest commandment in the law," posed by a Torah expert (22:34). Jesus cites two OT texts: Deuteronomy 6:5 and Leviticus 19:18. The former, recited twice daily as part of the Shema (Deut. 6:4–9), states that each member of the covenant community must love God with the totality of their being. The latter concerns the proper conduct of each Israelite within the nation (Lev. 19). Matthew does not divulge the response of the Torah expert, whereas Mark and Luke mention a favorable response (// Mark 12:32–33 // Luke 20:39). In omitting the positive response, Matthew may be setting up Jesus's castigation of the Jewish leaders in the following chapter.

Jesus turns the table on these troublemakers. It's time for *him* to trap *them*. He inquires about the ancestry of Israel's Messiah: "What do you think about the Messiah? Whose son is he?" (22:42a). At one level, the question isn't difficult, and they predictably answer with "the son of David" (22:42b). This is where things get interesting. Jesus cites Psalm 110:1, claiming that David acknowledges that the Messiah is "Lord" even *before* the Messiah is born! In other words, Jesus appears to be arguing that the Messiah must be preexistent (→Mark 12:35–37). From this close reading of Psalm 110:1, the Jewish leaders seem to have a too-narrow view of the Messiah. If the religious authorities rightly interpret Psalm 110:1, then they will grasp much of Jesus's identity and ministry. Although Matthew's Gospel opens with Jesus being identified as the "son of David" (1:1), we have learned that Jesus is much more than a physical descendant of David; he is Yahweh incarnate and thus David's supreme, cosmic "Lord."

The larger discourse of 21:33–22:46 contains four reactions from the Jewish elders, the first reaction motivating the subsequent three:

> They looked for a way to arrest him, but *they were afraid of the crowd* because the people held that he was a prophet. (21:46)

> When they heard this, *they were amazed.* So they left him and went away. (22:22)

> When the crowds heard this, *they were astonished* at his teaching. (22:33)

> No one could say a word in reply, and from that day on *no one dared to ask him any more questions.* (22:46)

By aligning these four reactions, we discover that despite their best attempts at trapping Jesus, the religious authorities are left stymied. Jesus's understanding of the OT is unparalleled because he is more than a mere interpreter of God's law. He speaks and acts with ultimate authority—as God himself. How can Israel's elders debate the one who authored their very Scriptures? Since the authorities' plans to have Jesus arrested are thwarted, they appear to move in a different direction, as we will learn in a few chapters. A public confrontation on the temple mount is off the table, so they will attempt to arrest him in private (26:3–5).

Judgment upon Israel's Religious Authorities (23:1–39)

Chapter 23 breaks down into two sections: 23:1–12 and 23:13–39. Jesus addresses the "crowds" and his "disciples" in the first section and then shifts to the religious authorities in the second. Jesus directs his scathing indictment toward the "teachers of the law and Pharisees." The "teachers of the law" or the "scribes" (*grammateis*) are the OT scholars of the day, professional interpreters of the Torah and a subset of the Pharisees (see Mark 2:16; cf. Matt. 5:20; 12:38; 15:1)[28] and the Sadducees.

Hypocrisy (23:1–12)

In the first section (23:1–12), Jesus contends that outward praise fuels the engines of the Jewish leaders (// Mark 12:38–39 // Luke 20:45–46). Matthew 23:5 reads, "Everything they do is done for people to see." Recall Jesus's words in 6:1: "Be careful not to practice your righteousness in front of others to be seen by them. If you do, you will have no reward from your Father in heaven." God will vindicate his people on the future day of judgment, whereas the Jewish leaders attempt to vindicate themselves in the present.

The following verses (23:8–12) highlight the disciples' radical devotion to and proclamation of God's revelation in the person of Jesus. The disciples should not seek to be called "Rabbi" and pursue worldly praise like the Jewish leaders do (23:5); instead, they should seek solidarity among their "brothers" (23:8). The hallmark of the new Israel of God is humility and service. The disciples must imitate the supreme servant of all—Jesus, who, as Isaiah's Suffering Servant, will be "exalted" at the resurrection (see 20:20–28; Isa. 53:10).

The Seven Woes (23:13–39)

In the following section (23:13–39), Jesus's attention turns from the "crowds and the disciples" (23:1) to the "teachers of the law and Pharisees," a group embodying the totality of Israelite leadership. This discrete passage, mostly unique to Matthew's narrative, is noteworthy for a few reasons. First, Jesus's tirade is marked by seven "woes" (23:13, 15, 16, 23, 25, 27, 29). These woe judgments, in keeping with the woe judgments found in the OT (e.g., Isa. 3:9, 11; Jer. 48:1; Ezek. 16:23), are a series of judgments against Israel's leaders and the nation whom they represent. Woe judgments are restricted to those whom God will judge with *finality*. John the Baptist's warning at the beginning of

---

28. D. A. Carson, "The Jewish Leaders in Matthew's Gospel: A Reappraisal," *JETS* 25 (1982): 166.

Matthew's Gospel is beginning to be fulfilled: "The ax is already at the root of the trees, and every tree that does not produce good fruit will be cut down and thrown into the fire" (3:10; see 3:11–12). The religious authorities have rejected God's revelation in his Son and have resisted Jesus's ministry from the very beginning. God is coming to burn "the chaff" of unbelief (3:12). The number seven in the Bible symbolizes completion or wholeness. The book of Revelation, for example, mentions seven spirits (1:4), seven churches (1:11), seven lampstands (1:12), seven seals (5:1), seven angels (8:2), seven thunders (10:3–4), and so on. The significance of the seven woes, then, is that God definitively judges Israel as a theocratic nation. There is no coming back from this eschatological judgment. The time has come for God to avenge the death of his righteous servants. Paul captures this idea in 1 Thessalonians 2:14–16 when he writes, "The Jews who killed the Lord Jesus and the prophets . . . always heap up their sins to the limit. The wrath of God has come upon them at last" (cf. Gen. 15:16; Dan. 8:23–25).

Second, judgment upon the religious authorities has two foci: hypocrisy and persecution of the righteous. Israel's leadership, while claiming to be righteous, are anything but. They claim to uphold God's law by erecting a fence of oral tradition around the Torah. In doing so, they have lost sight of the very point of God's law—loving him and one's neighbor (22:37–40)! The religious authorities have attempted to make the entire nation submit to their scrupulous teachings, all the while neglecting to submit their hearts to God's law. Blinded in their hypocrisy, they have persecuted God's prophets. The irony should not be missed here: Israel's leaders have attempted to earn God's righteousness by putting to death his righteous servants. In short, "Israel has rejected its prophets, and . . . by rejecting them Israel has failed to obey the law of Moses."[29] Jesus makes a strategic move in the seventh and final woe by aligning the current leadership with all those who have persecuted God's people "from the blood of righteous Abel [Gen. 4:8] to the blood of Zechariah son of Berekiah [2 Chron. 24:21; Zech. 1:1]" (23:35). The promise of Genesis 3:15 is truly coming to pass. The war between the offspring of the godly and the ungodly since the death of Abel will culminate in the death of Jesus.

Third, the seven woes in chapter 23 are the theological basis for the coming destruction of Israel's temple, outlined in chapter 24. The discourse shifts from the "teachers of the law and Pharisees" in 23:13, 15, 16, 23, 25, 27, 29 to "Jerusalem, Jerusalem" in 23:37. This critical move reveals that God holds *the entire nation of Israel culpable* (// Luke 13:34–35). The Jewish leaders

---

29. David L. Turner, *Israel's Last Prophet: Jesus and the Jewish Leaders in Matthew 23* (Minneapolis: Fortress, 2015), 284.

epitomize the spiritual condition of the majority of the nation (see 27:25). They are not acting alone in their rejection of him. The nation of Israel remains intractable and will do what they always do: persecute God's prophets. This time, though, they will kill God's Son, thereby incurring God's wrath. As a result, God will destroy Israel's temple, the hallmark of his covenant with them. To relate to God, to be reconciled to him and enjoy his glorious presence, one must now trust solely in Jesus.

Destruction of Israel's Temple and the Return of the Son of Man (24:1–25:46)

Jesus reserves the fifth and final teaching discourse, in 24:1–25:46, for the disciples (cf. 5:1–7:29; 10:5–11:1; 13:1–53; 18:1–19:1). This is the first time during passion week that Jesus teaches his disciples privately at length. We have noted that each teaching discourse focuses on a particular aspect of the kingdom: life within the kingdom (5:1–7:29), the proclamation of the kingdom (10:5–11:1), the unexpected or mysterious nature of the end-time kingdom (13:1–53), and relating to one another as kingdom citizens (18:1–19:1). The fifth discourse remains tethered to the other discourses on the kingdom in that it explains the *physical effects* of the kingdom. The spiritual dimension of the inauguration of the kingdom manifests itself mightily in the destruction of the temple in AD 70.

Jesus as the Crushing Stone (24:1–3)

The entire section of 21:23–23:39 has taken place in the shadow of the temple, and now Jesus decides to depart the area and venture east to the Mount of Olives. On their journey, the disciples draw Jesus's attention to the architectural splendor of the temple (24:1; →Mark 13:1). Jesus, though, is not impressed. The physical attraction of the temple in Jerusalem is only a veneer—the temple reeks of wickedness and idolatry. The time is ripe for it to be "thrown down" (24:2; cf. 26:61; 27:40).

The fifth teaching discourse in 24:1–25:46 (// Mark 13:1–37 // Luke 21:5–36) is no stranger to debate, as commentators struggle with tracing its general flow. Indeed, this section is one of the most contested portions of Matthew and the NT at large. Critical to the debate is the question posed by the disciples in 24:3: "When will this happen, and what will be the sign of your coming and of the end of the age?" R. T. France argues that the flow of the discourse rests upon the nature of the disciples' questioning. While the disciples appear to ask the same question from two different perspectives in Mark and Luke, France perceives two separate questions in Matthew's account. The first question, "When will this happen?" concerns the destruction of the temple, whereas the second question, "What will be the sign of your coming and of the end of the age?" refers to Jesus's second coming at the very end of history. Jesus answers the first question in 24:4–35 and then the second one in 24:36–25:46.[30] Observe that Matthew's version of the second question is also more specific than Mark's and Luke's versions:

> Tell us, . . . when will this happen, and what will be the sign of *your coming and of the end of the age*? (Matt. 24:3)

> Tell us, when will these things happen? And what will be the sign *that they are all about to be fulfilled*? (Mark 13:4)

> Teacher, . . . when will these things happen? And what will be the sign *that they are about to take place*? (Luke 21:7)

Mark's and Luke's versions are more or less synonymous and highlight the disciples' request to know the precise *timing* of the temple's destruction. Matthew's narrative underscores *Jesus's role* in the temple's destruction in the end times.

In the minds of the disciples, the overthrow of the temple must mean the ultimate destruction of the old age and the consummate arrival of the new age. In chapter 13 Jesus elucidates the nature of the arrival of the end-time kingdom to the disciples. He challenges their long-held views that the kingdom will arrive all at once and with great finality. Here in chapters 24–25, Jesus accents the destruction of the temple in the coming decades and then the ultimate destruction of wickedness and the consummate arrival of the new heavens and earth. The focus shifts, then, from the *arrival* of the kingdom in chapter 13 to its *consummation* in 24:36–25:46. Just as the arrival of the kingdom is a mystery (13:11), so also is its consummation in that judgment upon Israel's temple does not signal the ultimate destruction of the old age (24:4–35). "It is Jesus' task, then, to extend their horizons, to make them [the disciples] realize that a continuation without the temple until the 'close of the age' is possible, that the end of the temple . . . is not necessarily the end of all things."[31]

The broad structure of the Olivet Discourse is as follows:

30. France, *Gospel of Matthew*, 890.
31. France, *Gospel according to Matthew*, 340.

24:4–28	Events leading up to the destruction of the temple in AD 70
24:29–35	The arrival of the Son of Man
24:36–25:46	Unknown arrival of the Son of Man

While the discourse contains a host of allusions to the OT, the book of Daniel is baked into the Olivet Discourse, functioning as an interpretive framework for understanding Jesus's prophecy:[32]

Matthew 24:2: "Truly I tell you, *not one stone here will be left on another; every one will be thrown down.*"	Daniel 2:35 (NETS [OG]): "And the *stone that struck the image* became a great mountain, and it *struck the whole earth.*" Daniel 2:45 (NETS [OG]): ". . . just as you have seen a *stone* cut out of a mountain, without hands, and *it ground the earthenware and the iron and bronze and silver and gold.*"
Matthew 24:3: "What will be the *sign of your coming and of the end of the age?*"	Daniel 12:6 (NETS [OG]): "O Sir, *when then will you do the consummation of the wonders.*"
Matthew 24:6: "*Such things must happen,* but the end is still to come."	Daniel 2:45 (NETS [Theo.]): "The great God has made known to the king *what must happen* after this."
Matthew 24:15: "So when you see standing in the holy place '*the abomination that causes desolation,*' spoken of through the prophet Daniel."	Daniel 9:27 (NETS [OG]; cf. 11:31; 12:11): "In the temple *there will be an abomination of desolations.*"
Matthew 24:21 (NASB): "For then there will be a great *tribulation, such as has not occurred since* the beginning of the world until now."	Daniel 12:1 (Brenton [Theo.]): "And there shall be a time of tribulation, *such tribulation as has not been from the time* that there was a nation on the earth until that time."
Matthew 24:30: "Then will appear the sign of the *Son of Man* in heaven. And then *all the peoples of the earth* will mourn when they *see the Son of Man coming on the clouds of heaven,* with power and great glory."	Daniel 7:13–14 (NETS [OG]): "*A son of man was coming upon the clouds of heaven. . . . All the nations of the earth* according to posterity, and all honor was serving him."

This comparison leaves little doubt that Daniel is uppermost in Jesus's mind as he predicts the destruction of the temple and his return at the very end of history. One way in which NT authors cite the OT is by using the blueprint or prototypical model, wherein a NT writer arranges his material in light of a particular OT passage. We can see that technique here in Jesus's use of the book of Daniel. But what, then, is the significance? Why is Daniel critical to the Olivet Discourse?

---

32. Many of these allusions to Daniel are also proposed in Blomberg, "Matthew," 86–87.

The beginning of the discourse provides an important clue. When Jesus predicts that "not one stone here will be left on another; every one will be thrown down" (24:2), he is most likely alluding to Daniel 2:35 and 45, where the "stone"—that is, the Messiah or the eternal kingdom—smashes the statue. We ought to keep in mind that Jesus has already identified himself as the "stone" of Daniel 2 who breaks to pieces and crushes those who reject him (21:42–44). Since Israel will reject him in nailing him to the cross, he, the true temple or "stone," promises to crush the idolatrous stones of the Jerusalem temple. The prophecy of Daniel 2 is turned on its head. The *pagan* kingdoms in Daniel 2 that will be crushed by the enduring kingdom are equated with the nation of *Israel* in Matthew 24. Irony runs thick here.

As the Olivet Discourse unfolds, the basic outline of Daniel's narrative is maintained but with a twist: war between the kingdoms of the earth escalates into unparalleled tribulation, and a great antagonist arrives to deceive many within Israel (24:4–14), culminating in the "abomination of desolation" (24:15–28). The Son of Man arrives on the scene to bring swift judgment and vanquish the fourth beast (24:29–35). While Matthew doesn't explicitly mention the fourth beast, he expects his readers to supply the image from Daniel 7. Ironically, the fourth beast is not Rome but Israel! Much like he wielded the war machines of Assyria and Babylon when Israel forsook the covenant, God will deploy Rome in AD 70 to accomplish his purposes.

Judgment upon Israel's Temple (24:4–35)

The first portion of the discourse (24:4–14) informs the disciples that they should *not* be alarmed at false messiahs, political conflicts, famines, and earthquakes, since these occurrences are merely "the beginning of birth pains" (24:8). Even persecution, imprisonment, and the proclamation of the kingdom to the ends of the earth should not raise eyebrows (24:9–14; →Mark 13:5–13). What does raise a red flag, though, is the arrival of the "abomination that causes desolation" (24:15). The disciples should now take action and "flee to the mountains" (24:16), because the destruction of the temple is nigh.

Why does the "abomination that causes desolation" (24:15) occupy such a turning point in the discourse? While we could say much about this passage, we will focus on a few points. The phrase "abomination of desolation" stems from three passages in the book of Daniel: 9:27, 11:31, and 12:11. These three texts refer, at some level, to the defilement of the temple by Antiochus Epiphanes in 167 BC, when he sacrificed a pig upon the altar of the temple (1 Macc. 1:54). But, as several commentators argue, Daniel's prophecy was not exhausted in the second century BC. Jesus views the "abomination that causes desolation" as a future reality. It may be the case, then, that Daniel's prophecy is fulfilled in stages—by Antiochus Epiphanes in 167 BC, by the destruction of the temple in AD 70 (Matt. 24:15), and, finally, at the very end of history when the physical antichrist defiles God's sanctuary, the church (2 Thess. 2:4).

Scholars often argue that the Roman soldiers' profaning the temple by offering pagan sacrifices in the temple complex and erecting military banners in AD 70 fulfills Jesus's expectation of the "abomination that causes desolation" (see Josephus, *J.W.* 6.316).[33] But perhaps there's an additional dimension in mind. The expression "abomination that causes desolation" may also connote Israel's ungodly condition. Israel has become so wicked and vile that she is the culprit of impurity. Note that OT prophets often portray Israel's idolatry and unfaithfulness as an "abomination" or as "detestable" (e.g., Isa. 2:8; Hosea 9:10; Mic. 3:9; Nah. 3:6; Mal. 2:11). Deuteronomy 18:9 warns the Israelites to not "act according to *the abominations* [*ta bdelygmata*] of those nations" (NETS) living in the land of Canaan. If they do, then "anyone who does these things is *an abomination* [*bdelygma*] to the Lord" (Deut. 18:12). According to Deuteronomy 18, Israel will transform into the detestable thing she worships. The same point is likely in mind here in Matthew 24: Israel has worshiped the abominable temple, so she has become an abomination! "Whereas in the first instance the abomination which caused desolation was performed by a wicked pagan (Antiochus Epiphanes IV), now Israel, who rejects Yahweh's Messiah, typologically becomes 'the wicked, pagan nation' and, as such, suffers the fate of Yahweh's wrath."[34]

The flow of thought progresses with the phrase "immediately after the distress of those days" (24:29 // Mark 13:24). The Son of Man then arrives on the scene and pours out his judgment upon the wicked nation of Israel. But there is a ray of light in the darkness, as the Son of Man also restores the dispersed tribes of Israel—that is, true Israel (24:29–35; →Mark 13:24–31). The cosmic language in 24:29 symbolizes the destruction of one nation and the victorious emergence of another (e.g., Isa. 13:10–13; 24:1–6, 19–23; 34:4; Jer. 4:23–28; Ezek. 32:6–8). In this case, the cosmic language signifies the downfall of the nation of Israel and the rise of true Israel, composed of largely gentiles (see 21:43).

The Son of Man's enthronement is a critical theme in Matthew's narrative. We see it first in the wilderness temptation, where Jesus, faithfully submitting to his Father's will, defeats Satan and begins to rule as the Son of Man (4:1–11).

---

33. John Nolland, *Matthew*, NIGTC (Grand Rapids: Eerdmans, 2005), 971.

34. Michael P. Theophilos, *The Abomination of Desolation in Matthew 24.15*, LNTS 437 (New York: Bloomsbury, 2012), 127.

It crops up once more at the transfiguration (16:28; 17:2), where Jesus reveals himself to the disciples as the Son of Man who possesses the same qualities as the Ancient of Days (16:28; 17:2; →Mark 9:2–13). Again, Jesus reveals to the disciples that he will sit "on his glorious throne" as the "Son of Man" and judge "the twelve tribes of Israel" (19:28). Up to this point in the narrative, Matthew has been thoughtfully developing an important dimension to Jesus's identity as Daniel's Son of Man. Not only is Jesus the long-awaited descendant of Abraham and David (1:1); he is also the cosmic judge who rules at the Father's right hand.

The Second Coming (24:36–25:46)

The final section of the discourse (24:36–25:46) answers the second question of the disciples: "What will be the sign of your coming and of the end of the age?" (24:3b). The focus appears to shift from AD 70 to the unknown timing of the return of Jesus at the very end of history. Jesus claims that even he, in his humanity, remains ignorant of "the day or hour" of his coming (24:36). As the Lord incarnate, he temporarily submits to the Father's will (Phil. 2:5–8), but his ignorance of his return must be understood alongside the previous statement in 24:35, where he, in his divinity, explicitly places his words on par with his Father's: "Heaven and earth will pass away, but my words will never pass away" (cf. Isa. 40:8; 51:6).

Verse 36 is the thesis for the bulk of the remaining discourse (24:36–25:30).[35] "No one knows" when Jesus will return and consummately judge wickedness and establish the new heavens and earth. The second coming of Jesus is compared to "the days of Noah," when the unrighteous "knew nothing about what would happen until the flood came and took them all away" (24:37–39). The point is that the wicked endured judgment while the righteous were preserved in the ark (Gen. 7:6–23). Contrary to popular belief, being "left behind" is better than being swept away in the chaotic waters of judgment (24:40–41).

Since "no one knows" when Jesus will return (24:36), believers must "therefore keep watch" (24:42). Matthew repeats the expression "therefore keep watch" twice in this section (24:42; 25:13). Moreover, throughout the fifth discourse, Jesus commands the disciples to "watch out" (24:4), "understand" (24:15, 43), "learn" (24:32), "know" (24:33), and "be ready" (24:44). Vigilance is paramount, for judgment is imminent, and only those who are spiritually

---

35. Osborne, *Matthew*, 902.

attuned will recognize the signs of the times. Jesus then teaches his disciples four parables in 24:43–25:30 to tangibly illustrate the need for watchfulness.

The discourse ends with the final judgment, wherein the "Son of Man comes in glory and all the angels with him," and "he will sit on his glorious throne" (25:31). The wording here is strikingly similar to 24:30:

Matthew 24:30–31	Matthew 25:31–32
"Then will appear the sign of the *Son of Man* in heaven. And then all the peoples of the earth will mourn when they see the *Son of Man* coming on the clouds of heaven, with power and great *glory*. And he will send his *angels* with a loud trumpet call, and they will *gather* his elect from the four winds, from one end of the heavens to the other."	"When the *Son of Man* comes in his *glory*, and all the *angels* with him, he will sit on his glorious throne. All the nations will be *gathered* before him, and he will separate the people one from another as a shepherd separates the sheep from the goats."

In both passages, Daniel 7:13–14 is the controlling OT passage, but the central difference between the two is the consummate fulfillment of Daniel 7:13–14. Matthew 24:30–31 generally refers to AD 70, whereas 25:31–32 refers to Jesus's second coming.

Throughout the narrative, we have put our finger on Matthew's emphasis on the OT and Jewish cosmology, where God rules in the invisible heavens over his cosmic temple. Jesus reminds his audience in the Sermon on the Mount that "heaven" is "God's throne" (5:34). Later in 19:28 Jesus predicts that at his second coming "the Son of Man [will sit] on his glorious throne." Finally, 23:22 likewise states that "heaven" is "God's throne." By aligning these passages with 25:31–32, we surmise that Jesus, through his faithful ministry, death, and resurrection, will ascend to God's throne and rule with him over the cosmos.

At the second coming, at the very end of history, Jesus will "separate the people from one another as a shepherd separates the sheep from the goats" (25:32). Jesus's teaching on the mysteries of the kingdom anticipated this great event when the "Son of Man will send out his angels, and they will weed out of his kingdom everything that causes sin and all who do evil" (13:41; cf. 13:48). The righteous and the unrighteous will no longer live side by side. The righteous will inherit the new creation (25:34), whereas the unrighteous will be consigned to the "eternal fire prepared for the devil and his angels" (25:41; cf. Rev. 20:13–14).

One badge of righteous living is found in 25:35: "I [Jesus] was hungry and you gave me something to eat, I was thirsty and you gave me something to drink, I was a stranger and you invited me in." A few verses later, we discover that Jesus is referring to how kingdom citizens treat one another. When

God's people are persecuted and in need, genuine followers come to their aid (25:37–39). Since Jesus is united to his people, it's as though these true followers are ministering to Jesus himself (25:40). Much of what is found here has already been proclaimed in the fourth teaching discourse (18:1–19:1).

The Son of Man's Betrayal and Trial before the Sanhedrin (26:1–75)

Jesus as the Anointed King (26:1–16)

The beginning of chapter 26 transitions from the final teaching discourse to Jesus's impending death. Punctuating the end of the discourse, Jesus tells his disciples that the "Passover is two days away" and that "the Son of Man will be handed over to be crucified" (26:2). The destruction of the temple (24:2–35) is based upon Israel's ultimate rejection of her Messiah. Israel will crucify the "Son of Man" (26:2), only to be later judged by that very "Son of Man" (24:30). Matthew then mentions that the religious authorities, still intent on killing Jesus, now plan to execute their scheme "secretly" (26:4). Jesus, who remains popular among the people, did not fall for the Jewish authorities' public entrapments (22:15–40), so they must seize him in secret.

Unlike John, who places Jesus's anointing in Bethany at the beginning of passion week (John 12:1–8), Matthew and Mark delay the event until right before the Passover celebration (26:6–13 // Mark 14:3–9). In doing so, they tie Jesus's betrayal at the hands of Judas (26:14–16 // Mark 14:10–11) to what transpired at the anointing and deftly link the (messianic) anointing to the Passover celebration. We know little about Simon the Leper (26:6), but we can probably assume that he was healed by Jesus and subsequently integrated back into society. In all likelihood, he is one of the eyewitnesses of this startling account. From the parallel account in John, we learn that the woman who anointed Jesus is named Mary, and her two siblings are Martha and Lazarus (John 12:1–3). Perhaps Mark and Matthew omit the three names because of the family's intimate association with Jesus at this point in the early church. Associates of Jesus are the target of the Jewish authorities, and Matthew and Mark may be protecting their identity (see John 12:10–11; Acts 8:1–5).

Mary takes the "very expensive perfume" and pours it "on his head" (26:7). Anointing Jesus's head with precious oil appears to be a messianic gesture (e.g., Judg. 9:15; 1 Sam. 9:16; 16:13; Ps. 18:50). Mary likely understands that Jesus is the long-awaited Son of David (1:1) who will rule over his people and the nations. What she may lack, though, is a robust knowledge of how Jesus is both the Son of David *and* the Passover Lamb (26:26). The King is the atoning sacrifice.

Judas, whom we first met in 10:4, is appalled at Mary's actions. While John places the anointing at the beginning of passion week, as noted, Matthew follows Mark's lead in sandwiching the anointing at Bethany between the religious authorities' desire to put Jesus to death (26:3–5 // Mark 14:1–2) and Judas's betrayal (26:14–16 // Mark 14:10–11). The anointing is the catalyst for the betrayal, demonstrating that, in the eyes of Judas and the Jewish leaders, "Jesus and his disciples are planning an imminent messianic uprising."[36] The threat must be removed.

Jesus's Faithfulness as the Passover Lamb (26:17–46)

The narrative advances to the "first day of the Festival of Unleavened Bread," when the disciples inquire about where they will eat the Passover meal (26:17). That evening (Thursday night), Jesus and the disciples celebrate the Passover in Jerusalem (// Mark 14:12–25 // Luke 22:7–20; →Mark 14:12–31). Matthew is the only evangelist to include the line "My appointed time is near" (26:18). The disciples are to repeat that line to a "certain man." Its significance in the narrative is apparent: in the hours to follow, it will appear that Jesus is powerless, subject to the devious plots of wicked individuals. But nothing is further from the truth. Matthew's narrative opens with the expectation that Jesus, as the Son of David and the true Israel of God, will be put to death at the hands of wicked men. As a baby, Jesus escapes the foils of Herod (2:13–23), and as an adult, he deftly avoids the Jewish leaders' early attempts to kill him (12:14). But the time has now come for him to die. The Passover meal tangibly demonstrates Jesus's mission. Jesus is the definitive Passover Lamb, who will bear the sins of God's people with great finality.

The disciples' emotionally charged promise to die with Jesus (26:35) soon withers in Gethsemane. Perched on the slope of the Mount of Olives, Jesus and the disciples assemble to watch and pray (Luke 22:39). One striking element of the scene is the contrast between Jesus's faithfulness and the disciples' unfaithfulness. From the outset, Matthew has underscored Jesus's identity as the true and faithful Israel, who is intent on obeying his Father. Jesus rules over the devil in the wilderness temptation by submitting to his Father's will. Here again, Jesus reaffirms his commitment to his Father by drinking the "cup" of end-time suffering (26:42). The faithful one will drink the cup of God's eschatological wrath in order to liberate God's unfaithful people (see Isa. 51:17, 22; Jer. 25:15; 49:12).

36. Richard Bauckham, *Jesus and the Eyewitnesses: The Gospels as Eyewitness Testimony* (Grand Rapids: Eerdmans, 2006), 192.

Jesus's Arrest and Trial and Peter's Denial (26:47–75)

During the arrest (// Mark 14:43–50 // Luke 22:47–53 // John 18:1–14), Jesus tells one of his "companions" (or Peter), who has just struck one of the soldiers, to put down the sword (26:52; →John 18:10). There's no need for weapons, since Jesus has the authority to "call on" his "Father" who will "put at" his "disposal [*parastēsei*] more than twelve legions of angels" (26:53). Matthew is the only Gospel to include this saying. Why? While the OT mentions angels in military contexts (e.g., 2 Kings 6:17; Ps. 91:11), there may be a specific OT text in mind here. Daniel 7:13, a passage that is central to Matthew's narrative and is quoted in 26:64, reads, "He [the son of man] came as the Ancient of Days, and *attendants* [*hoi parestēkotes*] were with him" (AT). These "attendants" are the same group found in 7:10: "A thousand thousands were waiting on him [the Ancient of Days], and ten thousand times ten thousand stood *attending* [*pareistēkeisan*] him" (AT). The son of man, according to Daniel 7:13, earns the right to be "attended" by the angels of the Ancient of Days because of what he has accomplished in defeating the fourth and final beast. Jesus, too, because of his identity as the Son of Man who has vanquished the devil by faithfully adhering to God's will, has the right to summon the angels (see 24:30–31). But, despite having earned that right, Jesus's identity as the Son of Man is still, in some sense, unfinished. He must "fulfill" the OT expectations that God's servant must *first* suffer and die (e.g., Isa. 52:13–53:12). To summon angels is to get the end-time cart before the horse.

The soldiers transport Jesus from the Mount of Olives to the house of Caiaphas, the current high priest (26:57). It's here where the Sanhedrin, the ruling body of Israel composed of chief priests, scribes, and lay leaders, will preliminarily try Jesus. The Gospels disclose two trials by the Sanhedrin—one after midnight (26:59–66 // Mark 14:53–65) and one in the early morning (Luke 22:66–71). Much could be said about the first trial before the Sanhedrin (→Mark 14:53–65), but we will limit ourselves to two observations.

First, during the interrogation, Caiaphas breaks Jesus's silence and asks him a question: "Tell us if you are the Messiah, the Son of God" (26:63). Mark's version reads, "Son of the Blessed One" (Mark 14:61). While Caiaphas probably uses the title "Son of God" as synonymous with "Messiah" (notice how the two titles are paired in 26:63), Matthew's audience knows more about Jesus than Caiaphas. The term "Son of God," as we have argued throughout, takes on a prominent role in the First Gospel, particularly as it refers to Jesus's identity as true Israel, God's faithful, divine "son" (2:15; 3:17; 4:3, 6; 8:29; →16:13–20).

Second, Jesus affirms that he is indeed the "Messiah, the Son of God," but he then responds that he is also the "Son of Man" of Daniel 7. Prefacing the twin quotation from Daniel 7:13 and Psalm 110:1, Jesus tells the high priest, "*From now on [ap' arti]* you will see the Son of Man sitting at the right hand of the Mighty One and coming on the clouds of heaven" (26:64). Mark's narrative contains no such temporal phrase, so we need to give it some thought. While a handful of translations render "from now on [*ap' arti*]" as taking place in the distant future (HCSB, NLT, NIV 1984), other translations opt for an imminent understanding (ESV, NRSV, NIV [2011], KJV, NASB), and for good reason (cf. 23:39; 26:29 where *ap' arti* also occurs).

Matthew's narrative carefully tracks the cosmic ascension of Jesus, beginning with the wilderness temptation and culminating in the resurrection. The narrative has repeatedly drawn the readers' attention to the cosmos at various points and reminded them that Jesus has, through faithfully obeying God's law, begun to reign over it as the Son of Man from Daniel 7 (e.g., 5:34–35; 6:9–13; 16:17–19). Jesus's death and resurrection are at hand, and the time has come for him to sit on his Father's throne. Chapter 26 ends painfully with Peter's threefold denial (26:69–75; →Mark 14:66–72). It appears that Jesus's closest friends have nearly lost all hope. Peter has witnessed countless miracles and even confessed that Jesus is the "Son of God" in the midst of great peril on the Sea of Galilee (14:33). But will Peter and the others confess him as Lord at Jesus's defining moment on the cross? Peter and the disciples are eager to follow him at the beginning of Jesus's ministry, but will they do so at the end?

The Son of Man's Death (27:1-66)

The "Handing Over" of Jesus and the Death of Judas (27:1–10)

Chapter 27 opens with what appears to be the conclusion of the second trial before the Sanhedrin, a trial that only Luke records and that most likely took place within a chamber of the temple (→Luke 22:66–71; cf. Mark 15:1). The second trial formalizes the conclusion of the first: Jesus of Nazareth deserves death. The religious authorities "handed over" Jesus to Pilate on Friday morning (27:2). Recall that John the Baptist is "handed over" to Herod (4:12 AT), and Jesus predicted that he and his disciples would follow suit (10:17; 17:22; 20:18–19; 24:9–10; 26:2, 21, 23–25, 45).

Peter mentions Judas's hanging in his sermon in Acts 1:18–19, but Matthew is the only evangelist to describe the event in some detail (27:3–10). In 2 Samuel 15–16, Ahithophel, an advisor of King David, betrays him by giving tactical advice for Absalom's rebellion (2 Sam. 15:12, 31; 16:21–23; 17:1–4). Ahithophel soon hangs himself because his plans came to naught. Given the strong typological correspondence between Jesus and King David, there may be a typological connection between Ahithophel's betrayal of David and Judas's betrayal of Jesus. Both were at one time inner confidants of the king who failed to follow him in the end. Matthew also puts his finger on the OT's anticipation of the purchase of the "potter's field" in 27:6–10. The thrust of the composite quotation of Jeremiah 32:6–9 and Zechariah 11:12–13, clearly typological, demonstrates that "God is in fact sovereignly at work, even in the tragic events of Jesus' betrayal and Judas' death, just as he had been in the highly symbolic ministries of the prophets Zechariah and Jeremiah."[37]

Jesus's Trial and Sentencing before Pilate (27:11–26)

Pilate, maintaining residence in Jerusalem for the Passover festival, is Rome's prefect in Judea and responsible for preserving peace and security. If the Jewish leaders want to put Jesus to death, Pilate must agree and carry it out. They lead Jesus to the Praetorium, Herod's former palace in the Upper City of Jerusalem (// Mark 15:2–15 // Luke 23:2–3, 18–25 // John 18:29–19:16). The "chief priests and the elders" level a charge against Jesus—namely, that he claimed to be the "king of the Jews" (27:11). At one level, Jesus agrees with the charges when he states, "You have said so" (27:11). Matthew's Gospel has certainly demonstrated the legitimacy of Jesus's messiahship. But Jesus's messianic identity differs from expectations and Pilate's line of questioning. He is not attempting to liberate the nation and incite a rebellion. He is less concerned with political fallout and far more intent on vanquishing the devil and his demonic army. Jesus is king, but his rule far exceeds the physical boundaries of Palestine; it extends to the far reaches of the cosmos.

Jesus's Crucifixion and Burial (27:27–66)

Pilate's impression is that the religious authorities condemn Jesus "out of self-interest" (27:18), but his wife's curious dream that Jesus is "righteous" is telling (27:19 NASB). Pilate's wife, a gentile and possibly a God-fearer, displays more spiritual insight than those who boast in their righteousness (see 23:28). Just as Jesus predicted, these religious leaders, in claiming to be righteous, are bent on persecuting the truly "righteous" one (23:29, 35).

The trial continues, and the chief priests and the crowd demand the release of Barabbas (27:20–26a), a murderer and insurrectionist (Mark 15:7). Ironically, they would rather release an unrighteous individual who is truly guilty of the charges they brought against "righteous" Jesus. Pilate officially sentences Jesus to death by crucifixion (27:26b), and his soldiers then mock and beat him

37. Blomberg, "Matthew," 96.

in the Praetorium (27:27–31 // Mark 15:16–20). The soldiers smugly announce that Jesus is "king of the Jews," the second of four occurrences of the title in Matthew (2:2; 27:11, 29, 37). We first came across this title in 2:2, where the magi ask, "Where is the one who has been born king of the Jews?" At the end of Matthew's Gospel, we finally get the answer to their question. Here he is, some twenty-five chapters later—Israel's King, beaten and condemned. But it is precisely in this state that Jesus rules as Israel's King, for his kingship is principally marked by suffering and defeat.

Matthew 27:32–44 narrates Jesus's horrific crucifixion (// Mark 15:22–32 // Luke 23:33–43 // John 19:17–24). He is crucified at Golgotha between "two rebels" (27:38). In stacking several allusions to Psalm 22 throughout the event of the crucifixion (Matt. 27:35, quoting Ps. 22:18; Matt. 27:39, quoting Ps. 22:7; Matt. 27:46, quoting Ps. 22:1), Matthew is aligning Jesus's suffering with King David's suffering (→Mark 15:24–34). From the beginning to the end of the First Gospel, David's life typologically corresponds to Jesus's. From Bethlehem to Golgotha, Jesus repeats David's career but with a stark difference: Jesus is greater. There is no Bathsheba incident. No illicit census. No shred of transgression in Jesus's ministry. One could claim that Jesus is a greater David than David himself.

One stark feature of Matthew's Gospel is his inclusion of cosmic events in 27:51–53. Scholars have expended a great deal of energy on this difficult passage, but we will make a single point. This phenomenon should be understood in light of Matthew's insistence that the eschatological heavenly kingdom, the new creation, is beginning to irrupt on the earth (see Isa. 26:19; Ezek. 37:12–13; Dan. 12:1–2). We have traced this theme from the very beginning of Jesus's career until now. As the Son of Man from Daniel 7, Jesus begins to conquer the devil in his faithful adherence to the will of his Father and, as a result, begins to establish the heavenly kingdom on earth. The two locations—heaven and earth—are beginning to intersect through Jesus. The result of Jesus's atoning death for the sin of God's people is the in-breaking of the new creation. The rending of the veil in the temple symbolizes the tearing of the old cosmos (see Exod. 26:31–33) so that God's presence may descend and dwell with humanity (→Mark 15:33–41). Though Immanuel is God's glory on the earth in that he is now "with" humanity (1:23; 18:20; 28:20), his death opens access to heaven in a new and profound way (cf. John 1:51). Hebrews 12:22 captures this same thought: "You have come to Mount Zion, to the city of the living God, *the heavenly Jerusalem*. You have come to thousands upon thousands of angels in joyful assembly."

The crucifixion culminates in the soldiers' confession that Jesus is truly "the Son of God," a demonstration that God's glory is now advancing to the nations (27:54). Mark and Luke focus their attention only on the centurion (Mark 15:39 // Luke 23:47), whereas Matthew includes additional soldiers or "those with him." A key point is that participation within the kingdom does not depend upon converting to Judaism—all that is necessary is unwavering faith in Jesus. Three women, who "had followed Jesus from Galilee to care for his needs," stood "watching [the crucifixion] from a distance" (27:55–56). In pairing the centurion with these women, Matthew follows Mark in revealing a key component of the kingdom: all peoples, even gentiles and women, are prominent members through Jesus (→Mark 15:39–41).

Later that day, a member of the Sanhedrin (Mark 15:43) named Joseph of Arimathea pleads with Pilate for Jesus's body to be buried in his "own new tomb" (27:57–60 // Mark 15:42–47 // Luke 23:50–56 // John 19:38–42). The Sabbath is approaching, so Joseph must act quickly. Matthew identifies Joseph as a "disciple of Jesus" (27:57). True discipleship is a key theme running throughout the First Gospel (e.g., 16:24; 17:20; 26:31) and escalating during passion week. While the disciples are nowhere to be found (the last reference to Peter was in 26:75), Matthew shines the light on a devoted follower of Jesus. Joseph of Arimathea and the women in the preceding section (27:55–56) are cast in a better light than the original disciples. They are determined to follow Jesus to the end.

Chapter 27 finishes with an exchange that takes place the following day, the Sabbath, between the religious authorities and Pilate concerning Jesus's body (27:62–66). This incident is only found in Matthew's Gospel. The Jewish leaders accuse Jesus of being a "deceiver" (*ho planos*) by predicting that "after three days" he would "rise again" (27:63). Such an accusation is quite ironic because Jesus earlier told the disciples that "false prophets" would "mislead many" (*planēsousin*) within Israel (24:5, 24 NASB). The leaders admit that if Jesus's body is removed from the tomb, then the "last deception [the removal of Jesus's body] will be worse than the first [the prediction of Jesus's resurrection]" (27:65). In other words, an empty tomb would generate an incalculable number of disciples and turn the world upside down. They are right about that, of course, but they are wrong to say that Jesus is a "deceiver."

The empty tomb will testify to the veracity of Jesus's entire earthly ministry. Moreover, Matthew's inclusion of this exchange between the Jewish leaders and Pilate affirms the historicity of Jesus's resurrection. If the disciples are able to overpower the soldiers and steal Jesus's body in order to claim that Jesus rose from the grave, then they, too, are guilty of deception. Jesus's entire ministry— his kingdom message, his insistence that he was the Son of God and the Son of Man—would collapse like a house of cards. But if he truly rises from the dead in a physical, glorified body, then Jesus really is everything he claims to be.

The Exalted Son of Man and the Great Commission (28:1-20)

The Empty Tomb (28:1–10)

The four Gospels record various aspects of the resurrection (28:1–10 // Mark 16:1–8 // Luke 24:1–10 // John 20:1–8). Chapter 28 breaks down into three sections—the empty tomb (28:1–10), the conspiracy of the Jewish leaders (28:11–15), and the Son of Man's commission to the disciples (28:16–20). The first section takes place "at dawn on the first day of the week"—that is, early Sunday morning (28:1; →Mark 16:1–8). The two faithful women, Mary Magdalene and "the other Mary," were present at the crucifixion and burial (27:56, 61). Their fidelity to Jesus's ministry continues as they go "to look at the tomb." The narrative takes an odd turn here with the phrase *kai idou*, occurring at the beginning of 28:2 and translated as "suddenly" (HCSB). Matthew's use of the often-cited phrase, found some twenty-eight times throughout the narrative (e.g., 2:9; 3:16–17; 4:11; 8:24), prepares Matthew's audience for a surprising turn of events.

What have the women stumbled upon? Apparently, a "violent earthquake" accompanies "an angel of the Lord [coming] down from heaven" (28:2). It seems as though the earthquake has *already* happened and that the women are witnessing its effects. All three Synoptics mention earthquakes in the Olivet Discourse (Matt. 24:7 // Mark 13:8 // Luke 21:11), but only Matthew mentions two additional ones (27:54; 28:2). All three earthquakes should probably be understood as physical manifestations of God's judgment. We contemplated Matthew's use of earthquake language to describe the storm in 8:24 and noted its association with divine judgment upon the demonic forces (→8:23–27). Perhaps the presence of an earthquake at the crucifixion in 27:51 symbolizes God's judgment upon the old idolatrous cosmos and the one here in 28:2 represents God's definitive judgment upon death itself.

Another subtle yet profound detail is Matthew's description of the angel: "an angel of the Lord [who] came down *from heaven* [*ex ouranou*]" (28:2). Why mention his point of origin? One of the differences between this account of the resurrection and Mark's and Luke's is Matthew's description of what took place *outside* the tomb—Mark and Luke largely discuss what transpired *inside* it (// Mark 16:5–7 // Luke 24:3–8). A great deal of the First Gospel is the growth of the end-time kingdom through the proclamation of the gospel, resulting in God's glory emerging from heaven to earth (5:34; 6:9–10; 10:7; 16:19; 18:18–19; 26:64). As Matthew's Gospel progresses, so does the heavenly kingdom. Jesus's victory over the devil in the wilderness temptation, atoning death, and victorious resurrection result in the in-breaking of the kingdom. Heaven has come to earth! Reinforcing this suggestion is Matthew's description that the angel's "appearance was like *lightning* [*astrapē*]" (28:3). Lightning is often associated with God's heavenly presence (e.g., Exod. 19:16; Rev. 4:5; 8:5; 11:19; 16:18). So the angel's presence outside the tomb symbolizes God's heavenly presence on earth. Jesus is indeed "Immanuel" (1:23), so where Jesus goes in his earthly ministry, heaven goes with him. But the resurrection has brought about a critical change to God's presence among his people: God will dwell with his people *through the Spirit* (28:19). The faithful Son of Man has fashioned a new temple, and all those who trust in him enjoy God's unfettered presence.

The Great Deception (28:11–15)

Matthew's Gospel uniquely includes Pilate, at the request of the religious authorities, posting guards at the tomb to deter theft of Jesus's body (27:62–66). When the angel descended, the soldiers were "so afraid of him that they shook and became like dead men" (28:4; Rev. 1:17). Once the guards regained consciousness, they headed back to Jerusalem and informed the Jewish leaders of "everything that had happened"—that is, they testified to Jesus's resurrection (28:11). Despite hearing an irrefutable report that Jesus is alive, the authorities plan a cover-up. Why would the soldiers invent such a tale if they incurred guilt due to negligence? The same scheme they outline to Pilate in 27:64—that the disciples took the body—will be their official response. For this to work, everyone must be in on it. To seal the deal, the authorities pay the soldiers "a large sum of money" (28:12). This same group paid Judas thirty pieces of silver to betray Jesus (26:3, 14–16), and now they are paying a king's ransom to deceive the masses.

Such behavior demonstrates the utter wickedness of Israel's leaders. Discovering the truthfulness of the resurrection—the veracity of Jesus's identity and mission—does not lead the leaders to repentance; instead, they attempt to suppress and pervert the truth. The main point of the section ends on a bitter note: "And this story has been widely circulated among the Jews [*para Ioudaiois*] to this very day" (28:15). The word for "Jews" (*Ioudaioi*), while found nearly 150 times throughout John and Acts, occurs only five times in Matthew (2:2; 27:11, 29, 37; 28:15) and a handful of times in the other two Synoptics. This is telling. Could it be that Matthew's reluctance to use the term *Ioudaioi* underscores the nature of the genuine people of God, the true *spiritual* Jews? Only those who identify with Jesus, the embodiment of true Israel, are true Israel.

The Great Commission (28:16–20)

The final section in Matthew's Gospel is a fitting end to a dramatic narrative. In contrast to the religious authorities who commission the soldiers to spread lies and deceit (28:13), Jesus, as the faithful Son of Man, commissions the disciples to spread the message of salvation (28:19–20). The disciples meet him in Galilee, in fulfillment of the promise made earlier in 26:32 and then reiterated by the angel in 28:7 and Jesus himself in 28:10.

Like the women, when the disciples see Jesus, they worship him, a clear demonstration that Jesus is the Lord incarnate (28:17). Worship of Jesus is a central tenet of Matthew's Gospel. At the temptation, Jesus condemns the devil's desire for idolatrous worship (4:9–10, quoting Deut. 6:13). God alone deserves worship and adoration. Therefore, when Jesus is the object of worship throughout the First Gospel, the audience must assume that Matthew is identifying Jesus as Israel's God. To worship Jesus is to worship Yahweh, and monotheism remains intact. At Jesus's birth, "wise men" come to Bethlehem to "worship" him (2:2, 8, 11), and at key points in the narrative, Jesus is worshiped (8:2; 9:18; 14:33; 15:25; 20:20). Finally, at the end of the narrative, Jesus is once again "worshiped" (28:9, 17). Worship and adoration bookend Jesus's entire life. The "wise men" worship him because of who he is and what he *will accomplish*, whereas the disciples worship him because of who he is and what he *has accomplished*. But "some" of the disciples still wavered in their faith and "doubted," apparently lacking a full understanding of the nature of the kingdom and Jesus's full identity. Such insight will ultimately be grasped at Pentecost.

While this passage deserves much attention, we will focus on two points. First, Jesus commissions the disciples on a "mountain," so Matthew wants us to connect this event to all the previous events on mountains (4:8; 5:1; 8:1; 14:23; 15:29; 17:1, 9; 24:3; 26:30). We noticed in our discussion of the Sermon on the Mount that mountains in the OT are associated with God's presence among his people. The promise that Jesus will be "with" the disciples indicates how they will be empowered to carry out the commission (28:20). Whereas Adam and Eve, the patriarchs, and Israel fail to spread God's glory to the ends of the earth, Jesus succeeds in this endeavor. His faithfulness results in heaven and earth being joined together. The same divine presence that accompanied the patriarchs (Gen. 26:24; 28:15) and Israel (1 Chron. 22:18; Hag. 2:4–5) will now go with the disciples. Jesus came down and brought heaven with him. As the prophet Isaiah predicts, "Immanuel" or "God with us" has come in the person of Jesus (1:22–23, quoting Isa. 7:14). The glory that descended in Jesus and now dwells in the disciples will soon reach the nations. The main point of Matthew's final section, and arguably of the entire Gospel, is Jesus's promise to go "with" the disciples.

Second, Jesus commissions the disciples to "make disciples of all nations" as the victorious Son of Man of Daniel 7. Consider the prominent allusion to Daniel 7:14 in 28:18:

Matthew 28:18 (NASB): "All *authority* [*exousia*] *has been given* [*edothē*] to Me in heaven and on earth [*gēs*]."	Daniel 7:14 (NETS): "And *royal authority* [*exousia*] *was given* [*edothē*] to him, and all the nations *of the earth* [*tēs gēs*] according to posterity, and all honor was serving him. And his authority is an everlasting authority."

The verb "to give" (*didōmi*) is in the passive in Daniel 7:14 because it refers to the Ancient of Days (Dan. 7:9–10) conferring upon the son of man a right or "authority" to rule on account of his defeat of the fourth beast (Dan. 7:11–12). In attempting to make sense of Matthew's repeated allusions to Daniel 7, we have argued that Matthew presents Jesus as Daniel's Son of Man who initially yet decisively defeats the devil at the wilderness temptation. As the narrative marches forward, so does the kingdom. This "growth" of the kingdom is largely unique to Matthew's Gospel.

The narrative culminates when Jesus finally, through faithfully obeying his Father, earns the right to rule over the cosmos—that is, "heaven and earth" (see 6:10; 11:25; 16:19; 18:18–19). Perhaps not coincidentally, the LXX (OG) of Daniel 4:17 reads, "The Lord *of Heaven* [*tou ouranou*] has *authority* [*exousian*] over everything which is in *heaven* [*tō ouranō*] and which is on *earth* [*tēs gēs*]" (NETS). It appears that the son of man in Daniel 7:14 earns the right to rule alongside of the Ancient of Days according to one early Greek translation. Therefore, while Jesus begins to rule over "heaven and earth" at the wilderness temptation, his faithful life, death, and resurrection earn him the right to rule to an even greater degree at the right hand of his Father. Finally, when Jesus returns at the end of the age, his rule as the Son of Man will be consummated. The resurrected Jesus now enjoys "all authority." Before his death and resurrection, Jesus certainly possessed "authority" on account of his identity as God incarnate (7:29; 9:6, 8; 10:1; 21:23–24, 27), but now he has "all authority." This is not a far cry from Revelation's depiction of the Lamb, who is found "worthy" to open the seals of judgment because of his death and resurrection (Rev. 5:9, 12).

The Son of Man's cosmic rule is the basis for his commission to his disciples. They are to "go and make disciples of all nations" (28:19a). They are assured of success because glory will be "with" them and because they will be operating within the Son of Man's victorious rule. In the first commission in 10:1, Jesus gives the disciples "authority to drive out impure spirits and to heal every disease and sickness" but only within Israel. He specifically forbids them, "Do not go among the Gentiles or enter the town of the Samaritans" (10:5). The disciples are to proclaim to the Israelites that the "kingdom of heaven has come near" (10:6; cf. 3:2; 4:17). But here at the end of the narrative, the presence of the kingdom is more pervasive because of the Son of Man's success. So the disciples are now empowered with a greater degree of authority and are able to bring the message of the kingdom to the "nations." God's people are also to be marked by ultimate allegiance to the triune God in baptism (28:19b). All three persons of the Trinity have worked in harmony to bring God's glory to the ends of the earth!

Matthew: Commentaries

Albright, W. F., and C. S. Mann. *Matthew*. AB. Garden City, NY: Doubleday, 1971.

Allison, Dale C., Jr. *Matthew: A Shorter Commentary*. London: T&T Clark, 2004.

Blomberg, Craig L. *Matthew*. NAC. Nashville: Broadman, 1992.

Bruner, Frederick Dale. *Matthew: A Commentary*. Vol. 1, *The Christbook: Matthew 1–12*. Rev. ed. Grand Rapids: Eerdmans, 2004.

———. *Matthew: A Commentary*. Vol. 2, *The Churchbook: Matthew 13–28*. Rev. ed. Grand Rapids: Eerdmans, 2004.

Carson, D. A. "Matthew." In *Matthew–Mark*, vol. 9 of *Expositor's Bible Commentary*, edited by Tremper Longman III and David E. Garland, rev. ed., 23–670. Grand Rapids: Zondervan, 2010.

Davies, W. D., and Dale C. Allison Jr. *A Critical and Exegetical Commentary on the Gospel according to Saint Matthew*. Rev. ed. 3 vols. ICC. Edinburgh: T&T Clark, 1988–97.

Filson, Floyd V. *The Gospel according to St. Matthew*. 2nd ed. BNTC. London: Adam & Charles Black, 1971.

France, R. T. *The Gospel according to Matthew*. Rev. ed. TNTC. Grand Rapids: Eerdmans, 1985.

———. *The Gospel of Matthew*. NICNT. Grand Rapids: Eerdmans, 2007.

Garland, David E. *Reading Matthew*. Rev. ed. Macon, GA: Smyth & Helwys, 1999.

Gibbs, Jeffrey A. *Matthew 1:1–11:1*. CC. St. Louis: Concordia, 2006.

Green, Michael. *The Message of Matthew*. BST. Downers Grove, IL: InterVarsity, 2000.

Gundry, Robert H. *Matthew: A Commentary on His Handbook for a Mixed Church under Persecution*. Rev. ed. Grand Rapids: Eerdmans, 1994.

Hagner, Donald A. *Matthew*. 2 vols. WBC. Dallas: Word, 1993–95.

Harrington, Daniel J. *The Gospel of Matthew*. SP. Collegeville, MN: Liturgical Press, 2007.

Hauerwas, Stanley. *Matthew*. BTCB. Grand Rapids: Brazos, 2006.

Hill, David. *The Gospel of Matthew*. NCBC. Grand Rapids: Eerdmans, 1981.

Keener, Craig S. *A Commentary on the Gospel of Matthew*. Grand Rapids: Eerdmans, 1999.

———. *Matthew*. IVPNTC. Downers Grove, IL: InterVarsity, 1997.

Luz, Ulrich. *Matthew*. 3 vols. Hermeneia. Minneapolis: Fortress, 2001–7.

Mills, Watson E. *The Gospel of Matthew*. Rev. ed. Lewiston, NY: Mellen, 2002.

Morris, Leon. *The Gospel according to Matthew*. PNTC. Grand Rapids: Eerdmans, 1992.

Mounce, Robert H. *Matthew*. NIBC. Peabody, MA: Hendrickson, 1991.

Nolland, John. *The Gospel of Matthew*. NIGTC. Grand Rapids: Eerdmans, 2005.

Osborne, Grant R. *Matthew*. ZECNT. Grand Rapids: Zondervan, 2010.

Ridderbos, Herman N. *Matthew*. Bible Student's Commentary. Grand Rapids: Zondervan, 1987.

Turner, David L. *Matthew*. BECNT. Grand Rapids: Baker Academic, 2008.

Wilkins, Michael J. *Matthew*. NIVAC. Grand Rapids: Zondervan, 2004.

Witherington, Ben, III. *Matthew*. SHBC. Macon, GA: Smyth & Helwys, 2006.

Wright, N. T. *Matthew for Everyone: Part 1; Chapters 1–15*. Louisville: Westminster John Knox, 2004.

———. *Matthew for Everyone: Part 2; Chapters 16–28*. Louisville: Westminster John Knox, 2004.

Matthew: Articles, Essays, and Monographs

Allison, Dale C. *The New Moses: A Matthean Typology*. Minneapolis: Fortress, 1993.

Aune, David E., ed. *The Gospel of Matthew in Current Study*. Grand Rapids: Eerdmans, 2001.

Aus, R. D. *Matthew 1–2 and the Virginal Conception*. Lanham, MD: University Press of America, 2004.

Bacon, B. W. "The Five Books of Matthew against the Jews." *Expositor* 15 (1918): 56–66.

Barrett, C. K. "The House of Prayer and the Den of Thieves." In *Jesus und Paulus: Festschrift für Werner Georg Kümmel zum 70. Geburtstag*, edited by E. E. Ellis and E. Grässer, 13–20. Göttingen: Vandenhoeck & Ruprecht, 1978.

Baxter, Wayne. *Israel's Only Shepherd: Matthew's Shepherd Motif and His Social Setting*. LNTS 457. London: Bloomsbury T&T Clark, 2012.

Beare, Francis Wright. "The Mission of the Twelve and the Mission Charge: Matthew 10 and Parallels." *JBL* 89 (1970): 1–13.

Beaton, Richard. *Isaiah's Christ in Matthew's Gospel*. SNTSMS 123. Cambridge: Cambridge University Press, 2004.

Betz, H. D. *The Sermon on the Mount: A Commentary on the Sermon on the Mount, Including the Sermon on the Plain (Matthew 5:3–7:27 and Luke 6:20–49)*. Hermeneia. Minneapolis: Fortress, 1995.

Blomberg, Craig L. "Interpreting Old Testament Prophetic Literature in Matthew: Double Fulfillment." *TJ* 23 (2002): 17–33.

———. "Matthew." In *Commentary on the New Testament Use of the Old Testament*, edited by G. K. Beale and D. A. Carson, 1–110. Grand Rapids: Baker Academic, 2007.

Broadhead, Edwin K. *The Gospel of Matthew on the Landscape of Antiquity*. Tübingen: Mohr Siebeck, 2017.

Brown, Jeannine K. *The Disciples in Narrative Perspective: The Portrayal and Function of the Matthean Disciples*. AcBib 9. Boston: Brill, 2002.

Brown, Raymond E. *The Birth of the Messiah: A Commentary on the Infancy Narratives in the Gospels of Matthew and Luke*. 2nd ed. New York: Doubleday, 1993.

Caragounis, Chrys C. *Peter the Rock.* BZNW 58. Berlin: de Gruyter, 1990.

Carson, D. A. *The Sermon on the Mount: An Evangelical Exposition of Matthew 5–7.* Grand Rapids: Baker, 1978.

Carter, Warren. *Households and Discipleship: A Study of Matthew 19–20.* JSNTSup 103. Sheffield: JSOT Press, 1994.

———. *Matthew and Empire: Initial Explorations.* Harrisburg, PA: Trinity Press International, 2001.

Chae, Young S. *Jesus as the Eschatological Davidic Shepherd: Studies in the Old Testament, Second Temple Judaism, and in the Gospel of Matthew.* WUNT 2/216. Tübingen: Mohr Siebeck, 2006.

Charette, Blaine. *Restoring Presence: The Spirit in Matthew's Gospel.* JPTSup 18. Sheffield: Sheffield Academic, 2000.

———. *The Theme of Recompense in Matthew's Gospel.* JSNTSup 79. Sheffield: JSOT Press, 1992.

———. "'To Proclaim Liberty to the Captives': Matthew 11.28–30 in the Light of Old Testament Prophetic Expectation." *NTS* 38 (1992): 290–97.

Cope, O. Lamar. *Matthew: A Scribe Trained for the Kingdom of Heaven.* New York: Ktav, 1977.

Crowe, Brandon D. *The Obedient Son: Deuteronomy and Christology in the Gospel of Matthew.* BZNW 188. Berlin: de Gruyter, 2012.

Deutsch, Celia. *Hidden Wisdom and the Easy Yoke: Wisdom, Torah and Discipleship in Matthew 11.25–30.* JSNTSup 18. Sheffield: JSOT Press, 1987.

Donaldson, Terence L. *Jesus on the Mountain: A Study in Matthean Theology.* JSNTSup 8. Sheffield: JSOT Press, 1985.

Duling, Dennis C. *A Marginal Scribe: Studies in the Gospel of Matthew in Social-Scientific Perspective.* Eugene, OR: Cascade Books, 2012.

Dvořáček, Jiří. *The Son of David in Matthew's Gospel in the Light of the Solomon as Exorcist Tradition.* WUNT 2/415. Tübingen: Mohr Siebeck, 2016.

Edwards, Richard A. *Matthew's Narrative Portrait of the Disciples.* Valley Forge, PA: Trinity Press International, 1997.

Erickson, R. J. "Divine Injustice? Matthew's Narrative Strategy and the Slaughter of the Innocents (Matthew 2.13–23)." *JSNT* 64 (1996): 5–27.

France, R. T. *Jesus and the Old Testament.* Grand Rapids: Baker, 1982.

———. *Matthew: Evangelist and Teacher.* Downers Grove, IL: InterVarsity, 1998.

Garland, David E. *The Intention of Matthew 23.* NovTSup 52. Leiden: Brill, 1979.

Gench, Frances Taylor. *Wisdom in the Christology of Matthew.* New York: University Press of America, 1997.

Gerhardsson, Birger. *The Testing of God's Son (Matt 4:11 & Par.): An Analysis of an Early Christian Midrash.* Coniectanea Biblica: New Testament Series 2.1. Lund: Gleerup, 1966.

Gibbs, J. A. "Israel Standing with Israel: The Baptism of Jesus in Matthew's Gospel (Matt 3:13–17)." *CBQ* 64 (2002): 511–26.

Green, H. Benedict. *Matthew, Poet of the Beatitudes.* JSNTSup 203. Sheffield: Sheffield Academic, 2001.

Guelich, Robert A. *The Sermon on the Mount: A Foundation for Understanding.* Waco: Word, 1982.

Gundry, Robert H. *Peter: False Disciple and Apostate according to Saint Matthew.* Grand Rapids: Eerdmans, 2015.

———. *The Use of the Old Testament in St. Matthew's Gospel with Specific Reference to the Messianic Hope.* NovTSup 18. Leiden: Brill, 1967.

Gurtner, Daniel M. "The Gospel of Matthew from Stanton to Present: A Survey of Some Recent Developments." In *Jesus, Matthew's Gospel and Early Christianity: Studies in Memory of Graham N. Stanton,* edited by Daniel M. Gurtner, Joel Willitts, and Richard A. Burridge, 23–38. London: T&T Clark, 2011.

———. *The Torn Veil: Matthew's Exposition of the Death of Jesus.* SNTSMS 139. Cambridge: Cambridge University Press, 2006.

Gurtner, Daniel M., and John Nolland, eds. *Built upon the Rock: Studies in the Gospel of Matthew.* Grand Rapids: Eerdmans, 2008.

Hagner, Donald A. "Matthew: Christian Judaism or Jewish Christianity?" In *The Face of New Testament Studies: A Survey of Recent Research,* edited by Scot McKnight and Grant R. Osborne, 263–82. Grand Rapids: Baker Academic, 2004.

Ham, C. *The Coming King and the Rejected Shepherd: Matthew's Reading of Zechariah's Messianic Hope.* Sheffield: Sheffield Phoenix, 2005.

Hamilton, Catherine Sider. *The Death of Jesus in Matthew: Innocent Blood and the End of Exile.* SNTSMS 167. Cambridge: Cambridge University Press, 2017.

Hannan, Margaret. *The Nature and Demands of the Sovereign Rule of God in the Gospel of Matthew.* LNTS 308. London: T&T Clark, 2006.

Hare, Douglas R. A. *The Theme of Jewish Persecution of Christians in the Gospel according to St. Matthew.* Cambridge: Cambridge University Press, 1967.

Hengel, Martin. *The Charismatic Leader and His Followers.* Translated by J. Greig. New York: Crossroad, 1981.

Hood, Jason B. *The Messiah, His Brothers, and the Nations (Matthew 1.1–17).* London: T&T Clark, 2011.

Hubbard, Benjamin J. *The Matthean Redaction of a Primitive Apostolic Commissioning: An Exegesis of Matthew 28:16–20.* SBLDS 19. Missoula, MT: Society of Biblical Literature, 1974.

Huizenga, Leroy A. *The New Isaac: Tradition and Intertextuality in the Gospel of Matthew.* Leiden: Brill, 2012.

Jackson, Glenna S. *"Have Mercy on Me": The Story of the Canaanite Woman in Matthew 15:21–18.* JSNTSup 228. Sheffield: Sheffield Academic, 2002.

Jeremias, Joachim. *The Sermon on the Mount.* Translated by N. Perrin. Philadelphia: Fortress, 1963.

Jones, Ivor H. *The Matthean Parables: A Literary and Historical Commentary.* Studien zum Neuen Testament 80. New York: Brill, 1995.

Kingsbury, Jack Dean. *Matthew as Story.* 2nd ed. Philadelphia: Fortress, 1988.

————. *Matthew: Structure, Christology, Kingdom*. Philadelphia: Fortress, 1975.

————. "Observations on the 'Miracle Chapters' of Matthew 8–9." *CBQ* 40 (1978): 559–73.

————. *The Parables of Jesus in Matthew 13: A Study in Redaction Criticism*. London: SPCK, 1969.

Knowles, Michael. *Jeremiah in Matthew's Gospel: The Rejected-Prophet Motif in Matthean Redaction*. JSNTSup 68. Sheffield: Sheffield Academic, 1993.

Kupp, David D. *Matthew's Emmanuel: Divine Presence and God's People in the First Gospel*. SNTSMS 90. Cambridge: Cambridge University Press, 1996.

Kynes, W. *A Christology of Solidarity: Jesus as the Representative of His People in Matthew*. Lanham, MD: University Press of America, 1991.

Laansma, J. *"I Will Give You Rest": The "Rest" Motif in the New Testament with Special Reference to Mt 11 and Heb 3–4*. WUNT 2/98. Tübingen: Mohr Siebeck, 1997.

Lambrecht, Jan. *The Sermon on the Mount: Proclamation and Exhortation*. Wilmington, DE: Michael Glazier, 1985.

Leim, Joshua E. *Matthew's Theological Grammar: The Father and the Son*. WUNT 2/402. Tübingen: Mohr Siebeck, 2015.

Loader, W. R. G. "Son of David, Blindness, Possession, and Duality in Matthew." *CBQ* 44 (1982): 570–85.

Luz, Ulrich. *Studies in Matthew*. Grand Rapids: Eerdmans, 2005.

————. *The Theology of the Gospel of Matthew*. Cambridge: Cambridge University Press, 1995.

Marcus, J. "The Gates of Hades and the Keys of the Kingdom (Matt 16:18–19)." *CBQ* 50 (1988): 443–55.

Meier, J. P. *Law and History in Matthew's Gospel: A Redactional Study of Mt. 5:17–48*. Rome: Biblical Institute Press, 1976.

————. *The Vision of Matthew: Christ, Church, and Morality in the First Gospel*. New York: Paulist Press, 1979.

Menken, Maarten J. J. *Matthew's Bible: The Old Testament Text of the Evangelist*. Leuven: Leuven University Press, 2004.

Morosco, Robert E. "Redaction Criticism and the Evangelical: Matthew 10 as a Test Case." *JETS* 22 (1979): 323–31.

Moses, A. D. A. *Matthew's Transfiguration Story and Jewish-Christian Controversy*. JSNTSup 122. Sheffield: Sheffield Academic, 1996.

Moss, Charlene McAfee. *The Zechariah Tradition and the Gospel of Matthew*. BZNW 156. Berlin: de Gruyter, 2008.

Newport, Kenneth G. C. *The Sources and Sitz im Leben of Matthew 23*. JSNTSup 117. Sheffield: Sheffield Academic, 1995.

Neyrey, Jerome H. *Honor and Shame in the Gospel of Matthew*. Louisville: Westminster John Knox, 1998.

Novakovic, Lidija. *Messiah, the Healer of the Sick: A Study of Jesus as the Son of David in the Gospel of Matthew*. WUNT 2/170. Tübingen: Mohr Siebeck, 2003.

O'Leary, Anne M. *Matthew's Judaization of Mark: Examined in the Context of the Use of Sources in Graeco-Roman Antiquity*. LNTS 323. London: T&T Clark, 2006.

Olmstead, Wesley G. *Matthew's Trilogy of Parables: The Nation, the Nations and the Reader in Matthew 21:28–22:14*. SNTSMS 127. Cambridge: Cambridge University Press, 2003.

Orton, David E. *The Understanding Scribe: Matthew and the Apocalyptic Ideal*. JSNTSup 25. Sheffield: JSOT Press, 1989.

Overman, J. Andrew. *Matthew's Gospel and Formative Judaism: The Social World of the Matthean Community*. Minneapolis: Fortress, 1990.

Pennington, Jonathan T. *Heaven and Earth in the Gospel of Matthew*. NovTSup 126. Leiden: Brill, 2007.

Piotrowski, Nicholas G. *Matthew's New David at the End of Exile: A Socio-Rhetorical Study of Scriptural Quotations*. NovTSup 170. Leiden: Brill, 2016.

Powell, Mark A. *God with Us: A Pastoral Theology of Matthew's Gospel*. Minneapolis: Fortress, 1995.

Przybylski, Benno. *Righteousness in Matthew and His World of Thought*. Cambridge: Cambridge University Press, 1980.

Reeves, Rodney. "The Gospel of Matthew." In *The State of New Testament Studies: A Survey of Recent Research*, edited by Scot McKnight and Nijay K. Gupta, 275–96. Grand Rapids: Baker Academic, 2019.

Riches, John, and David C. Sim, eds. *The Gospel of Matthew in Its Roman Imperial Context*. London: T&T Clark, 2005.

Runesson, Anders. *Divine Wrath and Salvation in Matthew: The Narrative World of the First Gospel*. Minneapolis: Fortress, 2016.

Runesson, Anders, and Daniel M. Gurtner, eds. *Matthew within Judaism: Israel and the Nations in the First Gospel*. ECIL 27. Atlanta: SBL Press, 2020.

Saldarini, Anthony J. *Matthew's Christian-Jewish Community*. Chicago: University of Chicago Press, 1994.

Schreiner, Patrick. *The Body of Jesus: A Spatial Analysis of the Kingdom in Matthew*. LNTS 555. London: Bloomsbury T&T Clark, 2016.

———. *Matthew, Disciple and Scribe: The First Gospel and Its Portrait of Jesus*. Grand Rapids: Baker Academic, 2019.

Schweizer, Eduard. "Matthew's Church." In *The Interpretation of Matthew*, edited by G. Stanton, 129–55. Philadelphia: Fortress, 1983.

Senior, Donald P. *The Passion Narrative according to Matthew: A Redactional Study*. Leuven: Leuven University Press, 1982.

Sim, David C. *Apocalyptic Eschatology in the Gospel of Matthew*. SNTSMS 88. Cambridge: Cambridge University Press, 1996.

———. *The Gospel of Matthew and Christian Judaism: The History and Social Setting of the Matthean Community*. Edinburgh: T&T Clark, 1998.

Soares-Prabhu, George M. *The Formula Quotations in the Infancy Narrative of Matthew*. Rome: Biblical Institute Press, 1976.

Stanton, Graham N. *A Gospel for a New People: Studies in Matthew*. Edinburgh: T&T Clark, 1992.

———, ed. *The Interpretation of Matthew*. Rev. ed. Edinburgh: T&T Clark, 1995.

———. "The Origin and Purpose of Matthew's Gospel: Matthean Scholarship from 1945 to 1980." *ANRW*, part 2, *Principat*, 25.3:1889–1951.

Stendahl, Krister. *The School of St. Matthew and Its Use of the Old Testament*. Philadelphia: Fortress, 1968.

Stock, Augustine. *The Method and Message of Matthew*. Collegeville, MN: Liturgical Press, 1994.

Strecker, Georg. *The Sermon on the Mount: An Exegetical Commentary*. Translated by O. C. Dean Jr. Nashville: Abingdon, 1988.

Suggs, M. J. *Wisdom, Christology, and Law in Matthew's Gospel*. Cambridge, MA: Harvard University Press, 1970.

Thompson, William G. *Matthew's Advice to a Divided Community: Matt 17, 22–18, 35*. AnBib 44. Rome: Pontifical Biblical Institute, 1970.

Verseput, Donald J. "The Faith of the Reader and the Narrative of Matthew 13:53–16:20." *JSNT* 46 (1992): 3–24.

———. *The Rejection of the Humble Messianic King: A Study of Matthew 11–12*. Europäische Hochschulschriften 23. Frankfurt: Peter Lang, 1986.

Viviano, Benedict T. "Social World and Community Leadership: The Case of Matthew 23:1–12, 34." *JSNT* 39 (1990): 3–21.

Weaver, Dorothy J. *Matthew's Missionary Discourse: A Literary Critical Analysis*. JSNTSup 38. Sheffield: JSOT Press, 1990.

Wilkins, Michael J. *The Concept of Disciple in Matthew's Gospel as Reflected in the Use of the Term Mathētēs*. NovTSup 59. Leiden: Brill, 1988.

———. *Discipleship in the Ancient World and in Matthew's Gospel*. Grand Rapids: Baker, 1995.

Willitts, Joel. *Matthew's Messianic Shepherd-King in Search of "the Lost Sheep of the House of Israel."* BZNW 147. Berlin: de Gruyter, 2007.

Wilson, Alistair I. *When Will These Things Happen? A Study of Jesus as Judge in Matthew 21–25*. Milton Keynes, UK: Paternoster, 2004.

Yang, Yong-Eui. *Jesus and the Sabbath in Matthew's Gospel*. JSNTSup 138. Sheffield: Sheffield Academic, 1997.

Zacharias, H. Daniel. *Matthew's Presentation of the Son of David: Davidic Tradition and Typology in the Gospel of Matthew*. London: Bloomsbury T&T Clark, 2016.

CHAPTER TWO

The Gospel of Mark

Introduction[1]

Authorship and Date

Our Bibles bear the name Mark at the heading of this Gospel, yet Mark was not one of the original twelve disciples. How could Mark write a Gospel if he did not witness Jesus's earthly ministry (cf. Acts 1:21–22)? The answer probably lies in the comment made by the second-century church leader Papias when he recollects what he heard from the apostle John, or the "Presbyter":

> And the Presbyter [John] used to say this: Mark became Peter's interpreter and wrote accurately all that he remembered, not, indeed, in order, of the things said or done by the Lord. For he had not heard the Lord, nor had he followed him, but later on, as I said, followed Peter, who used to give teaching as necessity demanded but not making, as it were, an arrangement of the Lord's oracles, so that Mark did nothing wrong in thus writing down single points as he remembered them. For to one thing he gave attention, to leave out nothing of what he had heard and to make no false statements in them.[2]

From this quotation, we gain two key insights: (1) an individual named Mark wrote the Second Gospel; and (2) Mark did not witness these events firsthand but received eyewitness testimony through the apostle Peter. Though Mark was not part of the Twelve, he was a companion of Paul and Peter. It's

---

1. The introduction is an adaptation of Benjamin Gladd, "Mark," in *A Biblical-Theological Introduction to the New Testament: The Gospel Realized*, ed. Michael J. Kruger (Wheaton: Crossway, 2016), 65–66. Used with permission.

2. Eusebius, *Hist. eccl.* 3.39.15, in *Ecclesiastical History*, vol. 1, *Books 1–5*, trans. Kirsopp Lake, Loeb Classical Library (New York: Putman, 1926), 297.

likely that we should identify this Mark with John Mark in the book of Acts (Acts 12:12, 25; 13:5, 13; 15:37), the cousin of Barnabas who interacted closely with several apostles (Col. 4:10; 2 Tim. 4:11; Philem. 24; 1 Pet. 5:13). Though some modern scholars doubt that John Mark authored the Second Gospel, there's simply not enough evidence to overthrow a few internal hints within Mark's Gospel and the external witness of the early church.

The dating of Mark hinges on how we understand the relationship between the Synoptics, the nature of prophecy, and a handful of other details. Most contemporary scholars date Mark in the early to mid-70s largely because they view the Olivet Discourse, an event that largely predicts the destruction of the temple in AD 70, as a "prophecy after the event" (*vaticinium ex eventu*). If Jesus is God in flesh, coeternal with the Father, and creator of the cosmos, then he has the power to predict the destruction of the temple. Dating Mark to the late 50s and early 60s is preferred, then, because it allows enough time for Matthew and Luke to use Mark in composing their Gospels and because it retains the Olivet Discourse as a legitimate prophecy.

Purpose

Mark, probably writing from Rome, reworks OT and Jewish expectations of a messiah. Political triumph and physical triumph don't mark the messiah's reign, only suffering and defeat. Those who follow a suffering messiah will likewise follow in his footsteps and suffer in his wake. Jesus, the Messiah, is also Isaiah's Lord and Suffering Servant, who will redeem captive Israel from the shackles of sin and death and plant them in the land of the new creation. While Matthew emphasizes the *growth* of the kingdom and Luke underscores its *scope*, Mark develops the *preparation* and the mysterious *arrival* of the kingdom.

Outline

Generally speaking, Mark's narrative progresses geographically from Jesus's baptism in the Jordan to his ministry in Galilee and then on to Jerusalem. In Galilee, Jesus is welcomed by the populace, both Jews and gentiles. Jerusalem, ironically, is the place of suffering and death. Instead of embracing her Messiah, the city of David scorns him, eventually nailing him to a cross. One of the most distinctive features of Mark is his three-part "drama." R. T. France persuasively argues that Mark's Gospel falls into three "dramatic acts" (1:14–8:21; 8:22–10:52; 11:1–16:8).[3]

3. R. T. France, *The Gospel of Mark: A Commentary on the Greek Text*, NIGTC (Grand Rapids: Eerdmans, 2002), 11–15.

Prologue (1:1–13)
> Jesus as Messiah and Son of God (1:1)
> The Gospel as Told by Exodus, Malachi, and Isaiah (1:2–3)
> Baptism of Repentance (1:4–11)
> Cleansing Creation (1:12–13)

Act 1: Jesus in Galilee (1:14–8:21)

The Beginning of Jesus's Galilean Ministry (1:14–45)
> The Kingdom Is at Hand (1:14–15)
> The Summons to Follow (1:16–20)
> Cleansing the Synagogue (1:21–28)
> The Messianic Secret (1:29–39)
> Cleansing the Leper (1:40–45)

Jesus Gains Popularity in Galilee (2:1–3:6)
> Jesus Forgives the Paralytic (2:1–12)
> The Calling of Levi (2:13–17)
> Wineskins (2:18–22)
> Jesus as Priest-King (2:23–28)
> The Jewish Leaders Hatch a Plot (3:1–6)

Who Is Jesus of Nazareth? (3:7–35)
> The Calling of the Twelve (3:7–19)
> Rejection by Friends and Family (3:20–35)

The Nature of the Kingdom (4:1–41)
> Parables of the Kingdom (4:1–34)
> The Stilling of the Storm (4:35–41)

From Unclean to Clean (5:1–43)
> The Gerasene Demoniac (5:1–20)
> Healing the Woman with the Issue of Blood and Raising Jairus's Daughter (5:21–43)

Mounting Hostility in Galilee (6:1–56)
> Rejection at Nazareth (6:1–6)
> The Commissioning of the Twelve and the Martyrdom of John the Baptist (6:7–29)
> The Feeding of the Five Thousand (6:30–44)
> Jesus Walks on the Water (6:45–56)

Prologue (1:1–13)

Jesus as Messiah and Son of God (1:1)

The opening line of the Second Gospel sets the tone for the entire narrative: "The beginning of the gospel of Jesus Christ, the Son of God" (1:1 NASB). Before we define "gospel," we must first understand what Mark means by "beginning." Why does Mark relate "beginning" with the gospel? We can understand this in two ways: the "beginning" of the Gospel in a restrictive sense (the prologue [1:1–13]) or the "beginning" in a broad sense (the entire Gospel [1:1–16:8]). The narrow sense of "beginning" is likely in mind since Mark ties the OT quotations directly to John the Baptist's ministry in the prologue. That said, the prologue informs the entire narrative!

The word "gospel" is also an incredibly important word. Mark 1:1 states that it concerns "Jesus the Messiah." Narrowly, the term "gospel" refers exclusively to the message of Jesus's life, death, and resurrection (1 Cor. 15:2–4). But in a wider sense, the word also captures the death and resurrection of Jesus *and* the implications or effects. For example, in 1:15 the "good news" is paired with the "kingdom of God." The in-breaking of the kingdom of God is the *result* of what Jesus accomplishes in his death and resurrection. Craig Blomberg even suggests that "Mark may well have been the first Christian to use the word 'gospel' . . . as a term for the story about Jesus rather than for the message Jesus himself brought."[4]

The gospel is "about Jesus the Messiah, the Son of God" (1:1). First-century Jews had certain expectations about what their messiah would accomplish upon his arrival. Foremost among them was to overthrow the oppressive rule of Rome. The gentiles were to serve Israel, not vice versa. But Mark's portrayal (indeed, all the Gospels' portrayals) of Jesus's messiahship differs from what most anticipated. Though Jesus is genuinely Israel's Messiah, he comes not with a sword in hand as a conquering political king. He arrives as the Messiah who lays down his life as the sacrifice for his people (10:45). But here is the brilliance of Mark's narrative: in his atoning death, Jesus would indeed execute his reign as king. From the outside, Jesus's death appears to be an utter failure. But in reality, he rules in the midst of death and defeat. From beginning to end, Mark's Gospel explains how Jesus is simultaneously the King of Israel and the Suffering Servant of Isaiah. He is the royal Son of David (Isa. 9:6) *and* the sacrificial Lamb of God (Isa. 53:7).

In addition to being about "Jesus the Messiah," the gospel is also about Jesus as the "Son of God." Although there is some doubt whether the title "Son of God" is part of the original text, many commentators and most English translations include it (ESV, HCSB, NASB, NIV, NLT, etc.). The title "Son of God" makes good sense here, as it contains royal overtones in a handful of OT texts (2 Sam. 7; Ps. 2). Kings in the OT were viewed as being a "son" of God since they functioned on his behalf. The title "Son of God" also likely includes a divine dimension. Jesus is the unique "Son" of God (cf. John 3:16). Richard Bauckham rightly defines the title "Son of God" as referring "not merely to a status or office to which Jesus is appointed but to a profound relationship that binds Father and Son together."[5]

4. Craig L. Blomberg, *Jesus and the Gospels: An Introduction and Survey*, 2nd ed. (Nashville: B&H, 2009), 134.

5. Richard Bauckham, *Who Is God? Key Moments of Biblical Revelation* (Grand Rapids: Baker Academic, 2020), 98.

The two titles, Messiah and the Son of God, shape the entire narrative of the Second Gospel. Mark expects his audience to reflect upon these two titles and grasp the totality of Jesus's ministry in light of them. This two-fold purpose is not a far cry from the Fourth Gospel's purpose, outlined in John 20:31: "But these [signs] are written that you may believe that *Jesus is the Messiah, the Son of God*, and that by believing you may have life in his name." Of course, John's Gospel offers further reflection on Jesus's unique sonship, but much of the grist of the Fourth Gospel can be found in Mark.

The Gospel as Told by Exodus, Malachi, and Isaiah (1:2–3)

Three key OT references—Exodus 23:20, Malachi 3:1, and Isaiah 40:3—frame the prologue and set the trajectory for what follows. Mark is the only evangelist to pair these two OT quotations and one allusion. Matthew and Luke separate them, placing them in different contexts (Matt. 3:3, quoting Isa. 40:3; Matt. 11:10, quoting Exod. 23:20 and Mal. 3:1; Luke 3:4, quoting Isa. 40:3; Luke 7:27, quoting Exod. 23:20 and Mal. 3:1). Why does Mark uniquely wed Exodus 23:20, Malachi 3:1, and Isaiah 40:3, and why does he place them at the beginning of his Gospel?

We must first consider the precise relationship between verse 1 and verse 2. It appears that the phrase "Isaiah the prophet" (1:2) *explains* the entirety of the opening verse. Several translations unhelpfully separate these two verses by putting a period after verse 1 (ESV, HCSB, NASB, NRSV). The evangelist wants his audience to read the two verses as a single unit: "The beginning of the good news about Jesus the Messiah, the Son of God, *as* [*kathōs*] it is written in Isaiah the prophet" (cf. NLT). Here's the payoff: *the "gospel" depends upon and is explained by the book of Isaiah*. We will take our cue from 1:2 and thoughtfully consider how each major section of the narrative relates to Jesus as the end-time Messiah and the Son of God, as predicted in the book of Isaiah.

Adding another layer of difficulty to the prologue is the presence of "Isaiah the prophet" in 1:2a. Why only mention Isaiah by name? What about Exodus and Malachi? Mark tends to "sandwich" events in his narrative (e.g., 3:20–35; 5:21–43; 6:7–30; 11:12–25). This literary technique, known as intercalation, appears to be employed here with the Isaiah quotation.[6] Mark first mentions "Isaiah" but then cites Exodus 23:20 and Malachi 3:1:

As it is written **in Isaiah the prophet**: (1:2a)

> I will send my messenger ahead of you,
>> who will prepare your way (1:2b, quoting Exod. 23:20; Mal. 3:1)

6. Rikki E. Watts, *Isaiah's New Exodus in Mark* (Grand Rapids: Baker Academic, 2000), 89.

> A voice of one calling in the wilderness,
> "Prepare the way for the Lord,
>> make straight paths for him" (1:3, quoting Isa. 40:3)

The evangelist intends his readers to read Exodus 23:20 and Malachi 3:1 *in light of Isaiah 40:3*. We will now briefly examine the immediate context of these references and then relate our observations to Mark's Gospel.

EXODUS 23

According to Exodus 23:20–33, the "messenger," probably an angelic figure (see Exod. 3:2; 14:19; 32:34; 33:2; Josh. 5:13–15; Judg. 2:1–3; 6:11–24), will protect Israel along the way to the promised land: "I am sending an angel ahead of you to guard you along the way and to bring you to the place *I have prepared [hētoimasa]*" (Exod. 23:20). On account of their wickedness and idolatry, the messenger will fight Canaanites. The messenger's promise, though, is contingent upon Israel's behavior. If Israel listens to the messenger, then God will fight on their behalf and bless them (Exod. 23:22). If Israel conforms to the behavior of the pagan nations, then God will curse the nation (Exod. 23:32). The messenger is to escort them to the "place I have prepared." This language occurs earlier in Exodus 15:17 as a reference to the promised land as the future dwelling place of God's presence: "You will bring them in and plant them on the mountain of your inheritance—the place, LORD, you made for your dwelling, the sanctuary, Lord, your hands *established [hētoimasan]*."[7] So God promises Israel that he will graciously lead them to the promised land, vanquish their enemies, and dwell with them if they obey his commands.

MALACHI 3

Malachi 3 draws from Exodus 23 but refashions it in light of Israel's behavior in the postexilic era. God's people refuse to treat one another equitably and continue to break God's law in a variety of ways. According to Exodus 23, God sends his messenger to mete out punishment upon the Canaanites. Now, Malachi accuses Israel of injustice, and God will pour out judgment upon them (Mal. 1:6–10, 12–14, etc.). The messenger in Malachi 3:1–6 prepares Israel for the Lord's judgment. At the heart of Malachi's oracles is God's desire to refine the covenant community so that he can dwell with them:

7. T. Desmond Alexander rightly aligns Exod. 15:17 and 23:20. Alexander, *Exodus*, AOTC (Downers Grove, IL: InterVarsity, 2017), 533.

"I will send my messenger, who will prepare the way before me. Then suddenly the Lord you are seeking will come *to his temple*; the messenger of the covenant, whom you desire, will come," says the LORD Almighty.

But who can endure the day of his coming? Who can stand when he appears? For *he will be like a refiner's fire or a launderer's soap.* He will sit as a *refiner* and *purifier* of silver; he will *purify the Levites and refine them* like gold and silver. Then the LORD will have men who will bring offerings in righteousness, and the offerings of Judah and Jerusalem will be acceptable to the LORD, as in days gone by, as in former years. (Mal. 3:1–4)

According to his passage, God's judgment upon the wicked Israelites has a redemptive purpose—their holiness. A holy God cannot dwell with an unholy people, so he appoints an individual, a "messenger," to go before him and prepare Israel for his arrival. At the very end of history, the prophet Malachi predicts that the Lord will come to purify and redeem. Israel has become riddled with idolatry and social injustice (Mal. 1:6–10, 12–14, etc.), and the wicked Israelites, especially their leaders, who refuse to repent will be judged (Mal. 3:5; 4:1–3). But those within Israel who turn to the Lord will escape God's coming end-time judgment. The messenger in Malachi "prepares" Israel for the Lord's arrival. Only a few within Israel, a remnant, will repent and avoid God's wrath (4:6). The result of such purification is found in Malachi 3:3, when God finally dwells with humanity in the new creation: "*Then* the LORD will have men who will bring offerings in righteousness."

ISAIAH 40

Isaiah 40 marks a turning point in the book of Isaiah. Chapters 40–66, while anticipated in the first half of the book (e.g., Isa. 2:2–5; 24:1–25:12), predict Israel's release from Babylonian captivity and recast Israel's redemption as a second exodus (Isa. 40:10–11; 51:9; 52:10). God promises that, following a pattern he used in the first exodus, he will escort his people from Babylon to the promised land (49:9). Then he will create the new heavens and earth upon their arrival (Isa. 65:17–25; 66:22–23). The prophet Isaiah even predicts how God will bring about the new exodus—through the "servant(s)" (Isa. 42:1–9; 49:1–6; 50:4–9; 52:13–53:12). Isaiah 40:3 rests squarely in the prophetic expectation of God redeeming his people from Babylon and leading them through the desert and into the promised land: "A voice of one calling: 'In the wilderness prepare the way of the LORD; make straight in the desert a highway for our God.'" A handful of verses later, we arrive at the *goal* of Israel's redemption: "And *the glory of the* LORD *shall be revealed*, and all flesh shall see it together" (Isa. 40:5). God delivers his people from bondage so that he can dwell with them in the new creation (Isa. 65:17; 66:22).

CONCLUSION

By wedding Exodus 23, Malachi 3, and Isaiah 40 in 1:2b–3, Mark desires to achieve a few aims: (1) He underscores the eschatological dimension of his Gospel. Malachi 3 and Isaiah 40 are explicitly *end-time* prophecies in their respective contexts. Jesus's death and resurrection inaugurate the great tribulation, God's subjugation of the gentiles, deliverance of Israel from oppressors, Israel's restoration and resurrection, the new covenant, the promised Spirit, the new creation, the new temple, a messianic king, and the establishment of God's kingdom. (2) According to Malachi 3, the messenger must "purify" Israel for the arrival of God's holy presence. The Gospel of Mark must convince its readers that Israel needs such purification. At each major junction of the narrative, Mark underscores the unclean state of Israel, the nations, and all of creation. (3) The purification of humanity and the created order is the penultimate goal. The *ultimate* goal of purification is housing the glory of God. God purifies in order to dwell. So a major point of Mark's Gospel—if not *the* major point—is the following: *Jesus cleanses humanity and creation with the purpose of creating a dwelling place fit for the veritable presence of God.*

Now that we have filled in the background to the major contours of Mark's Gospel, we can more fully appreciate John the Baptist's role in the prologue (1:1–13). John stands in continuity with the "messenger" of judgment (Mal. 3:1) and the "voice" that proclaims the second exodus of Israel (Isa. 40:3). His purpose is twofold: prepare Israel for God's coming judgment (Exod. 23:20; Mal. 3:1) and announce the restoration of Israel and the arrival of the new creation (Isa. 40:3). To avoid judgment, Israel must repent of sinful behavior that sullied her garments and return to the Lord. John's appearance and diet are even in accordance with his oracles of judgment. They bring to mind Elijah's attire in 2 Kings 1:8: "He [Elijah] had a garment of hair and had a leather belt around his waist." Elijah ministered during the dark days of Israel's idolatry, calling Israel to repentance. But John also sees beyond divine judgment and heralds Isaiah's long-awaited new exodus of Israel and the restoration of the nations.

Baptism of Repentance (1:4–11)

According to 1:5, John the Baptist's ministry nets positive results: "The whole Judean countryside and all the people of Jerusalem went out to him.

Confessing their sins, they were baptized by him." This highly significant verse reveals that some Israelites are attaching themselves to John's baptism and turning their backs on Israel's now defunct institutions—her temple and its sacrifices. Ritual cleansing, according to the OT and Judaism, relates to God's presence in the midst of Israel to some degree (e.g., Lev. 15:5–27; CDa X, 10–14). For us to appreciate Mark's emphasis on ritual cleansing, let's consider in brief the geography of the Israelite camp in the wilderness.

At the center of the camp is the tabernacle, the place where God dwells.[8] The entire structure, including the courtyard, Holy Place, and Holy of Holies, is deemed "holy." But even within the holy tabernacle, only the back room is considered the *most* holy. Moving outside the courtyard of the tabernacle, Israel's camp is "clean," and everything outside the camp is "unclean." So there are three levels of gradation: holy, clean, and unclean. Determining what is unclean is tricky when we examine Israel's purity laws. On one level, uncleanness can refer to immoral activities (such as murder and theft) or to behavior tied to idolatry (such as drinking blood; Lev. 17–20). On another level, uncleanness can refer to anything that lacks perfection or is incomplete, such as skin diseases or the loss of bodily fluids (Lev. 11–15). In the latter case, the moral component isn't necessarily in view. The point of uncleanness in both scenarios is critical: God accepts only that which is pure, perfect, and ordered. But the issue of holiness is one notch above cleanness. Holiness is married to God's glory (→Mark 2:13–17).

So when John the Baptist offers a baptism of "repentance," he's challenging Israel's entire cultic system, and he's inviting Israel to enjoy complete ritual purity and the ability to dwell in the presence of a holy God. As Mark's narrative unfolds, we discover that Israel and her temple will now be reconstituted in a single person. According to 1:8, John confesses that a coming one will "baptize" Israel with the "Holy Spirit." As great as John's baptism is, "he [John] expresses the expectation that one will come soon who will wash with a newly available pneumatic detergent to perform a full purification."[9]

Mark then transitions from the baptism of Israel (1:4–8) to the baptism of Jesus (1:9–11 // Matt. 3:13–17 // Luke 3:21–22 // John 1:29–34). All four Gospels point out that those within Israel are baptized first, and then Jesus. The relationship between the two groups is worth pondering. Israel's baptism is preparation for his baptism; Jesus identifies with the Israelites. Though

---

8. This paragraph is an adaptation of Benjamin L. Gladd, *From Adam and Israel to the Church: A Biblical Theology of the People of God*, Essential Studies in Biblical Theology (Downers Grove, IL: InterVarsity, 2019), 16.

9. Matthew Thiessen, *Jesus and the Forces of Death: The Gospels' Portrayal of Ritual Impurity within First-Century Judaism* (Grand Rapids: Baker Academic, 2020), 23.

Jesus doesn't confess sin, he does identify with the need for purification. He who is already ritually clean will pass through the Jordan so that he may mercifully identify with the need for forgiveness of sin—a prescription that he himself will offer to the paralyzed man just a few paragraphs later (2:1–12).

According to 1:9–10, John baptizes Jesus in the Jordan River. At Jesus's baptism, the heavens are "torn open," an unusual phrase that portends his death and the tearing of the veil (15:38). When Mark's audience pondered the heavens "tearing," they would be drawn to apocalyptic texts such as Isaiah 13:10; 24:1–6; 34:4; Ezekiel 32:6–8; Joel 2:10, and so on. But chief among those texts is Isaiah 64:1 (63:19b MT/LXX):

> Oh, that you [Yahweh] would rend the heavens and come down,
>   that the mountains would tremble before you!

In Isaiah 63:15, Isaiah's lament transitions from a historical recollection of the first exodus to an expectation of a second exodus. The prophet pleads that Yahweh would "look down from heaven, and see from [his] holy and glorious habitation." A few verses later in 64:1, the prophet Isaiah asks that God repeat Sinai and "rend the heavens and come down." While the OG reads *anoixēs* ("to open") for the verb "rend" (cf. Matt. 3:16; Luke 3:21), other LXX recensions employ the verb *erēxas* ("to tear"), a reading much closer to Mark 1:10. At his baptism, then, Jesus initially fulfills the prophet Isaiah's wish that God would execute a new and final exodus.

The Spirit descends upon Jesus "like a dove." The Spirit's descent fulfills many OT texts that anticipate the arrival of the Spirit at the very end of history (e.g., Joel 2; Ezek. 37:4–14). Isaiah 32:15 even connects the descent of the Spirit with a "field" (*erēmos*). As true Israel, Jesus experiences his own personal Pentecost (cf. Acts 1–2). Mark describes the Spirit as a "dove," likely referring to the Genesis flood, when God created the world anew (Gen. 8:8–12). The evangelist presents Jesus, then, as the restored people of God—faithful Israel—at the cusp of the new creation.

When Jesus emerges from the water, God announces, "You are my Son, whom I love; with you I am well pleased" (1:11). The wording recalls at least two passages that prophesy the arrival of Israel's Messiah: Psalm 2:7 and 2 Samuel 7. At some level, Mark intends his audience to view Jesus's baptism as the formal commissioning of Jesus. God declares his Son to be the fulfillment of the long-awaited Messiah, so he sends him forth to be faithful where Adam and Israel were unfaithful. Jesus passes through the Jordan River as the first generation of Israelites passed through the Red Sea and the second generation trekked through the Jordan River. To lead Israel out of exile, he must repeat Israel's history.

The Spirit then "*drove [ekballei]* him into the wilderness" (1:12 HCSB). Mark's use of the verb "to drive out" (*ekballō*) strikes the reader as odd. Matthew and Luke employ the verb "to lead" (*agō*) for this event: "Jesus *was led* by the Spirit into the wilderness" (Matt. 4:1 // Luke 4:1). Mark's verb, "to drive out," occurs sixteen times in the Second Gospel, and ten of those occurrences refer to exorcisms. Perhaps Mark's preference for this verb stems from the redemptive-historical gravity of Jesus's wilderness temptation. In faithfully enduring the devil's temptation in the wilderness, Jesus gains the authority over the devil and his minions. So the Spirit *drives* Jesus into the wilderness so that Jesus can *drive out* unclean spirits. Further, Isaiah 63 recalls Israel's unfaithfulness in the wilderness, behavior that "grieved [the] Holy Spirit" (63:10; cf. Ps. 78:40). Perhaps the presence of the Spirit in Jesus's wilderness temptation recalls Israel's rebellion in the wilderness. Jesus, however, will not rebel against the Spirit, but instead will obey him. While the wilderness temptation occupies a single verse in the narrative, it profoundly shapes the remainder of the Second Gospel. As Israel's long-awaited king and incarnate Lord, Jesus wages a successful battle with Satan (→Luke 4:1–13).

Cleansing Creation (1:12–13)

As a result of Jesus's success, Mark mentions a strange detail: Jesus was among "the wild animals," and "angels attended him" (1:13 // Matt. 4:1–11 // Luke 4:1–13). Perhaps the inclusion of the animals is not so odd after all. A cardinal dimension of Jesus's ministry is his purging the environment of all wicked contaminants so that God may dwell with humanity and creation. By defeating the devil in the wilderness temptation, Jesus begins to purge the effects of Adam's fall from humanity and creation. If Mark regards demons as "unclean" (1:23, 27; 3:11, 30; 5:2; 6:7; 9:25), how much more is their leader, the devil, unclean? Perhaps we should view Jesus's victory over the devil against the backdrop of the various sacrifices contained in the book of Leviticus (→Luke 5:27–39). Jesus executes his messianic and priestly role by beginning to rid the cosmos of its longtime defiler.

One final detail: in mentioning the animals, Mark argues that the created order is beginning to be reconciled to God. The new creation has broken into history (Isa. 11:6; 65:25). That "angels attended him" also brings to mind the spiritual realm. The temptation sends shock waves throughout the entire created order, visible and invisible. So when Jesus successfully defeats Satan in the wilderness temptation, he has begun to reconcile God and the cosmos, including physical and spiritual realities (cf. Col. 1:20). It's hardly surprising, then, to find in the following section an overt emphasis on Jesus's victory over Satan's minions and the reversal of curses of the fall (1:21–45).

Another unique dimension of Jesus's identity in Mark 1 is evident in light of the two quotations from Malachi 3 and Isaiah 40. In Malachi 3, God follows the messenger and judges Israel: "Then suddenly the Lord you are seeking will come to his temple" (Mal. 3:1). According to Mark 1, it is Jesus who comes on the heels of the messenger—a clear identification with Israel's God. The same can be said for the Isaiah prophecy. Isaiah 40:3 announces that the Lord has come to redeem his people from captivity and begin the process of renewal; in Mark 1 Jesus serves in this identical capacity. Mark, from the very beginning of his Gospel, identifies Jesus with the God of Israel, affirming that Jesus is God in the flesh. He is the Son of God (1:1)!

◼ Act 1: Jesus in Galilee (1:14–8:21)

The Beginning of Jesus's Galilean Ministry (1:14–45)

The Kingdom Is at Hand (1:14–15)

With the use of the narrative device "and immediately" (*kai euthys*), the first phase of Mark's Gospel runs at a brisk pace. Matthew, Luke, and John employ *kai euthys* one time in their narratives, but Mark uses this unique phrase twenty-five times in his Gospel, especially in chapter 1 (1:10, 12, 18, 20, 21, 23, 29, 30, 42). To avoid repetition, English translations often do not translate each instance. This literary device pushes the narrative ahead quickly so that Mark's readers get to know Jesus through action.

According to 1:14, John is "put in prison" or, perhaps better, "handed over." This eerie detail sets the stage for Jesus to be handed over later on in the Gospel (3:19; 9:31; 10:33, etc.). If John is persecuted for preaching the arrival of Jesus, how much more will Jesus himself be persecuted? Immediately after John is imprisoned, Jesus flees north to Galilee, probably to avoid persecution. Jesus knows full well that he will eventually die at the hands of his countrymen (9:31; 10:33; 14:41), but there's work to be done.

Three parties have spoken thus far: the OT (Isaiah, Exodus, and Malachi), John the Baptist, and God. Now, for the first time, Jesus speaks. And what he proclaims is striking: "The time has come. . . . The kingdom of God *has come near.* Repent and believe the good news!" (1:15; see Isa. 52:7). Scholars have debated the precise nuance of the critical verb "has come near" (*ēngiken*), as it can entail a spatial or temporal idea (cf. 11:1; 14:42). It may be a touch of both. Many are now convinced that Mark is here referring to the already-not-yet aspects of the kingdom. Regarding the temporal nature of the kingdom, the end-time kingdom contains elements that are partially fulfilled or inaugurated in the first coming of Jesus (note the inclusion of the phrase "the time has come"). But the kingdom doesn't arrive in its fullness in the first century. When Jesus returns a second time, then God will consummately establish his eternal kingdom in the new heavens and earth. Regarding the spatial dimension, God's heavenly reign begins to invade the cosmos in Jesus of Nazareth at his first coming. At the very end of history, heaven will come down in its fullness.

The victory over Satan clears the way for Jesus to establish the kingdom of God on earth. The thick statement "kingdom of God" awaits further explanation in chapter 4, where we learn more about the nature of the kingdom and how it stands in continuity and discontinuity with the OT. For now, the readers of Mark must heed Jesus's message and believe in the "good news." The "good news" that opens Mark's Gospel in 1:1 is the same "good news" that Jesus proclaims.

The Summons to Follow (1:16–20)

Here in Mark, as in Matthew and Luke, we have the following arrangement of material: the temptation (1:12–13), the proclamation of the good news (1:14–15), and the calling of the disciples (1:16–20). It appears that Jesus's calling of the disciples is the result of his kingdom message (→Luke 5:1). The effective message inevitably generates a community of disciples. In all three Synoptics, Peter is listed first among the initial installment of disciples (Matt. 4:18–22 // Mark 1:16–20 // Luke 5:3–11). This is unsurprising given that Peter's voice is dominant in all three Gospels. We learn, too, that Peter is a fisherman by trade and probably lived in Capernaum (1:29–34). This explains why Mark's Gospel includes so many nautical details not found in the other two Synoptics and why the Gospel is stunningly aware of Jesus's movements around the northern portion of the Sea of Galilee.

At the beginning of his public ministry, Jesus calls Peter (Simon), Andrew, James, and John to follow him (1:16–20). Discipleship is a central concern of the Second Gospel. Mark's audience must contemplate the requirements of following Jesus of Nazareth. The more the narrative unfolds, the higher the stakes. What's the cost? Everything.

Jesus's summons to his disciples to "fish for people" may bring to mind Jeremiah 16:16: "'But now I will send for *many fishermen*,' declares the LORD, 'and they will catch them [Israelites in exile].'" According to Jeremiah 16, these fishermen have a twofold agenda: search out the scattered Israelites so that God can "restore them to the land" *and* hunt them down to "repay them double for their wickedness" (Jer. 16:15, 18). If Jeremiah 16 forms part of the background of Jesus's fishing metaphor, then Jesus's disciples will analogously function as heralds of restoration and judgment. God will restore those who respond positively to the disciples' message and judge those who don't.

Cleansing the Synagogue (1:21–28)

Mark packs the remainder of chapter 1 with several incidents of Jesus healing individuals and exorcising demons. The first event, in 1:21–28, may very well be paradigmatic; we discern themes here that are borne out elsewhere in the Gospel (// Luke 4:31–37). Peter Bolt suggests that Mark's Gospel presents "a group of thirteen suppliants" that "shows us a slice of life in the first-century world."[10] The overall point is that "together they illustrate a world in great need, a world under the shadow of death."[11] These individuals include the man with an impure spirit (1:21–28), a woman with a fever (1:29–31), a man with a withered hand (3:1–6), the Gerasene demoniac (5:1–20), the dying and then dead daughter of Jairus (5:21–23, 35–43), an unclean bleeding woman (5:24–34), the daughter of a gentile woman possessed by a demon (7:24–30), a deaf and mute man (7:31–37), a blind man from Bethsaida (8:22–26), a demon-possessed boy (9:14–29), and blind Bartimaeus (10:46–52).[12]

Mark provides his audience with clues about the timing and location of the first suppliant. The exorcism takes place in Capernaum, a notable fishing village with a Jewish population around one thousand[13] that functions as a hub for Jesus in his Galilean ministry (2:1; 9:33). Synagogues in the first century were the epicenter of local Jewish life and culture, where civil cases were adjudicated, children were educated, and, most of all, people prayed and worshiped. Mark points out that this incident took place on the Sabbath (1:21), perhaps because visiting speakers were often given the opportunity to lecture on the Sabbath (see Acts 13:15).[14]

We gain three significant insights from this paradigmatic event: (1) Jesus, as the Messiah and divine Son of God (1:24), has power to subdue and rule over

---

10. Peter G. Bolt, *The Cross from a Distance: Atonement in Mark's Gospel*, NSBT 18 (Leicester, UK: Apollos, 2004), 38.

11. Bolt, *Cross from a Distance*, 38.

12. Bolt, *Cross from a Distance*, 38.

13. Sharon Lea Mattila, "Capernaum," in *T&T Clark Encyclopedia of Second Temple Judaism*, ed. Daniel M. Gurtner and Loren T. Stuckenbruck (London: Bloomsbury T&T Clark, 2020), 2:130.

14. Craig S. Keener, *Acts: An Exegetical Commentary*, vol. 2, *3:1–14:28* (Grand Rapids: Baker Academic, 2013), 2045.

the demonic world because of his success in the wilderness temptation and the authority to speak as God himself, an unrivaled prophet (1:22); (2) in contrast to the demons possessing great insight into Jesus's identity, the Jewish people have difficulty grasping who Jesus truly is; and (3) the presence of demons in the house of worship (on the Sabbath, no less) indicates the spiritual state of Israel. If the synagogue embodies all of Jewish life and culture, then Israel's chief concern is being shackled not to Rome but to Satan!

The Messianic Secret (1:29–39)

Chapter 1 continues with a flurry of healings and further exorcisms (// Matt. 8:14–17 // Luke 4:38–41). Peter's mother-in-law is healed (1:30–31), and more demons are "driven out" (1:34). As king, Jesus is systematically establishing his kingdom on earth, purging the land of all opposition. In 1:34 we come across an enigmatic detail: "He would not let the demons speak because they knew who he was." We can make a similar observation in 8:30, which immediately follows Peter's accurate confession that Jesus is "the Christ" (i.e., the Messiah): "And he strictly charged them to tell no one about him" (ESV; cf. 1:44; 9:9). Why would Jesus forbid his disciples from telling others about his identity as Israel's long-awaited king? Does not Jesus want Israel to know that he's their Savior, who has come to liberate them from spiritual oppression? The answer rests on Jesus's fulfillment of Israel's expectations for the long-awaited Messiah. This well-known feature of Mark's narrative, labeled the "messianic secret," refers to Jesus altering and refocusing his audience's understanding of his messiahship (→4:1–20).

The following day, before dawn, Jesus leaves the house to find a secluded location to pray (1:35 // Luke 4:42–43). The disciples soon find him and urge him to return to the house because, they say, "Everyone is looking for you!" (1:37). The disciples want Jesus to return to Peter's house to continue to heal the sick and expel demons. But Jesus has other intentions. He desires to travel to "nearby villages" in Galilee and proclaim the good news of the kingdom's arrival, because that is precisely why he has come (1:38). In a word, God desires his eternal kingdom to extend to the far corners of the earth.

Cleansing the Leper (1:40–45)

The chapter ends with a curious event: Jesus healing a man stricken with leprosy (1:40–45 // Matt. 8:2–4 // Luke 5:12–14). Since this individual is deemed unclean, he is unable to be in contact with his fellow Jews (Lev. 13:45–46; 14:2–3). He is, quite simply, an outsider. When Jesus heals him (ironically, through touch!), he restores fellowship that was lost between this man and his community. True admittance to Israel, then, is only found through Jesus. In addition, notice that Jesus is the one who makes this leper "clean" (1:41). Israelites become clean through the various rites of the sacrificial system and a priestly declaration, but Jesus is now identifying himself as the true sacrifice who is able to provide true cleansing. But not only does Jesus purify the individual, he implicitly functions as a priest and Israel's true temple by pronouncing, "Be clean." Taken together, all the incidents in 1:21–45 demonstrate that Jesus is the end-time king (ruling over the demons), priest (making the leper clean), and prophet (speaking with unrivaled authority).

Jesus Gains Popularity in Galilee (2:1–3:6)

In chapter 1, news of Jesus's miracles and exorcisms naturally generates significant public attention (1:28, 33, 37, 45). Such a public commotion in chapter 1 lays the foundation for a conflict between Jesus and the Jewish leaders in chapters 2–3, climaxing in their decision to kill Jesus in 3:6. In each of the five upcoming episodes, Mark underscores the presence and hostility of the Jewish leaders (2:6–7, 16, 18, 24; 3:6).

Jesus Forgives the Paralytic (2:1–12)

The healing of the paralytic (2:1–12 // Matt. 9:2–8 // Luke 5:18–26) brings Jesus into direct contact with the Jewish authorities, something that was merely hinted at in 1:22. One theme that binds the healing of the paralyzed man in 2:1–12 with the previous context is reconciliation. The leper is miraculously pronounced "clean" (external) so that he may reintegrate with society, whereas the paralytic receives the forgiveness of sin through Jesus (internal). The leper receives reconciliation with his community, whereas the paralytic receives reconciliation with God. In both cases, reconciliation graciously flows from Jesus of Nazareth.

At the beginning of chapter 2, Jesus once more ministers in Capernaum, and a throng of people are not far behind. He "preached the word to them," though we are not given any details about the content of his message (2:2). Mark probably intends for the reader to connect Jesus's proclamation of the kingdom in 1:15, 21, and 39 with his teaching here. He is so popular that there is no more room for people to gather in the house, "not even outside the door" (2:2). In the first century, where living space was at a premium (in contrast to our Western culture), people had access to their roof from an outside staircase. Four individuals, so desperate to see their friend healed, hoist him up the staircase on a mat, dismantle a portion of the roof, and let him down where Jesus is teaching. Their faith is certainly on display (2:5).

Jesus forgiving the paralytic's sin is nothing short of breathtaking. Forgiveness entails two important aspects: (1) It was bound up with the sacrificial system and the temple. Quite simply, "without the shedding of blood there is no forgiveness" (Heb. 9:22; cf. Lev. 17:11). Forgiveness therefore requires a sacrifice. But where is the sacrifice here in Mark 2? It's certainly not found in the temple in Jerusalem (see 11:15–18). According to John the Baptist, there is a new, once-for-all sacrifice on the horizon. Recall that his baptism offered definitive "forgiveness of sins" (1:4). Though Mark hasn't divulged the specific identity of this sacrifice, as the narrative unfolds, we discover that it's none other than Jesus. The forgiveness offered here in 2:5 is based upon Jesus's future atoning death on the cross.

(2) Jesus offers forgiveness because he's God, and only God is the offended party. He alone has the right to pronounce a person innocent and declare a person to be in the right. In short, only God can justify. This is precisely what the Jewish leaders internally contemplate: "Why does this fellow talk like that? He's blaspheming! Who can forgive sins but God alone?" (2:7; cf. 11:25). Mark is beginning to fulfill his promise in 1:1 and demonstrate how Jesus is indeed the "Son of God"—Jesus has the authority to forgive. The ambiguous use of "God" here may even signal that Mark is identifying Jesus with Israel's Lord. The main point of the episode is found in 2:12 when the crowd "praises God" and declares, "We have never seen anything like this!"

The Calling of Levi (2:13–17)

The calling of Levi (or "Matthew"), the next episode, is provocative because of Levi's profession—he's a tax collector (2:13–17 // Matt. 9:9–13 // Luke 5:27–32). Tax collectors in the first century (no less than today!) were quite unpopular, as they ultimately answered to Rome. Jesus discovers Levi "sitting at the tax collector's booth" and abruptly commands him to "follow" him (2:14). Without recording a word of speech on Levi's part, Mark informs his audience that Levi, like Simon and Andrew, "got up and followed him" (2:15; cf. 1:17–18). The narrative then fast-forwards to Levi's house, where Jesus and his disciples are discovered communing with other tax collectors and sinners (2:15–16). In a world where strict Jews kept all those deemed unclean at arm's length, Jesus's intimate fellowship with these two groups is appalling in the eyes of the Jewish leaders (2:16). But since Mark has already presented Jesus as one who makes the unclean clean (1:40–45) and offers forgiveness to sinners (2:1–12), his fellowship with these groups makes marvelous sense.

The importance of this covenant meal should not be overlooked, and its location in Mark's narrative is all the more illuminating. But before we consider the meal in the immediate context, we must first recognize the nature of covenant meals in the book of Leviticus and how they relate to the discussion of sacrifices in general.

A dominant pattern in the Pentateuch, especially Leviticus, is the threefold cycle of sin/defilement → purgation/expiation → God's covenantal presence. Sin must be removed for a holy God to dwell with his people. The complex nature of Israel's sacrificial system should be understood as a movement from expiation (purification and reparation offerings—e.g., Lev. 4–5; 16), to consecration (burnt offerings—e.g., Lev. 6:8–13), to fellowship (tribute and peace offerings—e.g., Lev. 7:11–21).[15] The goal of the various sacrifices and offerings is dwelling with God *in a covenant meal*. "The cultic approach to God also explains the final sacrifice of the liturgy, the peace offering. *The highlight of the peace offering was a communion meal*. Some of the sacrificial meat would be returned to the worshiper who would then enjoy a sacred feast with family and friends in the presence of God. Having entered Yahweh's house, one then enjoys his unsurpassed hospitality."[16]

All three evangelists follow the basic movement of Jesus ridding the unclean devil from creation (Matt. 4:1–11 // Mark 1:11–12 // Luke 4:1–13), the subsequent cleansing of humanity from various internal and external effects of sin (Matt. 4:23–25; 8:1–9:8 // Mark 1:21–2:12 // Luke 4:31–44; 5:12–26), and finally, his eating with humanity in a covenant meal (Matt. 9:9–17 // Mark 2:13–17 // Luke 5:27–39). Meals in the Synoptics are central to Jesus's ministry in that they indicate Jesus's victory over Adam's sin and its effects; the covenant meals also anticipate *the* consummate meal in the new Jerusalem (Rev. 19:17–19).

Wineskins (2:18–22)

The time has come for the old to give way to the new. It's fitting, then, that the next section concerns old and new wineskins (2:18–22 // Matt. 9:14–17 // Luke 5:33–38). Much of Jesus's ministry is illustrated here. Throughout the OT and Second Temple Judaism, wine and feasting celebrate the establishment of the new creation (e.g., Isa. 25:6; Jer. 31:12–14; Hosea 14:7; Joel 3:18; Amos 9:13–14; 2 Bar. 29:5). By casting out demons, healing the broken, and forgiving sinners, Jesus announces that the new age has indeed arrived. So if the new age has arrived, then something must change. The various laws of

15. See L. Michael Morales, *Exodus Old and New: A Biblical Theology of Redemption*, ESBT 2 (Downers Grove, IL: InterVarsity, 2020), 92–98.

16. Morales, *Exodus Old and New*, 96 (emphasis added).

the Mosaic covenant and the way they regulate Israel's theocratic relationship to God and to the nations around them are now finding their ultimate fulfillment in Jesus of Nazareth. Jesus, Israel's Messiah and the Son of God (1:1), is now the only way in which humanity relates to God.

Jesus as Priest-King (2:23–28)

The Sabbath controversy in the following two sections tangibly addresses this very theme (2:23–28; 3:1–6 // Matt. 12:1–14 // Luke 6:1–11). One cardinal difference between Israel and her pagan neighbors is resting on the Sabbath. God commands Israel to refrain from their normal work week, meditate upon his sovereign power, and contemplate his own rest (Gen. 2:2; Exod. 20:8–11). The Lord alone is creator and sovereign king, and the Sabbath commandment concretely celebrates this precious truth. In the first Sabbath controversy, as Jesus and the disciples are strolling "through the grainfields," the Jewish leaders find fault with them (2:23–24). It's not clear if the Jewish leaders condemn the disciples for harvesting (cf. Luke 6:1) or traveling too far on the Sabbath. Whatever the case, the Jewish leaders accuse Jesus and the disciples of breaking a central tenet of the Mosaic law. Jesus's response is probably not what we would expect, for he justifies their actions with a seemingly odd incident in the life of King David.

The rhetorical question "Have you never read . . . ?" in 2:25 appears three times in Mark, and each of them rebukes the Jewish leaders for their failure to understand the meaning of the OT (2:25; 12:10, 26). Jesus claims that the Jewish leaders should have grasped his behavior because the OT itself expected it! Jesus draws from an incident in 1 Samuel 21:1–6, where David asks the priest Ahimelek if he can consume of the showbread in the temple—a privilege that only priests enjoy (Lev. 24:5–9). Curiously, Jesus mentions the priest Abiathar, whereas the high priest Ahimelek is found in 1 Samuel 21. Making matters more difficult is that the relationship between Abiathar and Ahimelek is not straightforward in the OT. On the one hand, 1 Samuel 22:20 and 30:7 state that Abiathar is the son of Ahimelek, but 1 Chronicles 18:16 claims that Ahimelek is the son of Abiathar. Which is it? Matthew and Luke's retelling of the event avoids this issue altogether by omitting any name. Instead of trying to resolve this issue through a number of historical reconstructions, perhaps we should conclude that Mark is being quite intentional here. He knows that the name Abiathar will throw the audience into confusion, eliciting the critical question, "Who is the true priest?" The answer is, as we've already seen in Mark, Jesus of Nazareth. But Jesus it not simply the true priest; he is the true priest-king.

To unlock another layer of significance, we must go back even further into the OT and consider the nature of the consecrated bread in its original context. According to Exodus 25:30, the "bread of the Presence" must be placed upon a table in the Holy Place "at all times." Then Leviticus 24:5–9 states that the priests must offer twelve loaves of bread, symbolizing the twelve tribes, on the table in the Holy Place in two stacks. The bread "belongs to Aaron and his sons," who must "eat it in a holy place" (Lev. 24:9 ESV). Further, and often overlooked, the bread rests next to various golden plates, pitchers, and bowls to be used in drink offerings (Exod. 25:29). Priests are to keep wine in these pitchers, as they accompany the drink offerings (Num. 15:7). What we have, then, in the bread and wine is a perpetual covenant meal that demonstrates God's faithfulness to and intimate presence with Israel. Lastly, Leviticus 24:8 mandates that the consecrated bread endure "Sabbath after Sabbath . . . as a lasting covenant." Two other items elsewhere receive the precise qualification of a "lasting covenant"—circumcision (Gen. 17:13, 19) and Sabbath (Exod. 31:16).[17]

In light of the OT, the Sabbath controversy in Mark 2:23–27 makes terrific sense and pulls together several of the threads in Mark's immediate context: (1) Just as David, a priest-king in his own right (2 Sam. 6:14), is granted the authority to eat the bread and give it to his fellow soldiers, so now Jesus, the descendant of David, authorizes his disciples to eat grain. Jesus's authority is predicated upon him being the Son of David and the "Son of Man" (cf. Dan. 7:13). By declaring himself the "Lord . . . of the Sabbath" (2:28), Jesus makes the staggering claim that all of creation is his temple or house and his disciples serve in it. The expression "house of God" is prominent in the book of Isaiah and often refers to Israel's eschatological temple (Isa. 2:2, 3; 56:7). As the message of the kingdom goes forth through Jesus and his followers, so the end-time temple of God expands to the ends of the earth (see Matt. 12:6). (2) Jesus also invokes 1 Samuel 21 because it involves a "lasting covenant," naturally correlating with Sabbath and circumcision. Sabbath observance and the bread of the Presence go hand in hand. If Jesus is the true temple, the true bread of the Presence, then he is also the true Sabbath rest. (3) The bread of the Presence is also wedded to wine. Taken together, both features symbolize a covenant meal between God and Israel. In the previous context, Jesus eats with "tax collectors" and "sinners" at the house of Levi (2:13–17) and then explains that one cannot pour "new wine" into "old wineskins" because of the arrival of the new age (2:18–22). The disciples, as they "pick some heads

17. Gordon J. Wenham, *The Book of Leviticus*, NICOT (Grand Rapids: Eerdmans, 1979), 310.

of grain" and presumably eat them, are enjoying a covenant meal with Jesus, the Lord incarnate.

The Jewish Leaders Hatch a Plot (3:1–6)

The Sabbath controversy comes to a head in 3:1–6, where Jesus (note the absence of his disciples) enters a synagogue on the Sabbath. This event in the synagogue serves as a fitting conclusion to this initial phase of his ministry, a ministry that began in the synagogues of Galilee (1:21, 29, 39). Mark sets the scene by mentioning a "man with a shriveled hand" (3:1). This man, like the woman with an issue of blood (5:25), suffers from a physical affliction. He is not whole (cf. 1 Kings 13:4).

The Jewish leaders were once again on the lookout and "watched him closely to see if he would heal him on the Sabbath" (3:2). In their minds, they have baited a trap, and they hope that Jesus will walk right into it. Jesus, knowing full well the intention of the religious leaders (cf. 2:8), summons the man to "stand up in front of everyone" (3:3). Little do they realize that *they* are walking into a trap! Before healing the man, Jesus asks his opponents a question: "Which is lawful on the Sabbath: to do good or to do evil, to save a life or to kill?" (3:4). If they respond with "to do good," then Jesus's actions will be vindicated and they will be proven wrong. If they respond with "to do evil," then they will also be wrong. Aware that either answer is self-incriminating, the leaders simply remain "silent."

The question Jesus poses to the leaders is thick with irony and presages the end of Mark's narrative. The connection between "killing" and "doing evil" certainly looks forward to Jesus's own death at the hands of the religious leaders, as the identical word (*apokteinō*) is found in key passages that refer to his death (9:31; 10:34; 12:7; 14:1). At the end of the passage—indeed, the main point of it—the religious leaders "plot" "how they might *kill* Jesus" (3:6). The word here for "kill" (*apollymi*) recalls 1:24, where the host of demons asks Jesus, "Have you [Jesus] come to *destroy* us?" In both contexts, the term contains military overtones. So the Jewish leaders are portrayed as laying the groundwork for a full-scale attack against Jesus the Messiah and the Son of God (11:18; 12:12; 14:1, 55; cf. John 5:18). They perceive him to be the enemy of Israel and, by implication, the enemy of God. But in reality, the tables are turned. Jesus is the genuine Son of God, and the Jewish leaders are the enemy. At the end of Mark's story, Jesus will be killed, yet his death will be the climactic life-giving act to others.

Mark divulges *why* the religious authorities are hostile to Jesus and his message in 3:5: "[Jesus] looked around at them in anger and, deeply distressed at *their stubborn hearts* . . ." The wording here is eerily similar to Isaiah 6:10, a passage that features prominently in 4:12: "Make the *heart* of this people *calloused*. . . . Otherwise they might see with their eyes, hear with their ears, understand with their hearts, and turn and be healed." As we will see shortly, Isaiah 6 is a judgment oracle against idolatrous Israel. Since Israel has adored false gods, the true God has transformed them into the very thing they worship. The point of the allusion to Isaiah 6:10 here in 3:5 is that Isaiah's oracle of judgment is alive and well in Jesus's time. Israel in the first century is just as idolatrous as she was in the eighth century BC (perhaps even more so). They were bowing down not to physical idols but to figurative ones, like human tradition (hence their preoccupation with preserving the Sabbath at the expense of life).

We must not lose sight, though, of the goodness of Jesus. If the leaders are bent on "doing evil" and "killing," then Jesus is characterized by "doing good" and "saving life." What we find here nicely summarizes Jesus's ministry thus far. Jesus is committed to restoring the entirety of a human being—body and soul. The new creation has broken into history, and Jesus is systematically transforming individuals to participate in the new age. The ability to completely restore this man's hand is unparalleled. Jesus does not perform this miracle as a prophet, acting on behalf of God on earth. He does so as God in the flesh, for granting life is something that God alone can do (Deut. 32:39; Neh. 9:6).

Who Is Jesus of Nazareth? (3:7–35)

The Calling of the Twelve (3:7–19)

The narrative shifts away from the synagogue to the Sea of Galilee, where Jesus "withdrew with his disciples" (3:7). In stunning contrast to the rejection by the Jewish elite, the general population from all over flocks to Jesus for healing (3:8; cf. 1:45). The Jewish leaders, who pride themselves in knowing Israel's Scriptures, are blind to Jesus's identity, whereas the crowd is quick to follow him (3:7). Mark, beginning south and working counterclockwise, divulges where the crowd is from: "Judea, Jerusalem, Idumea, and the regions across the Jordan and around Tyre and Sidon" (3:8). By mentioning these locations, Mark may be bringing the narrative to a climax thus far. Whereas only Jerusalem and Judea came out to follow John (1:5), a significant portion of Israel is responding positively to Jesus's kingdom message (// Matt. 12:15–16 // Luke 6:17–19).

Like his previous encounter with the crowd in 1:34, Jesus heals "many" and casts out demons. Here the title "Son of God" pops up once more. This is the second occurrence of the phrase and the second time demons explicitly identify Jesus:

> The beginning of the good news about Jesus the Messiah, *the Son of God.* (1:1)

> What do you want with us, Jesus of Nazareth? Have you come to destroy us? I know who you are—*the Holy One of God!* (1:24)

> Whenever the impure spirits saw him, they fell down before him and cried out, '*You are the Son of God.*' (3:11)

While the demons are certainly hostile to Jesus and his ministry, they possess keen insight into his identity as the divine Son of God (1:24). Because of this, Jesus forbids them to "tell others about him" (3:12). His identity and mission can be completely grasped only after the cross and resurrection. His ministry is marked not by political triumph but by suffering and defeat (→1:29–34).

In a scene laced with symbolism, Jesus assembles the twelve disciples "on a mountainside" (3:13–19 // Matt. 10:2–4 // Luke 6:14–16). While Mark's narrative has moved rather quickly up to this point, he often vividly recollects where Jesus and his companions are. They have been "beside the Sea of Galilee" (1:16; 2:13; 3:7), in many synagogues (1:21, 39; 3:1), in Peter's home (1:29), in another "home" (or perhaps Peter's home; 2:1), in Levi's house (2:15), and in the grainfields (2:23). For the first time, then, Mark mentions Jesus going up a mountain. In some sense, the narrative has been waiting for this profound event. The wording that Jesus "went up on a mountainside" in 3:13 may allude to Exodus 24, where Moses ascends Sinai (Exod. 24:12–13, 15, 18; 34:1–2) and the Lord finalizes his relationship with Israel (→Matt. 5:1–12).

Symbolically, the Twelve constitute true Israel—the twelve tribes in nucleus form. The replacement of Judas with Matthias in Acts 1:15–26 indicates that the Twelve symbolically reflect the twelve tribes descended from Jacob's sons (Gen. 29:32–30:24; 35:18). Just as Moses assembles the nation of Israel on Sinai and commands them to bless the nations, so now Jesus chooses the Twelve and charges them with the authority to proclaim the kingdom message and cast out demons (3:14–15). When the Israelites enter into a binding relationship with Yahweh at Sinai, Moses charges them to adhere to the covenant stipulations. A constitutive part of their identity as the people of God is their role in "blessing" the nations and welcoming them into the covenant community: "Now if you [Israel] obey me fully and keep my covenant, then out of all nations you will be my treasured possession. Although the whole earth is mine, you will be for me a kingdom of priests and a holy nation" (Exod. 19:5–6).

The tribes of Israel, however, fail to maintain covenant fidelity and fail to become a blessing to the nations. Jesus fulfills both of these obligations. He, as the last Adam and true Israel, faithfully adheres to God's law and guides gentiles into the people of God. Jesus then reconstitutes Israel in himself and summons twelve followers to identify with his faithfulness.

Regarding the content of the disciples' mission, we must consider why Jesus sends them out to "preach" and "have authority to drive out demons" (3:14–15). Preaching and exorcisms go hand in hand. Subjugation of the demonic forces takes place through the proclamation of the end-time reign of God that Jesus inaugurated at his forty-day wilderness temptation. What's curious is the placement of the appointment of the Twelve in Mark's narrative. Jesus has already preached and exorcized demons on multiple occasions (1:14, 21–28, 34, 39; 2:1; 3:10), but now the time has come for the disciples to extend, in an official capacity, the core of Jesus's ministry. In other words, Jesus's successful activity is the basis for the appointment of the Twelve. The commissioning of the disciples requires his success in the wilderness. In the first few chapters of Mark's Gospel, the disciples, though mentioned, have been background characters, but from here on out they will operate in the foreground.

Rejection by Friends and Family (3:20–35)

The remainder of chapter 3 focuses on the interplay between Jesus's family and the Jewish leaders. Mark once again uses his unique sandwich technique in presenting the material:

> Rejection by Jesus's family (3:20-21)
> Rejection by the Jewish leaders (3:22-30)
> Rejection by Jesus's family (3:31-34)

Mark's arrangement forces his readers to interpret Jesus's interaction with his family in light of the debate with the Jewish leaders. Despite Jesus's popularity (3:8), unbelief is running rampant. Even Jesus's family stands analogous to the Jewish leaders in that both parties have difficulty grasping Jesus's identity. Indeed, they are hostile toward him.

After Jesus appointed his twelve disciples on a mountain, he entered a house, where a "crowd gathered" (3:20). Mark introduces the readers to Jesus's family, and fortunately, first impressions are sometimes misleading. Mark is the only evangelist to disclose Jesus's family's motivation: "When his family heard about this, they went to take charge of him, for they said, 'He is out of his mind'" (3:21 // Matt. 12:46–50 // Luke 8:19–21). There's a growing sense of mystery surrounding Jesus's identity. If his own family, embarrassed by his ministry, cannot grasp his identity, then who can?

Immediately switching to the controversy with the Jewish leaders, Mark mentions the scribes' point of origin: "from Jerusalem" (3:22). Unlike Jesus's family, hailing from Nazareth, these religious authorities have traveled from Jerusalem, the city that will accuse Jesus of sedition and nail him to a cross. These leaders charge Jesus with being "possessed by Beelzebul" (3:22). While we are unsure of the precise meaning of this enigmatic title "Beelzebul" (cf. T. Sol. 3:2–5), Mark refines it with the phrase "prince of demons." So the Jewish leaders accuse Jesus of allying himself with a high-ranking demon in order to exorcise demons.

Jesus prefaces the following two parables with a question: "How can Satan drive out Satan?" (3:23). The first parable makes the point that a kingdom marked by division cannot endure (3:24). Civil war has no place in a successful military campaign. Jesus then transitions to the second parable, which features a "strong man" protecting his "plunder." To capture the prize, one must first bind the strong man (3:27). The strong man parable likely recalls Isaiah 49:24–26,[18] where the prophet Isaiah envisions Israel's return from Babylonian captivity. According to Isaiah 49:22–23, the nations will aid Israel's return to the promised land. Then, verse 24 asks the question: "Can plunder be taken from warriors, or captives be rescued from the fierce?" The answer to the question is a firm "No." No empire is more powerful than Babylon. But there's one in heaven who "laughs" at the plotting of rulers of the world (Ps. 2:4). His name is Yahweh, and he will rescue his people from the clutches of Babylon. Isaiah 49:25 prophesies the following: "Yes, captives will be taken from warriors, and plunder retrieved from the fierce." Israel's God promises to fight for his people at the very end of history and plant them in the new creation, where he will dwell with them for all of eternity.

According to the NT writers, the true enemy of Israel is not "Babylon" or Rome but Satan—the true, spiritual strong man. He's held Israel captive. Isaiah 49 identifies Yahweh as the one who conquers the strong man and releases the Israelites, yet Mark identifies Jesus as Israel's redeemer. Jesus is Israel's Lord incarnate who has come to liberate Israel from spiritual slavery. The time has come for Jesus to "bind" the strong man and release the bounty—the people of God. The parable of the strong man explains the significance of Jesus's exorcisms. It explains the true meaning of the exorcism in Capernaum in 1:21–25 and looks forward to the exorcism in the Gerasenes in 5:1–20.

18. Watts, *Isaiah's New Exodus*, 146–52.

The end of the chapter resumes Jesus's interaction with his family. Like the Jewish scribes, his own family does not understand the heart of Jesus's identity and mission. With his family standing "outside" the house (note the symbolic location) looking for him (3:31–32), his disciples encircle him *inside* the house. Jesus boldly claims that one's spiritual family trumps one's physical family, a most troubling claim in a tight-knit Jewish culture. The declaration that only those who "do God's will" are considered genuine participants of true Israel is the climax of the entire narrative thus far (3:35). Jesus has come to redeem Israel and bring her out of spiritual bondage, but only those who truly follow him will enjoy God's blessing. Allegiance to Jesus of Nazareth requires that one abandon all and follow him (1:16–20; 2:13–17). As Mark's narrative unfolds, his audience will learn more about what it means to be a true disciple.

The Nature of the Kingdom (4:1–41)

Mark opens his Gospel claiming that the book of Isaiah anticipates the "good news about Jesus." But if Isaiah (and the remainder of the OT) anticipates Jesus, then why do so many, particularly the Jewish scholars of the day, reject him? The ones skilled in studying the Scriptures that predict Jesus are the very ones fortified against him. At the end of chapter 3, we learned that even Jesus's family struggles mightily with his identity. What is so troubling about Jesus and his message of the kingdom? This measured tension is somewhat relieved here, as chapter 4 signals an important turn in Mark's narrative; this chapter is critical for understanding the nature of Jesus's teaching on the kingdom and how his disciples and others receive his message.

Parables of the Kingdom (4:1–34)

Up to chapter 4, the narrative has moved rapidly with Jesus and his followers bounding from one event to another. Finally, the narrative slows and Jesus speaks at length. In the previous chapters, Jesus has spoken only a few words, but here, in comparison, he speaks volumes. Three parables are given, with the first parable taking up nearly half of the chapter (4:3–20 // Matt. 13:1–23 // Luke 8:4–15). Functioning paradigmatically, the parable of the seeds (4:1–8, 13–20) answers the pressing question: If the person of Jesus genuinely fulfills OT expectations, then why do most reject him?

Again, Jesus teaches the crowd on the shore of Galilee. Since Peter, a fisherman by trade, is most likely the primary eyewitness behind the Second Gospel, Mark is sensitive to where Jesus is in relation to the Sea of Galilee

(1:16; 2:13; 3:7; 4:35–41; 5:1, 13; 6:47–49; 7:31). After Jesus delivers the parable of the seeds to the crowd (4:2–9), "the Twelve and the others around him" query Jesus privately, wanting him to interpret the parable for them (4:10). Jesus oddly answers, "The mystery of the kingdom of God has been given to you, but to those on the outside everything is said in parables" (4:11 AT). Yes, Jesus unveils the meaning of the parable to his disciples, but he refuses to interpret it for the outsiders.

Mark's Gospel famously draws a distinction between "insiders" and "outsiders." The insiders possess some level of understanding of Jesus's identity and message, whereas outsiders lack such insight. A distinctive of Mark's Gospel is his rather unvarnished appraisal of the disciples. At times the disciples appear ignorant of Jesus's identity, even obtuse (8:17–21). Yet the Twelve occasionally possess some insight (8:27–29). According to Mark, then, the disciples oscillate between identifying with the insiders and identifying with the outsiders. Mark's readers are encouraged to be mindful of how the disciples understand the nature of Jesus and his ministry in that they must hold fast to Jesus's words and trust his difficult teachings and acts. In a word, the audience must follow Jesus even when his teaching is painfully misunderstood by the eminent apostles. Mark encourages his audience to read and reread his narrative so that Jesus's teaching and deeds can be understood more deeply with each subsequent reading. Passion week unlocks the earlier portions of the narrative, and the earlier portions of the narrative unlock passion week.

Jesus formally quotes Isaiah 6:9–10, then applies it to the outsiders of 4:11. This group appears to be composed of three parties—the Jewish leaders, Jesus's family for the time being (3:20–21, 31–35), and all those who reject Jesus's message. The immediate context of Isaiah 6 fills in some of the details in Mark 4.

God informs the prophet Isaiah that Israel, like her idols, is blind and deaf (Isa. 6:9–10; cf. Deut. 29:3–4; Jer. 5:21; Ezek. 12:2; Ps. 115:4–8; 135:15–18). The Israelites have become like the objects they cherish. Earlier in the book of Isaiah, God likens Israel to an idolatrous tree:

> You will be ashamed because of the sacred oaks
> in which you have delighted;
> you will be disgraced because of the gardens
> that you have chosen.
> You will be like an oak with fading leaves,
> like a garden without water. (Isa. 1:29–30)

On account of the Israelites worshiping the "sacred oaks," God transforms them into "an oak with fading leaves." Therefore, God's commission to Isaiah in 6:1–13 entails profound judgment.

Israel cherishes her idols, so God promises to transform Israel into the very thing she adores—an idol! There's no coming back from this judgment under the same covenantal administration. When Israel does return from Babylonian captivity, it will be under different terms—under the new covenant and through the ministry of the long-awaited "servant(s)."

When the Jewish leaders accuse Jesus of partnering with demons, they are fully rejecting him. They are blind and deaf—not physically but spiritually. What are their idols, then? Instead of worshiping the Author of Israel's Scriptures, they worship the Scriptures themselves (see John 5:39); and instead of obeying the heart of the Mosaic covenant, they have built a fence around it (7:1–23). In applying Isaiah 6:9–10 to the Jewish leaders, Jesus locates his prophetic voice in the tradition of Isaiah. He is a second and greater Isaiah, and as such, he delivers an oracle of judgment that remains valid into the first century. What was true in the eight century BC is true in the first century. This explains why Mark's Gospel includes the purpose conjunction "so that" (*hina*) in 4:12 (cf. Matt. 13:13 // Luke 8:10 // John 12:38). Jesus speaks and acts in parables so that those on the outside will be *further* hardened in their idolatry and unbelief. Mark's use of Isaiah 6 in 4:12 is also, most likely, a combination of typology and verbal fulfillment. Isaiah's prophetic career typologically anticipates Jesus's ministry, and the calloused Israelites in the eighth century BC prophetically correspond to the calloused Jewish leaders in the first century AD. Further, since Isaiah's oracle was not exhausted in the eighth century BC but continues in the first century (and even today), we can also classify Mark's hermeneutical use as the direct fulfillment of a verbal prophecy.

Recall the quotations of Isaiah 40, Exodus 23, and Malachi 3 at the beginning of Mark's narrative. While the Isaiah 40 passage is exceedingly positive in predicting the return of Israel from captivity, the Malachi 3 quotation entails a considerable amount of judgment. The Lord is coming to judge wicked Israel: "Who can endure the day of his coming? Who can stand when he appears?" (Mal. 3:2–4; cf. 4:1). Mark identifies Jesus with the "LORD" of Malachi 3, so it makes sense that Jesus is continuing that role of divine judge. Mark's narrative has dropped hints of Jesus's role as eschatological judge thus far (2:8–10, 17). Mark even alludes to Isaiah 6:10 in 3:5, but for the first time here, divine judgment explicitly surfaces.

Many of Jesus's parables and deeds remain veiled, containing some level of hiddenness. Consider Jesus's command to the disciples in 4:9: "Whoever has ears to hear, let them hear." Believers, who have spiritual eyes to see, largely understand Jesus's message, whereas unbelievers, the spiritually blind, cannot. While the disciples oscillate between being insiders and outsiders, most of the Jewish leadership appear hardened from the start and unable to perceive. Consequently, for some, the nature of the kingdom is only temporarily hidden (the disciples), while for others it is permanently hidden (the Jewish leadership). Grant Osborne's comments on the nature of parables are quite relevant: "The parables encounter, interpret and invite the listener/reader to participate in Jesus' new world vision of the kingdom. They are a 'speech-event' that never allows us to remain neutral; they grasp our attention and force us to interact with the presence of the kingdom in Jesus, either positively (those 'around' Jesus in Mark 4:10–12) or negatively (those 'outside')."[19]

Like Daniel divulging the interpretation of Nebuchadnezzar's dream (Dan. 2:31–45; 4:19–27), Jesus interprets the parables for his disciples and some others (4:14–20). Only a handful of individuals can grasp his identity and mission because only a handful have genuine faith. The Jewish leaders lack such faith, and, at least at this juncture in the narrative, so does Jesus's family. Only those who truly trust and follow him will understand him.

The three following parables, though brief, explain the nature of the kingdom and Jesus's messiahship (→Matt. 13:1–52). The second parable could be an expansion or explication of the term "mystery" in 4:11: "Whatever is hidden [the kingdom of God] is meant to be disclosed, and whatever is concealed is meant to be brought into the open" (4:22). The reason why 4:11 is so tied to "mystery" lies in the book of Daniel.

The term "mystery" (*mystērion*) originates in the book of Daniel, particularly chapters 2 and 4. There, "mystery" constitutes eschatological wisdom that was previously hidden but now has been revealed. This revelation is divulged in two stages: an initial revelation and a subsequent interpretive revelation. According to Daniel, the content of the mystery entails God's end-time judgment upon the rebellious nations and the establishment of the eternal kingdom (Dan. 2:29–47; cf. 7:1–27).

New Testament writers employ *mystērion* to divulge revelation that contains new and surprising elements (e.g., Rom. 11:25; 16:25; 1 Cor. 2:7; 15:51; Eph. 3:3–4). God largely hides certain doctrines from his covenant community in the OT but has now revealed them in the NT. When Jesus asserts, then, that God has given the disciples the "mystery of the kingdom" (4:11), he means that they stand at a unique point in the history of redemption. The way in

---

19. Grant R. Osborne, *The Hermeneutical Spiral: A Comprehensive Introduction to Biblical Interpretation*, rev. ed. (Downers Grove, IL: InterVarsity, 2006), 294–95.

which the kingdom is unfolding in the ministry of Jesus is largely "hidden" in the OT.

The last two parables of Mark 4 further explain the "mystery." Old Testament prophets expected the establishment of the end-time kingdom to be a decisive overthrow of God's enemies at one consummate point at the very end of world history (e.g., Gen. 49:9–10; Num. 24:14–19; Dan. 2:35, 44–45), whereas Jesus explains that the kingdom he inaugurates is like seed in a field that gradually "sprouts and grows" (4:27) or like a mustard seed that slowly "grows" but later "becomes the largest of all garden plants" (4:32). Jesus stunningly claims that the latter-day kingdom does not arrive all at once. Paradoxically, two realms coexist simultaneously—those who belong to the kingdom and those who belong to the devil. God inaugurates the kingdom in his Son in the first century and will consummately establish the kingdom when his Son returns at the very end of history.

We can thus outline the three parables and the two analogies in chapter 4 as follows:

Parable	Meaning
Parable of the seeds (4:3–8, 13–20)	The nature of genuine faith
Analogy of the lamp (4:21–23)	The mysterious nature of the overlap of the ages
Analogy of the scales (4:24–25)	Responsibility of receiving the revelation of the kingdom
Parable of the seed (4:26–29)	The slow growth of the inaugurated kingdom
Parable of the mustard seed (4:30–32)	The slow growth yet eventual domination of the inaugurated kingdom

The parables could also apply to Jesus's identity as Israel's Messiah. While his messiahship is certainly the fulfillment of OT prophecies (1:1–3), the way in which he fulfills the OT is "mysterious." Herman Ridderbos is right to conclude, "This hidden greatness of Jesus Christ is, strictly speaking, the subject of the Gospels, and it is this greatness which determines the nature of the Kingdom."[20] As each Gospel makes clear—especially Mark's—Jesus is king in death. He rules *through* suffering. Though a suffering messiah is anticipated in a handful of passages (e.g., Isa. 52:13–53:12; Dan. 9:25–26; Zech. 12:10) and in various typological correspondences with notable figures such as King David (→John 2:13–25), messianic suffering does not play a central role in the OT. The vast majority of first-century Jews could not conceive that

20. Herman N. Ridderbos, *When the Time Had Fully Come: Studies in New Testament Theology* (Jordan Station, ON: Paideia, 1982), 16.

the Messiah could be crucified, bearing God's curse, much less be seen as a glorious divine ruler exercising ruling power while succumbing to defeat.

The last parable is capped with further instruction to the disciples, "as much as they could understand" (4:33). The word for "understand" (*akouein*) is the same word that is translated "to hear" throughout chapter 4 (4:3, 9, 12, 15–16, 18, 20, 23–24). The point is that the disciples and some within the crowd did indeed "hear" or understand the parables of the kingdom but only in a limited sense or "as much as they could." Verse 34 indicates that only the disciples were privy to the parables' interpretations: "When he [Jesus] was alone with his own disciples, he explained everything." This final verse mitigates some of the negative outlook on the disciples, as they alone are granted access to further revelation concerning some of the finer details on the nature of the kingdom. According to the analogy in 4:24–25, the more revelation one is given, the more one is responsible to grasp and heed its instruction. The disciples must "consider carefully" what Jesus has revealed to them concerning the nature of the kingdom. As the narrative of the Second Gospel marches along, the disciples alone will witness astounding revelatory events, but they are required to respond appropriately to the revelation and wholly trust Jesus. Experiencing revelation without following Jesus puts one's privilege at risk of being revoked (4:25).

The Stilling of the Storm (4:35–41)

Mark prefaces the next episode with "that day," forcing the reader to understand the nature of the kingdom in light of the stilling of the storm (// Matt. 8:23–27 // Luke 8:22–25). In some way, the inauguration of the kingdom informs the stilling of the storm and beckons the disciples (and the reader) to trust Jesus to an even greater degree. Although the disciples may have grasped a few elements of the kingdom from Jesus's parables and analogies, we will soon discover that they have a long way to go in comprehending his full identity.

Chapter 4 ends with Jesus commanding his disciples to venture to the "other side," or the southeastern portion of the Sea of Galilee (4:35). We will discover a bit later in chapter 5 why Jesus intends to head south. Importantly, Mark explains that Jesus and the disciples were "leaving the crowd behind" (4:36)—the same group that was not privy to the interpretation of the parables and additional revelation in the previous section (4:1, 10). So the introduction to the stilling of the storm subtly informs the reader that only the disciples are privy to what lies ahead. The question is, though, whether the Twelve will perceive or "understand" (*akouein*) the event and devotedly follow Jesus.

Soon, a storm raged upon the sea, "so that [the boat] was nearly swamped" (4:37). We learned from 1:16–20 that four of the disciples were fishermen by trade—Peter, Andrew, James, and John—and we would expect that they would be used to such inclement weather. But when the disciples wake Jesus and ask him, "Don't you care if we drown?" we discover that this is not a run-of-the-mill storm (4:38). The disciples know they are in great peril. The phrasing of the disciples' question suggests that they expect a positive answer; it could be rephrased as "You care that we are perishing, right?" At some level, the question is an attack on Jesus's identity and mission. If Jesus truly is who he claims to be, then why is he indifferent to their circumstances? And above all, why is he asleep?

We ought to consider the symbolic value of the storm in light of the OT. The stormy conditions on the sea symbolize the hostile forces arrayed against God's people (e.g., Ps. 74:13–14; Ezek. 32:2; Dan. 7:2). Although the disciples may not connect the dots in the midst of the storm, the squall on the Sea of Galilee represents the demonic host that opposes Jesus's program of inaugurating the kingdom.

Strikingly, Jesus is fast asleep "in the stern . . . on a cushion" (4:38). Why would Jesus behave this way, especially since the evangelists do not usually divulge such incidental details in narrating events? Whereas the storm symbolizes hostility toward God's people, sleep indicates trust in the midst of peril. Psalm 3:4–6 reads, "I [David] cried aloud to the LORD, and he answered me from his holy hill. *I lay down and slept*; I woke again, for the LORD sustained me. I will not be afraid of many thousands of people who have set themselves against me all around" (ESV; cf. Ps. 4:7–8). Deep, restful sleep embodies trust in God's sovereign hand. By sleeping during the storm, Jesus, the Son of David, demonstrates his perfect and unswerving trust in his Father's protection in the midst of grave physical and spiritual danger. Jesus is truly walking by faith and not by sight (2 Cor. 5:7). As commentators often point out, this story recalls Jonah's sleeping during the storm on his way to Tarshish in an attempt to run from God's call (Jon. 1). A close reading of the two accounts, though, leads to the conclusion that Jesus is quite *unlike* Jonah. Jonah sleeps for the wrong reason (fleeing from God's call [Jon. 1:1–6]), whereas Jesus sleeps for the right reason (trusting in the Lord). Jonah's failures prophetically anticipate Jesus's faithfulness.

Jesus is able to still the storm by uttering few words: "Quiet! Be still!" (4:39). According to the OT, God, as Israel's divine warrior, alone stills the raging seas. Psalm 89, for example, reads,

> For who in the skies above can compare with the LORD?
> Who is like the LORD among the heavenly beings?

In the council of the holy ones God is greatly feared;
  he is more awesome than all who surround him.
Who is like you, Lord God Almighty?
  You, Lord, are mighty, and your faithfulness surrounds you.

You rule over the surging sea;
  when its waves mount up, you still them.
You crushed Rahab like one of the slain;
  with your strong arm you scattered your enemies. (89:6–10; cf. Ps.
    65:5–7)

Identifying himself as Israel's divine warrior, Jesus calms the storm with two commands. These two imperatives are strangely directed *at the sea*. Why speak to the sea? Recall what the sea represents: the forces of evil who are gathered to oppose God's people. Jesus, therefore, is commanding the demons to evacuate the sea. The terms "be still" and "obey" occur in 1:25 and 27 in the context of exorcisms (// Luke 4:35). Just as he exorcised demons from people, Jesus is exorcising the demons from creation! This event on the Sea of Galilee is not so much about Jesus's actions toward the disciples as it is about *Jesus's actions toward creation as a whole.*

Jesus's victory over Satan in the wilderness temptation enables him to launch a full-scale, victorious attack. Recall that in 1:12–13 Jesus's success in the wilderness resulted in cleansing creation, allowing him to commune with the "wild animals" and the angels. Here Jesus purges evil from the sea. In 1:12–13 Jesus cleanses the *land*, whereas in 4:35–41 he cleanses the *sea*. In the Bible, land and sea function as a synecdoche for all of creation (e.g., Ps. 95:5; Jon. 1:9; Hag. 2:6; Matt. 23:15; Rev. 7:1–3; 10:2, 5, 8). What we discover is the beginning of the redemption of the entire created order, a redemption that will climax at the cross and resurrection.

As an aside, Mark's account of the stilling of the storm contains several details not included in Matthew's and Luke's narratives. For example, Mark mentions the presence of "other boats" in 4:36 and later remarks that Jesus was "in the stern, sleeping on a cushion" (4:38a). These clues suggest that Peter, a professional fisherman (1:16), is Mark's eyewitness source. One with an intimate knowledge of the Sea of Galilee would naturally point out these nautical details.

Matthew's retelling of the same event includes the line in Jesus's response "You of *little* faith" (Matt. 8:26), but Mark's narrative reads, "Do you still have *no* faith?" (4:40). The Second Gospel appears, at least on the surface, harsher on the disciples. The disciples are struggling a great deal with "hearing" or "understanding" (4:24) what has taken place in the stilling of the storm. The account ends with the question posed by the disciples: "Who is this? Even the wind and the waves obey him!" (4:41). Clearly, Jesus's identity and mission exceed their expectations.

Once more we find the two titles "Son of God" and "Messiah" coming together in the Second Gospel (1:1). Mark has skillfully identified Jesus with the divine warrior by showing him stilling the storm (Son of God) and has highlighted his royal descent as the Son of David by showing him sleeping (Messiah). If we seriously consider the Isaiah 40 quotation at the beginning of Mark to be paradigmatic for his Gospel as a whole, then Jesus is viewed here as Israel's Lord and Messiah, who is conquering Israel's enemies and leading them to the promised land in the Isaianic exodus (Isa. 43:2; 51:9–11). The disciples are not drowning, as they presume. Far from it! They (and creation) are being redeemed.

From Unclean to Clean (5:1–43)

The Gerasene Demoniac (5:1–20)

The physical storm on the Sea of Galilee may be over, but in a spiritual sense it is still brewing. The narrative continues seamlessly with Jesus and the disciples disembarking their boat "to the region of the Gerasenes" (5:1). There are three textual variants for locating Jesus's interaction with the demoniac: the region of the "Gerasenes," "Gadarenes," and "Gergesenes." The town of Gerasa (or Jerash) lies about thirty miles southeast of the Sea of Galilee; Gadara is about six miles southeast (cf. Matt. 8:28); and Gergesa is on the east side of the bank. The reading "Gerasenes" (*Gerasēnōn*) has the strongest textual support, "Gadarenes" (*Gadarēnōn*) is generally solid, and "Gergesa" (*Gergesēnōn*) is the weakest. All in all, the reading "Gerasenes" is to be preferred, and we should not lose sight of Mark's inclusion of the word "region" (*tēn chōran*). Though the town lies some thirty miles away, it could be conceived that the broad territory extends to where Jesus and the disciples disembark. At the end of the day, Mark's readers will immediately be struck by the broad location of the event—the Decapolis (5:20).

The connection between the exorcism here in 5:1–20 and the stilling of the storm is evident. In both events, Jesus is ruling over the demonic forces and is recapturing that which is lost in the fall. What makes this exorcism unique is the amount of space Mark dedicates to it—roughly half the chapter—and its location in the region of the Decapolis. From 1:15–4:34, the narrative situates Jesus and the disciples on the western side of the Sea of Galilee with the city of Capernaum serving as home base. Now, though, Jesus and company venture to the "other side" of the lake, a region populated by gentiles.

Though the disciples take on a prominent role in chapter 4, they fade into the background here in 5:1–20, and most of this material concerns only two individuals: Jesus and the demoniac (// Matt. 8:28–34 // Luke 8:26–39). By focusing the narrative on these two parties, Mark wants the reader to pay careful attention to their interaction. The exorcism in the synagogue in 1:21–28 bears remarkable similarity to the one here in 5:1–20:

Exorcism in 1:21–28	Exorcism in 5:1–20
Man with "impure spirit" (1:23)	Man with "impure spirit" (5:2)
Demon asks, "What do you want with us?" (1:24)	Demon asks, "What do you want with me?" (5:7)
Demon identifies Jesus as "Jesus of Nazareth" and "the Holy One of God" (1:24)	Demon identifies Jesus as "Jesus, Son of the Most High God" (5:7)
Jesus commands the demon, "Come out of him!" (1:25)	Jesus commands the demon, "Come out of this man!" (5:8)
Crowd responds in amazement (1:27)	Crowd responds in amazement (5:20)
Message of victory goes forth to Galilee (1:28)	Message of victory goes forth to the Decapolis (5:20)

Mark, therefore, wants us to read the two events together. The first took place in the house of worship of the Jews (the synagogue), and the second takes place in a land filled with pagan idolatry and uncleanness (the tombs of the Decapolis). The goal of both events is cleansing for the purpose of enjoying God's presence.

When Jesus and the Twelve disembark from the boat, a man "with an impure spirit" accosts Jesus (5:2). We have already seen that the word "impure" (*akathartos*) is a key term in Mark's Gospel, embodying the current state of people and creation—unfit for God's presence. One scholar remarks about the uniqueness of Mark's presentation of the demon, "This expression ["unclean spirit"] is without parallel in non-Jewish literature from pre-Christian times."[21] Mark devotes three whole verses to describing the dire situation of the demoniac (5:3–5). Two key themes immediately jump out at the reader: (1) The demoniac is unable to be subdued. The man, having been subdued by Legion, is a slave spiritually and physically to the devil. (2) The demoniac dwells in a place that reeks of defilement (tombs, pigs, etc.).

21. Loren T. Stuckenbruck, *The Myth of Rebellious Angels: Studies in Second Temple Judaism and New Testament Texts* (Grand Rapids: Eerdmans, 2017), 174.

Though no one can "subdue" him, the demoniac runs to Jesus and falls "on his knees" (5:6), a clear act of submission. Knowing that he is outranked, the demon asks, "What do you want with me, Jesus, Son of the Most High God?" (5:7). Like the demoniac in 1:23–26, this one also attempts to wrest control from Jesus by invoking his name. Announcing a person's name in the ancient world, especially in the context of an exorcism, is a tactic to gain authority over that person. The name "Son of the Most High God" is remarkable for a couple reasons. First, the title ironically answers the question the disciples pose in 4:41: "They were terrified and asked each other, 'Who is this? Even the wind and the waves obey him!'" The answer: the "Son of the Most High God," a title similar to the "Son of God" in 1:1. The demoniac possesses more insight into Jesus's identity than the disciples! Second, this title is found on a handful of occasions in the OT that refer exclusively to Israel's God (e.g., Gen. 14:18; Ps. 78:35). Jesus, then, is not just a man (4:41); he is God in the flesh. This is precisely why the demoniac recognizes Jesus's superiority. Jesus is not just Israel's Messiah; he is the sovereign ruler of the cosmos. The mystery of Jesus's messiahship is still being revealed.

As the ruler of the cosmos, Jesus turns the tables and asks the name of the demon. We discover that the demon's name is "Legion," a term that refers to a military division of six thousand soldiers. What we have, then, is all the trappings of a battle. But this is not just any battle—this is an end-time war between Yahweh in the flesh and the forces of evil. As the divine warrior, Jesus purposely ventures to a region that is markedly hostile to God's rule and authority. With a simple command, he triumphs over his enemies, sending them into a nearby "herd of pigs" (5:11–13a). Mark records some two thousand pigs rushing into the Sea of Galilee, where they "drowned" (5:13b). Keep in mind that we are on the heels of the stilling of the storm (4:35–41), where Jesus judged the hostile spirits by expelling them from the sea. So when the demon-possessed pigs crash into the lake, Mark concludes that these demons have joined their compatriots in judgment.

A thoughtful reader of Israel's Scriptures would also connect this event to the memorable drowning of Pharaoh's army. The conceptual parallels between the two accounts are striking:

Exodus from Egypt (Exod. 14:15–15:21)	Exorcism of the Demoniac (Mark 5:1–20)
Israel's physical enemy = Egyptian army (14:24, 28)	Israel's spiritual enemy = Legion (military division [5:9])
Enemy drowned in the sea (14:27–28)	Enemy drowned in the sea (5:13)
Yahweh, as Israel's warrior, judges Pharaoh's army (15:3)	Jesus, as Israel's warrior or "Lord," judges Satan's army (5:19)

Exodus from Egypt (Exod. 14:15–15:21)	Exorcism of the Demoniac (Mark 5:1–20)
Judgment of the Egyptians results in God receiving the glory (14:17–18, 31)	Judgment of Legion results in Jesus receiving the glory (5:20)
The nations admit to God's unrivaled power (15:14)	The people of the Decapolis admit to Jesus's unmatched power (5:20)

If Exodus 14–15 is in Mark's mind, then the exorcism here in chapter 5 is critical for his Gospel as a whole. Mark demonstrates that Jesus fulfills Isaiah's promise of a second exodus. As the Lord incarnate, Jesus redeems Israel from the clutches of the spiritual Egyptians; he has secured redemption by fulfilling Isaiah's prophecy of binding the strong man (i.e., Satan [3:27; Isa. 49:24–25]). This redemption has taken place primarily in Jewish territory. Now, as Jesus journeys into gentile territory, we learn that he is also concerned about reaching the nations and delivering them from spiritual oppression. Notice, too, the order of salvation: Jews first and then gentiles (see Acts 3:26; 13:46; Rom. 1:16). Isaiah's expectations of a second exodus are continuing to be fulfilled.

In this vein, Mark may also be alluding to Isaiah 65:4–7 in 5:5 and 11:

Isaiah 65:4, 7	Mark 5:5, 11
". . . who [idolatrous Israelites] sit *among the graves* and spend their nights keeping secret vigil; who eat the flesh of *pigs*, and whose pots hold broth of impure meat . . . because they burned sacrifices on the mountains and defied me on the *hills*."	"Night and day *among the tombs* and in the *hills* he would cry out and cut himself with stones. . . . A large herd of *pigs* was feeding on the nearby *hillside*."

Mark strategically takes a passage about idolatrous Israel and applies it to a demoniac. But what is significant is Isaiah's promise at the end of the oracle. The Lord assures Israel that he "will not destroy them all" and that he will "bring forth descendants from Jacob . . . and there will my servants live" (Isa. 65:8–9). If Isaiah 65 is in mind, then Jesus is fulfilling the prophecy of Isaiah when he expels the demons. Jesus, as *the* Suffering Servant (10:45), is creating a community of little "servants" (cf. Isa. 65:13–15). This man, representing all gentiles enslaved to the devil, is now considered to be part of redeemed Israel.

Healing the Woman with the Issue of Blood and Raising Jairus's Daughter (5:21–43)

Jesus accomplished what he set out to do in coming to the area of the gentiles, so now he and the disciples cross the Sea of Galilee and return to Jewish territory (5:21). This is the second crossing of the lake thus far (cf.

4:35). Here in the second half of chapter 5, we come across Mark's sandwich technique yet again:

Jairus's daughter (5:21-24)
Woman with the issue of blood (5:25-34)
Jairus's daughter (5:35-43)

All three Synoptics blend these two events so that the reader may interpret them together (// Matt. 9:18–26 // Luke 5:21–43).

Jesus's popularity among the Jewish people continues as he disembarks from the boat. One from the crowd named Jairus, a synagogue leader and a respected member of the community, pursues Jesus and falls "at his feet" (5:22; cf. 5:6). Curiously, this is the first nonpublic individual (and not one of the disciples [3:16–19]) to be named. Richard Bauckham persuasively argues that the unexpected disclosure of an individual's name in the Gospels indicates that that person is an eyewitness of the account.[22] This insight fits well here with Jairus (the daughter remains unnamed). As Mark researched his Gospel, he interviewed those who interacted with Jesus face-to-face. Jairus recognizes Jesus's ability to perform miracles and prostrates himself before Jesus, an act that acknowledges Jesus's superior status.

A woman "who had been subject to bleeding for twelve years" (5:25) suddenly interrupts the narrative. According to Leviticus 15:25–28, this woman would have been perpetually unclean, resulting in her ostracism from society. She has been suffering for twelve years (5:25, 26)—the same length of time as the sick daughter has lived (5:42). Her desperation is apparent from her desire to "touch" Jesus (cf. 3:10). After a single touch from her, Jesus would be rendered ritually unclean. But instead of *him* becoming *unclean* at her touch, *she* becomes *clean*. Her concrete display of faith results in her rejoining her community and integrating back into society. Climactically, Jesus commands her to "go in peace" (5:34). Peace between God and humanity is the driving force behind much of the OT, especially the book of Isaiah. This is not general peace but eschatological peace (Isa. 53:5; 54:13; 57:19; 66:12). Perhaps Isaiah 52:7 lies behind Jesus's statement: "How beautiful on the mountains are the feet of those who bring good news, who proclaim *peace*" (cf. Mark 1:15). Jesus restores this woman so that she may enjoy God's presence.

The narrative swings back to Jairus and his daughter. Jairus's worst nightmare is confirmed in 5:35 when he is informed that his daughter is now

22. Richard Bauckham, *Jesus and the Eyewitnesses: The Gospels as Eyewitness Testimony* (Grand Rapids: Eerdmans, 2006), 39–66.

dead. In his eyes and the eyes of the disciples, nothing further can be done. But Jesus breaks through their doubts and commands Jairus: "Don't be afraid; just believe" (5:36). Jairus must have the same faith that the woman with the issue of blood possesses (5:34; cf. 1:15; 2:5; 9:23; 10:52; 11:22–24). He must trust that Jesus alone holds the power to raise the dead. For the first time, Jesus permits only Peter, James, and John to join him for this miracle (5:37). What about the other nine disciples? In the Synoptics, Peter, James, and John are regarded as the inner three, those privy to extraordinary events (3:16–17; 9:2; 14:33). Recall that in 4:24–25 Jesus promises that those who receive more revelation are responsible to behave accordingly. More is expected of them. In the decades to come, Peter and John will become two pillars of the early Christian movement. Peter's influence on the Synoptics and the church in Acts is enormous, while Saint John will go on to write the Gospel that bears his name, three letters, and likely the book of Revelation.

Jesus takes his three disciples and the girl's parents into the room where she lies dead (5:40). Jesus takes the girl's hand and says in Aramaic, "*Talitha koum!*" Mark then gives us the translation: ". . . which means, 'Little girl, I say to you, get up!'" Aramaic was the dominant language in Palestine at this time, so Jesus primarily speaks in Aramaic throughout his ministry (3:17; 7:11, 34; 10:46; 14:36). But why would Mark feel compelled to disclose the Aramaic here? We cannot be sure, but it may partly be due to the significance of this event. Raising the dead is quite simply something that only God can do (cf. John 5:19–30). Whereas Elijah and Elisha raised people from the dead (1 Kings 17:19–22; 2 Kings 4:29–35), they only did so as mediators. The miracle here is qualitatively different. Jesus does not summon God's power. God's creative power, like the healing power found in 5:30, flows from Jesus himself, the life-giving Son of God (1:1). By bringing this girl back to life, Jesus is unequivocally claiming to be the Lord incarnate, and Mark preserves the Aramaic discourse to authenticate the miracle.

This miracle also anticipates Jesus's own resurrection at the end of Mark's narrative. If Jesus has the power to raise the dead because he is God in the flesh, then he also has the power to raise himself from the dead. Moreover, the NT affirms that all three persons of the Trinity participate in the resurrection (see Rom. 1:4; Gal. 1:1).

Mark then points out that the girl is a minor, approximately "twelve years old" (5:42). The woman with the issue of blood and the girl here, taken together, represent marginal figures in the first century. In addition to their low status, they are both unclean (Lev. 15:25–28; Num. 19:11). In both cases, then, Jesus declares clean those deemed unclean. God's presence is on the move.

Mounting Hostility in Galilee (6:1–56)

Rejection at Nazareth (6:1–6)

With so much success in the Decapolis, a gentile territory, one would assume that Jesus's success would extend to his home in Nazareth. But such is not the case. Jesus continues his ministry on the western side of Galilee as he heads southwest to his "hometown" of Nazareth (6:1). This is the first reference to Jesus's home. A similar acknowledgment occurs in 3:20–21 and 3:31–34, where his family appears to be at odds with his ministry. If Jesus's own family has difficulty grasping his identity, then it should be unsurprising that those in his hometown follow suit.

The narrative of 6:1–5 appears to be juxtaposed with Jesus's success in Capernaum in 1:21–28 (// Matt. 13:54–58 // Luke 4:14–30).

Mark 1:21–28	Mark 6:1–5
Capernaum (1:21)	Nazareth ("hometown" [6:1])
On the Sabbath (1:21)	On the Sabbath (6:2)
In the synagogue (1:21)	In the synagogue (6:2)
Crowd is "amazed" (1:22, 27)	Crowd is "amazed" (6:2)
Crowd asks one question (1:27)	Crowd asks six questions (6:2–3)
Jesus performs a miracle (1:23–26)	Jesus does not perform any miracles (6:5)

By narrating the episode of 6:1–5 in this manner, Mark signals to his readers that they should be struck with how those in Capernaum responded to Jesus's ministry in contrast to those in Nazareth. Ironically, those who know him best have the most difficulty accepting his claims. Whereas Jesus's family is unnamed in chapter 3, Mark divulges the names of his mother and brothers here: Mary, James, Joseph, Judas, and Simon (the sisters remain unnamed). Two of his half brothers, James and Judas, will eventually write two letters that are preserved in the NT. James even features quite prominently in the book of Acts and becomes the leader of the early church in Jerusalem (Acts 15).

The episode ends with Jesus being "amazed at their lack of faith" (6:6). Such unbelief stands in stark relief to those who demonstrate great "faith" in Jesus throughout Mark's narrative (2:5; 5:34, 36; 9:24; 10:52). Faith is required for miracles. But why are Jesus's family and community plagued by so much doubt? Shouldn't they be among the first to believe him? The answer lies in Jesus's response: "A prophet is not without honor except in his own town, among his relatives and in his own home" (6:4). Helpfully, in Luke's account of this event (Luke 4:25–27), Jesus goes on to cite two OT examples of Israel rejecting Elijah and Elisha, in contrast to two gentiles, the widow at Zarephath and Naaman, who embrace the prophets (1 Kings 17:7–24; 2 Kings 5:1–14). We should keep in mind, though, that Jesus did restore a remnant within Nazareth, as he laid "his hands on a few sick people and healed them" (6:5)

So Nazareth's unbelief fits squarely in the OT tradition of Israel rejecting her own prophets and gentiles coming to faith (5:1–20). One could even argue that these OT incidents prophetically anticipate Nazareth's rejection of Jesus and the greatest rejection of all—Israel's rejection of her own Messiah at the cross (cf. 12:1–12). Such rejection at Nazareth accents Jesus's strange messiahship, a messiahship that is breaking the Jewish mold.

The Commissioning of the Twelve and the Martyrdom of John the Baptist (6:7–29)

With rejection in the minds of Mark's readers, we now come across the disciples' second commissioning (// Matt. 10:1, 5–42 // Luke 9:1–6). In the earlier commissioning, each disciple is named (3:13–19) and all are granted "authority to drive out demons" (3:15). Here the commissioning is accompanied by "authority over *impure* spirits," who are defiling humanity and God's creation (cf. 1:23, 26–27; 3:30; 5:2, 8, 13; 7:25; 9:25). The disciples break up into groups of two (6:7). Why two? According to Deuteronomy, at least two individuals are required to testify in court, and the following verse explains the purpose of a legal testimony:

> On the testimony of *two or three witnesses* a person is to be put to death, but no one is to be put to death on the testimony of only one witness. The hands of the witnesses must be the first in putting that person to death, and then the hands of all the people. *You must purge the evil from among you.* (Deut. 17:6–7; cf. 19:15, 19)

The phrase "purge the evil from among you" is a central theme throughout Deuteronomy (13:5; 17:12; 19:13, 19; 21:21; 22:24; 24:7). The Israelites and particularly the priests must guard against all forms of defilement within the camp. Bearing legal testimony therefore exists for the preservation of the sanctity of God's people *so that* he may dwell in the midst of their community. A holy God cannot dwell among unholy people. Therefore, Jesus orders the disciples to be swift on their feet (6:8–9) and go out two by two so that they may hunt down "the evil" that is defiling the hearts of the Israelites. Following in the footsteps of John the Baptist, who proclaims a message of "repentance" in Judea (1:4–5), the disciples preach "that people should repent" (6:12).

As Mark's narrative moves forward, persecution and suffering gain more traction. The link between John the Baptist, Jesus, and the disciples is again formalized here in 6:14–29, where Mark spends a great deal of time explaining the death of John at the hands of Herod Antipas (// Matt. 14:1–12 // Luke 9:7–9). Jesus's ministry is so reminiscent of John's ministry that Herod wonders if John "has been raised from the dead" (6:16). The story of John's fate is packed with notable themes, but we will isolate two of them. (1) John's ministry, like the ministry of Jesus and the disciples, is characterized by calling Israel and her leaders (e.g., Herod) to repentance (6:17–18). John summons Judea to return to God so that God may come and dwell with them. The disciples, too, are commissioned to confront all forms of ungodliness. (2) John's fate serves as a model for the disciples and, ultimately, for Jesus. The future of the disciples is bleak, at least according to the world's standards. Since John is persecuted, the disciples must expect nothing less. The parallels between the death of John and the death of Jesus are many. Both are innocent yet killed (6:20 // 15:14); in both cases, the secular ruler is pressured into ordering an execution (6:21–25 // 15:15). John's and Jesus's bodies are taken and placed in tombs (6:29 // 15:46). Herod's mistaken belief that Jesus is John "raised from the dead" (6:16) anticipates Jesus's resurrection (16:6).

The Feeding of the Five Thousand (6:30–44)

Two important verses that set the tone for the entire account preface the feeding of the five thousand, the only miracle repeated in all four Gospels (// Matt. 14:13–21 // Luke 9:10–17 // John 6:5–13). Mark ties the feeding with the sending out of the twelve disciples in 6:6b–13. At the beginning of the account, the "apostles" eagerly related to Jesus "all they had done and taught" (6:30), presumably a reference to their success in driving out demons and healing others. In other words, the disciples explain that they have successfully carried out their mission in cleansing the region of "impure spirits" (6:7), clearing the way for God's presence to descend in Jesus at the feeding of the five thousand.

Intimate fellowship between Jesus and the disciples is prematurely cut short because of the pressing crowds, so Jesus suggests that they find a "deserted place [erēmon topon] . . . and rest [anapausasthe] a while" (6:31 NRSV). There is only one place in the entire OT (LXX) where these precise two words, "desert" (erēmos) and "rest" or "dwell" (anapauō), occur: Isaiah 32:16. Isaiah 32:15–20 predicts that the end-time Spirit will descend upon the cursed ground and establish the new, end-time creation. Isaiah 32:15–18 reads,

> . . . till the Spirit is poured on us from on high,
>   and the desert becomes a fertile field,
>   and the fertile field seems like a forest.
> The LORD's justice *will dwell* [*anapausetai*] in the *desert* [*erēmō*],
>   his righteousness live in the fertile field.
> The fruit of that righteousness will be peace;
>   its effect will be quietness and confidence forever.
> My people will live in peaceful dwelling places,
>   in secure homes,
>   in undisturbed places of rest.

Two chapters later in Isaiah, we learn more about the end result of the Spirit's coming and bringing about the new creation: "*The desert* [*erēmos*] and the parched land will be glad; *the wilderness* [*erēmos*] will rejoice and blossom. . . . They will see the glory of the LORD, the splendor of our God" (Isa. 35:1–2). The entire point of God reversing the covenant curses and bringing about the new creation is that Israel's God may dwell with humanity and creation. Consider that the term "wilderness" (*erēmos*) occurs five times in Mark 1 and is found in the programmatic Isaiah 40:4 quotation ("a voice of one calling in the *wilderness* [*erēmō*]"). If Jesus has Isaiah 32 and 35 in mind here, then we should perhaps understand the feeding of the five thousand as a fulfillment of Isaiah's prophecy.

The attempt by Jesus and the disciples to escape the crowd was thwarted, as the crowd "got there ahead of them" (6:33). When Jesus saw the multitude, he "had compassion on them, because they were like a sheep without a shepherd" (6:34). Jesus appears to quote a few OT texts (Num. 27:17; 2 Chron. 18:16), passages that are part of a larger trajectory of eschatological expectations of a coming Davidic ruler (Ezek. 34; Zech. 10). Jesus, as Israel's Messiah (1:1), recognizes that the time has come for him to unite the scattered tribes of Israel and rule over them in righteousness.

As the account advances, we discover that the crowd is in the "remote place" (*erēmos*), and there is understandably a lack of food (6:32–33 NRSV). Note that Luke states that Jesus and the disciples are in the vicinity of Bethsaida (Luke 9:10). While the disciples assume that the people will fend for themselves and buy food locally (6:36), Jesus intends to nourish them himself. For good reasons, commentators bridge Jesus feeding the five thousand in the wilderness with the Lord feeding the Israelites in the wilderness on their journey to Sinai and the promised land (cf. John 6:1–15, 25–71).

God's provision of manna in the wilderness stems from the Israelites grumbling to Moses and Aaron for lack of food; God graciously feeds them manna "from heaven" (Exod. 16:4). Exodus 16:6–7 explicitly states the purpose of God feeding his people: "You will know that it was the Lord who brought you out of Egypt, and . . . you will *see the glory of the* LORD" (cf. Exod. 16:12). Manna is a tangible expression of God's grace in the lives of the Israelites, and ultimately, God intends it to draw his people into his glorious presence. In feeding the five thousand (plus women and children) in the "wilderness," Jesus demonstrates that he is the Lord incarnate, who lovingly feeds and nourishes his people with his presence.

We should also contemplate how Jesus could be viewed typologically as a Moses figure who leads and serves God's people in the wilderness. Though he feeds them physically with bread and fish, he is symbolically feeding them with his glorious presence as the Son of God (1:1). This is the same presence that the OT has been promising from so long ago. In a second exodus, Jesus is leading his people out of the wilderness and guiding them to the true, spiritual promised land, where they will one day, at the resurrection, fellowship with him perfectly.

Jesus drops a subtle clue about how he will accomplish the redemption of his people: by offering up himself as a Passover lamb. According to 6:41, Jesus "*gave thanks* and *broke* the loaves.*" A similar expression is found at the Last Supper in 14:22, where Jesus "took bread, and when he had *given thanks*, he *broke* it and gave it to his disciples, saying, 'Take it; this is my body.'" So the feeding of the five thousand also enacts the annual Passover celebration and climaxes in the death of Jesus, the ultimate Passover sacrifice. The prophet Isaiah predicts that the suffering servant will secure the redemption of a remnant and trigger the new creation (Isa. 52:13–53:12).

At the end of the account, the disciples collect "twelve basketfuls of broken pieces of bread and fish" (6:43). Why twelve? The number twelve (*dōdeka*) occurs fifteen times in Mark, more than any other Gospel (Matthew = thirteen; Luke = twelve; John = six) and the second most of any NT book (Revelation = twenty-three). Twelve of the fifteen occurrences in Mark refer to the twelve disciples, and the remaining three refer to the woman with the issue of blood (5:25), Jairus's daughter (5:42), and the number of baskets here (6:44). In light of the overwhelming use of "twelve" in Mark, the number of baskets is significant and probably carries a great deal of symbolism. If the twelve disciples symbolize true Israel, then the twelve baskets here may symbolize the growth of true Israel through Jesus's feeding the five thousand and his sacrificial death. His life-giving presence produces a new creational remnant that begins to behold the glory of God.

Jesus Walks on the Water (6:45–56)

The narrative progresses from the feeding of the five thousand to Jesus famously walking on the water (// Matt. 14:22–32 // John 6:15–21). Mark joins these two accounts with his use of "and immediately" (*kai euthys*) in 6:45. Though these two episodes appear to be randomly aligned, the feeding of the five thousand is on Mark's mind throughout the account. Much of what we saw in Jesus stilling the storm in 4:35–41 is reiterated here in 6:45–52.

Jesus commands his disciples to "go on ahead of him to Bethsaida" (6:45). This is the third journey across the lake thus far and the second episode that focuses on Jesus's interaction with the disciples on the water. Many of the themes found in 4:35–41 are repeated here. We discovered in the first account that Mark recasts the stilling of the storm as a second exodus, wherein Jesus as Israel's God delivers the disciples from the clutches of the demonic forces (→4:35–41). This event in 6:45–52 tugs on many of those redemptive threads and weaves in a few more. The entire episode of Jesus walking on the water is quite reminiscent of God revealing himself to Moses and Israel in the exodus and at Sinai. Note a few general comparisons and three linguistic connections:

Sinai (Book of Exodus)	Walking on the Water (6:45–52)
Israel is divided into three camps at Sinai: the nation at the base (19:2), the elders halfway up (24:1), and Moses at the top (19:3)	The people are divided into three camps: the crowd remains on the land (6:45), the disciples in the boat (6:46), and Jesus on the mountain (6:46)
Moses ascends to the top of the mountain to meet with God (19:3)	Jesus goes up to the mountain to pray (6:46)
The "sons of Israel walked through dry land *in the midst of the sea* [*en mesō tēs thalassēs*]" (15:19 NETS; cf. 14:29; 15:8)	*The disciples are in a boat "in the middle of the lake* [*en mesō tēs thalassēs*]" (6:47)
Yahweh controls the sea (14:21–28)	Jesus controls the sea (6:48)
Yahweh promises Moses that he will *"pass by* [*pareleusomai*] before you in . . . glory"* (33:19 NETS); "I will cover you with my hand until *I pass by* [*parelthō*]" (33:22 NETS)	Jesus was "about *to pass by* [*parelthein*] them" (6:48)
Yahweh identifies himself as *"I am* [*egō eimi*] who I am" to Moses and to the Israelites (Exod. 3:13–14)	Jesus identifies himself to the disciples by saying, *"It is I* [*egō eimi*]" (6:50)

In the stilling of the storm, the emphasis is on Jesus's defeat of the demons as Israel's divine warrior and in fulfillment of Isaiah's expectations. Here, the emphasis is not so much on Jesus's defeat of the inimical forces—though it is certainly here (6:48)—as on the revelation of his identity to the disciples.

In the stilling of the storm, the focus is on Jesus cleansing creation *so that* God may dwell with creation and humanity. Here Mark highlights Jesus as Yahweh incarnate who *is presently* dwelling with creation. In the first exodus, God revealed himself to the Israelites as "Yahweh," and here in the second exodus, God once again reveals himself but in a more powerful and intimate way—in the person of his Son. God's revelation of himself in the first exodus prophetically anticipates Jesus's revelation of himself in the second exodus.

The disciples' reaction to such a bold revelation is, at least according to Mark's narrative, hardly surprising: "They were completely amazed, for *they had not understood about the loaves; their hearts were hardened*" (6:51–52). As when Jesus stills the storm, the disciples remain in the dark about who Jesus truly is. They are having great difficulty grasping Jesus's identity as Israel's suffering "Messiah" *and* the divine "Son of God" (1:1). According to 6:53, the disciples should have connected the dots in the feeding of the five thousand, but they were unable to because their "hearts were hardened." Mark's readers are confronted with a difficult question: Are the disciples outsiders and fulfilling the grave prophecy of Isaiah 6:9–10?

Though the disciples set course for Bethsaida, on the northeastern side of the lake (6:45), they land in Gennesaret, a coastal plain on the northwestern side. Is Mark's geography confused? Though some scholars believe so, a simpler answer is most sensible: the disciples' boat, because of the raging storm (6:48), is blown off course.

Defilement of the Heart and the Conversion of the Nations (7:1–37)

Hypocritical Leaders (7:1–13)

We have seen how the devil corrupts creation and humanity, barring them from God's presence. Now we discover another source of defilement—the human heart (// Matt. 15:1–20). The first half of chapter 7 is devoted to Jesus's interaction with the Jewish leaders "who had come from Jerusalem" (7:1). Since Jerusalem is characterized by suffering and death, the chapter opens with a note of hostility (cf. 3:6, 22). The Jewish leaders are astounded that some of the disciples are eating their food without washing their hands beforehand (7:2). According to Jewish oral tradition, this act makes one ritually impure.

Jesus cuts through such legalism and cites Isaiah 29:13 in fulfillment of Isaiah's words: "Isaiah was right when he prophesied about *you hypocrites*; as it is written: 'These people honor me with their lips, but their hearts are far from me'" (7:6). In Isaiah 29, the prophet rails against the spiritual leaders of Israel because of their inability to understand God's plans to judge wicked Israel and her surrounding nations yet deliver a righteous remnant (Isa. 29:10–12). These leaders are incapable of understanding God's program of redemption because of their superficial religion. Extraordinarily, Jesus claims that Isaiah ultimately had the first-century Jewish leaders in view! We should connect the Isaiah 29:13 quotation here in 7:6 to the earlier Isaiah 6:9–10 quotation in 4:12, as both Isaiah texts are bound up with idolatry. We discover here in chapter 7 *how* the people of Israel became enamored with idolatry in the first place (4:12)—they learned it from their idolatrous leaders (7:6–7). The leaders of Israel are guilty not of bowing down to physical idols crafted out of gold but of worshiping figurative idols—their own manufactured traditions.

True Defilement (7:14–23)

If human tradition does not make one truly impure, then what does? Jesus answers this question when he addresses the crowd in 7:15: "It is what comes out of a person that defiles them." This is a striking statement because of its implications. The Mosaic legislation teaches that one can become ritually impure because of external contaminants, but Jesus drills down to a deeper level of uncleanness—the human heart. Jesus is claiming that the Mosaic law is fundamentally unable to cleanse a sinful heart. But if the law cannot cleanse, what can? The answer lies not in *what* but in *who*. An animal sacrifice simply will not do. True holiness can only be found in the sacrificial death of Isaiah's servant (10:45; Isa. 52:13–53:12).

Mark's Gospel is, as we have seen repeatedly, intent on tracing Jesus's ministry against the backdrop of cleansing. John the Baptist, Jesus, and the disciples cleanse in order for God's glory to descend. Here in chapter 7, we learn about an important dimension to their ministry of cleansing: another source of pollution is the human heart. For God to dwell intimately with humanity, the heart must be purified from all evil. *Jesus's ministry is, first and foremost, directed at redeeming the inner person.* When he exorcises demons and heals, he is fundamentally intent on purifying the people of God.

One implication of Jesus's view of the law here is his declaration that "all foods" are now "clean" (7:19). Israel's dietary restrictions are fulfilled in Jesus and are no longer required for God's people in the new age. Such food restrictions separate the Israelites from their neighbors (Lev. 11; Deut. 14). The time has now arrived when God's people will no longer be marked by external regulations but by internal faith in Jesus, paving the way for Jews and gentiles to enjoy genuine fellowship with one another. The lifting of the dietary regulations is, not coincidentally, tied to the faith of a gentile woman in the following passage (7:24–30).

We must not gloss over an important dimension to Jesus's interaction with his disciples. In 7:17–18, he leaves the crowd and enters "the house." We are not told whose house this is, but we get the impression that Jesus is attempting to explain in more detail what he has already stated in 7:16 (like his instruction in 4:34). The disciples draw Jesus's ire when they ask him about "this parable" (7:17). He responds out of frustration with the question, "Are you so dull?" The wording is close to 4:13, where the disciples have difficulty in understanding the parable of the seeds: "Don't you understand this parable?" The disciples have struggled to comprehend Jesus's identity in his teaching and miracles at key junctures in the narrative (4:41; 6:37, 52), and they continue to do so here. When will they be cured of their blindness?

The Faith of a Syrophoenician Woman (7:24–30)

Jesus leaves from the northern part of the lake and heads for the region of Tyre (7:24), an area along the coast that is populated by gentiles (// Matt. 15:21–28). This is the second time Jesus has ventured into gentile territory (5:1–20), and his careful movement could be for a couple reasons: (1) since all foods are now "clean" (7:19), Jesus is tearing down the barriers between Jews and gentiles; and (2) since true defilement does not originate from the outside (7:15, 18–19), journeying to a gentile area will not ritually defile Jesus and his disciples. Jesus's pursuit of seclusion is quickly interrupted, as a gentile woman approaches him and pleads with him to exorcise an "impure spirit" from her daughter (7:25–26). Once again, Mark reveals the strong connection between demons and defilement (cf. 1:23, 26; 3:11, 30; 5:2, 8, 13; 6:7; 9:25).

Jesus is resistant to granting the woman's wish because "it is not right to take the children's bread and toss it to the dogs" (7:27). That is, Israelites (the children) deserve to be nourished *first* (*prōton*; // Matt. 15:24). Jesus is probably speaking in terms of the general order of salvation, an order that is anticipated in the OT: the salvation of Israel first and *then* the nations (e.g., Isa. 2:2–4; 60:1–14; Mic. 4:1–5). But the woman responds, "Even the dogs [the gentiles] under the table eat the children's crumbs" (7:28). Despite Israel's priority in the timing of salvation, the gentiles do become equals with the Israelites in the "latter days" (Isa. 56:6–7; 66:18–21). The gentile woman seizes on this redemptive-historical order and is rewarded for doing so. Seeing the incredible insight of this woman, Jesus immediately exorcises the demon from her daughter. With Jesus cleansing this young girl, God's glory is budding in gentile soil.

The Healing of a Deaf-Mute Man (7:31–37)

Oddly, Jesus and company first head north to Sidon, only to turn south to the Sea of Galilee as they make their way back to the Decapolis (7:31). Why take the long route? Though some scholars regard Mark's geography here as confused, perhaps Mark is being quite intentional about Jesus's travels. We have argued throughout that Jesus is systematically cleansing and preparing Israel and the nations for the arrival of God's presence. What if Jesus's march through Sidon, the northernmost city that the Gospels record Jesus visiting, signifies the extent of Jesus's restoration? Sidon and the Decapolis may function as a synecdoche (part for the whole), symbolizing the restoration of *all* the nations.

While in the Decapolis, Jesus heals a deaf and mute man (// Matt. 15:29–31). The placement of the healing in the narrative is remarkable. The man (probably gentile) was deaf and "could hardly talk" (7:32). Sensory obduracy in Mark's Gospel, as we have noted several times, springs from Isaiah 6:9–10. Outsiders, and especially the Jewish leaders, are characterized by their lack of hearing and stubborn hearts (3:5; 4:12; 7:6–7). Even the disciples are guilty of unbelief at times (4:12; 6:52; 8:17–18). What makes this miracle peculiar is Mark's description of the man. He uses the term *mogilalon* ("could hardly talk"), a term that occurs only once in the NT and the entire LXX. The term is found in Isaiah 35:5, where the prophet Isaiah predicts the reversal of curses and the in-breaking of the new creation. A few verses from the immediate context are illuminating:

> Say to those with fearful hearts,
> "Be strong, do not fear;
> *your God will come,*
> he will come with vengeance;
> with divine retribution
> *he will come to save you.*"
>
> Then will the eyes of the blind be opened
> and the ears of the deaf unstopped.
> Then will the lame leap like a deer,
> and the *mute tongue* [*glōssa mogilalōn*] shout for joy.
> Water will gush forth in the wilderness
> and streams in the desert. (Isa. 35:4–6)

If Isaiah 35 lies behind this healing, then Jesus, as the Son of God (1:1), should be identified with God "coming" and "saving" the mute man in fulfillment of Isaiah's prophecy. Moreover, the healing of the deaf-mute man also symbolizes the restoration of the nations and God's long-held desire to take up residence in their midst.

The Feeding of the Four Thousand and Continued Blindness (8:1–21)

The Feeding of the Four Thousand (8:1–10)

The feeding of the multitude in 8:1–10 continues Jesus's determination to see gentiles become part of the restored people of God (// Matt. 15:32–39). The soft link with the previous context in 8:1 ("During those days") encourages Mark's audience to read this miracle in light of his miracles in Tyre and the Decapolis (7:24–37). The purpose of the feeding is to confirm for Mark's audience that the gentiles are not second-class citizens in the end-time kingdom but fully participate in the restored Israel of God. What is generally true about the feeding of the five thousand rings true here in the feeding of the four thousand:

Feeding of the Five Thousand (6:30–44)	Feeding of the Four Thousand (8:1–11)
Crowd "gathered" (6:30)	Crowd "gathered" (8:1)
Jesus has "compassion" (6:34)	Jesus has "compassion" (8:2)
Miracle takes place in a "solitary place" (6:32)	Miracle takes place in a "remote place" (8:4)
The disciples doubt (6:37)	The disciples doubt (8:4)
Meal begins with five loaves of bread and two fish (6:38)	Meal begins with seven loaves of bread and "a few small fish" (8:5, 7)
Jesus gives "thanks" and breaks bread (6:41)	Jesus gives "thanks" and breaks bread (8:6)
Crowd eats and is "satisfied" (6:42)	Crowd eats and is "satisfied" (8:8)
Twelve baskets of food remain (6:43)	Seven baskets of food remain (8:8)

If Mark wants his readers to read the two miracles together, we have warrant to draw similar conclusions. As Israel's God incarnate, Jesus nourishes these gentiles with God's presence. Since Jesus began to cleanse the general area of the Decapolis of evil in 5:1–20, he now begins to fill it with his presence. In the feeding of the five thousand, Jesus fills the Jewish people with God's glory, granting them the status of end-time people of God. Jesus does the same here for the gentiles in the Decapolis.

The Continued Blindness of the Disciples (8:11–21)

Following the feeding of the four thousand, Jesus and company travel to "the region of Dalmanutha" (8:10). This is the fifth crossing of the lake in the narrative. Scholars are unsure about the location of Dalmanutha, though many suspect that it refers to somewhere along the northwestern side of the lake. The Pharisees approach Jesus, asking him to validate his ministry and perform a "sign from heaven" (8:11). Jesus will do no such thing, as he will not depend upon the whims of the unbelieving Jewish leaders. He is no circus act.

The sixth and final sea crossing brings Jesus to Bethsaida (8:22), but while they cross the lake, Jesus uses a parable about yeast to warn the disciples about the brewing hostility of the Jewish leaders and Herod (8:15 // Matt. 16:5–12). At the heart of the conversation is Jesus's claim that Herod and the Jewish leaders, because of their wicked hearts and antagonism toward the kingdom, are "yeast" or pollutants (see 3:6; 6:14–29; 8:11; 12:13). Yeast is often associated with influencing others, whether good (e.g., Matt. 13:33) or bad (e.g., 1 Cor. 5:6; Gal. 5:9). Mark's Gospel discloses yet another layer of contaminant that defiles God's people and the created order—corrupt leadership. Like yeast spreading through the entire loaf of bread, the wickedness of Israel's spiritual and political leaders has percolated into the covenant community so that the entire nation embodies the attributes of her leaders.

The disciples miss the spiritual significance of the parable of the yeast, focusing only on the physical dimension of the bread (8:16). Their lack of insight provokes Jesus to draw from the book of Isaiah once more: "Do you still not see or understand? Are your *hearts* hardened? Do you have *eyes* but fail to see, and *ears* but fail to hear?" (8:17–18; cf. Jer. 5:21; Ezek. 12:2). Jesus's words are riveting, as he applies the prophecy of Isaiah 6:9–10—a prophecy that the "outsiders" in Mark's Gospel begin to fulfill (3:5; 4:12; 7:6)—to his own disciples. This is also the second time Jesus has applied sensory obduracy language to the disciples (cf. 6:52). With Jesus's sobering words, Mark closes the first major section of his Gospel. It appears, then, that the yeast of the unbelieving Jewish leaders is beginning to permeate the hearts of the disciples. How can it be stopped? Will the disciples understand that Jesus is truly their Messiah and the Son of God (1:1)?

■ Act 2: Jesus Journeys to Jerusalem (8:22–10:52)

The Blind Can (Almost) See (8:22–9:1)

The Healing of the Disciples (8:22–30)

At Bethsaida, a group of individuals present a blind man to Jesus for healing, an event that only Mark records. This miracle is significant because of its placement within the narrative and the nature of the two-staged healing. In contrast to the other Synoptics, where Jesus often heals the blind (e.g., Matt. 11:5; 15:30; Luke 4:18; 7:21), there are only two healings of the blind in Mark's narrative (8:22–25; 10:46–52). Jesus attempts to heal the man, but his success is surprisingly limited: "He [the blind man] looked up and said, 'I see people; they look like trees walking around'" (8:24). So Jesus goes round two with this man, and this time the man is completely healed. Up to this point in Mark's Gospel, Jesus has cast out demons, healed scores of people, raised the dead, and stilled the raging sea. Why does it take two attempts to heal the man? Is Jesus's power petering out? Herein lies the answer: the placement of the miracle. Immediately before this healing, Jesus labels his disciples as being blind: "Do you still not see or understand? . . . Do you have eyes but fail to see?" (8:17–18). The healing of the blind man in two stages symbolizes the healing of the disciples' blindness in two stages.

The first stage of healing is found in the following account (// Matt. 16:13–16 // Luke 9:18–20), where Peter climactically confesses that Jesus is indeed the long-awaited Messiah: "He [Jesus] questioned his disciples, saying to them, 'Who do people say that I am?'" (8:27 NASB). After the disciples offer their list of prime candidates, Jesus pointedly asks Peter, "But who do you say that I am?" (3:29 NASB). The bell rings, and Peter declares, "You are the *Christ*" (8:29 NASB). The word for "Christ" is the Greek *christos*, meaning "anointed one" or "Messiah." Peter claims that Jesus is indeed the highly anticipated Messiah who has come to liberate Israel.

Notice that Peter identifies Jesus only as the "Messiah" and not as the "Son of God." Mark promises that he will demonstrate how Jesus is Israel's King *and* the Son of God (1:1; cf. Matt. 16:16), so there remains another dimension to the person of Jesus that Peter and the disciples must grasp. Peter's exuberance is quickly curbed as Jesus commands his disciples "not to tell anyone about him" (8:30). Jesus's identity as king must remain a secret because he breaks the mold (cf. 1:34; 5:43; 7:36; 9:9); he is a *suffering* Messiah who ushers in a kingdom marked by persecution and suffering. The first stage of healing the disciples' blindness is now complete. They now see Jesus more clearly, but only "like trees walking around" (8:24). In what follows, we discover additional blind spots.

The Son of Man Must Suffer (8:31–33)

Verse 31 is the first of three passion predictions in the second portion of Mark's narrative, shifting the tone from here onward:

Mark 8:31	Mark 9:31	Mark 10:33
"He then began to teach them that the Son of Man must suffer many things and be rejected by the elders, the chief priests and the teachers of the law, and that he must be killed and after three days rise again."	"The Son of Man is going to be delivered into the hands of men. They will kill him, and after three days he will rise."	"We are going to Jerusalem . . . and the Son of Man will be delivered over to the chief priests and the teachers of the law. They will condemn him to death and will hand him over to the Gentiles."

There is no riddle or parable here. Jesus "plainly" informs the disciples of his impending doom (8:32a). Although Mark has left traces of Jesus's suffering, death, and resurrection in the first section of his Gospel (2:5–10; 3:20–35; 6:1–6, 14–29), in his second act these three aspects of Jesus's final phase of ministry come into focus (// Matt. 16:21–28 // Luke 9:22–27).

Peter will have none of it (8:32b). According to Peter (and the disciples), Jesus was sent by God to rule over Israel and the nations, not to *be* ruled over by them. Instead of addressing Peter, Jesus addresses the true culprit—Satan. This is not to say that Peter is possessed by the devil; rather, Peter's objection conforms to a worldly outlook on Jesus's ministry. The disciples are having difficulty grasping that faithful suffering is the means by which Jesus will conquer Satan. So Peter objects to Jesus's suffering for two reasons: (1) it runs contrary to his own messianic and political aspirations, and (2) it hinders the devil's reign. Though Peter is obviously not aligned with Satan, he unwittingly supports Satan's agenda by objecting to Jesus's impending death.

Following the Suffering Son of Man (8:34–9:1)

If Jesus's identity as Israel's Messiah and the Son of God is bound up with suffering, then it follows that his disciples must follow suit. What is true of Jesus is true of his disciples. Every genuine disciple must be willing to "take up their cross and follow me" (8:34). For the disciples (and Mark's audience), this is a difficult pill to swallow because it entails rejection, persecution, and marginalization. To enter the kingdom of God, one must be willing to be ostracized in the kingdom of the world.

The saying ends with Jesus declaring, "If anyone is ashamed of me and my words in this adulterous and sinful generation, the *Son of Man* will be ashamed of them when he comes in his Father's *glory* with the holy angels" (8:38). This verse alludes to Daniel 7:13–14, where the "son of man," an enigmatic divine figure, is enthroned in heaven and granted "authority, glory and sovereign power." The Ancient of Days rewards the son of man for his defeat of the grotesque fourth beast (i.e., Rome; Dan. 7:11). Later on in Daniel 7, we discover that the remnant of righteous Israelites or the "holy people" are identified with the son of man. What is true of the son of man is true of the holy people (Dan. 7:18). Since the holy people suffer (Dan. 7:21–22, 25), we probably should infer that the son of man should also suffer (Mark 8:31; 9:31; 10:33). Just a handful of verses earlier, Jesus told the disciples that the "Son of Man must *suffer* many things" (8:31). Now, he claims that the "Son of Man . . . [will come] in his Father's *glory*" (8:38). Mark weds suffering and exaltation in this section, and Daniel 7 anticipates both of these realities, albeit dimly.

When Jesus "comes in his Father's glory" in the future, he will fulfill Daniel 7:13 and validate one's commitment to the kingdom, determining whether or not one fulfills the prophecy of the righteous "holy people." According to Daniel 7:21–22, the Ancient of Days pronounces "judgment in favor of the holy people," whereas in Mark 8:38, Jesus will pass judgment upon the holy people. Though remaining distinct, Jesus is functionally identified here with the Ancient of Days.

Within a single chapter, Mark portrays Jesus as a gracious healer (8:22–26) and sovereign end-time judge (8:38). The language in 8:38 is picked up later in 13:26–27, where Jesus foretells the destruction of the temple in AD 70 (and perhaps his second coming). Therefore, one could make a good case that Jesus has the destruction of the temple in mind here in 8:38. The entire point is that his followers must persevere in the midst of extraordinary suffering. Just as Jesus reigns in the midst of suffering, so too will his followers.

The Suffering Son of God (9:2–50)

The Transfiguration (9:2–13)

The enthronement of Daniel's son of man and his subsequent judgment remain at the forefront of Mark's mind as he details one of the most remarkable events in Jesus's ministry—the transfiguration. Mark prefaces this event with the temporal expression "after six days" (9:2). This is the only time in Mark that the number six appears, and it may not be incidental. According to Exodus 24:15–16, Moses waited at Sinai for six days until he was summoned on the seventh day (cf. Gen. 1–2). The account of the transfiguration is strongly reminiscent of Israel encamping at Sinai while Moses ascends to the top and experiences God's glory (Exod. 19–31). The temporal marker "after six days" also ties the previous section to the transfiguration. Jesus claims that he, as the Son of Man, will come "in his Father's glory" (8:38) and that some of his disciples will experience "the kingdom of God" coming "with power" (9:1). All three Synoptics place the same material before the transfiguration (Matt. 16:21–28 // Mark 8:31–9:1 // Luke 9:22–27). Therefore, somehow the transfiguration is a proleptic act of the arrival of the Son of Man to judge wickedness and vindicate his true disciples.

As with the raising of Jairus's daughter, only Peter, James, and John experience the transfiguration firsthand (cf. 5:37). Mark's description of Jesus's clothes is more vivid than Matthew's (17:2) and Luke's (9:29) accounts: "His clothes became *dazzling white, whiter than anyone in the world could bleach them*" (9:3). Why would Mark include such an odd detail about Jesus's clothes? If Daniel 7 forms part of the OT background of Mark's previous section (8:31, 38–9:1), then Jesus's "dazzling white" clothes may recall the attire of the Ancient of Days in Daniel 7:9: "Thrones were set in place, and the Ancient of Days took his seat. *His clothing was as white as snow.*" White clothes are common in the OT and Judaism, often referring to angelic messengers (e.g., 1 En. 71:1; 2 En. 37:1; cf. Matt. 28:3; Mark 16:5; John 20:12), but what makes Mark's description here unique is the prominence of Daniel 7 in Mark 8–9. Further, clothing in the OT is a mark of one's right to rule. The OT "uses YHWH's clothing to communicate establishing and confirming kingship."[23] As the Ancient of Days incarnate, Jesus is commissioned to rule over the nations and establish God's eternal kingdom (Dan. 2:44–45).

Consider God's declaration to the disciples concerning Jesus, the main point of the event: "This is my Son, whom I love. Listen to him" (9:7). The wording closely resembles Jesus's baptism (1:11), where God announces that Jesus is the true heir of David (Ps. 2:7; 2 Sam. 7:14). But there is a key difference between this declaration and the one at his public baptism. At the transfiguration, Jesus is clearly depicted as divine; glory radiates *from* him. He is the divine Son of God, whereas at his baptism, Jesus is viewed primarily as Israel's Messiah. Taken together, the two declarations of Jesus being God's "Son" encapsulate the two titles of 1:1.

Mark also adds that "Elijah and Moses . . . were talking with Jesus" (9:4). Though it's not completely evident why both of these figures are mentioned, perhaps these two prophets refer to the totality of the OT. Jesus is greater than both the Law and the Prophets. He is a greater Moses (lawgiver) and a greater Elijah (prophet). Furthermore, both Moses and Elijah experience theophanies on Sinai (Exod. 19; 1 Kings 19:8–18). Mark, though, strangely lists Elijah before Moses, whereas Matthew and Luke naturally place Moses before Elijah (Matt. 17:3 // Luke 9:30). It could be that Mark has not lost sight of Malachi 3–4. According to Malachi, the "messenger" figure is explicitly

23. Shawn W. Flynn, "YHWH's Clothing, Kingship, and Power: Origins and Vestiges in Comparative Ancient Near Eastern Contexts," in *Dress and Clothing in the Hebrew Bible: "For All Her Household Are Clothed in Crimson,"* ed. Antonios Finitsis, LHBOTS 679 (London: T&T Clark, 2019), 28.

identified with Elijah: "I will send the prophet *Elijah* to you before that great and dreadful day of the LORD comes" (Mal. 4:5; cf. Mal. 3:1). Immediately following the transfiguration, the disciples broach this very topic. The point is that Mark keeps his audience attuned to the critical theme of purifying God's people before the arrival of the great "day of the LORD."

Above all, we must not lose sight of the thrust of the transfiguration: Jesus as God in the flesh redeems, rules over, and dwells with humanity and creation in fulfillment of Isaiah's second exodus. Isaiah 64:1 is remarkably close to what transpires at the transfiguration, at least on a conceptual level, because the prophet Isaiah pleads with God to "rend the heavens and come down, that the mountains would tremble before" him. Jesus fulfills this prophetic expectation as Yahweh incarnate.

Mark doesn't disclose the precise location of the transfiguration (several contemporary scholars locate the event on Mount Hermon or Mount Meron), but we should probably assume that it took place north of Galilee. Mark 9:30 explains that Jesus "passed through Galilee" on his way to Capernaum. The bulk of Mark's narrative operates between two mountains: the mountain where Jesus is transfigured (9:2–8) and Mount Zion, where Jesus is crucified (15:21–41). On the first mountain, God declares Jesus to be his "Son" (9:7), whereas on the second mountain the centurion declares Jesus to be the "Son of God" (15:39). God's commission to Jesus on the first mountain—to redeem, rule over, and dwell with creation—is fulfilled at the cross on the second mountain.

Israel's Unbelief at the Mountain (9:14–50)

Coming down from the mountain, Jesus and the three disciples meet up with the remaining disciples (// Matt. 17:14–19 // Luke 9:37–45). A great crowd has gathered, and the "teachers of the law" are found "arguing with them" (9:14). At the heart of the discussion is the disciples' inability to cast out a demon (9:17–18). Jesus's frustration stems from his earlier commission to the disciples in 3:14–15 and 6:7. The disciples have enjoyed success in driving out demons (6:13, 30), so why do they fail here in chapter 9? Recall that at Sinai when Moses remains on the mountain, the Israelites grow restless and convince Aaron to manufacture a golden calf (Exod. 32:1–4). The effect of the Israelites' idolatry is that they transform into the very object of their worship—the golden calf. Moses appropriately labels the first generation of Israel as "stiff-necked" (Exod. 32:11; 33:3). Here Jesus in like manner refers to the disciples as idolatrous and an "unbelieving generation" (9:19). His wording is quite similar to Deuteronomy 32:20–21, where the Lord explains why he will withdraw his presence from the first generation of Israelites: "I will hide my face from them . . . for they are a *perverse generation*, children who are *unfaithful*. They made me jealous by what is no god and angered me with their *worthless idols*" (cf. Num. 14:27).

What is true of the first exodus is true of the second. Like the majority of the Israelites encamped at the base of the mountain who grow tired of waiting for Moses and the Lord and commit idolatry, so the remaining disciples grow restless in unbelief. As Jesus points out at the end of the miracle, the disciples are unable to exorcise the demon because of a lack of prayer (9:29; cf. 11:24). That is, they fail to trust in Jesus's authority over the demonic realm, which extends *through* their ministry to their fellow Jews and the surrounding nations. Instead of ministering in concert with Jesus, they attempt to act independently of Jesus by expelling the demon on their own terms. The disciples' partial blindness in the second exodus persists, preventing them from discerning God's acts of redemption.

Jesus then heads south, where he and the disciples will "pass through Galilee" (9:30). He relates his second passion prediction to the disciples (9:31; cf. 8:31; 10:33–34), but the disciples fail once more to comprehend his prediction (9:32 // Matt. 18:1–5 // Luke 9:46–48). The remainder of chapter 9 continues the theme of the disciples' misunderstanding concerning the nature of the end-time kingdom. The disciples are still expecting Jesus's reign to be marked by political might. Though the disciples' motivation is certainly misplaced, they are right to put their finger on the political dimension of the kingdom. But that dimension awaits the new heavens and earth (Rev. 21–22). During the overlap of the ages, the latter-day kingdom is not characterized by political or military might but by suffering and defeat.

We have come full circle to the "mysterious" nature of the eschatological kingdom outlined in 4:10–32. To gain entrance into the kingdom, one must embody the attitude of Jesus and become a "servant of all" (9:35). Jesus is the consummate Suffering Servant, who fulfills Isaiah's prophecy (Mark 10:43–45, quoting Isa. 52:13–53:12), and his true disciples will imitate his pattern of suffering. Even children, who lack status in society, are welcomed into the kingdom with open arms (9:36–37, 42). Admittance into the kingdom should be one's highest priority (9:43–47a), since unbelievers are sentenced to "hell, where 'the worms that eat them do not die, and the fire is not quenched'" (9:47b–48, quoting Isa. 66:24). The stakes could not be any higher.

Unbelief and Belief in Judea (10:1–52)

The Pharisees and Their Question on Divorce (10:1–16)

Leaving Capernaum, the last location mentioned in chapter 9 (9:33), Jesus again heads south and "into the region of Judea and across the Jordan"

(10:1). From 1:14–9:50, Mark has focused on Jesus's ministry in and around Galilee. Now Jesus resolutely turns south, knowing that he will die shortly. The Pharisees find him and begin to "test" (*peirazontes*) him by asking, "Is it lawful for a man to divorce his wife?" (10:2). The word here for "test" is found four times in Mark's Gospel. The first occurrence is in 1:13, where Satan "tests" or "tempts" Jesus, and the remaining three are associated with the Jewish leaders and their effort to trap Jesus (8:11; 10:2; 12:15). Perhaps, then, Mark is aligning Satan and the Jewish leaders in their attempt to overthrow Jesus (// Matt. 19:1–9).

Why would the Jewish leaders ask Jesus about divorce? In chapter 6 John the Baptist objects to Herod's divorce of the daughter of the king of the Nabateans and his subsequent marriage to his brother's wife, Herodias (6:17). John tells Herod, "It is not lawful . . . to have your brother's wife" (6:18; see Lev. 18:16; 20:21). So by asking Jesus about divorce, the Pharisees may be attempting to provoke Herod's ire toward Jesus.[24] This is not an innocuous question posed by the Pharisees, but a question that is politically motivated. In 3:6 the Pharisees team up with the Herodians to "plot . . . how they might kill Jesus." The question of divorce is a strategic means to that end.

The validity of divorce among the Jewish people in the first century was a settled matter. What was unsettled, though, was the grounds for divorce in the two schools of thought: the school of Hillel and that of Shammai (→Matt. 19:3). According to Deuteronomy 24:1, a man can divorce his wife on the grounds that "he finds something indecent about her." The phrase "something indecent" is difficult to nuance, and modern commentators offer a wide range of opinions. The point of Deuteronomy 24:1–4 is to protect the dignity of the woman so that she cannot be taken advantage of. David Garland argues, "The legislation on divorce certificates protected wives from brutal abandonment. It freed a wife from the accusation of adultery when she, out of necessity, remarried; and it prevented the first husband from destroying her new marriage by trying to reclaim her. It deterred anything that might look like wife-swapping. The law was therefore intended to keep the social upheaval associated with divorce to a minimum."[25]

Jesus responds to the disciples' question with a question of his own: "What did Moses command you?" (10:3). The Pharisees then refer to Deuteronomy 24 in support of divorce (10:4). Apparently, Moses is on their side. But Jesus makes a fascinating claim—"It was because your hearts were hard that Moses wrote you this law"—and then he goes on to cite Genesis 1:27 and 2:24.

24. Craig A. Evans, *Mark 8:27–16:20*, WBC 34B (Nashville: Nelson, 2006), 81.
25. David Garland, *Mark*, NIVAC (Grand Rapids: Zondervan, 1996), 379.

Though much could be said about Jesus's remarkable use of the OT in this passage, we will draw two brief conclusions.

(1) The permission of divorce in Deuteronomy 24 is not intended to be a long-term solution within the covenant community. Such a prescription was given "because [the Israelites'] hearts were hard." The fault does not lie in God's laws but in the hearts of the Israelites. Under the Mosaic economy, God's people, as a corporate community, were generally unable to preserve God's ultimate intention for marriage (Gen. 2:24). Jesus interprets Deuteronomy 24:1–4 through the lens of Genesis 1:27 and 2:24. The Spirit must circumcise the hearts of the Israelites so that they can fall in step with God's creational design (Deut. 30:5–6). Genesis 2:24, the model for the Israelite conception of marriage throughout the OT (Deut. 31:16–17; Mal. 2:15), is upheld in the NT as God's original design (1 Cor. 6:16; Eph. 5:31).

(2) Jesus identifies the Pharisees with the first generation of the Israelites when he says, "What did Moses command *you*?" and "It was because *your* hearts were hard" (10:3, 5). The sensory obduracy of the Jewish leaders is a key theme in Mark's Gospel, and it crops up once more here (3:5; 4:12; 7:6–7). According to Deuteronomy 29:2–4, the first generation of Israelites experienced God's unmatched display of power in the exodus, yet they failed to grasp its significance and trust in his promises. It reads, "*Your eyes* have seen all that the LORD did in Egypt to Pharaoh. . . . With *your own eyes* you saw those great trials, those signs and great wonders. But to this day *the LORD has not given you a mind that understands or eyes that see or ears that hear*." Like the first generation of Israelites, who failed to grasp the significance of the first exodus, the Jewish leaders fail to comprehend God's mighty acts in the second exodus.

Admittance to the Kingdom through Isaiah's Suffering Servant (10:13–45)

The following two sections broach the issue of who is worthy to inherit the end-time kingdom of God (// Matt. 19:13–30 // Luke 18:15–30). The first section concerns the admittance of children into the kingdom (10:13–16). Children are welcomed into the kingdom because they enjoy no special standing in society. They have nothing to offer, nothing to boast about. All they can do is cling to Jesus in utter dependence. Those attempting to "enter" the kingdom must do so "like a little child" (10:15). On the other end of the spectrum in the second section is the man who has "kept" all of God's commands since he was a child (10:17–21). This man, often referred to as the "rich young ruler," believes he has something to boast about—his own righteousness. But looks are often deceiving. Instead of using his wealth in service to others, he hoards it (10:21–22). In reality, this man has nothing firm to stand upon since he ultimately fails to love his neighbors. The disciples are still coming to grips with this basic issue. To gain entrance into the kingdom, one must abandon all and unswervingly follow Jesus (10:29–31). Mark is forcing his audience to reflect upon their personal commitment to Jesus and the kingdom here. They must ask themselves whether or not they have truly abandoned all and followed Jesus.

We come to the third and final passion prediction in 10:32–34 (// Matt. 20:17–19 // Luke 18:31–33). Mark mentions that Jesus and company are heading toward Jerusalem "with Jesus leading the way." The third passion prediction includes a few details that were not given in the first two. The prediction begins with Jesus outlining where he will be betrayed and put to death by Rome—in Jerusalem (10:32). According to John's Gospel, Jesus makes a handful of trips to Jerusalem during his ministry to celebrate Passover (John 2:13; 6:4; 12:1), whereas Mark (and the other two Synoptics) only includes one journey to Jerusalem.

According to 10:32, Mark relates *how* the procession is heading toward Jerusalem to celebrate Passover: Jesus is walking out in front of the group and "leading" them. Perhaps on a symbolic level, Jesus's actions may recall the messenger figure from Exodus 23:20: "I [Yahweh] am sending an angel [or "messenger"] *ahead of you* to guard you along the way and to bring you to the place I have prepared." The messenger in Exodus 23 is tasked with waging war against the pagan nations who occupy the land of Canaan and escorting the Israelites to the "place I have prepared"—that is, the promised land, depicted as a giant sanctuary (cf. Exod. 15:17). Since Exodus 23:20 is a controlling text for understanding the Second Gospel (1:2), Mark may very well have Exodus 23 in mind here. He is the only evangelist to mention the order of the procession to Jerusalem. So maybe Mark is portraying Jesus as a warrior headed for the eschatological battle where he will vanquish his enemies in his death and resurrection.

Following each passion prediction, the disciples struggle with a proper understanding of the nature of Jesus's identity and the kingdom (8:31–33; 9:31–37; 10:33–45). In response to James and John's preoccupation with inheriting a place of honor in the end-time kingdom (10:35–37), Jesus claims that the kingdom is unlike the rule of the nations. Those wanting to be in positions of honor must first be a servant (10:43–44). Jesus then alludes to Isaiah 53:10–12 in 10:45, one of the most important verses in the Second Gospel:

Mark 10:45	Isaiah 53:10–12
"For even the Son of Man did not come to be served, but to serve, and *to give his life* as a *ransom for many*."	"Yet it was the Lord's will to crush him and cause him to suffer, and though the Lord makes his life an offering for sin . . . my righteous servant *will justify many*, and he will bear their iniquities. . . . *He poured out his life unto death*, and was numbered with the transgressors. For *he bore the sin of many*."

This passage in the book of Isaiah is part of a larger group of "servant songs" (42:1–9; 49:1–6; 50:4–9; 52:13–53:12). This Isaianic servant figure represents the nation of Israel and suffers unjustly for "the many." God curses an individual so that he can bless the many. One dies for the sake of others. The servant's vicarious death is the means by which God redeems his people from captivity and restores them in the new creation.

The final act of Mark's three-part drama leaves the reader with a clearly defined portrait of Jesus in his role as Isaiah's servant.[26] He is the *suffering* Messiah, fulfilling Isaiah's expectations. All aspects of his ministry must be interpreted through his death and resurrection. Knowing the end of the story brings clarity to the beginning and middle portions. The series of Jewish confrontations in act one of Mark climax with one ultimate confrontation that leads to his death. But through suffering and defeat, Jesus is, in reality, executing his messianic rule. There is victory in the midst of defeat, glory in the midst of suffering, and power in the midst of weakness. In the words of Isaiah, in his death the servant will "divide the spoils with the strong" (Isa. 53:12).

Blind Bartimaeus (10:46–52)

Jesus's kingship remains at the forefront in the healing of blind Bartimaeus, or "son of Timaeus" (10:46–52 // Matt. 20:29–34 // Luke 18:35–43). The healing is the final event before the triumphal entry (11:1–10). *Before* Jesus heals him, Bartimaeus cries out, "Son of David, have mercy on me!" (10:48; cf. 11:10; 12:35). Mark narrates the healing of only two blind men in his Gospel—the two-stage healing of the blind man (8:22–25) and the healing of Bartimaeus (10:46–52). If the first healing symbolizes the two-stage healing of the disciples, then perhaps the healing of Bartimaeus symbolizes the eventual healing of a remnant of Jews (including the disciples) *and* gentiles.

Mark clearly associates the healing of Bartimaeus with Jesus's messiahship, but why? To ask the question another way, what is the relationship between healing the blind and the in-breaking of the kingdom? According to Isaiah 35:5, "The eyes of the blind [will] be opened and the ears of the deaf unstopped" *because* God is making his covenant community fit for the new creation. When he brings them out of exile, he reverses the effects of the fall, refashioning the bodies of his people so that they may dwell with him when they "see the glory of the LORD" (Isa. 35:2; cf. Isa. 61:1–2; Matt. 11:2–5). God's people must be

---

26. This paragraph is adapted from G. K. Beale and Benjamin L. Gladd, *The Story Retold: A Biblical-Theological Introduction to the New Testament* (Downers Grove, IL: InterVarsity, 2020), 91.

created anew, since they will dwell in the new heavens and earth. The healing of Bartimaeus, then, is a symbolic expression of Jesus undoing Adam and Eve's fall and admitting him into the kingdom.

The chapter ends with Bartimaeus leaving his garments behind and following Jesus, much like the disciples left their nets and followed him (1:18, 20; 10:28). But following Jesus in Mark's Gospel requires abandoning everything. Names in the Gospels may betray the identity of the eyewitnesses involved in the event (cf. 5:22), and the inclusion of his name may confirm his commitment to Jesus in the years that followed. Mark's audience is therefore encouraged to imitate Bartimaeus, confessing that Jesus is indeed the long-awaited "Son of David" and following him with no strings attached.

▨ Act 3: Jesus in Jerusalem (11:1–16:8)

Jesus as King and Judge of the Temple (11:1–26)

The first half of Mark's narrative (chs. 1–10) lays the foundation for what will transpire in the latter half (chs. 11–16). A central plank in Jesus's ministry is the judgment upon Israel's temple and the inauguration of the new temple. Chapters 1–10 anticipate this fundamental shift, and chapters 11–16 disclose how the transition from the old to the new occurs.

The Triumphal Entry (11:1–11)

Mark's Gospel has been anticipating the arrival of Israel's King in Zion at the triumphal entry (// Matt. 21:1–9 // Luke 19:29–38 // John 12:12–15). The enthronement of the long-awaited Messiah in Jerusalem is a key tenet of the book of Isaiah, for he is the pristine representative of God's cosmic rule on earth, centered in Jerusalem (e.g., Isa. 9:6–7). Isaiah 52:7 is representative of this prophetic hope: "How beautiful on the mountains are the feet of those who bring good news, . . . who say to Zion, 'Your God reigns!'" (cf. Isa. 2:2–5; Mic. 4:1–5; Zech. 14:16–21). As we consider Jesus's actions here in the triumphal entry in chapter 11, we must do so in light of the overwhelming expectation in the first century that God would one day restore his people and rule over them *in Jerusalem.*

On Sunday of passion week, one of the most public demonstrations in Jesus's ministry takes place. Situated on the Mount of Olives, Jesus sends his disciples eastward to Bethphage (11:1). In preparation for his entry into Jerusalem, Jesus orders two of his disciples to procure an unbroken colt (11:2–3). Jesus claims that the unbroken colt will be "tied," likely recalling Genesis

49:10–11: "The scepter shall not depart from Judah, nor the ruler's staff from between his feet, until Shiloh comes, and to him shall be the obedience of the peoples. *He ties his foal to the vine*, and his donkey's colt to the choice vine" (NASB). The prophecy of Genesis 49 finds its ultimate fulfillment in Jesus at the triumphal entry when he publicly announces his right to rule over Israel and the nations.

The triumphal entry clearly alludes to Zechariah 9. Indeed, Matthew's Gospel even quotes it (Matt. 21:4–5). The immediate context of Zechariah 9 helps us understand Jesus's actions more fully. According to Zechariah 9, God's undisputed sovereignty is on display. The prophet issues a judgment oracle against Israel's neighbors, wherein God dispossesses them of their territory (Zech. 9:1–7). The last verse of the oracle reads, "I [Yahweh] will encamp *at my temple* to guard it against marauding forces" (9:8). God will not let the nations defile his house, so he will do whatever it takes to preserve his holy name (cf. Zech. 2:5). Zechariah shifts gears in the following verses, where the prophet highlights the Messiah's rule in preserving Israel: "Rejoice greatly, O daughter of Zion! . . . Behold, your king is coming to you; he is just and endowed with salvation, humble, and mounted on a donkey, *even on a colt, the foal of a donkey*" (9:9 NASB). The manner in which the king arrives in Jerusalem is quite unique: "humble, and mounted on a donkey." We find the same behavior earlier in 1 Kings 1:32–33: "And they [Zadok, Nathan, and Benaiah] came into the king's presence. The king said to them, 'Take with you the servants of your lord, and have *my son Solomon ride on my own mule*, and bring him down to Gihon'" (NASB). Zechariah 9 and 1 Kings 1 aren't describing a weak or incompetent ruler but a *peaceful* one (see Zech. 9:10).

If the context of Zechariah 9 is retained in Mark's quotation, then Jesus's identity as Israel's Messiah shines brightly. By coming on a donkey, Jesus symbolically declares that the battle has initially been won and a time of messianic peace has arrived. The pilgrims who lay their palm branches and garments before Jesus (11:8) bring to mind similar behavior in the presence of royalty (2 Kings 9:13; 1 Macc. 13:51; 2 Macc. 10:7). But the enemies of Israel outlined in Zechariah 9:1–7 refer ultimately not to Rome but to Satan and his demons—the true enemies of God's people.

The messianic secret—a theme that is critical to Mark's narrative—is now unveiled for all to hear. No more hushed whispers. The time has come to shout from the rooftops that Jesus is Israel's long-awaited King. Why the change of approach? Why did Jesus spend the bulk of his ministry in Galilee silencing those proclaiming his messiahship only to announce it publicly at the triumphal entry? There are many good answers, but two will suffice.

(1) By keeping a lid on his identity as Israel's Messiah, Jesus creates an opportunity to refashion messianic expectations. Jewish messianic expectations in the first century, though incredibly diverse, do not feature a Messiah who claims to be divine or insists that his ministry is characterized by suffering. Now that the cross and resurrection are only days away, Jesus wants his followers to view his entire ministry through the lens of Israel's Messiah (and the divine Son of God).

(2) Since Jesus is unequivocally claiming to be Israel's Messiah in the triumphal entry, a political and religious clash is certain. Israel is still under Rome's thumb, and though Jews enjoy considerable religious freedom in worship, they must not attempt to usurp Rome's authority. As Jesus rides into Jerusalem, his kingship will inevitably lead to a conflict with Rome. In the eyes of the Romans, there is only one Caesar. We have also seen a growing hostility between Jesus and the Jewish leaders. Even at the beginning of Mark's narrative, we learn that the leaders are resolute in plotting to "kill Jesus" (3:6). In his words and actions, Jesus's claims to deity are inescapable (2:7). Healing on the Sabbath and his self-description as the "Lord . . . of the Sabbath" are deemed to be worthy of death (2:28). Jesus is striking at the very heart of their tightly held religious beliefs.

Josephus, a first-century Jewish historian, claimed that around three million visitors flocked to Jerusalem to celebrate Passover (*J.W.* 2.280, 6.425). Many scholars today, though, believe that the actual number was approximately two or three hundred thousand.[27] The bustling crowd that gathers around Jesus as he rides on the donkey soon causes a commotion. These people are arriving into town on Sunday to celebrate Passover that Friday, as it was common to arrive a week early. Mark divulges that pilgrims sang Psalm 118:25–26 (11:9–10), a passage from a collection of psalms called the Psalms of Hallel or the Egyptian Hallel (Ps. 104–6; 120–36; 146–50). Pilgrims sing these psalms during the Feast of Tabernacles, Pentecost, and the first day of Passover. These songs bear the name Egyptian Hallel because they recall Israel's exodus from Egypt and because they anticipate a second, greater redemption. When these pilgrims witness Jesus's symbolic gesture of riding on a donkey, clearly demonstrating his messianic identity, they are convinced that Jesus will ascend the throne of David right then and there and cast off the weighty yoke of Rome.

Mark's narrative abruptly moves from the pilgrims' recitation of Psalm 118 to Jesus entering the temple precinct. Matthew and Luke wed the triumphal

---

27. E.g., Eckhard J. Schnabel, *Jesus in Jerusalem: The Last Days* (Grand Rapids: Eerdmans, 2018), 157.

entry to Jesus judging the temple (Matt. 21:10–17 // Luke 19:45–46), whereas Mark uniquely includes Jesus entering the temple to look "around at everything," only to retreat out of the city and spend the night in Bethany with his disciples (11:11). The word here for "look around" (*periblepō*) is found only seven times in the NT, and six of those occurrences are in Mark's Gospel. Of those six, Jesus is the subject of all but one of them (3:5, 34; 5:32; 10:23; 11:11), and with the exception of 11:11, he only "looks around" at people. The point is that Mark often portrays Jesus examining those individuals situated around him. This time, however, Jesus is examining not people but his surroundings. As in 3:5, when he "looked around" at the Jewish leaders "in anger," here he evaluates the current state of the temple. Mark's readers are left wondering what will soon transpire.

Judgment upon the Fig Tree and Israel's Temple (11:12–26)

The narrative pushes forward to "the next day" (11:12)—that is, Monday of passion week. Matthew places the cursing *after* the temple judgment and narrates it as one event (Matt. 21:18–22), whereas Mark splits the cursing into two events and sandwiches it around the judgment of the temple.

Cursing of the fig tree (11:12–14)
Temple judgment (11:15–19)
Cursing of the fig tree (11:20–21)

Jesus's cursing of the fig tree is like a great deal of his ministry—a dramatized parable. The OT often compares the nation of Israel to a fig tree (e.g., Jer. 24:5; Hosea 9:10), so we should assume that Jesus is following suit. According to Jeremiah 8:13, God curses Israel for her idolatry (see Jer. 8:2), so he promises to deprive them of their harvest: "I will take away their harvest, declares the LORD. There will be no grapes on the vine. *There will be no figs on the tree, and their leaves will wither.* What I have given them will be taken from them" (cf. Jer. 29:17; Mic. 7:1). In the same way, then, when Jesus curses the fig tree, he's symbolically demonstrating the arrival of God's wrath upon the nation. Note that in 11:20–21 the tree withers, preserving the link to Jeremiah 8:13. God expects Israel to bear fruit, but she does not.

Old Testament prophets associate the cursing of the fig tree with Israel coming under God's curse and being sent into Babylonian exile. Here we discover the same line of reasoning: the nation of Israel, and especially her leaders, has committed idolatry by trusting in human tradition over God's word. Jesus will judge Israel's temple and judge the nation once for all. In sandwiching the episode of the fig tree with the temple judgment (11:15–19), Mark forces his readers to connect the two. Jesus brings down God's curse upon the nation *because* they have abused the temple and barricaded foreigners from worshiping there (11:17, quoting Isa. 56:7; Jer. 7:11).

Responding to this idolatry and exclusion, Jesus drives out the money changers from the courtyard and forbids "anyone to carry merchandise through the temple courts" (11:16 // Matt. 21:12–16 // Luke 19:45–47 // John 2:13–16). If one cannot purchase sacrifices, then one cannot be ritually cleansed and dwell in the presence of a holy God. Verse 15 states that Jesus was "*driving out [ekballein]* those who were buying and selling." Approximately two-thirds of the occurrences of the verb "drive out" (*ekballō*) are paired with exorcisms in the Second Gospel. For example,

> He also *drove out* many demons, but he would not let the demons speak because they knew who he was. (1:34)

> So he traveled throughout Galilee, preaching in their synagogues and *driving out* demons. (1:39)

> Jesus . . . began to speak to them in parables: "How can Satan *drive out* Satan?" (3:23)

> They *drove out* many demons and anointed many sick people with oil and healed them. (6:13)[28]

We have argued that exorcising demons is tied to Jesus's focused attention on expelling all unclean things *in order that God may dwell with humanity and creation*. What must be kept in mind is that exorcisms entail not only expulsion but also judgment, a judgment that is based upon Jesus's faithful obedience in the wilderness (1:13). Could it be that Jesus's expulsion of the money changers on a physical level is really an expulsion of demons on a spiritual level? After the wilderness temptation, the first exorcism in Mark's Gospel takes place in a synagogue, the local house of worship in Capernaum (1:21–28). If this connection is valid, then Mark bookends Jesus's ministry with two exorcisms. Jesus begins his work with an exorcism in Galilee and ends it with an exorcism in Jerusalem. This can hardly be happenstance.

The narrative in 11:17 progresses to Jesus teaching somewhere in the temple complex soon after the expulsion of the money changers. Obviously, the temple authorities would have immediately rectified the situation so that

28. Cf. 1:39; 3:15, 22; 5:40; 7:26; 9:18, 38.

business could carry on as usual. As Jesus teaches nearby, Mark discloses only a brief segment of his instruction to the crowd that gathers: "And as he taught them, he said, 'Is it not written: "My house will be called a house of prayer for all nations"? But you have made it "a den of robbers."'" Jesus draws from two significant OT passages: Isaiah 56:7 and Jeremiah 7:11. The pairing of these two texts resembles the pairing of Exodus 23, Malachi 3, and Isaiah 40 in 1:2b–3. One positive and one negative:

Reference (LXX)	Meaning
Isaiah 56:7 (NETS): "I will bring them into my holy mountain and make them joyful in my house of prayer; their whole burnt offerings and their sacrifices will be acceptable on my altar, *for my house shall be called a house of prayer for all the nations.*"	Gentiles will worship the Lord in the temple in the "latter days."
Jeremiah 7:11 (Brenton [Theo.]): "Is my house, whereon my name is called, *a den of robbers* in your eyes? And, behold, I have seen it, saith the Lord."	The Israelites will be exiled to Babylon because of their idolatry, trust in the temple, and lack of righteousness.

Isaiah 56:7 is an end-time prophecy that the temple will become a rallying point for the nations (Isa. 56:3–8). Ironically, the temple—a house intended to bless all the nations—was used in the first century to prevent the nations from worshiping. Instead of acting as a gateway to the Lord's presence, the temple had become an impregnable rampart. Jesus's actions in judging the temple on Monday of passion week fulfill the verbal prophecy of Isaiah. He simultaneously judges the temple in Jerusalem and establishes the end-time temple of the new creation. In this newly founded temple, foreigners and outcasts assemble in the presence of God and shout for joy (Isa. 56:3–8). God will no longer dwell partially in a physical structure; he will dwell in people and all of creation.

In the second OT quotation, Jeremiah castigates the Israelites for their misplaced trust in the temple and their spiritually derelict lives (Jer. 7:11). Jeremiah 7 is fulfilled in an immediate sense when the Lord exiles Israel to Babylon (Jer. 10:17–22), but the prophetic pattern of being sent into exile is picked up typologically here in Mark 11. The Jewish people in the first century are repeating the sins of their forefathers in the days of Jeremiah. Like their ancestors, the Jews have committed idolatry by trusting in the temple rather than the Lord.

Jesus's actions in judging the temple set forth a polarity that runs through chapters 11–16 and comprises the heart of passion week. In each major section,

Jesus judges the old idolatrous temple and simultaneously inaugurates the new end-time temple.[29]

Physical Temple in Jerusalem	New End-Time Temple
A "den of robbers" (11:17, quoting Jer. 7:11)	"House of prayer" (11:17, quoting Isa. 56:7)
"This mountain" (11:23)	Disciples must "stand praying . . . [and] forgive them" (11:25)
"A watchtower" in the vineyard (12:1)	Jesus as the "cornerstone" (12:10)
"All burnt offerings and sacrifices" (12:33)	The two love commands (12:30–31)
The teachers of the law "devour widows' houses" and "make lengthy prayers" (12:40)	
"Many rich people" who "threw in large amounts" of money in the "temple treasury" (12:41)	"A poor widow . . . put in two very small copper coins" (12:42)

The reaction of the Jewish leaders to Jesus's condemnation of the temple is identical to their response at the beginning of Mark's narrative: they intend to "kill him" (11:18; cf. 3:6). The three passion predictions are beginning to come to pass (8:31; 9:31; 10:33–34). Mark explains *why* the temple authorities and the "teachers of the law" are motivated to do so: "They feared him, because the whole crowd was amazed at his teaching." The leaders recognize Jesus's considerable popularity among the Jewish people. His miracles and teaching are unparalleled, and many Jews are convinced that he is who he claims to be. The problem, then, boils down to religious and political influence: Jesus's mission is at odds with the Jewish leaders, so if the populace sides with Jesus, then the leaders lose their influence on the nation. That is simply too much for the leaders to swallow.

Following the second half of the cursing of the fig tree (11:20), Jesus turns to his disciples, commanding them to "have faith in God" and to "not doubt" but believe when they say "to this mountain, 'Go, throw yourself into the sea'" (11:22–23 // Matt. 21:19–22). This seemingly odd teaching fits well with the OT conception of mountains. Often in the OT, God's presence is associated with mountains. The garden of Eden is the first mountain where God dwells with Adam and Eve (Gen. 2:8–14; Ezek. 28:13–14). Mount Sinai itself, too, is a grand temple (Exod. 3:5; 19–24). The prophet Isaiah even claims that Israel and the nations will stream to the "mountain of the Lord's temple" in the "last days" (Isa. 2:2; cf. Mic. 4:7). So the "mountain" here in 11:23 should be understood

29. For these comparisons and for many general insights about the temple in chs. 11–12, I am indebted to John Paul Heil, "The Narrative Strategy and Pragmatics of the Temple Theme in Mark," *CBQ* 59 (1997): 76–100.

as Israel's physical temple in Jerusalem. Jesus orders his disciples to embrace what has just transpired—the spiritual destruction of Israel's temple (11:15–17). Prayer and forgiveness in particular were bound up with the temple, but now Jesus empowers his disciples to enjoy both of these prerogatives independent of the physical temple in Jerusalem.

The True Purpose of the Temple (11:27–12:44)

The section 11:27–12:44 is a lengthy interaction between Jesus and the Jewish leaders that takes place in the temple complex on Tuesday of passion week. Each of these seemingly disparate conversations asserts the legitimacy and the presence of the end-time temple in the person of Jesus and his followers.[30]

Authority to Judge the Temple (11:27–33)

The Jewish leaders confront Jesus with the question, "By what authority are you doing these things?" (11:28 // Matt. 21:23–27 // Luke 20:1–8). They want to know why he denounces their place of worship, the centerpiece of God's covenant with them. Jesus responds with a clever riddle, leaving them no wiggle room (11:29–30). If the leaders admit that John the Baptist was indeed sent by God, then they indict themselves because they refused to accept his baptism, a baptism that was intended to replace a key function of the Jerusalem temple—forgiveness of sins. If the leaders claim that God didn't call John, they set themselves against many Jews who respond positively to John's prophetic summons. The leaders eventually plead ignorance, so Jesus refuses to answer them. Mark's audience is, however, in a great position to answer the leaders' question, "By what authority are you doing these things?" By now Mark's readers know that Jesus operates with the authority of Israel's Messiah and the divine Son of God (1:1). As such, Jesus has every right to judge Israel's idolatrous place of worship. Jesus is doing precisely what Malachi 3:1 anticipates: "Suddenly the Lord you are seeking *will come to his temple.*" As Israel's Lord incarnate, Jesus fulfills Malachi's prophecy in judging the temple.

The Parable of the Wicked Tenants (12:1–12)

Still in the temple precinct, Jesus continues to teach the crowds and the Jewish leaders (12:1). We learn in 12:12 that Jesus primarily directs the parable of the wicked tenants toward "the chief priests, the teachers of the law and the elders," not the crowd in general. This parable is prominent, and its

---

30. Heil, "Narrative Strategy," 81–89.

placement in the passion narrative is pronounced (12:1–12 // Matt. 12:33–46 // Luke 20:9–19). The parable describes the owner of a plot of land who planted "a vineyard" and then rented it to "some farmers" (12:1). The time came for the owner to collect "some of the fruit," so he sent a "servant" (12:2). But the tenants seized him, beat him, and sent "him away emptyhanded" (12:3). The owner sent more servants, but the tenants continued their pattern of wicked behavior (12:4–5). Then the owner sent his "son, whom he loved," thinking that the tenants would treat him differently (12:6). The tenants, though, seized and killed him and eventually threw "him out of the vineyard" (12:8). The son's death was the final nail in the coffin. The parable climaxes in the owner's decision to "give the vineyard to others" (12:9).

Once the OT background to the parable is understood, its meaning is illuminated. The OT often likens Israel to a vineyard (Ps. 80:8–18; Isa. 27:2–6; Jer. 2:21; 12:10; Ezek. 19:10–14; Hosea 10:1), but there are several points of contact between Isaiah 5 and Mark 12.

Isaiah 5	Mark 12	Meaning
God plants a vineyard (5:1–2)	A man plants a vineyard (12:1)	God establishes Israel as his covenant community
Vineyard fails to produce a harvest (5:2) on account of the failed leadership (3:14)	Tenants persecute the servants in order to inherit the vineyard (12:2–8)	The nation's leaders abuse God's people and rule selfishly
God removes the vineyard (5:5–6)	The vineyard is given to the "others" (12:9)	God will judge the nation and her leaders

Isaiah 5 is one of the most detailed accounts of God cultivating a vineyard (i.e., Israel):

> I will sing for the one I love
>   a song about his vineyard:
> My loved one had a vineyard
>   on a fertile hillside.
> He [Yahweh] dug it up and cleared it of stones
>   and planted it with the choicest vines.
> He built a watchtower in it
>   and cut out a winepress as well.
> Then he looked for a crop of good grapes,
>   but it yielded only bad fruit. (Isa. 5:1–2)

Why does the nation of Israel produce "only bad fruit," despite the Lord's cultivation? Isaiah answers that pressing question earlier in his book. According to 3:12–14, the nation's leaders are to blame: "Your guides lead you astray. . . . The LORD enters into judgment against the elders and leaders of his people" (cf. Isa. 1:10, 23–26). Isaiah 3:14 even mentions a vineyard: "It is you [elders] who have ruined my vineyard." But the vineyard in Isaiah 5 includes not only the leaders but also the entire nation (Isa. 5:7). The leaders corrupt the nation of Israel (Isa. 5:18–24), so God promises to "make it a wasteland" and rain down judgment upon it (Isa. 5:6; cf. Jer. 5:17; Amos 4:9; Mic. 1:6; Zeph. 1:13). The Aramaic translation of Isaiah 5:2–5 interprets the tower as the following: "I built my sanctuary in their midst, and I even gave my altar to atone. . . . I will break down the place of their sanctuaries" (cf. 4Q500, 2–4). This early Jewish interpretation claims that the "tower," or Israel's temple, will eventually be destroyed.

In both Isaiah 5 and Mark 12, God owns and establishes the vineyard, but the vineyard fails to generate the desired result. According to Isaiah 5, the vineyard does not produce fruit, whereas the vineyard in Mark's account bears fruit but is hindered by the tenants. Yahweh destroys Isaiah's vineyard, but in Mark the vineyard is given "to others" (12:9). Nevertheless, the parable of the wicked tenants provides theological rationale for the destruction of the temple: the Jewish leadership has led Israel astray, manifesting its despicable character by persecuting the prophets (the servants)—persecution that climaxes in the murder of the beloved son (cf. 1:11; 9:7). The wicked tenants attempt to gain possession of the vineyard through persecuting God's righteous servants (the OT prophets) and ultimately Jesus, so God will hand over possession of the vineyard to those who participate in the new temple (the "others"). The Jewish leaders, instead of serving the covenant community and mediating God's rule, attempt to rule over the nation and become independent of God. Mark 12:7 states their plan succinctly: "This is the heir. Come, let's kill him, *and the inheritance will be ours.*" One could make a good case that Mark draws on Isaiah 5 typologically. God's punishment of Israelite leadership and the nation entails Israel's exile in Babylon. This act of judgment sets a prophetic pattern of God sending the nation and the Jewish leaders into a permanent spiritual exile when they crucify his Son.

A quotation from Psalm 118 punctuates the end of the parable (12:10–11), demonstrating that Jesus's death is ironically the means by which God will establish his presence among his people. The temple in Jerusalem is no longer the locus of God's presence; the person of Jesus is. According to Psalm 118, the speaker is delivered from the hands of the "nations" (Ps. 118:5–14) because of God's faithfulness to his covenant (Ps. 118:1–4) and his righteousness (Ps. 118:19–21). Though the psalmist was initially rejected, God has fashioned him like a coping stone or cornerstone, which enjoys a preeminent position.

Considerable continuity exists between the context of Psalm 118 and Mark 12. The Lord will deliver Jesus from his enemies (the Jewish leaders) because of his righteousness, just as he delivered the psalmist on account of his faithfulness. Psalm 118:22 also includes the idea that what humanity rejects, God desires. The "rejected" "stone" that is ultimately exalted to the place of "cornerstone" by God communicates the idea of God constructing his temple with something or someone who is rejected by people but glorious in God's sight (Ps. 118:22–29). Nowhere in the parable of the tenants does exaltation or vindication appear. This concept is only brought forth through Mark's use of Psalm 118. Once more, Mark is probably thinking typologically here. God promises to exalt Jesus to a position of honor through his resurrection, an event that formally begins the construction of the end-time temple among his people (cf. Acts 4:11; 1 Pet. 2:7). In sum, according to Isaiah 5 and Psalm 118, the OT typologically anticipates God's judgment upon Israel and her leaders and the reestablishment of his people through the rejection and vindication of his Messiah.

The Jewish leaders immediately recognized the significance of the parable. Though their hearts remained calloused toward God's acts of redemption in Jesus (3:5; 7:6; 10:5), they still grasped the thrust of the parable, knowing "he had spoken the parable against them" (12:12). The presence of the crowd made it impossible for them to seize him right then and there, but something had to be done.

Foiled Entrapments (12:13–34)

The remainder of chapter 12 is largely the result of the parable of the wicked tenants, which is directed against the Jewish leadership (12:12). The following two episodes probably take place on Tuesday within the temple complex (12:13–27 // Matt. 22:15–33 // Luke 20:20–38). The religious authorities intend to trap Jesus so they may arrest him. If the leaders can "catch him in his words" (12:13), then they have the authority to arrest him in public despite the crowds. The first attempt is more political in nature and concerns the question of whether it's lawful to pay the Roman poll tax, a taxation that applies only to residents in Judea. Jesus, being from Galilee, would not be responsible to pay this tax. On one face of the denarius used to pay the tax is an imprint of Caesar with the inscription "Augustus Tiberius Caesar, son of the *deified Augustus*."[31] Such a claim is at odds with strict Jewish monotheism. On a political level, the coin is also a reminder of Rome's authority over Palestine,

---

31. Everett Ferguson, *Backgrounds of Early Christianity*, 3rd ed. (Grand Rapids: Eerdmans, 2003), 92.

an idea that would sit somewhat well with the Herodians (Rome appointed Herod to rule as a vassal) but agitate the Pharisees. In a deft move, Jesus asks the leaders to produce a denarius. The fact that the leaders are carrying these coins is revealing, for they are implicitly acknowledging Rome's authority. One of the more famous sayings of Jesus, "Give back to Caesar what is Caesar's and to God what is God's" (12:17), is a bit of a both/and. On the one hand, Jesus admits that one should live at peace with the governing authorities, while on the other, he insists that one should devote ultimate allegiance to God (cf. Rom. 13:1–7; 1 Pet. 2:13–14). The Pharisees and the Herodians attempt to catch Jesus, but Jesus turns the tables and traps them in their own scheme.

The second episode concerns the resurrection. The Sadducees, a group that considers only the Pentateuch to be Scripture and denies the resurrection, ask Jesus a complex question about the issue of levirate marriage. According to Deuteronomy 25:5–6, the brothers of the deceased must marry their sister-in-law if there is no heir in order to preserve the family name (cf. Gen. 38:8). So the Sadducees ask which of the seven husbands will be married to the wife in the new age (12:20–23). Jesus responds that the Sadducees are grossly mistaken because there will be no marriage in the new creation (12:25). Moreover, he then argues for the legitimacy of the resurrection based upon a well-known passage from the Pentateuch: Exodus 3. The resurrection is certain because God's faithfulness to his covenant ensures that he will raise the patriarchs to new life.

Jesus as Preexistent Priest-King; the Widow's Offering (12:35–44)

The interaction with "one of the teachers" concerning the greatest commandment demonstrates that not *all* the Jewish leaders are steeled in their resolve to kill Jesus (12:28–34; →Matt. 22:34–40). In 12:35–37 Jesus goes on the offensive (// Matt. 22:41–46 // Luke 20:41–44). He takes issue with the leaders' belief that "the Messiah is the son of David" (12:35). Now, the OT explicitly states that the Messiah will be a descendant of David (e.g., Isa. 11:1), and Mark's narrative has argued for that (10:47–48; 11:9–10). But Jesus puts his finger on Psalm 110:1 and advocates for a broader understanding of the Messiah—a *preexistent one*:

David himself, speaking by the Holy Spirit, declared:

> "The Lord said to my Lord:
>   'Sit at my right hand
>   until I put your enemies
>   under your feet.'" (12:36)

Scholars intensely debate the meaning of Psalm 110:1 and Jesus's use of it here. Psalm 110:1, the most-quoted OT passage in the NT, is enigmatic in its own right. A good argument, though, can be marshaled in favor of reading the second "Lord" (*'doni*) as an enigmatic divine figure (cf. Josh. 5:14). So in Psalm 110:1, David prophesies about an end-time event when Yahweh (*yhwh*) will address a divine figure (*'doni*) and install him as cosmic king at Yahweh's "right hand." Such a position of honor and power is reserved only for Israel's God. He alone possesses the right to rule the cosmos. For God to appoint another individual is unparalleled in the OT except for Daniel 7:13–14, where the son of man figure rides upon a cloud up to the Ancient of Days and inherits the right to rule (cf. Ezek. 1:26).

This is not the first passage in Mark's Gospel that points to Jesus's divinity. Throughout the narrative, Jesus is portrayed as Israel's Lord in his ability to forgive (2:7), exercise authority over the Sabbath (2:27–28), still the storm (4:35–41), raise the dead (5:41), multiply food (6:41; 8:7), walk on water (6:48), and reveal his glory at the transfiguration (9:2–6). Lest we forget, Mark intends to convince his readers that Jesus is the "Messiah" and the divine "Son of God" (1:1).

Jesus's use of Psalm 110:1 raises two noteworthy issues. First, in its original OT context, the precise meaning of the passage is quite enigmatic. The identity of the recipient ("my Lord") is ambiguous in the OT, but the NT makes clear that this person is Christ. So we should ultimately understand this passage as a reference to Jesus's preexistence (see Heb. 1:3, 13). Second, Psalm 110:1 is a prophecy concerning the enthronement of a preexistent divine figure. But this prophecy also includes a priestly aspect. Psalm 110:4 reads,

> The Lord has sworn
> and will not change his mind:
> "You are a *priest* forever,
> in the order of Melchizedek."

Therefore, Psalm 110 enigmatically anticipates the coronation of a preexistent figure who will one day rule over God's enemies and function in a priestly capacity (see Heb. 7:3, 17, 21).

Jesus's use of Psalm 110:1 is remarkable because it encapsulates much of his ministry. Jesus fulfills Psalm 110:1 because he is the "Lord" (*'doni*) who has come to inherit the right to rule over all forms of hostility. But what makes Psalm 110:1 paradigmatic is its already-not-yet anticipation of the eternal reign of God. The "Lord" (*'doni*) will rule "*until* [*'ad*] I make your enemies a footstool." Apparently, the figure "Lord" (*'doni*) here in 110:1 will sit at Yahweh's right hand (i.e., participate in the rule of God) *before* Yahweh consummately judges Israel's enemies. Psalm 110 therefore expects a twofold fulfillment of God's end-time kingdom. This is not a far cry from the "mystery of the kingdom" in 4:26–32. Jesus also fulfills the priestly aspect of Psalm 110:4. Mark has taken great pains to demonstrate how Jesus is a priest-king throughout the narrative. As such, he has just cursed the fig tree and judged Israel's temple, and now he ensures the inauguration of a new temple through his death and resurrection! Above all, Mark's readers must recognize that Jesus's identity as a preexistent priest-king is not a radically new doctrine but something that was enigmatically anticipated in the OT itself.

Chapter 12 climaxes with a seemingly odd account of a widow offering a few "copper coins" (12:42) in contrast to the rich giving vast sums of money (12:41; →Luke 21:1–4). The rich here should probably be identified with the rich man in 10:17–25 and the "robbers" in 11:17, who prey upon those who seek to buy sacrifices and worship at the temple in Jerusalem. Jesus encourages the disciples to imitate the widow, giving to God not out of a storehouse of money but out of faith.

Final Judgment upon Israel's Temple and the Second Coming (13:1-37)

Failure to Understand the New Temple and Destruction of the Old Temple (13:1–4)

Chapter 13, often referred to as the Olivet Discourse, takes place on the Mount of Olives (13:3) on Wednesday of passion week. All the material from 11:27 to 12:44 takes place at the temple. According to 13:1, Jesus and the disciples are now "leaving the temple." The disciples exclaim, "Look, Teacher! What massive *stones* [*lithoi*]! What magnificent buildings!" (13:1). A careful reader of Mark's narrative will immediately remember Jesus's earlier prediction where he identifies himself as the "stone the builders rejected" from Psalm 118:22–23:

Mark 12:10-11 (quoting Ps. 118:22-23)	Mark 13:1
"Haven't you read this passage of Scripture: 'The *stone* [*lithon*] the builders [*hoi oikodomountes*] rejected has become the cornerstone; the Lord has done this, and it is *marvelous in our eyes*'?"	"As Jesus was leaving the temple, one of his disciples said to him, 'Look, Teacher! What massive *stones* [*lithoi*]! What magnificent *buildings* [*oikodomai*]!'"

In 13:1 the disciples are agape at the "stones" and the "buildings" of the idolatrous Jerusalem temple; but in 12:10–11 the true temple, Jesus—the "stone"

rejected by the "builders"—deserves ultimate recognition. We can make two observations based on this comparison: (1) The disciples are marveling at the wrong thing! They remain partially hardened to God's mighty acts and have yet to understand fully that Jesus is the true temple and that the physical temple in Jerusalem has come under divine judgment. In a word, the disciples have largely missed the significance of Jesus's expulsion of the money changers and his teaching in the temple in 11:12–44. (2) Because Israel's leaders (and the majority of the nation) reject Jesus as God's precious "stone" and refuse to listen to him, God will in turn judge Israel's "stones," the Jerusalem temple.

The Olivet Discourse here in 13:1–37 (// Matt. 24:1–25:46 // Luke 21:5–36) is one of the most difficult and debated sections in all the NT. The difficulty lies in tracking the precise sequence of events, relating them to the OT, and, ultimately, linking them to Mark's narrative in 13:1–4. Though a full explanation is beyond the scope of this project, we can at least get our bearings.

In response to the disciples' glowing praise of the Jerusalem temple, Jesus throws a wet blanket on their admiration: "Do you see all these great buildings? . . . Not one stone here will be left on another; every one will be thrown down" (13:2). Clearly, Jesus is predicting the fall of the temple here, an event that took place several decades later at the culmination of the first Jewish revolt in AD 66–70. So Mark's audience should assume that the bulk of the Olivet Discourse must address the physical destruction of the temple. What follows, then, in chapter 13 extends Jesus's actions in the temple and his teaching (11:1–12:44). Jesus begins the process of judging the temple when he drives out the money changers (11:15–17), and in chapter 13 he promises to finish what he started.

The disciples are more than intrigued. Four disciples, Peter, James, John, and Andrew, want to know: "*When* will these things happen? And what will be the *sign* that they are all about to be fulfilled?" (13:4). The two questions posed by the disciples in 13:4 should be understood as synonymous.[32] That is, both questions seek an explanation of Jesus's statement in 13:2 about the destruction of the temple. The first question concerns the timing of the event, and the second refers to the "sign" preceding its arrival.

The discourse is divided up into three main parts, and we will briefly comment on each of them in turn:

13:5-23	The events leading up to the destruction of the temple in AD 70
13:24-31	The arrival of the Son of Man
13:32-37	The unknown arrival of the Son of Man

32. Robert H. Stein, *Jesus, the Temple, and the Coming Son of Man* (Downers Grove, IL: InterVarsity, 2014), 63–69.

The Events Leading Up to the Destruction of the Temple (13:5–23)

Many of the events anticipated in the Olivet Discourse take place within the lives of the disciples—the immediate audience of Jesus's teaching (13:1–4)—culminating in the destruction of Jerusalem by the Roman general Titus in AD 70. Moreover, the events depicted in 13:5–23, though preceding the destruction of the temple, are eschatological in nature. Generally speaking, *all* the events between the first and second comings of Christ should be understood as eschatological. Jesus's ministry inaugurates the great end-time tribulation. Drawing from a host of OT passages, Jesus explains in 13:5–23 that the tribulation is initially fulfilled in their lifetime. The inauguration of the end-time tribulation will manifest itself in two ways: false teaching and persecution. False messiahs will attempt to infiltrate the covenant community: "Many will come in my name, claiming, 'I am he,' and will deceive many" (13:6; cf. Dan. 9:27; 11:31–32). Associated with false teaching are warfare and cosmic disturbance (13:8, 24; Isa. 13:10; 34:4; Sib. Or. 12:157; 13:10; Josephus, *J.W.* 1.377; Philo, *Prov.* 2.41). Jesus warns his disciples that they should continue to persevere in their faith since these are merely the "beginning of birth pains" (13:8; cf. Isa. 13:8). That is, these eschatological realities are only the initial phase of God's judgment upon Jerusalem.

Moving from general realities to specifics, the discourse focuses on what eschatological realities of the tribulation will befall the disciples (13:9–13). Note the repetition of the second-person-plural "you" in this section. The language here of "handing over" (13:9) is used to describe the Jewish hostility toward John and Jesus.

John the Baptist	"After John *was put in prison* [*to paradothēnai*]" (1:14)
Jesus	"The Son of Man *is going to be delivered* [*paradidotai*] into the hands of men" (9:31)
Disciples	"*They will deliver* [*paradōsousin*] you to the courts, and you will be flogged in the synagogues" (13:9 NASB)

The disciples will participate in the pattern of suffering established by John the Baptist and ultimately Jesus. End-time hostility toward the covenant people will escalate before God pours out his wrath on the nation.

Mark 13:14 is a turning point in the discourse: "When you see '*the abomination that causes desolation*' standing where it does not belong—let the reader understand—then let those who are in Judea flee to the mountains." This is the first of two explicit references to the book of Daniel (13:14, 26). In Daniel 9:27, 11:31, and 12:11 the "abomination that causes desolation" is set up during the end-time tribulation of God's people when Israel's antagonist deceives the majority of the nation and persecutes the righteous (Dan. 8:23–25; 9:27; 11:31–35). This antagonist will defile God's temple and "exalt and magnify himself above every god" (Dan. 11:36).

The use of this enigmatic reference in Daniel makes good sense in Mark's narrative (→Matt. 24:4–35). Jesus in his Galilean ministry purifies and cleanses the created order and his people so that he may take up residence among them through the Spirit. What we discover here in 13:14 is, however, a consummate defilement in fulfillment of Daniel 9:27, 11:31, and 12:11. The defilement could be twofold: (1) it could refer to the Roman soldiers offering up pagan sacrifices in the temple in AD 70 (see Josephus, *J.W.* 6.316); and (2) it could refer to Israel itself becoming an abomination. Israel has worshiped the abominable temple, so she has become an abomination (→Matt. 24:15).

However we interpret the difficult phrase, this is an end-time defilement that cannot be undone. There is no cleansing of the nation here. Israel finds herself in the cauldron of God's wrath on account of her wickedness and unwillingness to listen to Jesus's message of deliverance. Escaping God's wrath is predicated upon responding positively to John the Baptist and Jesus (1:4, 15). But the majority of the nation and its leaders fail to do so. Soon they will crucify the very Son of God. Jesus, the Son of Man, will come in AD 70 to judge and bring an end to the theocratic nation of God.

The Arrival of the Son of Man (13:24–31)

The timing of the next section (13:24–31) is exceedingly difficult to determine. Some commentators argue that the arrival of the Son of Man will take place in the future at Christ's second coming, and they pair it with the following passage of 13:32–36. Others, though, contend that the Son of Man's arrival takes place in AD 70, appending it to the previous section of 13:5–23. At the end of the day, we may not have to choose a side, for the events contained within the Olivet Discourse interlock with one another. They are intentionally enigmatic. What is true about God's judgment upon the temple in AD 70 is also true about the final judgment upon the cosmos at the very end of history, since the temple symbolizes the cosmos. So in a very real sense, the Son of Man arrives in AD 70 to judge the idolatrous nation of Israel, but his arrival toward the end of the first century foreshadows his future arrival at the very end of history.

The cosmic language in 13:24 occurs in a number of places in the OT (e.g., Isa. 13:10–13; 24:1–6, 19–23; 34:4; Jer. 4:23–28; Ezek. 32:6–8), figuratively referring to the end of a pagan nation's existence and the establishment of another nation. The conflagration of heavens mirrors the chaos on earth as one historical epoch gives way to another. The language is appropriate here in chapter 13, where the nation of Israel has reached its theocratic end, eclipsed by a community of believers that find their identity in Jesus (cf. Acts 2:17–21, quoting Joel 2:28–32).

Mark 13:26 explains that "at that time people will see the Son of Man coming in clouds with great power and glory." This is a partial quotation of Daniel 7:13: "In my vision at night I looked, and there before me was one like a *son of man, coming with the clouds of heaven.*" The reference to Daniel 7:13 in Mark 13:26 signals the fulfillment of the Son of Man's end-time judgment upon the "fourth beast" (Dan. 7:7, 11–12, 26). According to the immediate context of Daniel 7, the Son of Man's judgment possibly takes place in Jerusalem, the "epicenter of all cosmic conflict . . . where God's enemies are judged and destroyed."[33] The fourth beast in Mark 13 is not a pagan nation, as Daniel envisions, but the nation of Israel and her temple. Ironically, Israel is identified as part of the pagan fourth beast, since she has become indistinguishable from the pagan nations!

But this judgment is not reserved for the disciples' distant future: the Son of Man's arrival in AD 70 ushers in the realization of the latter-day kingdom upon earth and the restoration of the true people of God (Dan. 7:22, 27). Mark 13:27 reads, "And he will send his angels and gather his elect from the four winds, from the ends of the earth to the ends of the heavens." A string of OT passages that refer to the ingathering of the dispersed tribes of Israel lies behind this statement (e.g., Deut. 30:4; Isa. 43:5). Those who follow Jesus of Nazareth will emerge victorious in AD 70 and constitute the restored Israel of God. One kingdom falls and another rises.

The Unknown Arrival of the Son of Man (13:32–37)

The final section of the Olivet Discourse seems to point forward to a time beyond AD 70: "But about *that day* or hour no one knows, not even the angels in heaven, nor the Son, but only the Father" (13:32). This is an incredibly rich yet difficult verse. Whereas 13:5–31 is marked by various "signs" and temporal indicators, this section is temporally opaque. Jesus's ignorance of the timing of "that day" strikes the reader as odd (cf. Acts 1:7). How can the divine Son of God be ignorant? Is he not all-knowing? Mark may be putting his finger on what theologians call the "economic" Trinity—how Jesus and the Father relate to one another in the history of redemption. While it is certainly true that the three persons of the Trinity are all God and possess the same divine

---

33. Crispin H. T. Fletcher-Louis, "The High Priest as Divine Mediator in the Hebrew Bible: Daniel 7:13 as a Test Case," *SBLSP* 36 (1997): 173.

essence (the "immanent" Trinity) outside time, the way in which they relate to one another is functionally different in the course of redemptive history. Here, Jesus is, in his humanity, temporally ignorant of his second coming. But such ignorance is held alongside the previous statement in 13:31, where he unabashedly places his words on par with God's: "Heaven and earth will pass away, but my words will never pass away" (cf. Isa. 40:8; 51:6).

The Final Hours (14:1-72)

Anointed as King (14:1-11)

Chapter 14 begins with the narrator marking the time of the Passover celebration: "Now the Passover and the Festival of Unleavened Bread were only two days away" (14:1). Passover begins at sunset on Nisan 14 (Exod. 12–13; Num. 9:1–15), and the festival brings to mind Israel's redemption from Egypt and God passing over those who painted the blood of a sacrificial lamb on their doorposts (→John 19:17–37). Mark frames the Jewish leaders' treachery with the Passover celebration. Ironically, by "killing" Jesus, these Jewish leaders will put to death the ultimate Passover sacrifice, who will liberate those who repent and trust in him.

In preparation for his impending death, the narrative progresses to the anointing in Bethany, where Jesus is dining at the "home of Simon the Leper" (14:3). This event probably took place on the previous Saturday night (Nisan 9), but Mark and Matthew push the event later in the week in order to bring Jesus into direct conflict with the Jewish leaders (// Matt. 26:2–16 // John 12:1–8).[34] In light of the symbolic significance of this event, the religious leaders must respond.

We may assume that Simon used to be a leper and that he had been healed by Jesus (cf. 1:40), later becoming an eyewitness of this event at Bethany. John's version of this event identifies the "woman" (14:3) as Mary and includes her siblings, Martha and Lazarus (John 12:3). In stark contrast to the unbelieving Jewish leaders, Mary anoints Jesus with a costly perfume, an act that demonstrates her appreciation of Jesus. By anointing him "on his head," she unflinchingly declares him to be the long-awaited Messiah, meaning the "anointed one" (14:3; cf. 1:1). Ironically, her anointing also prepares him for burial (14:8; cf. 16:1).

Mary's announcement that Jesus is Israel's end-times King catalyzes his betrayal (14:10–11). This is the second time Mark mentions Judas. The first was at the end of the list in 3:19, where he is described as the one "who betrayed

---

34. Schnabel, *Jesus in Jerusalem*, 155.

him [Jesus]." By slipping in that comment at the beginning of the narrative, Mark introduces an antagonist who has been lurking in the shadows ever since. Only now, on account of Mary's symbolic declaration, does he emerge into the spotlight. The evangelist weaves the anointing into his narrative to present Jesus as Israel's King who will die as a Passover sacrifice at the hands of the nation's leaders, betrayed by one of his closest allies (14:10). The account ends with the chief priests being "delighted" at Judas's commitment to their cause. It's only a matter of hours now.

The Last Supper (14:12–31)

Having established that Jesus is the ultimate Passover sacrifice and that Jesus will be betrayed by one of his disciples (14:1–11), the narrative progresses to the Passover celebration itself (// Matt. 26:17–35 // Luke 22:7–23). The meal is to begin Thursday night at sunset, yet scholars greatly debate the timing of the Last Supper and its relationship to the Passover celebration. Was the Last Supper a Passover meal? Was it held in advance? Do the Synoptics and John present conflicting narratives (cf. John 18:28; 19:14)? These are tricky questions, and commentators offer different theories. One theory is that at the Last Supper, Jesus celebrates Passover *without a lamb* a day early because he's inaugurating a new phase of redemptive history. He is the true Passover Lamb, so he purposely modifies the feast. His death on Friday coincides with the slaughtering of the Passover lambs at the temple. Other scholars argue that Jesus did indeed celebrate Passover on Nisan 14, which technically starts at sunset on Thursday. Finally and preferably, a good case can be made that Jesus celebrates the Passover meal a day early because he is a Galilean. Galileans were permitted to offer up the sacrifice a day early because of the crowds. Further, in AD 30 the Passover was likely celebrated on two different days because of the timing of the new moon (→John 13:1–17).

In any case, the disciples procure a sacrificial lamb and take it to the temple, where the priests offer it up, splashing its blood at the base of the altar (2 Chron. 35:15–20; Jub. 49:16–21). The disciples then take the carcass to the upper room, where they will eat it. Jesus and the disciples eat the Passover meal within the city walls at night (14:13; see Deut. 16:5–8; m. Pesah. 5.10).

As they eat, Jesus announces that one of them at the table will "betray" him (14:18). Though Judas is not named in Mark's account of this meal and the disciples are left in the dark (cf. // Matt. 26:25 // John 13:26), the audience knows full well that Judas was the betrayer. Jesus claims that the "Son of Man will go *just as it is written* about him. But woe to the man who betrays the Son of Man!" (14:21). Jesus here affirms the passion predictions (8:31; 9:31;

10:33–34) but adds an important element—"just as it is written." Jesus may have in mind a handful of OT passages that predict a suffering Messiah (e.g., Dan. 9:25–26; Zech. 12:10), or he may have in mind Daniel 7:21, where an end-time antagonist wages "war against the holy people" and defeats them. These holy people are represented by the "son of man" earlier in Daniel 7:13, who we ought to assume likewise suffers. God's sovereignty is held tightly together with human responsibility. This is evident here, where Judas is responsible for his actions in betraying Jesus.

Remarkably, Jesus identifies himself as the ultimate Passover Lamb. Mark's narrative has demonstrated that he is also Israel's Lord, who promised to liberate Israel from slavery. Jesus is both the sacrificial Lamb and Israel's God in the flesh. The main principle at work in the Passover celebration according to Exodus 12 is the holiness of God's people. The death of the sacrifice, the application of its blood to the doorposts, and eating it all achieve an ultimate purpose—consecration of Israel *for* God's presence. Each Israelite family rehearses the meal so that, collectively speaking, they function as priests who dwell in the presence of God.[35] When viewed through this lens, the final Passover fits marvelously in Mark's narrative. We have discovered through the narrative that Jesus systematically purifies and cleanses humanity and the created order so that heaven may come down.

Leaving the city, Jesus and company cross the Kidron Valley and head for the Mount of Olives (14:26). On the way, Jesus predicts a sobering reality: "You will all fall away . . . for it is written: '*I will strike the shepherd, and the sheep will be scattered*'" (14:27). This critical prediction is drawn from Zechariah 13:7; its use here is complex, but we will only make three observations: (1) the broad context of Zechariah 13 is the purification of the Israelites, where the Lord promises to "cleanse" the Israelites "from sin and impurity" (Zech. 13:1); (2) according to 13:7, God commands a "sword" to "awake . . . against my shepherd," whereas in Mark 14:27 God is the explicit agent: "*I* will strike the shepherd"; and (3) the "scattering" of the "sheep" refers to the confusion and turmoil of God's people because they lack the direction of their leader, the shepherd. The majority of the sheep are annihilated (Zech. 13:8), and the remaining ones are tested severely for the purpose of "calling on my [the Lord's] name" (Zech. 13:9).

The use of Zechariah 13:7 resonates with the themes of Mark's Gospel. The disciples have consistently struggled with understanding Jesus's message, his actions, and, ultimately, his identity. So it is not surprising that they will,

---

35. L. Michael Morales, *Who Shall Ascend the Mountain of the Lord? A Biblical Theology of the Book of Leviticus*, NSBT 37 (Downers Grove, IL: InterVarsity, 2015), 81–82.

in fulfillment of Zechariah's prophecy, abandon Jesus when God strikes his Son, the true Shepherd of his people (cf. 6:34). But their testing is for their refinement, their eventual realization of who Jesus truly is (see 1:2, quoting Mal. 3:1; Rev 1:7). At the resurrection of Jesus, they will finally confess that he is Lord.

Failure to Keep Watch in Gethsemane (14:32–42)

The disciples' pledge to never forsake their leader (14:29–31) is short lived. We now come to the garden of Gethsemane on the Mount of Olives (14:32), where they soon fail their leader (// Matt. 26:36–46 // Luke 22:40–46). Jesus divides the disciples into two groups. The first group is to "sit" while Jesus prays (14:32), and the second group, the inner three (Peter, James, and John), are to "keep watch" (14:34; cf. 13:37). Corresponding to Jesus's prediction that Peter would "disown" him three times (14:30), the disciples fall asleep three times (14:37, 39, 41). Why did the disciples have such difficulty staying awake in the face of great crisis? They struggled because "their eyes were heavy" (14:40). There's symbolism here. The disciple have been blind to Jesus's message and actions from the beginning, especially concerning his suffering (e.g., 4:41; 6:52; 8:18). Even when Jesus partially heals them of their blindness (8:27–30), they still see Jesus unclearly, like "trees walking around" (8:24). They are unaware of the redemptive-historical significance of the situation in Gethsemane. They should have recognized that Jesus is who he claims to be—the suffering King.

Arrest and Trial by the Sanhedrin (14:43–65)

Interrupting Jesus speaking to the disciples, Judas emerges out of the shadows (14:43) to play a pivotal role in Jesus's arrest (// Matt. 26:47–56 // Luke 22:47–50 // John 18:3–11). The pace of the narrative speeds up a bit as the phrase *kai euthys* ("and immediately") occurs in 14:43, 72, and 15:1. These passages are locked together, perhaps indicating that Jesus's death is nigh. Mark mentions that a "crowd" is ready for a fight and armed with "swords and clubs." Importantly, we also learn who dispatched this group: "the chief priests, the teachers of the law, and the elders" (14:43). All three parties represent the entire nation and make up the Sanhedrin, demonstrating that culpability rests squarely on the nation *and* on her leadership (cf. 8:31; 11:27; 14:53; 15:1). The narrator then reveals that Judas would ironically use a kiss—a gesture of friendship in the first century—to signal to the soldiers whom they should arrest (14:44). Judas is called here and in 14:42 the "betrayer" (*paradidous*), the antonym of a faithful follower or disciple. The man whom Jesus calls (3:19), commissions to cast out demons and proclaim the "good news" of the kingdom (6:7), and allows to witness countless miracles has now turned against him. Mark's audience should take the character of Judas to heart and ensure that they hold fast in their faith.

One of the disciples (John 18:10 identifies this person as Peter) brandishes a sword and cuts off the ear of one of the soldiers (14:47). This act provokes Jesus to address the angry crowd out of frustration: "Am I leading a rebellion . . . that you have come out with swords and clubs to capture me?" (14:48). The answer is no. Jesus is not leading a political rebellion; rather, he is leading a spiritual one. His kingdom does not expand through violence but through the proclamation of the gospel. Verse 50 is the sobering fulfillment of Jesus's words in 14:27, spoken just a few hours before: "Then everyone [the disciples] deserted him and fled." Indeed, his "sheep" have now "scattered" (Zech. 13:7). The account ends with an odd verse found only in the Second Gospel, and many commentators suspect that the fleeing "young man, wearing nothing but a linen garment," is Mark himself (14:51–52). He, too, is identified with the scattered disciples.

The trial before the Sanhedrin, the official ruling body of Israel, is preliminary in nature. There are two trials before the Sanhedrin: one after midnight (14:55–64 // Matt. 26:59–66) and one early Friday morning (Luke 22:66–71). The first takes place at night, and witnesses contradict one another and are riddled with false testimony (14:55–56). Eckhard Schnabel argues that "the members of the Sanhedrin knew what verdict they wanted. But they did not know how to obtain that verdict or when they would obtain it."[36] It the end, they still cannot "find any" "evidence against Jesus" (14:55). Recall that early in Mark's narrative the Jewish leaders began "to plot . . . how they might kill Jesus" (3:6; cf. 11:18). This trial is the culmination of their devious efforts. The account, too, is highly reminiscent of the Olivet Discourse when Jesus tells his disciples that they will "be handed over to the local councils . . . [and] stand before governors and kings as witnesses to them" (13:9). Jesus is beginning to fulfill his own words. This trial before the council is a key phase in the destruction of the Jerusalem temple.

Mark's audience is privy to a single line of "false testimony": "We heard him say, '*I will destroy* this *temple* [*katalysō ton naon*] made with human hands and *in three days* [*dia triōn hēmerōn*] *will build* [*oikodomēsō*] another, not made with hands'" (14:58). This statement, though certainly contorted, is true and will be fulfilled shortly. In 15:29 those in the vicinity of the cross

---

36. Schnabel, *Jesus in Jerusalem*, 251.

address Jesus as "you who are going to *destroy the temple* [*katalyōn ton naon*] and *build it in three days* [*oikodomōn en trisin hēmerais*]." The wording is nearly exact. Though Jesus never utters this line in Mark's account, it does appear in John 2:19. Jesus thrice claims in Mark's narrative that he will rise again "after three days" (8:31; 9:31; 10:34), that he is the "cornerstone" of the new temple (12:10), and that "not one stone" of the Jerusalem temple will be "left on another" (13:2). Taken together, much of Jesus's ministry hinges on these words. Through his death he will "destroy" the temple "made with human hands" (cf. Acts 7:48; 17:24; 19:26), and through his resurrection he will erect the end-time dwelling place of God, a sanctuary that only God can fashion—the community of saints.

The interrogation climaxes with the high priest asking Jesus if he is "the Messiah, the Son of the Blessed One" (14:61 // Matt. 26:63). We have come full circle to 1:1, where Mark promises to explore how Jesus is the "Messiah" and the "Son of God." The disciples have struggled mightily with identifying Jesus as both Israel's King and the divine Son of God. Yet the high priest clearly acknowledges both of these realities, much like the demons rightly identify Jesus (e.g., 1:24; 5:7). Confirming his identity, Jesus laconically states, "I am" (14:62). This is the same title that Jesus uses in 6:50 when he claims to be Yahweh incarnate, the great "I AM" of the exodus (Exod. 3:13–14). Pushing further, Jesus then quotes Daniel 7:13, which, as we have seen, refers to the enthronement of the divine enigmatic figure (cf. Ps. 110:1). This is the second time the destruction of the temple is paired with the arrival of the "son of man" from Daniel 7. In 13:26 the coming of the Son of Man occurs in AD 70 and then at the second coming.

> Daniel 7:13: "In my vision at night I looked, and there before me was one like *a son of man, coming with the clouds of heaven.*"
>
> Mark 13:26: "At that time *people will see the Son of Man coming in clouds with great power and glory.*"
>
> Mark 14:62: "*And you will see the Son of Man* sitting at the right hand of the Mighty One and *coming on the clouds of heaven.*"

Perhaps Mark wants his readers to pair Jesus's destruction of the temple and the establishment of the new temple in his death and resurrection with Daniel 7:13. If that is the case, then Jesus's enthronement over the cosmos reaches a new level with this death and resurrection. In 13:26 Jesus predicts that "people will see" (*opsontai*), whereas in 14:62 he states, "You will see" (*opsesthe*). The Jewish leaders have had enough. They can now charge Jesus with blasphemy (14:64), an offense that is worthy of death (Lev. 24:10–23).

Faithless Peter (14:66–72)

Chapter 14 ends with Peter in the courtyard of the high priest's house, where he denounces Jesus three times (// Matt. 26:69–75 // Luke 22:56–62 // John 18:16–18, 25–27). Apparently, Peter and John follow the arresting party to the house of Caiaphas (John 18:15), while the remaining disciples flee (to Bethany?). In the preceding passage, when Jesus was being interrogated inside the house, Peter "followed him [Jesus] at a distance" (14:54). Perhaps we are to take this statement literally and figuratively, as Peter soon sits "with the guards" and warms "himself at the fire" (14:54). Perhaps this is the group that arrested Jesus a few minutes prior, and now Peter is fellowshipping with them (cf. John 18:12, 18). In any case, Peter's denial stings on many levels. Despite his protestations that he would never forsake Jesus, even to the point of death (14:27–31), Peter counts his own life to be more valuable than following Jesus. Moreover, Peter's denial stands in stark contrast to Jesus's faithful testimony. Peter denies Jesus, whereas Jesus truthfully testifies to his identity. We will not hear a whisper about Peter and the disciples until after the resurrection (16:7). At this point in the narrative, Mark's audience must take inventory of their own lives and consider the cost of following Jesus of Nazareth. Will they imitate Jesus or Peter in the face of adversity?

The Death and Burial of Jesus (15:1–47)

Jesus, Pilate, and the Crucifixion (15:1–32)[37]

Friday morning, the following day, the Jewish leaders take Jesus before Pilate and attempt to put him to death for sedition against Rome (15:1–2; →John 18:28–40). All four Gospels record various facets of Pilate, on account of being provoked by the religious authorities, interrogating and sentencing Jesus (// Matt. 27:11–44 // Luke 23:1–5, 13–25 // John 18:29–19:24). At the core of the Jewish leaders' accusation is Jesus's claim to be divine (14:61–65; cf. John 19:7). The Jews are not permitted to carry out capital punishment, so they need Pilate's approval. Despite Pilate's ambivalence, the Jewish leaders remain steeled in their resolve to put Jesus to death (15:13–15).

Mark highlights Jesus's identity as Israel's Messiah by mentioning several royal features during his mocking and crucifixion: a purple robe, a crown of thorns, the Roman soldiers' taunt "Hail, king of the Jews," and the soldiers' sarcastic genuflecting (15:16–20). Taken together, these details leave a careful

---

37. My discussion of Ps. 22 in Mark 15 is taken from Benjamin L. Gladd, "Mark," in *A Biblical-Theological Introduction to the New Testament: The Gospel Realized*, ed. Michael J. Kruger (Wheaton: Crossway, 2016), 87–89. Used with permission.

reader of Mark's narrative with a poignant irony: in mocking Jesus, the soldiers acknowledge his true identity as king. The crucifixion occupies a central place in Mark's Gospel in that the entire narrative has been anticipating this event from the very beginning. Jesus's identity as God's royal Son is on display at the crucifixion (15:21–41). It is here where Jesus refashions Israel's expectations of their coming Messiah. Jesus executes his kingly rule, not by conquering the Romans with a sword, but by dying on a cross—the symbol of bearing God's covenant curse and sedition against the Roman government.

Psalm 22 plays a central role during the events leading up to the crucifixion and at the crucifixion itself. Within the span of one chapter, Psalm 22 is quoted three times.

Mark 15	Psalm 22
"And they crucified him. *Dividing up his clothes, they cast lots* to see what each would get" (Mark 15:24).	"They *divide my clothes* among them *and cast lots for my garment*" (Psalm 22:18).
"Those who passed by *hurled insults* at him, *shaking their heads* and saying, 'So! You who are going to destroy the temple and build it in three days'" (Mark 15:29).	"All who see me mock me; they *hurl insults, shaking their heads*" (Psalm 22:7).
"And at three in the afternoon Jesus cried out in a loud voice, '*Eloi, Eloi, lema sabachthani?*' (which means '*My God, my God, why have you forsaken me?*')" (Mark 15:34).	"*My God, my God, why have you forsaken me? Why are you so far from saving me, so far from my cries of anguish?*" (Psalm 22:1).

Matthew and Mark record Jesus quoting Psalm 22:1 while on the cross: "My God, my God, why have you forsaken me?" (Matt. 27:46; Mark 15:34), and the evangelists spell Jesus's words (most likely in Aramaic) slightly differently. The immediate context of Psalm 22 guides us in understanding Jesus's cry of dereliction. The psalm claims to be written by David, which is important to note given its notoriety in the passion narrative. But the various genres contained within the psalm make it all the more peculiar. The first part of the psalm is "prayer song," a genre in which the speaker is distressed and pleads with God to intervene. What ought to be kept in mind, too, is the relationship between the speaker ("I") and the Israelite community. The speaker often represents the community in his song. The community is expected to repeat the speaker's "prayer," thereby becoming participants in it.

Verses 1–21 are the prayer song, and verses 22–31 constitute a "thanksgiving," a literary form characterized by celebration of what the Lord has accomplished. In 22:2 David says, "You do not answer," but in verse 21 he says, "You answer me" (NASB). In other words, 22:22 marks the turning point at which God answers David's cry for help by acting decisively. (Notice that all three quotations in Mark 15 come from the first half of the psalm.)

Psalm 22:1 describes David's frustration with his predicament. In his moment of greatest need, God remains distant. David feels as though God has abandoned him. Though God does not "answer," David remains steadfast in his trust (22:4–5), confident that God still reigns over the cosmos (v. 3). Verse 8 describes the attitudes of David's enemies. His enemies mock him by saying, "Let the LORD rescue him [David]. Let him [the LORD] deliver him [David], since he [David] delights in him [the LORD]." Verses 17–18 describe David's enemies as treating him as though he is already dead.

In the latter portion of the psalm, there is something of a prophecy or expectation describing the conversion of the pagan nations: "All the ends of the earth will remember and turn to the LORD, and all the families of the nations will bow down before him, for dominion belongs to the LORD and he rules over the nations" (Ps. 22:27–28). Two elements are worth mentioning: (1) the conversion of the nations and (2) the cosmic rule of the Lord. Since all three quotations of Psalm 22 take place in Mark 15, it is likely that the psalm plays a central role in Mark's depiction of passion week—particularly Jesus's crucifixion. Often OT passages serve as a blueprint for a NT text. For example, we've seen how Isaiah 40–66 appears to serve as a blueprint for much of Mark's narrative. The same technique may be found here in chapter 15, where Mark arranges his material in accordance with a careful reading of Psalm 22.

The use of Psalm 22, a prominent Davidic psalm, is by no means coincidental. By quoting the psalm three times (15:24, 29, 34), Mark explicitly connects Jesus's actions to David's. It appears that David's enemies in Psalm 22, whoever they might be precisely in the historical context, prophetically correspond to the Roman soldiers (15:24) and "those who passed by" (15:29). The former are obviously pagan gentiles, whereas the latter probably include some Jews, even Jewish leaders. Moreover, Jesus's cry of abandonment corresponds to David's cry. David's feeling of abandonment typologically anticipates Jesus's same feeling, yet Jesus experiences it in a deeper and more significant way.

The overall context of Psalm 22 brings out the themes of vicarious suffering, Jesus's reign, and the conversion of the nations in Mark 15. In Psalm 22, David's suffering is somehow linked to the Israelites' suffering (present or future). In other words, David, as an individual, suffers on behalf of, or at least identifies with, the righteous, suffering Israelites. Much in the same way, Jesus suffers on behalf of his people. His suffering is vicarious for those who have faith in him and his message. Furthermore, Psalm 22's emphasis on God's supreme rule continues in Mark 15. This time, however, the focus has shifted to *Jesus's* supreme rule on the cross. Lastly, Psalm 22 predicts the conversion of the nations (22:27–28). It may not be a coincidence, then, that a pagan—a Roman soldier, no less!—makes a confession of faith at the cross following Jesus's quotation of Psalm 22:1.

The upshot of Mark's use of Psalm 22 is significant, particularly for this overall purpose of his Gospel. Mark informs his readers that this Jesus of Nazareth is indeed the long-awaited King of Israel and the descendant of David. In the throes of death and defeat, Jesus is simultaneously the supreme ruler over all expressions of authority, both physical and spiritual. David's experiences prophetically anticipate Jesus's own experiences throughout his earthly ministry, especially here at the crucifixion. As David rules over Israel *while* undergoing persecution from those around him, so too Jesus rules in the midst of defeat and despair by his own countrymen. Though faint and generally undeveloped in comparison, David's actions pave the way for Christ's experience on the cross. Indeed, it's surprising that Jesus, as Israel's Messiah, should be marked by suffering and death, but it's not without an OT precedent. And while some commentators are tempted to view Jesus as revealing a breach within the Trinity—namely, that the Father has turned his back upon the Son when Jesus prays Psalm 22:1 ("My God, my God, why have you forsaken me?")—we should understand Jesus, the God-man, as crying out to God *in his humanity* while bearing the divine curse.

The Death of Jesus and the Tearing of the Veil (15:33–39)

Jesus's death, recorded in all four Gospels (// Matt. 27:45–56 // Luke 23:44–49 // John 19:29–30), is prefaced with a temporal indicator: "At noon, darkness came over the whole land until three in the afternoon" (15:33). By divulging the time, Mark underscores the miraculous and symbolic nature of the darkness. The term for "darkness" (*skotos*) is rare in Mark. The noun occurs only here, and the verb form is found in 13:24: "the sun *will be darkened* [*skotisthēsetai*], and the moon will not give its light." We pointed out that the cosmic language of 13:24 finds its origin in the OT (e.g., Isa. 13:10–13; 24:1–6, 19–23; 34:4; Jer. 4:23–28; Ezek. 32:6–8), symbolically depicting the end of a sinful nation's existence and the establishment of another kingdom. Within this vein, darkness in the OT also contains overtones of judgment (e.g., Joel 2:2, 31; Zeph. 1:14–15). Indeed, the ninth plague in Egypt was absolute darkness over the land (Exod. 10:21–29). So in prefacing the account with darkness at midday, Mark frames the entire death of Jesus as God pouring out his end-time judgment upon his innocent Son so that all those who trust in him will be spared.

The cosmic dimension is also highlighted in the tearing of the veil immediately following Jesus's death. Once more, we discern a sandwich structure:

> Mark 15:33: "At noon, *darkness* came over the whole land until three in the afternoon."
>
> Mark 15:37: "With a loud cry, Jesus breathed his last."
>
> Mark 15:38: "The *curtain of the temple* was torn in two from top to bottom."

One of the major features of the Jerusalem temple is its symbolic representation of the cosmos. Those familiar with the symbolic significance of the inner veil in the temple would immediately make the connection between Jesus's death and the cosmos.

Israel's temple is composed of three parts: the outer courts, the Holy Place, and the Holy of Holies.[38] Each tier corresponds to a cosmic reality: the outer courts symbolize the earth (Exod. 20:24–25; 1 Kings 7:23–25), the Holy Place signifies the visible heavens (Exod. 25:8–9; Gen. 1:14), and the Holy of Holies represents the invisible heavens, where God dwells with his angels (Exod. 25:18–22; Isa. 6:1–7). The inner and outer veils, too, contain cosmic symbols woven into their fabric, such as cherubim, and the colors of the veil are blue, red, and purple to symbolize the sky (Exod. 26:31). Josephus, a first-century Jewish historian, comments, "It was a Babylonian curtain, embroidered with blue, and fine linen, and scarlet, and purple, and of a contexture that was truly wonderful . . . a kind of image of the universe" (*J.W.* 5.212). Philo, a contemporary of Josephus, follows suit: "He [the architect] chose the materials of this embroidery . . . choosing materials equal in number to the elements of which the world was made, and having a direct relation to them; the elements being the earth and the water, and the air and the fire" (*Vit. Mos.* 2.88). *The tearing of the veil, then, symbolizes the tearing of the old cosmos, permitting God's glorious presence to descend and dwell with humanity.* This explains why Luke's narrative explicitly pairs the rending of the veil with the dissolution of the cosmos: "It was now about noon, and darkness came over the whole land until three in the afternoon, for the sun stopped shining. *And the curtain of the temple was torn in two*" (Luke 23:44–45).

Jesus's ministry of cleansing and purifying the created order culminates in his death. The tearing of the veil symbolizes the totality of God's judgment upon creation, whereas his resurrection signals the beginning of the

---

38. This paragraph on the temple is conceptually dependent upon G. K. Beale, *The Temple and the Church's Mission: A Biblical Theology of the Dwelling Place of God*, NSBT 17 (Downers Grove, IL: InterVarsity, 2004), 38.

new eternal cosmos. The twin themes of judgment and new creation nicely summarize much of what we have seen in Jesus's ministry up to this point, especially in his victory over the devil in the wilderness temptation (1:12–13) and the stilling of the storm (4:35–41). These themes explain why he judges/ expels Satan and his demons and why he restores and purifies humanity and the created order. They also explain why Mark dedicates so much space to God judging the idolatrous temple in Jerusalem and establishing the new temple in Jesus and his followers. He judges in order to redeem.

Mark's account of the crucifixion climaxes in the confession of a soldier: "And when the centurion, who stood there in front of Jesus, saw how he died, he said, 'Surely this man was *the Son of God*!'" (15:39). Irony runs thick here. The first conversion after Jesus's death is likely a gentile. But not any gentile—a Roman soldier with a hundred men at his command! He and his soldiers most likely play some role in killing Jesus in the first place. The title "Son of God," as we have seen, contains connotations of divinity (1:1; 14:61). So it would appear that this soldier is acknowledging this reality, an idea that would generally fit his Roman worldview (Romans believed that Caesar Augustus was a god). Gentiles have featured prominently in the narrative (5:1–20; 7:24–30; 8:1–10), and it makes sense that this theme surfaces again. Jesus claims that the temple is supposed to "be called a house of prayer for all nations" (11:17, quoting Isa. 56:7), and we finally see that coming to fruition here. With God's presence bursting forth from heaven to earth, the first person who will enjoy his end-time presence is a Roman soldier.

Moreover, the centurion's confession is all the more stark given its context. When the Jewish leaders and the nation are satisfied that they have put to death a blasphemer and seditionist, this centurion sees Jesus for who he is. We would expect that the roles would be reversed. Finally, this confession rounds out the Second Gospel in that Mark intended to demonstrate that, according to 1:1, Jesus is the "Messiah, the Son of God." This title occurs at three critical junctures in the Second Gospel (1:11; 9:7; 15:39), and Joel Marcus righty recognizes the significance of the confession: "The centurion's confession is one of three architectonic acclamations of Jesus as the Son of God, which are similar in form and seem to structure the whole Gospel, appearing at its beginning, middle, and end."[39]

Though Jesus is rejected by humanity and cursed by God, Mark intends his audience to embrace Jesus as their Messiah, redeemer, and the divine Son of God. Jesus must bear humanity's curse, guilt, and shame so that his

---

39. Joel Marcus, *Mark 8–16: A New Translation with Introduction and Commentary*, AB (New York: Doubleday, 2000), 1059.

Father's wrath may be assuaged. The "outsiders" lack such spiritual perception (→4:11), for they view Jesus as a seditionist against Rome and a false messiah. In some sense, the cross itself is a dramatic parable, and its true meaning remains hidden from those who are spiritually blind. Only those who have eyes to see understand that Jesus is indeed the Messiah and the divine Son of God (see 1 Cor. 2:6–16).

Women at the Cross (15:40–41)

Following the conversion of a Roman centurion, Mark informs his audience of a group of women "watching from a distance" (15:40). These women are resolute in following Jesus. We learn the names of three of these indefatigable women: Mary Magdalene, Mary "the mother of James the younger and of Joseph," and Salome. Three observations are noteworthy: (1) This is the first time in the narrative where we learn of this group. Mark tells us that they "*had followed* [*ēkolouthoun*] him and cared for his [Jesus's] needs" while he was ministering in Galilee (15:41; cf. 1:18; 2:14; 8:34). We should assume, then, that these women are faithful. They appear to have traveled a great deal with Jesus and the disciples and have repented and believed the message of the kingdom. Their prominence in the resurrection narrative confirms this observation (16:1–8). (2) Because Mark names three of the women, we should probably assume that they become eyewitnesses of the crucifixion and resurrection. All four Gospels underscore their significance (Matt. 28:1 // Luke 8:2; 24:10 // John 20:1–18). (3) Mark weds the centurion's confession to the faithfulness of the women. Together, these two groups are socially inferior in first-century Judaism. The nature of the kingdom is precisely what Jesus claims it to be: a place where the last will be first and the first will be last (e.g., 9:35–37; 10:13–31).

The Burial of Jesus (15:42–47)

The last bit of chapter 15 features the burial of Jesus by "Joseph of Arimathea, a prominent member of the Council, who was himself waiting for the kingdom of God" (15:43 // Matt. 27:57–61 // Luke 23:50–56 // John 19:38–42). We probably should surmise that Joseph of Arimathea either objects to the Sanhedrin's verdict regarding Jesus or was not present (// Luke 23:51). At the very least, Joseph of Arimathea embodies a remnant of Jewish believers. The fact that he pleads with Pilate to procure Jesus's body and is described as "waiting for the kingdom" informs us that he is a true follower of Jesus. Pilate grants Joseph access to the body, which he wraps in "linen" and places "in a tomb cut out of rock" (15:46). Jews will celebrate Passover shortly at sundown, so it is imperative that Joseph make haste (15:42). Two of the three women mentioned in 15:40, Mary Magdalene and Mary "the mother of Joseph," take note of "where he [Jesus] was laid" (15:47).

An Empty Tomb (16:1–8)

Jesus's death may occupy the focal point of Mark's narrative, but it is certainly not the climax of his story. Though Mark's resurrection account is relatively brief (16:1–8), the account pulls a considerable amount of theological freight (// Matt. 28:1–8 // Luke 24:1–10 // John 20:1–18). Jesus's resurrection constitutes the dawn of the new heavens and earth. By rising from the dead, Jesus demonstrates that his kingship and resurrection are indeed true. Though many, including the nation of Israel as represented by its leaders, deemed Jesus's message scandalous, the resurrection vindicates Jesus's identity and mission.

The Empty Tomb and an "Angel Sitting at the Right Side" (16:1–5)

Early Sunday morning, "the first day of the week," the aforementioned three women arrive at the tomb in order to "anoint Jesus' body" (16:1–2). As the women approach the tomb, they ask one another "who will roll the stone away" from the tomb (16:3). Tombs in the first century were often used for burying multiple bodies, so it was not uncommon for men to roll away the rock that sealed the tomb. To their surprise, the women discover that the "very large" stone has already been moved (16:4). They enter the tomb, where they see "a young man dressed in a white robe sitting on the right side" (16:5).

The description of the angel "sitting on the right side" (lit. "sitting at the right") is an odd detail to include. While it probably refers to the right side of a stone bench inside the tomb, there may also be a symbolic dimension. The Fourth Gospel mentions that Mary Magdalene saw two angels dressed in white, sitting "one at the head and the other at the foot" where Jesus was buried (John 20:12), but Mark is the only evangelist to record an angel "sitting on the right side [of the bench]" (cf. // Matt. 28:2 // Luke 24:4). In Mark's Gospel the pairing of the words "sit" (*kathēmai*) and "right" or "right hand" (*dexios*) occurs in only three places:

> David himself, speaking by the Holy Spirit, declared: "The Lord said to my Lord: '*Sit* [*kathou*] at my *right hand* [*ek dexiōn*] until I put your enemies under your feet.'" (12:36)

"I am," said Jesus. "And you will see the Son of Man *sitting at the right hand* [*ek dexiōn kathēmenon*] of the Mighty One and coming on the clouds of heaven." (14:62)

As they entered the tomb, they saw a young man dressed in a white robe *sitting on the right side* [*kathēmenon en tois dexiois*], and they were alarmed. (16:5)

Mark 12:36 and 14:62 reference Psalm 110:1, a critical prophecy that anticipates the end-time arrival of an enigmatic divine figure who will be enthroned on God's cosmic throne. Jesus cites this prophecy twice in Mark and claims to be that figure on both occasions. The second passage (14:62) is especially significant because Jesus weds Daniel 7:13 with Psalm 110:1 and claims that the Jewish leaders will "see" this event take place—probably a reference to the destruction of the temple in AD 70 (→13:26). What if the angel "sitting" at the "right hand" symbolizes the Son of Man sitting at the right hand of God? Note that the angel's robe is "white," perhaps corresponding to Jesus's "white" garments at the transfiguration (9:3; 16:5 // John 20:12). In other words, the posture of the angel demonstrates precisely what Mark's Gospel has been attempting to disclose: through his death and resurrection, Jesus reigns as Israel's "Messiah" and the divine "Son of God" (1:1). Though the ascension is weeks away, his death and resurrection have qualified Jesus to assume the right to rule alongside his Father over the cosmos.

This line of thinking also resonates with several prominent OT passages where the "angel of the LORD," distinct from God ontologically, functions as his unique representative on earth (e.g., Exod. 3:2; Num. 22:22–27; Judg. 6:11–12; 13:20–21). The angel does what the Lord does. Matthew's Gospel even labels the angel who sits on the stone of the tomb an "angel of the Lord" (28:2). The resurrection account of Mark's Gospel has caused much consternation because of its abbreviated state and the lack of many details found in the other three Gospels, but when we consider the odd detail of the angel "sitting on the right side" in his account, it goes a long way in helping us make sense of the narrative.

Fear and Excitement (16:6–8)

The angel commands the women to inform the disciples, "[Jesus] is going ahead of you into Galilee. There you will see him, just as he told you" (16:7). The angel is referring here to 14:28, where Jesus promises that following his resurrection he "will go ahead of" the disciples "into Galilee." Why return to Galilee? Perhaps for a few reasons. By returning to Galilee, the location where

Jesus's public ministry begins (1:14), the disciples can now continue the work to which they have been called—calling people to repentance so that God may dwell in their midst. The disciples will circle back to their homeland and now proclaim the good news about Jesus of Nazareth. He is who he claims to be. Jesus begins the process of cleansing and renewal in Galilee. It's fitting, then, that their task should resume there.

Oddly, Mark's Gospel finishes with the three women "trembling and *bewildered* [*ekstasis*]" (16:8a). Such a reaction is not uncommon in the Second Gospel. When Jesus raised Jairus's daughter from the dead, those gathered "were completely *astonished* [*ekstasei*]" (5:42; cf. 4:41; 5:15, 33; 10:32). What is somewhat unexpected, though, is the silence of the women: "They said nothing to anyone, because they were afraid" (16:8b). Fear in Mark's Gospel is often associated with the disciples' reaction to Jesus exceeding expectations; he is the divine Son of God who has the power to still the storm (4:41), cast out demons (5:15), heal the woman with the issue of blood (5:33), and walk on water (6:50); he is also the Messiah who is characterized by suffering (9:32; 10:32). So perhaps the women are "afraid" because he once again exceeds the expectations of his followers. According to the OT, the general resurrection will occur at the very end of history, and all will be resurrected together. God will raise the righteous saints and restore them in the new creation, and he will raise the unrighteous and consign them to judgment (see Job 19:26–27; Isa. 25:7–8; 26:19; Ezek. 37:1–14, 26–35; Dan. 12:2–3). So the resurrection of a single individual would be quite unexpected.

Despite the angel commanding the women to tell Peter and the disciples that Jesus has risen from the dead, the women say "nothing to anyone" (16:8b). Are they disobeying the angel? Perhaps it's a mixed bag. Remember that the messianic secret runs through Mark's narrative. From the beginning, there has been a pervasive sense of mystery and enigma concerning Jesus's identity, and those who encounter Jesus often struggle with his identity. This is especially true in those instances where, ironically, the demons and gentiles have a better grasp on Jesus's identity than do his followers (e.g., 1:24; 5:7; 15:39). It would therefore not be altogether surprising if the three women shared some of the disciples' feelings. Also, many commentators argue that the end of Mark brilliantly summons the audience to pick up where the disciples and the women left off: follow Jesus earnestly and proclaim the gospel to the nations.

The Longer Ending (16:9-20)

One of the more pressing issues in Mark's Gospel is the longer ending of 16:9–20. Most contemporary English translations contain a handful of comments about it (cf. John 7:53–8:11). Four different endings of Mark's Gospel have come down to us, but we will discuss only two of them. The vast majority of commentators argue against the inclusion of 16:9–20 for many reasons, three of which are primary: (1) The manuscript evidence for the shorter ending (those manuscripts that omit 16:9–20) is particularly early and strong (e.g., Sinaiticus, Vaticanus). Early translations of Mark in Latin, Syriac, and Georgian also omit the longer ending, and some of the early church fathers show no awareness of it. (2) Scribes often expand and smooth out perceived difficulties in texts. One could see how the abrupt ending in 16:8 lends itself to such expansion. (3) The longer ending of Mark (16:9–20) contains several words and themes that are incongruent with Mark's style and narrative. For good reason, then, 16:9–20 shouldn't be included in Mark's Gospel.

Mark: Commentaries

Boring, M. Eugene. *Mark: A Commentary*. NTL. Louisville: Westminster John Knox, 2006.

Brooks, James A. *Mark*. NAC. Nashville: Broadman, 1991.

Cole, R. Alan. *The Gospel according to Mark*. Rev. ed. TNTC. Grand Rapids: Eerdmans, 1989.

Collins, Adela Y. *Mark*. Hermeneia. Minneapolis: Fortress, 2007.

Cranfield, C. E. B. *The Gospel according to Saint Mark*. Rev. ed. Cambridge: Cambridge University Press, 1977.

Culpepper, R. Alan. *Mark*. SHBC. Macon, GA: Smyth & Helwys, 2007.

Donohue, J. R., and D. J. Harrington. *The Gospel of Mark*. SP 2. Collegeville, MN: Liturgical Press, 2002.

Dowd, Sharyn. *Reading Mark: A Literary and Theological Commentary on the Second Gospel*. Reading the New Testament. Macon, GA: Smyth & Helwys, 2000.

Edwards, James R. *The Gospel according to Mark*. PNTC. Grand Rapids: Eerdmans, 2002.

Evans, Craig A. *Mark 8:27–16:20*. WBC. Nashville: Nelson, 2001.

France, R. T. *The Gospel of Mark*. NIGTC. Grand Rapids: Eerdmans, 2002.

Garland, David. *Mark*. NIVAC. Grand Rapids: Zondervan, 1996.

Guelich, Robert A. *Mark 1–8:26*. WBC. Dallas: Word, 1989.

Gundry, Robert H. *Mark: A Commentary on His Apology for the Cross*. Grand Rapids: Eerdmans, 1993.

Hooker, Morna D. *The Gospel according to Saint Mark*. BNTC. London: A & C Black; Peabody, MA: Hendrickson, 1991.

Hurtado, Larry. *Mark*. NIBC. Peabody, MA: Hendrickson, 1989.

Kernaghan, Ronald J. *Mark*. IVPNTC. Downers Grove, IL: InterVarsity, 2007.

Lane, William L. *The Gospel according to Mark*. NICNT. Grand Rapids: Eerdmans, 1974.

Marcus, Joel. *Mark 1–8: A New Translation with Introduction and Commentary*. AB 27. New York: Doubleday, 2000.

———. *Mark 9–16: A New Translation with Introduction and Commentary*. AB 27A. New York: Doubleday, 2009.

Stein, Robert H. *Mark*. BECNT. Grand Rapids: Baker Academic, 2008.

Strauss, Mark L. *Mark*. ZECNT. Grand Rapids: Zondervan, 2014.

Wessel, W., and M. L. Strauss. "Mark." In *Matthew–Mark*, vol. 9 of *Expositor's Bible Commentary*, rev. ed., edited by Tremper Longman III and David E. Garland, 671–988. Grand Rapids: Zondervan, 2010.

Witherington, Ben, III. *The Gospel of Mark: A Socio-Rhetorical Commentary*. Grand Rapids: Eerdmans, 2001.

Mark: Articles, Essays, and Monographs

Achtemeier, P. J. "'And He Followed Him': Miracles and Discipleship in Mark 10:46–52." *Semeia* 11 (1978): 115–45.

Ambrozic, A. M. *The Hidden Kingdom: A Redaction-Critical Study of the References to the Kingdom of God in Mark's Gospel*. CBQMS 2. Washington, DC: Catholic Biblical Society of America, 1972.

Anderson, Janice Capel, and Stephen D. Moore. *Mark and Method*. Minneapolis: Fortress, 2008.

Barrett, C. K. "The Background of Mark 10:45." In *New Testament Essays: Studies in Memory of T. W. Manson*, edited by A. J. B. Higgins, 1–18. Manchester: Manchester University Press, 1959.

Beavis, M. A. *Mark's Audience: The Literary and Social Setting of Mark 4.11–12*. JSNTSup 33. Sheffield: JSOT Press, 1989.

Best, Ernest. *Mark: The Gospel as Story*. Edinburgh: T&T Clark, 1983.

———. *The Temptation and the Passion: The Markan Soteriology*. 2nd ed. SNTSMS 2. Cambridge: Cambridge University Press, 1990.

Blount, Brian K. *Go Preach: Mark's Kingdom Message and the Black Church Today*. Maryknoll, NY: Orbis Books, 1998.

Bock, D. L. *Blasphemy and Exaltation in Judaism: The Charge against Jesus in Mark 14:53–65*. Grand Rapids: Baker, 1998.

Bolt, P. G. *The Cross from a Distance: Atonement in Mark's Gospel*. NSBT 18. Downers Grove, IL: InterVarsity, 2004.

Bond, Helen K. *The First Biography of Jesus: Genre and Meaning in Mark's Gospel*. Grand Rapids: Eerdmans, 2020.

Booth, R. P. *Jesus and the Laws of Purity: Tradition History and Legal History in Mark 7*. JSNTSup 13. Sheffield: JSOT Press, 1986.

Broadhead, Edwin K. *Naming Jesus: Titular Christology in the Gospel of Mark*. Sheffield: Sheffield Academic, 1999.

———. *Teaching with Authority: Miracles and Christology in the Gospel of Mark*. Sheffield: JSOT Press, 1992.

Camery-Hoggatt, Jerry. *Irony in Mark's Gospel: Text and Subtext*. New York: Cambridge University Press, 1992.

Casey, M. *Aramaic Sources of Mark's Gospel*. SNTSMS 102. Cambridge: Cambridge University Press, 1998.

Crossley, James G. *The Date of Mark's Gospel: Insights from the Law in Earliest Christianity*. JSNTSup 299. New York: T&T Clark, 2004.

Croy, N. Clayton. *The Mutilation of Mark's Gospel*. Nashville: Abingdon, 2003.

Danove, P. L. *The End of Mark's Story: A Methodological Study*. Leiden: Brill, 1993.

Derrett, J. D. M. "Christ and the Power of Choice (Mark 3:1–6)." *Bib* 65 (1984): 168–88.

———. "Contributions to the Study of the Gerasene Demoniac." *JSNT* 3 (1984): 2–17.

———. "He Who Has Ears to Hear, Let Him Hear (Mark 4:9 and Parallels)." *DRev* 119 (2001): 255–68.

Dewey, J. *Markan Public Debate: Literary Technique, Concentric Structure, and Theology in Mark 2:1–3:6*. SBLDS 48. Chico, CA: Scholars Press, 1980.

Driggers, Ira B. *Following God through Mark: Theological Tension in the Second Gospel*. Louisville: Westminster John Knox, 2007.

Dwyer, T. *The Motif of Wonder in the Gospel of Mark*. JSNTSup 128. Sheffield: Sheffield Academic, 1996.

Dyer, K. D. *The Prophecy on the Mount: Mark 13 and the Gathering of the New Community*. ITS 2. Bern: Peter Lang, 1998.

Edwards, J. R. "Markan Sandwiches: The Significance of Interpolations in Markan Narratives." *NovT* 31 (1989): 193–216.

Elliott, Scott S. *Reconfiguring Mark's Jesus: Narrative Criticism after Poststructuralism*. Sheffield: Sheffield Phoenix, 2011.

Evans, Craig A. "The Beginning of the Good News and the Fulfillment of Scripture in the Gospel of Mark." In *Hearing the Old Testament in the New Testament*, edited by Stanley E. Porter, 83–103. Grand Rapids: Eerdmans, 2006.

Fowler, Robert M. *Loaves and Fishes: The Function of the Feeding Stories in the Gospel of Mark*. SBLDS 54. Chico, CA: Scholars Press, 1978.

France, R. T. "Mark and the Teaching of Jesus." In *Studies of History and Tradition in the Four Gospels*, vol. 1 of *Gospel Perspectives*, edited by R. T. France and D. Wenham, 101–36. Sheffield: JSOT Press, 1980.

Garland, David. *A Theology of Mark's Gospel: Good News about Jesus the Messiah, Son of God*. BTNT. Grand Rapids: Zondervan, 2015.

Garrett, Susan R. *The Temptations of Jesus in Mark's Gospel*. Grand Rapids: Eerdmans, 1998.

Geddert, T. J. *Watchwords: Mark 13 in Markan Eschatology*. JSNTSup 26. Sheffield: Sheffield Academic, 1989.

Gray, Timothy C. *The Temple in the Gospel of Mark: A Study of Its Narrative Role*. Grand Rapids: Baker Academic, 2008.

Guelich, R. A. "'The Beginning of the Gospel': Mark 1:1–15." *Biblical Research* 27 (1982): 5–15.

Harrington, Daniel J. *What Are They Saying about Mark?* New York: Paulist Press, 2004.

Hatina, T. R. "The Focus of Mark 13:24–27: The Parousia or the Destruction of the Temple?" *BBR* 6 (1996): 43–66.

———. *In Search of a Context: The Function of Scripture in Mark's Narrative.* London: Sheffield Academic, 2002.

Hawkin, D. J. "The Incomprehension of the Disciples." *JBL* 91 (1972): 491–500.

Heil, J. P. *Jesus Walking on the Sea: Meaning and Gospel Functions of Matt 14:22–33, Mark 6:45–52 and John 6:15b–21.* AnBib 87. Rome: Pontifical Biblical Institute, 1981.

———. "A Note on 'Elijah with Moses' in Mark 9,4." *Bib* 80 (1999): 115.

Henderson, Suzanne W. *Christology and Discipleship in the Gospel of Mark.* Cambridge: Cambridge University Press, 2006.

Hengel, Martin. *Studies in the Gospel of Mark.* London: SCM; Philadelphia: Fortress, 1985.

Hooker, Morna D. "Mark." In *It Is Written: Scripture Citing Scripture; Essays in Honour of Barnabas Lindars, SSF,* edited by D. A. Carson and H. G. M. Williamson, 220–30. Cambridge: Cambridge University Press, 1988.

———. *The Son of Man in Mark: A Study of the Background of the Term "Son of Man" and Its Use in St. Mark's Gospel.* London: SPCK, 1967.

Horsley, R. A. *Hearing the Whole Story: The Politics of Plot in Mark's Gospel.* Louisville: Westminster John Knox, 2001.

Horsley, Richard A., Jonathan A. Draper, and John M. Foley. *Performing the Gospel: Orality, Memory, and Mark.* Minneapolis: Fortress, 2006.

Humphrey, Hugh M. *A Bibliography for the Gospel of Mark: 1854–1980.* New York: Mellen, 1982.

Hurtado, Larry W. "The Women, the Tomb, and the Climax of Mark." In *A Wandering Galilean: Essays in Honour of Seán Freyne,* edited by Z. Rodgers, 427–50. Supplements to the Journal for the Study of Judaism 132. Leiden: Brill, 2009.

Incigneri, Brian J. *The Gospel to the Romans: The Setting and Rhetoric of Mark's Gospel.* Leiden: Brill, 2003.

Iverson, Kelly R. *Gentiles in the Gospel of Mark.* New York: T&T Clark, 2007.

Iverson, Kelly R., and Christopher W. Skinner, eds. *Mark as Story: Retrospect and Prospect.* Atlanta: Society of Biblical Literature, 2011.

Iwe, J. C. *Jesus in the Synagogue of Capernaum: The Pericope and Its Programmatic Character for the Gospel of Mark; An Exegetico-Theological Study of Mark 1:21–28.* Tesi Gregoriana, Serie Teologia 57. Rome: Editrice Pontifica Università Gregoriana, 1999.

Juel, D. *Messiah and Temple: The Trial of Jesus in the Gospel of Mark.* SBLDS 31. Missoula, MT: Scholars Press, 1977.

Kealy, Seán P. *Mark's Gospel: A History of Its Interpretation from the Beginning until 1979.* New York: Paulist Press, 1982.

Kee, H. C. *Community of the New Age: Studies in Mark's Gospel.* Philadelphia: Westminster, 1977.

———. "The Function of Scriptural Quotations and Allusions in Mark 11–16." In *Jesus und Paulus,* edited by E. Earle Ellis and E. Grässer, 165–85. Göttingen: Vandenhoeck & Ruprecht, 1975.

———. "The Terminology of Mark's Exorcism Stories." *NTS* 14 (1967): 232–46.

———. "The Transfiguration in Mark: Epiphany or Apocalyptic Vision?" In *Understanding the Sacred Text: Essays in Honor of Morton S. Enslin on the Hebrew Bible and Christian Beginnings*, edited by J. Reumann, 137–52. Valley Forge, PA: Judson, 1972.

Kelber, W. H. *The Kingdom in Mark: A New Place and a New Time*. Philadelphia: Fortress, 1974.

Kingsbury, Jack Dean. *The Christology of Mark's Gospel*. Philadelphia: Fortress, 1983.

Kirchevel, G. D. "The 'Son of Man' Passages in Mark." *BBR* 9 (1999): 181–87.

Lambrecht, J. "The Relatives of Jesus in Mark." *NovT* 16 (1974): 241–58.

Lightfoot, R. H. *The Gospel Message of St Mark*. Oxford: Oxford University Press, 1962.

Magness, J. L. *Sense and Absence: Structure and Suspension in the Ending of Mark's Gospel*. Atlanta: Scholars Press, 1986.

Malbon, Elizabeth Struthers. *In the Company of Jesus: Characters in Mark's Gospel*. Louisville: Westminster John Knox, 2000.

———. *Narrative Space and Mythic Meaning in Mark*. San Francisco: Harper & Row, 1986.

Marcus, Joel. *The Mystery of the Kingdom of God*. SBLDS 90. Atlanta: Scholars Press, 1986.

———. "Son of Man as Son of Adam." *RB* 110 (2003): 38–61.

———. "Son of Man as Son of Adam, Part II: Exegesis." *RB* 110 (2003): 370–86.

———. *The Way of the Lord: Christological Exegesis of the Old Testament in the Gospel of Mark*. Louisville: Westminster John Knox, 1992.

Marshall, C. D. *Faith as a Theme in Mark's Narrative*. SNTSMS 64. Cambridge: Cambridge University Press, 1989.

Marshall, I. H. "Son of God or Servant of Yahweh? A Reconsideration of Mark 1:11." *NTS* 15 (1968–1969): 326–36.

Martin, Ralph P. *Mark: Evangelist and Theologian*. Grand Rapids: Zondervan, 1973.

Marxsen, Willi. *Mark the Evangelist: Studies in the Redaction History of the Gospel*. Translated by James Boyce. Nashville: Abingdon, 1969.

Matera, Frank J. "The Incomprehension of the Disciples and Peter's Confession (Mark 6,14–8,30)." *Bib* 70 (1989): 153–72.

———. *The Kingship of Jesus: Composition and Theology in Mark 15*. SBLDS 66. Chico, CA: Scholars Press, 1982.

———. *What Are They Saying about Mark?* New York: Paulist Press, 1987.

Mauser, Ulrich W. *Christ in the Wilderness: The Wilderness Theme in the Second Gospel and Its Basis in the Biblical Tradition*. SBT. London: SCM, 1963.

McLaughlin, J. L. "Their Hearts Were Hardened: The Use of Isaiah 6:9–10 in the Book of Isaiah." *Bib* 75 (1994): 1–25.

Miller, Susan. *Women in Mark's Gospel*. New York: T&T Clark, 2004.

Moloney, Francis J. *Mark: Storyteller, Interpreter, Evangelist*. Peabody, MA: Hendrickson, 2004.

Moule, C. F. D. "Mark 4:1–20 Yet Once More." In *Neotestamentica et Semitica: Studies in Honour of Matthew Black*, edited by E. Ellis and M. Wilcox, 95–113. Edinburgh: T&T Clark, 1969.

Myers, C. *Binding the Strong Man: A Political Reading of Mark's Story of Jesus.* Maryknoll, NY: Orbis Books, 1988.

Neirynck, F. *Duality in Mark: Contributions to the Study of Markan Redaction.* Rev. ed. BETL 31. Leuven: Leuven University Press, 1988.

Neyrey, Jerome H. "The Idea of Purity in Mark's Gospel." *Semeia* 35 (1986): 91–128.

———. "Questions, *Chreiai,* and Challenges to Honor: The Interface of Rhetoric and Culture in Mark's Gospel," *CBQ* 60, no. 4 (1998): 657–81.

Peterson, Dwight N. *The Origins of Mark: The Markan Community in Current Debate.* Leiden: Brill, 2000.

Phelan, J. E., Jr. "The Function of Mark's Miracles." *Covenant Quarterly* 48 (1990): 3–14.

Pimental, P. "The 'Unclean Spirits' of St. Mark's Gospel." *ExpTim* 99 (1988): 173–75.

Pryke, E. J. *Redactional Style in the Markan Gospel.* SNTSMS 33. Cambridge: Cambridge University Press, 1978.

Räisänen, H. *The "Messianic Secret" in Mark.* Translated by C. Tuckett. Studies of the New Testament and Its World. Edinburgh: T&T Clark, 1990.

Rhoads, D. *Reading Mark: Engaging the Gospel.* Minneapolis: Fortress, 2004.

Rhoads, D., J. Dewey, and D. Michie, *Mark as Story: An Introduction to the Narrative of a Gospel.* 3rd ed. Minneapolis: Fortress, 2012.

Riches, John K. *Conflicting Mythologies: Identity Formation in the Gospels of Mark and Matthew.* Edinburgh: T&T Clark, 2000.

Robbins, Vernon K. *Jesus the Teacher: A Socio-Rhetorical Interpretation of Mark.* Philadelphia: Fortress, 1984.

Roskam, H. N. *The Purpose of the Gospel of Mark in Its Historical and Social Context.* Leiden: Brill, 2004.

Rowe, R. D. *God's Kingdom and God's Son: The Background to Mark's Christology from Concepts of Kingship in the Psalms.* AGJU 50. Leiden: Brill, 2002.

Rudolph, D. J. "Jesus and the Food Laws: A Reassessment of Mark 7:19b." *Evangelical Quarterly* 74 (2002): 291–311.

Sabin, Marie Noon. *Reopening the Word: Reading Mark as Theology in the Context of Early Judaism.* New York: Oxford University Press, 2002.

Schildgen, Brenda D. *Power and Prejudice: The Reception of the Gospel of Mark.* Detroit: Wayne State University Press, 1999.

Schneck, R. *Isaiah in the Gospel of Mark, I–VIII.* BIBAL Dissertation Series 1. Vallejo, CA: BIBAL, 1994.

Shiner, Whitney Taylor. *Follow Me! Disciples in Markan Rhetoric.* SBLDS 145. Atlanta: Scholars Press, 1995.

———. *Proclaiming the Gospel: First-Century Performance of Mark.* Harrisburg, PA: Trinity Press International, 2003.

Shively, Elizabeth E. *Apocalyptic Imagination in the Gospel of Mark: The Literary and Theological Role of Mark 3:22–30.* BZNW 189. Berlin: de Gruyter, 2012.

Smith, S. H. *A Lion with Wings: A Narrative-Critical Approach to Mark's Gospel.* Sheffield: Sheffield Academic, 1996.

Stevens, B. A. "Divine Warrior in Mark." *Biblische Zeitschrift* 31 (1987): 101–9.

Stock, Augustine. *The Method and Message of Mark.* Wilmington, DE: Michael Glazier, 1989.

Strickland, Michael, and David M. Young. *The Rhetoric of Jesus in the Gospel of Mark.* Minneapolis: Fortress, 2017.

Sweat, Laura C. *The Theological Role of Paradox in the Gospel of Mark.* LNTS. London: Bloomsbury T&T Clark, 2013.

Tannehill, Robert C. "The Disciples in Mark: The Function of a Narrative Role." *Journal of Religion* 57 (1977): 386–405. Reprinted in *The Interpretation of Mark*, edited by W. R. Telford, 134–57. 2nd ed. Edinburgh: T&T Clark, 1995.

Taylor, Vincent. *The Formation of the Gospel Tradition.* London: Macmillan, 1935.

Telford, William R. *The Barren Temple and the Withered Tree: A Redaction-Critical Analysis of the Cursing of the Fig-Tree Pericope in Mark's Gospel and Its Relation to the Cleansing of the Temple Tradition.* JSNTSup 1. Sheffield: JSOT Press, 1980.

———, ed. *The Interpretation of Mark.* London: SPCK; Philadelphia: Fortress, 1985.

———. *The Theology of the Gospel of Mark.* New Testament Theology. Cambridge: Cambridge University Press, 1999.

———. *Writing on the Gospel of Mark.* Dorsett, UK: Deo, 2009.

Tolbert, Mary A. *Sowing the Gospel: Mark's World in Literary-Historical Perspective.* Minneapolis: Fortress, 1989.

Tuckett, C. M., ed. *The Messianic Secret.* Philadelphia: Fortress, 1983.

Upton, Bridget Gilfillan. *Hearing Mark's Endings: Listening to Ancient Popular Texts through Speech Act Theory.* Leiden: Brill, 2006.

van Iersel, B. M. F. "A Dissident of Stature: The Jesus of Mark 3.20–35." *Concilium* 2 (1999): 65–72.

———. *Reading Mark.* Collegeville, MN: Liturgical Press, 1988.

Watts, Rikki E. *Isaiah's New Exodus in Mark.* Grand Rapids: Baker Academic, 2000.

———. "Mark." In *Commentary on the New Testament Use of the Old Testament*, edited by G. K. Beale and D. A. Carson, 111–250. Grand Rapids: Baker Academic, 2007.

Weeden, T. J. *Mark: Traditions in Conflict.* Philadelphia: Fortress, 1971.

Williams, Joel F. *Other Followers of Jesus: Minor Characters as Major Figures in Mark's Gospel.* Sheffield: JSOT Press, 1994.

Winn, Adam. *The Purpose of Mark's Gospel: An Early Christian Response to Roman Imperial Propaganda.* WUNT 2/245. Tübingen: Mohr Siebeck, 2008.

———. "Resisting Honor: The Markan Secrecy Motif and Roman Political Ideology." *JBL* 133, no. 3 (2014): 583–601.

———. "Tyrant or Servant? Roman Political Ideology and Mark 10.42–45." *JSNT* 36, no. 4 (2014): 325–52.

Wrede, William. *The Messianic Secret.* Translated by J. C. G. Greig. Cambridge, MA: J. Clarke, 1971.

CHAPTER THREE

The Gospel of Luke

Introduction

Authorship and Date

The Gospel of Luke and the book of Acts are a single literary project. The first volume, the Third Gospel, details the ancestry, birth, life, death, and resurrection of Jesus. The second volume, Acts, describes how the apostles and early church proclaim the finished work of Christ. At the beginning of the first volume, angels announce the birth of a king in Bethlehem (Luke 2:8–16), and at the end of the second volume, the apostle Paul proclaims the "kingdom of God" in Rome (Acts 28:31). What begins in a little town in Judea in Luke will blossom to the "ends of the earth" in Acts (1:8).

The Third Gospel and Acts, because they are a single work, share the same author. The early church was convinced that a gentile bearing the name "Luke" authored both (e.g., Irenaeus, *Haer.* 1.23.1, 1.27.2; Clement of Alexandria, *Paed.* 2.1). While Luke was not one of the twelve disciples, he interviewed eyewitnesses and carefully documented their experiences (Luke 1:1–3). Within the book of Acts, commentators often note "we passages," several first-person-plural accounts that appear to be written by someone who traveled with Paul and witnessed his ministry (Acts 16:10–17; 20:5–15; 21:1–18; 27:1–28:16). Luke crops up in Paul's writings on a handful of occasions alongside Mark (Col. 4:10, 14; 2 Tim. 4:11; Philem. 24). If Luke and Mark were good friends, spending considerable time together and ministering with each other, then Luke may have gleaned information about Jesus's ministry from Mark (who gathered his from Peter).

Dating the Gospel of Luke often rests on three pillars: the dating of Mark's Gospel, the prophecy of the fall of Jerusalem (Luke 21:5–36), and the events recorded at the end of Acts (Acts 28:17–31). Luke likely depends on the Gospel of Mark, a Gospel probably published in the late 50s/early 60s. In Luke 21, Jesus prophesies Jerusalem's ruin at the hand of the Romans, events that occurred in AD 70. While many contemporary scholars deny Jesus's ability to predict the future, the entire thrust of the Olivet Discourse in all three Synoptics rests upon his power to do so. Luke presents Jesus as the one who ascends to the Father's right hand, where he presently rules over the cosmos. If he can rule over every inch of the cosmos, then he certainly has the ability to predict what will transpire. Finally, at the end of Acts, Luke records Paul's Roman imprisonment that ended in AD 62. The window of time for Luke to publish his Gospel, then, is from AD 62 to AD 70, making a date in the mid to late 60s most favorable.

Purpose

According to Luke 1:4, the evangelist writes his Gospel so that his largely gentile audience "may know the certainty of the things" they "have been taught" (1:4). What have they been taught? Jesus is Israel's Spirit-anointed king, who conquered Satan and his demons, died on the cross, rose to new life, and ascended to the Father's heavenly throne. He offers forgiveness of sin and life in the new creation to those who trust in him. Every believer, regardless of race or ethnicity or social standing, participates in restored true Israel, the end-time people of God. Matthew emphasizes the *growth* of the kingdom, Mark highlights the *preparation* and *arrival* of the kingdom, and Luke underscores its *scope*—vertical and horizontal dimensions. The kingdom topples rulers, physical and spiritual (vertical), and welcomes those from all walks of life (horizontal).

Outline

Following Mark, Luke outlines his material geographically. Jesus is born in the small town of Bethlehem in Judea and then baptized in the Jordan by John the Baptist. After his temptation in the wilderness of Judea, he heads north and ministers in the villages and towns of Galilee. The journey from Galilee to Jerusalem comprises about a third of Luke's Gospel (9:51–19:44). His ministry climaxes in Jerusalem, where he is condemned, crucified, and raised from the dead. Luke's account ends with the Son of Man ascending to the Father, the Ancient of Days, to govern every molecule of the universe.

The Promises of Deliverance (1:1-80)

The Prologue: The Purpose of Luke's Gospel (1:1–4)

Luke's Gospel opens with a purpose statement: "I too decided to write an orderly account . . . so that you [Theophilus] may know the certainty of the things you have been taught" (1:3b–4; cf. Josephus, *Ag. Ap.* 1.1–3, 2.1–2). We know next to nothing about "most excellent Theophilus." He very well could be the patron or financial backer of the production of Luke's Gospel, as writing in the ancient world was costly. The expression "most excellent" could indicate that he's a prominent official (see Acts 23:26; 24:3; 26:25). Though Luke mentions only one individual in 1:1–4, a wider audience is certainly in view. Luke's emphasis on the incorporation of gentiles into the covenant community suggests that Luke's audience is largely gentile Christians.

The "things" that Theophilus learned according to 1:1 likely refer to the other literary accounts of Jesus's life (the Gospel of Mark?), and the description that these things "have been fulfilled" stresses the fulfillment of Israel's Scriptures. Putting it all together, Theophilus appears to have learned about the broad contours of the life of Jesus, his death, and his resurrection, so Luke writes his Gospel to affirm the truthfulness of these events that *fulfill* OT expectations and that have been communicated by apostolic eyewitnesses (see Acts 1:3, 21–22). It may not be a stretch, then, to conclude that a key component of all four Gospels is to give confidence to God's people, to Christians, that Jesus's ministry is indeed true and that he is precisely who he claims to be.

The Angelic Prediction of the Births of John and Jesus (1:5–38)

Matthew narrates Jesus's birth through Joseph's perspective, whereas Luke recounts the birth through the eyes of Zechariah, Elizabeth, and Mary. Luke's narrative begins with two angelic visitations. Running through chapters 1–2 is a comparison between John and Jesus. While John is great, Jesus is greater. Note some of the more apparent differences:

John	Jesus
Elizabeth is barren and old (1:7)	Mary is young and a virgin (1:34)
Zechariah is slow to believe Gabriel's prediction (1:20)	Mary immediately believes Gabriel's prediction (1:38)
John is of priestly descent and identifies with Elijah (1:5, 17)	Jesus is of royal descent and identifies with David (1:27)
John is a "prophet of the Most High" (1:76)	Jesus is the "Son of the Most High" (1:32)
John prepares Israel for Jesus's arrival (1:17b, 76-79)	Jesus is God in the flesh (1:31-32)

Luke first focuses on John the Baptist, who will "go on before the Lord . . . to turn the hearts of the parents to their children and the disobedient to the wisdom of the righteous—to make ready a people prepared for the Lord" (1:17). His life will be especially devoted to the Lord, and he will refrain from drinking wine (1:15; see Num. 6:3; cf. Luke 5:37–38; 7:33). Luke, like Matthew and Mark, draws a line from Malachi's "messenger" figure to John the Baptist. Malachi prophesies that in the latter days the "messenger" will prepare rebellious Israel for the arrival of the Lord. Israel is in a state of unbelief and rebellion, so the messenger is tasked with summoning Israel to repentance (Mal. 3:1–2; 4:5–6). The Lord's arrival is at hand, and Israel must be ready.

Following the angelic announcement concerning John, the angel Gabriel visits Mary and promises that, though a virgin, she will bear a son (1:26–38; →Matt. 1:22–23). Although the Third Evangelist underscores the person of John in the story of Israel's redemption (1:13–17; 1:67–80), he reserves his highest praise for Jesus. Luke heaps several key descriptions on top of one another that find their point of origin in the OT: "Jesus" (lit. "Joshua" [1:31]), "Son of the Most High" (1:32), "holy one" (1:35), and "Son of God" (1:35). As Joshua, he will save his people from the plight of sin (→Matt. 1:21–22). Each title addresses a unique aspect of Jesus's identity and mission, especially his identity as the divine Son of God and true Israel. In 1:32–33 Gabriel announces a principal characteristic of Jesus's mission: "The Lord God will give him the throne of his father David, and he will reign over Jacob's descendants forever; his kingdom will never end." In fulfillment of OT texts such as 2 Samuel 7:12, Isaiah 9:6, and Daniel 7:13–14, Jesus's ministry will entail the establishment of God's eternal kingdom.

The Songs of Mary and Zechariah and the Birth of John (1:39–80)

One of Luke's unique contributions in faithfully retelling the life of Jesus is the inclusion of several hymns in the first two chapters (1:46–55; 1:68–79; 2:14; 2:29–32). Within each song are conspicuous themes that resound throughout the Third Gospel. We encounter the first hymn when Mary visits her "relative" Elizabeth in the "hill country of Judea" (1:36, 39, 65). Whereas Joseph is from Nazareth in Galilee (1:26), Zechariah and Elizabeth live in Judea. When Mary enters Elizabeth's house, Luke narrates that "the baby [John] leaped in her womb" (1:41). Later, Elizabeth recounts, "The baby in my womb leaped *for joy*" (1:44). John the Baptist's joyous reaction, even within the womb, flows from the hope that the new age will, at the very end of history, dawn with the Messiah's coming. That day has come, so joy is the only fitting response (see Isa. 49:13; 51:11; 60:15; 61:10–11; 65:18–19; Luke 1:14, 58; 10:17, 21; 15:5; 19:37; 24:41, 52).

The exchange between Mary and Elizabeth is also remarkable in that Elizabeth calls Jesus "my Lord" (*kyriou mou*; 1:43). The term "Lord" (*kyrios*) has occurred ten times in the narrative so far, and each occurrence refers to Israel's God (e.g., 1:6, 16, 32). In Elizabeth's confession that Jesus is her "Lord," Luke thoughtfully identifies Jesus as Israel's Lord incarnate. Verse 45 confirms this observation when Elizabeth declares, "Blessed is she [Mary] who has believed that the *Lord* [*kyrios*] would fulfill his promises to her" (cf. 1:38). This line prompts Mary's well-known response in the following section (1:46–55).

The first song (1:46–55), often referred to as the Magnificat, extols God for the incarnation. The hymn is largely reminiscent of Hannah's prayer in response to the birth of Samuel (1 Sam. 2:1–10). Many points of contact exist between the songs of Hannah and Mary, but one of the more prominent ones is their insistence that God exalts the poor and humble yet overthrows the rich and the proud (1 Sam. 2:4–5, 7–8; Luke 1:51–53). Mary is "blessed" *because* God recognizes her "humble state" (1:48) and accomplishes "great things" for her (1:49). Further, we should consider the larger context of Hannah's prayer and the overall thrust of 1–2 Samuel. The prophet Samuel is instrumental in establishing the Davidic dynasty (e.g., 1 Sam. 16:1–13). While David is certainly a remarkable king in many ways, his reign is marked by internal strife and personal and administrative failings. In the end, David is not Israel's solution to defeating God's enemies and overcoming wickedness—that is reserved for one of his descendants (2 Sam. 7). Mary's song, therefore, is the ultimate realization of Hannah's requests. Jesus, the true heir of David, will finally secure the throne and vanquish evil.

Mark's Gospel highlights the *preparation* for and mysterious *nature* of the kingdom, whereas Matthew underscores the *growth* of the heavenly kingdom on earth. Luke retraces much of the same themes but displays unique *vertical* and *horizontal* concerns. The Third Gospel (and Acts) can be summarized in two key verses, both of which occur in the birth narrative:

> He [God] has brought down rulers from their thrones
> but has lifted up the humble. (1:52)

> [Jesus will be] a light for revelation to the Gentiles,
> and the glory of your people Israel. (2:32)

The person of Jesus, through his faithfulness, defeats all forms of "powers," especially the devil and his cohorts. This explains why Luke often mentions the toppling of Satan's power and influence, mediated through his demons (e.g., 4:1–13, 33, 41; 8:2, 27, 29; 9:1; 10:17; 13:32). The defeat of these authorities kicks the door wide open for those whom the devil has long held captive—the marginalized and the gentiles.

John's birth is yet another reason for rejoicing (1:58), and though the baby was to be named Zechariah (1:59), Elizabeth and Zechariah heed the angel's command and name him John (1:61, 63). The song of Zechariah (1:68–79), the Benedictus, is a wonderful illustration of restoration among God's people. It answers the question posed by Zechariah and Elizabeth's friends and family in 1:66: "What then is this child going to be?" Some nine months prior,

Zechariah doubts Gabriel's message, so the angel strikes him mute. Now, though, Zechariah cannot help but extol God's marvelous work of redemption. Gabriel's promise of deliverance has come to pass! The song splits into two halves: the first half details the significance of the coming Messiah's rule (1:68–75), whereas the second half focuses on John and the Messiah (1:76–79). The last few lines of the song state the result of their ministry:

> . . . the *rising sun* will come to us from heaven
>   to *shine* on those living in darkness
>   and in the shadow of death,
>   to guide our feet into the path of peace. (1:78–79)

The wording here likely reflects Isaiah 60 and the end-time restoration of Israel, the nations, and God's heavenly descent in new creation: "Arise, *shine, for your light has come*, and the glory of the LORD rises upon you. . . . Nations will come *to your light*. . . . *The sun* will no more be *your light* by day, nor will the brightness of the moon *shine on you*, for the LORD will be your everlasting *light*, and your God will be your glory" (Isa. 60:1, 3, 19; cf. LXX: Jer. 23:5; Zech. 3:8; 6:12). Zechariah has good reason to sing of God's redemption, for the promise of Isaiah 60 will soon come to pass. The final verse of chapter 1 reveals that John becomes "strong in spirit" and remains in the Judean wilderness until his public ministry (cf. 2:40). We could even translate this expression as "strong in the Spirit," a reference to the Spirit's work in John's life. Even before Jesus arrives on the scene, the Spirit is preparing for his arrival.

The Arrival of the King (2:1–52)

The Birth of Jesus (2:1–21)

Luke famously time-stamps Jesus's birth: "In those days Caesar Augustus issued a decree that a census should be taken of the entire Roman world. (This was the *first* [*prōtē*] census that took place while Quirinius was governor of Syria.)" (2:1–2; cf. 1:5). We are presented with a thorny historical issue because Quirinius ruled Judea from AD 6 to 7, ten or so years later than the birth of Jesus. There are a few ways to resolve the tension, and one of the most attractive ones is to render the phrase "This census was *before* [*prōtē*] Quirinius governed" (cf. John 1:15, 30).[1] However we resolve the issue, why mention Rome's census? It demonstrates Israel's subjugation under Rome.

---

1. David E. Garland, *Luke*, ZECNT (Grand Rapids: Zondervan, 2011), 117–18.

Notice also how Luke opens chapter 2: "In those days *Caesar Augustus*." The point is that Jesus, while he is the long-awaited Messiah (1:27, 32–33, 69), is born *under* Rome's authority, *under* Caesar Augustus.

Joseph, while from Nazareth, heads south to Bethlehem to "register" (2:5). He may have owned land there, but we cannot be sure. What is important is the redemptive-historical connection between Joseph and Bethlehem, a town with strong Davidic roots (Mic. 5:2, 4; →Matt. 2:5–6). While in Bethlehem, Mary gave birth to Jesus, wrapping "him in cloths" and placing "him in a manger, because there was no *guest room* [*katalymati*] available for them" (2:7). Contrary to popular belief, Jesus was most likely born in a house (NIV [2011], NLT), not an inn (NASB, NRSV, NIV 1984, KJV). The word for "guest room" (*katalyma*) occurs later in Luke's narrative as a reference to the place where Jesus and the disciples will celebrate Passover (22:11 // Mark 14:14). Apparently, the guest room is unavailable at a (relative's?) house in Bethlehem, so Mary and Joseph are forced to share space with animals. In contrast to Caesar's spectacular wealth and palatial accommodations, Jesus is born in the humblest of circumstances. Remember, God promises to bring down "rulers from their thrones" but lift up "the humble" (1:52).

Not far from the guest room, an "angel of the Lord" appears to shepherds and announces the birth of Jesus, "the Messiah, the Lord" (2:11). The angel clearly identifies Jesus as Israel's King and God (see 1:42–45). Further, since the angel is identified as an "angel *of the Lord*," does not the angel ultimately serve Jesus, its "Lord"? More angels arrive on the scene and praise God in what is the third hymn (Gloria in Excelsis): "Glory to God in the highest of heaven, and on earth peace to those on whom his favor rests" (2:14). In contrast to Rome's promise of peace throughout the empire, the *pax Romana* (2:1), true peace is only found in Jesus—a peace that extends beyond the empire to the farthest corners of the cosmos. The shepherds were ecstatic at the news, and once they saw the birth of Jesus for themselves (2:16), they "spread the word concerning what had been told them about this child" (2:17). In what will become a major point of emphasis in Luke-Acts, this is the first explicit reference to the proclamation of the good news.

Matthew's narrative highlights the arrival of the magi to visit baby Jesus (Matt. 2:1–12), whereas shepherds are prominent in Luke. Why shepherds? This connection may bring Jesus's identity as the long-awaited Davidic heir to the forefront. Recall that David was a shepherd from Bethlehem (1 Sam. 17:15; 2 Sam. 5:2; Ps. 78:70–72), and shepherding is often associated with the Messiah in the OT (e.g., Ezek. 34:23). Both Jesus and David have inauspicious beginnings, minister during great political oppression, liberate Israel from that oppression, and, finally, experience a great deal of suffering.

Before we discuss the remainder of chapter 2, let us pause and consider Luke's presentation of angels thus far. The "angel of the Lord" (1:11), later identified as the angel Gabriel, appears to Zechariah and Mary (1:11–20; 1:26–38), and then an "angel of the Lord," presumably Gabriel again, visits the shepherds in the field (2:9–12). Finally, a "great company of the heavenly host" surrounds the shepherds (2:13–14). The angel Gabriel appears in Daniel 8:16 and 9:21, where he interprets Daniel's vision. The angel in Daniel 10, while not explicitly identified, is most likely Gabriel.[2] This is important because the angel in Daniel 10 takes on a military role as the "prince of the Persian kingdom," or an evil angel, resists him; the archangel Michael then comes to Gabriel's aid (Dan. 10:13). The War Scroll at Qumran describes how the names Michael and Gabriel are written on some of the shields to be used in the final eschatological battle (1QM IX.14–18; cf. 4Q529 1, 2–4).[3] The military dimension to Gabriel's role fits well here in Luke's Gospel, where he informs Mary that Jesus will be the "Son of the Most High" who will inherit an everlasting kingdom (1:32–33). Luke's graphic description of the "great company of the heavenly host" is undoubtedly military in nature (2:13; see LXX: 1 Kings 22:19; 2 Chron. 33:3; Neh. 9:6).

Putting all the pieces together, we see that the first few chapters of Luke's narrative present the angels as mighty warriors preparing for battle. Their mighty, divine king has arrived, and because they are convinced that he will win the battle, they announce his success well before he begins to fight. Whereas Matthew's Gospel highlights the convergence of heaven and earth in the person of Jesus—God's heavenly presence is now dwelling in the midst of humanity—Luke's Gospel underscores Jesus's victory over the entire cosmos. His victory subdues all invisible enemies. The effect of Jesus's cosmic victory is *peace* or reconciliation (Eph. 1:10, 20–23; Col. 1:20). At Jesus's birth the angels declare, "Glory to God in the highest of heaven, and *on earth peace* to those on whom his favor rests" (2:14). At the triumphal entry, the pilgrims exclaim, "Blessed is the king who comes in the name of the Lord! *Peace in heaven* and glory in the highest!" (19:38). Jesus's ministry, from beginning to end, is the pursuit of end-time cosmic peace.

Jesus's Presentation at the Temple (2:22–40)

The law stipulates that parents are to dedicate their firstborn sons and livestock (Exod. 13:2, 11–16). While the narrative does not explicitly mention

---

2. J. J. Collins, *Daniel*, Hermeneia (Minneapolis: Fortress, 1993), 373.

3. See J. J. Collins, "Gabriel," in *Dictionary of Deities and Demons in the Bible*, ed. Karel van der Toorn, Bob Becking, and Pieter W. van der Horst (Grand Rapids: Eerdmans, 1999), 338–39.

the dedication of the firstborn, we should assume that Joseph and Mary obeyed this important rite, for the firstborn was an incredibly important pillar of Israelite society, for they represented the entire family. When God pours out the final plague upon the firstborn of Egypt and Israel (Exod. 12:12–13), he claims a legal right to the firstborn. "Every person and animal that was divinely saved from death now belongs to YHWH in a special way."[4] When a firstborn is "devoted" or set apart to the Lord, it is as though the entire family unit is devoted. Even the Levites function as a corporate "firstborn," representing the whole nation (Num. 3:12; cf. Exod. 4:22). So when Joseph and Mary devote their "firstborn" to the Lord, they declare that Jesus is holy and set apart to God. As we will soon see, Luke's narrative casts Jesus not only as the firstborn of his family but as the firstborn of the children of God (cf. Heb. 2:11–13). He is the true Israel of God and the one identified with the Passover lamb (2:41; 22:14–22).

Soon after Jesus's birth, Joseph and Mary present him at the temple (2:22–24), where a "righteous" individual named Simeon warmly takes Jesus in his arms and utters the fourth and final hymn, the Nunc Dimittis (2:29–32). Luke describes the man as "waiting for the consolation of Israel" (2:25), an eschatological term that refers to Israel's restoration (cf. Isa. 40:1; 49:13; 61:2). At the end of the song, he declares that Jesus will be a "light for revelation to the Gentiles, and the glory of your people Israel" (2:32). Filled with the Spirit (2:25), Simeon alludes to a handful of passages in Isaiah where the "servant" will restore God's people and minister to Israel's neighbors. Isaiah 49:3–6 reads, "You are my servant, Israel. . . . It is too small a thing for you to be *my servant* to restore the tribes of Jacob and bring back those of Israel I have kept. I will also make you a *light for the Gentiles*, that my salvation may reach to the ends of the earth" (cf. Isa. 42:6). Isaiah understands the "servant," a single individual, as "Israel," who will trigger the restoration of an Israelite remnant and usher gentiles into the covenant community. In weaving Isaiah 49 into his pronouncement, Simon anticipates that Jesus will fulfill these promises of restoration by saving the remnant of Israelites. But salvation is not only reserved for a remnant of ethnic Jews; it extends to the nations. Simeon's predictions echo throughout Luke-Acts, as he presents Jesus as true Israel who heralds salvation to Israel and the gentiles (e.g., Luke 3:6; Acts 1:8; 9:15; 13:7).

The narrative continues with the introduction of another character, Anna. She is described as a "prophet" who spent most of her life as a widow (2:36–37). Upon meeting Jesus and his parents, she immediately speaks about Jesus

---

4. Desmond Alexander, *Exodus*, AOTC (Downers Grove, IL: InterVarsity, 2017), 253.

"to all who were looking forward to the redemption of Jerusalem" (2:38). Like Simeon, who anticipates the "consolation of Israel," this group eagerly awaits the end-time kingdom and the Messiah's reign. What is common to Simeon and Anna is that they both view baby Jesus as the catalyst for the latter-day restoration of God's people. What should not be missed at this point in the narrative is the sheer amount of revelation that has accompanied Jesus's birth. God has spoken a great deal *to* and *through* quite a diverse crowd: an angel to Zechariah (1:11–20), an angel to Mary (1:28–38), Mary to Elizabeth (1:46–55), Zechariah to his relatives (1:67–79), angel(s) to shepherds (2:9–14), Simeon to Joseph and Mary (2:29–32), and Anna to those gathered in the temple (2:38). It has been some four hundred years since God has spoken, but Luke 1–2 breaks the silence with a flurry of revelation.

Jesus as a Boy in the Temple (2:41–52)

Paralleling John growing and becoming strong (1:80), Jesus also "grew and became strong" (2:40). A double helix, the lives of these two individuals are intertwined. Jesus, the Lord incarnate, becomes a human being, and Luke highlights his humanity throughout his narrative. In this vein, Luke is the only evangelist to mention an event between Jesus's birth and his public ministry (2:41–52). The event takes place in Jerusalem when Jesus, a twelve-year-old, celebrates the Passover with his family (2:42; cf. Exod. 12:24–27; 23:15; Deut. 16:1–6). The Passover gains prominence here in the narrative as it anticipates the final Passover at the end of passion week, a Passover that will inaugurate the second and final exodus of God's people (cf. 3:4–6, quoting Isa. 40:3–5; 4:18–19, quoting Isa. 61:1–2).

Joseph and Mary, unaware that Jesus stays behind in Jerusalem, trek north toward Nazareth (2:43–44). Once they realize Jesus is missing from their caravan, they venture back to Jerusalem and discover Jesus in the temple "sitting among the teachers, listening to them and asking them questions" (2:46). Oh, to be a fly on the wall of Solomon's colonnade! While we are in the dark as to what precisely they discuss, we can be confident that it had to do with the OT at some level. The passage focuses not on the content of Jesus's message but on its effect: "Everyone who heard him was amazed at his understanding and his answers" (2:47). Jesus, as far as we know, was not formally trained. He learned a great deal of Israel's Scriptures from his parents and local synagogue (see 4:14–30). But what we have here is completely unheard of. Jesus, as a twelve-year-old boy, confounds Israel's elite scholars. No wonder Luke frames this event with Jesus being "filled with wisdom" (2:40) and growing "in wisdom" (2:51). He is all-wise with respect to his divinity, and he grows in wisdom with respect to his humanity. He is fully God and fully human.

We should note Jesus's reaction to his parents: "Didn't you know I had to be in my Father's house?" (2:49). While Joseph is his earthly "father" (2:48), Jesus claims to be in his "Father's house," evincing his submissive role to the Father even as a boy. The word "house," though not found in Greek, is probably implied (see NIV, HCSB, NASB, ESV, NLT, NRSV). The temple has been the focus of three significant events up to this point: the narrative opens with Zechariah ministering in the Holy Place (1:5–22), then Joseph and Mary dedicate Jesus at the temple (2:22–40), and finally Jesus interacts with Israel's teachers in the temple (2:46–47). As the narrative unfolds, we will discover that the temple will become a centerpiece of Jesus's ministry, as it is here.

The account ends with Luke reminding the reader of Jesus's obedience to his parents: "He [Jesus] went down to Nazareth with them and *was obedient* [*hypotassomenos*] to them" (2:51). Only found three times in Luke, this term occurs elsewhere in 10:17 and 10:20, both references to demons submitting to Jesus's reign (cf. Ps. 8:7 LXX; 1 Cor. 15:27–28; Eph. 1:22; Heb. 2:8). Perhaps Luke wants his readers to bring both passages together. For Jesus to gain the victory over the demonic realm, resulting in their "submission" to him, he must willfully "submit" to and obey his Father and his parents. In a word, he must *earn* the right to rule over the demons.

The Baptism of John; Jesus as the Last Adam (3:1–38)

John the Baptist and Jesus's Baptism (3:1–22)

Chapter 3 begins with another time stamp: "In the fifteenth year of the reign of Tiberius Caesar" (3:1). Tiberius, the stepson of Augustus (see 2:1), ruled from AD 14 to 37, and Luke appears to be starting the clock when Tiberius begins his coregency with his stepfather Augustus in AD 11/12. Therefore, the year is most likely AD 26/27, when Jesus is in his early thirties (3:23). The death of Herod the Great (4 BC) brought about a shift in how Rome ruled Palestine. The territory was split into four parts, and each son ruled over a particular region. Herod Antipas ruled over Galilee from 4 BC to AD 39. Another son, Archelaus, ruled over Judea, Samaria, and Idumea; but he was particularly inept, so Rome deposed him (AD 6) and established his territory as a province. This enabled Rome to govern Israel more directly through prefects, the most famous of whom is Pontius Pilate (AD 26–36).

The last we heard of John the Baptist was at the end of chapter 1, when we learned that he "lived in the wilderness until he appeared publicly to Israel"

(1:80). Well, this is his public appearance (→Mark 1:1–8). John paves the way for Yahweh's coming to restore and judge (// Matt. 3:1–12 // Mark 1:1–8). As the bridge between the old age and the new age, John must prepare Israel for the inauguration of the latter days. Those who repent and identify with John's baptism will participate in the new covenant community—that is, true Israel—but those who refuse will bear God's end-time wrath.

Luke's quotation of Isaiah 40:3–5 differs from Mark and Matthew in that he cites two additional verses from Isaiah, so the inclusion of Isaiah 40:5 is noteworthy: "And *all people* will see God's salvation" (3:6). The emphasis is clear: Jesus, who has already been identified as "salvation" (1:71, 77; 2:11, 30), is the object of the hope of all nations. The deliverance of the nations is a significant part of Isaiah's message. The Lord will raise up faithful "servant(s)" who will forge a remnant within the nation of Israel. The remnant of ethnic Israel will, in turn, escort the surrounding nations to Jerusalem, where all humanity will experience God's end-time presence (Isa. 2:1–5; 49:6; 66:18–24). Luke has already identified Jesus as Yahweh's pristine "servant" (2:32) and as Yahweh himself (1:42–45; 2:11). So Luke wants his readers to understand that Isaiah's prophecies will be inaugurated in the ministries of John and Jesus. The time has come for Israel's God to visit his people and establish a new covenant community based upon the faithfulness of Jesus. Jesus is both the God who visits and the God who serves.

John commands the emerging "crowds" to turn from their sins and not rest upon their status as physical heirs of Abraham. Becoming a child of God and gaining admittance into eschatological Israel do not depend upon one's lineage but upon the condition of the heart (3:7–11 // Matt. 3:7–10). Luke uniquely includes two contemptable parties, tax collectors and soldiers, who inquire about how they should respond to John's message (3:12, 14). In both cases, John commands them to be just in their dealings with others. The thrust of John's message is that righteous behavior toward one another is an expression of a right relationship with God. By including these two groups, Luke continues to draw attention to individuals who were traditionally pariahs in Palestine but who now receive prominence in end-time Israel (cf. 5:27–30; 7:8; 29, 34; 15:1; 18:10–13). Note that John does not tell the two groups to convert, taking on the physical markers of Israel (food laws, Sabbath, etc.), but to identify themselves with his renewal in the wilderness. Cleansing and purification mark John's baptism, whereas the coming Spirit and the new creation mark Jesus's baptism (3:15–18; →Mark 1:4–8). John prepares the new covenant community for God's glorious presence.

Jesus's baptism by John officially marks the beginning of Jesus's earthly ministry. God declares him to be his "Son," the object of his favor, and the long-awaited ruler of Israel (3:22; cf. 2 Sam. 7:14; Ps. 2:7). The Spirit descending "in bodily form like a dove" recalls several OT passages that herald the new creation (e.g., Gen. 8:8–12; Isa. 32:15–16; Ezek. 36:26–30). The appearance of the dove (3:22) and Jesus's identification as a son of Adam (3:38) demonstrate that much of Jesus's ministry will entail the dawn of a renewed cosmos (→Matt. 3:13–17).

The Genealogy (3:23–38)

Luke's genealogy differs from Matthew's in several ways, but two of them are pronounced: the genealogy follows Jesus's baptism (3:21–22) and traces Jesus's lineage all the way to Adam (3:38). Matthew begins his genealogy at the beginning of his Gospel, whereas Luke places the genealogy between Jesus's baptism (3:21–23) and wilderness temptation (4:1–13). Luke's genealogy informs, then, these twin events. Certainly, Jesus's august ancestry is an essential component of Luke's genealogy, with the inclusion of David (3:31), Jesse (3:32), and Judah (3:33). But the last string of names—including Shem, Noah, Enoch, Seth, and Adam—draws the readers' attention to Genesis 1–11, where the godly line of Adam and Eve is preserved. The entire genealogy ultimately testifies to God's commitment to keep the original promise of Genesis 3:15:

> And I will put enmity
>   between you [the serpent] and the woman [Eve],
>   and between your offspring and hers;
> he will crush your head,
>   and you will strike his heel.

According to Genesis 3:15, redemption is guaranteed. A godly king, in the pristine, perfected image of God, will vanquish the serpent, the embodiment of evil, at the very end of history. In Genesis 3:15 God promises that the divine commission of Genesis 1:28 will be accomplished. God will see to it that his glory will extend to the ends of the earth and that all of creation worships him.

■ Phase 1: Jesus in Galilee (4:1–9:50)

The Beginning of the Last Adam's Victory and Hometown Rejection (4:1–44)

The Wilderness Temptation (4:1–13)

The wilderness temptation, recorded in all three Synoptics (// Matt. 4:1–11 // Mark 1:12–13), follows Jesus's baptism in Matthew and Mark, whereas Luke includes this event after the genealogy. Why stitch together the temptation with Jesus's identity as the "son of Adam" (3:38)? Jesus is the second Adam, who has come to do what Adam, Noah, Abraham, and Israel failed to do—that is, perfectly trust God's promises, subdue evil, and ensure that God's glorious presence reaches the far corners of the earth. The time has come for the promise of Genesis 3:15 to be set in motion.

The devil appears to have tempted Jesus at the end of a forty-day fast in the wilderness, when Jesus is most vulnerable (4:2 // Matt. 4:2). The two prominent pieces of information—forty-day duration and wilderness location—recall Israel's own temptation in the wilderness. Numbers 14:34 states, for example, "For forty years—one year for each of the forty days you explored the land—you will suffer for your sins and know what it is like to have me against you" (cf. Ezek. 4:4–5). Israel's forty years of restlessness illustrates Israel's unbelief in God's promises. So Jesus's forty days of faithful endurance in the wilderness is a typological microcosm of Israel's experience. Their unfaithfulness anticipates a redeemer's faithfulness. Jesus, as true Israel, must retrace the steps of the nation. Perhaps we could peel away another redemptive-historical layer: the forty-day allotment of time and fasting also echoes Moses's forty-day stint on Sinai, when he fasts (Exod. 24:18; 34:28). If the connection exists, then Jesus's temptation is truly a turning point in Israel's career. He takes it upon himself to reconstitute the people of God, live on their behalf, and faithfully carry out the divine commission given to Adam and Eve in the garden (Gen. 1:28; 2:15).

God commands Adam and Eve to "be fruitful and increase in number; fill the earth and subdue it" (Gen. 1:28). A constitutive part of subduing the created order is eliminating all forms of opposition that stand against God and his people. Upon seeing the serpent enter the garden, the first couple should have immediately subdued and cast it out. Because they do not and subsequently succumb to the serpent's temptation, God casts out Adam and Eve from his presence (Gen. 3:24–25). But Genesis 3:15 promises that a coming redeemer will one day decisively subdue the serpent. While the OT contains a host of rulers defeating Israel's enemies (e.g., David, Solomon), not one fully vanquished them. Old Testament writers promised the arrival of the messiah who would ultimately fulfill Genesis 1:28 and 3:15 (e.g., Gen. 49:8–10; Num. 24:17; 2 Sam. 7:12–14; Pss. 2; 89; 110; Isa. 9:6–7; 11:1–5; Jer. 23:5). Here in the wilderness temptation, Jesus assumes the mantle of Adam and Israel and achieves what all his predecessors failed to accomplish: the defeat and banishment of *the* enemy of God and his people.

Matthew and Luke record the first temptation as the devil attempting to break Jesus's reliance upon his Father's provision: "If you are the Son of God, tell this stone to become bread" (4:3–4 // Matt. 4:3). Like the serpent tempting Adam and Eve to function independent of God and partake of the tree of the knowledge of good and evil (Gen. 3:1–5), the devil intends to upend Jesus's trust in his Father so that Jesus emerges independent of him. Jesus will have none of it, and he responds by citing Deuteronomy 8:

> [Israel,] Remember how the LORD your God led you all the way in the desert these forty years, to humble you and to test you in order to know what was in your heart, whether or not you would keep his commands. He humbled you, causing you to hunger and then feeding you with manna, which neither you nor your ancestors had known, to teach you that *man does not live on bread alone but on every word that comes from the mouth of the LORD.* (Deut. 8:2–3)

God requires Israel to trust him solely, for he and he alone provides for her needs, both spiritual and physical. The moment Israel attempts to become independent of God, she immediately falls into chaos (e.g., Num. 11:1–9). Jesus endures the same test that Adam and Eve and the nation of Israel experienced, but instead of seeking independence from the Father, he rests in his sovereign and gracious provision.

The second and third temptations are switched in Luke and Matthew (4:5–12 // Matt. 4:5–10). In the Third Gospel, the devil then takes Jesus to a "high place" where they could view "all the kingdoms of the world in a moment of time." We can't say for sure, but Jesus may have experienced the second and third temptations in the form of a vision (4:5–8; cf. Rev. 4:1; 17:3; 21:10). In any case, the devil claims to have "domain" over the kingdoms of the earth and vows to give the earthly kingdoms over to Jesus if Jesus worships him. The wording here in the second temptation closely resembles the LXX (OG) of Daniel 7:14:

Luke 4:6	Daniel 7:14
"*I will give* [*dōsō*] you all their *authority* [*tēn exousian*] and *splendor* [*tēn doxan*]"	"And royal *authority* [*exousia*] *was given* [*edothē*] to him, and all the nations of the earth according to posterity, and all *honor* [*doxa*] was serving him. And his *authority* [*exousia*] is an everlasting *authority* [*exousia*]" (NETS [OG])

The NT affirms that the devil is indeed given the right to rule over the earth (e.g., Job 1:6–12; 2:17; Rev. 12:7–12), and Jesus even claims that the devil is the "prince of this world" (John 12:31; 14:30). But as a result of Jesus's faithfulness in the temptation and on account of his death and resurrection, Satan begins to lose his grip of authority (e.g., Luke 10:17–20; John 12:31; Rev.

12:7–12). In some sense, then, Satan is right to claim that he has "authority" but is wrong to claim that he can "give it to anyone" he wishes (4:6), for God alone is sovereign over the cosmos. Further, the devil may be parodying the prophecy of Daniel 7, where the "son of man" is "given" "authority" and "honor" upon defeating the fourth beast. The devil has no right to bestow upon Jesus cosmic authority. Such bestowal is reserved only for the Ancient of Days (Dan. 7:9–10). But in resisting the wiles of the devil, Jesus initially fulfills the prophecy of Daniel 7 and commences his ascent to his Father, the Ancient of Days (see Matt. 28:18; Rev. 13:2). Jesus's ascent to the throne of the Ancient of Days begins here in the Judean wilderness.

In the second temptation, Jesus is enticed to accept a perpetual state of submission to and ruling alongside Satan. The devil desires worship, the same devotion that God deserves and requires. Jesus quotes the book of Deuteronomy once more: "*Fear the LORD your God, serve him only* and take your oaths in his name" (Deut. 6:13). Deuteronomy 6:13 insists that Israel maintain allegiance to God and to no one else, despite pressure from the surrounding nations. Unfortunately, Israel repeatedly succumbs to idolatry by worshiping other gods alongside the Lord. This results in the Lord judging the nation and casting them into exile. Jesus repeats the same test but refuses to give in to Satan's devices.

For the third and final temptation, the devil and Jesus journey to the "highest point of the temple" (4:9). It may be that the two physically traverse to the top of the Jerusalem temple, but we are most likely again encountering a vision. Satan solicits Jesus to leap from the temple's ledge, triggering God to send for his angels. For the third temptation, the devil supplements his assault by quoting Psalm 91:11–12: "For he will command his angels concerning you to guard you in all your ways; they will lift you up in their hands, so that you will not strike your foot against a stone." The devil desires to control God's provision by forcing him to protect the Son. At the core of this temptation is Satan's desire for Jesus to *manipulate* his Father—to force his hand against his will. Jesus responds by quoting Deuteronomy yet again: "Do not follow other gods, the gods of the peoples around you; for the LORD your God, who is among you, is a jealous God and his anger will burn against you, and he will destroy you from the face of the land. *Do not put the LORD your God to the test* as you did at Massah" (Deut. 6:14–16). The quotation from Deuteronomy 6:16 refers back to Exodus 17:1–7, where Israel demanded water from God. The nation should trust in God's gracious provision, being confident that God will nourish them. The devil desires Jesus to follow suit—to imitate his forefathers and demand that God deliver him from the fall from the precipice of the temple.

The devil's quotation of Psalm 91 is rife with irony, for the passage goes on to read, "You will tread on the lion and the cobra; you will trample the great lion and the serpent" (Ps. 91:13). Psalm 91 interprets Genesis 3:15: "And I will put enmity between you and the woman, and between your offspring and hers; *he will crush your head, and you will strike his heel.*" Here's the irony: Jesus in the wilderness temptation initially and decisively defeats the devil or crushes his head, thereby fulfilling the prophecies of Genesis 3:15 and Psalm 91:13! In the words of J. Christiaan Beker, "D-Day is over and the powers of evil have received a blow from which they can never recover."[5] The temptation ends on an ominous note: "When the devil had finished all this tempting, he left him until an opportune time" (4:13). Though Satan loses the cosmic battle and Jesus secures his defeat, Satan will continue to fight and inflict as much damage as possible through his emissaries (cf. 22:3, 53).

Jesus's Expulsion from Nazareth (4:14–30)

After he stakes claim to the cosmos, Jesus's public ministry begins in Galilee when he visits two synagogues (4:15, 33). Luke is the only evangelist to place Jesus's rejection at Nazareth at the beginning of Jesus's public ministry (// Matt. 13:53–58 // Mark 6:1–6). In doing so, Luke sets the tone for the remainder of Jesus's ministry. What happens in Nazareth serves as a template for what will generally take place throughout Luke-Acts—Jesus's own people reject him, yet the nations welcome him with open arms.

With a population of about five hundred, Nazareth was an unimpressive town built on a hill of limestone just west of the Sea of Galilee.[6] As is his custom, Jesus visits the synagogue in Nazareth on the Sabbath to worship with his fellow Jews and longtime friends. Jesus stands up and reads from Isaiah 61, a passage that squarely focuses on the arrival of the end-time Year of Jubilee. But before we consider Isaiah 61, we must learn a bit about the Year of Jubilee in the Pentateuch.

Leviticus 25:8–55 instructs the Israelites to observe the "Year of Jubilee." Not only must the Israelites obey a Sabbath rest one day a week; the land must "rest" every seventh year (Lev. 25:4). On the seventh Sabbath rest of the land (forty-nine years in total), a Year of Jubilee is declared on the Day of Atonement (Lev. 25:9). The fiftieth year celebrates God's gracious provision, and

---

5. J. Christiaan Beker, *Paul the Apostle: The Triumph of God in Life and Thought* (Minneapolis: Fortress, 1980), 159.

6. Richard A. Freund and Daniel M. Gurtner, "Nazareth," in *T&T Clark Encyclopedia of Second Temple Judaism*, ed. Daniel M. Gurtner and Loren T. Stuckenbruck (New York: Bloomsbury T&T Clark, 2020), 2:539.

the entire year is considered "holy" (Lev. 25:12). Land is to be returned to its original owner (Lev. 25:13). Debts are to be forgiven, allowing the downtrodden within Israel to be restored. Two key principles characterize the Year of Jubilee: (1) Israel must recognize that the promised land is not theirs. They are merely tenants. According to Leviticus 25:23, "The land must not be sold permanently, because the land is mine and you reside in my land as foreigners and strangers." (2) The Israelites should not be indebted to one another in the form of slavery. Everyone is equal. Leviticus 25:42 states, "Because the Israelites are my servants, whom I brought out of Egypt, they must not be sold as slaves." Taken together, these two principles demonstrate that the cosmos is being realigned with Israel's God.[7] Order is restored, and Israel must function as a corporate, faithful Adam who mediates God's rule over the promised land.

We have no record of Israel ever keeping the Jubilee, but we do know that the Year of Jubilee is picked up later in the OT and cast as a prophecy associated with the release of the Israelites from Babylonian captivity. According to Isaiah 61, the promised "servant" heralds "freedom for the captives" and announces the "year of the LORD's favor" (Isa. 61:1–2; cf. Ezek. 46:16–17; Dan. 9:20–27). The Year of Jubilee corresponds with the release of captive Israelites, since Israel is destitute in Babylon. All hope of restoration has waned. But Isaiah prophesies that the coming Messiah will herald the victory of God's people. Isaiah thus envisions the return of Israel from Babylon as an end-time Year of Jubilee.

Luke then narrates Jesus's reaction to the reading of Isaiah 61: "Then he rolled up the scroll, gave it back to the attendant and sat down. The eyes of everyone in the synagogue were fastened on him. He began by saying to them, '*Today this scripture is fulfilled in your hearing*'" (4:20–21). Jesus explicitly identifies himself and his ministry with the prophetic figure of Isaiah 61, who announces the end of Israel's exile and the arrival of the new creation. We now realize the significance of Jesus quoting Isaiah 61 in the synagogue. The poor and outcast are given hope. Though Luke's audience may be economically poor and marginalized in their communities, they can rest assured that Jesus liberates them from spiritual poverty and accompanies them into the promised land of the new creation, where they can enjoy incalculable wealth. What is so striking about this text is *where* the prophecy is fulfilled. Nazareth, an unassuming town—a place not given much attention—marks the beginning of the new age.

Jesus, though, is not only the *herald* of Isaiah 61; he is also the *object* of what he proclaims. At the fall, Satan gains a foothold over the cosmos. Of

7. J. B. Green and N. Perrin, "Jubilee," *DJG*, 450.

course, God rules over Satan, who cannot thwart God's decrees. When Jesus withstands Satan's temptations in the wilderness, Jesus overthrows Satan's domain. Jesus is now the ruler, and he has realigned the cosmos under the reign of God and brought all of creation into a Sabbath rest.

The crowd, amazed at Jesus's conviction, quickly comments, "Isn't this Joseph's son?" (4:22). Jesus responds with the unvarnished truth, disclosing the true intent of their hearts: "Surely you will quote this proverb to me, 'Physician, heal yourself! . . . Do here in your hometown what we have heard that you did in Capernaum'" (4:23). The crowd wants Jesus to prove his kingship and dazzle them with a circus act. But he refuses to cave in to their demands. Regardless of what Jesus says and does, the Nazarenes will reject him (4:24).

In 4:25–27 Luke uniquely includes two examples of prophets who were unwelcome in their native homeland and who ministered to gentiles: Elijah (1 Kings 17:1–24) and Elisha (2 Kings 5:1–14). Luke draws extensive connections to these two prophets in his narrative (→7:11–17). Both Elijah and Elisha possess zeal for God and his law, stand opposed to Israel's idolatry, reach out to and care for gentiles, and perform a host of miracles. There are also parallels between Elijah's opponents and those who reject Jesus. The wording "out of town and [they] took him" (*exō tēs poleōs kai ēgagon auton*) occurs in 1 Kings 20:13 (LXX), where Jezebel hires "two transgressors" who take Naboth "outside the city" (*exēgagon auton exō tēs poleōs*) and stone him. The idea may be that those in Nazareth are falling in step with their idolatrous ancestors, either analogically or typologically. At the outset of Jesus's ministry in Nazareth, Luke wants his audience to view Jesus's ministry through the lens of Elijah and Elisha. What is true of the famed prophets will be true of Jesus. History will repeat itself.

Demonic Expulsion from Capernaum (4:31–44)

Jesus's rejection in Nazareth (4:16–30) is contrasted with his successful ministry in Capernaum (4:31–44 // Mark 1:21–38). While Jesus was born in Bethlehem and then raised in Nazareth, he uses Capernaum as the base of his operations during his ministry. In Nazareth, Jesus's own community attempts to drive him out of the area (4:29), whereas in Capernaum Jesus expels a multitude of demons (4:35–36, 41). The word "to drive out" in 4:29 is used elsewhere in the Third Gospel for the expulsion of demons (9:40, 49; 11:14, 18–20; 13:32). Ironically, Jesus's longtime friends have treated him like a demon by expelling him from their midst! Perhaps this explains why Luke includes the odd detail about the crowd taking him to the "brow of *the hill* [*tou orous*] . . . *to throw* him *off the cliff* [*katakrēmnisai*]" (4:29).

Later on in the narrative, pigs graze on "the hillside" (*tō orei*) and then, possessed by demons, rush "*down the steep bank* [*kata tou krēmnou*] into the lake" (8:32–33). Not coincidentally, Jewish crowds in the Fourth Gospel accuse Jesus on three different occasions of possessing a demon (John 7:20; 8:48; 10:20).

At the synagogue in Capernaum, a hostile demoniac confronts Jesus: "Go away! What do you want with us, Jesus of Nazareth? Have you come to destroy us? I know who you are—the Holy One of God!" (4:34; →Mark 1:21–28). Jesus commands the demon to depart from the man, and the demon immediately complies (4:35). Since Jesus gains the decisive victory over Satan in his wilderness temptation, the demons remain subject to him. The demonic expulsion utterly surprises the crowd in the synagogue: "All the people were amazed. . . . News about him spread throughout the surrounding area" (4:36–37; cf. 4:22). Chapter 4 ends with Jesus healing Simon Peter's mother-in-law (4:38–41 // Matt. 8:14–15 // Mark 1:29–31) and the proclamation of the kingdom throughout the region (4:44).

Jesus as "Lord" and the First Disciples (5:1–39)

The Call of Peter, James, and John (5:1–11)

The kingdom is taking root, and now the time has come to call the disciples. Luke narrates the calling of Simon Peter at length but covers James and John only in brief (5:1–11 // Matt. 4:18–22 // Mark 1:16–20 // John 1:40–42). Peter is clearly the focus of the account, and a number of noteworthy themes mark his call: (1) The narrative opens with Jesus proclaiming the "word of God" on the "Lake of Gennesaret," or the Sea of Galilee (5:1). The message of the kingdom or the "word of God" in Luke-Acts is effective, often eliciting faith and resulting in a community of believers (e.g., 1:2; 8:11–15, 21; 11:28; 21:33; Acts 4:4, 31; 6:2, 7; 8:14; 11:1; 12:24; 13:44, 48–49). In a mere two chapters, the proclamation of the kingdom has stimulated a great deal of response (4:14, 37, 40; 5:1, 15; cf. 7:17). (2) Peter's reaction to the miracle is remarkable on two levels: he recognizes Jesus as Israel's "Lord" (*kyrie*) who alone possesses divine power over the created order (5:8; cf. 1:43, 45; 2:11), and he even calls himself a "sinner" (cf. Gen. 18:27; Exod. 3:6; Isa. 5:18). In reporting Peter's actions, Luke associates him with all other "sinners" in Luke-Acts, who are in dire need of God's grace and mercy (5:30, 32; 7:34, 37; 15:7, 10; 18:13, 19:7). (3) The great catch of fish that accompanies Peter's calling is likely symbolic of his fruitful ministry that Luke narrates in the book of Acts (→Mark 1:16–18 and John 21:1–23).

A *Leper and a Paralytic (5:12–26)*

After the calling of the first few disciples, the narrative advances to the healing of two individuals—a leper (5:12–16) and a paralytic (5:17–26)—then the calling of Levi, a tax collector (5:27–32), and, finally, the discussion of wineskins (5:33–39). Matthew and Luke follow Mark's lead in the general sequence of these four accounts (// Matt. 8:2–4; 9:2–8; 9:9–13; 9:14–17 // Mark 1:40–44; 2:3–12; 2:14–17; 2:18–22), leaving the reader with a strong impression as to the *extent* and *nature* of the end-time kingdom.

The healing of the leper (5:12–16) is paradigmatic for many subsequent miracles. Luke uniquely adds that the man is "covered with leprosy," underscoring his dreadful situation (5:12 // Matt. 8:2 // Mark 1:40). Leprosy, as Hannah Harrington points out, tangibly "illustrates the process of decay"[8] and ritual defilement (Lev. 14:3). The unnamed man falls to his knees and cries out, "*Lord* [*kyrie*], if you are willing, you can make me clean" (5:12). Luke is also the only evangelist to include this divine title here. After Jesus heals the man so that he may fully participate in the covenant community (→Mark 1:40–44), word travels fast and a crowd of sick individuals descends upon him (5:15). At the end of the episode, the narrative depicts Jesus as "often" withdrawing "to lonely places" for prayer (5:16; cf. 3:21; 6:12; 9:18, 28–29; 11:1; 18:1; 22:41, 44). Luke holds Jesus's identity as Israel's God incarnate together with his identity as a human who radically depends upon his Father at every moment. Jesus is the Lord in the flesh who cares for outsiders and restores them for admittance into the kingdom, all the while obediently relying upon his Father's will. He truly is God *and* man.

The healing of the paralytic once again showcases Jesus's concern for the weak (5:17–26 // Matt. 9:2–8 // Mark 2:3–12). Luke introduces the account by mentioning the Jewish leaders who "had come from every village of Galilee and from Judea and Jerusalem" (5:17). Word of Jesus travels fast, and they want to see the miracles for themselves (4:14, 37; 5:15). As the event unfolds, Jesus's interaction with the religious authorities reveals that their presence in the home is not merely to observe but to evaluate and judge (5:21–24). The reader also discovers that "the power of the Lord was with Jesus to heal the sick" (5:17). Only Yahweh possesses the ability to heal (e.g., Exod. 15:26), so when Jesus heals the broken, he does so as Israel's "Lord." Peter cries out to Jesus as "Lord" in his calling (5:8), and the leper follows suit just a few verses later (5:12). This is the third occurrence of "Lord" (*kyrios*) in the first half of chapter 5. The point is obvious: God is visiting his people and fashioning them

---

8. Hannah K. Harrington, "Purity," in *Eerdmans Dictionary of Early Judaism*, ed. John J. Collins and Daniel C. Harlow (Grand Rapids: Eerdmans, 2010), 1123.

for the new creation. The healing of the paralytic also demonstrates Jesus's concern for an individual's spiritual condition. While healing the man of his physical infirmity is quite remarkable in its own right, what is truly noteworthy is Jesus's authority to forgive sins (5:20; →Mark 2:1–12).

The Call of Levi and New Wine Skins (5:27–39)

The calling of Levi brings several themes in chapter 5 to a head (// Matt. 9:9–17 // Mark 2:14–22). Levi, also called Matthew (Matt. 9:9), is a tax collector. Tax collectors were quite disliked in the first century, as they typically are in any century, yet they feature prominently in Luke's Gospel (3:12; 7:29, 34; 15:1; 18:10–13). Rome taxed the Jewish people directly and indirectly. On the one hand, Rome used the Jewish leaders to procure tribute directly on their behalf—a tax that manifested itself in a land tax (*tributum soli*) and a head tax (*tributum capitis*). Rome also indirectly outsourced a taxation to a group called tax farmers or tax collectors.[9] This group collected taxes on goods at ports and tax booths along a road or at the entrance to a city. These tax collectors paid the tribute ahead of time—in full—and then turned around and collected payment as they accosted those passing by. This is how they made their living. Charging exorbitant rates and fees, however they deemed fit, would not be out of the ordinary. According to early Jewish tradition, tax collectors were associated with thieves and murderers (m. Ned. 3.4). It's not difficult to imagine the disdain all would have for these tax collectors.

In calling a tax collector and four fishermen to be numbered among the twelve disciples, the nucleus of true Israel, Jesus symbolically announces that the kingdom is largely composed neither of the socially elite nor of the religiously and ritually observant but of ordinary and scorned individuals. Luke mentions that Levi hosts a "great banquet." The combination of a tax collector (an outsider), a "great banquet," and "new wine" (5:37–39) evokes Isaiah 25:6 (cf. Gen. 21:8; Rev. 19:9):

> On this mountain the LORD Almighty will prepare
> *a feast* of rich food for *all peoples,*
> a banquet of *aged wine*—
> the best of meats and *the finest of wines.*

If Isaiah 25 is in view, then Jesus's actions are eschatological. Fulfilling the expectation of Isaiah 25, he is, as Yahweh in the flesh, fellowshipping with

---

9. T. E. Schmidt, "Taxation, Jewish," in *Dictionary of New Testament Background*, ed. Craig A. Evans and Stanley E. Porter (Downers Grove, IL: InterVarsity, 2000), 1165.

all of humanity. Isaiah 25 also mentions that the banquet takes place "on this mountain" (25:6, 7), a likely reference to the new Jerusalem as the eschatological temple (cf. Isa. 2:2). According to Luke 5, God's glory has arrived in the person of Jesus, and the nations are now enjoying intimate communion with him. Ironically, those who are hostile to God's work of redemption are not "sinners" (5:30) but the Jewish leaders—the OT scholars of the day. Instead of embracing Jesus and his message, the religious authorities are marked with the maxim "The old is better" (5:39; →Mark 2:18–22).

Life in the New Age (6:1-49)

Luke continues to follow Mark's ordering of events. The two events on the Sabbath (6:1–11) follow the discourse on old and new wine (5:33–39), demonstrating that the Sabbath regulations are tied to the larger question of the relationship between the old age and the new age. If Jesus has ushered in a new stage of redemption, then how do the external particulars of the covenant (Sabbath, food laws, etc.) relate to eschatological Israel? Since Jesus is the true high priest, the one who determines who is "clean" and fit for end-time Israel (4:36; 5:14), then other aspects of the Mosaic covenant must relate to him.

Lord of the Sabbath (6:1–11)

We have covered these two events in our discussions of Matthew 12:1–14 and Mark 2:23–3:6, so we will only highlight three observations: (1) Jesus's identity as the true temple and priest is the hermeneutical key to unlocking this section. By invoking King David's consumption of the consecrated bread and giving it to his soldiers, an event that testifies to the royal and priestly dimension of David, Jesus, to an even greater degree, demonstrates that he is able to consume and give it to his disciples. The same could be said for the healing of the man with the "shriveled hand" (6:8). Jesus intentionally restores a person, transitioning him from unclean to clean, so that he can fully participate in the new covenant community and live in the presence of God's glory (see Lev. 21:16–20). Jesus is the only way to enjoy deep Sabbath rest (→Matt. 11:28–30).

(2) The consecrated bread on the table must be understood in relation to the pitcher next to it, where priests kept wine for the drink offerings (Exod. 25:29; Num. 15:7). Bread and wine in the Holy Place signify close fellowship with Yahweh. The Sabbath controversy (6:1–11) makes good sense in light of the previous two incidents in the narrative. We saw that Levi holds "a great banquet" (5:29) and that "new wine must be poured into new wineskins"

(5:38). Here in the Sabbath controversy, Jesus once again enjoys a covenant meal with his disciples, who pick "some heads of grain" (6:1).

(3) The religious authorities are on the offensive, for this is the third event where the Pharisees and the "teachers of the law" have assembled together to evaluate Jesus (5:17, 21, 30; 6:2). In 6:7 they are "looking for a reason to accuse Jesus . . . to see if he would heal on the Sabbath." Instead of recognizing Jesus as the long-awaited descendant of David and the Lord in the flesh, they actively pursue his ruin.

Appointing Twelve Disciples (6:12–16)

Luke is the only evangelist to place the calling of the Twelve right after the two episodes that take place on the Sabbath (6:1–11 // Matt. 10:2–4 // Mark 3:16–19). First Samuel 21 may still be on Luke's radar, because according to Leviticus 24:5 the twelve loaves of bread are prepared on the table in the Holy Place. The twelve loaves obviously symbolize the twelve tribes of Israel, who dwell in God's presence. Could it be that Jesus is designating his twelve disciples here as the true bread of Israel, which dwells in the presence of Jesus, the true priest and temple?

The appointment of the Twelve in the immediate context could also involve the theme of hostility. Luke 6:11 ends with the acrimonious leaders debating how they will secure Jesus's demise, and 6:12–16 comprises the appointment of the disciples. If the Jewish leaders set themselves against Jesus, then they will certainly set themselves against his followers.

Another unique dimension of Luke's narrative here is the prominence of Jesus's prayer life: "Jesus went to a mountainside to pray, and spent the night praying to God" (6:12). Prayer in the Third Gospel is, as we have seen, quite prominent (3:21; 5:16; 6:12; 9:18, 28–29; 11:1; 18:1; 22:41, 44). Jesus often prays to the Father for strength and wisdom. Here Jesus depends upon the Father, perhaps inquiring for wisdom in calling the remaining disciples. The first crop of disciples—Peter, Andrew, James, and John—are summoned in 5:1–11, but here Luke furnishes the complete list. The three evangelists all designate the disciples as "apostles" (*apostolous*) in this passage (Matt. 10:2 // Mark 3:14 // Luke 6:13), but Luke is the only one to maintain that appellation throughout the narrative (9:10; 11:49; 17:5). He likely preserves the term "apostles" so that his audience can trace their missional activity through Acts, where it occurs some twenty-nine times. What begins here on a mountain in Galilee will reach the ends of the earth in just a few decades. The calling of the twelve disciples on a mountain certainly symbolizes the restoration of end-time Israel (Matt. 10:2–4; →Mark 3:16–19). Just as Moses assembles the twelve tribes of Israel at Sinai, so Jesus assembles twelve followers. Jesus is clearly the antitype of Moses. Further, the narrative portrays Jesus as Yahweh, who dwells on top of Sinai in a thick cloud among his people (Exod. 19:11, 18).

The Sermon on the Plain (6:17–49)

The narrative presses on with Jesus descending the mountain to a "level place" (6:17). In the first several chapters, Luke underscores *where* the events have taken place: the temple (1:5; 2:22, 41), private homes (1:39; 2:7; 4:38; 5:18, 29), the Jordan River (3:3), the wilderness (4:1), synagogues (4:16, 33, 38), the Sea of Galilee (5:1), a grainfield (6:1), and a mountain (6:12). Here the setting is on a "level place." While the sermon here, known as the Sermon on the Plain, contains a number of remarkable similarities to Matthew's Sermon on the Mount (chs. 5–7), this sermon appears to be distinct. The setting is different, the sermon is more compact, and it contains additional elements.

Luke mentions that a "large crowd of his disciples" has gathered along with "a great number of people from all of Judea, from Jerusalem, and from the coastal region around Tyre and Sidon" (6:17; cf. Acts 1:8). The audience is most likely composed of Jews and some gentiles who are curious about Jesus and his miracles. For the next several passages, the presence of the crowd becomes an important dimension to Jesus's ministry (6:17; 7:1, 9, 11, 12). He often directs his attention to them, imploring them to be true followers rather than mere observers. Why does Luke sandwich the episode of healing in 6:17–19 with the calling of the Twelve (6:12–16) and the sermon (6:20–49; cf. Matt. 4:18–7:29)? The appointment of the Twelve is a significant step in the expansion of the kingdom, a kingdom that is marked by the arrival of the new creation and the subjugation of demonic forces. The Sermon on the Plain could be Jesus's explanation of how to live *within* the expanding kingdom.

In general contrast to Matthew's Sermon on the Mount, Luke sharpens the audience of Jesus's sermon. The blessings and curses are directed toward "you" (plural): "Blessed are *you* who are poor, for *yours* is the kingdom of God. . . . But woe to *you* who are rich, for *you* have already received *your* comfort" (6:20, 24). While 6:20 states that Jesus is "looking at his disciples," 7:1 notes that he "finished saying all this to the people who were listening." Most likely, then, Jesus is directing his sermon to the throng mentioned in 6:17–19. The reader should assume that all within the crowd will fall into one of two categories—blessed or cursed. If they follow King Jesus, then they are blessed. If not, then they will bear God's curse (see Deut. 27:9–28:68).

Four blessings earmark the first section of the sermon (6:20–22), and four curses or "woes" distinguish the second (6:24–26). The blessings in 6:20–22 are, like those in Matthew 5:3–12, eschatological in nature. Those who obey Jesus are "blessed" or shown divine favor (e.g., LXX: Ps. 1:1; 32:12; 33:9; Dan. 12:12). The sermon highlights several themes that Luke has set in place since the beginning of the narrative. For example, the poor, hungry, despondent, and persecuted are "blessed" (6:20–22; cf. 1:52b–53a), whereas the rich, well fed, jubilant, and highly esteemed are cursed (6:24–26; cf. 1:52a, 53b). The presence of the kingdom inverts the world's ethics. For example, Mary and Joseph, though poor (2:7, 24), find their joy in God's promises and receive eschatological blessing (1:45; 11:27).

Life in the new age is marked by two dimensions: radical love for one another (6:27–36) and, subsequently, withholding judgment (6:37–42). Loving one's neighbor has always been a central component to being part of God's family (see Lev. 19:18), but, because of the internal work of the Spirit, the command to love is ramped up in the new covenant community (Jer. 31:31–34; Ezek. 36:25–27; Matt. 5:43–44; 1 John 4:7–8). The imperative to "not judge" has to do with assuming God's unique position of authority (6:37). When individuals "judge" one another, they become the absolute arbiter of right and wrong. This type of sin is reminiscent of God's prohibition to Adam and Eve to not eat from the tree of the knowledge of good and evil (Gen. 3:17; cf. Matt. 7:1–5; James 4:11–12). God alone possesses the ultimate right to decide what is right and what is wrong.

The sermon ends with two examples of responding to Jesus's message (6:43–49). Fruit is inevitable, but what kind of fruit will be produced? Those within the crowd who respond positively will "bear good fruit," whereas those who do not will bear "bad fruit" (6:43 // Matt. 7:16–20). The contents of the heart will ultimately be manifest on the outside for all to see. The end of the sermon is stunning: "Why do you call me, 'Lord, Lord' [*kyrie kyrie*] and do not do what I say?" (6:46 // Matt. 7:21). Acknowledging Jesus as "Lord" (*kyrios*) has been an extraordinary feature of Luke's Gospel, for it recognizes that Jesus is Israel's God incarnate (e.g., 1:43, 45; 2:11; 5:8a, 12, 17). But we discover here that it is possible for one to acknowledge Jesus as divine yet ultimately deny him with one's actions. This is not a far cry from James 2:19: "You believe that there is one God. Good! Even the demons believe that—and shudder." Spirit-empowered works must always accompany faith.

The Arrival of End-Time Blessing (7:1–50)

The Faith of the Centurion (7:1–10)

Chapter 7 contains two key miracles—the healing of the centurion's servant (7:1–10) and the raising of the widow's son (7:11–17)—that force the reader to reflect upon the precise nature of Jesus's identity, mission, and the kingdom. The story of the centurion immediately follows the sermon, forcing Luke's audience to read them together. The Sermon on the Plain (6:20–49), especially the last few verses, has significant bearing on how we are to understand the present passage (7:1–10). Luke's retelling of the event includes several details that are absent from Matthew's narrative (// Matt. 8:5–13). We discover here that this centurion is a prominent member of his community. Though likely a gentile, he has great admiration for Israel and even financed the construction of the local synagogue in Capernaum. He is a God-fearer, an individual who follows a great deal of the Torah but probably remains uncircumcised (7:5). His level of influence must be extensive, for he orders "some elders of the Jews" to Jesus to inquire about his servant (7:3). Luke's version also claims that the servant is "about to die" (7:2 // Matt. 8:6).

What is common to both Matthew and Luke is the centurion's unparalleled faith. Jesus even exclaims, "I tell you, I have not found such great faith even in Israel" (7:9). The themes of hearing and obeying resound in this section. Genuine "hearing" is always wedded with works:

But to you *who are listening* [*tois akouousin*] I say: Love your enemies, do good to those who hate you. (6:27)

As for everyone who comes to me and *hears* [*akouōn*] my words and puts them into practice, I will show you what they are like. (6:47)

But *the one who hears* [*ho akousas*] my words and does not put them into practice is like a man who built a house on the ground without a foundation. (6:49)

When Jesus had finished saying all this to the people who were *listening* [*tas akoas*] . . . (7:1)

The centurion *heard* [*akousas*] of Jesus and sent some elders of the Jews to him, asking him to come and heal his servant. (7:3)

If we are right in putting these occurrences of listening together, then the centurion is the "listener" par excellence. He hears about Jesus, believes that he has the power to heal, and acts accordingly; he is a wise builder (6:48; 7:5). In emphasizing the centurion's status as a God-fearer, Luke may be laying the foundation for the inclusion of Cornelius, another God-fearer, in Acts 10:23–48. Also, we would be remiss to forget Naaman, who is likewise a gentile official who renounces his gods and turns to the Lord (2 Kings 5; Luke 4:27). In fulfillment of OT expectations and shadows, gentiles are now joining true Israel (e.g., Isa. 2:2; 25:6), but according to this passage, they are doing so through faith in Jesus and not by adherence to the external stipulations of the Mosaic covenant.

Raising the Widow's Son (7:11–17)

Rounding out the section of 6:17–7:17, Luke once again attunes his readers to the crowds. They have been present throughout, and now they will witness Jesus's greatest miracle up to this point. Occurring only in Luke's Gospel, the event takes place in the town of Nain (7:1), a city (*polis*) that lies some six miles southeast of Nazareth. The parallels in the LXX between this event and raisings performed through Elijah and Elisha are pronounced:

Elijah	Elisha	Jesus
Elijah meets a woman at the "town gate" (*ton pylōna tēs poleōs*; 1 Kings 17:10)		Jesus meets a woman at the "town gate" (*tē pylē tēs poleōs*; 7:12)
The woman is a widow (*chēra*; 1 Kings 17:10)	The woman is married (2 Kings 4:9)	The woman is a widow (*chēra*; 7:12)
Son dies (1 Kings 17:17)	Son dies (2 Kings 4:20)	Son is dead (7:12)
Elijah "gave him [the son] to his mother" (*edōken auton tē mētri autou*; 1 Kings 17:23)	Elisha commands the Shunammite woman, "Take your son" (2 Kings 4:36)	Jesus "gave him [the son] back to his mother" (*edōken auton tē mētri autou*; 7:15)
The woman recognizes that Elijah is indeed a "man of God" (1 Kings 17:24)	Shunammite woman "fell at his [Elisha's] feet" and did obeisance (2 Kings 4:37)	The crowd recognizes that Jesus is a "prophet" (7:16)

Why would Luke overtly allude to these two narratives, especially to the Elijah narrative? Perhaps for three reasons: (1) In contrast to Elijah and Elisha, Jesus performs this miracle with his own life-giving authority. Elijah and Elisha are quick to call upon God's power (1 Kings 17:20–21; 2 Kings 4:33), whereas Jesus unflinchingly heals the boy. The point is clear—Jesus performs this miracle as God in the flesh. Notice the crowd's reaction: "*God* has come to help his people" (7:16; see 1:68, 78). (2) Jesus is not only the Lord incarnate; he also identifies with the long-awaited Elijah messenger. The prophet Malachi predicts that an Elijah-like messenger will arise immediately preceding the eschatological day of the Lord, unifying the covenant community (Mal. 4:5–6). So, while the Gospels view John the Baptist as certainly fulfilling Malachi's prophecy, there are points of continuity between Jesus and Elijah. (3) Traces of typological fulfillment are probably in mind, too, since Elijah and Elisha minister to gentiles.

Exceeding Expectations (7:18–35)

The healing of the widow's son pulls Jesus's identity to the forefront. The reaction of the crowd in 7:16 that "a great prophet has appeared among us" sews the raising of the widow's son to John's inquiry in 7:19. The disciples of John relate to the imprisoned John the Baptist "all these things" (7:18), and certainly a portion of "these things" must be the miracle in 7:11–17. We last heard about John when Herod locked him up in 3:19–20. From prison, John wondered if Jesus was truly the "one who is to come" (7:20). Why would John doubt Jesus's identity? Probably for a few reasons. John, like his fellow Jews, expects that the Messiah will overthrow the Romans and establish the kingdom of God right then and there. If Jesus is the king, then where is the kingdom? John suffers and is imprisoned at the hands of Herod! He should be ruling with Israel's Messiah. He has yet to grasp the mysterious nature of the overlap of the ages. Suffering and kingdom oddly overlap. Further, Jesus is more than a king—he is God in the flesh. So John is still trying to wrap his head around how Jesus simultaneously fulfills OT expectations as Israel's God and her Messiah while establishing a kingdom that runs parallel to the end-time tribulation. The mounting tension running throughout 4:14–7:50 is somewhat relieved in the discourse of the "mysteries of the kingdom" in 8:1–18.

In curing "many who had diseases, sicknesses and evil spirits," and giving "sight to many who were blind" (7:21), Jesus tangibly reveals to John's disciples that he is indeed the long-awaited King of Israel. He then alludes to a swath of passages from Isaiah that prophetically anticipate Jesus's actions of restoration (Isa. 26:19; 29:18–19; 35:5–6; 42:7, 18; 61:1). The discourse ends with a blessing to the audience: "Blessed is anyone who does not stumble on account of me" (7:23). The Sermon on the Plain opens with four blessings (6:20–22), and it is hardly a coincidence that Luke includes one here. True end-time blessing and admittance into the new age can be procured only through a proper understanding of Jesus.

Jesus then presses further into his relationship with John in the remainder of the section, contending that John's ministry stands in continuity with the OT. John is a transitional figure, caught between the end of the old age and the beginning of the new (→Matt. 11:7–15). While much of this section mirrors Matthew's account (Matt. 11:2–19), Luke juxtaposes the reaction of the tax collectors with the reaction of the religious authorities: "All the people, even the tax collectors . . . acknowledged that God's way was right. . . . But the Pharisees and the experts in the law rejected God's purpose for themselves" (7:29–30). Once again, those on the fringes of society, even tax collectors (3:12; 5:27, 30; 7:34; 15:1; 18:10–13), are in better shape than those who lay claim to God's covenant with Israel.

Jesus Anointed King (7:36–50)

While it is tempting to align the anointing here with the anointing in Matthew 26:6–13 // Mark 14:3–9 // John 12:1–8, this event appears distinct. Its placement within the narrative, the setting, and the characters involved are different. The significance of anointing Jesus with precious perfume is unmistakable—Jesus is anointed as the long-awaited King of Israel (e.g., Judg. 9:15; 1 Sam. 9:16; 16:13; Ps. 18:50). His identity has been under discussion for much of chapter 7, and this section serves as a fitting capstone. Luke displays a concern about *who* anoints Jesus and *where*. The *who* is a woman "who lived a sinful life" (7:37). The *where* is the home of "one of the Pharisees" (7:36), an individual well on his way to becoming a follower of Jesus. This is the first of three meals with Pharisees (7:36–50; 11:37–54; →14:1–24).

Table fellowship is close to the heart of Luke's Gospel. Spanning most cultures, sharing a meal demonstrates a level of intimacy and identity. In the Greco-Roman world, "such meals became public markers of a group's identity, and thus social boundaries could be more or less defined in terms of inclusion or exclusion from the table fellowship associated with these events."[10] So Jesus appears to invert social conventions by realigning one's ultimate identity. To become part of God's family, his covenant community, is not founded upon social standing, wealth, or family, but upon following the Son of Man.

That Simon is named (7:40) perhaps indicates that he later became an eyewitness of this account. The pairing of a ritually clean Pharisee and an unclean sinful woman (a prostitute?) is riddled with irony, for Pharisees were fastidious about maintaining ritual purity at all times. Here we have a sinner— a woman, no less—anointing Jesus with her most prized possession and publicly announcing that Jesus is the end-time king. She is truly committing to following Jesus as Lord. No wonder Jesus declares that her "faith has saved" her and that she is now at "peace" with God (7:50). The woman embodies the outcasts who respond positively to John the Baptist's summons to repentance, whereas Simon represents those who rebuff it.

The Odd Reception of the Kingdom (8:1–56)

Redeemed Women (8:1–3)

The beginning of chapter 8, while unique to the Third Gospel (8:1–3; cf. Matt. 13:1–2 // Mark 4:1–2), is hardly unsurprising given Luke's intention to demonstrate the *scope* of the kingdom. The kingdom is available to all

---

10. M. A. Powell, "Table Fellowship," *DJG*, 926.

who follow Jesus, even "sinful" women (7:37). Recall that Mark highlights the *cleansing* of the created order for the kingdom's mysterious arrival, and Matthew underscores the *growth* of the kingdom. Luke tightly joins 8:1–18 to the preceding context of 7:36–50 with the expression "after this" (*en tō kathexēs*) in 8:1 so that his readers connect the prominent women in 8:1–3 to the "sinful" woman anointing Jesus in the house of Simon. The women listed—Mary Magdalene, Joanna, and Susanna—all share something in common: they "had been cured of evil spirits and diseases" (8:2; cf. 7:21; 11:26). It is not entirely clear what is meant by "cured of evil spirits." Luke could be referring to the means by which Satan and his demons afflict humanity as a result of the fall (sickness, etc.). At the very least, Luke suggests that nothing can impede the advancement and extent of the kingdom, not even Satan himself. The women are also named, perhaps demonstrating that they eventually testified to portions of Jesus's ministry. Mary Magdalene is found at the crucifixion (Matt. 27:56 // Mark 15:40), the burial of Jesus (Matt. 27:61 // Mark 15:47), and the resurrection (Matt. 28:1 // Mark 16:1). We also learn that the women support Jesus and the Twelve as they proclaim the gospel from town to town. They may have helped advance the kingdom through financial means. The same principle that is on display in 7:36–50 operates here: these women have been forgiven much, so they love much (7:41–47).

The Parable of the Soils and the Mystery of the Kingdom (8:4–18)

Luke's discussion of the nature of the kingdom in 8:4–18 is, in some sense, a bare-bones exposition of the end-time rule of God on earth. While resembling much of the discourse on the kingdom in Mark 4:1–20, Luke 8:4–15 lacks the emphasis on the "messianic secret" that runs through the Second Gospel. In comparing Luke 8:4–15 to Matthew 13:2–53, many parables on the nature of the kingdom are absent in Luke's account. This is unsurprising given that the growth of the kingdom is at the heart of Matthew's narrative. Nevertheless, we should not discount the prominence of the parable of the soils (8:5–15) and the inclusion of the "mysteries of the kingdom" (8:10 AT) in the narrative of Luke.

Since we have already covered this discourse in some detail in Matthew 13:2–23 and Mark 4:1–20, we need only to recognize here that the parable of the soils explains why some accept Jesus's kingdom message and many do not. The theological basis for the parable lies in the quotation of Isaiah 6:9 in 8:10. In fulfillment of Isaiah's prophecy, many do not accept Jesus because of their idolatrous hearts.

One unique feature of the narrative is worthy of contemplation. In Luke's account, the seed that falls "along the path" is immediately snatched away because of "the devil" (*ho diabolos*). The devil prevents the seed from growing, "so that they may not believe and be saved" (8:12). The seed that falls along the rocky ground is unable to take root, because "in the time *of testing* [*peirasmou*] they fall away" (8:13). We can perceive shades of Jesus's wilderness temptation here: "When *the devil* [*ho diabolos*] had finished all this *tempting* [*peirasmon*], he left him until an opportune time" (4:13). Though conquered and unable to win the war, Satan exerts influence in the world and assails the covenant community. In a word, Satan uses the same bag of tricks in tempting the covenant community (cf. 11:4; 22:28, 40, 46). But if God's people are to vanquish the devil, they must persevere and imitate the Son of Man's faithfulness in trusting God's promise of deliverance, a promise that is now fully revealed in his Son.

The Unbelief of Jesus's Family and the Disciples (8:19–25)

A brief account of Jesus and his family follows the parables of the kingdom (// Matt. 12:46–50 // Mark 3:20–21, 31–35). Mark 3:21 discloses *why* Jesus's family wants to talk with him: "They said, 'He is out of his mind.'" But Matthew and Luke do not explicitly state the basis for the family's actions, perhaps because the messianic secret is not a major feature of their narratives. It is certainly discernable but not a primary characteristic. At the very least, Jesus's family is unwilling to follow him at every turn. Luke pairs the account of his mother and brothers (8:19–21) with the parables of the kingdom (8:4–18), encouraging his audience to ponder the connection between the soils and Jesus's family. Are they the rocky soil that will not persevere? Or will they trust in Jesus's message and bear fruit? The inclusion of Mary here is all the more striking in light of Luke's portrayal of Mary in the birth narratives, where she demonstrates remarkable faith in God's promises.

The same theme of hesitancy continues in the following passage of the stilling of the storm (// Matt. 8:23–27 // Mark 4:36–41), where the disciples, upon witnessing Jesus's identity as Yahweh incarnate and the last Adam, fail to fully grasp his identity (→Matt. 8:23–27). We are approximately a third of the way through Luke's narrative, and Jesus's closest associates—his family and disciples—still struggle with the nature of his messiahship and the kingdom. Luke wrote his Gospel to provide an "account of the things that have been fulfilled" (1:1), yet the way in which the OT is being fulfilled differs from long-held expectations.

The Gerasene Demoniac and the Raising of Jairus's Daughter (8:26–56)

Luke juxtaposes the unbelief of Jesus's family and his disciples with the following two accounts in 8:26–56 of individuals trusting in Jesus (// Matt. 8:28–34 // Mark 5:1–20). In 8:22 Jesus and the disciples set sail to cross the Sea of Galilee from Capernaum to Geshur. According to 8:26, they arrive in the "region of the Gerasenes," an area that most likely includes the Decapolis and thus many gentiles (// Mark 5:20). Luke uniquely describes the demoniac as a man who "had not worn clothes or lived in a house" (8:27) and whose demon kept him "under guard," broke "his chains," and drove him "into solitary places" (8:29). By heightening the dire circumstances of the man and the nearly indomitable power the demon exerts over him, Luke underscores the gravity of his redemption (→Mark 5:1–43). His restoration is top-down—Jesus redeems him without any initiation from the demoniac.

In contrast to Jesus's family and the disciples, the demon rightly identifies Jesus as the "Son of the Most High God" (8:28 // Matt. 8:29 // Mark 5:7). This same title appears throughout the Third Gospel (1:32, 35, 76; 2:14; 6:35; 19:38; cf. Acts 7:48; 16:17). The "Most High" (*hypsistos*) or "Most High God" (*ho theos hypsistos*) occurs only thirteen times in the NT, and ten of those occur in Luke-Acts. The title is found in the LXX as a reference to God's exclusive identity as sovereign Lord over the world (e.g., Gen. 14:22; 2 Sam. 22:14; Ps. 18:13; 47:2). So Luke presents Jesus as absolute King who governs over every tract of the cosmos. But he is not a distant ruler in a far-off land, aloof from the needs of his people, but a ruler who has drawn near to save those who cannot save themselves.

Following the Son of Man at All Costs (9:1–50)

Empowered to Conquer (9:1–9)

Jesus's rule over Satan and his domain ties the broad previous context of 4:1–8:56 (especially 8:22–56) to the present section of 9:1–9. Jesus stills the storm (8:22–25), symbolizing Jesus's overthrow of demonic influence from the created realm; exorcises demons from the Gerasene demoniac (8:26–39); and conquers death itself (8:40–56). Jesus calls the first crop of disciples in 5:1–11 and 5:27–32 and then assembles the full contingent of twelve in 6:12–16. Here in 9:1–9 he commissions them to proclaim the arrival of the end-time kingdom and to continue the overthrow of Satan's territory (// Matt. 10:9–15 // Mark 6:8–11). The twelve disciples appropriate the kingdom not with a physical sword but with the proclaimed word (9:2; cf. Acts 1:3, 4, 8). Earlier in Luke's narrative, Satan tests Jesus by giving (*dōsō*) him "authority" (*tēn exousian*) over the cosmos (4:6; cf. Dan. 7:14 LXX). Jesus now gives (*edōken*) "authority" (*exousian*) to the disciples as a result of his faithfulness in the wilderness (9:1; cf. 4:6; 10:19; 20:2; Acts 8:19). But the disciples should expect resistance as they will, like John, endure great hardship (9:7–9).

The Feeding of the Five Thousand, Peter's Confession, and the First Passion Prediction (9:10–27)

The disciples return, and by all indications they enjoyed a successful campaign, so Jesus and the Twelve retreat to a region north of the Sea of Galilee in the general vicinity of Bethsaida (9:10). The feeding of the five thousand, taking place "in a remote place" (*en erēmō topō*), looks back to Israel's wilderness wanderings, where God fed them with manna (Exod. 16:4; →Mark 6:32–44). Found in all four Gospels (// Matt. 14:13–21 // Mark 6:30–44 // John 6:5–13), the miracle demonstrates that Jesus is the true nourishment of God, the life-giving presence of Yahweh. Luke's emphasis on the crowd sitting down or reclining to eat (9:14–15) aligns this event with other meals in the narrative (e.g., 5:29–39; 7:36–50; 10:38–42; 14:1–23; 19:5–10; 22:7–38; 24:36–49), suggesting that the eschatological banquet is at hand and God is redeeming end-time Israel through a second exodus (see Isa. 25:6–8).

Luke places Peter's confession immediately following the feeding of the five thousand (// Matt. 16:21–28 // Mark 8:31–9:1). While it is not immediately clear why these two events are joined, the disciples perceive, on account of his spectacular miracle, that Jesus is indeed Israel's long-awaited Messiah (cf. John 6:14–15). Peter's confession that Jesus is "God's Messiah" (9:20) nicely bookends Peter's first run-in with Jesus. The calling of Peter in chapter 5 climaxes with Peter confessing that Jesus is "Lord" (5:8), and now he confesses that Jesus is "God's Messiah." On the lips of Peter lies the key to unlocking Jesus's identity: Jesus of Nazareth is both Yahweh incarnate and the anointed King of Israel. He is the Son of God and the Son of David. The angel Gabriel was right to predict, "He will be great and will be called the *Son of the Most High*. The Lord God will give him the throne of *his father David*" (1:32).

Jesus immediately sets the record straight: "the Son of Man must suffer many things" (9:21). This is the first of six passion predictions (9:44; 12:50; 13:32–33; 17:25; 18:32–33).[11] The suffering dimension of Jesus's messiahship, though not entirely absent from the narrative, picks up considerable steam going forward. The religious authorities and Jesus's own community have opposed Jesus from the beginning (4:14–30; 5:17–39; 6:1–11), but Jesus has largely ministered without impediment. That will soon change.

11. Garland, *Luke*, 699.

The Transfiguration and the Disciples' Failed Exorcism (9:28–50)

All three Synoptics include the transfiguration (// Matt. 17:1–8 // Mark 9:2–8), and because we have explored a handful of prominent OT themes contained in the event, we have little reason to reproduce all of them here (→Matt. 17:1–8 and Mark 9:2–8). We need only to recall that all three evangelists underscore Jesus's identity as the exalted Son of Man who possesses the attributes of the Ancient of Days (note the possible allusion to Dan. 7:9 in 9:29–30) and who fulfills the prophecy of Daniel 7 (note the allusion to Dan. 7:13–14 in 9:26 and Acts 7:56). Fused with Jesus's identity as the resplendent Son of Man is an overt attempt to cast the transfiguration as a recapitulation of Sinai, where God gives Israel his law and commissions the nation to be a "kingdom of priests" to their neighbors (Exod. 19:6). Commentators often point out Luke's emphasis on a second exodus in 9:30–31 when Jesus discusses "his departure" (*tēn exodon autou*) with Moses and Elijah (cf. Exod. 19:1 LXX; Heb. 11:22). The gist of the transfiguration is that the Father announces his Son's initial success as the faithful, divine Son of Man, the true representative of Israel.

The disciples continue to struggle with Jesus's identity in the following account, where they are unable to exorcise a demon (9:37–41 // Matt. 17:14–18 // Mark 9:14–27). They are like an "unbelieving and perverse generation" (9:41; see Deut. 32:20–21 LXX). Their unfaithfulness is starkly juxtaposed with Jesus's faithfulness on display at the transfiguration. Instead of expanding the kingdom by the power of Jesus, they attempt to expel the demon on their own terms. Frustrated with his disciples, Jesus exorcises the demon himself (9:42–43).

Luke transitions into the second passion prediction (9:44; cf. 9:22; 12:50; 13:32–33; 17:25; 18:32–33), and even though the Messiah's death is anticipated in the OT, the disciples still have difficulty comprehending it: "It [Jesus's passion] was hidden from them, so that they did not grasp it" (9:45; cf. 10:21–23). Although the OT predicted that the Messiah would suffer, first-century Jews did not anticipate that suffering would *characterize* his ministry. Like the hidden nature of the kingdom, dimensions of Jesus's messiahship remain hidden, only to be revealed after the cross and resurrection (24:25–27; John 2:21–22).

◼ Phase 2: The Journey to Jerusalem (9:51–19:27)

Resolved to Suffer (9:51–62)

The section of 9:51–62, unique to Luke, is a critical hinge in the narrative. Up to this point, Jesus has ministered in and around Galilee. Now, though, the time has come for him to head south to Jerusalem. The latter-day storm of persecution is brewing. Two observations are illuminating here: (1) While the journey to Jerusalem is critical to the narrative, Luke never loses sight of the goal. He prefaces Jesus's firm decision to turn south: "*As the time approached for him to be taken up to heaven*, Jesus resolutely set out for Jerusalem" (9:51). The ultimate goal of Jesus's ministry is his resurrection and enthronement to the Father's right hand as the royal Son of Man (24:51; Acts 1:9). To achieve that end, he must first suffer. A U-shaped pattern emerges. Jesus must go down (to Jerusalem) in order to go up (to heaven). Fulfilling his role as the suffering servant, he must first suffer and then be exalted (Isa. 52:13–53:12). (2) Matthew and Mark merely specify that Jesus turns south (// Matt. 19:1 // Mark 10:1), whereas Luke states that Jesus "resolutely" (lit. "set his face") heads toward Jerusalem (9:51; cf. Isa. 50:7). Such resolution explains why Luke sets aside nearly ten chapters for this leg of the journey. All of 9:51–19:44 takes place during the trek to Jerusalem.

The book of Isaiah forms the blueprint for Jesus's journey to Jerusalem. Luke ponders Isaiah, particularly chapters 40–66, and then recounts the journey in light of it. At the beginning of his narrative, the term "way" (*hodos*) occurs twice in the context of Zechariah's prediction about his son, John the Baptist: "You, my child, will be called a prophet of the Most High; for you will go on before the Lord to prepare *the way* [*hodous*] for him . . . to guide our feet into *the path* [*hodon*] of peace" (1:76, 79). A few chapters later, Luke quotes from Isaiah 40:3–5:

> The voice of one crying in the wilderness:
> "Prepare *the way* [*tēn hodon*] of the Lord,
>   make his paths straight.
> Every valley shall be filled,
>   and every mountain and hill shall be made low,
>   and the crooked shall become straight,
>   and the rough places shall become level *ways* [*hodous*],
> and all flesh shall see the salvation of God." (3:4–6 ESV; cf. 7:27)

In our discussion of Mark 1:2–3, we learned that John the Baptist's ministry triggers the long-awaited restoration of the Lord's people from Babylonian captivity. Remarkably, the Synoptics identify Jesus with Israel's "Lord," who redeems Israel from spiritual captivity. The term "way" (*hodos*), while occurring throughout the Third Gospel, appears often throughout the journey (9:3, 57; 10:4, 31; 11:6; 12:58; 14:23; 18:35; 19:36). Could it be that Jesus and the disciples' journey to Jerusalem symbolically embodies restored Israel's journey or "way" to the promised land, fulfilling Isaiah's promise? It makes sense, then, that Luke would allocate nearly a third of his narrative to Jesus the Lord leading his people out of spiritual bondage and into the new creation by his death and resurrection. According to Acts 9:2, 19:9, 23, 22:4, 24:14, and 22, the word "way" (*hodos*) is a technical Isaianic term referring to the church as end-time Israel.[12]

Further still, much of Jesus's teaching in 9:51–19:44 is an expansion of the Sermon on the Plain in 6:17–49. The same principles are worked out and paired with engaging parables that seize the readers' attention. The narrative slows, forcing the reader to take to heart and consider the various layers of meaning each parable figuratively conveys. The brilliance of parables is how they beckon the reader to read again and again so that their meaning may be unlocked. True followers of the Son of Man will read the parables with great care, and while they may not grasp their meaning at first, they will eventually do so and receive the blessing and restoration of the new creation. Luke encourages his readers to join Jesus in his journey of redemption. Conversely, outsiders and those who follow Jesus out of convenience will never truly discover the intent of the parables, finding themselves on the receiving end of God's judgment. All who reject his summons to join him on the journey will never set foot in the promised land of the new creation. At the end of the Gospel, Jesus symbolically retraces the journey once more on the "road" (*hodos*) to Emmaus, but this time he teaches not in riddles but in plain speech (24:32, 35).

The first section of Luke (1:5–9:50) introduces the audience to the nature of Jesus's identity and the end-time kingdom, whereas the teaching on the road to Jerusalem explores the challenges and sacrifices believers will face if they desire to follow Jesus of Nazareth to the new creation. We can break down the teaching into three general sections: expansion of the kingdom (10:1–11:13), inevitable conflict with the kingdom (11:14–54), and life within the kingdom (12:1–19:44). So as we unpack the following chapters, we must never lose sight of where we are in the Third Gospel.

After encountering resistance from the Samaritans, who view the temple in Jerusalem as a rival sanctuary (9:52–56), Jesus explains to three unidentified individuals that participating in the kingdom means sacrificing everything (9:57–62). The kingdom must be prized above family and community, and those who want to follow Jesus will imitate his U-shaped ministry—suffering, then exaltation.

12. David W. Pao, *Acts and the Isaianic New Exodus*, WUNT 2/130 (Tübingen: Mohr Siebeck, 2000), 66.

Expansion of the Kingdom (10:1–11:13)

The Seventy-Two Disciples (10:1–24)

The sending out of the seventy-two disciples, an event only recorded by Luke, marks the expansion of the kingdom. The faithfulness of seventy-two in heralding the kingdom exemplifies what true devotion or "service" (9:62) to the kingdom looks like. At the beginning of chapter 9, Jesus commissions the Twelve; but here he charges seventy-two disciples. Why a second commissioning? Clearly the two are connected:

Twelve Disciples	Seventy-Two Disciples
Jesus commissions them to proclaim the "kingdom of God" (9:2)	Jesus commissions them to proclaim that the "kingdom of God has come near" (10:9)
The disciples are empowered to "drive out all demons" (9:1)	The seventy-two report that "demons submit" to their authority (10:17)
The disciples must "shake the dust off" their feet if they are rejected (9:5)	The seventy-two must "wipe" the "dust . . . from [their] feet" if they are rejected (10:11)

Jesus appoints seventy-two additional disciples (10:1). The term "appointed" (*anedeixen*) occurs in the LXX in contexts of royal nominations (e.g., 1 Esd. 1:32, 35, 41, 44; 2 Macc. 9:25), so Jesus deputizes the seventy-two disciples to wage warfare against the onslaught of demonic forces (see 10:18).

Why seventy-two? These seventy-two disciples recall Genesis 10, where God splits humanity into seventy-two people groups: "These are the clans of Noah's sons, according to their lines of descent, within their nations. From these the nations spread out over the earth after the flood" (Gen. 10:32). The LXX includes seventy-two nations in the list of nations in Genesis 10:2–31, whereas the MT has seventy. This explains why some manuscripts read "seventy" and others read "seventy-two" in Luke 10:1.

According to Genesis, the nations of the world gather together in "one language and a common speech" (Gen. 11:1). Their goal: construct a massive structure to boast in their accomplishments and manipulate God (11:3–4). God originally charged Adam and Eve to spread throughout and bring his glory to the ends of the earth (1:28). Instead of obeying that divine commission, rebellious humanity assembles together and does just the opposite. Judgment ensues and God comes down to scatter the nations throughout "the whole earth" (11:8).

Luke sets the commissioning of the seventy-two against the backdrop of Genesis 10–11. These seventy-two disciples symbolize the seventy-two nations of the world—the new humanity. The commissioning of the twelve disciples in 9:1–6 represents the proclamation of the gospel to Israel, whereas the commissioning of the seventy-two in 10:1–17 symbolizes the proclamation of the gospel to the nations. This pattern fits well with Luke's larger program, encapsulated in Acts 1:8—Israel first, Samaria next, and then the nations (cf. Rom. 1:16). The commissioning of the seventy-two also takes place immediately after Jesus's resolution to head south and suffer. So we should assume that the gospel will flourish in the midst of suffering and rejection.

Acts 8 narrates the dispersion of the believers in Jerusalem on account of persecution (8:1). Their dispersion is, strangely, the catalyst for the gospel going forth into neighboring regions, resulting in the salvation of Samaritans (8:4–25) and gentiles (8:26–40). What we have, then, is a reversal of a reversal. The seventy-two disciples reverse Genesis 10–11, only to be dispersed again. But crucially, Luke 10 and Acts 8 underscore the propagation of the gospel in both situations.

Coming back to Luke 10: the disciples ecstatically report, "Lord, even the demons submit to us in your name" (10:17), but Jesus responds in a seemingly unusual manner: "I saw Satan fall like lightning from heaven. I have given you authority to trample on snakes and scorpions and to overcome all the power of the enemy; nothing will harm you" (10:18–19). While commentators debate the precise time of Satan's fall, its tight connection to the mission of the seventy-two suggests that it occurs during or at the end of their mission. Jesus's response resembles Isaiah 14:12: "How you have fallen from heaven, morning star, son of the dawn! You have been cast down to the earth, you who once laid low the nations!" In the immediate context of Isaiah 14, the Babylonian king attempts to ascend to the same heights as God, but God will cast him down (Isa. 14:15–21). The whole of Luke 10, then, demonstrates that the seventy-two disciples continue to dismantle the kingdom of Satan. What takes place on earth in the success of the seventy-two disciples is reflected in the heavens (cf. 21:25–28; Rom. 16:20; Rev. 12). The physical and the spiritual dimensions are interlaced. Jesus's victory over Satan in the wilderness empowers his followers to continue the expansion of God's eternal kingdom and the overthrow of Satan, thereby fulfilling the OT expectation that the great antagonist of God's people would finally be defeated (Gen. 3:15; Num. 24:17–19).

Crucially, the fall of Satan in 10:18 continues Jesus's program of extending peace throughout the cosmos. The seventy-two disciples herald "peace" (*eirēnē*) to the nations (10:5), the same eschatological peace that the angels announced at Jesus's birth (2:14) and the pilgrims in Jerusalem proclaim at the triumphal entry (19:38).[13] Further still, Satan's defeat, achieved in 4:1–13

---

13. Ming Gao, *Heaven and Earth in Luke-Acts* (Carlisle, UK: Langham Monographs, 2017), 52–56.

and reiterated in 10:18, swings open the door for the gospel to flourish among the nations. According to the OT, Satan and his angels blind the nations, enticing them to commit idolatry (cf. Deut. 4:19; 1 Cor. 10:20; Rev. 20:2–3). But now that Jesus has triumphed over the demons, the truth of the gospel is unveiled, allowing the nations to stream to restored Israel so they may learn the righteous decrees of God.

The Parable of the Good Samaritan; Mary and Martha (10:25–42)

The nature of the kingdom, specifically the overthrow of Satan, has largely been "hidden . . . from the wise and the learned" (10:21). It is beyond coincidence that the following account concerns an "expert in the law" who identifies with the "wise and learned" and possesses a warped view of Jesus's program (10:25; cf. 7:30; 11:45–46, 52; 14:3). He is not making a neutral inquiry into the nature of the kingdom but wants to "test" (*ekpeirazōn*) Jesus (10:25). The same word is found in Luke 4:12, where the devil tempts Jesus to "test" God. Perhaps Luke wants his readers to view this testing in 10:25–37 as an extension of the devil's schemes, for the NT often ties false teaching to the devil.

Jesus asks a question and the scholar answers correctly by quoting Deuteronomy 6:5 and Leviticus 19:18 (// Matt. 22:34–40 // Mark 12:28–31). So far, so good. Jesus affirms his answer but then drills to the heart of the matter: "Do this and you will live" (10:28; cf. Lev. 18:5). If the expert in the law truly believes that following the Lord entails absolute devotion to God and one's neighbor, then he must act on it. "Faith without deeds is dead" (James 2:26). Can he walk the talk?

The narrator takes his audience inside the motives of the religious scholar and reveals that he wants "to justify himself" (10:29)—that is, he wants to earn his righteous stance before a holy God. Instead of living a life of faith in the promises of the Lord, he chooses to earn a right standing before God and exclude those around him. He has chosen poorly. A truly devoted heart will manifest love toward others, regardless of their social standing. In reciting Deuteronomy 6:5 ("Love the Lord [*kyrion*] your God"), Luke shows his readers an additional layer of the episode: the expert also fails to identify Jesus as his Lord (cf. 10:17, 39).

The famous parable of the good Samaritan (10:30–36) answers the question posed by the expert in the law: "Who is my neighbor?" (10:29). The parable contains four notable characters: the beaten man (Jew? gentile?), a priest, a Levite, and a Samaritan. The priest and the Levite embody the upper echelon of Jewish culture, whereas the Samaritan is an individual despised by the Jews (→John 4:1–26). The priest and the Levite pass by "on the other side" of the beaten man (10:31, 32). Commentators often point out that these two individuals are probably maintaining ritual purity (see Lev. 22:4; Num. 19:13; 31:19). They are far more concerned about the scruples of ritual than about the life of an individual. We are not far removed from Jesus's question to the Pharisees in 6:9: "Which is lawful on the Sabbath: to do good or evil, to save life or to destroy it?"

The parable must also be understood in light of the successful mission of the seventy-two disciples (10:1–17) and Luke's Gospel at large. The kingdom is blooming among the nations, and all those within the covenant community must recognize God's new phase of redemption. After Jesus delivers the parable, he asks the expert in the law, "Which of these three do you think was a neighbor . . . ?" (10:36). Perhaps reluctantly, the expert is forced to admit that the neighbor is the Samaritan, the "one who had mercy" on the beaten man (10:37a). The parable is prefaced with the imperative to "do this" (10:28)—the commandments of Deuteronomy 6:5 and Leviticus 19:18—and concludes with another imperative, "Go and do likewise" (10:37b). Leviticus 19, too, requires the Israelites to care for a "foreigner" residing among them and to "love them" (Lev. 19:33–34). In sum, while this scholar many know the ins and outs of the OT, he must practice what he preaches, regardless of a person's ethnicity. An obedient reader of Israel's law would have.

Luke places the account of Mary and Martha following Jesus's interaction with the expert in the law. While Luke identifies the location only as "a village," this account probably takes place in Bethany, where Lazarus, Mary, and Martha live (John 11:1–44; 12:1–11). The juxtaposition of the two women arrests the reader. Martha's frenetic behavior stands in contrast to Mary sitting "at the Lord's feet listening to what he said" (10:39). We find the same idea in Acts 22:3, when Paul recounts his upbringing in Jerusalem "at the feet of Gamaliel" and being "educated" (ESV, NASB). In both cases, sitting at the feet is associated with learning. In stark contrast to the expert in the law who interrogates Jesus (10:25), Mary sits at the feet of her Lord and submits herself to his kingdom message. Two women who do not enjoy a great deal of social standing in first-century Jewish culture stand in sharp relief to the popular expert in the law.

The Lord's Prayer and the Expansion of the Kingdom (11:1–13)

Chapter 11 begins with the disciples asking Jesus to instruct them on how they should pray (// Matt. 6:9–13). The Third Gospel highlights Jesus's prayer life more than any other Gospel, and we discover Jesus praying at key moments (3:21; 5:16; 6:12; 9:18, 29; 22:41, 44). His ministry opens with him praying at the

Jordan River (3:21) and ends with him praying on the cross (23:46). What is so remarkable about the disciples' request is that the disciples, like many Jews, would have enjoyed a robust prayer life. For example, the recitation of the Shema (Deut. 6:5–9) took place in the morning and evening, and Jews often prayed in their local synagogues. The disciples must have noticed something peculiar about Jesus's prayer life. Was it *when* Jesus prayed, *how* he prayed, or *what* he prayed? Was it all three?

The model prayer opens with Jesus calling God "Father" (11:2). Right away, Luke's readers would perceive an oddity: typical Jews would not call God their "Father." The OT primarily casts God as Israel's covenant-keeping King who rules over the cosmos and graciously commits himself to preserving a people group. This explains why the typical names are, for example, "Lord," "Yahweh," and "God." While the OT presents Israel's God as Father on a few occasions (Exod. 4:22–23; Deut. 1:29–31; 32:6; Ps. 103:13–14; Prov. 3:11–12; Isa. 63:16; 64:8; Mal. 2:10), it is rare. In the four Gospels, Jesus's favorite term for addressing God is "Father" (e.g., Matt. 10:32; Mark 8:38; Luke 2:49; John 5:17). Further, Jesus, on a number of occasions, claims that God is also the "Father" of the disciples (e.g., Matt. 5:16, 48; 6:1; Mark 11:25; Luke 6:36; 11:13; 12:32; John 14:7, 21). What accounts for the shift of language from the OT to the NT? Richard Bauckham argues that "Jesus may have understood Abba to be the new name of God that corresponded to the new beginning, the new exodus, the new covenant with his people that God was initiating."[14] Just as God gives Israel a distinct name in the exodus (Exod. 3:14–15), so now God receives another name in the second exodus. Perhaps the term "Father" includes not only a new dimension of intimacy but also a new revelatory description of Israel's Lord. God, the Father, will now be known by his work of redemption in his Son. The Lord's Prayer, then, is primarily marked by pleading to God to continue working out the new eschatological phase in his program—the long-awaited second exodus.

Five requests stud the prayer. The first two requests are nearly synonymous, since they entail the expansion of God's presence throughout the cosmos. The disciples should pray for the outworking of the second exodus in the setting apart ("hallowed") of God's "name" and the establishment of his kingdom on the earth (11:2). The remaining three petitions may be the manner in which the first two are carried out. That is, the requests for provision (11:3), forgiveness of sin, and deliverance from temptation (11:4) entail the responsibilities of the disciples in the ever-expanding kingdom. While God is sovereign over

14. Richard Bauckham, *Jesus: A Very Short Introduction* (Oxford: Oxford University Press, 2011), 67.

all the affairs of his kingdom, his followers remain responsible for advancing the kingdom. The disciples may be tempted to underestimate the effectiveness of prayer in this regard, but Jesus assures them that they should "ask" and "it will be given" to them (11:9).

Inevitable Conflict with the Kingdom (11:14–54)

With the success of the seventy-two disciples (10:1–24) and faithful prayer (11:1–13), the eternal kingdom is gaining traction. But as the kingdom grows, so does hostility. The message of the kingdom is always confrontational—everyone either submits to the Son of Man or rejects him. There is no middle ground. The present section of 11:14–54 describes the ramifications of unbelief and opposition.

Luke sets apart 11:14–13:8 as a broad, discrete section in which Jesus interacts at length with the "crowds" (*ochlos*; 11:14, 27, 29; 12:1, 13, 54). In the midst of this interaction, Jesus dines with the religious authorities (11:37–52), only to return to the crowds (11:53–12:1). The crowds have featured prominently in the narrative, often responding well to Jesus's message (e.g., 5:1, 15; 6:17; 8:40; 9:11, 12), but ever since Jesus turned south toward Jerusalem, the crowds are becoming increasingly hostile toward his message. *The crowds, then, embody the general perception of the nation of Israel.* Some within the crowd will respond favorably to the kingdom message, but by and large, the crowd will ultimately reject him.

The Beelzebul Controversy (11:14–36)

Jesus's faithfulness as the last Adam and true Israel broke Satan's grasp on the cosmos; but while the nature of the kingdom is largely spiritual, the kingdom has considerable physical effects. One effect is the restoration from demonic possession. Freedom from demonic enslavement brings about an incontrovertible change to a person's physical, emotional, and spiritual dimensions. The general populace and the Jewish leaders cannot deny the physical effects of the in-breaking of the kingdom. But instead of acknowledging Jesus's lordship and identity as the end-time Messiah, some within Israel pursue another route: they attribute Jesus's power to Satan himself.

Luke places the Beelzebul controversy (11:14–22 // Matt. 12:22–32 // Mark 3:22–29) after Jesus's teaching on prayer (11:1–13), so there must be an organic connection between the two. Since prayer plays an instrumental role in the expansion of the kingdom, conflict inevitably arises between believers and unbelievers—those who submit to Jesus's rule and those who reject it. This does not mean that some believers will not struggle to grasp Jesus's full identity; indeed, the disciples and Jesus's own family have yet to embrace all the aspects of his messiahship (8:19–21; 9:37–43). But what separates Jesus's family and the disciples from some within Israel is that the latter continually and willfully reject Jesus's message. We have already examined the controversy in some detail (→Mark 3:22–29), so we need only point out that Luke presents Jesus as Israel's divine warrior, who is liberating captive Israel in fulfillment of prophetic expectations (e.g., Isa. 49:24–26).

In Matthew and Mark, the controversy lies between two parties: Jesus and the religious authorities (Matt. 12:24 // Mark 3:22). Luke broadens Jesus's audience to include "some of them [the crowd]" (11:14–15). The narrative also includes a key statement: "But if I drive out demons by *the finger of God*, then the kingdom of God has come upon you" (11:20). We have stumbled upon an allusion to Exodus 8:19: "The magicians said to Pharaoh, '*This is the finger of God*.' But Pharaoh's heart was hard and he would not listen, just as the LORD had said" (cf. Exod. 31:18; Deut. 9:10 LXX). What is true of the first exodus is true of the second: God's enemies remain stubborn despite tangible signs (→John 2:1–12). Pharaoh and the Egyptians remain obstinate during the great plagues of Egypt, refusing to submit to Yahweh's acts of redemption.

In addition to a typological use of the OT here, there also may be a hint of irony. The unbelievers within the "crowd" are aligned not with the redeemed Israelites but with recalcitrant Pharaoh. Just as Pharaoh rejects the Lord in the face of the "signs" of the first exodus, so also these first-century unbelievers reject "*the sign [to sēmeion] of* Jonah" and the arrival of a "greater" Solomon in the second exodus (11:29–32 // Matt. 12:39–42). At Jesus's birth, Simeon is right to predict that Jesus is "destined to cause the falling and rising of many in Israel, and to be *a sign [sēmeion]* that will be spoken against" (2:34; cf. 2:12; 21:7, 11, 25; 23:8).

Judgment upon the Religious Authorities (11:37–54)

We now come to the result of rejecting Jesus's ministry of redeeming his people in the second exodus. Luke transitions from Jesus condemning the crowds to his eating in the home of a Pharisee (11:37–54), an episode found only in the Third Gospel. This is the second of three meals with Pharisees (7:36–50; 11:37–54; →14:1–24). In progressing from the unbelief of the crowds to the Jewish leaders, we learn that the unbelief of the crowds largely stems from their corrupt leaders. We are not privy to the motivations of this particular Pharisee; we know only that he invites Jesus to dine with him at his home along with "experts in the law" (11:45). It does not take long for conflict to arise between the two groups: "The Pharisee was surprised when he noticed that Jesus did not first wash before the meal" (11:38).

Washing one's hands before meals in first-century Jewish culture is tied to ritual purity (cf. Matt. 23:25–26), so the Pharisee is incredulous that Jesus is not obeying tightly held oral traditions. Since Jesus recently interacted with the crowds (11:37), he would be considered unclean and in need of cleansing.[15] Jesus responds with a series of scathing woes quite similar to what we find in Matthew 23 (→Matt. 23:13–36). Old Testament prophets reserve woes for those whom God will judge with finality (e.g., Isa. 3:9, 11; Jer. 48:1; Ezek. 16:23). Jesus directs the first three woes toward the Pharisees (11:39–44) and the second three toward the experts in the law (11:46–52).

Jesus first indicts the Pharisees for neglecting a fundamental principle of being created in God's image: "Did not the one who made the outside make the inside also?" (11:40). Each individual is composed of physical and spiritual dimensions, but the Pharisees, in emphasizing the external, have marginalized the heart. Godly living begins internally and then proceeds externally. Further, with the incarnation, true ritual purity—inside and out—can now only be found in Jesus (→Mark 7:1–16). Individuals must wash themselves in the fount of Jesus, who does what sacrifices and ritual washings could never accomplish—make an individual clean and acceptable before God (Heb. 9:13–14).

The first three woes concern the external behavior of Pharisees and how they are consumed with hollow obedience toward the law (11:42; Lev. 27:30; Deut. 14:22) but miss the thrust of it—namely, to love God and one another (10:27). The acclaim of others kindles their hypocritical behavior (11:43). As a result, their preoccupation with maintaining ritual purity has, ironically, caused them to be a filthy contaminant, a veritable well of uncleanness. They are "like unmarked graves" that transmit uncleanness to those who interact with them (11:44; Lev. 22:4; Num. 19:13; 31:19). The Pharisees have become like the beaten man in the parable of the good Samaritan (10:31–32), the very one they try to avoid!

The second three woes against the experts in the law (11:46–52) intensify the judgments outlined in the first three. What we learn here, though, is the culpability of the Jewish leaders and the nation as a whole. Jesus warns, "This generation will be held responsible for the blood of all the prophets that has been shed since the beginning of the world" (11:50; cf. 1 Thess. 2:14–16). Instead of instructing the covenant people to live wisely in a fallen world, the religious leaders have erected barriers that prevent others from entering into

---

15. John Nolland, *Luke 9:21–18:34*, WBC 35B (Grand Rapids: Zondervan, 1993), 663.

God's family (11:52; cf. 19:46). Such exclusion runs against the grain of Luke's message, a message that is devoted to the inclusion of the nations into true Israel. But not only are these religious leaders preventing the gentiles from joining God's people; they are even making it difficult for their fellow Jews to enjoy the blessing of God's covenantal presence!

The chapter climaxes with the reaction of the Jewish leaders when they verbally assault Jesus and "besiege him with questions . . . to catch him in something he might say" (11:53–54; cf. 6:7). Their forefathers killed the righteous prophets of old, and now they are resolute in slaughtering *the* Righteous One.

Summons to Respond to the End-Time Kingdom (12:1–19:27)

The final block of material (12:1–19:27) on the journey to Jerusalem is a summons for the religious authorities, the crowds, and the disciples to embrace the kingdom. Since Jesus inaugurates the end-time kingdom through his faithfulness as the last Adam and true Israel, all people, regardless of social standing, wealth, or ethnicity, must respond accordingly.

Warning against Hypocrisy and Material Gain (12:1–34)

After Jesus dines with the religious authorities (11:37–54), a throng of people surround him and begin "trampling on one another" (12:1a). But Jesus focuses his attention away from the crowd and addresses the disciples in 12:1b–12 (// Matt. 10:26–33). He warns them to avoid the "yeast" or "hypocrisy" of the intractable Pharisees, who are arrayed against God's righteous servants (11:37–54). God is the creator of all things, and only he can plumb the depths of the human heart and determine who truly fears him. In contrast to many within the crowd who are part of a "wicked generation" (11:29), the disciples are deemed Jesus's "friends" (12:4). They must not "be afraid of those who kill the body" but rather "fear him who, after your body has been killed, has the authority to throw you into hell" (12:4, 5). If the Jewish authorities persecute the prophets and the governing authorities set themselves against God's people, then the disciples should expect the same fate. Whereas God's enemies can only kill the body, he alone possesses the "authority" to sentence a person to hell (cf. Heb. 10:31).

A man from the crowd interjects, asking whether or not he should receive an additional slice of his brother's inheritance (12:13). While Luke's audience is unaware of the man's motivations, we should assume, on the basis of the parable that follows (12:16–21), that the request concerns material gain. Jesus responds with a governing principle: "Watch out! Be on your guard against all kinds of greed; life does not consist in an abundance of possessions" (12:15). Not only should believers "guard against" hypocrisy (12:1); they should also "guard against" greed (12:15). Material possessions are not unbiblical, but hoarding and yearning for more promotes greed and idolatry. The wealthy have great difficulty in staving off the corrupting influence of money. In 12:16–21 Jesus illustrates this with the parable of the rich man who hoards his crops and attempts to store a surplus, only to die before reaping the benefits. He is a "fool" because he invests in himself rather than in God (12:20). Indeed, he is rich on earth but "not rich toward God" (12:21; cf. 1:53).

Since believers invest their time and energy in the kingdom, they must not fret about food or clothing, for God promises to meet their needs (12:22–34 // Matt. 6:25–33). If God cares for the animals and the grass of a field, then how much more will God nourish those in his image (12:23–29; cf. Job 38:41; Ps. 147:9)? Luke is mindful of the poor and the outcast, so we are hardly surprised to find this theme crop up here. Recall that part of the Lord's Prayer is a request that God provide believers with "*daily* bread" (11:3). In the wilderness, the devil first tests Jesus, the last Adam and true Israel, by tempting him to turn a stone into bread (4:3–4). Unlike Adam in the garden and Israel in the wilderness, Jesus faithfully rests in his Father's care and provision. In the same way, those who belong to restored Israel and participate in the kingdom must imitate Jesus and trust in the goodness of the Father. Believers enjoy the "already" dimension of the end-time kingdom. Indeed, the Father has given them the kingdom (12:32; cf. 9:1; 10:19; 20:2; Acts 8:19; Dan. 7:14). Yet believers still await its future consummate fulfillment, so they are required to "seek" it (12:31). One "not yet" dimension that will take place in the eternal new cosmos is the believers' physical inheritance, in which all of the redeemed will share and enjoy the wealth of the new creation (Rev. 21:24).

Prepared for the Son of Man's Arrival (12:35–48)

The second half of chapter 12 hinges on Jesus's return as the "Lord" (*kyrios*) and Son of Man to judge all of humanity. God rewards those who soberly pursue the advancement of the kingdom but judges those who slumber and neglect its priority (cf. Rev. 3:20). Luke uses the term "Lord" or "master" (*kyrios*) nine times in 12:35–48 and in all three parables, so it is hardly a coincidence that Jesus is called "Lord" in 12:41 and 42. He should at least be indirectly identified as the "master" in the first and third parables.

In the first parable, the servants are "dressed" and "ready for service" (cf. Exod. 12:11; Eph. 6:14) because they anticipate the arrival of their master (12:35–38 // Matt. 25:1–13 // Mark 13:33–37). The second illustration concerns a house owner who fails to prepare for a thief (12:40). Together with the crowd, Peter pipes up and wonders if he and his fellow disciples will be spared the Son of Man's evaluation or if Jesus is targeting only the crowd (12:41). Jesus refuses to give Peter a direct answer, only to press on with a third parable (12:42–48). The third parable repeats the same principle: the "wise" and "faithful" manager prepares for the master's arrival, so he treats his servants well (12:42). The foolish manager grows weary and mistreats the servants (12:45 // Matt. 24:43–51). At the close of the parable, we discover two categories of foolish servants, represented by the one who "knows the master's will" yet disregards it (12:47) and the one who "does not know" the will of the master at all (12:48). The former will receive greater judgment. The disciples, the crowd, and Luke's audience must determine the correct course of action. The question is not "*Will* Jesus return and evaluate their lives?" but "*When* will the Son of Man return?"

Judgment on Those Who Refuse to Submit (12:49–13:9)

The next section further explains the nature of the Son of Man's return and reinforces the overall point of the three parables in 12:35–48. As we come across one of the most sobering passages in all of Luke, the discourse shifts from third person to first person in 12:49–53. Jesus claims to "have come to bring fire on the earth" and desires that "it were already kindled" (12:49; cf. 9:54–55). Such a statement is connected to John the Baptist's prediction that Jesus would "baptize" unbelievers with "fire" (3:16). The OT employs such language to refer to God's latter-day divine judgment upon the wicked (e.g., Isa. 9:18–19; Amos 5:6; Mal. 3:2). So when Jesus claims that he has arrived on the scene to "bring fire," he may very well be identifying with Yahweh here.

John the Baptist emerges in the wilderness precisely to prepare Israel for God's coming fiery judgment (1:76; 3:3–20). Now that John has been imprisoned, the period of preparation is nearly over, leaving little time for repentance. Jesus's audience must turn from their wickedness, lest they bear the Son of Man's end-time wrath. End-time judgment and restoration are fused together in the person of Jesus. As the Son of Man, Jesus establishes the eternal reign of God on the earth *and* executes judgment upon those who stubbornly refuse. This explains why the shepherds announce in 2:14 that there is "peace to those on whom his favor rests," but here in 12:51 Jesus explicitly claims that he has not come to "bring peace on earth."

The largely spiritual arrival of Jesus's reign is a difficult pill to swallow. Whereas the OT generally expects the kingdom and tribulation to arrive in its fullness (first the tribulation and then the kingdom), the NT authors argue that both end-time realities strangely overlap with one another. This explains why in the following passage Jesus claims that the majority of his audience is unable to discern such mysterious eschatological realities (12:54–59 // Matt. 16:2–4). They lack eyes to see and ears to hear so that they may grasp the unusual state of affairs.

A few from the crowd probe Jesus, wondering if Pilate's recent atrocities are related to Jesus's teaching concerning the Son of Man's coming in judgment (13:1). This account, unique to Luke's Gospel, contains the second mention of Pilate (3:1), where he is explicitly tied to persecution of the Jews. We have evidence of several historical accounts of Pilate provoking the Jews on a number of occasions (e.g., Josephus, *Ant.* 18.55–59), so this example in 13:1 is hardly surprising. But the discussion of Pilate's oppression of the Jews here in chapter 13 may suggest that it is a portent of things to come, as Jesus will soon suffer under his jurisdiction (ch. 23). We are, after all, on the road to Jerusalem. Jesus responds to those in the crowd, denying that the Galileans who perished at the hands of Pilate did so because of unbelief (13:2). The same principle applies for those who died when the tower in Siloam fell upon them (13:4). They weren't worse sinners than anyone else. They died because it was their time. But if the audience refuses to respond appropriately to Jesus's message, then they will suffer to a far greater degree—eternal torment (13:5). The parable of the fig tree in 13:6–9 aptly captures this principle.

The Consequence of Refusing to Believe (13:10–35)

The narrative breaks as Jesus ends his interaction with the crowd, and we move into the setting of a local synagogue, where Jesus teaches on the Sabbath (13:10). Luke's audience is privy to a concrete example of the unbelief that Jesus has warned about. Apparently, a woman from the crowd suffers a debilitating condition and cannot straighten her back. Her malady is attributed to a demon that has held her captive for eighteen years. We may make two observations: (1) Luke once again weds physical pain and suffering to demonic influence (cf. 6:18; 7:21; 8:2, 29; 9:39). As the successful Son of Man, Jesus has vanquished the devil and is in the process of overthrowing his kingdom. He seeks the full restoration of the created order. (2) The significance of this event lies in *when* Jesus heals the woman. The synagogue leader takes offense at Jesus healing the woman because it is the Sabbath—a day set apart for rest. But the leader's view of the Sabbath is skewed, along with his understanding of Jesus (→Matt. 11:27–30). The account ends with two contrasting reactions: the crowd is "delighted" on account of what Jesus has accomplished (13:17; cf. 1:14, 28; 6:23; 10:20; 15:5, 32; 19:6, 37), whereas the religious authorities are "humiliated."

How can Israel's leaders reject the very one they are expecting? Unbelief is running rampant among the nation's elite, and Luke continues to probe this issue with the two parables immediately following the healing on the Sabbath (13:18–21 // Matt. 13:31–33 // Mark 4:30–32). The parables of the mustard seed and the yeast communicate the idea that the end-time kingdom mysteriously begins small but then grows over time (→Matt. 13:24–52). It doesn't look like the kingdom has arrived (hence unbelief), but Jesus assures his audience that he has truly inaugurated the kingdom. Luke's audience must embrace the already-not-yet reality of the kingdom despite what their eyes see and their ears hear.

Jesus is on the move as he journeys "through the towns and villages" and makes "his way to Jerusalem" (13:22; cf. 8:1). Suffering and betrayal are at hand, so his message comes with a sense of urgency. One individual asks him, "Lord, are only a few people going to be saved?" (13:23). Again, the issue at hand is the lack of belief among those who hear Jesus's message. Is it true that the majority of Israel will reject their Messiah? Jesus affirms that "many . . . will try to enter [the kingdom] and will not be able to" (13:24). The illustration of the narrow door bears this out (13:24–28). Just as most Israelites have rejected a long line of prophets, the nation of Israel will not believe that Jesus is indeed the Son of God. Despite unexpected elements to Jesus's identity and kingdom, Israel is still held responsible.

In a section not dissimilar to Paul's argument in Romans 9–11, the final two verses focus on the restoration of a "few" within Israel (13:23) and the influx of the nations. According to 13:29, "people will come from east and west and north and south, and will take their places at the feast in the kingdom of God." Luke alludes to a smattering of passages from Isaiah that predict the restoration of the remnant of exiled Israelites from the four corners of the world (Isa. 43:5–7; 49:12) and the salvation of the nations. Their participation in a "feast" also fulfills Isaiah 25:6–8, where the nations enjoy an end-time covenant meal with the Lord. Both groups find their complete deliverance in trusting in the Son of Man's message and his work, resulting in their status as the true Israel of God (→5:27–39).

Luke somberly ends chapter 13 with the assured fate of the nation, the result of continued unbelief. A group of Pharisees warn Jesus that Herod perceives Jesus as a threat to his rule and wants him dead (13:31). But Jesus remains un-deterred, promising to press on: "Go tell that fox, 'I will keep on driving out demons and healing people today and tomorrow, and *on the third day* I will reach my goal" (13:32; cf. 9:22, 44; 12:50; 17:25; 18:32–33). Jesus's faithfulness in his wilderness temptation initially defeats Satan's rule over the cosmos, and then, through his teaching, exorcisms, and healings, he continues the systematic overthrow of the devil's dominion. What Jesus begins, he must complete. The ultimate goal is not the cross, as necessary and important as it is, but his resurrection/ascension, when he sits at the Father's right hand and rules to an even greater degree. But in order for Jesus to inherit his Father's cosmic rule, he must first suffer (13:34–35). Jerusalem, the very city that epitomized King David and Solomon's rule, is the city that will kill their long-awaited descendant. Consequently, divine judgment is all that remains (→19:28–44 and Matt. 23:37–39).

Feasting with the Son of Man (14:1–23)

A great deal of chapter 14 appears only in the Third Gospel, and Luke's emphasis on table fellowship is glaring. This is the third meal Jesus eats with Pharisees (7:36–50; 11:37–54; 14:1–24), and all three appear to be unique to the Third Gospel. The three meals share a few characteristics:

	Evaluation	Issue	Condemnation
7:36–50	Pharisee "saw" (7:39)	Jesus associating with an unclean sinful woman (7:37–38)	Pharisees lack love and devotion for Jesus (7:47)
11:37–54	Pharisee "noticed" (11:38)	Jesus eating with unwashed hands (11:38)	Pharisees lack purity of heart (11:39–41)
14:1–24	Pharisees "carefully watched" (14:1)	Jesus healing on the Sabbath (14:3)	Pharisees lack proper understanding of the Sabbath (14:5) and pursue positions of honor (14:8-14)

Table fellowship is seemingly an odd context for these indictments of the Jewish leaders, since meals embody deep friendship and common identity. In all three meals, Pharisees take notice of Jesus's actions. The Pharisees merely watch (*idōn*) Jesus in the first two, but during the third and final meal they "carefully watch" (*paratēroumenoi*) him (14:1). The term "carefully watch" (*paratēreō*) often occurs in the context of individuals spying on someone for the purpose of entrapment (e.g., Dan. 6:12 LXX-Theo; Sus. 12, 15–16). The same term occurs two other times in the Third Gospel, and both concern the religious leaders' desire to trap Jesus (6:7; 20:20; see Mark 3:2; Acts 9:24). Further, all three meals in Luke's narrative follow hostility between Jesus and the Jewish leaders or crowds (7:30–35; 11:29–32; 13:15–16). Perhaps, then, the religious authorities exploit table fellowship in the third instance as a place for judgment and evaluation. They never intend to enjoy sweet fellowship with Jesus. Much like Haman being hung on his own gallows (Esther 7:10), Jesus uses table fellowship as an opportunity to condemn and evaluate *them*!

The miracle in 14:1–6 is the fourth miracle Jesus performs on the Sabbath (see 4:31–35; 6:6–11; 13:10–17), and many of the same themes surface here. The religious authorities have abused the Sabbath by oppressively restricting nearly every aspect of Jewish life during it. There is no Sabbath rest here. In 14:1 the Pharisees "carefully watch" Jesus, whereas in 14:7 he notices them. Jesus draws their attention to how they "picked the places of honor at the table." Their behavior during the meal is a microcosm of their behavior in all of life. Instead of pursuing God's glory and adoration, they pursue their own by oppressing the weak. The time has come for God to invert their way of life. This man's dropsy, a condition associated with greed and gluttony where the body swells due to the buildup of liquid, embodies the Pharisees. They "need to be healed of their moral dropsy, their greedy desire for personal wealth and honor. There is one in their midst who can heal them of their unquenchable selfish social and material ambition."[16]

After healing the man and silencing the Pharisees (14:4–6), Jesus issues two parables to his audience. The first parable entails a wedding celebration where the guests should pursue the "lowest place" and not the "place of honor" (14:8–10; cf. Prov. 25:6–7). Verse 11 could very well be viewed as a summary of the entirety of Luke's Gospel: "All those who exalt themselves will be humbled, and those who humble themselves will be exalted." Luke may be alluding to Ezekiel 21:26 here, as commentators often suggest (cf. James 4:10; Sir. 3:19; Let. Aris. 263). The point of the OT allusion is that "the source of honor (*doxa*; 14:10) in God's kingdom is derived not from the social order described by affluent friends, siblings, relatives, or rich neighbors (cf. 14:12), but from the judgment of God."[17] Divine judgment is poured out upon the proud who refuse to submit to Jesus's authority, whereas end-time restoration awaits those who bow the knee before the Son of Man. In contrast to the religious authorities, Luke sets forth Jesus as the supreme example of one who humbles himself so that God will "exalt" him:

Jesus: Prototype of Humility Leading to Exaltation	Jewish Leaders: Prototype of Exaltation Leading to Humiliation
Born in humble circumstances (2:12)	Assume positions of honor (11:43; 20:46)
Serves others (22:27)	Exploit their position of wealth and influence (11:46)
Welcomes outsiders (5:30; 7:34; 15:2; 19:7)	Marginalize outsiders (10:30–37)
Exalted to the right hand of the Father (Acts 2:33; 5:31)	Judged at the very end of history (11:46–52)

16. Garland, *Luke*, 567.
17. David W. Pao and Eckhard J. Schnabel, "Luke," in *Commentary on the New Testament Use of the Old Testament*, ed. G. K. Beale and D. A. Carson (Grand Rapids: Baker Academic, 2007), 339.

To identify with the exalted and vindicated Son of Man, one must first put one's trust in him and then pursue a life of service to others. At the resurrection, God will publicly vindicate and exalt believers before the world. According to the second parable, Luke's audience should welcome the marginalized (14:12–14) instead of inviting members of their own elite social standing. Both parables reflect Luke's unique vertical and horizontal perspective on the kingdom (→1:52).

The meal at the Pharisee's house continues as one individual announces, "*Blessed* is the one who will eat at the feast in the kingdom of God" (14:15). As a response, Jesus relates a third parable to the group at the table. The thrust of the parable of the banquet (14:16–24 // Matt. 22:2–14) is that while those who participate in the end-time feast will indeed be "blessed," only those who respond rightly to the invitation will enjoy its benefits. Blessing in Luke's narrative is largely tied to eschatological restoration in the new eternal cosmos, a condition reserved solely for those who follow Jesus throughout their life (e.g., 6:20–22; 11:28; 12:37; 14:14).

One by one, the invited guests are unable to attend the banquet. The first two guests are more concerned about material possessions (14:18–19), and the third turns down the invitation on account of a recent marriage (14:20). Jesus has already spoken about the crippling effects of wealth (12:13–34) and the priority of the kingdom over the bonds of family (9:60; 11:28), so there are no surprises here. The parable takes a startling turn, however. Instead of canceling the feast, the man offers the invitation to the downtrodden—"the poor, the crippled, the blind and the lame" (14:21). It probably doesn't take long for those seated at the table with Jesus to connect the dots. The first three invitees are the Pharisees; because they cherish their positions of honor and pursue their status over following Jesus, they are denied entrance to the feast. They pursue blessing, but they receive a curse. The marginalized, on the other hand, commit themselves to following Jesus and receive great blessing. This parable encapsulates the heart of Luke's two-volume project: the insiders (the Israelites) are outsiders, and the outsiders (gentiles and social outcasts) are insiders.

Chapter 14 ends with a fitting block of teaching concerning the nature of true perseverance within the kingdom. The narrative shifts from Jesus dining with the Pharisees (14:1–24) to him traveling on the road to Jerusalem with "large crowds" (14:25). All three Synoptics include the parable of the seeds (Matt. 13:1–15 // Mark 4:1–12 // Luke 8:4–10) to stress one basic principle: though some are attracted to the message of the kingdom and begin to follow Jesus, they often do not—on account of wealth, persecution, family, and so on—persevere to the end. Gaining entrance into the eternal new heavens and earth requires absolute devotion to Jesus, from start to finish (5:11; 6:47; 9:24; 17:33; 18:29).

After discussing one's commitment to the kingdom, even above family (14:26–27 // Matt. 10:37–38), Jesus gives two short parables that illustrate the importance of measuring one's obligation to the kingdom. Just as one calculates the cost of building a tower and a king estimates the number of soldiers needed for battle, so also those within the crowd need to measure the cost of following Jesus (14:28–33). But how much does it cost? Everything.

The discourse ends with a command: "Whoever has ears to hear, let them hear" (14:35). This exact clause occurs earlier in 8:8b immediately following the proclamation of the parable of the seeds to the crowd (8:4–8a). In both cases, Jesus's audience must have spiritual perception to fully grasp his parabolic teaching (cf. Deut. 29:3–4; Isa. 6:9–10; →Mark 4:1–20). Only those who are truly devoted to the kingdom will understand Jesus's difficult teaching, whereas the casually committed will remain ignorant. The parables cut two ways—blessing for believers and cursing for unbelievers.

Joy over Repentance (15:1–32)

In 15:1 the narrative progresses as Jesus shifts his focus back to the religious authorities (cf. 14:1, 25). The section opens with "tax collectors and sinners . . . *drawing near* to him" (15:1 ESV), hinting that ritual purity is likely in mind; it would be scandalous for a Jew to fellowship with unclean individuals ("sinners"). While we are not told the precise identity of the sinners, only that they are paired with tax collectors (cf. 5:30; 7:34, 37), we should assume that they comprise any individuals who are not conforming to the oral tradition of the Pharisees. Further, according to their oral tradition, a house becomes unclean when tax collectors enter it (m. Hag. 3.6; m. Tehar. 7.6). So the three parables in 15:1–32 appear to address one issue: How can a holy God dwell with unclean sinners? Answer: through repentance. Turning from sin and clinging to Jesus is the way in which believers enjoy God's presence. All three parables stress, above all, God's joy over those who repent. Not only does a holy God dwell with humanity through his Son; he takes pleasure in it. A good case can be made that all of 15:1–17:10 takes place at an undisclosed location where Jesus fellowships with tax collectors, sinners, Pharisees, and his disciples. The first three parables (15:3–32) primarily target the Pharisees, whereas the next three parables are addressed to the disciples (16:1–13, 19–31; 17:6–10).

The parable of the lost sheep (15:3–7) mirrors the parable found in Matthew 18:12–14, but there the focus is on the worth of children in the kingdom (Matt. 18:1, 6, 10). Here in Luke 15, Jesus draws his audience's attention to the worth of repentant "sinners" (15:1, 10, 18). Though the same parable occurs in Matthew 18 and Luke 15, the differences in Luke's account underscore a few themes that frame much of the chapter. First, Luke emphasizes joy: "He *joyfully* [*chairōn*] puts it on his shoulders. . . . '*Rejoice with* [*syncharēte*] me.' . . . There will be more *rejoicing* [*chara*] in heaven" (15:5–7). From the beginning of Luke's Gospel, joy remains an important and unique element of the narrative, for it tangibly illustrates the in-breaking of the new creation and the fulfillment of God's promises (e.g., 1:14; 2:10; 10:17).

Second, Luke also highlights repentance: "one sinner who *repents* . . . ninety-nine righteous persons who do not need to *repent*" (15:7). Certainly, the restoration of the nations and those on society's fringes strikes a major chord within the narrative, but it does so with an important qualification—all must turn from their sin and embrace Jesus as Savior (e.g., 3:3, 8; 5:32; 13:3, 5; 24:47). Access to the end-time kingdom is restricted to those who renounce sin and embrace Jesus.

The parable of the lost coin (15:8–10) rehearses the same ideas. A woman, upon discovering her lost coin, summons her friends to "rejoice" with her (15:9). Just as the shepherd and the woman rejoice in discovering what had been lost, so also heaven itself erupts with joy over the conversion of a sinner (15:7, 10). In contrast to the religious leaders, who grumble (15:2), the angels rejoice (15:10). What is true on earth is true in heaven. The covenant community on earth is represented by the angels assembled before the throne of God (see Rev. 1:20).

The parable of the prodigal son (15:11–32) is one of the most well-known passages in all of Luke. The point of the first two parables is rehearsed here but in more detail. In addition, a third party enters the picture. The basic flow of the story is easy to follow: A Jewish father has two sons. The older appears to remain faithful to his family and God, whereas the younger receives an early inheritance only to squander it on sinful living. The younger son, after finding himself in the worst of circumstances—eating with the pigs—repents and returns home. The father is quick to recognize the son's repentance and immediately celebrates his return. The older son, the firstborn, grows jealous since he never left the fold, so to speak. The final line—the climax of the parable of the prodigal son and the main point of all three parables—is the recovery of what was lost. God rejoices over those who repent.

Identifying the main characters is a bit tricky. Since there is "rejoicing" in heaven in the first two parables (15:7, 10), we should assume that the father, who is eager to "celebrate" and "be glad" (15:23, 24, 32), is God. The older son, the firstborn, is analogous to the religious authorities who bank on their covenantal identity to save them, not on a soft heart for God (15:2). The prodigal son, though, is harder to determine. He could refer to a wayward Jew who behaves like pagan gentiles, only to repent and return to God. Or he could refer to a gentile who belongs to God's larger family of humanity, repents, and then becomes a true child. Or the prodigal could embody the outsiders—a chief theme of the Third Gospel. His identity could even be a blend of all three. No matter how we slice it, the point is that the prodigal son is a *sinner*. Recall that Luke applies the term "sinner" to Jews, gentiles, and even Peter (5:8; 7:37; 13:2; 19:7; 24:7).

The parable rotates around two contrasting reactions to the prodigal's return:

Father (God)	Older Son (Religious Authorities)
"Filled with compassion" (15:20)	"Became angry" (15:28)
"Ran to his son" (15:20) and "began to celebrate" (15:24)	"Refused to go in [the house]" (15:28)
Refers to the prodigal as "your [older son's] brother" (15:27)	Refuses to be called the prodigal's brother and instead labels him "this son of yours [father's]" (15:30)

The brilliance of the parable is its summary of a great deal of Luke's message: God is quick to welcome sinners but resolutely hostile toward those who refuse to turn from sin. God's compassion for sinners is tangibly on display when Jesus welcomes the broken. But as the kingdom extends to outsiders, unbelieving Jews and especially the Jewish authorities grow more and more antagonistic toward Jesus's mission. Grace is met with animosity. Note, though, that Jesus still invites the Jewish authorities to repent and accept his invitation. Luke's audience must pause and consider how they will respond. Will they admit to and turn from their sin and embrace Jesus, or will they refuse what he offers?

Three reflections on this profound parable are in order. First, the father's treatment of the prodigal son is laden with symbolic language. The parable associates the younger son with pigs, which makes him ritually unclean (Lev. 11:7; Deut. 14:8; Isa. 65:4; 66:3, 17). Not only is the son the pigs' caretaker; he yearns to eat with the pigs (15:15–16). Luke's pervasive emphasis on table fellowship in his narrative is now all the more striking. The son is, at some level, identified with the putrid swine. Upon recognizing his condition, the son comes "to his senses," repents, and heads home (15:17–18).

Second, the father's treatment of his prodigal son is remarkable in its similarities to the Joseph narrative. He clothes the son in his "best robe" and puts a ring on his finger and sandals on his feet (15:22). The language is close to Genesis 41:42, when Pharaoh gives Joseph a ring and dresses "him in robes of fine linen." A few verses earlier, the prodigal son is forced to work with pigs because "there was a severe famine in that whole country" (15:14). According to Genesis 41, Pharaoh dreams that seven years of famine would descend upon Egypt after seven years of prosperity (Gen. 41:25–32). The combination of these plot points refers Luke's audience back to the Joseph narrative. The donning of clothes in the OT and Judaism symbolizes the right to inherit and rule (e.g., Gen. 3:21; 37; Num. 20:24–28; 1 Kings 11:30–31; 19:19–21; Isa. 22:21; 1 En. 62:15–16). The prodigal son, after recognizing his sin, comes and receives a great deal of inheritance and rule over the estate, just as Joseph is given the right to rule over Egypt. The father elevates his prodigal son to the status of ruler. The restoration of the prodigal son, the sinner, symbolizes all the outsiders within Luke's narrative and their new identity as the true Israel of God. They are all identified with the great patriarch Joseph. The father twice announces that the son "was dead" but is now "alive again" (15:24, 32). Life here should be understood as *resurrection* life, the new creational act of God whereby he spiritually resurrects those who trust in Jesus (see John 5:25; Rom. 6:11, 13; 1 Pet. 1:3; Rev. 1:18; 2:8; 20:5).

Third, a key feature of the parable lies in how the older son relates to the younger and the older one's lack of joy over the prodigal's return. Upon seeing Jesus's compassion toward outsiders, the Jews should have responded kindly and joyfully welcomed the repentant sinners into the family of God. But that never materialized. The parable of the prodigal son stings Jesus's hearers, for they must repent of their legalism and identify with the younger son if they are to be clothed in God's finest attire.

Wealth for the Sake of the Kingdom (16:1–31)

One scholar comments on the parable of the unjust steward, "The parable suggests numerous connections, nuances, and possibilities—most of them dead ends."[18] The parable of the "unjust steward," or the parable of the "shrewd manager" (16:1–13), is difficult on multiple levels. To name a few, it's not clear where the parable ends, the thematic link that ties the present parable with the previous parable is not readily apparent, and, perhaps most importantly and unexpectedly, the master applauds the dealings of his dishonest manager.

Klyne Snodgrass sensibly argues that the parable runs from 16:1 to 16:8a, while 16:8b interprets the parable and 16:9 applies it.[19] After delivering three

18. Klyne R. Snodgrass, *Stories with Intent: A Comprehensive Guide to the Parables of Jesus* (Grand Rapids: Eerdmans, 2008), 402.
19. Snodgrass, *Stories with Intent*, 411.

parables to the Pharisees (15:1–32), Jesus primarily addresses the Twelve in 16:1–17:10. We transition from the parable of the prodigal son (15:11–31) to the parable of the shrewd manager (16:1–15). While it may seem odd to jump from one to the other, we discover a key link in 16:9: "I tell you, *use worldly wealth to gain friends* for yourselves, so that when it is gone, you will be welcomed into eternal dwellings." The prodigal son squanders his inheritance on himself (15:13–14), but when he repents, the father entrusts the younger son with his wealth (15:22–24). The son is now in a position to use his wealth wisely. The parable of the shrewd manager is then the logical outflow of the parable of the prodigal son. Chapter 16 largely concerns wealth and how the Pharisees are identified as those "who loved money" (16:14).

Luke presents the Pharisees as collectively setting themselves against Jesus for a variety of reasons (5:21, 30; 6:7; 11:53, etc.). But while readers can infer that the Pharisees are wealthy (see 14:1), this is the first instance where they are explicitly identified with great wealth. Although Jesus addresses his disciples in 16:1, the parable of the shrewd manager (16:1–8a) and the parable of the rich man and Lazarus (16:19–31) are a direct attack against the Jewish leaders. It may not be far off the mark to suggest that Jesus is warning the Twelve to not accrue wealth with the same motivation as the religious authorities (see 12:1–48).

The parable of the shrewd manager opens with the manager "*wasting* [*diaskorpizōn*] his [the rich man's] possessions" (16:1), just as the prodigal son "*squandered* [*dieskorpisen*] his wealth" (15:13; cf. 1:52). The rich man is right to be angry, for the manager has abused his estate. While we expect the master to punish the steward, the parable takes an unusual turn: the steward approaches two of his master's debtors and settles the debts for a fraction of what is owed (16:5–7). So the steward doubles down by reducing the debt, forcing the master to lose even *more* money. Oddly, "the master" (*ho kyrios*) commends the "dishonest manager" because he acts "shrewdly" (16:8).

The key to understanding the parable is found in 16:9, which can be paraphrased, "Put yourself in a good position through your use of money, which so easily leads you astray, so that when this age is over God will receive you into his eternal dwelling."[20] The last clause of 16:9, "they may welcome you into eternal dwellings" (HCSB), is critical. The same idea is found in 16:4 as the motivating factor of the steward's actions: "People will welcome me into their houses." The savvy actions of the steward, though unjust, are the means by which he gains entrance into these homes. The phrase "eternal dwellings" is unique and most likely refers to the new heavens and earth—the "eternal

---

20. Snodgrass, *Stories with Intent*, 415.

dwelling" place of God and humanity. The term "dwellings" occurs often in the context of the tabernacle/temple in both Testaments (e.g., Exod. 25:9 LXX; Matt. 17:4 // Mark 9:5 // Luke 9:33; Acts 15:16; Heb. 8:2, 5; Rev. 21:3). If Jesus's audience wants to gain admittance into the new cosmic temple, then they must, like the unjust steward, use their wealth, possessions, social standing, connections, employment—all of life—for the sake of the kingdom and not for themselves.

The following section (16:10–15) reinforces this principle and outlines the Pharisees' reaction. Though Jesus addresses the parable to his disciples in 16:1, the Pharisees take umbrage at the meaning of the parable (16:14). They do so because they would rather use their wealth to build their own kingdom on earth—an empire that will soon fade—than to serve God's eternal kingdom. They choose corruptible possessions over the incorruptible new cosmos. In between the parable of the unjust steward and that of the rich man and Lazarus is a brief section that, while knotty in its details, concerns two central points: (1) The kingdom that Jesus inaugurates truly fulfills OT expectations. The entire OT, at some level, anticipates Jesus and his kingdom message (24:27). (2) Jesus's audience must therefore do whatever it takes to gain admittance, "forcing their way into it" (16:16; cf. Matt. 11:12) and remaining faithful to their spouse (16:18 // Matt. 5:32; 19:9 // Mark 10:11).

The parable of the rich man and Lazarus (16:19–31), perhaps one of the most poignant and engaging parables in Luke's narrative, explains the outcome of a life devoted to wealth and pleasure. Jesus uses the parable of the unjust steward (16:1–8) to motivate his audience to use their wealth wisely, whereas this parable explains what will befall those who refuse to do so. The characters in parables usually remain unnamed, but here the poor man is called Lazarus. Why? Lazarus is the Greek name for the Hebrew Eliezer, a name that means "God helps" (see Exod. 18:4), and commentators often suggest that "God helps" the poor man in contrast to the rich man, who helps himself. The rich man is clearly juxtaposed with Lazarus on multiple levels, before and after death:

Rich Man before Death	Lazarus before Death
Dresses "in purple and fine linen" (16:19)	Bedecked with sores (16:20)
Dines sumptuously (16:19)	Begs for food (16:21)
Receives "good things" (16:25)	Receives "bad things" (16:25)
Rich Man after Death	**Lazarus after Death**
Endures an unquenchable fire (16:24)	Dines with Abraham (16:23)
Lives "in torment" (16:23, 25)	Lives in comfort (16:25)

A great reversal occurs after death. Lazarus, the beggar, gains the inheritance of the new heavens and earth, where he dwells with Abraham. The rich man, on the other hand, finds himself destitute and in eternal agony.

Moreover, the fact that the rich man calls Abraham his "father" upon death and that Abraham calls him his "son" is striking (16:24, 25, 27). John the Baptist's words to the crowds ring true once again: "Do not begin to say to yourselves, 'We have Abraham as our father.' For I tell you that out of these stones God can raise up children for Abraham" (3:8). Robust faith in Jesus is the true defining characteristic of God's people, not lineage.

In between the rich man and Lazarus a "great chasm has been set in place" (16:26), not permitting either party to join the other (cf. 1 En. 18:11–12; 22:8–13). The rich man, now living in fiery torment (cf. Isa. 66:24; Matt. 13:40, 42; Jude 7; Rev. 20:10), asks Abraham if Lazarus could inform his five brothers of what will transpire if they remain engrossed in wealth (16:28). Their very lives depend on it. Abraham tells him that there is no need for Lazarus to do so because the entire OT bears witness to this message (16:29). The rich man pleads one last time, asking if perhaps someone "from the dead" will testify—surely then his brothers will have a change of heart (16:30). Abraham's final response is stunning: "If they do not listen to Moses and the Prophets, they will not be convinced even if someone rises from the dead" (16:31). Clearly Jesus's own resurrection has now entered the picture. We can glean two principles here: (1) The truthfulness and reliability of the OT is just as sure as Jesus's resurrection. So to doubt the OT is to doubt the resurrection, and to doubt his resurrection is to doubt the OT. Further still, the OT itself anticipates Jesus's resurrection, so the two notions are inextricably bound together (24:25–27, 45–46). (2) Despite Jesus's resurrection being reliable and utterly true, many will inevitably doubt it (→Matt. 27:62–66).

The main idea of the parable of the rich man and Lazarus, then, reinforces the thrust of the parable of the unjust steward: money and possessions must be used as tools for the sake of the kingdom; otherwise, eternal torment awaits. If the religious authorities remain greedy and marginalize outsiders, then they will, like the rich man, endure estrangement from God. The poor, however, must continue to rely upon "God's help" in every aspect of life so that they may "inherit the earth" at the resurrection (Matt. 5:5).

Faithfulness in the Present and Future Kingdom (17:1–37)

Chapter 17 continues to probe the question of what faithful devotion to Jesus entails. While chapter 16 focuses on *wealth and devotion*, chapter 17 centers on *true, persevering faith*. We can subdivide chapter 17 into four broad sections: (1) the first section concerns a faith that falls prey to false teaching (17:1–4); (2) instead, genuine faith promotes the growth of the kingdom (17:5–10); (3) such faith is available to all, even a Samaritan leper (17:11–19); and (4) genuine faith will persevere until the second coming of the Son of Man (17:20–37).

The first section begins with Jesus addressing his disciples (17:1; cf. 16:1). Recall that his address in 16:1 was interrupted by the Pharisees in 16:14. Resuming his discourse aimed at the disciples, Jesus claims that "things that cause people to stumble are bound to come, but woe to anyone through whom they come" (17:1; →Matt. 18:6–9). The phrase "things that cause people to stumble" is one word in Greek (*ta skandala*), often referring to some sort of trap or enticement, especially idolatry and false teaching (see, e.g., LXX: Josh. 23:13; Judg. 2:3; 8:27; Pss. 105:36; 140:9; Hosea 4:17; Wis. 14:11; 1 Macc. 5:4; Pss. Sol. 4:23; see also Rom. 14:13; 16:17; Gal. 5:11). It is likely, then, that Jesus is denouncing the deception of the Jewish leaders (16:14; 17:22). False teaching is inevitable, yet God promises to judge severely those who proclaim it.

In order to withstand false teaching, the disciples respond with a desire for Jesus to "increase" their "faith" (17:5); they want "bigger" faith. But more is not always better. It is the quality of the faith that counts. The second section demonstrates that a little faith, the size of a mustard seed, has great power—enough to uproot and plant a mulberry tree (17:6). Several chapters earlier, Jesus compares the growth of the kingdom to that of a mustard seed that, though incredibly small, becomes a powerful tree (13:19; cf. Ezek. 17:23; Dan. 4:20–22). The kingdom, too, begins with a single person, Jesus, but eventually expands to the ends of the earth (Acts 1:8). The disciples must not succumb to the wiles of the religious authorities but must possess genuine faith in the advancement of the kingdom that is rooted in Jesus.

After furnishing a parable on the nature of faithful service (17:7–10), Luke reminds his readers once more that Jesus is still on his journey to Jerusalem (17:11; cf. 9:51, 53; 13:33; 18:31; 19:11). Suffering awaits. As Jesus heads south, he enters into a town near or in Samaria, where ten lepers meet him (17:12). Samaritans and Jews did not get along for several reasons (→John 4:1–26). Earlier in Luke's narrative, Jesus dispatches a few disciples to a particular Samaritan town, only to be rebuffed (9:52–53). This time, though, Jesus seeks an audience with lepers. The term "leper" (*lepra*) entails a wide variety of skin diseases,[21] but the essence of the offense is that it ritually defiled the individual, consigning them to a life outside the Israelite community (see 5:12–14). Until the individual was cleansed, he or she could not participate in

---

21. BDAG, λέπρα, 592.

society, let alone worship. Jesus points out that the Samaritan is the only one to respond with worship when he is cleansed, noting that his "faith" made him "well" or, better, "saved him" (17:19).

The key to unlocking the significance of the miracle lies in the response of the lone man who returned, "praising God" (17:15). Praising God is a key response in Luke-Acts in that it rightly recognizes God's gracious act of deliverance (e.g., Luke 2:14, 20; 5:25, 26; 7:16; 13:13; 18:43; Acts 4:21; 11:18; 21:20; cf. Acts 12:23). Faith in Jesus leads to restoration and deliverance, regardless of ethnicity. While the other nine lepers are healed physically, this one is healed physically *and* spiritually.

The fourth and final dimension of faith is that it perseveres until the second coming of Jesus (17:20–37). The section opens with the Pharisees questioning Jesus about the establishment of the eternal kingdom (17:20). They probably assume that the end-time kingdom will arrive all at once and with great suddenness, a belief that is generally in line with the OT (→Matt. 13:24–52). But Jesus claims that the arrival of the kingdom first takes place primarily (but not exclusively) on a spiritual level—"the coming of the kingdom of God is not something that can be observed" (17:20b; cf. 8:10; 13:18–20; 19:11). Indeed, he argues, "the kingdom of God is in your midst" (17:21; cf. 11:20; 16:16). The kingdom is already but not yet.

Turning to his disciples, Jesus then focuses on the "not yet" future, physical dimension of the kingdom. He states, "The time is coming when you will long to see one of the days of the Son of Man, *but you will not see it*" (17:22). The disciples will not witness the arrival of the consummation, the full-blown fulfillment of the eternal kingdom, an event that will take place at the very end of history. Much of the material of 17:22–37 is found in Matthew 24:17–18, 23–27, and 37–39. Matthew 24:4–35 concerns the destruction of the temple in AD 70 and the events leading up to it, whereas Luke focuses on the end of world history, outlining the second coming of Jesus and the events leading up to it. As we discussed in Matthew 24:36–25:46, the events of AD 70 serve as an eschatological template for Jesus's second coming. The title "Son of Man" occurs some twenty-five times in Luke, and many of its occurrences are associated either with Jesus's death (9:22, 44, 58; 18:31; 24:7) or with his second coming (9:26; 12:8, 40; 17:22, 24, 26, 30; 18:8; 21:27; 22:69). Not coincidentally, the son of man figure of Daniel 7 brings together both of these dimensions—suffering (7:21, 25) and exaltation/judgment upon wickedness (7:12–14). During Jesus's journey to Jerusalem, Luke has emphasized God's judgment upon those who are consumed with wealth and possessions (e.g., 12:20; 16:9), whereas this section largely focuses on the role of the Son of Man as judge (cf. 12:40). Judgment awaits all who neglect the Son of Man's message.

The disciples must resist false teachers who claim to be the Messiah (17:23 // Matt. 24:23–26). Jesus's arrival, unlike the presence of these false teachers, will radiate throughout the cosmos (17:24; cf. Rev. 6:14). In the fifth passion prediction, Jesus once more reminds the disciples of what must transpire before his return: "but first he must suffer many things and be rejected by this generation" (17:25; cf. 9:22, 44; 12:50; 13:32–33; 18:32–33). Luke compares, probably typologically, the coming of the Son of Man to the "days of Noah" (17:26) and the "days of Lot" (17:28). The descriptions of both OT events in Luke 17 are intriguing, since it is not altogether clear why the Third Evangelist taps Genesis 6–7 and Genesis 19. We can probably assume that Luke has in mind at least a moral dimension: Noah and Lot lived during times of notable wickedness (see 2 Pet. 2:5–6; Jude 7). But in both cases, Luke underscores how groups carried out their normal daily living,[22] completely oblivious to looming judgment (17:27–28). Such behavior is utterly antithetical to Jesus's teaching on the road to Jerusalem, where he repeatedly calls his audience to a life of sobriety and attentiveness. Spiritual lethargy has no place in the overlap of the ages. The last section outlines the sense of urgency attached to the second coming (17:30–37). Worldly possessions and status are straw in light of God's fiery judgment (Isa. 5:24). As with the great flood in Genesis 7, those who are consumed with this world will be "taken" away in judgment, while the faithful will be "left" (17:34–35).

Persevering Faith (18:1–43)

During the interadvent period, the covenant community will endure great hardship and persecution, so the parable of the persistent widow motivates believers to persevere. Unlike other parables in Luke's Gospel, this one is prefaced with a purpose statement: "that they [the disciples] should always pray and not give up" (18:1; cf. 5:36; 6:39; 12:16; 13:6, etc.). The phrase "give up" occurs often in the New Testament in the context of bearing up under end-time persecution (2 Cor. 4:1, 16; Gal. 6:9; Eph. 3:13; 2 Thess. 3:13).

The general flow of the parable is easy enough: a widow steadfastly pleads with a pagan judge to grant her justice. Nearly all the details of the parable are vague—we know nothing of why or how the widow was wronged, nothing about the "adversary," and nothing about where this took place except for "in a certain town" (18:2a). But we do learn something about the nature of the judge: he "neither feared God nor cared what people thought" (18:2b), and, on account of the widow's persistence, he hands down a favorable verdict (18:5).

22. See discussion in Pao and Schnabel, "Luke," 347–48.

The parable turns on two key themes: justice and perseverance. Luke goes out of his way to highlight the unbelieving status of the judge. Why? The idea is that if an unrighteous judge hands down a favorable verdict for persistence, how much more will a righteous judge do so? The noun and verb forms for "justice" are riddled throughout the parable, occurring in 18:3, 5, 7, and 8. This is not the generic form for "justice," though. The term here is found in a number of passages that describe acts of retribution or vengeance—justice for a person who has been victimized (see Rom. 12:19; 13:4; Heb. 10:30; 1 Pet. 2:14; Rev. 6:10, etc.). The widow in the parable, then, is seeking retribution and vindication. She desires that the judge punish the one who has unjustly wronged her.

In the previous context, much of Jesus's teaching concerns the believers' perseverance before his second coming (17:22–37). As history unfolds, hostility increases between God's people and the world. Participating in the kingdom inevitably results in great hardship and persecution. True believers must "lose" their lives for the sake of the kingdom (17:33). They will be wronged, and the world will do its worst. But because the widow perseveres, the judge avenges her. Because true believers press on in their faith, God promises to avenge them (see Rev. 6:9–10).

Whereas the parable of the persistent widow underscores persevering faith, a faith that endures until the end (18:1–8), the parable of the Pharisee and the tax collector highlights the quality of faith that initially brings one into a relationship with God (18:9–14). Jesus addresses the parable to "some who were confident of their own righteousness and looked down on everyone else" (18:9). This Pharisee boasts in his identity as a member of the covenant community (18:11–12). His horizontal behavior—that is, his exclusion of sinners—affects his vertical relationship with God. In his eyes, he *deserves* God's affection and presence because of his external conformity to God's law and because of his adherence to human tradition. In vivid contrast, a tax collector has no leg to stand on; all of his works dissolve like quicksand. But God looks upon the tax collector and justifies him because of the inner disposition of the man's heart—he recognizes that he is estranged from God, a "sinner" (18:13). Luke often pairs Pharisees and sinners, and one could argue that this parable embodies all that has come before and all that follows (see 5:30, 32; 7:37, 39; 15:1–2).

In the explanation of the parable, Jesus asserts that God justifies the tax collector because "all *those who exalt* [*ho hypsōn*] themselves *will be humbled* [*tapeinōthēsetai*], and *those who humble* [*ho tapeinōn*] themselves *will be exalted* [*hypsōthēsetai*]" (18:14). The wording here evokes a programmatic verse in the Magnificat: "He [God] has brought down rulers from their thrones but *has lifted up the humble [hypsōsen tapeinous]*" (1:52). The Pharisee exults in his own merit and attempts to rule over outsiders, so God cuts him down. On the other hand, the tax collector recognizes his lowly position, so God raises him up.

The following two passages reinforce the principle of God exalting the lowly and humbling the proud (18:15–30). According to 18:15, many were "bringing *infants* to him so he might touch them" (HCSB). Luke often associates touching in his narrative with healing (e.g., 5:13; 6:19; 7:39; 8:44–47; 22:51), so it's possible that parents brought their infants to Jesus on account of a physical issue with their children. Whatever the case, the point of 18:15–17 is that Jesus admits *all* into the kingdom, regardless of age. Whereas Matthew's and Mark's accounts read "children" (*paidia*; Matt. 19:13 // Mark 10:13), Luke's reads "infants" (*ta brephē*; 18:15). Why the difference? Luke may be furthering the contrast between the Pharisee in 18:9–14 and the infants in 18:15. Jesus opens the door of the kingdom for those who, like babies, have nothing to offer; but he bolts the door shut to those who, like the Pharisee, think they have earned it.

The next section rounds out Jesus's insistence that following him is the only requirement for the end-time kingdom (→Mark 10:17–22). God condemns the Pharisee in 18:9–14 because he boasts in his superiority over others, and here a "certain ruler" stands condemned because he boasts in his adherence to God's law (18:18, 20–21 // Matt. 19:16–29 // Mark 10:17–30). The unwillingness of the rich young ruler to love God above his extensive wealth is an indictment of many of the religious authorities who have interacted with Jesus on his journey to Jerusalem (→12:1–34 and 16:1–31). It is beyond coincidence that Jesus devotes a great deal of his journey to the subject of wealth and possessions. In the end, God detests both expressions of boasting—horizontal (18:14) and vertical (18:21). Notice, too, Luke's three descriptions of what is at stake: justification (18:14), entrance into the kingdom (18:16), and eternal life (18:18). While all three are not synonymous expressions and entail slightly different spiritual realities, they are tightly bound up with one another.

As Jerusalem draws near, Jesus issues his sixth and final passion prediction (18:32–33; see 9:22, 44; 12:50; 13:32–33; 17:25). The prediction is prefaced with Jesus taking "the Twelve aside" (18:31). With the exception of 17:25, each passion prediction is spoken exclusively to the disciples, and even in 17:25 the prediction is rather cryptic. The idea, then, is that Jesus chooses to reveal this key aspect of his ministry to a chosen few. The crowds are unable to grasp Jesus's suffering, death, and resurrection. Their expectations make little room for a messiah who bears God's curse and subsequently rises from the dead. The disciples, too, have difficulty wrapping their heads around Jesus's death and resurrection. Luke is the only evangelist to place the prediction immediately before the healing of the blind man and the only author to mention the ignorance of the disciples (// Matt. 20:17–19 // Mark 10:32–34). This is also the second time Luke describes the disciples as lacking understanding and states that Jesus's passion prediction remains "hidden" from them (9:45; 18:34). The tension (not contradiction) in all four Gospels is that Jesus's messianic identity shatters long-held expectations, all the while fulfilling OT expectations (1:1; 24:25–27, 45–46).

The spiritual blindness of the disciples is juxtaposed with the healing of the blind man in 18:35–43 (// Matt. 20:29–34 // Mark 10:46–52). We learn that Jesus and the disciples are nearing the end of the journey as they close in on Jericho. In narrating the journey, Luke has not generally tracked Jesus's movement to Jerusalem with geographic precision (cf. 17:11), since he is primarily concerned to convey Jesus's teaching in the context of his symbolic journey as Israel's Lord to the new creation (→9:51). The healing of the blind man (named Bartimaeus or "son of Timaeus" in Mark 10:46) demonstrates, above all, Jesus's identity as the royal "Son of David" (18:38–39; →Mark 10:46–52) and Yahweh incarnate (note the blind man's use of "Lord" in 18:41).

Luke uniquely records the reaction of the blind man and the crowd: "Immediately he received his sight and followed Jesus, *praising God. When all the people saw it, they also praised God*" (18:43). Effusive joy and praise, common in Luke's narrative, is the result of the in-breaking of the new age and the end of exile (Isa. 49:13; 51:11; 60:15; 61:10–11; 65:18–19; Luke 2:20; 4:15; 5:26; 7:16; 13:13; 17:15; 23:47). Israel's Lord is redeeming his people from spiritual exile, and worship is the only sensible response.

Zacchaeus and the Parable of Ten Minas (19:1–27)

In 18:35, Jesus "approached Jericho," whereas in 19:1 he "entered Jericho and was passing through." Jesus presses on in his journey to Jerusalem. An individual from Jericho named Zacchaeus is a "chief tax collector" (*architelōnēs*; 19:2), an extremely rare title in Greek literature. Tax collectors occupy no small role in Luke's narrative, and he is the only evangelist to include this event, so we should assume that this episode is significant. Since these tax collectors made a living off taxing goods by bullying and accosting people, we can assume that Zacchaeus is widely held in disrepute (→5:27–36).

Luke names the tax collector, suggesting that Zacchaeus continued to follow the Son of Man and later became an eyewitness. Further, Luke describes him as "short in stature" (19:3 NRSV). Why mention his height and narrate the man climbing "a sycamore-fig tree" (19:4)? Perhaps his small stature symbolizes a key theme running throughout the Third Gospel: God exalts the lowly or the "short in stature" (see 1:52). The theme of exaltation of the lowly may explain the odd detail in 19:8 when Zacchaeus "stood up" after the meal.

The story of Zacchaeus also mirrors several points made in the parable of the Pharisee and the tax collector in 18:10–15. The chief tax collector Zacchaeus, like the tax collector in 18:13–14, admits his sinful behavior and is subsequently exalted before the Lord. Zacchaeus's response leads to Jesus's declaration: "Today salvation has come to this house, because this man, too, is a son of Abraham" (19:9; cf. 1:69, 71, 77). Becoming part of *true* Israel, as Luke clearly demonstrates in his Gospel, is never dependent upon ethnic descent but upon one's identification with Jesus. God curses those who rest upon their ethnic descent for deliverance but blesses those who solely identify with his Son and confess their sin. Mary's prediction in 1:55 that God will be merciful to "Abraham and his descendants" is coming to fruition in a most unexpected manner—the salvation of a chief tax collector!

The parable of the ten minas in 19:12–27 is complicated on several levels, so we will make only a handful of observations. The parable in Matthew 25:14–30, while possibly the same material, differs at several points (cf. Mark 13:34). While not contravening Jesus's use of the parable, Matthew and Luke employ it at different points in their narratives to suit their own purposes. Luke includes two plots in his parable. The first plot concerns a nobleman who distributes ten minas each to ten servants (one mina is approximately three months' wages) and charges them with putting his "money to work" until he returns (19:13). Upon his return, he evaluates three of those servants. The first two wisely invest the man's money and yield financial gains (19:16, 18). But the third servant buried the money, so he has nothing to show (19:20). The master rewards the first two servants (19:17, 19) but punishes the third (19:22–26). Intertwined with this plot is a second plotline that describes the same nobleman leaving to be "appointed king" (19:12). While the nobleman was away, the "subjects . . . sent a delegation after him to say, 'We don't want this man to be our king'" (19:14). His subjects vehemently oppose his appointment. When the nobleman returns, he rounds up the rebellious subjects to "kill them" in his presence (19:27).

David Garland cogently argues that this parable is not about Jesus's reign during the interadvent period, as is often thought, but about an earthly, pagan rule. Jesus relays the parable to his hearers—that is, to all those gathered around him in Jericho—so that they may grasp what his messiahship and his kingdom are *not* like.[23] Jesus will soon enter Jerusalem on a donkey as Israel's true king, a king who ushers in peace and mercy upon all who identify with him, regardless of their social standing—even a chief tax collector. In

23. Garland, *Luke*, 758–64.

a word, "the parable prepares for a contrast between the rulers of this world and Jesus, who is poised to enter Jerusalem as a king."[24]

Phase 3: Jesus in Jerusalem (19:28–24:53)

Coming in the Name of the Lord (19:28–48)

The triumphal entry (19:28–38) and the response of the Jewish leaders (19:39–44), probably both taking place on Sunday, are the climax of Jesus's journey to Jerusalem. What began in 9:51 comes to a head here. We study this event in some detail in our discussions of Matthew 21:1–9 and Mark 11:1–10, so we need only consider its placement within Luke's narrative.

The Triumphal Entry (19:28–38)

As he nears the Mount of Olives, Jesus orders two disciples to procure a colt for his entrance into Jerusalem (19:29–31). Upon securing the colt, Jesus rides the colt into Jerusalem, publicly demonstrating his identity as Israel's King (see Zech. 9:9). Those who presumably witnessed the healing of the blind man (Bartimaeus) in 18:35–43 and the restoration of Zacchaeus in 19:1–9 declare,

> Blessed is the *king* who comes in the name of the Lord!
> Peace in heaven and glory in the highest! (19:38)

Luke's narrative reads "the king" (*ho basileus*), whereas Matthew and Mark say, "Blessed is he who comes" (*eulogēmenos ho erchomenos*; Matt. 21:9 // Mark 11:9). Luke makes explicit what Matthew and Mark imply—the arrival of Israel's King (see Ps. 118:26).

Two salient elements of Luke's Gospel also converge here. Luke often attunes his readers to angels and the invisible realm. Why? It may be that a central dimension to Jesus's ministry involves his sovereign rule not just over the earth but over the entire cosmos. His successful reign overthrows all rebellion, spiritual and physical. The effect of his ministry is, therefore, "peace" and reconciliation. At his birth, angels announce peace "on earth" (2:14), and at the triumphal entry, the pilgrims declare "peace in heaven." Earth and heaven, then, encapsulate the entire universe.

God's Judgment upon Jerusalem and the Temple (19:39–48)

Luke is the only evangelist to narrate the response of the Pharisees immediately following Jesus's triumphal entry (19:39–40 // Matt. 21:15–16) and his

24. Garland, *Luke*, 763.

subsequent weeping over Jerusalem (19:41–44). Hostility between Jesus and the Pharisees, who probably represent the entire nation, has been brewing for some time as Jesus travels to Jerusalem from Galilee (e.g., 11:37–43, 53; 12:1; 14:1–3; 15:2; 16:14; 18:10–11). If we are correct to see Jesus's journey to Jerusalem as Yahweh redeeming his people from spiritual bondage and leading them to the promised land of the new creation, then the Pharisees' rejection is all the more poignant. They are not simply rejecting Jesus's messiahship; they are rejecting the Lord's great act of redemption (note the use of "Lord" [*kyrios*] in 19:34 and 38). This final denunciation will manifest itself publicly at the crucifixion.

The Pharisees' utter rejection of God's mercy leads to Jesus famously weeping over Jerusalem in the following passage (19:41–44). The nation of Israel, represented by the religious authorities, was indeed looking for peace. But they wanted political peace more than anything else. What they did not realize is that political independence is not their chief concern. They need peace with God; they are estranged, slaves to the devil and the fallen world. Ironically, by rebuffing Jesus throughout his ministry and climactically at his triumphal entry, they reject the very thing they long for. Israel, by and large, "did not recognize the time of God's coming" or his "visitation" (19:44 HCSB, NASB, ESV). Jesus's redemption is "now . . . hidden from your [the nation's] eyes" (19:42; cf. 2:30; 10:23). At the triumphal entry, Jesus arrives as the prince of peace, but in the near future, he promises to come again as the Son of Man in judgment, laying waste to Jerusalem. Luke 19:43–44 anticipates the destruction of Israel's temple in the Olivet Discourse (21:5–36; cf. Ps. 137:9; Hosea 10:14).

During Jesus's Galilean ministry, Luke does not feel it necessary to keep his readers attuned to the precise geographic details of Jesus's whereabouts. But once Jesus's journey to Jerusalem draws to a close, Luke divulges his location. Notice the Third Gospel's geographic progression as Jesus nears and then enters Jerusalem:

Now on his way to Jerusalem . . . (17:11)

As Jesus approached Jericho . . . (18:35)

Jesus entered Jericho . . . (19:1)

He was near Jerusalem . . . (19:11)

He went on ahead, going up to Jerusalem. (19:28)

As he approached Jerusalem . . . (19:41)

When Jesus entered the temple courts . . . (19:45)

The climax of the journey, then, is Jesus's actions in the temple. The events of 19:45–21:38 take place within the temple complex, where we discover Jesus teaching the crowds. Luke carefully mentions the crowds repeatedly in this section (19:47–48; 20:1, 9, 16, 45; 21:37–38), so we should assume that, while Jesus interacts with the religious leaders and his disciples, they remain within earshot. The people need to overhear these difficult conversations. If they desire to follow the Son of Man at all costs, they must know what they are getting into.

Jesus, as Israel's Lord, is now visiting his temple, probably on Monday of passion week (// Matt. 21:12–16 // Mark 11:15–18 // John 2:13–16). And what does he discover? Instead of the temple functioning as a "house of prayer" (19:46a, quoting Isa. 56:7) that welcomes the nations into the presence of God, the nation of Israel has transformed it into a "den of robbers" (19:46b, quoting Jer. 7:11; →Mark 11:15–18). The juxtaposition of what transpires in the Jerusalem temple with Zacchaeus in the previous section is stunning. Because Zacchaeus, a chief tax collector, admits to his sinful ways, Jesus comes to his "house" and offers him "salvation" (19:5, 9). On the other hand, because the nation of Israel refuses to lead the nations to God's glory, Jesus comes to Israel's "house" in judgment (19:46). The Israelites assiduously preserve their covenant identity by keeping the gentiles at arm's length while neglecting to cultivate a warm relationship with God. But not only does Jesus come to Israel's temple as the Lord incarnate; he also comes as the Son of Man who is continuing to overthrow the fourth beast (Dan. 7:7–8, 13–27). In driving out (*ekballein*) "those who were selling," he resumed his prerogative of "driving out" demons (see 9:40, 49; 11:14–15, 18–20; 13:32).

The religious authorities immediately grasp Jesus's symbolic actions in the temple. To judge the temple is to judge the nation. Just who does Jesus think he is? Jesus's behavior in 19:47–48 mirrors his conduct as a twelve-year-old boy in 2:46–48:

> They [Jesus's parents] found him *in the temple courts*, sitting among the *teachers*, listening to them and asking them questions. *Everyone who heard him was amazed* at his understanding and his answers. . . . "Didn't you know I had to be in my Father's house?" (2:46–49)

> Every day *he was teaching at the temple*. But the *chief priests, the teachers of the law and the leaders* among the people were trying to kill him. Yet they could not find any way to do it, because *all the people hung on his words*. (19:47–48)

At the beginning of Luke's Gospel, Jesus, even as a boy, teaches in his "Father's house" (2:49), whereas in 19:46 he arrives at "my house." In the immediate context of Isaiah 56:7, "my house" explicitly refers to Yahweh's temple (note the phrases "my covenant" [Isa. 56:4, 6], "my temple" [Isa. 56:5], "my holy mountain" [Isa. 56:7], and "my altar" [Isa. 56:7]). A good case can be made that "my house" in 19:45 refers to Jesus's house, since Luke's narrative repeatedly identifies him as Israel's Lord (see 19:34, 38). The shift from my "Father's house" in 2:49 to "my house" in 19:46 may allude to Jesus's perfect obedience to the Father's will. Jesus has earned the right to judge Israel's temple.

Debating Israel's Authorities (20:1-47)

Jesus's Authority Questioned (20:1–8)

Perhaps on Wednesday of passion week, the religious authorities, now convinced that Jesus deserves death (19:47), ask him, "Who gave you this authority [to judge the temple]?" (20:2). Luke mentions three groups assembled in the temple listening to Jesus: "the chief priests, the scribes, and the leaders of the people" (19:47 HCSB). Here we witness the inception of the clash between Jesus and the high priests. To the north, in Galilee, the Pharisees and the scribes carry a great deal of authority, but in Jerusalem the Sadducees and the high priests are the power brokers. They control the inner workings of the temple and ultimately occupy a mediatorial role between Rome and Israel. As passion week unfolds, the high priests emerge on the scene alongside the Pharisees and the scribes (20:19; 22:2, 4, 50, 52, 54, 66; 23:4, 10, 13; 24:20).

All three Synoptics follow up Jesus's actions in the temple with an interrogation by the authorities (Matt. 21:23–27 // Mark 11:27–33 // Luke 20:1–8; cf. John 2:18–22). By condemning the temple and rendering it obsolete, Jesus is, in effect, pulling out the rug from underneath the high priests. Their job descriptions are now obsolete. Aghast at Jesus's actions, they inquire, "Tell us by what authority you are doing these things? . . . Who gave you this authority?" (20:2). The two key words, "give" and "authority," ring throughout the Third Gospel:

> And he said to him, "I *will give* [*dōsō*] you all their *authority* [*tēn exousian*] and splendor; *it has been given* [*paradedotai*] to me, and I *can give* [*didōmi*] it to anyone I want to." (4:6)

> When Jesus had called the Twelve together, *he gave* [*edōken*] them power and *authority* [*exousian*] to drive out all demons and to cure diseases. (9:1)

> I *have given* [*dedōka*] you *authority* [*tēn exousian*] to trample on snakes and scorpions and to overcome all the power of the enemy; nothing will harm you. (10:19)

"Tell us by what *authority* [*exousia*] you are doing these things," they said. "Who *gave* [*ho dous*] you this *authority* [*exousian*]?" (20:2)

Without exception, Luke pairs "giving" and "authority" only in the context of demonic activity. He is also the only evangelist to wed "give" and "authority" during the wilderness temptation. As we argued in our discussion of 4:1–13, the devil alludes to Daniel 7:14 when he tempts Jesus. He parodies the Ancient of Days handing over or "giving" the eternal kingdom to the Son of Man. Ironically, because Jesus does not fall prey to the devil's lie, the Ancient of Days does indeed begin to hand over the kingdom to Jesus at the end of the temptation. As the successful Son of Man, Jesus then empowers the Twelve (9:1) and the seventy-two disciples (10:19) to participate in his program of extending his kingdom. Therefore, when the Jewish authorities ask Jesus, "Who gave you this authority?" Luke's audience knows full well the answer to the question—the Ancient of Days. The Father rewards the Son of Man for his obedience in defeating the fourth beast, the devil. So a great deal of the basis for Jesus's actions in the temple lies in his identity as the divine Son of Man (see 20:41–44). This is precisely what he claims at his interrogation only a few days later when he states, "From now on, the Son of Man will be seated at the right hand of the mighty God" (22:69). If Jesus discloses his full identity on Wednesday of passion week, he will never make it to Friday.

Jesus responds to the question by posing a question of his own: "Tell me: John's baptism—was it from heaven, or of human origin?" (20:3). The authorities soon realize they are trapped. If they admit that John's ministry flows from divine unction, then they stand guilty before God because they refused to submit to John's baptism (20:5; see 7:30–35) and rejected his prophetic testimony regarding Jesus (3:16–17, 21–22; see John 1:6–8, 19–34). On the other hand, if they claim that John was a fraud, then they will fall out of favor with the populace (20:6). Not wanting to fall on their own sword, the officials plead ignorance (20:7).

The Parable of the Wicked Tenants (20:9–19)

All three Synoptics generally place the parable of the wicked tenants after Jesus's judgment upon the temple (Matt. 21:33–46 // Mark 12:1–12 // Luke 20:9–19), and Luke closely follows Mark in placing it immediately after the religious leaders question Jesus's authority. As we mentioned in our discussion of Mark 12:1–12, the dominant OT backdrop of this passage lies in Isaiah 5:1–7, where Yahweh cultivates a vineyard and readies it for production. But Israel, the vineyard, "yielded only bad fruit" (Isa. 5:2). As a result, the Lord swears to destroy it and "make it a wasteland" (Isa. 5:5–6). In the same way, perhaps even in a typological manner, the nation of Israel in the first century, represented by the religious authorities, refuses to bear fruit: "The tenants . . . sent him [the servant] away empty-handed" (20:10). God mercifully sends his "servants," or prophets, to Israel, yet they continue to reject them (see 11:49–51; 13:34–35; 19:41–44; cf. 2 Chron. 36:15–19). Finally, God sends his prized "son," the one whom he loves, and Israel consummately rejects him (20:13). As a result, God promises to hand over the vineyard "to others," most likely gentiles (20:16a). The religious authorities, knowing the significance of the parable, respond, "God forbid" (20:16b). They realize what is at stake in this parable; their idolatrous actions have led to God forsaking Israel and his temple.

The discourse ends climactically when Jesus quotes Psalm 118 in conjunction with an allusion to Daniel 2:34–35 in 20:17–18: "Then what is the meaning of that which is written: 'The stone the builders rejected has become the cornerstone'? [Ps. 118:22] Everyone who falls on that stone will be broken to pieces; anyone on whom it falls will be crushed [Dan. 2:34–35]." By associating these two texts, Luke, like Matthew, suggests that Jesus is simultaneously the end-time temple and the crushing messianic "stone" from Daniel 2. He is the stone of the new cosmic sanctuary and the stone of judgment. *He is simultaneously the beginning of a new house of God and the instrument of divine wrath.* Further, the stone in Daniel 2:34–35 parallels the "son of man" in Daniel 7:13–14, since they both conquer the fourth and final kingdom. Here in Luke 20, the object of judgment is the religious authorities (and the theocratic nation of Israel), so it may not be a stretch to surmise that they are ironically identified with the idolatrous colossus and the fourth beast (Dan. 2:44–45; 7:11). The passage ends with the leaders unable to arrest Jesus because of his popularity among the people. This is the second time they are unable to do so (see 19:47–48).

Paying Tribute to Caesar and the Question on the Resurrection (20:20–40)

The religious authorities are not giving up in their quest to "kill" Jesus (19:47). Immediately following the indictment of the parable of the wicked tenants (20:9–18), the Jewish leaders attempt to pit Jesus against Pilate in the question over taxation (20:20–26 // Matt. 22:15–22 // Mark 12:13–17). Following the first line of inquiry, the leaders then pit Jesus against the crowd over the issue of the resurrection (20:27–40 // Matt. 22:23–33 // Mark 12:18–27).

Luke's interest in the book of Daniel shows little sign of abating as he moves into the discussion concerning paying tribute to Rome (20:20–26). Luke is the only evangelist to characterize the authorities as commissioning "spies" who "pretended to be sincere" while intending to "*hand* him *over* [*paradounai*] to *the power* [*tē archē*] and *authority* [*tē exousia*] of the governor" (20:20 // Matt. 22:15 // Mark 12:13). While this verse certainly fulfills, at least to some degree, Jesus's passion predictions about being handed over (see 9:44; 18:32; cf. 9:22; 12:50; 13:32–33; 17:25), the language is most peculiar; and we have seen this exact wording before. In the temptation narrative we read, "I [the devil] will give you all their *authority* [*tēn exousian*] and splendor; *it has been given* [*paradedotai*] to me, and I can give it to anyone I want to" (4:6). Above we discussed the prominence of "giving" and "authority" in the broad and immediate context of Luke's Gospel and its relationship to Daniel 7 (see 20:2). The point is that these religious authorities are doing to Jesus what their master, the devil, tries to do in the wilderness. They are unwittingly parodying the Ancient of Days in handing Jesus over to the authority and power of Pilate. As in his response to the devil's wiles in the wilderness, Jesus sees through such "duplicity" (*tēn panourgian*; 20:23). Strengthening this line of interpretation, we discover that the same term for duplicity (*panourgian*) occurs in 2 Corinthians 11:3 in the context of Eve succumbing to the serpent's "craftiness" (*tē panourgia*; NASB).

The issue at hand in 20:20–26 concerns paying tribute to the Roman Empire. Rome procured tribute from Judea directly and indirectly. When Archelaus, the son of Herod the Great, was deposed in AD 6, Rome established Judea as a province, requiring the Jews to pay a tribute tax to the governor. While Luke's narrative often mentions tax collectors, this passage here involves something of a different sort. Rome required the leadership of Israel to collect tribute directly from the people, either the land tax or the head or poll tax. In this passage, the religious authorities question Jesus's commitment to Israel. If Jesus supports Israel paying tribute to Rome, then he aligns himself with a pagan ruler, Caesar. But if he denounces the tribute, then the Jewish leaders can drag him before Pilate for insubordination. Joel Green rightly observes, "The resulting portrait has Jesus in a vice [*sic*] between Pilate and the people. If Jesus answers one way, he stands condemned by Rome as a dissident; if the other, he depletes his capital with the populace."[25]

Jesus famously responds, "Give back to Caesar what is Caesar's, and to God what is God's" (20:25). The thrust of this saying is that the Jews must obey Rome *and* God. This is not far from Paul's exhortation that believers must "be subject to the governing authorities" (Rom. 13:1; cf. 1 Pet. 2:13–14). While it is tempting to understand this principle in isolation, we must consider Jesus's admonition in light of his teaching on the kingdom elsewhere. The

25. Joel B. Green, *The Gospel of Luke*, NICNT (Grand Rapids: Eerdmans, 1997), 712.

fulfillment of the end-time kingdom must be understood in an already-not-yet manner. That is, the kingdom arrives in the first century in a broadly spiritual manner, whereas its consummation will occur at Jesus's second coming. The kingdom, then, mysteriously overlaps with the old age (→Matt. 13:1–52 and Mark 4:1–34). Jesus's presentation of the kingdom is odd in that believers are caught in the middle of two domains. On the one hand, they must abandon all, trust in Jesus, and persevere in the spiritual kingdom of God. On the other, they still remain in the old age, an age that is physically ruled by pagans. Until the Son of Man returns, his followers must always identify with the kingdom of God, yet not cast off the yoke of pagan rule. At the heart of the issue is God's providence and sovereign decree in establishing pagan rulers over his people during the interadvent period. The Jewish leaders in 20:20–26, since they are not followers of Jesus, will not grasp the deeper significance of Jesus's response. What they do understand is that Jesus brilliantly affirms a commitment to God's people *and* to government, a position that is grounded in his confidence in God's sovereign might.

The leaders fail to pit Jesus against Pilate, so now they attempt to defame him in the public arena. Luke shines the spotlight on the Sadducees in 20:27. He explicitly mentions the Sadducees only once in his Gospel but three times in Acts (4:1; 5:17; 23:6). It appears that this Jewish group wielded considerable political power in Jerusalem (see Josephus, *Ant.* 13.297–98), and all the high priests belong to the Sadducees.[26] They were also known for denying the resurrection (20:27; Acts 23:6–7; Josephus, *Ant.* 18.16) and God's providence (Josephus, *Ant.* 13.173; Josephus, *J.W.* 2.164), and they treated only the Pentateuch as Scripture. We can assume that the Sadducees are colluding with the other Jewish leaders, such as the Pharisees and the scribes (20:1, 19). They ask Jesus a hypothetical question about the nature of the resurrection based upon Deuteronomy 25:5–6.

Jesus responds with a principle found in the Pentateuch itself, affirming that there will indeed be a resurrection in the new creation but that marriage will not play a part in the new age (20:34–38). Luke details only the response of the scribes: "Some of the teachers of the law responded, 'Well said, teacher!'" (20:39 // Matt. 22:33). The scribes, who believe in the resurrection (Acts 23:6–9), could not have said it any better. Luke ends the debate over tribute in the previous passage with, "And astonished by his answer, they [the teachers of the law and the high priests] became silent" (20:26). Now, at the end of this debate, "no one dared to ask him any more questions" (20:40). According to Matthew and Mark, the Jewish leaders ask a third question about the greatest

---

26. C. Fletcher-Louis, "Priests and Priesthood," *DJG*, 701.

commandment following this debate over the resurrection (Matt. 22:34–40 // Mark 12:28–34), but Luke includes no such question. Jesus has definitively silenced the religious authorities.

Jesus as David's Lord (20:41–47)

The Jewish leaders have asked him two questions thus far, so now Jesus asks them a question of his own: "Why is it that the Messiah is the son of David? . . . David calls him [the Messiah] 'Lord.' How then can he be his son?" (20:41–44). This saying, along with the following portions of Luke's narrative, likely takes place on Wednesday or Thursday of passion week (20:41–22:6). While all three Synoptics include this prominent saying (Matt. 22:41–45 // Mark 12:35–37 // Luke 20:41–44), the passage takes on an additional layer of meaning in the Third Gospel.

We covered this difficult text in our discussion of Mark 12:35–37, so we will only point out how Luke employs it in his narrative. The early chapters of Luke unambiguously identify Jesus as the long-awaited heir of David who will rule over God's eternal kingdom (1:27, 32, 69; 2:4, 11; 3:31; cf. 18:38–39). At the same time, we have tracked Luke's penchant for aligning Jesus with Yahweh, Israel's "Lord" (e.g., 1:43, 45; 2:11; 5:8, 12, 17; 6:46). The inclusion of this saying is unique in that Luke's readers, at this point in the narrative, have come to realize that both figures—Israel's Lord and the Messiah—exist in the person of Jesus. Luke has spent twenty chapters answering the second question, found in 20:44 ("David calls him 'Lord.' How then can he be his son?"). The answer: Jesus is simultaneously Israel's King *and* her divine Lord.

One dimension of Psalm 110 is clear enough, as enigmatic as the psalm is in its original context. Yahweh promises to rule through David's "Lord" and vanquish his enemies. The promise that God will "judge the nations, . . . crushing the rulers of the whole earth" (Ps. 110:6) may still be in mind, perhaps ironically, in the following verses when Jesus states that the religious authorities will be "punished most severely" for taking advantage of the weak—that is, the widows (see 1:52). Many of Israel's leaders spent their careers looking outward, praying that God would punish the pagan nations. Little did they know that God would soon come and punish them.

The Coming Destruction of Israel's Temple (21:1–38)

The Offering of a Widow (21:1–4)

Luke, following Mark's sequence, uses the widow's offering in 21:1–4 to bridge Jesus's condemnation of the scribes in 20:45–47 and his judgment upon the temple in 21:5–36 (// Mark 12:41–13:36). On the surface, its placement seems odd, but Luke's logic remains intact once we grasp the flow of the narrative. The widow is most likely in the court of women, where, according to early Jewish tradition, a series of thirteen "shofar chests," or trumpet treasury boxes, stood (m. Sheqal. 6.1–5). These chests collected money for a variety of offerings related to the temple, such as bird offerings, wood, frankincense, "gold for the Mercy seat," and freewill offerings (m. Sheqal. 6.5). Luke does not disclose what offering in particular she was contributing toward, as it makes no difference; the point is that she gave a very meager amount (21:2). Since she is a widow, she most likely has great difficulty in making ends meet.

The widow's poverty stands in contrast to the wealth of the teachers of the law, who "walk around in flowing robes" and sit in the "most important seats in the synagogue" and in the "places of honor at banquets" (20:46). They give to the temple "out of their wealth" (21:4). There is no true sacrifice here. The nub of the issue is the pride of the rich, particularly the religious authorities; the condition of their heart manifests itself on the outside. They use their wealth to promote themselves. The widow, though, uses what little she has to serve God. Because of her heart condition, she has "put in more than all the others" (21:3). While Luke does not explicitly allude to Isaiah 66:1–2 here, it may be conceptually in mind: "Where is the house you will build for me? . . . These are the ones I look on with favor: those who are humble and contrite in spirit." God hides his glory from those who attempt to earn it, but gives it freely to those who serve him.

Judgment upon the Temple and the Coming of the Son of Man (21:5–38)

The narrative transitions immediately to the Olivet Discourse. We are still about midway through passion week. While all three Synoptics include this section, only the Third Evangelist omits the location where Jesus delivers it. Matthew and Mark explicitly state that Jesus and the disciples leave the temple complex and travel outside Jerusalem to the Mount of Olives (Matt. 24:1–3 // Mark 13:1–3). In keeping Jesus's location ambiguous, Luke keeps his readers' attention on the temple precinct, where Jesus has been teaching a great throng since 19:47; he will continue to do so until 21:38.

The disciples gleefully pointed out "how the temple was adorned with beautiful stones and *with gifts dedicated to God [anathēmasin]*" (21:5). If we keep the immediate context in mind, we can conclude that the temple, like the Jewish leaders, is ostentatious and beautiful on the outside (20:46–47). But, spiritually, the temple reeks of a pungent odor. Luke peculiarly remarks on the "gifts dedicated to God." This expression is one word in Greek (*anathēmasin*) and often found in contexts regarding various offerings given to the temple. Josephus, a first-century Jewish historian, boasts that the rebuilt temple was "adorned . . . gloriously by fine ornaments, and with great magnificence, in the use *of what has been given them* [*tōn anathēmatōn*]" (Josephus, *J.W.* 7.45; cf. Josephus, *Ant.* 8.99). The contributions of the rich in the preceding passage (21:1) likely fall under the umbrella of "gifts dedicated" to the temple. The promised judgment that will befall Israel's temple in 21:5–36 is tied to the behavior of the rich in 21:1–4. The whole of Luke's narrative makes clear that the rich boast in wealth, power, and externals—the very things God despises. God promises in 1:52–53 to bring "down rulers from their thrones" and send "the rich away empty." So according to the Gospel of Luke, divine judgment upon Israel's temple largely (but not exclusively) stems from pride and the idolatry of wealth (11:37–54; 13:34–35; 19:41–44).

We cover the Olivet Discourse in our discussion of Matthew 24:1–25:46 and Mark 13:1–37, so we will limit our discussion of this passage to a few lines. We must be mindful that the Olivet Discourse is, on account of its rich and complex imagery, exceedingly difficult to interpret with great precision, so we ought to remain cautious in our conclusions. The disciples ask Jesus two questions: "When will these things [the destruction of the temple] happen? And what will be the sign that they are about to take place?" (21:7). Mark's and Luke's accounts appear to ask the same question from two different perspectives (Mark 13:4 // Luke 21:7). The first question relates to the timing of the temple's destruction, whereas the second concerns a "sign" that signals its arrival. In contrast, the two questions posed by the disciples in Matthew's account seem to be two distinct questions, first concerning the timing of the temple's destruction, then concerning the sign of Jesus's second coming at the consummation of the age (// Matt. 24:3).

Luke follows the broad outline of the other two evangelists:

| 21:8-19 | Events leading up to the destruction of the temple in AD 70 |
| 21:25-36 | The arrival of the Son of Man |

The main difference between Luke and the other two Synoptics is the lack of a discrete section predicting the second coming of Jesus. Mark and Matthew include a section prefaced with "But about that day or hour no one knows, not even the angels in heaven, nor the Son, but only the Father" (Matt. 24:36 // Mark 13:32). That line signals a break between the events predicting the destruction of the temple in AD 70 (Matt. 24:15–35 // Mark 13:14–30) and the second coming of Jesus (Matt. 24:36–25:46 // Mark 13:32–36). Several commentators interpret Luke 21:25–36 as a reference to the second coming, but it may refer to the destruction of the temple. Since Luke's account includes no such transition, it seems that he is primarily concerned with the destruction of the temple in AD 70 in his use of the material. That said, God's judgment upon Israel in AD 70 serves as a template for his judgment upon unbelieving humanity at the very end of history, immediately preceding the new eternal cosmos. In some sense, then, we may be splitting eschatological hairs.

The section of 21:8–19 explains events that *precede* the destruction of the temple—false teaching (21:8–9), political instability (21:9–10), and persecution (21:12–19). While each of these is an expression of the latter-day tribulation, they do not signal the imminent destruction of the temple. The turning point lies in 21:20: "When you see Jerusalem being surrounded by armies, you will know that its desolation is near." Matthew and Mark reference Daniel 9:27, 11:31, and 12:11 with the phrase "the abomination that causes desolation" (Matt. 24:15 // Mark 13:14). Israel has, on account of her idolatry with the idolatrous temple, transformed into an abomination herself (→Matt. 24:15). Luke focuses not so much on Israel's idolatry as on Rome's siege that eventually leads to the "desolation" of Jerusalem. "In fulfillment of all that has been written" (21:22)—that is, in fulfillment of several OT predictions—the theocratic nation of Israel has reached her definitive end (e.g., Deut. 32:35; Jer. 46:10; Dan. 9:26; Hosea 9:7; Mic. 3:12).

Verse 25 fits marvelously well with what we have seen thus far in Luke's narrative: "There will be signs in the sun, moon and stars. On the earth, nations will be in anguish and perplexity at the roaring and tossing of the sea." The language here, while similar to Matthew 24:29 and Mark 13:24, suggests an angelic dimension to the Son of Man's arrival. In apocalyptic literature, especially Daniel, stars symbolize angels, who represent people or nations on earth (e.g., Judg. 5:20; Dan. 8:10; 10:13, 20–21; 12:1; Rev. 1:20). The idea, then, is that judgment on earth reflects judgment in heaven. Revelation 12, a text that shares several affinities with Luke 21, states the matter with some clarity: "Its [the dragon's] tail swept a third of the *stars* out of the sky and flung them to earth. . . . Then war broke out in heaven. *Michael* and his *angels* fought against the *dragon*, and the *dragon* and *his angels* fought back. But he was not strong enough, and they lost their place in heaven" (Rev. 12:4, 7–8). Though John probably has Christ's death and resurrection largely in mind in Revelation 12, the point is that angels wage a cosmic battle. What takes place on earth reflects conflict in the heavens. Could it be that the Son of Man's judgment upon Jerusalem through the Roman soldiers corresponds to a heavenly battle between good and bad angels? This may explain why Luke has consistently referenced angelic activity throughout his narrative (1:11–20, 26–38; 2:9–15;

4:1–13, 33–37; 10:18; →2:11). Jesus intends to bring peace throughout the cosmos, so all forms of opposition must be subdued.

Luke caps the discourse with a note about Jesus's traveling patterns: "Each evening he went out to spend the night on the hill called the Mount of Olives" (21:37; cf. 22:39). Matthew and Mark mention that Jesus and the disciples lodge in Bethany during passion week (Matt. 21:17 // Mark 11:11), and Luke states that he sleeps on the Mount of Olives. While some may see a contradiction between the accounts, it is quite possible that Jesus spent the night in two locations throughout the week.[27]

The Last Supper, Jesus's Betrayal, Arrest, and Trial (22:1–62)

Judas and the Religious Authorities (22:1–6)

All three Synoptics place Judas's interaction with the religious leaders after the Olivet Discourse as the Passover draws nigh (Matt. 26:1–5, 14–16 // Mark 14:1–2, 10–11 // Luke 22:1–6). While the "chief priests" and the "teachers of the law" are still looking for an opportunity to exterminate Jesus (22:2), Judas arrives on the scene. Luke is the only evangelist to mention the spiritual dimension of Judas's intentions: "*Satan entered Judas* . . . and Judas went to the chief priests and the officers of the temple guard and discussed with them how he might betray Jesus" (22:3–4; cf. John 6:70; 13:2).

Three brief comments are in order: (1) Although Jesus defeats Satan at the wilderness temptation (4:1–13), Satan still possesses power to deceive and oppress God's people. At the end of the temptation, the narrative reads, "When the devil had finished all this tempting, he left him [Jesus] until an opportune time" (4:13). Despite his defeat, Satan has been active throughout Jesus's ministry, particularly during passion week. (2) By mentioning Satan's influence on Judas, Luke once again draws the readers' attention to the spiritual dimension. The spiritual and the physical are intertwined with one another. (3) Although Satan enters Judas and influences his decision to betray Jesus, Judas still remains responsible for his decision. This is clear from 22:22: "Woe to that man [Judas] who betrays him [Jesus]" (see 6:16; Acts 1:16–20; 2:23). Satan and Judas *both* bear responsibility for Jesus's death.

The Last Supper (22:7–38)

Jesus and the Twelve celebrate Passover in the city of Jerusalem, probably Thursday night (→Mark 14:12–31). After Peter and John follow Jesus's

27. I. Howard Marshall, *The Gospel of Luke: A Commentary on the Greek Text*, NIGTC (Grand Rapids: Eerdmans, 1978), 784.

instructions and prepare the Passover meal (22:8–13), they all recline at the table in the upper room (22:14). Table fellowship, as we have seen, plays a considerable role in Luke's Gospel. At the beginning of Jesus's ministry, he dines at the house of Levi (or Matthew) and enjoys a "great banquet" (5:29). He eats three meals with Pharisees (7:36–50; 11:37–54; 14:1–24), feeds five thousand (9:10–17), and delivers a handful of parables and sayings that feature banquets and feasting (13:29; 14:7–14, 16–24; 15:22–32). The Passover, then, is likely the culmination of all these gatherings. Jesus tells his disciples that he has "eagerly desired to eat this Passover" with them because it is the last one "until it [the Passover] finds fulfillment in the kingdom of God" (22:15–16). A few verses later he explains, "I will not drink again from the fruit of the vine until the kingdom of God comes" (22:18). The Passover celebration is not merely anticipatory of Jesus's atoning death but a foreshadowing of his rich fellowship with his disciples in the new creation (22:29–30; Isa. 25:6–8; Rev. 19:9). Each time Jesus eats with his disciples and followers, they enjoy a taste of what lies ahead in the new cosmos (cf. Acts 2:42; 20:7).

In a passage found earlier on in Matthew's and Mark's narratives (Matt. 19:28; 20:24–28 // Mark 10:41–45), the disciples get ahead of themselves and argue over who will "be greatest" in the eternal kingdom (22:24). It could be at this juncture that Jesus washes the disciples' feet, a symbolic act of servitude, and then imparts the Farewell Discourse (John 13:1–17:26). In any case, the disciples still do not grasp that Jesus (and they) must suffer (22:27). *If* the disciples faithfully endure persecution, *then* they will inherit the kingdom. In fulfillment of Daniel 7:13–14, 22, and 27, on account of the Son of Man's faithfulness, the Ancient of Days will hand over the kingdom to him. And on account of the disciples' faithfulness, the Son of Man will bestow upon them the right to rule with him (22:29; see 12:32; Rev. 3:21).

As the night grows darker, Jesus discloses to Peter during the meal, "Satan has asked to sift all of you as wheat" (22:31). Satan is on the prowl, and one of his chief characteristics is accusing God's people of being in the wrong when they are, in reality, in the right. The classic example is Satan's request to test Job in order to determine that Job is ultimately unrighteous (Job 1:11; 2:5; cf. Zech. 3:2; Jude 7). In the end, Job maintains his faith in God despite extreme adversity. Analogous to Satan falsely accusing Job before God, Satan lodges a formal request to "sift" the disciples "as wheat" and break the faith of *all* the disciples to bring God's condemnation upon them. He succeeds with Judas (22:3), but what about the other eleven? Why do they not succumb to Satan's allurements? Their security lies in Jesus's priestly intercession for his disciples. The Jesus who calls, saves, and delivers Peter (5:1–11) is the same Jesus who preserves the faith of his followers (see John 17:9–15; Rom. 8:33–34). Jesus reassures Peter that he prays for him so that his "faith may not fail" (22:32). Peter, overconfident in his own faith, swears that he will follow Jesus at all costs (22:33), a promise that he will soon break (22:54–62).

Luke uniquely mentions Jesus ordering the disciples to ready themselves for a journey and buy a sword (22:36; cf. 10:4 // Matt. 10:9–10 // Mark 6:8). The physical sword here is figurative for "preparedness"[28] because Jesus will, in fulfillment of Isaiah 53:12, be "numbered with the transgressors." The disciples must be prepared for the coming persecution. The quotation of Isaiah 53 is significant, for it is the only explicit reference to the fourth servant song of Isaiah in the Third Gospel (Isa. 52:13–53:12; cf. Acts 8:32–33; 1 Pet. 2:22–25). While the doctrine of atonement is certainly discerned in Luke-Acts, it's not a major feature of the narrative, so Luke's reference to Jesus's identity as Isaiah's suffering servant is worth considering. Jesus here is clearly identified with Isaiah's suffering "servant" (*pais*; Isa. 52:13), but without hesitation his disciples also call him "Lord" (*kyrios*; 22:33, 38). Jesus, then, is simultaneously Isaiah's suffering servant, who vicariously atones for the sin of his people in his humanity, and Israel's Lord, who redeems them from spiritual exile in his divinity.

Gethsemane and the Trial before the Sanhedrin (22:39–62)

Jesus leaves late Thursday night for the Mount of Olives to pray in the garden of Gethsemane (22:39 // Matt. 26:36–56 // Mark 14:32–52). After he commanded his disciples to pray and submitted himself to the will of his Father (22:40–42), "an angel from heaven appeared to him and strengthened him" (22:43). It may not be a matter of coincidence that the devil tempts Jesus to cast himself down from the temple's precipice so that God will, in fulfillment of Psalm 91:11–12, "command his angels . . . to guard [him] carefully" (4:10). According to Psalm 91, God does offer angelic protection for the righteous, who "rest in the shadow of the Almighty" and "trust" in God (Ps. 91:2). Jesus clearly trusts in his Father in Gethsemane, despite the unimaginable horrors at hand, so this unusual insight may allude to Psalm 91 (cf. Deut. 32:43 LXX; Judg. 6:12, 14; Dan. 10:18–19).

While Jesus prays in Gethsemane, on the slope of the Mount of Olives, Judas leads the Jewish authorities and their band of soldiers and betrays Jesus with a kiss (22:47–48). Jesus asks the crowd why they did not arrest him while he was publicly teaching in the temple. He then explains that this is their "hour—when darkness reigns" (22:53). The idea is that Judas, the

---

28. James R. Edwards, *The Gospel according to Luke*, PNTC (Grand Rapids: Eerdmans, 2015), 640.

soldiers, and the religious leaders belong to the kingdom of Satan. The wording resembles what we find in Ephesians 6:12: "For our struggle is not against flesh and blood, but against the rulers, against *the authorities* [*tas exousias*], against the powers of this *dark* [*tou skotous*] world and against the spiritual forces of evil in the heavenly realms" (cf. Acts 26:18; Col. 1:13). The physical darkness (it is late Thursday evening) and the figurative darkness coalesce here in the narrative. The following section details Peter's threefold denial of Jesus in the courtyard of the high priest's palace (22:54–62 // Matt. 26:69–75 // Mark 14:66–72 // John 18:15–18, 25–27).

John's Gospel describes an unofficial examination of Jesus at the palace of Annas (John 18:13–24), and the Synoptics provide two trials before the Sanhedrin—one after midnight at the residence of either Caiaphas or Annas (Matt. 26:59–66 // Mark 14:55–64) and one early Friday morning, probably in the chamber of the Jerusalem temple in the Hall of Hewn Stone with Caiaphas presiding (22:66–71). Jewish law requires that a formal trial must be held during the day: "In capital cases, they [the judges] try the case by day and complete it [by] day" (m. Sanh. 4.1).[29] This explains why Luke prefaces the trial in 22:66 with "at daybreak." The Sanhedrin find Jesus guilty of blasphemy in their initial examination (// Matt. 26:66 // Mark 14:64), so the council seeks only to charge him officially and deliver him to Pilate. They ask Jesus if he is the Messiah so that they may formally convict him of rebellion against Rome (22:67a).

Jesus's response in 22:67b–68 is twofold. At first he does not answer their question about his messianic identity directly, saying only that they will certainly not "believe" him. On the one hand, on account of their idolatry, they are incapable of fully grasping his identity and trusting in him. Sin has hardened their hearts. On the other, while Jesus is the long-awaited Messiah and has demonstrated it on many occasions, his messianic claims exceed their expectations. After expressing that they cannot grasp his messianic identity, he later claims to be the "Son of Man . . . seated at the right hand of the mighty God" (22:69). Two OT texts come to mind: Daniel 7:13–14 and Psalm 110:1. In referencing these two passages, Jesus argues that he is not simply Israel's Messiah but her divine, preexistent Lord (→Matt. 26:64).

The council then asks Jesus to confirm his identity as the "Son of God." After Gabriel informs Mary that she will give birth to the "Son of the Most High," who will be called the "Son of God" (1:32, 35), every occurrence of "Son of God" in Luke's Gospel occurs in the context of demonic activity:

---

29. Jacob Neusner, ed., *The Mishnah: A New Translation* (New Haven: Yale University Press, 1988).

The devil said to him, "If you are the *Son of God*, tell this stone to become bread." (4:3)

"If you are the *Son of God*," he [the devil] said, "throw yourself down from here." (4:9)

Moreover, demons came out of many people, shouting, "You are the *Son of God!*" (4:41)

When he [the demoniac] saw Jesus, he cried out and fell at his feet, shouting at the top of his voice, "What do you want with me, Jesus, *Son of the Most High God?*" (8:28)

This is a title that connotes the highest position imaginable—the ruler of all things. The title is found on the lips of the devil and his demons because it refers to Jesus's cosmic authority. To be the Son of God, then, is to rule from the very throne of God, a reign that is above all physical and spiritual authorities. The council does not believe that Jesus truly possesses such authority, but they do comprehend, at some level, what his claim entails.

Jesus's Sentencing, Death, and Burial (23:1–56)

Jesus before Pilate and Herod (23:1–25)

The Jewish leaders depart the chamber of the temple and escort Jesus to the Praetorium (or palace) in the Upper City, where Pilate resides for the Passover (23:1 // Matt. 27:11–44 // Mark 15:1–32 // John 18:19–24). Once they arrive, the chief priests officially file charges against Jesus, stating that he "claims to be Messiah, a king" (23:2). Luke's Gospel uniquely mentions Jesus "subverting [the] nation" and opposing "payment of taxes to Caesar." The latter accusation, in light of the debate about paying taxes in 20:20–26, is hardly surprising. But the former accusation is. They accuse Jesus of seducing Israel as one who "stirs up" and incites "the people to rebellion" (23:5, 14). The language here is reminiscent of a false teacher or a deceiver (LXX: Num. 32:7; 1 Kings 18:17–18; Sus. 9; see also 1 En. 99:2; T. Jud. 14:1). Apparently, the chief priests "merge religious and political concerns."[30] According to them, Jesus's false teaching is the way in which he attempts to establish his kingdom, a domain that stands in conflict with Rome.

30. Eckhard J. Schnabel, *Jesus in Jerusalem: The Last Days* (Grand Rapids: Eerdmans, 2018), 282.

As Pilate deliberates, he interviews Jesus personally and directly: "Are you the king of the Jews?" (23:3a), to which Jesus replies, "You have said so" (23:3b). Pilate remains unpersuaded that Jesus is a threat, so he tells the chief priests that he finds "no basis for a charge against this man" (23:4). The leaders will not give up so easily, so they press on in their charge that Jesus has been systematically deceiving Israel from "Galilee . . . all the way here" (23:5). Galilee, at this time, was not under direct Roman rule. Herod Antipas, who had governed Galilee and Perea since 4 BC, was in town staying in the Hasmonean palace to celebrate Passover. So it makes sense for Pilate to confer with Herod about this purported insurrectionist, since Jesus had spent the bulk of his career in Galilee. If anyone should know whether Jesus is a threat to Rome, it is Herod.

The chief priests and the soldiers then bring Jesus to the palace to be examined by Herod, an examination that is unique to the Third Gospel. Though Jesus spends a few years ministering in Galilee, the two have never met face-to-face. Herod "hoped to see him [Jesus] perform a sign of some sort" (23:8). No doubt Herod heard about Jesus's famed miracles, and perhaps he is in the mood to be entertained. But Jesus is not a circus spectacle, carried about by the whims of others. He remains silent during the interrogation, drawing Herod's displeasure. As a result, Herod commands his soldiers to mock Jesus by "dressing him in an elegant robe" (23:11). We cannot help but notice the irony here. In mocking Jesus as a king, they unwittingly affirm his status as *the* king. Unconvinced that Jesus is a seditionist, Herod sends him back to Pilate.

The setting shifts back to outside the Praetorium as Pilate stands before the chief priests. He declares to the leaders that he and Herod find "no basis for [their] charges against him" (23:14–15a; cf. Acts 3:13). It was customary to release a guilty individual at Passover, and Pilate probably believes that the leaders would rather release Jesus than Barabbas, who is guilty of murder and sedition against Rome (23:19). But he is wrong. Despite Pilate's repeated attempts to exonerate Jesus, the Jewish leaders and the crowd force his hand: "Pilate decided to grant their demand . . . and surrendered Jesus to their will" (23:24–25).

The Innocent Crucified (23:26–43)

Luke describes a portion of Jesus's journey to Golgotha or "the place called the Skull" (23:33). As Simon from Cyrene, perhaps an eyewitness to this event, carries the cross for Jesus, a crowd follows Jesus, particularly "women who mourned and wailed for him" (23:27; cf. 8:52; Zech. 12:10–14). At the beginning of Luke's Gospel, women are overjoyed at Jesus's birth because he will conquer Israel's enemies (1:42; 2:10, 38). Now, though, it appears that Jesus himself is being conquered. But Jesus refocuses their lament: "Do not weep for me; weep for yourselves and for your children" (23:28). The wording of 23:28–31 corresponds to what Jesus says earlier about God's judgment upon Jerusalem (19:41–44; 21:20–36). Why would Jesus raise the issue of Israel's judgment as he makes his way to Golgotha? The answer lies in Jesus's interaction with the nation of Israel and her leaders throughout his career, climaxing in the parable of the wicked tenants (20:9–18). Since the majority of Israelites reject Jesus as their king and savior, God will pour out his wrath upon them.

At Golgotha, Jesus is crucified between two criminals, fulfilling his role as David's long-awaited descendant and Isaiah's suffering servant, "numbered with transgressors" (22:37; // Matt. 27:45–56 // Mark 15:33–39 // John 19:29–30). On the cross, Luke records him saying, "Father, forgive them, for they do not know what they are doing" (23:34). While it is difficult to grasp fully the nuance of Jesus's prayer, the thrust of it is that Israel, her leaders, the Roman soldiers, and Pilate do not completely understand Jesus's identity, for if they did, "they would not have crucified the Lord of glory" (1 Cor. 2:8; cf. Acts 3:17). So Jesus prays that God would extend a measure of mercy to them. Luke's second volume will reflect Jesus's forgiving heart in his faithful witness, Stephen, whose prayer for his murderers echoes his Master's (Acts 7:60).

The Third Gospel narrates a discussion between Jesus and the criminals. One of the criminals mocks Jesus (23:39), whereas the other reprimands the mocker and admits that the two of them are receiving their due. Jesus, on the other hand, "has done nothing wrong" (23:41). The criminal then turns to Jesus, asking him to "remember" him when he arrives in his "kingdom" (23:42). In doing so, the criminal recognizes that Jesus is truly who he claims to be and innocent of all charges. Jesus grants his request: "Truly I tell you, today you will be with me in *paradise* [*paradeisō*]" (23:43). The term "paradise" (*paradeisos*) often refers to the garden of Eden, where God dwells intimately with Adam and Eve (e.g., LXX: Gen. 2:8, 9, 10, 15, 16; Ezek. 28:13; see also 1 En. 20:7; 32:3; Sib. Or. 1:24, 26, 30). So why does Jesus refer to heaven as the earthly garden of Eden? The answer lies in the relationship between the garden and God's presence in heaven.

The garden of Eden is God's sanctuary on earth, a microcosm of the cosmos itself. In commenting on 23:43, G. K. Beale states, "That he and the believing criminal would be together 'in Paradise [or the Garden]' immediately after their death, suggests . . . that Jesus' death was in fact a pathway leading to a new creational Eden, apparently beginning to fulfil the intention of the primeval garden sanctuary."[31] In other words, Jesus promises the criminal intimate fellowship in the eternal new cosmos (2 Cor. 12:3–4; Rev. 2:7). Such a promise must be understood in light of Jesus's larger prerogative of communing with outsiders in Luke's Gospel. Repentance and trust in Jesus are the way in which tax collectors, women, sinners, and now an insurrectionist enjoy God's presence in the new age. A few chapters earlier, Jesus promises Zacchaeus that he will dwell in his "house today" (19:5). Now, Jesus promises an insurrectionist that he will "today" dwell in God's heavenly house.

Jesus's Death and Burial (23:44–56)

The emergence of the new creation and the destruction of the old cosmos continue in Luke's narrative, as he is the only evangelist to mention darkness "over the whole land" and the ceasing of the sun to shine with the tearing of the veil (23:44–45). The destruction of the temple parallels the destruction of the cosmos (→Mark 15:33–41). Jesus cries out, "Father, into your hands I commit my spirit," demonstrating that even in death he submits to the Father's will (23:46). At every point of his ministry, from beginning to end, Jesus rests in the Father's sovereign hand (3:21; 4:1–13; 5:16; 6:12; 9:29; 22:39–46).

From the world's perspective, it appears that God's plan is in chaos—the Messiah has come under God's curse, the Jewish and Roman leaders have succeeded in silencing him, and demons revel in victory. But this is precisely how God intends for history to unfold. The immediate result of the crucifixion is the conversion of the centurion in 23:47: "The centurion, seeing what had happened, praised God and said, 'Surely this was a righteous man.'" While all three Synoptics include the centurion's response, Luke's narrative is the only account to mention that he "*praised* God." The same reaction echoes throughout the narrative when individuals experience miracles or extraordinary events (2:20; 4:15; 5:25–26; 7:16; 13:13; 17:15; 18:43), revealing that God is truly at work. So, when the centurion reacts in effusive praise, he sees beyond the externals of the cross and understands it for what it is—God's unrivaled wisdom and redemption manifested in Jesus (see 1 Cor. 1:18).

The narrative shifts to Joseph of Arimathea requesting the body of Jesus from Pilate (23:50–54 // Matt. 27:5–61 // Mark 15:42–47 // John 19:38–42). Joseph, a prominent member of the Sanhedrin, symbolizes the remnant of believing ethnic Jews (→John 19:38). Pilate grants the request, and the body is placed in Joseph's personal tomb. It is nearly sundown on Friday, and the Sabbath is about to begin. At the end of the passage, Luke mentions how

31. G. K. Beale, *The Temple and the Church's Mission: A Biblical Theology of the Dwelling Place of God*, NSBT 17 (Downers Grove, IL: InterVarsity, 2004), 190.

"women who had come with Jesus from Galilee followed Joseph and saw the tomb and how his body was laid in it" (23:55). The same group of women, some of whom are named in 24:10, are also found in the previous passage observing the crucifixion "at a distance" (23:49). They most likely include those mentioned in 8:1–3. The point is that these women have witnessed a great deal of Jesus's miracles and followed him at various junctures throughout his ministry. They accompany him on the journey to Jerusalem to celebrate Passover, behold his death on the cross, and now shadow his body to Joseph's tomb. Their devotion to Jesus is unparalleled.

The Resurrection, the Road to Emmaus, and the Ascension (24:1–53)

The Resurrection (24:1–12)

Luke, falling in line with the other Gospels, records Jesus's resurrection (24:1–12 // Matt. 28:1–8 // Mark 16:1–8 // John 20:1–18). Early Sunday morning, the women, intent on anointing the body, discover that the stone has been "rolled away from the tomb" (24:2). As they go inside, they are unable to locate the "body of the *Lord* Jesus" (24:3). Whereas Mark's account reads, "Jesus' body" (Mark 16:1), Luke once again draws his readers' attention to Jesus as Israel's "Lord" (cf. John 20:2). The account then introduces two characters who were dressed "in clothes that gleamed like lightning" (24:4; cf. Acts 1:10). Their white attire probably reflects their heavenly origin (→Matt. 28:2). They are clothed in white because they, like Gabriel, stand before God's throne representing the saints (1:19; cf. Acts 10:4; Rev. 4:4). As divine messengers, they state that Jesus is "living" or, better, "the living one" (*ton zōnta*; 24:5). Revelation 1:18 also identifies Jesus as "the Living One" (*ho zōn*) who was "dead" but now "holds the keys of death and Hades." The body of Jesus is not simply revivified but is the physical inauguration of the new creation. After believing that Jesus indeed fulfilled his prophecies about his death and resurrection (24:8; see 9:22, 44; 18:32–33), the women relate his resurrection to the disciples and other followers (24:9–10). The disciples, though, remain skeptical of Jesus's resurrection. Peter sprints to the tomb and notices "strips of linen lying by themselves" instead of wrapped around Jesus's body (24:12; see 23:53).

The Road to Emmaus (24:13–35)

One of Luke's most well-known passages is his unique account of two disciples traveling to Emmaus from Jerusalem. The evangelist time-stamps the journey with the phrase "now that same day" (24:13; cf. 23:12). What day? Sunday, the day the women discovered the empty tomb (24:1–8). Two options exist for pinpointing the precise location of the city of Emmaus (see Josephus, *Ant.* 12.306; Josephus, *J.W.* 5.42), and though commentators are unsure which one is in view, the point is that Luke frames this event as a journey. The journey to Jerusalem, occupying more than a third of Luke's narrative (9:51–19:27), is a period of instruction, confrontation, and summons to enter the kingdom. The journey to Emmaus is the capstone of Luke's Gospel, for it aligns Jesus's career with the OT and beckons the reader to grasp the totality of Jesus's ministry. In a word, *the road to Emmaus tangibly demonstrates how Jesus's life, death, and resurrection fulfill the entire sweep of redemptive history—the very thing Luke promised to do at the beginning of his Gospel (1:1–4).*

The two journeying disciples appear distinct from the eleven disciples (24:33; see 24:9). Luke names one as Cleopas but leaves the other one unnamed (24:18). Cleopas perhaps became an eyewitness who related this event to Luke (1:2). These two minor characters could embody Luke's audience, for it may be difficult for his readers to reconcile Jesus's death and resurrection with OT expectations. If the OT anticipates his ministry, death, and resurrection, then why did Israel and her leaders resolutely reject the one they were expecting?

Luke tells us that the two of them were "talking with each other about everything that had happened" (24:14). On the road, Jesus approached the two individuals, but they failed to recognize him, for "their eyes were prevented from recognizing him" (24:16 NASB). Their lack of recognition probably stems from spiritual stubbornness, diagnosed by Jesus as slowness of heart to believe the Scriptures (24:25); but God has ultimately withheld full comprehension of Jesus's identity. The two disciples, although they witnessed Jesus's miracles and listened to countless parables, have yet to grasp his identity in its fullness. The two appear to be among those who distrust the women's report about Jesus's resurrection (24:11) and, ultimately, disbelieve Jesus's repeated passion predictions (9:22, 44; 12:50; 13:32–33; 17:25; 18:32–33; see 24:44). Their "downcast" demeanor in 24:17 manifests the condition of their heart. All hope is lost. We have reached a fundamental problem in Luke's narrative. Jesus staked his mission on his resurrection. If he is not raised, then there's no redemption, no forgiveness of sins for Jews and gentiles, no restoration of end-time Israel, nothing to rejoice over, no kingdom, no Messiah, no success as the Son of Man, no undoing of the first Adam's failure, and no fulfillment of OT promises.

Jesus asks the two followers what they are discussing. To their surprise, he remains ignorant of what transpired in Jerusalem the last few days. In 24:19–24 the two disciples recount Jesus's career, especially passion week. They confess that he "was a prophet, powerful in word and deed before God and all the people" (cf. Acts 7:22), that the Jewish leaders "handed him over to be sentenced to death, and they crucified him," and that they believed "he was the one who was going to redeem Israel" (24:19–21). The disciples' appraisal of Jesus is not altogether incorrect. Indeed, they put their finger on a handful of important aspects of his identity—Jesus is a mighty prophet (4:14, 24; Acts 2:22), and the Jewish leaders did betray him (Luke 23:1–2). But they want a messiah who will liberate them from Rome, not one who is characterized by suffering and bearing God's curse. Further, the two make no mention of Jesus as Israel's Lord incarnate.

Jesus reacts strongly to their appraisal:

> He said to them, "How unwise and slow you are to believe in your hearts all that the prophets have spoken! Didn't the Messiah have to suffer these things and enter into His glory?" Then beginning with Moses and all the Prophets, He interpreted for them the things concerning Himself in all the Scriptures. (24:25–27 HCSB)

There is much to unpack here, but we will restrict ourselves to two points. First, Mark (and Matthew to a lesser degree) underscores the spiritual obstinacy of the disciples throughout his account. The Twelve are unable to perceive fully the nature of Jesus's identity and the end-time kingdom (→Matt. 13:1–52 and Mark 4:1–34). Luke, though, while he quotes Isaiah 6:9 in 8:10, refrains from applying the disciples' ignorance until the end of his Gospel. There are pockets of ignorance, of course (see 9:45), but the explicit obduracy language of "seeing" and hard "heart" and its connection to Isaiah 6 as it relates to the disciples is notably absent in the Third Gospel until chapter 24. The presence of sensory language in 24:16, 25, 31, 32, and 45 is noteworthy and likely recalls that critical passage from the key passage of Isaiah (see Acts 28:26–27, quoting Isa. 6:9–10).

Second, the disciples' ignorance stems from a misreading of the OT—and not just a handful of OT passages but the OT *at large*. We could rework 24:25–27 as the following: "Moses and all the Prophets predicted that the Messiah had to suffer and enter into his glory." If the two disciples had read the OT correctly by grasping the various layers of prophetic types and patterns, aligning Israel's prophecies to the person of Jesus, they would not have been taken aback by the events of passion week. The category of mystery is helpful here: "In a very real sense, a complete or full meaning of large swaths of the Old Testament was partially and sometimes mostly 'hidden' but now has been fully revealed, particularly as it relates to Christ. The incarnation of

Christ, the embodiment of God's full revelation, sheds new light on the Old Testament, bringing about a fuller meaning of the prior revelation. . . . Full or complete meaning was 'hidden' in the Old Testament but has now been 'revealed' in light of Christ."[32]

Daylight is quickly fading, so the two disciples ask Jesus to dine with them at an unknown residence (24:28–29; cf. John 20:19–23). As Jesus reclined, he "took bread, gave thanks, broke it and began to give it to them" (24:30). His words are nearly identical to what we find at the Last Supper in 22:19, a covenant meal where Jesus explicitly predicts his suffering. This is not déjà vu. At this moment, the two followers immediately realize Jesus's identity as their suffering king: "Then their eyes were opened and they recognized him" (24:31). The passive voice of the verb "were opened" (*diēnoichthēsan*) probably, like "prevented" (HCSB) in 24:16, is a divine passive, where God is the agent (cf. 24:45). God is the one who opens the disciples' minds for a correct understanding of Jesus (see Acts 16:14). This is an important point for Luke's readers, as they must recognize that their grasp of Jesus's life, death, and resurrection is ultimately a divine gift. After Jesus supernaturally vanishes from the two disciples (24:31), they are emboldened to spread the good news to the eleven in Jerusalem (24:33).

Jesus's Appearance to the Eleven and His Ascension (24:36–53)

The final section of Luke's narrative caps many of the themes embedded throughout his Gospel and builds a bridge to Acts. These same themes flourish throughout Acts. Jesus appears to the disciples and announces, "Peace be with you" (24:36 // John 20:19). Peace in the Third Gospel is no small matter, occurring at critical junctures. Angels proclaim peace "on earth" at Jesus's birth (2:14), Jesus himself declares peace to many he encounters (7:50; 8:48), and he commands his disciples to extend peace (10:5–6). And at the triumphal entry, the pilgrims even declare "peace in heaven" (19:38). In declaring peace here to the eleven disciples, Jesus acknowledges that his death and resurrection have ushered in eschatological unity, both physical (Jews and gentiles) and spiritual (humanity and God). Later in Acts, Peter characterizes God's eschatological message to the Roman centurion Cornelius as "good news of peace through Jesus Christ, who is Lord of all" (Acts 10:36).

Despite Jesus's physical appearance, the disciples remain in disbelief (24:37–39 // John 20:19–23). To allay their doubts, Jesus eats a piece of "broiled fish" (24:42). Consumption of food demonstrates physicality. An ethereal

---

32. G. K. Beale and Benjamin L. Gladd, *Hidden but Now Revealed: A Biblical Theology of Mystery* (Downers Grove, IL: InterVarsity, 2014), 292–93.

spirit or an angel has no need for such things (see Tob. 12:15–19). This is one of many "convincing proofs" that Jesus performs so that his apostles may become reliable eyewitnesses of his resurrection (Acts 1:3, 8; 2:32, etc.; cf. Luke 1:4). Eating in the presence of the disciples may also connect to other instances of table fellowship (e.g., 5:29; 7:36; 9:13; 14:15; 22:8–38; 24:30).

Jesus proceeds to tell the eleven what he told the two disciples on the road to Emmaus—namely, that the OT anticipates his suffering and exaltation (24:46–47). He orders them to remain in Jerusalem until they receive the promised Spirit or the "power from on high" (24:49; Acts 2:1–4). The Spirit will empower the disciples to testify to what has transpired during the course of Jesus's life, death, and resurrection—and, through repentance, to offer forgiveness of sins in his name to all nations (see Acts 1:8; 2:32; 3:15; 5:32; 10:39, 41; 13:31; 22:15; 26:16). So the "glory" into which the Messiah enters after his suffering (Luke 24:26) entails the spread of God's eschatological kingdom to embrace *all people groups* across the world. The global advance of God's kingdom, by the power of God's Spirit, burrows deep into the book of Acts.

Luke finishes his Gospel with a nice summary of Jesus's ascension (24:50–53). According to Acts 1:3, Jesus further instructs his disciples on the nature of the kingdom for forty days and then he ascends. Why omit the period of instruction? Luke probably jumps right to the ascension because it rounds out his Gospel quite well. A central tenet of Luke's Gospel is bringing "down rulers from their thrones" and lifting "up the humble" (1:52). The U-shaped movement from Jesus's death to his exaltation falls in line with this theme (see 9:51). It is precisely in Jesus's humility on the cross that he overthrows the "rulers from their thrones." Paul puts the matter this way: "And having disarmed the powers and authorities, he made a public spectacle of them, triumphing over them by the cross" (Col. 2:15). The cross is the means by which God exalts his Son and the means by which Jesus conquers his enemies. Jesus ascends to the right hand of his Father as the vindicated Lord, where he rules over the cosmos, intercedes for his people, pours out the Spirit upon the church, and executes judgment upon wickedness.

The last two verses of the Third Gospel describe the disciples' reaction to Jesus's ascension: "Then they [the disciples] *worshiped* [*proskynēsantes*] him and returned to Jerusalem with great joy. And they stayed continually at the temple, praising God" (24:52–53 // Matt. 28:17). The term "worship" (*proskyneō*) is found here and one other time in Luke's Gospel—when the devil tempts Jesus to worship him (4:7). Jesus's response to the devil's temptation is worth quoting: "It is written: 'Worship [*proskynēseis*] the Lord your God and serve him only'" (4:8, quoting Deut. 6:13). The point is obvious: when the disciples worship Jesus at the end of the narrative, they celebrate Jesus as the enthroned Lord who has accomplished precisely what he and the OT anticipate. If Luke's audience desires to follow the risen Lord, then they, too, must be willing to retrace Jesus's U-shaped ministry. Life during the overlap of the ages is characterized by persecution, suffering, and humility. But at the end of history, God will cry out to his people, "Come up here," and vindicate them before the world (Rev. 11:12; cf. 1 Thess. 4:16–17).

Luke: Commentaries

Bock, Darrell L. *Luke*. 2 vols. BECNT. Grand Rapids: Baker, 1994–96.

———. *Luke*. IVPNTC. Downers Grove, IL: InterVarsity, 1994.

———. *Luke*. NIVAC. Grand Rapids: Zondervan, 1996.

Bovon, François. *Luke 1: A Commentary on the Gospel of Luke 1:1–9:50*. Translated by Christine M. Thomas. Minneapolis: Fortress, 2002.

Caird, G. B. *Saint Luke*. PNTC. London: Penguin, 1963.

Carroll, John T. *Luke: A Commentary*. NTL. Louisville: Westminster John Knox, 2012.

Edwards, James R. *Luke*. PNTC. Grand Rapids: Eerdmans, 2015.

Ellis, E. Earle. *The Gospel of Luke*. NCBC. Greenwood, SC: Attic, 1977.

Evans, C. F. *Saint Luke*. London: SCM; Philadelphia: Trinity Press International, 1990.

Evans, Craig A. *Luke*. NIBC. Peabody, MA: Hendrickson, 1990.

Fitzmyer, Joseph A. *The Gospel according to Luke*. 2 vols. AB. Garden City, NY: Doubleday, 1981–85.

Garland, David. *Luke*. ZECNT. Grand Rapids: Zondervan, 2011.

Green, Joel B. *The Gospel of Luke*. Rev. ed. NICNT. Grand Rapids: Eerdmans, 1997.

Johnson, Luke T. *The Gospel of Luke*. SP. Collegeville, MN: Liturgical Press, 1991.

Leaney, A. R. C. *The Gospel according to St Luke*. 2nd ed. BNTC. London: Adam & Charles Black, 1976.

Lieu, Judith. *The Gospel of Luke*. Epworth Commentaries. London: Epworth, 1997.

Marshall, I. Howard. *The Gospel of Luke*. NIGTC. Grand Rapids: Eerdmans, 1978.

Nolland, John. *Luke*. 3 vols. WBC. Dallas: Word, 1989–93.

Schweizer, Eduard. *The Good News according to Luke*. Atlanta: John Knox; London: SPCK, 1984.

Stein, Robert H. *Luke*. NAC. Nashville: Broadman, 1992.

Talbert, Charles H. *Reading Luke*. Rev. ed. Reading the New Testament. Macon, GA: Smyth & Helwys, 2002.

Tannehill, Robert C. *Luke*. Abingdon New Testament Commentaries. Nashville: Abingdon, 1996.

Vinson, Richard B. *Luke*. SHBC. Macon, GA: Smyth & Helwys, 2008.

Luke: Articles, Essays, and Monographs

Achtemeier, Paul J. "The Lukan Perspective on the Miracles of Jesus." In *Perspectives on Luke-Acts*, edited by C. H. Talbert, 153–67. Danville, VA: Association of Baptist Professors of Religion, 1978.

Adams, Sean A., and Michael Pahl, eds. *Issues in Luke-Acts*. Piscataway, NJ: Gorgias, 2012.

Alexander, Loveday. *The Preface to Luke's Gospel: Literary Convention and Social Context in Luke 1.1–4 and Acts 1.1*. SNTSMS 78. Cambridge: Cambridge University Press, 1993.

Baltzer, K. "The Meaning of the Temple in the Lukan Writings." *Harvard Theological Review* 58 (1965): 263–77.

Barrett, C. K. "Luke/Acts." In *It Is Written: Scripture Citing Scripture; Essays in Honour of Barnabas Lindars, SSF*, edited by D. A. Carson and H. G. M. Williamson, 231–44. Cambridge: Cambridge University Press, 1988.

Bartholomew, Craig G., Joel B. Green, and Anthony C. Thiselton, eds. *Reading Luke: Interpretation, Reflection, Formation*. Grand Rapids: Zondervan; Milton Keynes, UK: Paternoster, 2005.

Blomberg, Craig L. "Midrash, Chiasmus, and the Outline of Luke's Central Section." In *Studies in Midrash and Historiography*, vol. 3 of *Gospel Perspectives*, edited by R. T. France and D. Wenham, 217–59. Sheffield: JSOT Press, 1983.

Bock, Darrell L. "Jesus as Lord in Acts and in the Gospel Message." *BSac* 143 (1986): 146–54.

———. *Proclamation from Prophecy and Pattern: Lucan Old Testament Christology*. JSNTSup 12. Sheffield: JSOT Press, 1987.

———. *A Theology of Luke and Acts: God's Promised Program, Realized for All Nations*. BTNT. Grand Rapids: Zondervan, 2012.

Bovon, François. *Luke the Theologian: Fifty-Five Years of Research (1950–2005)*. Waco: Baylor University Press, 2006.

———. "The Role of the Scriptures in the Composition of the Gospel Accounts: The Temptations of Jesus (Lk 4:1–13 par.) and the Multiplication of the Loaves (Lk 9:10–17 par.)." In *Luke and Acts*, edited by G. O'Collins and G. Marconi, 26–31. New York: Paulist Press, 1993.

Braun, Willi. *Feasting and Social Rhetoric in Luke 14*. SNTSMS 85. New York: Cambridge University Press, 1995.

Brawley, Robert L. "Canon and Community: Intertextuality, Canon, Interpretation, Christology, Theology, and Persuasive Rhetoric in Luke 4:1–13." *SBLSP* 31 (1992): 419–34.

———. *Centering on God: Method and Message in Luke-Acts*. Louisville: Westminster John Knox, 1990.

———. *Luke-Acts and the Jews: Conflict, Apology, and Conciliation*. SBLMS 33. Atlanta: Scholars Press, 1987.

———. *Text to Text Pours Forth Speech: Voices of Scripture in Luke–Acts*. Indiana Studies in Biblical Literature. Bloomington: Indiana University Press, 1995.

Bridge, Steven L. *Where the Eagles Are Gathered: The Deliverance of the Elect in Lukan Eschatology*. JSNTSup 240. New York: Sheffield Academic, 2003.

Brodie, T. L. "The Departure for Jerusalem (Luke 9:51–56) and a Rhetorical Imitation of Elijah's Departure for the Jordan (2 Kings 1:1–2:6)." *Bib* 70 (1989): 96–109.

———. *Luke the Literary Interpreter: Luke-Acts as a Systematic Rewriting and Updating of the Elijah-Elisha Narrative.* Rome: Pontifical University of St. Thomas Aquinas, 1987.

Brown, Schuyler. *Apostasy and Perseverance in the Theology of Luke.* AnBib 36. Rome: Pontifical Biblical Institute, 1969.

Buckwalter, H. Douglas. *The Character and Purpose of Luke's Christology.* Cambridge: Cambridge University Press, 1996.

Cara, Robert J. "Luke." In *A Biblical-Theological Introduction to the New Testament: The Gospel Realized*, edited by Michael J. Kruger, 94–113. Wheaton: Crossway, 2016.

Carroll, J. T. *Response to the End of History: Eschatology and Situation in Luke-Acts.* SBLDS 92. Atlanta: Scholars Press, 1988.

Chance, J. Bradley. *Jerusalem, the Temple and the New Age in Luke-Acts.* Macon, GA: Mercer University Press, 1988.

Coleridge, Mark. *The Birth of the Lukan Narrative: Narrative as Christology in Luke 1–2.* JSNTSup 88. Sheffield: Sheffield Academic, 1993.

Conzelmann, Hans. *The Theology of St. Luke.* Translated by Geoffrey Buswell. London: Faber & Faber, 1960.

Cosgrove, C. H. "The Divine ΔΕΙ in Luke-Acts: Investigations into the Lukan Understanding of God's Providence." *NovT* 26 (1984): 168–90.

Crump, D. *Jesus the Intercessor: Prayer and Christology in Luke-Acts.* WUNT 2/49. Tübingen: Mohr Siebeck, 1992.

Culpepper, R. Alan. "The Gospel of Luke." In *The New Interpreter's Bible*, edited by Leander E. Keck et al., 9:3–490. Nashville: Abingdon, 2003.

Dahl, N. A. "The Story of Abraham in Luke-Acts." In *Studies in Luke-Acts: Essays Presented in Honor of Paul Schubert*, edited by L. E. Keck and J. L. Martyn, 139–59. Nashville: Abingdon, 1966.

Darr, John A. *Herod the Fox: Audience Criticism and Lukan Characterization.* JSNTSup 163. Sheffield: Sheffield Academic, 1998.

Daube, D. "Inheritance in Two Lukan Pericopes." *Zeitschrift der Savigny-Stiftung für Rechtsgeschichte* 72 (1955): 326–34.

Denaux, A. "Old Testament Models for the Lukan Travel Narrative: A Critical Survey." In *The Scriptures in the Gospels*, edited by C. M. Tuckett, 271–305. BETL 131. Leuven: Leuven University Press, 1997.

Denova, R. I. *The Things Accomplished among Us: Prophetic Tradition in the Structural Pattern of Luke-Acts.* JSNTSup 141. Sheffield: Sheffield Academic, 1997.

Dicken, Frank, and Julia Snyder, eds. *Characters and Characterization in Luke-Acts.* London: Bloomsbury T&T Clark, 2016.

Dillon, Richard J. *From Eye-Witnesses to Ministers of the Word: Tradition and Composition in Luke 24.* AnBib 82. Rome: Pontifical Biblical Institute, 1978.

Dinkler, Michal Beth. *Silent Statements: Narrative Representations of Speech and Silence in the Gospel of Luke.* Berlin: de Gruyter, 2013.

Doble, Peter. *The Paradox of Salvation: Luke's Theology of the Cross.* SNTSMS 87. Cambridge: Cambridge University Press, 1996.

Dollar, Harold E. *St. Luke's Missiology: A Cross-Cultural Challenge*. Pasadena, CA: William Carey, 1996.

Egelkraut, H. L. *Jesus' Mission to Jerusalem: A Redaction-Critical Study of the Travel Narrative in the Gospel of Luke, Lk. 9:51–19:48*. Europäische Hochschulschriften 23/80. Frankfurt: Peter Lang, 1976.

Esler, Philip F. *Community and Gospel in Luke-Acts: The Social and Political Motivations of Lucan Theology*. Cambridge: Cambridge University Press, 1987.

Evans, Craig A., and J. A. Sanders, eds. *Luke and Scripture: The Function of Sacred Tradition in Luke-Acts*. Minneapolis: Fortress, 1993.

Farris, Stephen. *The Hymns of Luke's Infancy Narratives: Their Origin, Meaning and Significance*. JSNTSup 9. Sheffield: JSOT Press, 1985.

Fitzmyer, Joseph A. *Luke the Theologian: Aspects of His Teaching*. Eugene, OR: Wipf & Stock, 2004.

———. "The Use of the Old Testament in Luke-Acts." In *To Advance the Gospel: New Testament Studie*s, 295–313. 2nd ed. Biblical Resource Series. Grand Rapids: Eerdmans, 1998.

Fletcher-Louis, Crispin H. T. *Luke-Acts: Angels, Christology and Soteriology*. WUNT 2/94. Tübingen: Mohr Siebeck, 1997.

Frein, B. C. "Narrative Predictions, Old Testament Prophecies and Luke's Sense of Fulfillment." *NTS* 40 (1994): 22–37.

Gagnon, R. A. J. "Luke's Motives for Redaction in the Account of the Double Delegation in Luke 7:1–10." *NovT* 36 (1994): 122–45.

Garrett, Susan R. *The Demise of the Devil: Magic and the Demonic in Luke's Writings*. Minneapolis: Fortress, 1989.

Giblin, Charles H. *The Destruction of Jerusalem according to Luke's Gospel: A Historical-Typological Moral*. AnBib 107. Rome: Pontifical Biblical Institute, 1985.

Grangaard, Blake R. *Conflict and Authority in Luke 19:47 to 21:4*. Studies in Biblical Literature 8. New York: Peter Lang, 1999.

Green, Joel B. *The Theology of the Gospel of Luke*. Cambridge: Cambridge University Press, 1995.

Gregory, Andrew, and C. Kavin Rowe, eds. *Rethinking the Unity and Reception of Luke and Acts*. Columbia: University of South Carolina Press, 2010.

Harrington, Jay M. *The Lukan Passion Narrative: The Markan Material in Luke 22,54–23,25: A Historical Survey, 1891–1997*. New Testament Tools and Studies 30. Leiden: Brill, 2000.

Harris, Sarah. *The Davidic Shepherd King in the Lukan Narrative*. London: Bloomsbury T&T Clark, 2016.

Hartsock, Chad. *Sight and Blindness in Luke-Acts: The Use of Physical Features in Characterization*. Leiden: Brill, 2008.

Hays, Christopher M. *Luke's Wealth Ethics: A Study in Their Coherence and Character*. WUNT 2/275. Tübingen: Mohr Siebeck, 2010.

Heil, John Paul. *The Meal Scenes in Luke-Acts: An Audience-Oriented Approach*. SBLMS 52. Atlanta: Scholars Press, 1999.

Henrichs-Tarsenkova, Nina. *Luke's Christology of Divine Identity*. London: Bloomsbury T&T Clark, 2016.

Hills, J. V. "Luke 10.18—Who Saw Satan Fall?" *JSNT* 46 (1992): 25–40.

Jipp, Joshua W. "Luke's Scriptural Suffering Messiah: A Search for Precedent, a Search for Identity." *CBQ* 72, no. 2 (2010): 255–74.

Johnson, L. T. *The Literary Function of Possessions in Luke-Acts*. SBLDS 39. Missoula, MT: Scholars Press, 1977.

Kimball, Charles A. *Jesus' Exposition of the Old Testament in Luke's Gospel*. JSNTSup 94. Sheffield: JSOT Press, 1994.

Kinman, B. R. *Jesus' Entry into Jerusalem: In the Context of Lukan Theology and the Politics of His Day*. AGJU 28. Leiden: Brill, 1995.

Kirk, A. "'Love Your Enemies,' The Golden Rule, and Ancient Reciprocity (Luke 6:27–35)." *JBL* 122 (2003): 667–86.

Klutz, Todd. *The Exorcism Stories in Luke-Acts: A Sociostylistic Reading*. SNTSMS 129. Cambridge: Cambridge University Press, 2004.

Knight, Jonathan. *Luke's Gospel*. London: Routledge, 1998.

Kurz, W. S. *Reading Luke-Acts: Dynamics of Biblical Narrative*. Louisville: Westminster John Knox, 1993.

Lampe, S. J. *Abraham in Luke-Acts: An Appropriation of Lucan Theology through Old Testament Figures*. Rome: Pontificia Universitas Gregoriana, 1993.

Liefeld, Walter L., and David W. Pao. "Luke." In *Luke–Acts*, vol. 10 of *Expositor's Bible Commentary*, rev. ed., edited by Tremper Longman III and David E. Garland, 9–355. Grand Rapids: Zondervan, 2007.

Litwak, Kenneth D. *Echoes of Scripture in Luke-Acts: Telling the History of God's People Intertextually*. New York: T&T Clark, 2005.

Longenecker, R. N. "Luke's Parables of the Kingdom (Luke 8:4–15; 13:18–21)." In *The Challenges of Jesus' Parables*, edited by R. N. Longenecker, 125–47. McMaster New Testament Series. Grand Rapids: Eerdmans, 2000.

Maddox, Robert. *The Purpose of Luke-Acts*. Edinburgh: T&T Clark, 1982.

Mánek, J. "The New Exodus in the Books of Luke." *NovT* 2 (1957): 8–23.

Marshall, I. Howard. *Luke: Historian and Theologian*. Downers Grove, IL: InterVarsity, 1998.

McComiskey, Douglas S. *Lukan Theology in the Light of the Gospel's Literary Structure*. Carlisle, UK: Paternoster, 2004.

McKnight, Scot, and Nijay K. Gupta, eds. *The State of New Testament Studies: A Survey of Recent Research*. Grand Rapids: Baker Academic, 2019.

Méndez-Moratella, Fernando. *The Paradigm of Conversion in Luke*. JSNTSup 252. New York: T&T Clark, 2004.

Menzies, Robert P. *The Development of Early Christian Pneumatology with Special Reference to Luke-Acts*. JSNTSup 54. Sheffield: Sheffield Academic, 1991.

Minear, Paul S. *To Heal and to Reveal: The Prophetic Vocation according to Luke*. New York: Seabury, 1976.

Miura, Yuzuru. *David in Luke-Acts*. WUNT 2/232. Tübingen: Mohr Siebeck, 2007.

Moessner, David P., ed. *Jesus and the Heritage of Israel: Luke's Narrative Claim upon Israel's Legacy*. Harrisburg, PA: Trinity Press International, 1999.

———. *Lord of the Banquet: The Literary and Theological Significance of the Lukan Travel Narrative*. Minneapolis: Fortress, 1989. Repr., Harrisburg, PA: Trinity Press International, 1998.

———. *Luke the Historian of Israel's Legacy, Theologian of Israel's "Christ": A New Reading of the "Gospel of Acts" of Luke*. Berlin: de Gruyter, 2016.

Moxnes, Halvor. *The Economy of the Kingdom: Social Conflict and Economic Relations in Luke's Gospel*. Philadelphia: Fortress, 1988.

Müller, Mogens, and Jesper Tang Nielsen, eds. *Luke's Literary Creativity*. London: Bloomsbury T&T Clark, 2016.

Nave, Guy D., Jr. *The Role and Function of Repentance in Luke-Acts*. AcBib. Atlanta: Society of Biblical Literature, 2002.

Neagoe, Alexandru. *The Trial of the Gospel: An Apologetic Reading of Luke's Trial Narratives*. SNTSMS 116. Cambridge: Cambridge University Press, 2002.

Neale, David A. *None but the Sinners: Religious Categories in the Gospel of Luke*. JSNTSup 58. Sheffield: JSOT Press, 1991.

Nelson, Peter K. *Leadership and Discipleship: A Study of Luke 22:24–30*. SBLDS 138. Atlanta: Scholars Press, 1994.

Neyrey, Jerome. *The Passion according to Luke: A Redaction Study of Luke's Soteriology*. New York: Paulist Press, 1985.

———, ed. *Social World of Luke-Acts*. Peabody, MA: Hendrickson, 1991.

Nielsen, Anders E. *Until It Is Fulfilled: Lukan Eschatology according to Luke 22 and Acts 20*. WUNT 2/126. Tübingen: Mohr Siebeck, 2000.

O'Toole, Robert F. *Luke's Presentation of Jesus: A Christology*. Rome: Biblical Institute Press, 2004.

Pao, David W. *Acts and the Isaianic New Exodus*. WUNT 2/130. Tübingen: Mohr Siebeck, 2000.

Pao, David W., and Eckhard J. Schnabel. "Luke." In *Commentary on the New Testament Use of the Old Testament*, edited by G. K. Beale and D. A. Carson, 251–415. Grand Rapids: Baker Academic, 2007.

Parsons, Mikeal. *Body and Character in Luke and Acts: The Subversion of Physiognomy in Early Christianity*. Grand Rapids: Baker Academic, 2006.

———. "The Place of Jerusalem on the Lukan Landscape: An Exercise in Symbolic Cartography." In *Literary Studies in Luke-Acts: Essays in Honor of Joseph B. Tyson*, edited by R. P. Thompson and T. E. Phillips, 155–71. Macon, GA: Mercer University Press, 1998.

Patella, Michael. *The Death of Jesus: The Diabolical Force and the Ministering Angel; Luke 23,44–49*. Cahiers de la Revue Biblique 43. Paris: J. Gabalda, 1999.

Powell, Mark A. *What Are They Saying about Luke?* New York: Paulist Press, 1991.

Ravens, David. *Luke and the Restoration of Israel*. JSNTSup 119. Sheffield: Sheffield Academic, 1995.

Resseguie, James L. *Spiritual Landscape: Images of the Spiritual Life in the Gospel of Luke*. Peabody, MA: Hendrickson, 2004.

Roth, S. John. *The Blind, the Lame, and the Poor: Character Types in Luke-Acts.* JSNTSup 144. Sheffield: JSOT Press, 1997.

Rowe, C. Kavin. *Early Narrative Christology: The Lord in the Gospel of Luke.* BZNW 2/139. New York: de Gruyter, 2006.

Sanders, James A., and Craig A. Evans, eds. *Luke and Scripture: The Function of Sacred Tradition in Luke-Acts.* Eugene, OR: Wipf & Stock, 2001.

Scaer, Peter J. *The Lukan Passion and the Praiseworthy Death.* Sheffield: Sheffield Phoenix, 2005.

Senior, Donald. *The Passion of Jesus in the Gospel of Luke.* Wilmington, DE: Michael Glazier, 1989.

Shillington, George V. *An Introduction to the Study of Luke-Acts.* London: T&T Clark, 2007.

Strauss, Mark L. *The Davidic Messiah in Luke-Acts: The Promise and Its Fulfillment in Lukan Christology.* JSNTSup 110. Sheffield: Sheffield Academic, 1995.

Talbert, Charles H. *Reading Luke: A Literary and Theological Commentary on the Third Gospel.* Macon, GA: Smyth & Helwys, 2002.

Tannehill, Robert C. *The Narrative Unity of Luke-Acts: A Literary Interpretation.* Philadelphia: Fortress, 1986.

———. *The Shape of Luke's Story: Essays in Luke-Acts.* Eugene, OR: Cascade Books, 2005.

Tiede, David L. *Prophecy and History in Luke-Acts.* Philadelphia: Fortress, 1980.

Tilborg, Sjef van, and Patrick Chatelion Counet. *Jesus' Appearances and Disappearances in Luke 24.* Biblical Interpretation. Leiden: Brill, 2000.

Turner, Max. *Power from on High: The Spirit in Israel's Restoration and Witness in Luke/Acts.* JPTSup 9. Sheffield: Sheffield Academic, 2000.

Walton, Steve. "The State They Were In: Luke's View of the Roman Empire." In *Rome in the Bible and the Early Church*, edited by Peter Oakes, 1–41. Grand Rapids: Baker Academic, 2002.

Weatherly, Jon A. *Jewish Responsibility for the Death of Jesus in Luke-Acts.* JSNTSup 106. Sheffield: Sheffield Academic, 1994.

Wilson, Stephen G. *Luke and the Law.* SNTSMS 50. Cambridge: Cambridge University Press, 1983.

Woods, Edward J. *The "Finger of God" and Pneumatology in Luke-Acts.* JSNTSup 205. Sheffield: Sheffield Academic, 2001.

Zwiep, Arie W. *The Ascension of the Messiah in Lukan Christology.* NovTSup 87. Leiden: Brill, 1997.

CHAPTER FOUR

The Gospel of John

Introduction

Authorship and Date

The authorship of the three Synoptics is complex, but the authorship of the Fourth Gospel is especially so. At the end of the narrative, an individual known as the "disciple whom Jesus loved," who "leaned back against Jesus at the supper," claims to have testified to the contents of the book and "[written] them down" (21:20, 24). The issue is connecting this person with one of the Twelve or with another esteemed individual in the early church. In tracing the "disciple whom Jesus loved" throughout the narrative (13:23; 19:26; 20:2; 21:20), we find that this person appears to be one of the disciples, an insider— one who witnesses countless miracles and follows Jesus from the beginning.

The narrative discloses that the beloved disciple participates in the Passover feast at the end of passion week in the upper room (13:23). Although it's possible additional guests attended, the Synoptics mention only the twelve disciples attending (Matt. 26:17–30 and par.), confining our investigation to the Twelve. We should then attempt to differentiate him from the named disciples. For example, the beloved disciple surfaces in the narrative along with several disciples in chapter 21 when Jesus appears to them on the shore. "That he is one of the seven who go fishing in chapter 21 and, by implication, is not Peter, Thomas, or Nathanael, suggests he is one of the sons of Zebedee or one of the other two unnamed disciples (21:2)."[1] James and John are the "sons of Zebedee" (Matt. 10:2 and par.), and since James is martyred in Acts 12:1–2, John the apostle is the only remaining option. Furthermore, there is a

---

1. D. A. Carson and Douglas J. Moo, *An Introduction to the New Testament*, 2nd ed. (Grand Rapids: Zondervan, 2005), 237.

good possibility that John the apostle, the son of Zebedee, is Jesus's cousin on his mother's side (19:25–27; Matt. 20:20–28; 27:56; see also Papias, frag. 10.3). Taking a look at the evidence external to the Fourth Gospel, we observe that many within the early church identified the author as John, the son of Zebedee. For example, Irenaeus states, "John, the disciple of the Lord, who also had leaned upon His breast, did himself publish a Gospel during his residence at Ephesus in Asia" (*Haer.* 3.1.1; see also 3.8.3, 3.11.2). Some scholars suggest that a minor figure in the early church known as John the elder wrote the Fourth Gospel, but the evidence is meager. Therefore, the author of the Fourth Gospel is most likely the apostle John, the son of Zebedee.

Since Peter's death is narrated retrospectively 21:18–19, the Fourth Gospel must have been written after AD 65, the approximate time of Peter's death. Another line of argumentation is the absence of any discussion of the destruction of the temple in AD 70. Whereas the Synoptics include this event in the Olivet Discourse (Matt. 24:1–25:46 // Mark 13:1–37 // Luke 21:5–36), its omission in John's Gospel is noteworthy. So either the destruction of the temple remains in the near future or significant time has passed since its destruction. Finally, the Fourth Gospel appears to be tied to the three epistles that bear John's name, as identical themes and wording are found in them. If John's Gospel is read with the Johannine Epistles in mind, we can interpret the three epistles as a response to an aberrant interpretation of this published Gospel. Taken together, these three observations suggest that the Fourth Gospel was probably published in the 80s.

Purpose

Two of the four Gospels include a purpose statement. At the beginning of the Third Gospel, Luke tells us that he writes his Gospel so that Theophilus "may know the certainty of the things" he has been "taught" (1:4). At the end of the Fourth Gospel, we find something similar: "These [things] are written that you may believe that Jesus is the Messiah, the Son of God, and that by believing you may have life in his name" (20:30–31). John purposes to deepen the faith of Jewish Christians and reach unbelievers by setting forth Jesus of Nazareth as Israel's Messiah and the divine Son of God, *with the result that* his audience may enjoy life in the eternal new cosmos.

Outline

John organizes his material differently from the Synoptics at several points. The general movement of the Synoptics progresses from Judea to

Galilee, then on the road to Jerusalem, and finally to the city of Jerusalem. The Fourth Gospel appears to be more sensitive to a chronological retelling of events, splitting Jesus's ministry into two halves: the Book of Signs (1:19–12:50) and the Book of Glory (13:1–20:31). Each Synoptic also includes a host of miracles, whereas John surgically selects only seven "signs" (or eight miracles if we include 21:6) to explain Jesus's identity and mission. John even devotes more material to Jewish festivals and passion week. At the end of passion week, too, we are privy to an intimate discourse with the disciples in the upper room on the night of Jesus's betrayal (13:1–17:26) and then a Roman trial before Pilate (18:28–19:16). As a result, the audience of the Fourth Gospel is left pondering Jesus's unique relationship to the Father and the Spirit, the mission of the disciples in the world, and the glory of the cross and resurrection.

Prologue (1:1–18)

> The Beginning of a New Cosmos (1:1–5)
>
> Jesus as the Light and Temple (1:6–18)

The Book of Signs (1:19–12:50)

Testifying to the Son of God (1:19–51)

> John's Testimony and Jesus as the Son of God (1:19–34)
>
> The Testimony of the First Disciples and Jesus as the Gateway to Heaven (1:35–51)

The In-Breaking of the New Age and Conflict in Jerusalem (2:1–25)

> The First Sign and the Beginning of the New Cosmos (2:1–12)
>
> Jesus and Israel's Temple (2:13–25)

Light and Darkness—the Conflict Continues (3:1–36)

> Jesus and Nicodemus (3:1–21)
>
> The Testimony of John the Baptist (3:22–36)

Believing Samaritans and Unbelieving Galileans (4:1–54)

> Jesus and the Samaritan Woman (4:1–42)
>
> Healing the Official's Son (4:43–54)

Healing on the Sabbath and Jesus's Identity as the Son of God (5:1–47)

> Healing at the Pool of Bethesda (5:1–15)
>
> The Theological Significance of Healing on the Sabbath (5:16–47)

Prologue (1:1-18)

The Beginning of a New Cosmos (1:1–5)

The prologue of John's Gospel (1:1–18) contains some of the richest descriptions of Jesus in all the New Testament. Mark's Gospel opens with Jesus as a full-grown man, Matthew begins with a genealogy (Matt. 1:1–16), and Luke begins his account with an announcement of John's and Jesus's births (Luke 1:5–38). The Gospel of John, though, goes well beyond Jesus's birth—into eternity past. The first phrase in John's Gospel, "In the beginning," alludes to Genesis 1:1, setting the timeframe for Jesus's activity and identity (cf. 1 John 1:2). Verses 1–5 identify Jesus, the "Word" (*ho logos*), as the eternal God, and his role as the creator of "all things" (1:3). Genesis 1 presents God speaking the cosmos into existence: "And God said, 'Let there be light.' . . . God called the light 'day'" (Gen. 1:3, 5; cf. Gen. 1:6, 8, 9, 10, 11, 14, 20, 24, 26, 29; Ps. 33:6). In some sense, John is rereading the creation account and placing Jesus squarely within it. John is careful not to collapse Jesus and the Father into the same person. They remain distinct persons, yet they are coeternal, participating in the same divine activity. By underscoring Jesus's role in the first creation, John sets the stage for his role in the new creation (see Col. 1:15–17; Rev. 3:14). He is the great Life-giver, the only one who has the power to overcome the "darkness" (1:5). The Fourth Gospel opens with a reference to the very beginning of the first cosmos (1:1–4) and ends with the very end of history, when Jesus returns to take his people into the new heavens and earth (21:23). John narrates Jesus's earthly ministry, then, not simply within the history of Israel or earthly kingdoms but within the history of the universe itself. This is "metahistory" in its fullest sense.[2]

Jesus as the Light and Temple (1:6–18)

John uniquely presents Jesus as the "light" (1:4–9), a description that runs throughout the Fourth Gospel and that stands in contrast with "darkness" (3:19–21; 8:12; 9:5; 11:9; 12:35–36, 46). The Dead Sea Scrolls contain language of light and darkness in several sectarian documents, demonstrating the pervasiveness of such dualism (e.g., 1QS III, 3, 19, 25; 1QM I, 1, 11; XIII, 5). Ultimately, light and darkness stem from the creation account and Israel's exodus (e.g., Gen. 1:3; Exod. 13:21; 14:20). The prophets expect God to once again create his people anew and bring them out of exile (e.g., Isa. 9:2; 42:16; 45:7). If darkness symbolizes humanity's ignorance and rebellion and the fallen state of the "world" or cosmos, then light symbolizes revelation and deliverance.

2. Richard Bauckham, "Historiographical Characteristics of the Gospel of John," *NTS* 53 (2007): 26.

Jesus is the light who pierces the steeled resolve of rebellion, imparting new life to those who trust in him, regardless of race or ethnicity (1:9–13). Jesus is the great overcomer.

John then progresses from depicting Jesus as the light of salvation to representing him as God's glory in Israel's tabernacle. The connection is a natural one, for fire, a bright light, symbolizes God's glorious presence (e.g., Exod. 3:2; 13:21; 24:17; Lev. 9:24; Num. 9:15). John 1:14 is central to John's prologue and his Gospel as a whole: "The Word became flesh and *made his dwelling* [*eskēnōsen*] among us. We have seen his glory, the glory of the one and only Son, who came from the Father, full of grace and truth." The verb "made his dwelling" (*skēnoō*) is tricky to translate, having no exact English equivalent. It means something like "to tabernacle," bringing to mind the exodus. The mobile sanctuary, where God dwells with Israel during the wilderness wandering, is a prophetic pattern of Jesus dwelling with his people as they wander in the spiritual wilderness. The glory that fills Israel's tabernacle/temple (Exod. 40:34–35; 1 Kings 8:10–11 // 2 Chron. 5:13–14) is the same glory that descends in the person of Jesus. But what the Israelites enjoyed in part, the disciples enjoy in full. In dwelling intimately with humanity, Jesus more fully discloses the very nature of God. John says that he "explained" the Father (1:18 NASB). God graciously reveals himself in many ways in the OT—in creation, in a person's conscience, and in the Torah—but he reveals himself more fully in his Son (Heb. 1:1–2). So as his narrative unfolds, John wants his readers to see Jesus as the life-giving Son of God who graciously dwells with his people, all the while disclosing the God of the OT. Jesus is the great revealer.

◼ The Book of Signs (1:19–12:50)

Testifying to the Son of God (1:19–51)

John's Testimony and Jesus as the Son of God (1:19–34)

The remaining portion of chapter 1 focuses on various characters bearing witness to Jesus, preeminently John the Baptist. All the events in 1:19–42 appear to take place "on the other side of the Jordan" (1:28; cf. 3:26; 10:40), a location that is notoriously difficult to pin down but could be northeast of the Sea of Galilee in Batanea.[3] John the Baptist downplays his own role by refusing to view himself as an Elijah figure (cf. Matt. 11:14) or the long-awaited "prophet" of Deuteronomy 18:15 (1:19–21). Instead, he sees himself as "the

---

3. Benjamin A. Foreman, "Locating the Baptism of Jesus," in *Lexham Geographic Commentary on the Gospels*, ed. B. J. Beitzel and K. A. Lyle (Bellingham, WA: Lexham, 2017), 71.

voice of one calling in the wilderness, 'Make straight the way for the Lord'" (1:23). Here John quotes Isaiah 40:3 and asserts his function: to make preparations for the Lord's coming in a second exodus (→Mark 1:1–3). In baptizing the people with water, symbolizing ritual purity and forgiveness of sin, he readies them to house the glory of God. John the Baptist's behavior threatens the established cult of the temple in Jerusalem, provoking the "priests" and "Levites" to confront him (1:19).

The following day, John sees Jesus approaching and declares, "Look, the Lamb of God, who takes away the sin of the world" (1:29). John the Baptist perceives that Jesus, Israel's Passover sacrifice, will liberate captive Israelites (1:29). These Israelites are enslaved not to a physical enemy but to sin and darkness. In 1:23 John declares the arrival of the new exodus, and in 1:29 he announces *how* that exodus will take place. God instituted the Passover in Exodus 12 to remind the Israelites of his passing over the homes with smeared blood on the lintels (Exod. 12:7; cf. 29:38–46). Only those who obeyed were spared the tenth plague of judgment when God killed the firstborn of each family (Exod. 11:1–8). The lamb, in the place of the firstborn and ultimately the family, temporarily and partially bore God's wrath. This institution set the stage for Isaiah to connect the lamb with an individual who would bear God's end-time wrath fully and with great finality (Isa. 53:7–12; cf. Dan. 9:26; Zech. 12:10–14). Jesus would serve as the substitute not only for the sins of the household but for the "sin of many" (Isa. 53:12). The Jesus who redeems Israel in the second exodus is the same Jesus who gives himself up as ultimate sacrifice (see 19:36).

John recollects that at Jesus's baptism in the Jordan River, Jesus received the Spirit and was identified as the "Son of God" (1:34 ESV). While it is tempting to see the title "Son of God" simply as a functional term that refers to Jesus strictly as a human messianic figure on the basis of texts such as 2 Samuel 7:14 and Psalm 2:7, the title also encompasses his divine identity. He is God's "Son" because he shares the same divine substance as his Father (see 1:14b; 5:16–30) and because he is true Israel (→Matt. 3:13–17). It could be said that Jesus's identity as the Son of God, the climax of John's testimony, embraces all of John the Baptist's previous descriptions of Jesus—the one who is "before" him (1:15), the "Lamb of God" (1:29), the divine King, and true Israel (1:34).

The Testimony of the First Disciples and Jesus as the Gateway to Heaven (1:35–51)

In the following section, John's testimony generates further testimony among the first few disciples (1:35–45). The theme of testimony (*martyria*), a key characteristic of the Fourth Gospel, is part of a "cosmic trial motif" that Andrew

Lincoln popularized two decades ago.[4] He argues that John's peculiar use of words such as "truth," "witness"/"testimony," and "judgment" displays an awareness of a covenantal lawsuit. The trial in John's narrative, Lincoln argues, depends upon Isaiah 40–55, where Yahweh enters into judgment with rebellious Israel and the pagan nations (Isa. 42:18–25; 43:22–28; 50:1–3). A careful reader of John's Gospel can discern seven signs, seven discourses, and seven witnesses.

The seven witnesses are as follows: John the Baptist (1:19, 32, 34; 3:26, 28), Jesus himself (8:14), Jesus's works (5:36), the Father (8:18), the OT (5:39), the Samaritan woman (4:39), and the crowd at Lazarus's raising (12:17). The point of these seven witnesses appearing one after another in the narrative is for the "various characters in the narrative, most notably the leaders of the Jewish people . . . to decide whether they will believe Jesus' witness or the witness about him."[5] But Jesus is not only the cardinal witness in the trial—he is *the judge* (5:22). Jesus is Israel's Messiah and the divine Son of God, who perfectly reveals the Father in the seven "signs" or evidences of this reality. By believing this "truth," a message that Jesus sets forth and bears witness to, John's audience will inherit eternal life. In turn, John's readers will then go out into the world and testify to the truth of Jesus through the power of the Spirit, the advocate of truth (14:16, 26; 15:26). While we should be careful not to subsume all of the Fourth Gospel under this rubric, Lincoln helpfully puts his finger on a chief characteristic of John's narrative.

Returning now to John the Baptist's "testimony" about Jesus, we notice that John asserts that Jesus is the long-awaited Messiah and Son of God who will atone for the sins of many (1:34). This point is reaffirmed throughout the entire sequence of events in 1:35–51. According to 1:45, arguably the high point of the testimony, the entire OT prophetically anticipates these various strands of Jesus's identity. While some pit the call of the disciples in the Synoptics (Matt. 4:18–22; 9:9 and par.) against the call of the disciples in the Fourth Gospel, both can be true. Jesus's initial summons to "come" (1:39) could be reinforced later with the official call in the Synoptics.[6] John goes on to mention the whole cadre of the twelve disciples in 6:67 and 20:24.

The setting then shifts from "beyond the Jordan" (northeast of the Sea of Galilee) to Bethsaida in Galilee (1:43–44). Immediately following Nathanael's confession, Jesus claims that Nathanael will see something "greater" (1:50) and then aligns himself with Genesis 28:12 in 1:51: "You will see heaven open, and the angels of God ascending and descending on the Son of Man."

---

4. Andrew T. Lincoln, *Truth on Trial: The Lawsuit Motif in the Fourth Gospel* (Peabody, MA: Hendrickson, 2000).

5. Lincoln, *Truth on Trial*, 23.

6. D. A. Carson, *The Gospel according to John*, PNTC (Grand Rapids: Eerdmans, 1991), 154.

According to Genesis 28, Jacob dreams about angels ascending and descending on a "stairway" that functions as "the gate of heaven" (Gen. 28:12, 17). The location of Jacob's dream earns the name Bethel or "house of God" (Gen. 28:17, 19), and the place later functions as a place of worship in Israel's history (Judg. 20:26; 1 Sam. 10:3). There may be various layers of typology between Genesis 28 and John 1:51. By identifying himself as the gateway to heaven, Jesus is making a handful of critical claims: (1) He is the locus of God's glory, the true temple (1:14). (2) He is also the true bridge between the two realms—heaven and earth. One of the First Gospel's emphases is the descent of heaven to earth, whereas John explores how the two realms are fused in Jesus. (3) As a consequence of the first two points, if Jesus is the true temple and the true gateway to heaven, then the Jerusalem temple is neither of those.

By the end of chapter 1, John has made several remarkable assertions about Jesus. Some of the more prominent ones are that he is the divine creator (1:3), temple (1:14a), revealer of the Father (1:18), true Israel (1:34), Spirit-anointed Messiah (1:34), unique "Son" of God (1:14b, 34), atoning sacrifice/Isaiah's suffering servant (1:29, 36), and gateway to heaven (1:51). Chapter 1 is clear yet challenging. John's language and images clearly communicate Jesus's identity. Yet the way he heaps one description on top of another makes it difficult to relate all of them to one another. Jesus is the creator *and* the sacrificial Lamb of God! Jesus is the God-man: he is all that is God and all that is (unfallen) man. John will spend the next twenty chapters unpacking what he introduces here. No wonder the early church used the symbol of an eagle to describe the Fourth Gospel. It is truly a thing to behold.

The In-Breaking of the New Age and Conflict in Jerusalem (2:1–25)

The First Sign and the Beginning of the New Cosmos (2:1–12)

Chapter 2 begins with a time reference: "on the third day" (2:1). The time stamp may seem odd at first, but clarity comes when we align it with the previous temporal markers:

1:19-28	Day 1
1:29	Day 2 ("the next day")
1:35	Day 3 ("the next day")
1:43	Day 4 ("the next day")
2:1	Day 6 ("on the third day" or two days later)

Adapted from Edward W. Klink III, *John*, ZECNT (Grand Rapids: Zondervan, 2016), 160.

Edward Klink rightly argues that John frames the first week of Jesus's ministry in accordance with the six days of creation in Genesis 1. John opens his Gospel with an explicit reference to Jesus as the creator of the first cosmos (1:3), so "the first six days of the work of Jesus at the beginning of his ministry are equivalent in nature and force to the first six days of the work of God at the beginning of time."[7] Jesus's ministry begins with a calculated week (1:19–2:11) and ends with a calculated week (12:1–20:25).[8] This is hardly coincidental. His first week of ministry anticipates his final week of passion.

Jesus and his disciples attend a wedding in Cana, probably a city to the west of the Sea of Galilee (2:1). The first and fourth signs take place here (2:1–11; 4:46–54), and according to 21:2, Nathanael is from there. Excluding the location, details of the wedding are scant. We can probably assume that a relative of Jesus is a participant, explaining why his mother, Mary, bears some responsibility for administering the feast (2:2). John does not offer his readers the names of the bride and groom, and no mention of the guest list is made. Those tidbits are irrelevant to John's main point. The narrative focuses on three characters: Jesus, his mother, and the "master of the banquet." Mary informs Jesus that "they have no more wine," likely requesting that Jesus and his disciples procure some from a nearby market (2:3). Jesus, though, views his entire life and ministry through his program of redeeming humanity and the cosmos; he only acts at the right moment or "hour" (2:4). As John's Gospel progresses, his "hour" of suffering and exaltation grows nigh (cf. 12:23, 27; 13:1; 16:2; 17:1; →17:1–5).

John discloses to his readers that "six stone water jars" are on hand—"the kind used by the Jews for ceremonial washing, each holding from twenty to thirty gallons" (2:6; cf. 11:55). According to purity laws, clay jars transmit uncleanness and are to be avoided (e.g., Lev. 11:33; 15:12). Stone jars, however, do not (e.g., m. Miqw. 4.1; b. Shabb. 58a). John has already identified Jesus as the true temple, and as such, he is the means by which one enjoys God's glory. Purity and cleanness are now bound up with following Jesus of Nazareth. Further, these purification jars are massive, each holding around twenty to thirty gallons.

After the jars are filled with water, Jesus then charges the servants to bring the wine to the headwaiter (2:9–10). To his surprise, this new wine is far better than what the guests were served earlier. What we have, then, is an abundance of choice wine. Wine and banquets are a major feature in all four Gospels, and we have discussed their significance (→Mark 2:18–22 and

---

7. Edward W. Klink III, *John*, ZECNT (Grand Rapids: Zondervan, 2016), 161.
8. Bauckham, "Historiographical Characteristics of the Gospel of John," 24.

Luke 5:27–32). Old Testament prophets expect a great banquet at the end of history with God in the new heavens and earth, a covenant meal that signals the arrival of God's presence among the restored Israelites and the nations (see Isa. 25:6; Jer. 31:12–14; Hosea 14:7; Joel 3:18; Amos 9:13–14). Jesus's miraculous transformation of water into wine tangibly affirms that the new creation and the restoration of all things have arrived on the climactic sixth day of his ministry.

At the end of the miracle in Cana, John's readers learn that this is "the first of the signs through which he revealed his glory" (2:11). The Fourth Gospel is often divided into two halves: the Book of Signs (1:19–12:50) and the Book of Glory (13:1–20:31). The term "sign" (*sēmeion*) occurs at critical points in the narrative (2:23; 4:48, 54; 6:2, 14, 26; 9:16; 12:18; 20:30), tangibly demonstrating that Jesus is the divine Son of God and Israel's long-awaited King. According to 1:34–45, John the Baptist and the first disciples bear witness to Jesus's identity. Now, Jesus manifests his identity through his own works.

Commentators generally agree that the Fourth Gospel contains seven signs; and six of those seven are often agreed upon, but the seventh sign is difficult to pin down. Brandon Crowe, refining Marc Girard's proposal, persuasively argues for a chiastic structure:[9]

Sign 1 A. Water, wine, purification, and eschatological life (2:1–11)

   Sign 2 B. Healing of the official's son (4:43–54)

      Sign 3 C. Healing of the lame man (5:1–15)

         Sign 4 D. Feeding of the five thousand (6:1–15)

      Sign 5 C'. Healing of a blind man (9:1–12)

   Sign 6 B'. Raising of Lazarus (11:1–44)

Sign 7 A'. Water, blood, purification, and eschatological life (19:1–20:31)

The seventh and final sign is Jesus's death and resurrection. In this arrangement, the first six signs anticipate the ultimate and perfect seventh sign. The cross and resurrection, then, are the full demonstration of Jesus's identity as the divine Son of God and Israel's Messiah. Mark contains a total of eighteen miracles, Matthew twenty, and Luke eighteen, whereas John lists only eight (including 21:6).[10] The point is that John has carefully chosen eight miracles or seven signs to present his depiction of Jesus. To understand the nature and purpose of the signs, we must take a step back.

---

9. Brandon Crowe, "The Chiastic Structure of Seven Signs in the Gospel of John: Revisiting a Neglected Proposal," *BBR* 28 (2018): 65–81.

10. Bauckham, "Historiographical Characteristics of the Gospel of John," 28.

The seven signs in John are ultimately derived from the book of Exodus, where we discover two sets of "signs." The first set, composed of three signs (Exod. 4:1–9), is designed to convince the Israelites that Moses is God's appointed agent in redeeming his people. The second set of signs targets Pharaoh and the Egyptians. God promises to "harden" Pharaoh's heart *so that* God might dispense the ten plagues upon Egypt (Exod. 3:19–20; 4:21–23). The purpose of the plagues is manifold: (1) Above all, they display God's unique character as the only true and sovereign Lord. Exodus 7:3–5 illustrates this nicely: "I [the Lord] will harden Pharaoh's heart, and though I multiply my *signs* [*ta sēmeia*] and wonders in Egypt, he will not listen to you. Then I will lay my hand on Egypt and with mighty acts of judgment. . . . And *the Egyptians will know that I am the* LORD" (cf. Exod. 4:8–9, 17; 7:3, 9; 10:1–2; 11:9–10; 12:13). (2) The plagues also indicate divine judgment upon unbelief (Exod. 6:6; 7:4; 12:12). (3) God uses the plagues to forge a community that exclusively worships him. He redeems a people for himself *through* the plagues of judgment. Notice the language of Exodus 7:4: "I will lay my hand on Egypt and with mighty acts of judgment I will bring out my divisions, my people the Israelites."

The immediate and broad context of John's Gospel contains several points of typological contact between Jesus's ministry and Israel's exodus from Egypt. For example, Jesus is the true tabernacle in contrast to the earthly tabernacle (1:14; Exod. 40:34–38), the ultimate revelation in contrast to God's revelation at Sinai (1:17; Exod. 20:1), the perfect Passover sacrifice in contrast to an animal sacrifice (1:29; Exod. 12:3), true Israel who passes through the Jordan River in contrast to unfaithful Israel (1:32–34; Josh. 3), and the one ultimately lifted up in contrast to the snake in the wilderness (3:13–14; Num. 21:8–9). What is true of Israel's first exodus will be true of Israel's second exodus, but in a greater and escalated way. Signs accompany the first and second exoduses, but the signs that accompany the second exodus are greater than those that attended the first. So the seven signs in the Fourth Gospel are an unparalleled manifestation of God's holy, sovereign, and gracious character that takes place in his Son. They also contain elements of judgment upon those who continue to rebel. And, finally, the seven signs are the means by which God will preserve a godly remnant.

One more item regarding the *effect* of the seven signs is in order. In the first exodus, the ten plagues or signs always generated a response—belief or unbelief. Indeed, the majority of the nation of Israel did not grasp the significance of the ten plagues. If they had, they would have trusted in the Lord and entered into the promised land. Deuteronomy 29:2–4 sets forth a principle that operates throughout the rest of Scripture: "Your [the first generation of Israelites] eyes have seen all that the LORD did in Egypt to Pharaoh, to all his officials and to all his land. With your own eyes you saw those great trials,

The In-Breaking of the New Age and Conflict in Jerusalem (2:1–25)

those *signs* [*ta sēmeia*] and great wonders. But to this day the LORD has not given you a mind that understands or eyes that see or ears that hear." Psalm 106:7 is even more explicit:

> *Our fathers in Egypt did not grasp*
> *the significance of Your wonderful works*
> or remember Your many acts of faithful love;
> instead, they rebelled by the sea—the Red Sea. (HCSB)

True perception of signs and wonders operates on a spiritual level. Only a few of the first generation of Israelites genuinely "grasp the significance" of the ten plagues of Egypt. The same principle operates once more in John: Jesus, as Israel's God incarnate, is once again bringing his people out of bondage through signs and wonders, and as during the first exodus, many Israelites will perceive that Jesus is unique yet fail to trust his message. Only a few will truly perceive the meaning of the signs and wonders and trust his claims. Here in 2:11 the disciples do recognize Jesus's uniqueness on account of the miracle and believe "in him," and this recognition functions as the main point of 2:1–12. *Therefore, the seven "signs" in the Fourth Gospel manifest Jesus's identity as the glorious divine Son of God and result in giving the Father glory, eliciting belief or further unbelief, and accomplishing the redemption of his people.*

Jesus and Israel's Temple (2:13–25)

Jesus, his disciples, and his family then travel to the prominent fishing village of Capernaum (2:12), a town that functions as a hub for Jesus's ministry in Galilee (6:17, 59). Jesus and the disciples head south to Jerusalem, where he will celebrate the Passover festival. The Synoptics more or less arrange their material geographically—Jesus ministers in and around Galilee, he journeys to Jerusalem, and finally, he celebrates Passover in Jerusalem, dies, and rises from the grave. John, though, narrates Jesus's ministry differently. While living in Capernaum, he travels to Jerusalem to celebrate several feasts:

2:13, 23	Passover
5:1	"One of the Jewish festivals"
6:4	Passover
7:2	Tabernacles or Booths
10:22	Dedication or Hanukkah
11:55; 12:1; 13:1	Passover

Adapted from Andreas J. Köstenberger, *A Theology of John's Gospel and Letters: The Word, the Christ, the Son of God*, BTNT (Grand Rapids: Zondervan, 2009), 413.

Why does John go out of his way to connect Jesus to these festivals? Andreas Köstenberger puts the matter succinctly: "John taps deeply into the matrix of OT traditions in his effort to show Jesus as the fulfillment of the major institutions of Judaism . . . such as the Sabbath as well as festivals like Passover and Tabernacles."[11]

According to the Synoptics, Jesus "cleanses" or, better, judges the temple at the end of his ministry (Matt. 21:12–13 // Mark 11:15–17 // Luke 19:45–46), whereas John frontloads the event. Some scholars see a contradiction between the accounts, and others argue for one cleansing that John places at the beginning of Jesus's ministry for emphasis. Still others argue for two cleansings: one at the beginning of Jesus's ministry and one at the end. There is little need to see a contradiction between the accounts as the latter two options are quite plausible. In the end, it probably makes little difference if there is one cleansing or two, as the general point remains the same: the temple in Jerusalem is outdated with the coming of Jesus, the true temple (1:14, 51), and it reeks of pride and idolatry (→Mark 11:15–17). Further, in fronting the temple judgment, John sets the tone for Jesus's *public* ministry. Richard Bauckham rightly adds, "He [Jesus] is a pre-eminently public figure, engaged almost from the start with the leaders of the Jewish theocracy in the Temple, ultimately engaged with Rome itself in the person of Pilate."[12]

In the previous three passages, John ropes the disciples into his plot (1:35–42, 43–51; 2:1–12), but in the clearing of the temple (2:13–25) and in Jesus's exchange with Nicodemus (3:1–15), there is not a whisper about the disciples. The narrative focuses solely on Jesus's confrontation with the religious authorities. Is there any redemptive-historical significance to this observation? Perhaps. In contrast to the Synoptics, the Fourth Gospel oddly contains not a single exorcism, nor does John include Jesus's temptation. In all three Synoptics, the narratives progress immediately from Jesus's baptism to his wilderness temptation (Matt. 3:13–4:11 // Mark 1:9–13 // Luke 3:21–4:13) and then reference a flurry of exorcisms (Matt. 4:24 // Mark 1:21–28 // Luke 4:31–37). Although Jesus's baptism in John's Gospel does not immediately precede his actions in the temple, Jesus clearly confronts Israel's failed leadership. Perhaps the conflict between Jesus and Jewish leadership in the temple and at night with Nicodemus should be viewed along similar lines: Jesus, as the unique and faithful Son of God, is overcoming the devil and the forces of evil.

---

11. Andreas J. Köstenberger, *A Theology of John's Gospel and Letters: The Word, the Christ, the Son of God*, BTNT (Grand Rapids: Zondervan, 2009), 422.
12. Bauckham, "Historiographical Characteristics of the Gospel of John," 26.

Jesus enters the "temple courts" or the court of the gentiles (2:14), where animals are sold for sacrifices. Diaspora Jews traveling to Jerusalem purchased sacrifices at the temple and needed to exchange their currency for the requisite Tyrian coinage. To exchange currency, though, was costly, as the temple authorities heavily taxed the exchange. Jesus fashions a whip and drives out "all from the temple courts" (2:15). John then discloses that the disciples watched the event unfold and "remembered" Psalm 69:9: "Zeal for your house will consume me." Whether they connect Psalm 69 to Jesus's actions in the temple immediately or after his resurrection (cf. 12:16) is unclear. Psalm 69 concerns David's righteous behavior in the midst of unjust accusations by his enemies (Ps. 69:4) and his passion for the temple or "house" (Ps. 69:9). King David's "zeal" for the temple and his unjust persecution typologically relate to Jesus's passion for God's dwelling place and his inevitable conflict with the Jewish leaders (2:19).

The religious authorities (lit. "the Jews"; see 1:19; 5:10, 15, 16, 18; 7:11, 13, 15, etc.) burn with anger and ask, "What *sign* [*sēmeion*] can you show us to prove your authority to do all this?" (2:18). Jesus responds enigmatically: "Destroy this temple, and I will raise it again in three days" (2:19). The answer is brilliant because Jesus, in the first clause, simultaneously refers to the destruction of the physical temple *and* the destruction of his own body. In the second, though, he refers only to the raising of his body. His death and resurrection, taken together, are the seventh and final sign in 19:20–20:31. John divulges two different responses to Jesus's words. On the one hand, the Jewish leaders are unable to grasp its meaning—they wrongly attribute it solely to the Jerusalem temple (2:20). Judgment upon the temple is not formally a "sign," but it is still very much connected to the miracle at Cana and the seventh and final sign. So it is unsurprising that some cannot perceive its true meaning. On the other hand, the disciples, while not comprehending Jesus's reply immediately, did understand it "after he was raised from the dead" (2:21). John's readers are fortunate to gain immediate insight as the event unfolds through the parenthetical comment in 2:21: "But the temple he had spoken of was his body."

John ends chapter 2 by connecting the Passover celebration with "signs" and purported belief among "many people" because they "saw the signs he was performing" (2:23). Like the first generation of Israelites who recognize Yahweh's uniqueness in the exodus but eventually fail to trust him, these first-century Jews follow suit in that they, while observing Jesus's unique identity, fail to commit their lives to him (cf. 6:2, 14; Luke 4:22–30). In turn, Jesus refuses to "entrust" himself to them because he, as God in the flesh, sees through the veneer of their faith (2:24–25; cf. 16:30; Mark 2:8 // Luke 5:22). At the end of chapter 2, John catalogues three types of responses to Jesus's signs: true faith (disciples; 2:11), hostility (Jewish leaders; 2:18), and hypocritical faith (the crowds; 2:23). If the first sign generates a wide range of responses, what about the remaining six? John therefore encourages his readers to identify with the disciples' response and unswervingly place their faith in Jesus.

Light and Darkness—the Conflict Continues (3:1–36)

Jesus and Nicodemus (3:1–21)

The three categories of response set forth in chapter 2 continue into chapter 3, particularly with respect to Nicodemus. Is he hostile to Jesus's ministry? Will he initially believe in Jesus and then fall away at some point in the future? Or will he believe in Jesus and persevere to the end? Connecting Jesus's exchange with Nicodemus in chapter 3 with Jesus's previous interaction with the Jewish leaders in the temple is critical. It is possible, even likely, that Nicodemus is confronting Jesus.[13] We should assume that Jesus and the disciples continue to remain in or around Jerusalem for all of 3:1–15. Once again, no mention is made of the disciples in 3:1–15. The narrative zooms in on Jesus and Nicodemus.

John describes Nicodemus as a "member of the Jewish ruling council" (lit. "a ruler of the Jews"; 3:1). Three critical points are in order: (1) Not all Pharisees possess political capital, but a handful of wealthy Pharisees participate in the Sanhedrin, the ruling body in Jerusalem that governs the nation (→Mark 14:43–65). (2) Nicodemus may be part of the well-known Gurion family, who embodies Jerusalem's aristocracy and core beliefs.[14] What we have, then, is Jesus interacting not with any Jew but with *the* Jew, one who represents a great deal of Judaism (notice the plural "you" in 3:7). (3) John notes that Nicodemus comes to Jesus "at night." Nearly at the end of John's Gospel, Nicodemus is again described as one who "visited Jesus at night" (19:39). The time of day is significant, for John opens his Gospel with an antithesis between light and darkness (1:4–5, 8–9; 11:9–10). Jesus is the light of the new creation that overcomes the darkness of the fallen old age. By associating Nicodemus with darkness, John urges his readers to view the encounter between Jesus and Nicodemus along redemptive-historical lines—as a *conflict* between light and darkness.

Nicodemus admits that no "teacher" could do such "signs" (*sēmeia*) "if God were not with him" (3:2). Herein lies a problem: true, Jesus's signs are

---

13. Klink, *John*, 192–204, rightly connects Nicodemus's exchange with the conflict in 2:13–25.

14. Richard Bauckham, *The Testimony of the Beloved Disciple* (Grand Rapids: Baker Academic, 2007), 137–72.

miraculous and God is at work in him, but Jesus is more than a "teacher" (cf. 1:38; 11:28; 13:13–14; 20:16)—he is God in the flesh and the King of the cosmos. The exchange centers on Nicodemus's misunderstanding of the nature of what it means to be "born again" (3:3 NIV, HCSB, ESV) or "born from above" (NRSV). The expression "born again" is multifaceted, encompassing layers of Jewish eschatology and apocalypticism. To be "born again" is nearly equivalent to the verb "to live" or the noun "life" in the Fourth Gospel and means to become part of the dawning of the new creation that will ultimately be fulfilled in the eternal new cosmos (e.g., 3:15, 16, 36; 4:10; 5:21, 39; 6:33, 40). It is a robust, already-not-yet term that taps into much of what we find throughout the NT (e.g., 2 Cor. 5:17; Eph. 2:5; Col 3:1–4).

The problem is that Nicodemus, ironically a "teacher" himself and quite knowledgeable in the OT, remains hostile to Jesus and lacks a robust understanding of the nature of regeneration. In a word, "he should have understood the need for a God-given new birth, and God's promise that he would give his people a new heart, a new nature, clean lives and a full measure of the Spirit on the last day."[15] The dominant OT background is Ezekiel 36, where the prophet predicts that God will, in the latter days, cleanse his people from their idolatry and give them a "new heart" so that they might obey his law (Ezek. 36:24–27). But not only will God restore his people; he will also transform the land itself "like the garden of Eden" (Ezek. 36:35) and create a massive eschatological city-temple (Ezek. 40–48). Nicodemus appears to have a deficient understanding of prophetic anticipation of personal and corporate renewal. He is not reading the OT correctly. Further, he fails to see that such end-time renewal takes place solely through faith in God's Son. The lifting up of "the snake in the wilderness" for Israel's deliverance prophetically prefigures Jesus being "lifted up" and exalted on the cross and resurrection so that all those who trust him will be saved (3:14–15; see Num. 21:8–9).

The narrator probably takes over at this point, so we should view all of 3:16–21 as explanatory reflection on what transpires between Nicodemus and Jesus. The thrust of this section is that God graciously and lovingly sent his "one and only Son" (*ton huion ton monogenē*). One Greek term (*monogenēs*) stands behind the description "one and only," a term found four times in the Fourth Gospel and each referring to Jesus (1:14, 18; 3:16, 18; cf. 1 John 4:9). The word generally means "only one of its kind or class."[16] The term often but not exclusively applies to a parent having an "only" child, whether a boy

15. Carson, *John*, 197.
16. BDAG, μονογενής, 658.

or girl (e.g., Judg. 11:34; Tob. 3:15; 6:11; Luke 7:12; 8:42; 9:38; Heb. 11:17). The idea, then, is not that God gave birth to Jesus, but that he commissioned his *unique* Son to enter into a dark and rebellious "world" (*ton kosmon*) with the purpose of bringing new creational life to those who trust in him (3:16). Light overcomes the darkness. If Nicodemus believes that Jesus is the great Life-giver and turns from his sin, then he will become part of God's true family (3:21). Keep in mind that Jesus has been God's Son from eternity past before the incarnation, and there was never a point in time in which Jesus was not God's Son (→5:16–47).

The Testimony of John the Baptist (3:22–36)

Jesus and the disciples leave Jerusalem and head to the "Judean country-side" so that he may baptize. While Jesus himself is not physically baptizing people (see 4:2), he sanctions it. In the same breath, the Fourth Gospel mentions that John the Baptist, too, is baptizing "at Aenon near Salim," a region probably east of Mount Gerizim (3:23).[17] Why does baptism crop up here in the narrative? Baptism is prominently on display in 1:19–34, where John baptizes the crowds so that "he [Jesus] might be revealed to Israel" (1:31). The central aim of both baptisms is to purify true Israel of her sin and prepare her for God's glory in Jesus. John the Baptist's disciples point out that Jesus is also baptizing (3:26), but John doesn't flinch. In contrast to Nicodemus, he understands Jesus's identity and mission. The two baptisms do not compete with each other; rather, John's baptism is preparation for Jesus's arrival. John the Baptist's role is to prepare true Israel, the "bride," for Jesus, the "bridegroom" (3:29; →Mark 2:19–22).

The remainder of chapter 3 (3:31–36) is another explanatory reflection upon John's testimony in 3:27–30 and, in particular, Jesus's exchange with Nicodemus in 3:11–13.[18] The narrator identifies Jesus as the "one who comes from above" and John the Baptist as "the one who is from the earth" (3:31). As faithful as John the Baptist is, he is not the Light of heaven (1:8). According to 3:32, Jesus "testifies to what he has seen and heard, but no one accepts his testimony." Jesus is the ultimate witness of the Father, who testifies to his holy and gracious character (cf. Rev. 1:5; 3:14), but such testimony is largely rebuffed by those reveling in the darkness (1:10–11; 2:18–20; 3:11). Verse 33 is critical to Jesus's mission and John's Gospel as a whole: "Whoever has accepted it

17. Craig S. Keener, *The Gospel of John: A Commentary* (Peabody, MA: Hendrickson, 2003), 1:576.
18. Colin G. Kruse, *John: An Introduction and Commentary*, TNTC 4 (Downers Grove, IL: InterVarsity, 2003), 123.

[Jesus's testimony] has certified that God is truthful" (3:33). Trusting in Jesus's identity and his message ultimately upholds the Father himself and, in effect, the OT (5:31–40). Failure to accept Jesus's testimony is a failure to believe the Father and Scripture. A few verses earlier in 3:27–30, John the Baptist faithfully bears witness to Jesus, so he naturally falls into this category of one who accepts Jesus's testimony and affirms "that God is truthful." John's readers are challenged with the same admonition: believe that Jesus is the light who reveals the fullness of the Father. At this stage in the narrative, the readers are to imitate John the Baptist, not Nicodemus.

Believing Samaritans and Unbelieving Galileans (4:1–54)

Jesus and the Samaritan Woman (4:1–42)

Jesus and his disciples left the "countryside" of Judea (3:22) and headed north for Galilee because the Pharisees "had heard he was gaining and baptizing more disciples than John" (4:1). Jesus's baptism of eschatological renewal threatens the Jewish status quo. He could have taken a few routes to Galilee, but he chooses to pass through Samaria for its symbolic significance. He and the disciples stop at Sychar, "near the plot of ground Jacob had given to his son Joseph" and close to "Jacob's well" (4:5–6). John weds two important and related concepts: land and water.

This is also the second time the patriarch Jacob moves into the foreground of John's narrative. According to Genesis 33:19–20, Jacob purchased land on the fringes of Shechem and, importantly, "set up an altar and called it El Elohe Israel." The word here for "set up" recalls Genesis 28:12–13, where the stairway to heaven was "resting" (*mutstsob*) on the ground and the Lord "stood" (*nitstsob*) above it.[19] Erecting the altar at Shechem is tied to what transpires earlier in the Genesis narrative at Bethel when Jacob envisions the stairway to heaven. What binds both of these texts together is God's covenantal presence dwelling with Jacob.

There is considerable debate concerning the precise origin of the Samaritans and the nuances of their cherished beliefs in the first century AD. Two generally agreed-upon points are worthy of consideration: (1) the Samaritans established a rival priesthood and built a separate temple on Mount Gerizim (Josephus, *Ant.* 11.310, 340–46), a sanctuary that John Hyrcanus in the early second century BC demolished; and (2) the Samaritans held to the exclusive use of the Pentateuch (à la the Sadducees) and, in that vein, the eschatological

---

19. Victor P. Hamilton, *The Book of Genesis, Chapters 18–50*, NICOT (Grand Rapids: Eerdmans, 1995), 349–50.

expectation of the arrival of a "prophet like Moses" from Deuteronomy 18:18 (see John 4:25–26).

Jews and Samaritans did not, on the whole, get along well. For example, one famous early Jewish text reads, "Samaritan women are deemed menstruants from their cradle" (m. Nid. 4.1). That is, Samaritan women are ritually unclean from birth. Nevertheless, Jesus approaches the well "about noon" (lit. "the sixth hour"; 4:6). Perhaps John's point in detailing the time of day lies in its stark contrast with Nicodemus, who met with Jesus "by night" (3:2). Jesus asks the woman to draw him some water, but she is taken aback because of the cultural friction between Jews and Samaritans (4:7–9). In 4:10, Jesus turns the table, asserting that she should be asking him for water because "he [Jesus] would have given you living water." Living water, a rich biblical-theological concept that begins in Genesis 1–2 and ends in Revelation 21–22, refers to God's life-giving presence that nourishes creation and humanity (e.g., Isa. 35:6; 41:17–18; 44:3; Jer. 2:13; Ezek. 36:25–27; 47:1–12; Zech. 14:8). The idea, then, is that Jesus claims to be the locus of God's glory, the true temple (in contrast to the temple in Jerusalem and the rival site on Mount Gerizim). The OT prophetic types and shadows of the physical temple find their ultimate fulfillment in Jesus—the living water—and all those who trust in him (see 3:5; 7:38; 19:34). Jesus offers this unclean, adulterous Samaritan woman the opportunity to participate in God's true sanctuary—the person of Jesus.

The disciples return to Jesus with food (cf. 4:9), but Jesus responds cryptically, "My food . . . is to do the will of him who sent me" (4:34). What is the Father's sustenance or "will" for his Son? That question is succinctly answered later in the narrative: "This is the will of him who sent me, that I shall lose none of all those he has given me, but raise them up at the last day. . . . *Everyone who looks to the Son and believes in him shall have eternal life*, and I will raise them up at the last day" (6:39–40; cf. 5:19–23). So the Father appoints the Son to redeem, preserve, and resurrect those whom the Father has chosen. All aspects of Jesus's career must be filtered through this mission—his actions, teaching, interactions, death, and resurrection. Quite simply, Jesus came to save, preserve, and glorify his saints and plant them in the new creation. Jesus's disciples, therefore, must align their role with his mission (4:35–38).

John caps Jesus's ministry in Samaria with extensive belief: "Many of the Samaritans from that town believed in him because of the woman's testimony" (4:39). This woman, a pariah at some level, testifies to the truth of Jesus's identity. In a word, she "accepted" Jesus's identity and "certified that God is truthful" (3:33). The passage ends with Jesus himself teaching the Samaritans for two days, resulting in further belief. At the end of the account, the villagers testify that "this man really is the Savior of the world" (4:42).

Healing the Official's Son (4:43–54)

John narrates Jesus journeying from Samaria to Galilee and then explains why: "For Jesus himself had testified that a prophet has no honor in the prophet's own country" (4:44 NRSV; cf. Mark 6:4 and par.). What is Jesus's own country? As several commentators point out, the answer is Galilee *and* Judea—all Jewish territory. Notice the pairing of Judea and Galilee in 4:54. Jews in Jerusalem reject him in 2:13–25, and now Jews in Galilee will follow suit. The believing Samaritans are sandwiched between the two accounts. The Galileans, on the surface, "welcomed him" with open arms (4:45). Why such a strong reception? These Galileans are likely included in the group described in 2:23 that sees Jesus's "signs" in Jerusalem but eventually fails to believe. Their allegiance is only skin deep.

The healing of the official's son contains several remarkable (typological?) parallels with the tenth and final Egyptian plague and with the exodus as a whole:

First Exodus	Second Exodus in John 4:43-54
Institution of Passover (Exod. 12:1-28)	Recalls belief at the first "Passover Festival" (4:45; cf. 2:23)
The blood of the Passover sacrifice is a "sign" (Exod. 12:13)	Healing becomes "the second sign" (4:54)
Israel recognizes God's "signs and wonders" yet fails to trust in him (Deut. 4:34; 6:22; 29:3-4)	The Jewish Galileans will not believe in Jesus unless they see "signs and wonders" (4:48)
Firstborn dies unless a Passover sacrifice is offered (Exod. 12:12-13)	Official's son will die unless Jesus intervenes (4:47)
Pharaoh fails to trust in Yahweh despite the death of his firstborn (Exod. 12:29)	Official believes Jesus and rescues his son despite not seeing signs and wonders (4:51)
Pharaoh is called a "king" (*basileus*; Exod. 6:27, 29; 14:5)	The son's father is called a "royal official" (*basilikos*)

Some of these connections may seem tenuous, but when we put all of them together, a picture emerges: the Jews in Galilee, like the Jews in Judea, recognize Jesus's miraculous power in his signs, but they fail to recognize the true significance of the signs. The signs point to Jesus's identity as the "one and only" Son of God—Yahweh incarnate, who entered into creation in order to redeem his people in the second and final exodus by bearing God's wrath as *the* Passover sacrifice. John nearly places the official in the same category as the disciples. In 2:11 the disciples "believed" in Jesus *after* the "sign" of turning the water into wine. Here, the official "believed" *before* the "sign" of healing the boy (4:50 NASB). After the miracle, though, the official's "whole household believed" (4:53). Though we know nothing about the ethnicity of the "royal official," he, at the very least, symbolizes a faithful remnant in Jesus's "country" (4:44). *If* the exodus is broadly in view in 4:43–54, then the faith of the "royal official" (*basilikos*) plausibly stands in sharp relief because Pharaoh, the "king" (*basileus*) of Egypt, refuses to believe even after seeing signs and wonders.

On a literary and theological level, the first and second signs reinforce one another. Not only does true faith accompany both (2:11; 4:53), but both are tied to Jesus's life-giving mission. Turning water into wine and bringing life to the nearly dead (2:9; 4:51) are functionally equivalent. Both miracles or signs bear witness to Jesus as the light of the new creation that penetrates the darkness of the fallen world. Furthermore, according to Exodus 4:8, God gives Moses two signs—turning Moses's rod into a snake and making his hand leprous—because "if they [the Israelites] do not believe . . . the first sign, they may believe the second." We see something similar here throughout the Fourth Gospel: God graciously gives Israel multiple signs that attest to his glory in his Son.

Healing on the Sabbath and Jesus's Identity as the Son of God (5:1-47)

Healing at the Pool of Bethesda (5:1–15)

The narrative progresses as Jesus heads south to Jerusalem to celebrate "one of the Jewish festivals" (5:1). John doesn't disclose which festival Jesus celebrates (Booths? Passover?), but that's not critical to the story. He does give attention to where Jesus goes—a pool close to the "Sheep Gate" that "is surrounded by five covered colonnades" (5:2). Scholars generally agree that the pool in Bethesda should be identified with the two pools underneath St. Anne's Monastery, north of the temple complex. A collection of "disabled people" bathed at the pool for healing on account of Jewish folklore. It's unclear how this worked precisely, but that's of little interest to the narrative. The point is that "Jesus replaces not only John's baptism (1:31–33), ritual purity (2:6), proselyte baptism (3:5), and the Samaritan water of Jacob's well (4:14) but also the water of a popular healing cult."[20]

---

20. Keener, *Gospel of John*, 1:638.

Jesus approaches a man who has been disabled for thirty-eight years and asks if he wants "to get well" (5:7). Yes, of course! Instead of carrying the man to the pool, Jesus heals him on the spot: "Get up! Pick up your mat and walk" (5:8; cf. Mark 2:11; Acts 3:7). The narrator then reveals that the miracle (the third "sign") occurs on the Sabbath (5:9). This is the first mention of the Sabbath in the Fourth Gospel, and its importance cannot be overstated (see 7:22; 9:14, 16; 19:31). Rather than celebrating the man's restoration, the Jewish leaders accuse him of breaking the Sabbath by carrying his mat. Transporting items on the Sabbath is strictly prohibited (Num. 15:32; Neh. 13:15–19; Jer. 17:21).

The man, not unlike Eve in the garden and Aaron at Sinai, shifts the blame (5:11). It's not his fault he's carrying his mat. At the behest of the Jewish leaders, he attempts to locate Jesus, but to no avail, for "Jesus had slipped away into the crowd" (5:13). Sometime later, Jesus hunts down the man in the temple, warning him, "See, you are well again. Stop sinning or something worse may happen to you" (5:14). Despite being made well, this man refuses to follow Jesus at all costs. He has already caved in to the demands of the Jewish leaders in 5:13 and will eventually give up Jesus in 5:15—behavior eerily similar to Judas betraying Jesus (cf. 13:21; 18:2). The nub of the issue is this man's ultimate desire to please the Jewish leaders over Jesus of Nazareth. In his eyes, Jesus is, quite simply, not who he claims to be. The healing of the invalid stands in razor-sharp contrast to the later healing of the blind man who confesses to the Jewish leaders that Jesus is a "prophet" (9:17) and "from God" (9:33; →9:1–34).

The Theological Significance of Healing on the Sabbath (5:16–47)

The narrative shifts from Jesus's interaction with the invalid to the Jewish leaders' (*hoi Ioudaioi*) interaction with Jesus. They "persecute him" on account of what transpires on the Sabbath (5:16). Jesus's relation to the Sabbath is difficult to summarize, but the thrust of it is that Jesus brings the institution of the Sabbath to its fulfillment. True and eschatological rest finds its substance in Jesus (→Matt. 11:28). Jesus, as the Son of God, possesses the divine right to heal on the Sabbath because he is the true Sabbath. Profaning the Sabbath threatens one of the most treasured characteristics of Judaism; it threatens Israel's identity as God's covenant community. No wonder Jesus's action draws the ire of the religious authorities. If they could grasp Jesus's identity as the life-giving Son of God, who inaugurates the new age (2:1–11), houses the glory of God (1:14), fulfills Israel's feasts (2:13, 23; 4:45), and offers eschatological life and participation in the new temple through the

Spirit (3:5–8; 4:13–14), then they would have no issue with his conduct on the Sabbath. We must also never lose sight of the bigger picture. Sabbath is part of a much larger program of reflection and enaction, as Gordon Wenham wisely comments:

> During these [seven Israelite] festivals there were seven days of rest, first and seventh unleavened bread, weeks, solemn rest day, day of atonement, first of booths, first day after booths. The majority of these festivals occur in the seventh month of the year. Every seventh year is a sabbatical year (Exod. 21:2ff.; Lev. 25:2ff.; Deut. 15:1ff.). After forty-nine (7 x 7) years there was a super-sabbatical year, the year of jubilee (Lev. 25:8ff.). Through this elaborate system . . . the importance of the sabbath was underlined. Through sheer familiarity the weekly sabbath could come to be taken for granted. But these festivals and sabbatical years constituted major interruptions to daily living and introduced an element of variety into the rhythm of life. *In this way they constantly reminded the Israelite what God had done for him, and that in observing the sabbath he was imitating his Creator, who rested on the seventh day.*[21]

Jesus's action on the Sabbath and during one of the Jewish festivals (5:1), then, is significant. He stunningly divulges the basis for this action on the Sabbath: "My Father is always at his work to this very day, and I too am working" (5:17). Two points are critical: (1) Jesus refers to the temple as "my Father's house" to those selling doves (2:16), but here he explicitly uses the expression "my Father" with the Jewish leaders. Addressing God as "Father" or "my Father" is extraordinary within a first-century Jewish context (→Luke 11:1–4). Jesus uses the term "Father" to describe Israel's God, and remarkably, he encourages his followers to do so. Further, the Fourth Gospel, from the prologue on, describes Jesus as the "one and only" Son of God (e.g., 1:14, 18, 49; 3:16–18, 35–36). He enjoys a unique relationship with the Father, a relationship that no created being shares. For all of eternity, Jesus has always related to the Father as his Son, and in the incarnation we are privileged to see how this sonship is fleshed out. (2) The claim that the Father is at "work" and that Jesus is also "working" in the same way refers to Jesus's identity as the creator of all things (Gen. 1–2). While God's image-bearers work in an analogous fashion to God's six-day creative work (Gen. 1:28; 2:15), the two parties remain distinct. But Jesus, as the Son of God, participates in God's unique creative work. This is precisely the point of 1:3: "Through him [Jesus] all things were made." Taken together, these two points demonstrate that Jesus

---

21. Gordon J. Wenham, *The Book of Leviticus*, NICOT (Grand Rapids: Eerdmans, 1979), 301–2 (emphasis added).

is undoubtedly divine. In case John's readers miss the implication of Jesus's declaration, the narrator states, "For this reason they tried all the more to kill him; not only was he breaking the Sabbath, but *he was even calling God his own Father, making himself equal with God*" (5:18). This is a watershed moment in the narrative. The Jewish leaders will never be at ease until they put him in a grave (see 10:33; 19:7).

The next section of chapter 5 explains in greater detail some of the mechanics of Jesus's relationship with his Father (5:19–30), and then the final section confirms the veracity of that relationship (5:31–47). There is much to unpack in 5:19–30, but we will concern ourselves with only a handful of observations. This passage upholds two basic principles: in the incarnation, Jesus is simultaneously equal with and functionally subordinate to the Father (→Mark 13:32–37).[22] In a word, "the Father initiates, sends, commands, commissions, grants; the Son responds, obeys, performs his Father's will, receives authority."[23] The section of 5:19–23 flows from one premise, followed by one ground clause and three explanatory clauses,[24] all supporting the idea that the Son cannot act independently of the Father.

Premise: "The Son can do nothing by himself" (5:19a)

Ground: "*because (gar)* whatever the Father does the Son also does" (5:19b AT)

Explanation 1: "*for (gar)* the Father loves the Son and shows him all he does" (5:20)

Explanation 2: "*for (gar)* just as the Father raises the dead and gives them life, even so the Son gives life to whom he is pleased to give it" (5:21)

Explanation 3: "*for (gar)* the Father judges no one but has entrusted all judgment to the Son" (5:22 AT)

The second explanation is worthy of contemplation, as it's fundamental to the Fourth Gospel.[25] The "Father raises the dead" (5:21) means that God is committed to the great act of redeeming all of creation and humanity. Verse 21 ends with the Son also giving life and implicitly raising the dead. Just as the Father raises the dead, so does Jesus, because he, too, is divine. The beginning

---

22. Andreas J. Köstenberger and Scott R. Swain, *Father, Son and Spirit: The Trinity and John's Gospel*, NSBT 24 (Leicester, UK: Apollos, 2008), 88.

23. Carson, *John*, 251.

24. Klink, *John*, 286n8.

25. My discussion of 5:21–30 is adapted from Benjamin L. Gladd and Matthew S. Harmon, *Making All Things New: Inaugurated Eschatology for the Life of the Church* (Grand Rapids: Baker Academic, 2016), 48.

of verse 24 highlights the need for faith in Jesus in order to obtain "eternal life." But how is "eternal life" defined here in chapter 5 and John's Gospel as a whole? Verse 24b explains that the one who believes "will not be judged but has crossed over from death to life." According to this verse, eternal life in the Fourth Gospel must be understood along redemptive-historical lines—that is, the transfer from death in the old age to life in the new age (see 3:15, 16, 36; 4:14, 36; 5:39; 6:27, 40, 47, 54, 68; 10:28; 12:25, 50; 17:2–3). Vital to Jesus's program is his intention, as Yahweh incarnate, to give new creational life to all who believe. The Synoptics certainly accent this dimension, but John's Gospel places this theme at the heart of Jesus's ministry. According to 10:10, Jesus came that believers may enjoy eschatological or resurrection "life, and have it to the full."

The theme of crossing over "from death to life" sets the tone for the next several verses, as 5:25–29 further unpacks John's definition of eternal life. Verse 25 begins with an odd yet gripping description: "An hour is coming, and is now here" (HCSB). It's easy to overlook this statement, but doing so misses the point of the verse, for the next clause tells us that this is the hour "when the dead will hear the voice of the Son of God." The term "hour" (*hōra*) plays no small role in John (4:21, 23; 12:23; 16:25, 32; 17:1) and ultimately stems from the book of Daniel (Dan. 8:17, 19; 11:6, 35, 40).[26] Of special interest to us is Daniel 12:1–2:

> At that *time* [lit. "hour"; Gk. *tēn hōran*] Michael, the great prince who protects your people, will arise. There will be a time of distress such as has not happened from the beginning of nations until then. But at that time your people—everyone whose name is found written in the book—will be delivered. Multitudes who sleep in the dust of the earth will awake: some to everlasting life, others to shame and everlasting contempt.

Notice the close connection between the key word "hour" and resurrection in 5:25 and Daniel 12:1–2 (→17:1–5). What confirms the allusion to Daniel 12:1–2 is the following verses. In 5:28–29, John continues to allude to Daniel 12 when he states, "A *time* [lit. "hour"; Gk. *hōra*] is coming when all who are in the graves will hear His voice and come out—those who have done good things, to the resurrection of life, but those who have done wicked things, to the resurrection of judgment" (HCSB).

So when we read Jesus's statement that "an hour is coming and is now here," we can appreciate the gravity of his statement. The resurrection has

---

26. Stefanos Mihalios, *The Danielic Eschatological Hour in the Johannine Literature*, LNTS 436 (New York: T&T Clark, 2011).

broken into history. That explains the "now" part, but there is still a side of the resurrection that has yet to arrive. Notice the phrase "is coming" in 5:25a. Though the resurrection and new creation have broken in, the bodily resurrection of believers has yet to occur. John 5, therefore, teaches a two-stage resurrection. Jesus initially gives life or raises believers from the dead on a spiritual level in fulfillment of Daniel 12:1–2. But Jesus will one day raise believers from the dead in their fullness at the very end of history (1 Cor. 15:12–54; Rev. 20:13).

The final section of chapter 5 concerns Jesus's identity as the Son of God as corroborated by several key witnesses. The entire section is a legal indictment upon the Jewish leaders for their refusal to believe in Jesus. They set out to kill because of their wrong perception of him (5:16–18). The point of 5:31–47 is that the Jewish leaders stand in the wrong because of their failure to believe the witness of the Father (5:32, 36), John the Baptist (5:33), and the OT Scriptures (5:39–40). Jesus is not untethered to the history of redemption; he is its climax. If the religious authorities read the OT Scriptures rightly, then they would believe him, for "he [Moses] wrote about me [Jesus]" (5:46).

Jesus Feeds True Israel in Anticipation of His Death (6:1–71)

The Feeding of the Five Thousand (6:1–15)

The narrative advances to the feeding of the five thousand, the fourth sign and the only miracle repeated in all four Gospels (Matt. 14:13–21 // Mark 6:32–44 // Luke 9:10–17 // John 6:1–15). We examined this miracle in our discussion of Mark 6:32–44, so we will only make a handful of observations. John sets the scene with a description of Jesus leaving Jerusalem "some time after" the events of 5:1–47 and then heading north to cross the Sea of Galilee (6:1). The Fourth Gospel uniquely adds that Jesus goes up "on a mountainside" and sits down "with his disciples" (6:3). Mountains are not a major feature of John's narrative (cf. 4:20–21; 8:1), and the language here is akin to what we find in the Sermon on the Mount that strongly portrays Jesus as a Moses figure (cf. Exod. 19; Matt. 5). It is fitting that John casts Jesus as the true Moses in light of the significant exodus themes contained within the feeding of the five thousand. Notice the following parallels: the Passover celebration (6:4 // Exod. 12), eating bread or manna in the wilderness (6:11, 32 // Exod. 16:4, 31), and the Jews beginning to "grumble" (6:41 // Exod. 16). John puts his finger on two main issues in his retelling of the miracle: Jesus's relationship to the Passover and the repeated failure of Israel to trust God's promises of provision.

After noticing the great throng of people on their way to Jerusalem to celebrate the Passover, Jesus summons Philip and asks, "Where shall we buy bread for these people to eat?" (6:5). The narrator then discloses that this question is a "test" (6:6; cf. Exod. 16:4; Deut. 8:2). Philip should have recognized that Jesus, on the basis of his identity as the divine Son of God, is the great Life-giver and will provide for the crowd. Philip bore witness to Jesus turning water into wine (2:1–12) and countless other miracles, so he should have put two and two together. The same can be said of Andrew, who also fails the test (6:8–9). These two disciples, probably representing the remaining ten, have yet to grasp the full extent of Jesus's identity. They should have applied what they saw Jesus accomplish previously to the present situation. In the same way, the nation of Israel, despite witnessing Yahweh's unique acts in redeeming his people from Egypt, immediately fails to bring those acts to bear on their present situation in the wilderness (Exod. 16). But because Jesus is Yahweh incarnate, he is merciful and gracious; he overcomes the disciples' unbelief, multiplies the bread, and creates a new people of God, founded upon his future death and resurrection.

According to 6:14–15, the fourth sign elicits an incredible reaction and the crowd confesses, "Surely this is the Prophet who is to come into the world" (6:14). Like the Samaritan woman, who also confesses that Jesus is the Messiah-prophet (4:19) from Deuteronomy 18:15–18, the crowd believes that Jesus is the long-awaited King of Israel who has arrived on the scene to usher in political peace and establish the eschatological kingdom. But Jesus's kingship breaks the mold of what many first-century Jews believed. His kingship is marked not by political triumph but by suffering and death (→18:36). He does indeed bring peace, but not primarily political peace. He brings spiritual peace to the cosmos. In the second half of chapter 6, we discover that the crowd's belief is only skin deep. They are dazzled by the miracle, but like the crowd in 2:23–25, this group is unwilling to swallow Jesus's true identity as the life-giving God in the flesh.

Jesus Walks on Water (6:16–24)

Matthew, Mark, and John include Jesus walking on the water following the feeding of the five thousand (Matt. 14:22–33 // Mark 6:47–51 // John 6:16–24), so it is likely that all three evangelists describe the same event. Relating the fourth sign to Jesus walking on the water may seem odd at first but makes good sense once we get a handle on what transpires on the Sea of Galilee. John emphasizes the timing of the event ("when evening came") and that it was "dark" (6:16–17). Darkness, as we've mentioned before, is a major component of the Fourth Gospel. Jesus is the great light who enters the fallen, dark world in order to redeem it (1:5; 8:12; 12:35, 46).

In walking on the water and using the self-description "It is I" (lit. "I am"), Jesus aligns himself with Yahweh, the unrivaled Liberator of people from darkness (see Exod. 3:14; Job 9:8; Isa. 41:4; →Mark 6:47–51). What we have then, on account of the crowd's misunderstanding of Jesus's identity at the end of the feeding of the five thousand (6:14–15), is a corrective. The crowds (and possibly the disciples) view Jesus's miracle as a demonstration of his messianic identity. It's true, Jesus is a king, but he's more than a king. He's the King of the universe—the great "I am"—who will redeem his people out of spiritual exile. In the feeding of the five thousand, the crowds and the disciples witness the miraculous sign, whereas only the disciples are privy to the miracle on the water.

The Bread of Life Discourse and the Reaction of the Disciples (6:25–71)

The section 6:25–59, referred to as the Bread of Life Discourse, is a complex yet critical portion of the Fourth Gospel. Things are coming to a head. Jesus has performed four "signs" thus far: turning water into wine (2:1–11), healing the official's son (4:43–54), healing the lame man (5:1–11), and feeding the five thousand (6:1–15). The first and second signs, both taking place in Cana, immediately result in belief (2:11; 4:53), whereas the third and fourth signs are accompanied by unbelief (5:14–18; 6:15, 25–59). In the third sign the unbelief among the Jewish leaders is pronounced, but here in the feeding of the five thousand, unbelief characterizes the masses. What is more, the Fourth Gospel is the only Gospel to exclude the Last Supper from the narrative. This omission together with some of the eucharistic language in the Bread of Life Discourse warrants, in the eyes of many commentators, the view that John incorporates a good deal of sacramentalism into the narrative. That is, John consciously invites his readers to read this section in light of the Eucharist or Lord's Supper. On the one hand, we should be careful about importing too much sacramentalism into this passage. But on the other, how could we not discern echoes of it upon a second and third reading of John's narrative?

At the end of the discourse, John discloses that the entire block of discourse takes place in a synagogue in Capernaum (6:59; cf. Mark 1:21). Following the feeding of the five thousand, Jesus and the disciples leave for Capernaum (6:16), a location that features prominently in all four Gospels as it is Jesus's home during his ministry (see 2:12; 4:46; Matt. 4:13; Mark 2:1; Luke 4:23). The discourse breaks down into six exchanges between Jesus and the crowd

The Gospel of John
Jesus Feeds True Israel in Anticipation of His Death (6:1–71)

gathered in the synagogue.[27] The thrust of the exchange is the crowd's unwillingness to embrace Jesus as the divine Son of God, the true life-giving presence of God on earth. They desire a messiah-prophet who will liberate them from Rome's oppression (6:15), but what they need is the Son of God, who will deliver them from the oppression of sin.

The first two exchanges concern the superficiality of the crowd's perception of Jesus (6:25–29). They ultimately seek Jesus for personal gain—"you are looking for me . . . because you ate the loaves and had your fill" (6:26). This is not the attitude of a true follower of Jesus. One's life ought to be centered upon the Son of Man, who grants "eternal life" to those who believe in him (6:27; cf. 1:51; 5:27; 6:53, 62; 8:28; 9:35; 12:23; 13:31). Careful readers would discern an allusion to Daniel 7, where the Ancient of Days grants the son of man possession of the eternal kingdom on account of his successful defeat of the fourth beast (Dan. 7:13–14). According to Daniel 7, the son of man also represents the righteous Israelites who persevere under persecution, who are also "given" the kingdom (Dan. 7:18, 22, 27). Jesus's audience must understand that he is indeed offering them the eschatological kingdom but only if they trust in him (6:29).

The third and fourth exchanges focus on the audience's demand for Jesus to perform a "sign" that verifies his identity as the Son of God (6:30–40). They even appeal to a combination of Exodus 16:4 and Psalm 78:24: "Our ancestors ate the manna in the wilderness. . . . 'He [Moses] gave them bread from heaven'" (6:31). The crowd, in their use of "our ancestors," identify themselves with the first generation of Israelites in the wilderness—not a good thing! The first generation of Israelites, with the exception of Caleb and Joshua, never set foot in the land of Canaan precisely because they grumbled and failed to trust in Yahweh. Furthermore, the crowd appears to identify the pronoun "he" in the quotation as Moses (6:32), but it instead refers to Yahweh. Yahweh is the ultimate source of nourishment for the Israelites, not Moses. Taken together, the crowd gathered in the synagogue is ironically repeating the sins of their ancestors in the wilderness—ignoring the true life-giving presence of God in their midst.

In the fifth and sixth exchanges (6:41–58), the crowd's unbelief reaches a climax. John labels the crowd (6:2, 5, 22, 24)—the same group that Jesus fed in 6:1–14 and now engages in the synagogue—as "the Jews" (*hoi Ioudaioi*; 6:41, 52). We perceived earlier in the narrative that John reserves this title for the Jewish leaders, who represent the nation at large (see 1:19; 2:18; 3:1; 5:10, 15, 16). Now, the nation and her leaders have fallen in sync. Both groups have

27. Klink, *John*, 323.

341

willfully rejected Jesus's signs that display his identity as God's unique Son. Jesus then discloses the ultimate reason for their lack of understanding: "All those the Father gives me will come to me" (6:37), and, "No one can come to me unless the Father who sent me draws them" (6:44). The Jews' misunderstanding ultimately stems from God willing it so (cf. 10:29; 12:37–40; 17:2, 6–9; 18:9). True perception of Jesus, then, rests in the Father's sovereign will.

The implications of the Bread of Life Discourse are difficult to swallow, as the following verse explains: "On hearing this, many of his disciples said, 'This is a hard teaching. Who can accept it?'" (6:60). Jesus goes on to say that the most difficult teaching is still to come—Jesus's resurrection and ascension (6:62). Fallen humanity (or "the flesh") is simply unable to grasp fully God's revelation in his Son, and only those who possess the Spirit can comprehend it (6:63; cf. 1 Cor. 2:6–16). At this, "many of his disciples" leave Jesus and never return (6:66). Continuing in this vein, Jesus then broaches the topic of Judas, who fails to understand (6:70; →13:2). Peter, though, acknowledges that Jesus possesses "the words of eternal life" and that he and the others "have come to believe and to know that you are the Holy One of God" (6:69). God has drawn the eleven disciples to himself, and though they still struggle with Jesus's identity at times, they have sufficiently grasped it.

The Feast of Booths (7:1–8:59)

John's coverage of the Feast of Booths is lengthy (7:1–8:59), focusing on Jesus's teaching in the temple complex (7:14, 28; 8:20). As we wade deeper into this section we will probe various facets of the festival, but for now a brief overview will suffice. Adult males were generally required to attend three major festivals annually in Jerusalem—Passover (2:13; 6:4; 11:55), Weeks, and Booths (7:2). The Jews celebrated the Feast of Booths in the autumn for seven days, plus a day of rest at the beginning of the festival. Moses commands the Israelites to rehearse the wilderness wanderings by dwelling in booths and offering up various sacrifices (Lev. 23:34–43; Num. 29:12–38; Deut. 16:13; cf. Ezra 3:1–4; Neh. 8:13–18). They are also to procure the "product of majestic trees—palm fronds, boughs of leafy trees, and willows of the brook" (Lev. 23:40 HCSB). Over time, the feast became more elaborate, but these two elements were retained and provide the backdrop for Jesus's teaching.

Jesus and the Feast of Booths (7:1–13)

The section 7:1–13 takes place in the region of Galilee, whereas all of 7:14–8:59 appears to occur in Jerusalem during the Feast of Booths. The entirety of 7:1–8:59 stands in the wake of Jesus healing the invalid, the third sign, in 5:1–15. The Jewish leaders' unbelief, which manifests itself so starkly when they desire to kill Jesus because he breaks the Sabbath and identifies himself with Israel's God in 5:18, has not abated by the time we get to 7:1–8:59. John informs his readers that Jesus, despite the Feast of Booths (or Tabernacles) drawing near, remains to the north in Galilee because "the Jewish leaders there [in Judea] were looking for a way to kill him" (7:1). The wording in 7:1 corresponds to 5:18. Further, chapter 7 picks up where chapter 6 leaves off—continued unbelief. But this time around, it touches Jesus's own family.

John mentions Jesus's brothers, a detail which is hardly surprising given that Jesus is likely still near his home in Capernaum (6:59). This is the second time John has brought Jesus's relatives into view. According to 2:12, his brothers witness the first sign in Cana. Crucially, though, John doesn't state that they believe in Jesus as a result of the miracle—only his disciples believe (2:11). The brothers, named James, Judas, Joseph, and Simon (Matt. 13:55 // Mark 6:3), tell Jesus, "Go to Judea, so that your disciples there may see the works you do. No one who wants to become a public figure acts *in secret* [*kryptō*]. Since you are doing these things, *show* [*phanerōson*] yourself to the world" (7:3–4). The brothers pine for Jesus to cease acting in "secret" and to unveil himself to the world.

Jesus's signs function as acted-out mysteries at some level. The biblical definition of "mystery" is the unveiling or disclosure of God's previously hidden wisdom (→Mark 4:1–34). The Synoptics explicitly attribute mystery to the already-not-yet arrival of the end-time kingdom (Matt. 13:11 // Mark 4:11 // Luke 8:10), and while John never uses the term "mystery" in his Gospel, a careful reader can discern its presence throughout the narrative. The Synoptics invoke mystery when describing the paradoxical arrival of the kingdom, whereas John uses the *concept* of mystery to describe many of Jesus's acts, and especially his signs. When Jesus performs a sign, he unveils a unique and unexpected aspect about himself and, ultimately, his Father. But as Jesus reveals himself in the signs, there is still a sense of hiddenness; he often remains veiled to those around him. It is not until Jesus appears three times to his disciples *after* his resurrection that he fully reveals himself (20:20, 26; 21:1).

Jesus's brothers, perhaps unwittingly, demand that Jesus reveal himself yet again in a hidden-but-now-revealed manner. The two key terms, "secret" and "show," and their cognates are often paired with mystery in the LXX (Dan. 2:47 [OG]) and NT (1 Cor. 4:5; 14:25; Eph. 3:9; Col. 1:26).[28] Jesus responds

---

28. See Benjamin L. Gladd, *Revealing the* Mysterion: *The Use of Mystery in Daniel and Second Temple Judaism with Its Bearing on First Corinthians*, BZNW 160 (Berlin: de Gruyter, 2008), 178–79.

almost predictably: "My time is not yet here. . . . My time has not yet fully come" (7:7–8). This line demonstrates that Jesus will indeed unveil himself and disclose his identity for all the world to see, but that will take place only on the cross and in the resurrection—the seventh and final sign.

Jesus Teaches at the Feast in Jerusalem (7:14–39)

Again, John presents a series of exchanges between Jesus and the crowd in the temple in Jerusalem. Some of the same themes that are found in Jesus's previous exchange with the crowd in the synagogue in Capernaum reverberate here as Jesus teaches the crowd in the temple. Midway through the feast, Jesus makes his way to Jerusalem, where he teaches a crowd of "the Jews" (*hoi Ioudaioi*) in the temple complex (7:14–15). The Jews are flummoxed at Jesus's unrivaled knowledge "without having been taught" (7:15). Such a conclusion betrays their lack of belief in Jesus as the unique Son of God, who reveals what the Father discloses (7:16–18). As a result, Jesus states that they are "trying to kill" him (7:19). Aghast, the crowd responds, "You are demon-possessed. . . . Who is trying to kill you?" (7:20). The Fourth Gospel stands unique in that it doesn't contain any exorcisms. This is the first of three accusations that Jesus is demon-possessed (see 8:48–52; 10:20). A chapter earlier, Jesus claims that Judas, the betrayer, is a "devil" (6:70). Here the crowd flips the script and attaches an eerily similar title to Jesus. The point of the irony is that the crowd grossly misjudges Jesus. Jesus deftly responds to the Jewish crowd and aligns them with the Jewish leaders who reject him after the healing of the invalid (7:21–24; cf. 5:1–15). The "Jewish leaders" (*hoi Ioudaioi*) in 5:1–15 and the crowd or "the Jews" (*hoi Ioudaioi*) gathered in Jerusalem in 7:14–24 are consonant in their evaluation of Jesus.

The following section of 7:25–36 turns on the reaction of several parties to Jesus's claim to be the Son of God, the one whom the Father "sent" (7:28–29). "Some of the people of Jerusalem" (lit. "some of the Jerusalemites") wonder if their leaders have changed their appraisal of Jesus and now believe that he is the long-awaited Messiah (7:25). In their eyes, Jesus is teaching in public, and the Jewish authorities have yet to confront him in the temple (7:26). John's description of the Jerusalemites' messianic views in 7:27 is cryptic, and commentators struggle to explicate it. Whatever the precise background, the point is that they are unwilling to believe that Jesus is who he claims to be—the sent one, the divine Son of God (7:28–29). The crowd, presumably composed of Jerusalemites and Galilean pilgrims, attempts to "seize" Jesus but is unable to do so "because his hour had not yet come" (7:30; cf. 2:4; 8:20; 12:23; 13:1; 17:1).

John then introduces the following section with the third temporal marker, "On the last and greatest day of the festival" (7:37a; cf. 7:2, 14), and it appears that all of 7:37–8:59 takes place on this same day. John records Jesus proclaiming, "Let anyone who is thirsty come to me and drink. Whoever believes in me, as Scripture has said, rivers of living water will flow from within them [believers]" (7:37b–38; cf. NRSV). The Greek here is ambiguous, and other translations prefer this reading: "The one who believes in Me, as the Scripture has said, will have streams of living water flow from deep within him [Jesus]" (HCSB; cf. NASB, ESV). It is somewhat unclear whether Jesus or believers are the focus of the last part of 7:38, and both may be in mind. In any case, according to early Jewish tradition, a priest filled a golden pitcher with water from the Pool of Siloam and then traversed to the Water Gate and poured out the water into one of two silver bowls. The other bowl was filled with wine, and then both bowls were poured out at the altar (m. Sukkah 4.9–10). Jesus most likely has this Jewish ritual in mind when he identifies himself (and/or believers) as "living water."

He further states that Scripture anticipates his claim, and though no quotation is provided, a string of OT prophetic texts connect the abundance of water with God's end-time presence among his people (e.g., Isa. 43:19; 58:11; Ezek. 36:25–27; 47:1–12; →4:13–14). One text in particular strikes at the heart of Jesus's message: "On that day [the Feast of Tabernacles] HOLY TO THE LORD will be inscribed on the bells of the horses, and the cooking pots in the LORD's house will be like the sacred bowls in front of the altar. Every pot in Jerusalem and Judah will be holy to the LORD Almighty" (Zech. 14:20–21). The expression "holy to the Lord" means devoted or set apart for God's presence. Zechariah predicts, then, that at the end of history the nations will stream to Jerusalem and enjoy God's unfettered presence in their midst. Jesus offers the Jews gathered at the temple the opportunity to enjoy intimate fellowship with God—the very thing the Jews were celebrating at the festival. A few chapters earlier, Jesus offers a Samaritan woman God's life-giving presence (4:13–14) through faith and not by worshiping on Mount Gerizim. Similarly, Jesus offers these Jews access to God's glory—and not by worshiping on Mount Zion. The narrator takes over in 7:39 and connects the coming Spirit with Jesus as the end-time temple (cf. 3:5–8; 14:15–31).

The Reaction of the Crowd and the Jewish Leaders (7:40–52)

The last section of chapter 7 describes various reactions of the crowd and the religious authorities to Jesus (7:40–52). Chapter 7 as a whole contains a host of reactions to Jesus, and here is an attempt to catalogue many of them:

Believers	Unbelievers	Ambivalent
Disciples (7:3)	Jesus's brothers (7:5)	Nicodemus (7:50)
"Many" of the crowd (7:31)	The crowd (7:30, 32)	Soldiers (7:46)
	Some Jerusalemites (7:25)	
	Chief priests and Pharisees (7:11, 32, 45)	

A consensus regarding Jesus's identity has yet to emerge among the populace—a situation that, we can assume, stems from Jesus breaking the mold of long-held expectations (7:40–43). Is he a prophet? Yes. Is he the Messiah? Yes. But Jesus is more than a prophet and more than the Messiah—he is the divine Son of God, the creator of the cosmos, the true temple, and the atoning sacrifice.

At the end of the chapter, the Jewish leaders come into focus. Earlier in 7:32, the chief priests and the Pharisees ordered soldiers to arrest Jesus; but after listening to Jesus speak, the soldiers disobey their orders because "no one ever spoke the way this man does" (7:46). Nicodemus, an esteemed Pharisee who has secretly sought Jesus at night (3:1–15), interjects and asks his colleagues to give Jesus a fair hearing (see Deut. 1:16–18). Is Nicodemus breaking rank and starting to grasp Jesus's identity? Perhaps.

Jesus as the Great "I AM" (8:12–30)

The majority of contemporary translations omit 7:53–8:11 because of the lack of textual support.[29] Several manuscripts flag this section, revealing that the scribes who copied it doubted its veracity. Even when Erasmus was in the process of compiling manuscripts into a collection that would become the base text of the KJV, he was apprehensive as to whether 7:53–8:11 should be included.[30] This doesn't mean that the account is untrue; indeed, some careful and wise commentators believe it is historical. For well over a thousand years, the church at large benefited from it. That said, we will not discuss 7:53–8:11 since we are primarily concerned with John's narrative in its original setting.

Jesus continues to teach while in the temple during the Feast of Booths. The crowd gathered in the temple moves to the purview, and the remaining portion of chapter 8 is largely directed toward unbelieving Jews and the hostile religious leaders. Great opposition lies ahead. Jesus utters, "*I am the light of the world. Whoever follows me will never walk in darkness, but will have the*

---

29. See the wise discussion in Bruce M. Metzger, *A Textual Commentary on the Greek New Testament*, 2nd ed. (New York: United Bible Societies, 1994), 187–88.

30. Peter J. Williams, *Can We Trust the Gospels?* (Wheaton: Crossway, 2018), 114.

light of life" (8:12). This is the second of seven "I am" statements followed by a predicate nominative:

John 6:35, 41, 51	"I am the bread of life"
John 8:12	"I am the light of the world"
John 10:7, 9	"I am the gate for the sheep"
John 10:11, 14	"I am the good shepherd"
John 11:25	"I am the resurrection and the life"
John 14:6	"I am the way and the truth and the life"
John 15:1, 5	"I am the true vine"

With the possible exception of 15:1 and 5, each statement occurs in the midst of a polemic or some misunderstanding. The number seven often symbolizes completeness in the Bible, and it fits well here. Jesus claims to be the substance, the true reality of *all* OT expectations. In the immediate context of 8:12, Jesus, "the light of the world," may correspond to the lighting ceremony during the Feast of Booths. The festival included a ceremony whereby priests lit candles at the temple, so that "there was not a courtyard in Jerusalem which was not lit up" on account of its brilliance (m. Sukkah 5.3).[31] If Jesus has this Jewish ritual in mind along with a band of texts from the OT that associate light with the new age (see Isa. 9:1; 42:6; 49:6; 60:1), then he claims to be the source of the new creation itself—God incarnate (see Gen. 1:3).

The Pharisees press Jesus, wanting to know how he can make such claims without proper "testimony," since at least two parties are required to bear legal witness (8:13; Deut. 19:15). John's readers are once again confronted with the cosmic lawsuit theme. Jesus argues that he, because of his status as God's Son, possesses the right to bear witness concerning himself. The Father, too, bears witness to his identity as the "light of life" (8:12, 18). The religious authorities then ask, "Where is your father?" (8:19a). They have fundamentally missed Jesus's point: he's not talking about his earthly father, Joseph, but his heavenly Father. The Pharisees once again display an ignorance of Israel's God (8:19b, 27).

Jesus teaches the crowd "once more" at the festival (8:21; cf. 8:12). He predicts that his audience will "die" in their "sin" and consequently be unable to follow him when he ascends into heaven (8:21). A great gulf exists between heaven ("above") and the world ("below"), and unless the crowd believes in Jesus, they will never inherit eternal life (8:23). Confusion continues to set

31. Jacob Neusner, ed., *The Mishnah: A New Translation* (New Haven: Yale University Press, 1988).

in as Jesus predicts, "When *you have lifted up* [*hypsōsēte*] the Son of Man, then you will know that *I am* [*egō eimi*]" (8:28 AT). This is an extremely rich text, and many Johannine themes intersect here. "Lifting up" in the Fourth Gospel refers to Jesus's being lifted up physically on the cross and, ironically, to Jesus being lifted up in an exalted sense (see 3:14; 8:28; 12:32). Jesus also fulfills the role of the suffering servant of Isaiah 52:13–53:12. At the beginning of Isaiah's final servant song, the text of the LXX reads,

> See, my servant shall understand,
>> and *he shall be exalted and glorified exceedingly*
>> [*hypsōthēsetai kai doxasthēsetai sphodra*]. (52:13 NETS)

This song couples glory and exaltation or lifting up. Isaiah's audience must interpret the totality of the servant's suffering and death as ironic and paradoxical. He's exalted in the midst of suffering.[32] Bauckham avers, "Building on this exegetical foundation [of Isa. 52:13], John uses the verb 'to lift up' (*hypsoō* [as in Isaiah]) in riddling references to Jesus' death (3:14; 8:28; 12:32), implying that his physical elevation above the earth on the cross (12:32–33) is at the same time his exaltation to heaven, where he returns to the Father to share his glory. . . . He is viewing the cross as exaltation rather than humiliation—or rather, as exaltation in humiliation."[33]

Furthermore, in 8:28 Jesus also alludes to Isaiah 43:10:

Isaiah 43:10 LXX	John 8:28
"I too am a witness, says the Lord God, and the servant whom I have chosen so that *you may know* [*gnōte*] and believe and understand *that I am* [*synēte hoti egō eimi*]. Before me there was no other god, nor shall there be any after me." (NETS)	"When you have lifted up the Son of Man, then *you will know that I am* [*gnōsesthe hoti egō eimi*]." (AT)

In the immediate context of Isaiah 43:10, Yahweh summons his people to be his "witnesses," and his "servant" will testify to Yahweh's unrivaled identity as the only God in contrast to the nations, who worship their idols in vain (Isa. 43:9, 12; cf. 45:5–6). Yahweh is the great "I AM" who redeems the Israelites out of Egypt in the first exodus (Exod. 3:14), and because he is still the great "I AM," he will do so once more in a second exodus (e.g., Isa. 41:4; 43:10; 45:18–19; 46:9; 47:8; 48:12). According to Isaiah 43:25, just a handful of verses later in the LXX, Yahweh once again states, "*I am, I am* [*egō eimi egō*]

---

32. Richard Bauckham, *Gospel of Glory: Major Themes in Johannine Theology* (Grand Rapids: Baker Academic, 2015), 73.
33. Bauckham, *Gospel of Glory*, 73.

eimi] the one who blots out your acts of lawlessness" (NETS). The formula "I am, I am" is quite rare, occurring only three times in the LXX (Isa. 43:25; 45:19; 51:12). Jesus's allusion to Isaiah 43 is all the more significant then. As Jesus hangs on the cross and "blots out" sins, his identity is fully disclosed as the great "I AM," the divine Son of God. And it is precisely in the cross and resurrection that Jesus will lead his people out of darkness and into the light of a new exodus.

The Seed of the Godly and Ungodly (8:31–59)

The final half of chapter 8 drills down into what it means to be a true child of God (8:31–47), but the Jews react strongly to Jesus's teaching on the matter (8:48–59). John's prologue sets forth an important principle found not only within the Fourth Gospel but in the NT as a whole: one's identity with Jesus, not ethnic descent, is the sole determining factor for salvation. John states it succinctly: "To all who did receive him [Jesus], to those who believed in his name, he gave the right to become children of God—children born not of natural descent . . . but born of God" (1:12–13). Here in 8:31 Jesus claims that his audience, even the ones who have initially "believed" but are not genuine believers (8:30), is enslaved to sin (see 8:24; cf. Rom. 6:18). They must grasp the "truth" in order to be "set . . . free." The Jews disagree: "We are Abraham's descendants and have never been slaves of anyone" (8:33; cf. Luke 3:8).

Jesus responds with some of the most gripping language found in the Gospels. Not only is his audience shackled to sin (8:34–38) and not *true* descendants of Abraham (8:39–41); they are part of the ungodly line that goes all the way back to Genesis 3:15. They are not the godly descendants of Adam and Eve through the line of Seth (Gen. 5:1–3) but descendants of the serpent who wage war against the godly seed. They "belong to . . . [their] father, the devil" (8:44). Sons behave in accordance with their fathers (see 5:19–30), and here the sons of the devil embody his attitude. Sons are in the image of their father. The devil "was a murderer from the beginning" (8:44), and his offspring follow suit in attempting to kill Jesus (8:40). The Jews have difficulty grasping Jesus's identity as the Son of God because they do not "belong to God" (8:47). True understanding is ultimately predicated upon God's gracious election. The reaction of the Jewish crowd at the temple is fierce. They accuse Jesus of being a "Samaritan and demon-possessed" (8:48; cf. 7:20; 10:20). The chapter ends with Jesus claiming that he existed "before Abraham was born" and that he is the great "I am" (8:58; cf. 1:1), two statements that reinforce his identity as Yahweh incarnate. Jesus then furtively flees the scene, "slipping away from the temple grounds" (8:59).

Healing the Blind Man and Further Jewish Conflict (9:1–10:42)

The Fifth Sign (9:1–12)

The combination of a soft transition ("As he [Jesus] went along" [9:1]) at the beginning of the chapter with the lone geographic reference to the Pool of Siloam (9:7, 11), a pool inside Jerusalem that was used for the pouring-out ritual during the Feast of Booths (m. Sukkah 4.9–10), suggests that the setting is still Jerusalem. Since the final day of the Feast of Booths (a fall feast) is mentioned in 8:37 and the Festival of Dedication or Hanukkah (a winter feast) is mentioned in 10:22, this healing likely occurs in the intervening months. The Fourth Gospel juxtaposes the healing of the lame man in chapter 5 with the healing of the blind man in chapter 9. Here are some of the most notable connections:

Healing of Lame Man (5:1–18)	Healing of Blind Man (9:1–41)
History of individual described (5:5)	History of individual described (9:1)
Pool associated with healing (5:6)	Pool associated with healing (9:7)
Jesus heals on the Sabbath (5:9)	Jesus heals on the Sabbath (9:14)
Jews accuse him of violating the Sabbath (5:10)	Pharisees accuse Jesus of violating the Sabbath (9:16)
Man doesn't know where or who Jesus is (5:13)	Man doesn't know where or who Jesus is (9:12)
Man betrays Jesus to the Jews (5:15)	The Jews cast the man out of the synagogue (9:34–35)
Jesus works as his Father is working (5:17)	Jesus must do the works of one who sent him (9:4)

Adapted from Craig S. Keener, *The Gospel of John: A Commentary* (Peabody, MA: Hendrickson, 2003), 1:639.

The central difference between the two is the positive response of the blind man in chapter 9, which stands in stark contrast to the negative response of the lame man in chapter 5. The key common denominator, though, is the rejection of the Jewish leaders.

Jesus asserts that the man's blindness is neither because of his personal sin nor because of the sins of his parents (9:3a) but because God intends to "display" his "works" through him (9:3; cf. 2:11; 5:36). The Father has sovereignly purposed that this man become blind so that Jesus may heal him, thus manifesting his identity as the unique Son of God. In other words, this man is beset with blindness *in order* that God may bring glory to himself.

The Reaction to the Fifth Sign (9:13–34)

The response to the healing of the blind man is exceptionally complex, as it brings to a head many themes that John has discussed thus far. Scholars have allegorized this text to reconstruct the ostensible schism between Jews and Jewish Christians at the end of the first century. A far better approach is to read this passage in light of the whole of the Fourth Gospel and take the account at face value—Jesus of Nazareth really did heal a blind man, an event that deepens the fissure between Jesus and the Jewish leaders during his ministry. This fifth sign further strains the relationship between Jesus's followers and the religious authorities, even before passion week.

This section turns on two interviews by the Pharisees. In the first interview, the man's neighbors bring him to the Pharisees for a formal interrogation (9:13–23). While the narrator doesn't divulge why the neighbors do so, we can probably infer that they want to maintain a good relationship with the religious authorities (cf. 9:22). In any case, the Pharisees once again take umbrage at Jesus performing the miracle on the Sabbath (9:14). Commentators note that Jesus's use of spittle and dirt in healing the blind man (9:6) recalls God forming "man from the dust of the ground" (Gen. 2:7; cf. Mark 7:33; 8:23). Since John has already identified Jesus in 1:1–4 as the agent of creation, the one who created Adam in the first creation, it's reasonable for him to perform another creative act in the new creation. The Pharisees are not unified in their opposition to Jesus, as some of them note the sign's validity (9:16). They then summon the man's parents, who, while testifying to the miracle, are unwilling to attribute it to Jesus (9:20–21). As it turns out, the parents fear being "put out of the synagogue" more than being put out of God's presence (9:22; cf. 12:42; 16:2).

As the second interrogation unfolds, the man born blind is still unwilling to condemn Jesus. He bravely rebukes the Jewish leaders for not believing in the fifth sign, for "if this man [Jesus] were not from God, he could do nothing" (9:33). While the Pharisees claim to be "disciples of Moses" and the man born blind a "disciple" of Jesus, little do they realize that Moses himself anticipates Jesus (9:28; see 5:46–47). Confronted with the reality that this man has been truly healed yet unconvinced that Jesus is who he claims to be, the leaders "threw him out" (9:34). That is, they are excluding him from fellowship with his community. They have audaciously claimed to be the arbiters of who participates in the true people of God and who does not. The problem is that Jesus alone has that authority (see 1:12–13).

The Explanation of Healing (9:35–41)

News of the man's expulsion reaches Jesus, so Jesus finds him and asks, "Do you believe in the Son of Man?" (9:35). Though the man born blind is unsure whom Jesus is speaking about (9:36), Jesus explicitly identifies himself as the Son of Man (9:37). At this point the man confesses, "I believe," and "he worshiped" (*prosekynēsen*) Jesus (9:38). Worship (*proskyneō*) in the Fourth Gospel is not a dominant theme, and the closest text is Jesus's interaction with the Samaritan woman in chapter 4, where Jesus claims that "*true worshipers will worship* [*hoi alēthinoi proskynētai proskynēsousin*] the Father in the Spirit and in truth" (4:23). It may be that John wants us to connect the man born blind here with the Samaritan woman, for in both cases the two outsiders are now participating in God's end-time temple by acknowledging the "truth" of Jesus's identity. Chapter 9 ends with a scathing indictment of the religious authorities. They may "see" physically, but they remain "blind" to the Father's work in his Son (9:39–41).

The Parable of the Good Shepherd (10:1–21)

The following section in 10:1–21 contains what Jesus describes as a "figure of speech" (*tēn paroimian*; 10:6), a term that is close to the common word "parable" (*parabolē*) in the Synoptics (see Sir. 39:3; 47:17; cf. John 16:25, 29). This discourse shares several features with parables, so it's probably appropriate to label it as such. Whatever the precise literary category, we can divide the parable into two halves, 10:1–5 and 10:7–18. The first half introduces key themes within the parable, and the second half develops some of those themes.[34] While the parable may seem disjointed within the flow of the narrative, it resonates with the religious leaders' behavior in the previous context. In 9:13–34, they reject the fifth sign, the healing of the blind man, and "throw him out" of the Jewish community (9:34). Scores of OT texts are likely in mind in the parable, and much of it concerns Jesus, the good shepherd, as a faithful leader over against Israel's faithless leaders (see below). Jesus nourishes his flock, whereas the Jewish leaders plunder theirs.

Sandwiched between the two halves of the parable is the narrator's explanation of why Jesus gives them a parable: "Jesus used this figure of speech, but the Pharisees did not understand what he was telling them" (10:6). Often in the Synoptics, Jesus speaks in parables so that his words may remain veiled to outsiders and the majority of the Jewish leaders (→Mark 4:33). A parable at this juncture in John's narrative seems odd. A handful of verses earlier, Jesus states, albeit indirectly, that the Pharisees are "blind" to his identity (9:41). Blindness and ignorance go hand in hand, so we should not be surprised that the Jewish leaders are having a difficult time grasping the true significance of the parable. Indeed, Jesus gives the parable in order to further harden them (see 12:39–40, quoting Isa. 6:10).

34. Carson, *John*, 384.

There are several characters and dimensions to the parable, but we will only comment on two. (1) Jesus identifies himself as the "gate" of the sheep pen in 10:7. This is the third of seven "I am" statements with a predicate nominative (6:35, 48, 51; 8:12; 10:7, 9; 10:11, 14; 11:25; 14:6; 15:1, 5), and there's great christological significance here. In claiming to be the gate, Jesus asserts that he is the entrance to the covenant community. To state it another way, one cannot become *a* child of God without being identified with *the* Son of God (cf. 1:12–13). (2) According to 10:11, Jesus is also "the good shepherd" who "lays down his life for the sheep." Standing behind much of this language is Ezekiel 34, where God condemns Israel's leaders or "shepherds" for their lack of care. In the immediate context of Ezekiel 34, Israel's leaders, instead of patterning their behavior on God's shepherding, use their position to "take care of" only themselves (Ezek. 34:2) and rule God's flock "harshly and brutally" (Ezek. 34:4; cf. Jer. 23:1; 50:6; Zech. 11:16). In contrast to Israel's failed leadership, God will raise up his own shepherd—a Davidic figure who will faithfully care for the flock of Israel (Ezek. 34:16–24; cf. Ps. 78:70–71; Isa. 11:6–9; Jer. 23:4–5; Mic. 5:4). Jesus inaugurates this promise and deems the current Jewish leaders to be analogous to the unfaithful leaders in Ezekiel's day.

The response to the second portion of the parable is again confusion: "The Jews who heard these words were again divided. Many of them said, 'He is demon-possessed and raving mad'" (10:19–20). Notice the switch in opponents from Pharisees in 9:40 immediately before the parable to "the Jews" (*tois Ioudaiois*) in 10:19. The Pharisees represent the totality of Israel's leadership and embody the attitude of the nation (→3:1 and 6:41–58). Therefore, on the one hand, many Jews deny that Jesus is who he claims to be—the unique Son of God. On the other, some within the nation appear convinced that the fifth sign confirms his identity, for, they ask, "Can a demon open the eyes of the blind?" (10:21; cf. 7:20; 8:48–49, 52). The answer is an emphatic no.

The Feast of Dedication (10:22–42)

The following event takes place some months later, during the "Festival of Dedication" or Hanukkah in the winter (10:22). This annual feast in Jerusalem celebrates the purification and refurbishment of the temple after Antiochus IV Epiphanes defiled it in 167 BC (1 Macc. 4:36–59). As Jesus teaches in the temple, "walking in Solomon's Colonnade," the "Jews" (*hoi Ioudaioi*) urge Jesus to reveal his true identity in plain terms (10:24). No more parables, veiled communication, or concealed signs. But Jesus affirms that he already has revealed his identity: "The works I do in my Father's name testify about me" (10:25). At the very least, Jesus has in mind the third sign, the healing of

353

the lame man (5:1–15), which discloses Jesus's identity as the unique Son of God. The Jews are unable to grasp the true significance of Jesus's "works" or signs because of God's decree: "You do not believe because you are not my sheep. My sheep listen to my voice; I know them, and they follow me" (10:26–27). Jesus is tapping into a theme of the recent parable and the Fourth Gospel at large—the Father elects and preserves his flock, those who fully comprehend Jesus's identity (10:4; cf. 6:37–39, 65). Jesus then proceeds to identify himself with the Father when he states, "I and the Father are one" (10:30). Signs demonstrate the unique relationship between the Father and the Son (see 5:16–30).

Arming themselves with stones, the Jews prepare to kill Jesus right then and there on account of his claim to be "one" with the Father (cf. 5:18; 8:59). In their eyes, Jesus commits blasphemy because he is a "mere man" who declares himself "to be God" (10:33). Jesus follows up their accusation with a notoriously complex quotation from Psalm 82:6: "Is it not written in your Law, '*I [Yahweh] have said you are "gods"*'? If he called them '*gods*,' to whom the word of God came—and Scripture cannot be set aside—what about the one whom the Father set apart as his very own and sent into the world? Why then do you accuse me of blasphemy because I said, 'I am God's Son'?" (10:34–36). Identifying the "gods" (*'elohim/theoi*) of Psalm 82 is no easy task, and commentators generally list three options: (1) Israel as a nation; (2) Israel's unrighteous rulers; or (3) rebellious angelic rulers. While a good case can be made for all three, the third option is preferred since there is a tight connection between angelic rulers governing the nations in the OT and in the Gospels (cf. LXX: Deut. 32:8; Dan. 10:12–13; →Luke 10:1–24). However we identify the "gods" in Psalm 82, Jesus's point is that if the OT itself makes room for Yahweh calling someone besides himself "god," *how much more* should we allow Jesus to call himself "God"? The abiding authority of the OT is used here along with an a fortiori (lesser to greater) argument.[35]

Once more the Jews attempt to "seize" Jesus, but he miraculously escapes (10:39). The "hour" or time for his betrayal, death, and resurrection has not arrived. On four occasions Jesus slips away from arrest:

> At this they tried to seize him, but no one laid a hand on him, because his hour had not yet come. (7:30)

> Yet no one seized him, because his hour had not yet come. (8:20)

35. See discussion in Köstenberger, "John," 465–67.

At this, they picked up stones to stone him, but Jesus hid himself, slipping away from the temple grounds. (8:59)

Again they tried to seize him, but he escaped their grasp. (10:39)

According to 7:30 and 8:20, the Jews were unable to arrest him "because his hour had not yet come" (cf. Luke 4:29–30). Such language speaks to the triune God's sovereign plan of redemption. John keeps his audience attuned to the comfort of knowing that nothing can thwart any divinely purposed thought, decision, event, or interaction. Jesus will be betrayed, killed, and cursed at God's chosen moment—not a nanosecond sooner or later.

The chapter ends with Jesus retreating "across the Jordan," where "John had been baptizing in the early days" (10:40). We mentioned in 1:28 that the region "across the Jordan" likely refers to Batanea, a location northeast of the Sea of Galilee. If this is correct, then we can conclude that Jesus's departure from Jerusalem at the end of the Feast of Dedication is symbolic: his public ministry, bracketed by John's baptism and testimony to Jesus, is drawing to a close. He is leaving Jerusalem not simply because the feast has ended but because he has been rejected by Jerusalem itself. In contrast, notice the positive response of the Galileans at the end of the chapter, the main point of chapter 10: "In that place [Batanea] many believed in Jesus" (10:42). The Jews in Jerusalem seek to kill Jesus, whereas the Galileans trust in him. The next time Jesus arrives in Jerusalem, he will not slip away. At that "hour," he will submit himself to the crowds, to the soldiers, to Pilate, and to the devil. But in giving himself up, he will vanquish sin and death and be raised to new life.

The Raising of Lazarus as the Sixth Sign (11:1–57)

The Death of Lazarus (11:1–16)

Now that Jesus has returned to Galilee, the narrator shifts the audience's attention south to Bethany (11:1). This town lies to the east of Jerusalem, on the eastern side of the Mount of Olives. Bethany functions as Jesus's hub of operations during passion week (Matt. 21:17 // Mark 11:11) and is the home of Simon the Leper (Matt. 26:6 // Mark 14:3) and the home of the three siblings—Mary, Martha, and Lazarus (cf. Luke 10:39–42). After mentioning the setting, John isolates one of the three siblings before launching into the event: "This Mary, whose brother Lazarus now lay sick, was the same one who poured perfume on the Lord and wiped his feet with her hair" (11:2). While John describes Mary anointing Jesus in the next chapter (12:1–11), it seems as though his audience is already familiar with this Mary. She, while unnamed, anoints Jesus in Matthew 26:6–13 // Mark 14:3–9 during passion week, but in Luke 10:38–39 she is named with her sister Martha (Lazarus is absent). There, Jesus visits the home of Mary and Martha in a "village" (i.e., Bethany) earlier in his ministry. John's audience, then, may know her personally or through reading the accounts of the other evangelists. Further, Mary and Martha appear to be good friends with Jesus, because they send word to him in 11:3: "The one you love is sick." John's narrative coheres well with the Third Gospel.

Jesus, after receiving word that Lazarus is ill, predicts, "This sickness will not end in death. No, it is for God's glory so that God's Son may be glorified through it" (11:4). Once more the formula of "signs" in the Fourth Gospel is repeated: signs manifest Jesus's identity as the glorious, divine Son of God that results in giving the Father glory, eliciting belief or further unbelief (2:11; 9:3; 10:38; 11:15, 40; 17:24). Jesus responds to Lazarus's sickness on two levels: (1) He's truly grieved over Lazarus's condition because Lazarus, a dear friend, is ravaged by the effects of Adam and Eve's fall. Jesus, a perfect human, responds with incredible emotion and tenderness. (2) Jesus will overcome one of the fall's greatest enemies—death itself. And in doing so, he will perform the sixth sign and bring glory to his Father. In raising Lazarus from the dead, Jesus lays the groundwork for the seventh and final sign—his own death and resurrection. If Jesus displays his glory and in turn gives glory to his Father in the sixth sign, how much more will he do so in the seventh sign?

The Raising of Lazarus (11:17–44)

Jesus and his disciples approach Bethany, but before they arrive, Martha runs out to greet Jesus. She says, "If you had been here, my brother would not have died. But I know that even now God will give you whatever you ask" (11:22). She's probably not expecting Jesus to raise her brother from the dead, but she firmly believes that Jesus could have miraculously prevented it. Jesus then predicts that Lazarus will "rise again" (11:23). Martha, like most Jews in the first century, believes in the general resurrection at the end of history (e.g., Dan. 12:1–2), so she expects to be reunited with him in the new eternal cosmos. But Jesus responds with a startling declaration: "I am the resurrection and the life. The one who believes in me will live, even though they die; and whoever lives by believing in me will never die. Do you believe this?" (11:25–26).

This is the fifth "I am" statement with the predicate nominative and arguably the most riveting (see 6:35, 48, 51; 8:12; 10:7, 9; 10:11, 14; 11:25; 14:6; 15:1, 5).

Jesus's claim to be "the resurrection and the life" is predicated upon his divinity as the creator (1:1–4) and his mission to make all things new. Jesus is not simply saying that he has the power to raise Lazarus from the dead, which, of course, he possesses as the divine Son of God, but he is also claiming to be the source and agent of the *new creation*. Martha's response is profound and exemplary: "Yes, Lord, . . . I believe that you are the Messiah, the Son of God, who is to come into the world" (11:27). This is precisely why John has written his Gospel—to convince Jews that Jesus is the Son of God and to affirm the faith of Christians with the assurance that Jesus is precisely who he claims to be (20:30–31). John's audience must follow suit and respond in belief to the seven signs of the Fourth Gospel. Martha then returns home and informs Mary of Jesus's arrival (11:28–30). Mary, like her sister, believes that Jesus could have prevented Lazarus's death (11:32).

The details of Jesus raising Lazarus from the dead echo Jesus's own resurrection. Here are some of the more prominent ones:

Resurrection of Lazarus	Resurrection of Jesus
Presence of a "tomb" (11:38)	Presence of a "tomb" (20:1)
Removal of "stone" (11:39, 41)	Removal of "stone" (20:1)
Dead for "four days" (11:39)	Dead for "three days" (19:31; 20:1)
Body wrapped with "strips of linen" (11:44)	Body wrapped with "strips of linen" (19:40; 20:5)
"Cloth [wrapped] around his face (11:44)	"Cloth . . . had been wrapped around Jesus' head" (20:7)
Raising elicits belief (11:42, 45)	Resurrection elicits belief (20:19–23, 29)

In reading the account of Jesus raising Lazarus from the dead, John's audience would have certainly recalled Jesus's earlier promise that the "time . . . has now come when the dead will hear *the voice* [*tēs phōnēs*] of the Son of God and those who hear will live. . . . All who are in their graves will . . . *come out* [*ekporeusontai*]" (5:25–29). Not coincidentally, Jesus shouts in a "loud voice" (*phōnē megalē*) for Lazarus to "come out" (*deuro exō*; 11:43). In a word, the sixth sign is an incredibly significant eschatological event in Jesus's ministry, as it presages his own death and resurrection. Of the first six signs—turning water into wine, healing the official's son, healing the lame man, feeding the five thousand, healing the blind man, and raising Lazarus from the dead—this sign is certainly the greatest.

We should, however, distinguish between the raising of Lazarus and the resurrection of Jesus. While Jesus receives his glorified body, a body fit for the new heavens and earth, Lazarus isn't transformed into a glorious existence.

He will die again. Only at the resurrection at the very end of history will Lazarus receive his new creational body (1 Cor. 15:35–57; 1 Thess. 4:13–18).

The Decision to Kill Jesus (11:45–57)

As we come to the last section in chapter 11, we witness two responses of the Jews gathered at the tomb. Not a whisper is said about Mary and Martha's reaction and the response of the disciples. We can assume that their faith in Jesus only deepened. John mentions the belief of "many of the Jews" (11:45) but focuses on the unbelief of a few who subsequently informed the Pharisees of "what Jesus had done" (11:46). The greatest sign thus far in the narrative sets the stage for the greatest antagonism.

The Jewish leaders meet together as the Sanhedrin, the ruling body of Israel (11:47). They recognize that Jesus's signs are generating significant belief from the populace, and if he continues, "everyone will believe in him, and then the Romans will come and take away both our temple and our nation" (11:48). This is not the first time the religious authorities have attempted to exterminate Jesus. The Jewish leaders, and especially the Pharisees, seek to kill him on a handful of occasions on account of blasphemy (5:18; 7:1, 19, 25, 30; 8:37, 40). But here the Sanhedrin formally meets to plot his demise. The issue at hand in 11:48 appears to be political insurrection. If Jesus garners enough followers, then Rome will act swiftly and take direct control of Jerusalem, and as a result, the religious authorities will lose their jobs. Self-preservation is at stake here.

Caiaphas, the high priest at the time, famously states to the Sanhedrin, "You do not realize that it is better for you that one man die for the people than that the whole nation perish" (11:50; cf. 18:14). John's readers would have quickly noted the irony: Caiaphas has unwittingly identified the heart of Jesus's ministry! The Father has sent Jesus into the world to die, granting life to all those who believe. The narrator then unpacks Caiaphas's comment and claims that the high priest is unaware that he is prophesying about Jesus's death on behalf of not only the Jewish people but also the nations (cf. 1 John 2:2). Caiaphas's words are persuasive, so the council formally conspires "from that day on" to kill Jesus (cf. 12:10; Matt. 26:4; Acts 9:23). With the Jewish leaders now on the prowl, Jesus "no longer moved about publicly among the people of Judea" but "withdrew to . . . a village called Ephraim, where he stayed with his disciples" (11:54). While commentators are unsure about the precise locale of this "Ephraim," the point is that Jesus must retreat in order to avoid conflict. His "hour" will arrive soon enough.

Jesus Anointed as King and the Triumphal Entry (12:1–50)

Mary Anoints Jesus as King (12:1–11)

At the end of chapter 11, the religious authorities order the Jews to divulge Jesus's whereabouts during Passover should he be discovered (11:57). Chapter 12 opens with Mary, Martha, and Lazarus serving a meal "in Jesus' honor," probably in the home of Simon the Leper (12:1–2; cf. Matt. 26:6 // Mark 14:3). The anointing in 12:1–8 is also recorded in Matthew 26:6–13 and Mark 14:3–9 (not in Luke 7:37–39, as some suppose). John notes that this event took place "six days before the Passover" (12:1), a reference to Saturday evening, communicating that "the countdown to Passover and to Jesus' crucifixion has begun."[36] Recall that John carefully tracks the first week of Jesus's ministry (1:19–2:11), and he will now track his final, climatic week (12:1–20:25).

We discuss this event in our comments on Matthew 26:6–13 and Mark 14:3–9, so we need only to reaffirm what we say there. In anointing Jesus's head (Matt. 26:7 // Mark 14:3) and feet with expensive perfume, Mary acknowledges that Jesus is the long-awaited King of Israel (cf. 1 Sam. 10:1; 2 Kings 9:3). But John's narrative uniquely adds that Mary anoints Jesus's feet and wipes them with her hair (12:3). Washing feet is associated with servants, so Mary views herself to be in a position of service to her King (→13:4–17). Further, it was common to anoint a dead body (2 Chron. 16:14; Mark 16:1; Luke 23:56; 24:1; John 19:39–40), so Mary's behavior contains yet another layer of significance—she anoints a *suffering* King. Reinforcing the symbolism, Mary's anointing leaves Simon's house "filled with the fragrance of the perfume" (12:3). The word "fragrance" (*osmē*) may recall the various sacrifices of the temple cult (e.g., Exod. 29:18, 25, 41), and "perfume" (*myron*) is associated with the construction of Israel's tabernacle (Exod. 30:25). Both details may indicate that Jesus is the true Passover sacrifice and the cornerstone of the true temple.

After the anointing takes place, Judas, who is first introduced in 6:71 as the betrayer, objects to such a lavish use of perfume: "Why wasn't this perfume sold and the money given to the poor?" (12:5). The narrator then unmasks Judas's true intent: he was a "thief" at heart. A thief, in contrast to a servant (i.e., Mary), is marked by a wholly selfish way of life (see 10:1, 8, 10). A thief brings only destruction and ruin. Jesus then rebukes Judas for attempting to undermine Mary (12:7–8). The account ends with many Jews coming to Simon's house because "Jesus was there" and because they want to see Lazarus

---

36. Eckhard J. Schnabel, *Jesus in Jerusalem: The Last Days* (Grand Rapids: Eerdmans, 2018), 153.

(12:9). The sixth sign continues to reap a great harvest of belief (see 12:17–18). But the religious leaders will have none of it, so they now conspire to put Lazarus to death as well. In their eyes, he, too, is a threat to political stability.

The Triumphal Entry and the Passion Prediction (12:12–36)

The triumphal entry, while present in all four Gospels (Matt. 21:1–9 // Mark 11:1–10 // Luke 19:28–40 // John 12:12–19), is a somewhat bare-bones account in John's Gospel. John does include the timing of the event ("the next day," or on Sunday) and the two prominent OT quotations—Psalm 118:25 and Zechariah 9:9 (and possibly Zeph. 3:14–16)—but omits the preparation for the colt (cf. Mark 11:1–3 and par.), so the connection to Genesis 49:10–11 may not be as strong here. Nevertheless, John, like the other three evangelists, presents Jesus as the long-awaited Messiah, who has come to Jerusalem one final time. He will be crowned as king and fulfill many OT promises, but not the way his followers expect—he will don a crown of thorns and be lifted up on a cross, where, in the midst of suffering, he will rule over all creation (→Mark 11:1–10).

The Fourth Gospel uniquely includes the narrator's comments on this event: "At first his disciples did not understand all this. Only after Jesus was glorified did they realize that these things had been written about him and that these things had been done to him" (12:16). Two thoughts: (1) The disciples do not fully grasp the significance of the triumphal entry as it unfolds in real time. There is a sense in which *this event and other critical aspects of Jesus's ministry remain hidden from them until the cross and resurrection*. The cross and resurrection shed light on Jesus's previous acts. In other words, latter revelation of the cross/resurrection explains the earlier revelation of Jesus's ministry. The seventh sign explains in greater detail the first six signs. The hidden-but-later-revealed nature of these two events brackets his ministry.

John 2:22	John 12:16
"After he was raised from the dead, his disciples [*hoi mathētai autou*] recalled [*emnēsthēsan*] what he had said. Then they believed *the scripture* [*tē graphē*] and the words that Jesus had spoken."	"At first *his disciples* [*autou hoi mathētai*] did not understand all this. Only after Jesus was glorified *did they realize* [*emnēsthēsan*] that *these things had been written about him* [*tauta ēn ep' autō gegrammena*] and that these things had been done to him."

This doesn't mean that the disciples are completely ignorant of certain events and sayings of Jesus. John 2:22 states that they "believed"! The disciples understand partially but lack *full* comprehension. (2) When John connects Jesus's acts to the OT in 2:22 and 12:16, we can assume that these OT passages are fulfilled in unique and unexpected ways, and this is why the disciples do not fully grasp these events immediately. Therefore, certain aspects of Jesus's identity, acts, and mission *mysteriously* fulfill OT expectations (→Matt. 13:1–52, Mark 4:1–33, and Luke 24:13–35).

The next section includes Jesus's passion prediction, announcing that the "Son of Man" will be "glorified" in the "hour" of his death (12:23, 28; cf. Dan. 7:13–14; 12:1). The long-awaited "hour" in the Fourth Gospel has now arrived (see 2:4; 7:30; 8:20). As Jesus talks to his disciples, presumably in Jerusalem, he cries out to his Father, "Father, glorify your name!" (12:28), and then the Father immediately responds, "I have glorified it, and will glorify it again." The Son has "glorified" the Father's "name" in performing six signs, and he will do so again in a greater way in his death and resurrection, the seventh and final sign.

Isaiah Saw the Glory of Jesus and the Stubbornness of Unbelieving Jews (12:37–50)

As the Book of Signs comes to a close, the remainder of chapter 12 is incredibly important to the Fourth Gospel and the other three Gospels at large. The narrator quotes two prominent passages from Isaiah. The first, Isaiah 53:1, is drawn from the fourth servant song of Isaiah, in 52:13–53:12 (cf. Isa. 42:1–9; 49:1–6; 50:4–9), and the second is from Isaiah's commissioning in Isaiah 6:1–13. We've noticed the prominence of Isaiah 6 in Matthew, Mark, and Luke. All four evangelists quote Isaiah 6 as judgment upon those who reject Jesus's message (see Matt. 13:11–15 // Mark 4:10–12 // Luke 8:10 // John 12:38–40; Acts 28:25–28). Matthew, Mark, Luke, and John broadly apply Isaiah 6 to unbelievers within Israel, and Luke even targets the Jewish leaders at the end of Acts. The Synoptics quote Isaiah 6 during Jesus's Galilean ministry, whereas John waits until passion week and Luke nestles the quotation in Paul's Roman imprisonment.

According to Isaiah 6, Israel is corrupt to its very core. In Isaiah 6:9–10, Israel is blind and deaf, reflecting their idolatrous practices. Israel has become blind and deaf like the idols they worship (cf. Deut. 29:3–4; Pss. 115:4–8; 135:15–18; Jer. 5:21; Ezek. 12:2). The nation of Israel in the first century, as represented by the Jewish leaders, has rejected Jesus's message because they have committed idolatry by worshiping Torah and oral tradition (5:39). Jesus stands in continuity with Isaiah by reiterating the prophet's words. Isaiah's prophetic act continues into the first century. Further, when Israel rejects Jesus's signs, Isaiah's prophecy is fulfilled (12:38). While the Father is the one who sovereignly gives individuals the ability to comprehend the signs or draw people to himself (6:44), the Jews are still held responsible for believing in Jesus.[37]

At the end of the Isaiah quotations, the narrator comments, "Isaiah said this because he saw Jesus' glory and spoke about him" (12:41). Incredibly, John claims that the prophet Isaiah witnessed Jesus in his vision of Yahweh in Isaiah 6. Isaiah 6:1 reads, "I saw the Lord, *high and exalted* [*ram wenissa'*], seated on a throne." The exact language is then applied to the suffering servant in 52:13, who will also be "*raised and lifted up* [*yarum wenissa'*] and *highly exalted* [LXX: *doxasthēsetai sphodra*]." Within the book of Isaiah, the servant's atoning work corresponds to Yahweh's sovereign status as cosmic King. This insight fits remarkably well with the immediate context and the Fourth Gospel as a whole (→8:28). A few verses earlier, the Father promises to "glorify" (*doxasō*) his Son and fulfill Isaiah's prophecy. But John merges both figures in the person of Jesus. Jesus is simultaneously the exalted Lord of Isaiah 6 *and* Isaiah's suffering servant. Daniel Brendsel puts his finger on the significance of the two Isaiah quotations: "For John, Isaiah 'saw' one possessing true 'glory' (John 12:41). Isaiah saw a Servant whose humiliation is his glory, whose suffering reveals the identity of Yahweh, and whose death becomes the means whereby Israel and the nations might experience the eschatological second exodus for their good."[38] This is not a far cry from the prologue, where John affirms Jesus as the creator of the cosmos (1:1–3) and the atoning "Lamb of God" (1:29, quoting Isa. 53:7).

The Book of Glory (13:1–20:31)

Isaiah's Suffering Servant Forms Little Suffering Servants (13:1–38)

With the conclusion of the Book of Signs (1:19–12:50), chapter 13 transitions into the Book of Glory (13:1–20:31), and 13:1–30 introduces a smaller literary unit called the Farewell Discourse (13:31–16:33).

Washing the Disciples' Feet (13:1–17)

John sets the stage for Jesus's final words with his disciples (13:1–3) and mentions that the "meal was in progress" (13:2). The Synoptics affirm that

37. Carson, *John*, 448–49.
38. Daniel J. Brendsel, *"Isaiah Saw His Glory": The Use of Isaiah 52–53 in John 12*, BZNW 208 (Berlin: de Gruyter, 2014), 213.

Jesus and the disciples (probably accompanied by other followers) celebrate the Passover at sunset Thursday night (Nisan 14) in the upper room in Jerusalem (Matt. 26:17–18 // Mark 14:12 // Luke 22:7). But according to John 18:28 and 19:14, the Jews celebrate Passover on Friday night (Nisan 15) at sunset *after* Jesus's death. While several good options exist that reconcile the differences without seeing a contradiction, two stand out: (1) Galileans, on account of traveling to Jerusalem and in an attempt to avoid the crowds, offered up their Passover sacrifices and celebrated the meal a day early; and (2) in AD 30 a disagreement broke out between the Sadducees and the Pharisees regarding the precise date of the new moon and, therefore, when the Passover should be celebrated. Pharisees celebrated the Passover evening on Nisan 14 (Thursday night), and Sadducees celebrated it on Nisan 15 (Friday night).[39]

John mentions that "the Devil had already put it into the heart of Judas, Simon Iscariot's son, to betray Him [Jesus]" (13:2 HCSB). Such eschatological conflict has been building throughout the narrative (e.g., 3:1; 5:16; 8:59; 10:39; 11:53), and here, at the beginning of the Book of Glory, the conflict will come to a head. Satan will use Judas to accomplish his nefarious plan, and though we may be tempted to let Judas off the hook, he remains culpable for his actions (18:2–5; cf. Luke 22:3, 22; Acts 1:16–20). The devil, too, only operates under the sovereign hand of God yet still remains responsible for his actions. Before the horrific events of the passion unfold, Jesus remains confident of two guiding principles outlined in 13:3: (1) "the Father had put all things under his power" (cf. 3:35; 5:20; 17:2; Matt. 11:27; 28:18), and (2) "he had come from God and was returning to God." The sovereignty of the Godhead reminds Jesus that the plan of redemption will unfold precisely the way it was planned in eternity past and that he will ascend to the throne.

Jesus then proceeds to wash the disciples' feet in one of the most memorable passages in all of John's Gospel (13:4–5). John is the only evangelist to record this event, and since it occurs just prior to the Farewell Discourse, it must be important. While all three Synoptics record the Last Supper (Matt. 26:17–30 // Mark 14:12–26 // Luke 22:7–23), it is absent in John. This is all the more striking given John's portrayal of the feeding of the five thousand (6:1–15) and the Bread of Life Discourse (6:25–58) as anticipations of the Last Supper.

Washing feet, a menial task, is commonly reserved for servants. But Jesus's servitude is not generic—he is not any servant but *the* long-awaited Servant. By washing the feet of the disciples, Jesus consciously aligns himself with Isaiah's suffering servant. The prophet Isaiah predicts that God's "righteous servant," as a result of his atoning sacrifice, "will justify many" (Isa. 53:11). Further,

---

39. These two options are found in Schnabel, *Jesus in Jerusalem*, 145–47.

the word "servant" (Heb. *'ebed*; Gk. *pais/doulos*) occurs nearly twenty times in Isaiah 40–66 and refers to the idolatrous nation of Israel, who repeatedly disobeys God and fails to bring salvation to the nations. But within this section of Isaiah 40–66, a righteous servant comes on the scene who obeys God, suffers on behalf of the covenant community, stimulates belief within the nations, and brings Israel out of exile (Isa. 42:1–9; 49:1–13; 50:4–11; 52:13–53:12). Following the servant's faithful obedience, Isaiah 55–66 switches to the plural "servants" (Heb. *'abadim*; Gk. *douloi*) to describe a righteous group of Israelites and gentiles that fully identify with the one faithful servant (Isa. 56:6; 63:17; 65:8–9, 13–15; 66:14).[40] When Jesus washes the disciples' feet and then commands the disciples to "wash one another's feet" (13:14), he's creating a community of little suffering servant figures (cf. Acts 13:47; Col. 1:24). What is true of Jesus will be true of the disciples. Just as he suffers, they too will suffer. Just as he is lifted up, they too will be lifted up.

Washing the disciples' feet (13:4–5) also touches on John's larger theme of purification, a theme that runs from the beginning of the narrative all the way to the end. Water signifies cleansing, new creation, and the presence of the end-time Spirit (1:33; 2:6; 3:5; 4:14, 23; 7:38; 9:7; 19:34). If we combine our insights from Isaiah with John's emphasis on water, then we can summarize this incredibly important event as follows: Jesus, as Isaiah's Suffering Servant, creates and purifies a group of faithful servants who constitute true and faithful Israel. And since they are cleansed, they are now prepared for the Spirit's descent so that they may be the end-time temple of God.

The Betrayer (13:18–30)

In contrast to Jesus, who serves and purifies his followers, Judas, the betrayer, has selfishly "turned against" Jesus in typological fulfillment of Psalm 41:9 (13:18). King David pens Psalm 41 to lament the enemies who are arrayed against him (Ps. 41:5–8). But there's an enemy *within* the ranks, as David explains: "Even my close friend, someone I trusted, one who shared my bread, has turned against me" (Ps. 41:9; cf. Job 19:13–14, 19; Ps. 55:12–13). Just as David is betrayed by those closest to him (even his own son, Absalom), so also Jesus is betrayed in a greater way by Judas. Jesus is not only Isaiah's Suffering Servant but also the suffering Son of David.

John then discloses an exchange between Peter and "the disciple whom Jesus loved" (13:23), who probably should be identified with John, the son of Zebedee and the author of the Fourth Gospel (cf. 19:26; 20:2; 21:7, 20). The

---

40. Brendsel, *"Isaiah Saw His Glory,"* 56–60.

disciples are perplexed at the possibility of betrayal, especially at the hands of one of their own (// Matt. 26:20–25 // Mark 14:17–21 // Luke 22:21–22). After Jesus's death and resurrection, the apostles likely reread portions of the OT, specifically the Psalms, and discerned a prophetic anticipation of what transpired in their midst Thursday evening.

Earlier, the devil merely "prompted" Judas to betray Jesus (13:2), but now the devil has "entered into him" (13:27). While the Fourth Gospel lacks exorcisms, it still highlights the spiritual dimension, particularly warfare between Jesus and the devil. Satan enters Judas to betray Jesus in order to affix him to the cross. Satan believes that if he can put Jesus to death, then he will gain the upper hand and rule over him. The Synoptics narrate Jesus's wilderness temptation (Matt. 4:1–11 // Mark 1:12–13 // Luke 4:1–13), whereas the Fourth Gospel lacks this event. In the Synoptics, Jesus progressively drives out Satan's kingdom, and the cross is the culmination of spiritual conflict between Jesus and Satan. John, though, focuses the cosmic and eschatological conflict between Jesus and the devil *at the cross* (cf. 1 Cor. 2:8; Eph. 1:21; Col. 2:15; 1 Pet. 3:22). The passage ends on an ominous note: "As soon as Judas had taken the bread, he went out. *And it was night*" (13:30). "Night" and "darkness" symbolize the fallen, ignorant, and hostile old age in the Fourth Gospel (1:5; 3:2, 19; 6:17; 8:12; 9:4; 11:10; 12:35, 46; 19:39). Judas embodies this dark, old age. He, like the old age, remains hostile to Jesus—the true light.

The Prologue to the Farewell Discourse (13:31–38)

The Farewell Discourse (13:31–16:33) includes six critical statements of Jesus. Edward Klink outlines the Farewell Discourse in the following manner:[41]

Prologue (13:31–38)

Statement 1: "I Am the Way and the Truth and the Life" (14:1–14)

Statement 2: "I Will Give You the Paraclete" (14:15–31)

Statement 3: "I Am the True Vine" (15:1–17)

Statement 4: "I Have Also Experienced the Hate of the World" (15:18–27)

Statement 5: "I Will Empower You by the Paraclete" (16:1–15)

Statement 6: "I Will Turn Your Grief into Joy" (16:16–24)

Epilogue (16:25–33)

Scholars note similarities between the Farewell Discourse and the "testament" genre that is found in a few places in the OT and is subsequently

41. Klink, *John*, 574.

developed in Judaism. This type of literature narrates prominent figures, such as Joseph, Joshua, and David, gathering their sons or followers together before their imminent death and giving them a final word of comfort and exhortation (e.g., Gen. 49; Deut. 33; Josh. 24; 1 Chron. 28–29; T. 12 Patr.; T. Adam; T. Mos.).

Fortunately at the end of chapter 16, Jesus reveals the purpose of the entire discourse: "I have told you these things, so that in me you may have peace. In this world you will have trouble. But take heart! I have overcome the world" (16:33). He promises the disciples that they will enjoy "peace" through their union with him and that although they will encounter great end-time affliction and tribulation, they can "overcome the world" on account of their identification with him, the great Overcomer. As we progress through the Farewell Discourse, we must never lose sight of its ultimate purpose. Every verse, every paragraph in some way encourages the disciples to withstand the end-time trials that will befall them in the coming days.

In the prologue, the major themes of the Farewell Discourse are outlined: (1) The Son and the Father are glorified in the cross and resurrection (13:31–32). According to 13:31, "The Son of Man *is glorified* [*edoxasthē*] and God *is glorified* [*edoxasthē*] in him." This is the last occurrence of Jesus as the "Son of Man" and the second occurrence of him explicitly receiving glory or being "glorified" in the Fourth Gospel (cf. 12:23). Daniel 7:13–14 associates the "son of man" with "glory," and the other evangelists allude to Daniel 7:13–14 when they pair "Son of Man" with "glory" (see Matt. 16:27; 19:28; 24:30; 25:31; Mark 8:38; 13:26; Luke 9:26; 21:27). The point, then, is that the cross and resurrection are an eschatological event that establishes the eternal kingdom and begins to overthrow all forms of hostility, particularly sin and the devil.

(2) The disciples must love one another (13:34–35). Jesus addresses his disciples as "children," issuing them a "new command" that they might "love one another" (13:33–34; cf. 1 John 2:1, 12, 28; 3:18; 4:4; 5:21). The OT certainly admonishes God's people to love one another (e.g., Lev. 19:18), and a great deal of the Mosaic covenant is bound up with that admonition. But God's people in the new age are now commanded to love more deeply with the Spirit's power (e.g., Matt. 5–7; 1 John 4:7–8; 1 Pet. 1:22–23).

(3) The Son will depart to heaven (13:36). After the crucifixion and resurrection, Jesus will arrive in heaven, where he will return to the Father and a chorus of angels and begin to construct the new heavens and earth (→14:1–4). The idea isn't that the disciples will be restricted from accessing the new creational temple, but that their time hasn't come (see 7:34; 8:21; 13:36). They have work to do!

(4) Peter will betray Jesus (13:37–38). Peter is shocked that he will not immediately follow Jesus, for he promises to "lay down" his "life" for Jesus (13:37).

Jesus sees through Peter's hollow promise, predicting that Peter will instead betray him "three times" (cf. 18:15–18, 25–27). Jesus, though, will "lay down" his own "life" for Peter and restore him (10:11, 15, 17–18; 15:13).

The Disciples of Jesus Participate in the Father's Commission (14:1-31)

Preparing the New Creational Temple (14:1-4)

Jesus commands the disciples to not lose heart when he returns to the Father as the vindicated Son of Man (14:1) *because* he is "going there [his Father's house] to prepare a place for" them (14:2; cf. 2:16–17). While most consider Jesus's words to be a general reference to heaven, Steven Bryan perceptively connects this language with other passages that prophesy the in-gathering of God's people into the eschatological temple (Exod. 15:17; Isa. 2:2; 2 Macc. 2:17–18; 1 En. 39:4; 71:16). One passage from the Dead Sea Scrolls mentions how the tribes of Israel will inherit "chambers" and "rooms" in the end-time temple (11Q19 44.1–16). Bryan then concludes, "Jesus' words . . . are not so much concerned with the removal of his followers from earth to heaven as they are about the dissolution of the divide between heaven and earth. . . . Jesus displaces the earthly dwelling place of God and also goes to the Father to prepare the heavenly dwelling of God to be the dwelling place of his people."[42]

These observations resonate well with John's presentation of Jesus in his narrative. Jesus is the ladder or portal between two realms (1:51), with his resurrection spearheading and founding the new cosmos. After his death and resurrection, he emerges into the heavenly realm to continue constructing the new cosmic temple. This new cosmic temple begins at the incarnation (1:14) and extends to his followers as Jesus's earthly ministry unfolds. This explains why the Fourth Gospel continues to highlight the new creation, water, the presence of the Spirit, and Jesus's departure. Jesus isn't simply departing because his work in creating the new temple is finished. Herein lies a unique dimension of John's Gospel: the Synoptics emphasize Jesus's ascension to the right hand of the Father as the Son of Man to rule over creation, whereas John underscores Jesus's continual role in creating the cosmic sanctuary. He promises to "come back" and "take" his disciples, so that they "may be where" he is (14:3). When Jesus returns at the very end of history, his preparations will be complete and the new eternal cosmos will be ready for his followers. Not coincidentally, John's final message to the church in Revelation 21:1–22:5

---

42. Steven M. Bryan, "The Eschatological Temple in John 14," *BBR* 15 (2005): 198.

assures believers that heaven and earth will finally be joined together and all God's people will enjoy his presence for all eternity.

Jesus as the Way, Truth, and Life (14:5–14)

The structure of the next two sections (14:5–14 and 14:15–31) flows from the three questions of Thomas (14:5), Philip (14:8), and Judas (14:22). The disciples are still struggling with aspects of Jesus's ministry and teaching. As the discourse progresses, the disciples probe various angles of Jesus's teaching (cf. 16:17, 18). The first question, by Thomas, reveals a lack of understanding concerning Jesus's return to the Father: "Lord, we don't know where you are going, so how can we know the way?" (14:5). Jesus's often-quoted response, the sixth "I am" statement, is riveting: "I am the way and the truth and the life" (14:6). These three predicate nominatives pull together a great deal of Jesus's identity and mission in the Fourth Gospel.

The term "way" (*hodos*) occurs first in 1:23 as part of the Isaiah 40:3 quotation and then three more times here in 14:4–6. If the term's meaning is consistent, it lines up very well with the use of "way" or "the Way" in the Synoptics and especially Luke-Acts (e.g., Luke 9:3, 57; 18:35; 19:36; Acts 9:2; 19:9, 23; 22:4; 24:14, 22). When John calls Israel to "prepare the way for the Lord," he's declaring the end of the exile and the return of God's people to the promised land (→Mark 1:2–3). In telling Thomas that he is the way, Jesus pronounces that the long-awaited redemption flows *through* him. Consummate fulfillment of the OT's anticipation of the promised land is the new cosmic temple, a place that Jesus will make ready for his followers upon his death and resurrection.

Verse 6 also states that Jesus is the "truth," reflecting once again John's cosmic trial motif (e.g., 1:14, 17; 5:33; 8:32, 40, 44; 15:26; 16:7; 18:38). At the core of "truth" in John's Gospel is that *Jesus is Israel's Messiah and God incarnate, coeternal with the Father*. His relationship with the Father unfolds yet again in the next several verses. The thrust of his response to Philip's inquiry is, "Anyone who has seen me has seen the Father" (14:9). Those who believe that Jesus is the divine Son of God, the "truth," based "on the evidence of the works themselves" (14:11), will participate in the new cosmic sanctuary. Those who fail to believe are judged, but those who believe enter into the new cosmos.

Finally, Jesus presents himself as the "life" in 14:6. A chief aspect of Jesus's career is giving "life" to his followers. Life in the Fourth Gospel is none other than new creational life that begins during Jesus's earthly ministry (e.g., 1:4; 3:15, 16; 4:14, 36; 5:24; 20:31; →5:19–30). Eschatological life in the new, cosmic sanctuary finds its point of origin in Jesus himself. Therefore, the incredible statement that Jesus is "the way and the truth and the life" largely entails his threefold mission to create the new heavens and earth as the new dwelling place for God and humanity—all taking place *through* him.

The Gift of the Advocate (14:15–31)

At the end of the previous section, Jesus promises that he will "do" "anything" his disciples ask in accordance with his "name" (14:14; cf. Matt. 18:19). Such a request largely entails obeying God's perfect will, which honors the three persons of the Trinity.[43] So the pouring out of the Spirit empowers the disciples to glorify God as they bear witness to him in a hostile world. Jesus petitions the Father to furnish them with "another advocate" (14:16).

The term "advocate" (*paraklētos*; NIV, NRSV, NET, NLT), occurring four times in John (14:16, 26; 15:26; 16:7), is variously rendered as "counselor" (NIV 1984, HCSB), "helper" (NASB, ESV), and "comforter" (KJV). Scholars debate the precise nuance of the term with great vigor. The following verse clues us in on how to understand the term; John describes the *paraklētos* as "the Spirit of truth" (14:17). Truth and *paraklētos* must then be related in the Fourth Gospel. Truth in John's narrative, from beginning to end, is bound up with God putting the world on trial over the person of Jesus. The word "advocate," then, is likely a good fit in light of the immediate context of the Fourth Gospel and its wider usage (see 1 John 2:1; Philo, *Ios.* 239; Philo, *Vit. Mos.* 2.134; Philo, *Praem.* 166; Philo, *Flacc.* 22–23, 151, 181).

The cosmic trial that began with the coming of Jesus into the world extends into the lives of Jesus's followers. The disciples are tasked with carrying out the same trial that Jesus began. But they are assured that they have an "advocate." Recall that two witnesses are required for a legal conviction (Num. 35:30; Deut. 19:15; John 8:17; 2 Cor. 13:1), so the Spirit will aid the disciples in their prosecution. Andrew Lincoln concludes, "They are not alone as they play their role in the lawsuit of history. . . . This Advocate will be with the disciples (14:16, 17). He will aid them in their witness to the truth, because, as the Spirit of truth, he will guide them into all truth."[44]

Since the disciples are promised "another advocate," they must already possess an advocate. This is none other than Jesus, who has been guiding them into the "truth" or a right understanding of his identity and mission. Jesus has spent the entirety of his career demonstrating his identity to his followers through various signs, so when he departs for heaven, the Spirit will continue to attest to Jesus's identity. We can frame a great deal of John's theology as

43. Kruse, *John*, 297.
44. Lincoln, *Truth on Trial*, 27.

the following: *The Father sends the Son, and the Father and the Son send the Spirit. The disciples, too, are then sent by the triune God to attest to the Son's identity*. The first half of John's Gospel concerns the Son's identity with the Father and the fulfillment of the divine commission, and the second half brings the disciples into fulfilling that same mission.[45]

The third question, from Judas (or Thaddaeus; see Matt. 10:3 // Mark 3:18), concerns Jesus's restriction of his self-disclosure to his disciples and his withholding it from the "world" (14:22). Jesus reveals himself only to those who love him. Love and knowledge go hand in hand. An individual cannot have one without the other. Furthermore, in stark contrast to the Spirit, who empowers the disciples to fulfill the mission of the Father and the Son, the "prince of this world" empowers Judas Iscariot, Pilate, and the Jewish leaders to fulfill his devilish commission (14:30). We can discern a divine commission and a satanic anticommission. Earlier, in 13:27, Satan entered Judas so that he might betray Jesus and accomplish his plan. This is eerily similar to the Spirit living in the disciples and being in them (14:17). The coming Spirit empowers the disciples to testify to and fulfill Jesus's life-giving mission, whereas the "prince of this world" empowers his disciples to deceive and fulfill his life-destroying mission (cf. 8:44). Paul labels Satan an "angel of light" for good reason because he imitates the truth (2 Cor. 11:14). The book of Revelation also presents a satanic trinity, one that is patterned after Daniel 7. The satanic trinity is bent on imitating the triune God, but eventually the devilish trinity, unable to sustain its imitation, will collapse within itself (Rev. 13; 17:5–18).

This section of the discourse ends with Jesus's seemingly odd command to the disciples: "Come now; let us leave" (14:31). The problem is that the Farewell Discourse continues through chapter 17. It's not until 18:1 that Jesus and his disciples leave the upper room. Several decades ago, many commentators argued that the Farewell Discourse is a composite of several discourses haphazardly stitched together. But in recent years, scholars have rightly recognized the unity of the Farewell Discourse. What commentators believed were earmarks of highly redacted material are, in reality, sophisticated literary devices. One of these occurs here in 14:31. The imperative "Come now; let us leave" is quite similar to what we find in Mark 14:42 when Jesus tells his disciples in Gethsemane to awaken from slumber and "Rise! Let us go! Here comes my betrayer!" Both imperatives come in the midst of conflict—here in John 14:30–31 the devil is coming, and in Mark 14:42 the "betrayer is near" (HCSB). Perhaps in John 14:31 Jesus is commanding his disciples not to arise physically from the table but to arm themselves figuratively for spiritual

45. Köstenberger and Swain, *Father, Son and Spirit*, 106–7.

conflict. As the Farewell Discourse progresses, the disciples will become more aware that the world "hates" them (15:19), that they will suffer grave persecution from within the covenant community (16:1), and that the "evil one" will pursue them (17:15).

In Union with the Son (15:1–27)

Jesus as the True Vine (15:1–17)

The previous section ends with an imperative for the disciples to prepare for battle (14:31), and this passage explains why. The disciples stand united with Jesus, and since he and the devil will soon clash, the disciples must expect the same eschatological antagonism. The seventh and climactic "I am" statement is found in 15:1: "I am the true vine." Here we find one of Jesus's most captivating and theologically pregnant discourses in the Fourth Gospel. The agricultural metaphor of a vine recalls several OT passages that symbolically depict Israel as a vine (e.g., Isa. 5:1–7; Ps. 80:9–20; Jer. 8:12–14). So when Jesus says that he's the "vine" and his Father is the "gardener," he's claiming to be the people of God—Israel itself. But Jesus also claims to be the *"true [hē alēthinē] vine."* John's narrative contains several similar statements:

The *true [to alēthinon]* light that gives light to everyone was coming into the world. (1:9)

Yet a time is coming and has now come when the *true [alēthinoi]* worshipers will worship the Father in the Spirit and in truth. (4:23)

It is not Moses who has given you the bread from heaven, but it is my Father who gives you the true *[ton alēthinon]* bread from heaven. (6:32)

I am the *true [hē alēthinē]* vine, and my Father is the gardener. (15:1)

Now this is eternal life: that they know you, the only *true [alēthinon]* God, and Jesus Christ, whom you have sent. (17:3)

John ties the noun "truth" (*alētheia*) and the adjective "true" (*alēthinos*) to his larger cosmic trial motif, and the adjective cuts two ways: (1) The adjective "true" lies in contrast to that which is false. So when Jesus asserts that he is the "true vine" or true Israel, he stands over against a false vine or an idolatrous Israel (cf. 12:37–41). The only way for the disciples and John's readers to participate in the genuine covenant community is to join themselves to

Jesus and produce "much fruit" by loving one another deeply (15:5, 9–17; cf. Gal. 5:22–26). Those who fail to do faithful works wither and will be "thrown into the fire and burned" (15:6). (2) The adjective "true" also functions on a redemptive-historical plane. The OT contains institutions, persons, and events that anticipate Jesus and his followers. They are a shadow (the type) of something greater (the antitype or that which is "true"). There's a sense in which the covenant community in the OT typologically anticipates the covenant community in the NT.

While one people of God spans both Testaments, the NT covenant community enjoys a more intimate relationship with God. Why? This is another unique aspect of the Gospels and the NT at large—that the Messiah embodies true Israel and reconstitutes the covenant community within himself. Paul claims in Ephesians 3:6 that Jews and gentiles mysteriously participate in true Israel through union with Christ: "This mystery is that through the gospel the Gentiles are heirs together with Israel, members together of one body, and sharers together in the promise *in Christ Jesus.*" Gentiles, together with Jewish believers, have now become true Israelites through faith alone in Christ, the embodiment of true Israel, and not by identifying with the externals of the Mosaic covenant. Therefore, the major thrust of 15:1–17 is that God, the gardener of Israel, considers to be part of true Israel, the true vine, those who belong to his Son by trusting in and following him alone.

Opposition from the World (15:18–27)

According to 15:1–17, being united to Jesus entails participating in true Israel, as Jews and gentiles stand on equal footing through Israel's Messiah. Union with him also entails participating in his suffering: "If the world hates you, keep in mind that it hated me first" (15:18). In the introduction to the Farewell Discourse, as Jesus washes the disciples' feet, he symbolically furnishes them with a new identity as little "suffering servants" of Israel (13:1–17). They are so united to Jesus, *the* Suffering Servant, that they are now included in his suffering and mission. What is true of Jesus is true of his followers. Of course, they are qualitatively different from Jesus—they will not suffer vicariously for sin, nor are they coeternal with the Father. Nevertheless, Jesus's Isaianic mission is the disciples' Isaianic mission. Notice in 15:20 that Jesus draws the disciples' attention to his previous statement in 13:16 that "a *servant* is not greater than his master." All those joined to Jesus embody his life, suffering, and mission.

The "world" (*tou kosmou*), Jesus states, "hates" believers (15:19). The "world" here is composed of all, Jews or gentiles, who disavow Jesus's identity, mission, and followers. We've seen how John consistently presents the world (*kosmos*) as hostile toward Jesus and his disciples (see 1:9, 29; 3:16–17, 19; 4:42; 12:31). The world and the newly formed Israel of God stand in opposition to one another, an antagonism that begins in the garden of Eden and continues until the second coming of Christ. But contrary to popular belief, such suffering is not general but eschatological. The antagonism of the world between the first and second comings of Christ is an escalated, more profound persecution than what previously occurred in the OT.

Verse 22 discloses the results of God's trial of the world: "If I had not come and spoken to them [the world], they would not be guilty of sin; but now they have no excuse for their sin." Jesus's ministry in the Fourth Gospel is largely public in nature because he plays a key role in God's cosmic trial. God sends his Son to perform signs to determine who will be judged or declared in the right. The world, by and large, has rejected Jesus as Israel's Messiah and the unique Son of God, and as a result, God declares them "guilty of sin" (cf. 7:7; 9:41; Rom. 1:20).

Verse 25 reveals the ultimate reason for their rejection of Jesus: "This is to *fulfill* what is written in their Law: 'They hated me without reason.'" The guilty verdict has been anticipated from long ago. The fulfillment formula is attached to one implicit OT quotation (17:12, quoting Ps. 41:9?) and five explicit ones: 12:38 (Isa. 53:1), 13:18 (Ps. 41:9), 15:25 (Ps. 35:19; 69:4), 19:24 (Ps. 22:18), 19:36 (Ps. 34:20). All but one of these quotations are drawn from the book of Psalms—specifically, Davidic psalms (cf. 2:17, quoting Ps. 69:9). Consider, too, that John ramps up OT quotations in general as passion week unfolds. We can draw an important conclusion, then: Jesus's suffering and death fall very much in line with the OT, particularly King David's experiences. David's life contains patterns that prophetically anticipate the sufferings of the long-awaited Messiah, his ultimate heir. David suffered innocently at the hands of his enemies, and now that same injustice is repeated in the life of Jesus.

The final two verses of chapter 15 repeat many of the themes contained in 14:15–31. This section explains why the world has denied the truth of the Son. The Father and the Son send the "Spirit of truth" or the "Advocate" so that he may "testify" to Jesus's identity and mission. The Spirit is the great revealer of God's work of redemption. This is especially true of apocalyptic and eschatological realities. The apostle Paul picks up on this theme in the lengthiest treatment of wisdom in the NT: 1 Corinthians 1–2. There he vigorously argues that only those who possess the Spirit can fully grasp God's work. According to 1 Corinthians 2:10, the Spirit reveals the wisdom of the cross, "the deep things of God" (cf. Dan. 2:22; 4:9; 5:11; 11:33; Rev. 2:7, 17, 29; 3:6, 13, 22). Only God's people possess the revelatory Spirit (1 Cor. 2:6–16) and can truly grasp the Son's identity. The world, on the other hand, does not possess the Spirit and is therefore unable to grasp the salvific implications of God's revealed wisdom in the Son. Much of the first half of John's Gospel develops the presence of the Spirit as he relates to the new creation, the temple, and the new covenant (1:32, 33; 3:5–6, 8; 4:23–24; 6:63), whereas the Spirit in the Farewell Discourse is often tethered to testifying to and revealing the Son (15:26; 16:13). The end-time Spirit reveals the truth of the Son to the disciples, empowering the disciples to testify about the Son to the world (15:27).

End-Time Suffering and a Suffering Messiah (16:1–33)

Final Preparation for Suffering and the Spirit's Work to Convict and Inform (16:1–15)

The first verse in this section states the purpose of the previous section: "All this [15:18–27] I have told you so that *you will not fall away [mē skandalisthēte]*" (16:1; cf. Luke 7:23). The only other occurrence of the verb "to fall away" or "to cause to offend" is in 6:60–61, where Jesus asks the disciples if the "hard teaching" of the Bread of Life Discourse "offends" (*skandalizei*) them. This word refers to some sort of trap or enticement, often related to idolatry and false teaching (e.g., LXX: Josh. 23:13; Judg. 2:3; 8:27; Pss. 105:36; 140:9; Hosea 4:17; Wis. 14:11; 1 Macc. 5:4; Pss. Sol. 4:23; see also Rom. 14:13; 16:17; Gal. 5:11). The two occurrences in John, though, aren't tied to false teaching but to a teaching that is incredibly difficult to swallow. Jesus's suffering and death should not cause the disciples to retreat from their devotion to him; instead, their loyalty will be galvanized through end-time suffering.

God's people are no strangers to persecution and affliction. Indeed, persecution broke out between the first two descendants of Adam and Eve when Cain murdered his brother, Abel! While suffering and unjust persecution are a staple of Israel's story, the OT predicts that the righteous within the covenant community will endure an escalated state of persecution or tribulation in the "latter days" (e.g., Jer. 30:7; Ezek. 38–39; Dan. 11:36–45; 12:10). Such end-time persecution first befalls Jesus and then extends to the disciples. This end-time suffering is in mind when Jesus informs the disciples that they will be "put . . . out of the synagogue" (16:2). Earlier, in chapter 9, the blind man's parents, fearing the Jewish leaders, did not want to be "put out of the synagogue" (9:22), whereas the Jewish leaders "threw . . . out" the blind man from the community on account of his devotion to Jesus (9:34). The same fate awaits the disciples. As the history of the church unfolds in the coming decades, the majority of the Jewish nation will persecute the apostles. Jesus warns the disciples in the Olivet Discourse that they will be "handed over to the local councils and flogged in the synagogues" (Mark 13:9 // Matt. 10:17 // Luke 21:12). Of course, a remnant of ethnic Jews embrace the gospel (e.g., Acts 2:41; Rom. 11:5), but Israel, by and large, will reject it (e.g., Rom. 11:3). The readers of John's Gospel, living some five decades after Jesus's earthly ministry, are still in the throes of conflict. The end-time persecution that began with Jesus and the apostles continues into the early church, extending even to today.

Jesus's departure paves the way for the Spirit's arrival, as the Spirit's ministry is an extension of Jesus's ministry. According to 16:8, the coming Spirit will "*prove [elengxei]* the world to be in the wrong about sin and righteousness and judgment." These three aspects of the Spirit's work in 16:7–11 comport with Jesus's own ministry.[46] The term "prove" is variously understood, since it can mean to "expose" in a neutral sense (e.g., 3:20; Eph. 5:11), or it can mean to "reprove" or "convict" in a negative sense (e.g., 1 Cor. 14:24; 1 Tim. 5:20). In the latter sense, the term can also mean to bring shame and guilt for the purpose of repentance (e.g., LXX: 2 Sam. 7:14; Prov. 3:11; Rev. 3:19).[47] The idea, then, is that the coming Spirit graciously convicts the world of wrongdoing *so that those within the fallen world may turn from their rebellious ways.* The Spirit in the Fourth Gospel is nearly synonymous with the new creation and the temple (3:5–6, 8; 4:23–24; 6:63). Here in 16:9–11 his life-giving work is on display once more, but this time John accents his future role of restoration in convicting individuals of their sin.

Verses 9–11 unpack what Jesus means by "sin," "righteousness," and "judgment" (16:9–10). First, the Spirit searches the hearts of humanity and convicts unbelievers of unbelief or "sin." That is, they refuse to believe Jesus's signs that demonstrate his identity as Israel's Messiah and the divine Son of God (see 8:24; 15:22). The world is held accountable for failing to recognize Jesus during his earthly ministry. Once John publishes his Gospel, a book that contains the seven signs that point to his identity, God still holds the world accountable because the Fourth Gospel preserves these signs. But the Fourth Gospel was partly written so that unbelievers will recognize the truth of the seven signs and trust in Jesus (20:30–31).

Second, the Spirit also convicts the world of "righteousness." This is probably not God's perfect righteousness but the world's *false* righteousness. From the beginning of John's narrative, Jesus challenges the Jews' external religiosity. They may appear to be right before God, but inwardly they are "full of the bones of the dead" (Matt. 23:27). Nicodemus is a terrific example of one

---

46. Carson, *John*, 537. I'm largely indebted to his view in my explanation of 16:7–11.
47. Carson, *John*, 537.

who transitions from this category of legalism (3:1–15) into a right relationship with God (19:39–42). When Jesus returns to the Father, the Spirit will convict many of their dead works in order that they may enjoy fellowship with God.

Third, the Spirit will reveal how wrong are those who denounce Jesus. The "prince of the world" misguides, blinds, and deceives the world into thinking that Jesus is not who he claims to be (16:11). But the devil "now stands condemned," so the Spirit will soften the hearts of some who decry Jesus.

From Grief to Joy (16:16–33)

The Farewell Discourse shifts from the Spirit's work of conviction (16:8–11) and revelation (16:12–15) to the disciples' response to Jesus's death and resurrection (16:16–33). The Spirit reveals the "truth" of Jesus's identity (16:13) and opens the eyes of the disciples to the full significance of his death and resurrection, for one cannot understand Jesus as the Messiah and the unique Son of God apart from his death and resurrection. Jesus informs the disciples that they will soon "see" him "no more" (a reference to his death), and then "after a little while" they will "see him" (a reference to his resurrection) (16:16). The disciples, though, remain perplexed at Jesus's words: "What does he mean by saying, 'In a little while you will see me no more, and then after a little while you will see me,' and 'Because I am going to the Father'? . . . We don't understand what he is saying" (16:17–18). This is one of the last recorded exchanges between Jesus and the disciples, and it's reasonable that Jesus would broach the issue of his death and resurrection one final time (cf. 7:33; 12:35; 13:33; 14:19). The disciples recognize Jesus's identity from the first "sign" and believe in him from that point on (2:11). Yet the Twelve continue to struggle with Jesus's claim to be Israel's *suffering* Messiah. This is a salient aspect of the Synoptics and Mark's Gospel in particular (→Mark 8:22–30).

Within the Synoptics, especially Mark, Jesus insists that his disciples and others conceal his identity. This is known as the "messianic secret." Mark 1:34 says, for example, "Jesus healed many who had various diseases. He also drove out many demons, but he would not let the demons speak because they knew who he was." Once more, Mark 8:30, a passage that immediately follows Peter's accurate confession that Jesus is indeed "the Christ" (i.e., the Messiah), says, "Jesus warned them not to tell anyone about him" (cf. Mark 9:9). Why does Jesus prohibit his disciples from telling others his identity as Israel's long-awaited King?

Several OT texts anticipate a coming king who will deliver Israel and redeem her from her plight, recapturing that which was lost in the garden. The messiah would emerge on the scene as an anointed Adamic figure who would rule consummately over evil, restore humanity's fortunes, and usher in the eternal new cosmos (e.g., Gen. 3:15; 49:8–10; Num. 24:17; 2 Sam. 7; Pss. 2; 78; 132; Isa. 9:6–7; 11:1–5; Jer. 23:5; Dan. 2:44–45). A persecuted messiah also appears to be anticipated in a few passages. Daniel 9:25–26, for example, seems to suggest that the messiah will eventually be put to death: "From the time the word goes out to restore and rebuild Jerusalem until the Anointed One, the ruler, comes, there will be seven 'sevens,' and sixty-two 'sevens.' . . . After the sixty-two 'sevens,' the Anointed One will be put to death and will have nothing" (cf. Isa. 52:13–53:12; Zech. 12:10).

According to all four Gospels, the disciples have difficulty wrapping their heads around Jesus's coming death and resurrection because they are largely expecting a messiah who will vanquish the Roman Empire, not suffer at the hands of the "world"—their own citizens, the Jewish authorities, Pilate, and Rome. Jesus must refine their understanding of his messiahship. It is marked first not by political, earthly, physical triumph but by end-time suffering and death. Jesus indeed fulfills OT expectations, but the way in which the OT is fulfilled in the person of Jesus differs from the disciples' expectations. The disciples must learn to read and reread the Hebrew Scriptures rightly (→Luke 24:13–35).

In 16:25, Jesus states that he has "been speaking figuratively" up until this moment but that "a time is coming" when he will "no longer use this kind of language" (cf. 10:6). A good case can be made that Jesus is describing not only his teaching in the Farewell Discourse but his entire teaching ministry. There's a sense in which Jesus's teaching has always been veiled, even to his disciples. Sometimes it's thinly veiled, and other times it's shrouded in a cloud of mystery. The disciples will only be able to grasp Jesus's rich identity *after* the crucifixion and the resurrection. The disciples will fully understand Jesus's identity as the King of Israel and the divine Son of God at Pentecost in Acts 2. While they certainly catch glimpses of it throughout Jesus's earthly ministry (16:29), they must await the fullness of Spirit for proper understanding.

Chapter 16 ends with the purpose of the entire Farewell Discourse: "I have told you these things, so that in me you may have peace. In this world you will have trouble. But take heart! I have overcome the world" (16:33). The last testament of Jesus to the disciples offers them comfort in the difficult days ahead. They are assured of "peace." But this peace is not a reference to political or social circumstances; it is spiritual and eschatological. This category of peace refers to reconciliation with God, a peace that only Jesus offers to those who follow him (see 14:27; Luke 2:14; 19:38; Eph. 1:10, 20–23; Col. 1:20). The fall fractures humanity and creation's relationship with God, but Jesus restores this long-lost fellowship.

Further, Jesus commands his disciples to "take heart" *because* he has "overcome the world." "To overcome" (*nikaō*) is nearly a technical term in John's letters and the book of Revelation, where it refers to the world overcoming believers physically but believers overcoming the world spiritually (e.g., 1 John 2:13–14; 4:4; 5:4; Rev. 2:7; 11:7; 12:11; 13:7; 21:7). The world does its worst—persecuting, mocking, pillaging, and marginalizing God's people—but persevering believers conquer these expressions of eschatological "trouble" or tribulation. This pattern of behavior is ultimately modeled after Christ, who, like a Passover lamb, is conquered physically on the cross, but who, like a royal lion, spiritually conquers all forms of evil (Rev. 5:5–6; cf. Gen. 3:15; Rom. 16:20).

Curiously, the Fourth Gospel is the only Gospel that lacks exorcisms and the wilderness temptation, an event that begins the overthrow of the devil's kingdom. Why? John views the totality of Jesus's conflict with the devil at the cross. So when Jesus says to the disciples that he has "overcome" the world, he's anticipating his death and resurrection. In a word, the arrival of the new creation expressed in turning water into wine, healing the official's son, healing the lame man, feeding the five thousand, healing the blind man, and raising Lazarus is predicated upon a successful journey to the cross and resurrection from the grave.

The High Priestly Prayer (17:1–26)

Jesus's Personal Prayer (17:1–5)

The Synoptics, especially Luke, record Jesus praying often and at key junctures in his ministry (e.g., Matt. 14:23; 26:36; Mark 6:46; Luke 6:12). The Fourth Gospel, though, records Jesus praying three times (11:41–42; 12:27–28; 17:1–26). And while some view the prayer in chapter 17 to be at odds with Jesus's prayer in Gethsemane (Matt. 26:36–44 // Mark 14:32–39 // Luke 22:41–45), they nicely complement each other. The prayer in Gethsemane accents Jesus's suffering and endurance in the midst of tribulation, whereas this prayer in chapter 17 underscores the outcome and goal of the cross—the Son's glorification of the Father and the Father's glorification of the Son—and the preservation and mission of the disciples and all subsequent believers.

The prayer, traditionally known as the "high priestly prayer" on account of its intercessory tenor, likely encapsulates the entire Fourth Gospel.[48] We can discern three major sections: 17:1–5, 17:6–19, and 17:20–26. In the first section

---

48. Carson, *John*, 551.

(17:1–5), Jesus asks his Father to glorify him in his coming death and resurrection so that the Son will, in turn, glorify the Father. Jesus has succeeded in carrying out his Father's work by granting life to those whom the Father has chosen. As the faithful Adam, the true Israel, and the unique Son of God, he finished "the work" the Father "gave" him to accomplish (17:4). The first words out of Jesus's mouth set the tone for his death and resurrection: "Father, the hour has come" (17:1; cf. 12:23). We've seen the importance of "hour" (*hōra*) in John's Gospel and how it relates to a number of critical themes:

Reference	Theme
John 2:4: "My *hour has not yet come* [*oupō hēkei hē hōra mou*]" (cf. 7:30; 8:20; 12:23; 13:1).	Jesus's death and resurrection
John 4:23: "*A time is coming and has now come* [*erchetai hōra kai nyn estin*] when the true worshipers will worship the Father in the Spirit and in truth" (cf. 4:21).	Establishment of the end-time temple
John 5:25: "*A time is coming and has now come* [*erchetai hōra kai nyn estin*] when the dead will hear the voice of the Son of God and those who hear will live" (cf. 5:28).	Resurrection of saints
John 16:2: "They will put you out of the synagogue; in fact, *the time is coming* [*erchetai hōra*] when anyone who kills you will think they are offering a service to God."	End-time persecution of the disciples and subsequent followers

Often the narrative weds "hour" with the common verb for "coming" or "arrival," and because "hour" is profoundly eschatological, John likely has fulfillment in mind. The book of Daniel and other prophetic and Jewish texts use similar language to refer to eschatological tribulation and restoration (e.g., Jer. 30:23–24; Dan. 8:17, 19; 11:35, 40, 45; 12:1; Joel 4:1; Zeph. 1:7; 1QM I, 4).[49] The "hour" of fulfillment has now arrived in Jesus's earthly ministry and especially in his death and resurrection. While the OT and Second Temple Judaism generally understand tribulation to *precede* restoration, both eschatological periods oddly overlap. The hour of end-time persecution is at hand, but so is the hour of resurrection and the new creation.

Jesus's Prayer for the Disciples (17:6–19)

Much of the second section of the prayer reflects on Jesus's success in preserving the disciples, whom God chose and "gave" to the Son "out of the world" (17:6). When the Son discloses the Father through signs, the disciples

---

49. Mihalios, *Danielic Eschatological Hour*, 74, 170–71.

rightly recognize that Jesus is the divine Son of God and the one "sent" from the Father. In contrast to the Jewish leaders and Judas (17:12), they believe Jesus's words and deeds (17:8).

The prayer ultimately turns on the Son's twofold request that the Father "protect" the disciples from the devil as they continue to persevere in a hostile "world" (17:15–16) and that the Father "sanctify" the disciples in "truth" (17:17). While the disciples are not to find their identity in the rebellious world, they nevertheless remain within it (17:11; cf. 15:19). Throughout Jesus's earthly ministry, Jesus is "protecting" and guarding them (17:12 HCSB). But *how* does Jesus protect and guard? He does so in the "name" of the Father. The Fourth Gospel repeatedly weds Jesus's "name" to revealing his Father (e.g., 1:12; 2:23; 3:18; 5:43; 10:25; 12:13, 28), for one's name is often associated with one's identity. To be guarded in Jesus's name, then, is to be found in him. We find something akin to this in Paul, where he refers to believers being "in Christ." *True* members of the covenant community, true Israel, are so tightly bound to Christ through the Spirit that nothing can breach their relationship with God. The often-quoted Romans 8:39 states that nothing can "separate" believers "from the love of God that is in Christ Jesus." The world cannot separate true believers from Jesus, but Jesus can separate individuals from the world.

The second part of 17:12 specifies a key opponent of the covenant community: "Not one of them is lost, except *the son of destruction* [*ho huios tēs apōleias*], so that the Scripture may be fulfilled" (HCSB). The reference here to Judas falling away from the flock demonstrates that he was never truly part of God's people (cf. 6:64, 71; 1 John 2:19–20). He never genuinely believed the signs. John labels him the "son of destruction"—the antithesis of Jesus, the "Son of God," the great Life-giver. God is marked by giving life, whereas the devil is marked by stealing it (cf. Isa. 57:4 LXX; Jub. 10:3; 2 Thess. 2:3). Judas's betrayal, while it may seem surprising on the surface, has been anticipated for a long time. The OT, especially Daniel, anticipates the arrival of an antagonist who will infiltrate the covenant, seduce many within by manipulating the law, and oppress the righteous (Dan. 7:25; 8:24–25; 9:26–27; 11:30–35; 12:10). Paul claims that this "mystery of lawlessness" is "already at work" in the covenant community (2 Thess. 2:7 NASB). And according to 1 John 2:18–19, "many antichrists have come" because it is the eschatological "last hour." So while the NT expects a final, physical antichrist or opponent to arrive at the very end of history immediately preceding Jesus's second coming, Judas is the first in a long train of antichrist figures who assault the covenant community. Jesus asks his Father to protect the disciples from one of their closest friends and confidants—Judas Iscariot. Betrayal indeed.

Jesus's Prayer for Future Disciples (17:20–26)

The third and final section of Jesus's high priestly prayer transitions from a prayer concerning the disciples (17:6–19) to a request for all believers (17:20–26). The governing principle is easy enough to grasp: the unity of God's people, Jew and gentile, demonstrates the intimate unity between the Father and the Son; when believers concretely reflect such harmony in their lives, the world becomes attracted to it (17:23). In a word, the bond between the Father and the Son fuels missions. This present section is one of the most theologically pregnant passages in the NT because it probes the unique relationship between the persons of the Trinity, especially the relationship between the Father and the Son, and how believers relate to that unique relationship.

According to 17:21, the triune God graciously includes believers in his fellowship: "May they also be in us." While believers obviously do not enjoy the same type of fellowship with the three persons of the Trinity that the Father, Son, and Spirit enjoy with each other, the Godhead, in some sense, opens up and allows believers to enjoy fellowship with them. The central theme in Scripture is God's commitment to dwell with humanity in the eternal new cosmos. The OT opens with this expectation in Genesis 1–2, and the NT closes with this expectation met. There's a reason why John sees the "new Jerusalem" "coming down out of heaven" (Rev. 21:2). God decreed in eternity past that creation and humanity would one day behold his "glory" for all of eternity (17:24).

The World Puts Jesus on Trial and Jesus Puts the World on Trial (18:1-40)

Jesus Betrayed and Arrested (18:1–11)

After praying, Jesus and the disciples leave the upper room in Jerusalem and head for the Mount of Olives, passing through the Kidron Valley. Matthew and Mark specify Gethsemane as a general "place" (*chōrion*; Matt. 26:36 // Mark 14:32), whereas John forgoes the name Gethsemane and calls it a "garden" (*kēpos*; 18:1), the same term found in the context of Jesus's burial (19:41). Why does John use this unusual term? Perhaps it recalls Genesis 1–3. While the Greek term *paradeisos* stands behind the word for "garden" or "paradise" in the LXX of Genesis 2–3, this term for garden (*kēpos*) occurs in Jewish literature as a reference to the garden of Eden (Josephus, *Ant.* 1.38, 45, 51; Sib. Or. 1:26, 23:48). Jesus's betrayal and arrest in the garden of Gethsemane parallels his wilderness temptation in the Synoptics. On the slopes of the Mount of Olives, a "detachment of soldiers" confronts him, "carrying torches, lanterns and weapons" (18:3). They are ready for battle.

In addition, John peppers the final chapters of his Gospel with several subtle references to Genesis 1–3:

Genesis 1-3	John 18-20
The serpent tempts Adam and Eve in the garden of Eden (Gen. 3:1-7)	Judas, embodying the serpent, betrays Jesus, the last Adam, in a garden (18:3)
Adam should have waged war over the serpent in the garden of Eden (Gen. 1:28; 2:15)	Judas, embodying the serpent, leads soldiers to wage war against Jesus in the garden (18:3)
God commands Adam to function as a gardener of Eden (Gen. 2:15)	Mary Magdalene believes the resurrected Jesus, who is buried in a garden, is a "gardener" (20:15)
God "breathed" into Adam "the breath of life" (Gen. 2:7)	Jesus breathes on the disciples and imparts the Spirit (20:22)

Consider that John, too, numbers the days of the first and last week of Jesus's ministry (1:19–2:11; 12:1–20:25), paralleling the seven days of Genesis 1–2. If creation and new creation bookend Jesus's career, we should expect that John would supply other connections to the Genesis account. But what's the significance? Why draw parallels between the Fourth Gospel and Genesis? John introduces Jesus by alluding to Genesis 1:1 and connecting him to the creation of all things in 1:1–5, but Jesus is not only God; he is the God-*man*. He embodies true Israel—he is the vine (15:1–8). But he also embodies true humanity—he is true Adam. He must bear the sin, guilt, and penalty of the first Adam in order to bring about the creation of the new cosmos and redeem humanity.

Addressing the soldiers and Judas in 18:6, Jesus claims to be the great "I AM" (AT). The readers of John's narrative know the significance of this claim (→8:12–30). Rooted in Exodus 3:14, it is a claim to be Yahweh in the flesh, the great Redeemer of Israel. This explains the odd response of the detachment of soldiers: "They drew back and fell to the ground" (18:6; cf. Job 1:20; Dan. 2:46). The wording here suggests that the soldiers recognize something entirely unique about Jesus's identity, although they proceed to arrest him (18:12).

The Interrogation of Peter and Jesus (18:12–27)

The soldiers then lead Jesus to the house of Annas, the previous high priest and father-in-law of Caiaphas (the current high priest). John is the only evangelist to record the trial of Jesus at Annas's house. When we examine the four Gospels as whole, we learn that Jesus is tried a total of four times: an unofficial Jewish trial before Annas (18:13–24), an official Jewish trial before the Sanhedrin with Caiaphas presiding that reaches a preliminary indictment (Matt. 26:59–66 // Mark 14:55–64), an official Jewish trial before the Sanhedrin with Caiaphas presiding that concludes with a formal indictment (Luke 22:66–71), and a Roman trial before Pilate (Matt. 27:11–26 // Mark 15:1–15 // Luke 23:1–25 // John 18:28–19:26).

Peter's denial of Jesus brackets the unofficial trial before Annas:

18:15–18	Denial #1
18:19–24	Jesus's trial before Annas
18:25–27	Denials #2 and #3

The Synoptics present Peter's threefold denial as a whole (Matt. 26:69–75 // Mark 14:66–72 // Luke 22:54–62), whereas John splits the event into two. Why? Peter's unfaithfulness is starkly juxtaposed with Jesus's faithfulness. Jesus affirms his identity as Jesus of Nazareth with the statement "I am" (*egō eimi*; 18:5), but Peter denies his identity as a disciple by announcing "I am not" (*ouk eimi*; 18:17).

We also discover that Peter is not alone but is accompanied by "another disciple" (18:15). This is likely John the apostle and the son of Zebedee, the author of the Fourth Gospel (cf. 13:23; 19:26–27; 20:2–4, 8; 21:4, 7, 20). John is apparently "known" in some way to Caiaphas. The narrative is silent concerning the precise relationship, but according to Mark 1:19–20 and Luke 5:9–10, the sons of Zebedee, James and John, are involved in a fishing enterprise with Peter in Capernaum. It's not a stretch to envisage their fishing business finding its way to Jerusalem. Whatever the case, John and Peter's presence here in the courtyard at the palace of Annas gives the audience strong eyewitness testimony of these critical events.

Inside the palace, Annas opens the unofficial trial with a general line of questioning concerning Jesus's "disciples" and "his teaching" (18:19). Perhaps Annas concerns himself with the disciples to determine whether they are also a threat to Israel's political stability.[50] If Jesus threatens Israel's relationship with Rome, then his followers should also be investigated. Regarding Jesus's "teaching," Annas may have in mind a great deal of what the Fourth Gospel has outlined during Jesus's ministry, for a distinctive of the Fourth Gospel is the public nature of Jesus's discourses concerning the condemnation of the temple (2:13–22), his unique relationship with his Father (3:1–15; 5:16–47; 7:28–36; 8:14–30), particulars of the Mosaic covenant and the Sabbath (5:16;

---

50. Schnabel, *Jesus in Jerusalem*, 236.

6:25–59; 7:21–24, 37–38; 8:12; 9:14), his claim to be the true leader of God's people (10:1–18), the raising of Lazarus (11:45–57), and his self-identification as the Messiah at the triumphal entry (12:12–19).

Jesus responds by framing his entire ministry in terms of the cosmic trial motif: "I have spoken openly *to the world* [*tō kosmō*]. . . . I always taught in synagogues or at the temple, where all the Jews come together" (18:20). God put the world on trial in the person of Jesus to condemn those who refuse to believe but to impart life to those who believe. Here Annas believes that he's putting Jesus on trial, but in reality, Jesus is the one who puts him on trial. Part of Jesus's point is that since his ministry is deeply public, even cosmic, Annas can ask anyone who heard him. This unofficial trial is the only *Jewish* trial recorded in John's Gospel. While that may strike the reader as odd at first, it makes sense in light of the fact that the Fourth Gospel casts the entirety of Jesus's career as a trial before the Jewish people.

One of Annas's soldiers then slaps Jesus for disrespecting the "high priest" (18:22; cf. 19:3), but Jesus tells the soldier (or Annas) to "testify as to what is wrong" (18:23). This soldier is oblivious to the fact that he stands before Jesus—the judge of the cosmos, to whom the Father has "entrusted all judgment" (5:22). The account ends with Annas sending Jesus to Caiaphas (18:24), who will find Jesus guilty of blasphemy in a preliminary trial (Matt. 26:59–66 // Mark 14:55–64).

Jesus Stands before Pilate (18:28–40)

Verse 28 picks up right after the Sanhedrin meets in one of the rooms of the temple and concludes that Jesus is guilty of blasphemy and sedition (→Luke 23:1–25). The material that the Fourth Gospel devotes to Pilate outstrips what we have in the Synoptics, for John allocates nearly thirty verses to this event, whereas the Synoptics contain about half of that. Why spend so much time on Pilate's interaction with Jesus? Perhaps for a few reasons. Many of Jesus's discourses in the Fourth Gospel are lengthy, likely reflecting the eyewitness testimony of John the apostle, the author. Further, Jesus's extensive interaction with Pilate is the climax of the cosmic lawsuit. Pilate, as prefect of Judea, represents the Roman Empire, and the Roman Empire represents all the nations of the world. The point, then, is that all of humanity, Jew and gentile, tries Jesus and finds him guilty. He stands guilty of claiming something he is not: according to these two parties, he is not Israel's king and he is not the unique Son of God. Their conclusions are diametrically opposed to the purpose of John's Gospel—to convince the readers that "Jesus is the Messiah, the Son of God" (20:31).

In this vein, John often uses the description "the Jews" (*hoi Ioudaioi*) from Jesus's arrest to his burial (cf. 18:35),[51] whereas the Synoptics prefer the labels "chief priests," "elders of the people," "Pharisees," and "teachers of the law" at the end of passion week (e.g., Matt. 26:47; 27:1, 12, 62; Mark 14:43; 15:1, 3, 10; Luke 22:52, 66; 23:13). John's Gospel often (but not exclusively) uses the plural "the Jews" to draw a tight connection between the actions and views of Israel's leaders and the nation itself. What is true of her leaders is generally true of the populace. Keep in mind, though, that not all the Jewish leaders or the entire nation stand in opposition to Jesus; sometimes the term "the Jews" is positive (see 11:45; 12:11).

Since the Jews are not allowed to put anyone to death (18:31), the Jewish leaders must submit to Rome and convince Pilate to convict, sentence, and crucify Jesus. It is early Friday morning, the day of Passover, and in order to "avoid ceremonial uncleanness" and participate in the feast, the Jewish leaders "did not enter the palace" (18:28). This verse is rife with irony. The Jewish leaders are more concerned about keeping Passover (→13:1–17) than they are about killing Jesus, the true temple (2:21). Their bodies may be ritually clean on the outside, but their hearts are ritually impure on the inside.

After the leaders file charges (// Matt. 27:11–12 // Mark 15:1–2 // Luke 23:2), Pilate remains reluctant about trying Jesus (18:31a). They press on in their case against Jesus, demanding that Pilate alone can put him to death (18:31b). At this point in the narrative John interjects, reminding his readers that these events "took place to fulfill what Jesus had said about the kind of death he was going to die" (18:32). It may appear, at least externally, that there is no justice in the world, but God ordained these unjust events before time (Rev. 13:8). Pilate agrees to determine whether Jesus is indeed worthy of death. In 18:33–38, a section not found in the Synoptics, we are privy to what transpires during this initial hearing inside the palace. This is the exchange we've been waiting for.

While this section is critical to John's Gospel and deserves a full treatment, we will draw our attention to two chief points: (1) Pilate's first question to Jesus is unambiguous: "Are you the king of the Jews?" Is Jesus a threat to Rome? Will he incite a rebellion? According to 20:31, John pens his Gospel to demonstrate that Jesus is in fact Israel's "Messiah." But Jesus doesn't fit Pilate's (or the Jewish leaders') category of messiahship. Jesus argues that his "kingdom is not of this world" but is "from another place" (18:36). The idea is that Jesus's kingship and territory are not confined to a plot of land or territory. His kingdom is derived from an entirely different order and origin. He is not simply the king of Israel but the King of the universe.

---

51. John 18:12, 14, 20, 31, 33, 36, 38, 39; 19:3, 7, 12, 14, 19, 20, 21, 31, 38, 40, 42; 20:19.

(2) Jesus's identity is ultimately bound up with his mission. He put on flesh to disclose through seven signs that he is the divine Son of God who perfectly reveals the identity of the Father. This is the "truth" or the purpose of his coming (18:37). The next verse captures the heart of Pilate's (and Israel's) ignorance: "What is truth?" (18:38). The "truth" (*alētheia*) word group in John contains more saturation than any NT book and the second most in comparison to the LXX (Psalms uses the word group sixty-one times). For example, John uses "truth" terms fifty-five times, while the Synoptics use it eighteen times in total. Predictably, John's letters make use of these terms twenty-eight times, and Revelation ten times. It is clearly a Johannine favorite, pulling the cosmic trial motif into its orbit. When Pilate asks "What is truth?" he reveals that he is on the wrong side of the legal aisle; for only those who can grasp Jesus's identity possess the spiritual capacity to receive the truth of Jesus (18:37). Pilate stands guilty before the cosmic Judge. John's audience must recognize that Pilate is in the wrong and must ensure that they confess that Jesus is King and the unique Son of God, who atones for their sins.

According to Luke's Gospel, Pilate confers with Herod between 18:38a and 18:38b. John's narrative continues the scene with Pilate, whereas Luke transitions to Herod's interrogation (Luke 23:6–12). Pilate returns outside to the religious authorities, announcing that he finds "no basis for a charge against" Jesus (18:38b). In Pilate's estimation, Jesus is confused or perhaps a little misguided, but he is no threat to the might of Rome. The Jewish leaders refuse to abandon their plans, even after Pilate suggests the release of Barabbas, a well-known seditionist (18:40). The irony of the Fourth Gospel is relentless—Barabbas truly is a threat to Rome.

The Sentencing, Death, and Burial of Jesus (19:1–42)

Pilate Sentences Jesus (19:1–16)

Pilate, unconvinced that Jesus stands guilty (19:4), orders the soldiers to flog Jesus (19:1 // Matt. 27:27–31 // Mark 15:16–20). Perhaps flogging Jesus would placate the leaders. While the soldiers fashion a "crown of thorns" and clothe Jesus in a "purple robe" (19:2) to mock him, they are, in reality, confirming his true identity as King. When Pilate presents Jesus to the leaders as "the man" (19:5), they are incensed: "As soon as the chief priests and their officials saw him, they shouted, 'Crucify! Crucify!'" (19:6).

According to 19:7, Pilate discovers the real reason why the religious authorities are pursuing the death of Jesus: "He claimed to be the Son of God." We've come full circle to the healing of the lame man that transpired on the

Sabbath in 5:1–18, the third sign. There the leaders rightly perceive that Jesus is indeed claiming to be the divine Son of God (5:18), but they wrongly label it blasphemy. It isn't blasphemy because Jesus is God! The chief priests finally reveal their true motivation behind Jesus's arrest (→Mark 14:53–65).

The scene shifts back inside the palace, where Pilate interrogates Jesus a second time. This time around, Pilate is "even more afraid" (19:8) because in his pagan, polytheistic worldview it is possible for gods to come down "in human form" (Acts 14·11). Is Jesus one of these gods? Notice another layer of irony here. Pilate, clearly a pagan, has more insight into Jesus's identity than the Jewish leaders, who possess the OT and have witnessed Jesus's signs. Verse 11 contains two interlocking principles that must be held together: God's sovereignty and human responsibility. God has ordained the course of history, even the horrendous death of Jesus. That is, God entrusts Pilate with the authority or "power" to convict Jesus. Pilate's actions are not independent of God's purposes. On the other hand, individuals are still responsible for their actions: "The one [Caiaphas? Judas?] who handed me over to you is guilty of a greater sin." Although God ordained Jesus's betrayal at the hands of Judas and the Jewish leaders, they are still held responsible for their wicked behavior (cf. Acts 2:23).

Pilate is now even more resolute to release Jesus (19:12), yet the Jewish leaders won't take no for an answer. They decide to play their trump card—allegiance to Caesar. To release Jesus is, ultimately, to betray Tiberius Caesar, for there can be only one "king" (19:12). The Jews know full well that Pilate is in a precarious position with Tiberius Caesar and has been for some time. Pilate, after hearing the Jews' response, caves in and officially passes judgment upon Jesus at the "Stone Pavement" (*bēmatos*; 19:13). John time-stamps this event: "It was the day of Preparation of the Passover; it was about noon" (19:14a). It's early Friday afternoon of Passover on the fourteenth day of Nisan in AD 30. What makes this Passover peculiar is that the Sabbath is just a few hours away, at sundown. The Jewish people will soon celebrate Passover and then observe the Sabbath. Pilate continues taunting the Jewish authorities by announcing, "Here is your king," and, "Shall I crucify your king?" (19:14b–15a). The Jews make the audacious claim, "We have no king but Caesar" (19:15b). They would rather align themselves with a pagan king than confess that Jesus is their Lord and savior.

Jesus as the Passover Sacrifice (19:17–37)

The soldiers lead Jesus out to the "place of the Skull," or Golgotha (19:17–22), an area outside the city that should probably be identified with the Church of the Holy Sepulchre. Jesus, according to 19:17, carries the crossbeam (Latin *patibulum*) as far as the city gate, and then Simon of Cyrene brings it to Golgotha (// Matt. 27:32 // Mark 15:21 // Luke 23:26). Pilate orders that Jesus's indictment be mounted on a cross in three languages (Aramaic, Latin, and Greek): "Jesus of Nazareth, the King of the Jews" (19:19–20). Clearly, Pilate executes Jesus for sedition against Rome. The chief priests object, however, for they wanted the sign to read, "This man claimed to be king of the Jews" (19:21). But Pilate refuses to give in; he wants the last word. From beginning to end, Pilate remains convinced that Jesus is innocent of charges. In affixing the placard on the cross, he taunts the Jewish leaders, but more importantly, he unwittingly reveals Jesus's identity as Israel's Messiah. The seven signs of John's Gospel are designed to elicit belief or further unbelief, and here at Jesus's death and resurrection, the seventh and final sign, unbelief is running rampant. Even when Jesus's identity is plainly visible for the world to see—written in three languages!—his true identity remains largely hidden to its onlookers.

The narrative then transitions to four Roman soldiers casting lots to determine who should keep Jesus's garment. At this juncture, the narrator cites Psalm 22:18: "This happened that the scripture might be fulfilled that said, 'They divided my clothes among them and cast lots for my garment'" (19:24 // Matt. 27:35 // Mark 15:24 // Luke 23:34). By quoting Psalm 22:18, the Fourth Gospel stresses that Jesus of Nazareth is indeed the long-awaited King of Israel. In the throes of death and defeat, Jesus is the supreme ruler over all authorities, physical and spiritual. David's experiences of suffering, especially in Psalm 22, typologically foreshadow Jesus's own experiences throughout his earthly ministry, especially here at the crucifixion (→Mark 15:21–32). As David rules over Israel while undergoing persecution from those around him, so too Jesus rules in the midst of despair and defeat by his own people. At the beginning of Jesus's ministry when he clears the temple of the merchants, the narrator quotes Psalm 69:9. And then during passion week, Jesus himself quotes three Davidic psalms—Psalm 41:9 (13:18), and Psalm 35:19 and Psalm 69:4 (15:25). It is fitting, then, that these four Davidic psalms that stress suffering explain Jesus's ministry. John assures his readers that Jesus's sufferings do not invalidate his Davidic messiahship, as some may suppose, but *prove* it (20:31).

The Fourth Gospel contains the most vivid description of the soldiers stripping off Jesus's outer garment or mantle. Presumably, Jesus was still dressed in the purple robe that he acquired in 19:2. Clothing in the OT symbolizes throne rights (see Gen. 37; Num. 20:24–28; 1 Kings 11:30–31; 19:19–21). So when the four soldiers strip him of his royal robe, they are symbolically and outwardly divesting him of his right to rule. But nothing could be further from the truth.

The four Gospels report several women witnessing the crucifixion (Matt. 27:56 // Mark 15:40 // Luke 23:49 // John 19:25). While the number of women is disputed, John appears to mention four: two unnamed ("his mother [Mary]" and "his mother's sister [Salome?]") and two named ("Mary the wife of Clopas" and "Mary Magdalene"). It's possible to identify "his mother's sister" with Salome, the mother of the two famed "sons of Zebedee" (see Matt. 20:20–28; 27:56; Papias, frag. 10.3). If this is correct, then Salome is Jesus's aunt on his mother's side. This would make the author of the Fourth Gospel, the apostle John and the "beloved disciple," Jesus's cousin. Consequently, we have three relatives of Jesus gathered at the cross (19:25–26). In this light, the exchange between Jesus, his mother, and John is much more natural. Jesus asks John to care for his mother, presumably because John's father, Joseph, has died and his brothers are not yet followers of Jesus (7:5). According to the narrative, the last time Jesus spoke to his mother was during the first week of his public ministry when he informed her that his "hour [had] not yet come" (2:4) and then later performed the first sign. Here in the final week of his earthly ministry, his hour has arrived in the seventh and final sign.

John stresses the nature of Jesus's body on the cross much more than the other evangelists. Two observations are in order. First, instead of breaking Jesus's legs, the soldiers pierce his body, resulting in a "sudden flow of blood and water" (19:34). Blood and water, while certainly affirming a physical death, carry a symbolic value. Following the OT, Jesus often associates water with new life, the coming Spirit, the new eschatological temple, and the new covenant (3:5; 4:10–15; 7:38; 13:5; →3:5–8). So when the soldiers pierce his side, the flow of water confirms that Jesus is the wellspring of new life at the very moment of death. He gives end-time life, actualizes the new covenant, offers forgiveness of sin, and establishes the new temple while hanging on the cross. Nothing quite captures Jesus's work of redemption better than John's famous line "It is finished" (19:30).

Second, the Passover theme comes to the forefront of the narrative once more as John alludes to Exodus 12:46 in 19:36: "These things happened so that the scripture would be fulfilled: 'Not one of his bones will be broken'" (cf. Num. 9:12). Recall that John the Baptist testifies that Jesus is the "Lamb of God, who takes away the sin of the world" (1:29), setting Jesus on a trajectory as the Isaianic suffering servant and the ultimate Passover sacrifice (Isa. 53:7). Stated simply, animal sacrifices are unable to assuage God's wrath and deliver individuals from their plight. Even though the OT doesn't explain how this will work with great precision, the great, eschatological sacrifice will be a person. According to Psalm 34:20, a Davidic psalm, God promises to protect "all his [a righteous person's] bones, not one of them will be broken." Notice that the ordinance of Exodus 12:46 in Psalm 34:20 is applied to an individual, but not just any person—a Davidic figure. Once again, Davidic typology bubbles to the surface. In reading the beginning and end of the Fourth Gospel together, we discover that Jesus is simultaneously Isaiah's Suffering Servant and a suffering Davidic King.

Pushing further, we must understand the broad redemptive scope of the Passover sacrifice. According to the OT, this sacrifice triggers Israel's redemption and new birth, the means by which God brings his people from death to life. Michael Morales rightly captures the thrust of it: "The Passover sacrifice was for the sake of Israel's departure out of Egypt (death to the old life), and the sea crossing symbolized Israel's rebirth (or resurrection), with the ascent to God's presence at Sinai. . . . Jesus was transformed through his crucifixion-death, burial, and resurrection, that is, his exodus was *out of* the old creation, under the judgment of God, and *into* the new creation of glory."[52] In the first exodus, God killed Pharaoh's "firstborn son" because Pharaoh attempted to kill God's "firstborn son" (Exod. 1:16, 22; 4:22–23; 11:1–10). In the second exodus, though, God sacrifices his own "beloved Son" so that he may liberate true Israel, his "firstborn son."

The Burial of Jesus (19:38–42)

The Sabbath is nigh, so Jesus must be buried with haste. All four Gospels outline the basic contours of Jesus's burial (Matt. 27:57–61 // Mark 15:42–47 // Luke 23:50–56 // John 19:38–42), most notably Joseph of Arimathea asking Pilate for permission to bury the body. John, though, brings two additional elements into focus: Joseph's fear of the Jews and Nicodemus's assistance. While it's tempting to think that Joseph lacks a robust commitment to Jesus in light John's comment that he "feared the Jewish leaders," the very fact that he goes to Pilate and pleads for the body of Jesus, a God-cursed man, informs the reader that he has the type of faith that endures. There appear to be moments when Joseph's faith wavers, but at the end of the day, his faith perseveres. Where are the disciples? Judas, the betrayer, is off the scene, and John boldly stands by the Jesus at the cross, but what about the other ten? As the ten disciples cower in fear, Joseph and Nicodemus, two wealthy and prominent members of the Sanhedrin, stand by Jesus.

---

52. L. Michael Morales, *Exodus Old and New: A Biblical Theology of Redemption*, ESBT 2 (Downers Grove, IL: InterVarsity, 2020), 165 (emphasis original).

The most surprising element of this account is Nicodemus's participation. He's a remarkably complex character in the Fourth Gospel. Each time John introduces Nicodemus, he names and describes him in the same breath: "Now there was a Pharisee, a man named Nicodemus who was a member of the Jewish ruling council" (3:1); "Nicodemus, who had gone to Jesus earlier and who was one of their own number" (7:50); and "Nicodemus, the man who earlier had visited Jesus at night" (19:39). When we first meet Nicodemus, he comes to Jesus "at night" (3:2), the same description we find here in 19:39. In their first encounter, Nicodemus appears to stand in opposition to Jesus's actions in the temple (3:2), but later in 7:50–52 Nicodemus questions the other Jewish leaders about judging Jesus too hastily. The third and final time we come across Nicodemus, he assists Joseph in Jesus's burial—a bold act of faith. We are probably right to conclude, then, that Nicodemus has become a disciple of Jesus. The fact that John names him each time could reveal that he is an eyewitness of critical events. Further, Nicodemus's inclusion in the Fourth Gospel is a sign of hope for a remnant of ethnic Jews. While Nicodemus is first identified with darkness, Jesus has come in order to shine "in the darkness" (1:5). Jesus, the great Light-giver, has overcome Nicodemus's darkened heart.

Testifying to the Risen Son of God (20:1–31)

Jesus Raised from the Dead (20:1–10)

Chapter 20 opens with Mary Magdalene arriving at the tomb Sunday morning (20:1). Although John only mentions Mary Magdalene, Salome and Mary the mother of James and Joseph are probably with her (// Matt. 28:1 // Mark 16:1–2 // Luke 24:1). Mary Magdalene discovers that the stone of the tomb has been rolled away and then hastens to Peter and the "other disciple" (John), informing them that the tomb is empty (20:2). John beats Peter to the tomb but stays outside and peers into it. While John remains outside, Peter enters the tomb, noticing that there is no body—only "the strips of linen lying there, as well as the cloth that had been wrapped around Jesus' head. The cloth was still lying in its place, separate from the linen" (20:6–7 // Luke 24:12). The narrative's attention to the physical materials is remarkable. If individuals stole Jesus's body, wouldn't they have also taken the burial cloths (cf. 11:44)? According to 20:8, John, upon entering the tomb, "saw and believed." The seventh and final sign is eliciting belief. Note that many of these odd details surrounding the empty tomb, such as John and Peter "running" and bending over, are not fabricated to add color to the narrative, as some may suppose, but indications of careful eyewitness testimony.

Verse 9 grips the reader: "They [John and Peter] still did not understand from Scripture that Jesus had to rise from the dead" (cf. 2:22). While John believes that Jesus is the Son of God in the resurrection, he is still coming to grips with how the OT anticipates the momentous event and how Jesus's resurrection fits into the wider story of redemption. The OT expects the resurrection to occur at the very end of history, when *all* people will be resurrected together. God will physically restore righteous individuals in the new creation and consummately punish the unrighteous (Job 19:26–27; Isa. 25:7–8; 26:19; Ezek. 37:1–14, 26–35; Dan. 12:2–3), so the resurrection of a single individual would be quite unexpected (→Luke 24:25–26).

Jesus Appears to Mary Magdalene (20:11–18)

Peter and John leave the tomb and then Mary Magdalene arrives a second time at the tomb, where she gazes into it and sees "two angels in white, seated where Jesus' body had been" (20:11 // Mark 16:5). The two angels ask why she is crying, to which she responds: "They have taken my Lord away" (20:13). Mary, still outside the tomb, turns around and notices someone in close proximity. She sees Jesus but doesn't recognize him, mistaking him for a "gardener" (20:15). Recall that Jesus is betrayed in a garden (18:1), and his tomb is in a garden in close proximity to the site of the crucifixion (19:41). Now the narrator describes him as a "gardener." Taken together, these details seem to indicate that John has in mind Genesis 1–2 (→18:1). John presents Jesus as the inaugurator of the new eternal cosmos—the new and better garden. Genesis 1–2 presents Adam as a king, priest, and prophet who is responsible for extending the cultic boundaries of Eden, eliminating all unclean things (e.g., the serpent) and producing a progeny that images God in all facets of life (Gen. 1:28; 2:15). In his death and resurrection, Jesus has emerged victorious as a greater Adam in a glorified existence. He pays the price for the first Adam's transgressions and offers life to his followers. To stand before God, it is not enough to be innocent of sin; one must also possess perfect righteousness—the righteousness that the first Adam was to earn in the garden and the righteousness that the last Adam did earn in his faithful life. Believers enjoy both benefits by in trusting in Jesus.

According to 20:16, when Jesus utters her name, Mary *then* recognizes him, much like the sheep who "listen" to the "voice" of the gatekeeper (10:3). Apparently Jesus's glorified, physical existence contains elements of continuity and discontinuity. He's different but the same (cf. 1 Cor. 15:35–38). Verse 17 continues to elude many: "[Mary,] do not hold on to me, for I have not yet ascended to the Father. Go instead to my brothers and tell them, 'I am ascending to my Father and your Father, to my God and your God.'" Commentators have wrestled with the meaning of this verse for some time, and there may not be a single interpretation. We may be working with layers of meaning here. There are at least two possibilities. On the one hand, the way in which Jesus and Mary relate to each other has changed in light of the resurrection, yet the new way of relating to one another has yet to come (i.e., the pouring out of the Spirit). The two individuals are caught in the middle between epochs. Keep in mind, though, that a few verses later Jesus commands Thomas to touch Jesus's side (20:27). On the other hand, there may also be a pragmatic reason: Mary needs to stop clinging to Jesus and inform the disciples of Jesus's resurrection. Notice the progression of the commands: "Do not hold on to me. . . . Go instead . . . and tell them." Jesus is alive; make haste!

Jesus's First Appearance to the Disciples (20:19–23)

John tracks Jesus's three appearances to the disciples (21:14), with the first appearance taking place later on Easter Sunday evening at an undisclosed location "with the doors locked for fear of the Jewish leaders" (20:19a). If the Jewish leaders kill their leader, then what will they do to his followers? Luke's Gospel also includes this event in 24:36–43. Two important details are found in both Gospels: (1) Jesus miraculously appears to the disciples and declares, "Peace be with you" (20:19b // Luke 24:36). The OT looks forward to the eschatological peace that marks the new age. Unity is the hallmark of the new creation—reconciliation between God and humanity/creation and reconciliation between the various people groups. The Aaronic blessing, a prayer that embodies a great deal of this expectation, reads,

> The LORD bless you
>   and keep you;
> the LORD make his face shine on you
>   and be gracious to you;
> the LORD turn his face toward you
>   and give you *peace*. (Num. 6:24–26)

Consider how peace correlates with God's glorious presence. For God to dwell intimately with his people in creation, there must be peace. But for peace to occur, there must be reconciliation (Pss. 4:8; 29:11; 37:11; Isa. 9:6–7; 14:7; Jer. 33:6). Jesus's atoning death and end-time resurrection reconciles humanity to God *so that* God may dwell with creation. Jesus, the "tabernacling" Word,

393

now dwells more intimately with his people through the power and mediation of the Spirit.

(2) Jesus commands the disciples to examine his body with their own eyes (20:20 // Luke 24:39). Jesus is not a revivified spirit but the resurrected, physical Lord. He puts on flesh and blood in the incarnation, a status that he will possess for all of eternity. At the resurrection, he obtains a physical existence that is now fit for the new eternal cosmos (1 Cor. 15:47). He is, in the words of Revelation 3:14, the "Originator of God's [new] creation" (HCSB). The Fourth Gospel opens with Jesus creating the original creation, and it concludes with him inaugurating the new creation.

What takes place next is riveting: "And with that he breathed on them and said, 'Receive the Holy Spirit. If you forgive anyone's sins, their sins are forgiven; if you do not forgive them, they are not forgiven'" (20:22–23). Genesis 2:7 is the clearest OT background for this perplexing text:

Genesis 2:7	John 20:22
"And God formed man, dust from the earth, and breathed [*enephysēsen*] into his face a breath of life, and the man became a *living* [*zōsan*] being." (NETS)	"And with that *he breathed* [*enephysēsen*] on them and said, 'Receive the Holy Spirit.'"

Genesis 2:7 is a pregnant text in its own right. In Genesis 1, Adam is created in the image and likeness of God (1:26–28), whereas in the second account Adam receives the "breath of life" (2:7). These two creative acts parallel each other. Further, Ezekiel 37 picks up on the theme of God's life-giving "breath" in Genesis 2:7 and associates it with Israel's reunification, their latter-day resurrection, and the Spirit: "And he said to me, Prophesy to the breath; prophesy, son of man, and say to the breath, This is what the Lord says: Come from the four winds, and *blow* [*emphysēson*] into these corpses, and *they shall live* [*zēsatōsan*]" (Ezek. 37:9 NETS; cf. 1 Kings 17:21).

If the Fourth Gospel indeed alludes to Genesis 2:7 and possibly Ezekiel 37:9, then we have a very significant redemptive-historical event: Jesus, as God incarnate, passes on the Spirit to the disciples, creating them in his own restored image—much like Adam passes on his image to Seth (Gen. 5:3). Jesus promises that his followers will receive the Spirit when he departs (7:39; 14:16), and here Jesus is making good on that promise. As a result of the Spirit's presence in the disciples, they begin to form true Israel and the true temple. Their identity as the new humanity is intimately tied to the forgiveness of sin in the following verse (20:23). What strikes the reader as odd at first glance actually makes wonderful sense: *temporary* forgiveness of sin was bound up with the physical temple and its sacrificial system in Jerusalem, but now that Jesus has died as the once-for-all sacrifice, he offers definitive and permanent forgiveness to those who trust him. As in the Great Commission in Matthew 28:19–20, Jesus charges the disciples to proclaim the gospel to unbelievers so that they, too, can enjoy a new identity and the indwelling Spirit. The disciples' reception of the Spirit here in 20:22 is, on the surface, hard to square with their reception of the Spirit at Pentecost in Acts 2. Do they receive the Spirit here or at Pentecost? The disciples appear to experience a proleptic installment of the Spirit of Pentecost. What takes place in 20:22 is a foretaste of what is to come several weeks later in Acts 2.

Jesus's Second Appearance to the Disciples and the Purpose of the Fourth Gospel (20:24–31)

The narrative progresses to the second appearance of Jesus to the disciples and the famous incident with Thomas, who, for whatever reason, is not with the other disciples when Jesus appears to them the first time (20:24). Despite the disciples telling Thomas that they have "seen the Lord," he is unwilling to "believe" (20:25). Thomas is not a major figure in the Synoptics, as he's only present in the list of the Twelve (Matt. 10:3 // Mark 3:18 // Luke 6:15). The Fourth Gospel, though, mentions him on four occasions: 11:16, 14:5, 20:24–29, and 21:2. The first time we meet Thomas, he's eager to follow Jesus to Jerusalem and "die with him" (11:16). So, on the one hand, Thomas is to be congratulated for his willingness to stand with Jesus even in the face of grave danger. But now that Jesus has died, and even despite the eyewitness testimony of his peers, he's reluctant to believe.

The narrative then ticks forward a week, when Thomas and the disciples assemble in the same place (20:26). Jesus once again appears to his disciples, but this time Thomas is present. After seeing Jesus in the flesh, Thomas finally and famously admits that Jesus is his "Lord" and "God" (20:28). Thomas's belief prompts Jesus to acknowledge that although Thomas does indeed believe, "blessed are those who have not seen and yet have believed" (20:29). The seventh and final sign—Jesus's death and resurrection—engenders a response. In this case, Thomas believes the sign and his faith deepens.

Now, at the end of the body of the Fourth Gospel, John states his purpose in writing it: "These [things] are written that you may believe that Jesus is the Messiah, the Son of God, and that by believing you may have life in his name" (20:31). Verse 31 is the main point of the entire Gospel. John pens every paragraph, every verse to demonstrate that Jesus is Israel's Messiah and the Son of God. John spent decades reflecting on the life and ministry of Jesus, and he selects with the greatest care seven signs to present Jesus as the unique Son of God and King of Israel. John, as a key eyewitness to these signs, intends these seven signs to persuade unbelievers that Jesus is who he claims to be and to affirm the faith of believers. The *ultimate* purpose of the Fourth Gospel is that John's readers may "have life in his [Jesus's] name." Jesus is a life-giving God, and this is a life-giving Gospel. Belief in Jesus leads to end-time life in the present that will reach its fullness in the eternal new cosmos.

Epilogue (21:1–25)

The epilogue begins with Jesus's third and final appearance to the disciples. While John has carefully tracked the events of passion week (13:1; 18:28; 19:31; 20:1, 19) and mentioned Jesus's appearance to the disciples "a week later" (20:26), he merely divulges to his readers that what transpires in 21:1–23 takes place "after this," or after Jesus's appearance to Thomas in 20:26–29. Since Acts 1:3 records that Jesus "appeared" to the disciples during a stint of forty days, we should assume that 21:1–23 takes place within this forty-day period.

Jesus's Third Appearance to the Disciples (21:1–14)

The opening line in 21:1 is crucial for grasping the significance of Jesus's actions: "Afterward Jesus *appeared* [*ephanerōsen*] again to his disciples, by the Sea of Galilee. *It happened* [*ephanerōsen*] this way" (21:1). The verb "to appear" (*phaneroō*) is a notable feature of the Fourth Gospel (1:31; 2:11; 7:4; 9:3). We suggested in our discussion of 7:1–13 that "signs" in the Fourth Gospel are acted-out mysteries—they simultaneously unveil Jesus's identity and conceal it. The three appearances of the resurrected Christ fall into this category, but the accent is on *unveiling*. Jesus's threefold disclosure to the disciples in 20:19–23, 20:24–29, and 21:1–14 contributes to the disciples' understanding of his identity as Israel's Messiah and the divine Son of God. At the end of the first appearance, the disciples receive the Spirit (20:22–23), the one who reveals "mysteries" to God's people (see Dan. 2:20–23; 5:14; 1 Cor. 2:1–16; 14:2; Eph. 1:9, 17; 3:3–5). Through the agency of the Spirit, the disciples can now grasp the full significance of all the signs, especially the seventh. Thomas's confession that Jesus is the "Lord" in 20:28 matches Peter's realization that he is "Lord" in 21:7 (cf. 21:12). It is no coincidence, then, that both disciples who previously struggle with Jesus's identity (18:15–18, 25–27; 20:25) now come to grips with the truth that Jesus is indeed the Son of God.

The scene opens with six disciples joining Peter at night to fish on the Sea of Galilee, but to their dismay, they came up empty (21:1–3). Matthew

28:16 and Mark 14:28 and 16:7 mention Jesus meeting with his disciples in Galilee, so it may very well be that the event in chapter 21 takes place during this period. The next morning, Jesus, standing on the shore, instructs them to cast their net on the right side of the boat (21:6). While the disciples are unaware that it is Jesus standing on the shore, they obey without hesitation. The result is astounding. They haul in a "large number of fish"—153, to be exact (21:6, 11). At this, John informs Peter, "It is the Lord," prompting Peter to jump into the water and head for the shore (21:7). When the remaining disciples catch up, they all enjoy a meal together, where Jesus feeds them with fish and bread (21:13).

Why does John finish his narrative with an odd account of Jesus eating with the disciples on the shore? The answer lies in its relationship with the feeding of the five thousand (6:1–15), Jesus walking on the water (6:16–24), and the Bread of Life Discourse (6:25–71). Consider the parallels between the accounts:

Chapter 6	Chapter 21
Presence of fish and bread (6:9)	Presence of fish and bread (21:9)
Multiplication of fish (6:11)	Multiplication of fish (21:6, 11)
The disciples on a boat on the Sea of Galilee at night (6:16)	The disciples on a boat on the Sea of Galilee at night (21:3)
Jesus feeds the five thousand (6:11)	Jesus feeds the seven disciples (21:13)
Peter confesses that Jesus is the "Holy One of God" (6:69)	Peter realizes that Jesus is the "Lord" (21:7)

Herein lies the difference between the two events: the disciples' confusion and hesitancy mark the feeding of the five thousand (6:7, 9), whereas their obedience and illumination characterize the second account. It's unclear if Jesus intends to draw connections between himself and the "bread" in 21:9 like he does with the "bread" in 6:35. The point is that in both cases Jesus shares a meal with his true disciples. In the Bread of Life Discourse (6:25–59) and in the following discourse (6:60–70), many of the "Jews" (6:41, 52) and "his disciples" (6:60) are unwilling to embrace Jesus and his message. At the end of the Gospel, only a handful of devoted disciples remain. But though only a few in number, these disciples constitute true and faithful Israel and will take the gospel of Jesus to the ends of the earth.

Peter's Faithfulness and Mission (21:15–25)

The final section of the Fourth Gospel concerns Peter, who, along with John, has played no small role in the narrative. At the beginning of the narrative, Jesus declares that he (Simon) will be called "Peter" (1:42). Though John doesn't disclose the significance of the change of name, Matthew's Gospel does: "And I tell you that you are Peter, and on this rock I will build my church, and the gates of Hades will not overcome it" (Matt. 16:18; cf. Mark 3:16). Peter, then, will play a significant part in the establishment of the end-time people of God. Later on in chapter 6 when several disciples decide to no longer follow Jesus, Peter reaffirms his commitment to Jesus, who has "the words of eternal life" and is identified as the "Holy One of God" (6:68–69). In the upper room at the end of passion week, Peter promises to "lay down" his "life" for Jesus (13:37). This hollow promise prompts Jesus's prediction that Peter will deny him three times before the night is over (13:38). Peter comes into focus one more time in chapter 18 when he fulfills the prophecy (18:15–18, 25–27).

Their present interaction begins with Jesus asking Peter if he loves him "more than these" (21:15). The antecedent of "these" is difficult to pin down. Commentators often put forward two options: (1) Jesus is asking Peter if he loves him more than his fishing career; or (2) Jesus asks Peter if he loves him more than the other disciples love Jesus. While the immediate context may better suit the former (21:1–14), the latter makes the most sense in light of the broad context of the Fourth Gospel. God's love for the world (3:16; 13:1), intra-Trinitarian love (3:35; 10:17; 15:9), and believers' love for God (13:34–35; 14:15, 23; 15:17) are integral to the narrative. Indeed, Jesus himself tells the disciples that their lives must be, above all, marked by a love for God and one another (15:12).

In 21:15, Jesus asks Peter if he "loves" (*agapas*) him, and Peter responds with, "You know that I love [*philō*] you." Though it has become fashionable to highlight the two Greek verbs *agapaō* and *phileō*, "to love," in 21:15–17 and discern subtle differences between the two, they are best viewed as synonymous (see Prov. 8:17 LXX; 1 Pet. 1:22; 5:14; 2 Pet. 1:7). Jesus's threefold line of questioning must be understood in light of Peter's threefold betrayal of Jesus in 18:15–18 and 25–27. Over a fire, the high priest's servant girl and his soldiers ask Peter if he is a follower of Jesus. Now, apparently over another fire, Peter is asked about his devotion to Jesus.

The pastoral metaphor that Jesus uses (lambs and sheep) refers to God's people, the flock. Both Testaments liken the people of God to a flock and Israel's kings to shepherds (e.g., 2 Sam. 5:2; Ps. 78:71; Ezek. 34). Jesus, the "good shepherd" (10:11), is entrusting the church to Peter, who must embrace his role as an apostle. He (and the other apostles) is charged with preserving the health of end-time Israel, the church. In reading 1 Peter 5:2–4, one can almost overhear Jesus's words to Peter a handful of decades earlier: "[Elders,] be shepherds of God's flock that is under your care. . . . When the Chief Shepherd appears, you will receive the crown of glory."

Jesus even predicts that Peter will "stretch out" his "hands" and will "glorify God" in his death (21:18–19). Peter, like Jesus, would be crucified. According to early church tradition, Peter was crucified upside down under Nero around AD 65 (Eusebius, *Hist. eccl.* 2.25.5, 3.1.2). By the time John published the Fourth Gospel, Peter is dead and the church scattered throughout is well aware of it. But John presents Peter as one who gave up his life for the sake of Christ and his church. Such humility and self-sacrifice will no doubt inspire believers to follow suit.

The narrative ends with the narrator, John, identifying himself as "the disciple who testifies to these things and who wrote them down" (21:24). The readers of the Fourth Gospel, those in the first century and today, can be confident that the whole of John's testimony about Jesus is "true" (21:24; cf. 19:35; 1 John 1:1–4). History and theology are not distant cousins but the best of friends. We would not be far off the mark to say that John the apostle bears witness to the seven "witnesses" in the narrative—John the Baptist (1:19, 32, 34; 3:26, 28), Jesus himself (8:14), Jesus's works (5:36), the Father (8:18), the OT (5:39), the Samaritan woman (4:39), and the crowd at Lazarus's raising (12:17). John is highly selective about what he sets forth in his Gospel. Indeed, "even the whole world would not have room for the books" that could be written about Jesus (21:25). The entirety of John's Gospel should be considered a testimony to the person of Jesus. Because John and the other apostles take their role as eyewitnesses seriously, even as divinely sanctioned, we can be confident that what we read in the Gospels really happened. Their message is true because their apostleship is true, and their apostleship is true because their Commissioner is true.

Two of the four Gospels end with a commission at some level. An emphasis of the First Gospel is the growth of the kingdom, so it makes sense that Matthew would punctuate his Gospel with the Great Commission (Matt. 28:16–20). As the resurrected Son of Man, Jesus empowers his disciples to subdue all forms of antagonism and proclaim the gospel to the nations so that he may dwell with them. John's Gospel ends not so much on the growth of the kingdom as on its *preservation*. The exhortation that Peter "feed" and "take care" of God's people (21:15–17) alludes to Peter nourishing the church with sound doctrine and protecting it from false teachers. It's hardly coincidental that the two epistles in the NT that bear Peter's name do just that.

John: Commentaries

Barrett, C. K. *The Gospel according to St. John*. Rev. ed. London: SPCK; Philadelphia: Westminster, 1978.

Beasley-Murray, George R. *John*. Rev. ed. WBC. Nashville: Nelson, 1999.

Borchert, Gerald L. *John*. 2 vols. NAC. Nashville: Broadman & Holman, 1996–2002.

Brant, Jo-Ann. *John*. Paideia Commentaries on the New Testament. Grand Rapids: Baker Academic, 2011.

Brodie, Thomas L. *The Gospel according to John: A Literary and Theological Commentary*. New York: Oxford University Press, 1993.

Brown, Raymond E. *The Gospel according to John*. 2 vols. AB. Garden City, NY: Doubleday, 1966–70.

Bruner, Frederick Dale. *The Gospel of John: A Commentary*. Grand Rapids: Eerdmans, 2012.

Bultmann, Rudolf. *The Gospel of John: A Commentary*. Edited by R. W. N. Hoare and J. K. Riches. Translated by G. R. Beasley-Murray. Philadelphia: Westminster, 1971.

Burge, G. M. *John*. NIVAC. Grand Rapids: Zondervan, 2000.

Carson, D. A. *The Gospel according to John*. PNTC. Grand Rapids: Eerdmans, 1991.

Edwards, Mark. *John*. Blackwell Bible Commentaries. Malden, MA: Blackwell, 2004.

Keener, Craig S. *The Gospel of John: A Commentary*. 2 vols. Peabody, MA: Hendrickson, 2003.

Klink, Edward W., III. *John*. ZECNT. Grand Rapids: Zondervan, 2016.

Kruse, Colin G. *The Gospel according to John*. Rev. ed. TNTC. Grand Rapids: Eerdmans, 2004.

Lincoln, Andrew T. *The Gospel according to Saint John*. BNTC. London: Continuum; Peabody, MA: Hendrickson, 2005.

McHugh, John F. *A Critical and Exegetical Commentary on John 1–4*. ICC. London: T&T Clark, 2009.

Michaels, J. Ramsey. *The Gospel of John*. NICNT. Grand Rapids: Eerdmans, 2010.

———. *John*. NIBC. Peabody, MA: Hendrickson, 1989.

Milne, Bruce. *The Message of John*. BST. Downers Grove, IL: InterVarsity, 1993.

Moloney, Francis J. *The Gospel of John*. SP. Collegeville, MN: Liturgical Press, 1998.

Morris, Leon. *The Gospel according to John*. Rev. ed. NICNT. Grand Rapids: Eerdmans, 1995.

Ridderbos, Herman N. *The Gospel of John: A Theological Commentary*. Grand Rapids: Eerdmans, 1997.

Schnackenburg, Rudolf. *The Gospel according to St. John*. 3 vols. New York: Herder and Herder, 1968–82.

von Wahlde, Urban C. *The Gospel and Letters of John*. 3 vols. ECC 3. Grand Rapids: Eerdmans, 2010.

Whitacre, Rodney A. *John*. IVPNTC. Downers Grove, IL: InterVarsity, 1999.

Witherington, Ben, III. *John's Wisdom: A Commentary on the Fourth Gospel*. Louisville: Westminster John Knox, 1995.

John: Articles, Essays, and Monographs

Anderson, Paul N. *The Christology of the Fourth Gospel: Its Unity and Disunity in the Light of John 6*. WUNT 2/78. Tubingen: Mohr Siebeck, 1996.

———. *The Fourth Gospel and the Quest for Jesus: Modern Foundations Reconsidered.* London: T&T Clark, 2006.

———. *The Riddles of the Fourth Gospel: An Introduction to John.* Minneapolis: Fortress, 2011.

Anderson, Paul N., Felix Just, and Tom Thatcher, eds. *John, Jesus, and History.* Vols. 1–3. SBLSymS 44; ECIL 2; ECIL 18. Atlanta: SBL Press, 2007, 2009, 2016.

Arterbury, Andrew E. "Breaking the Betrothal Bonds: Hospitality in John 4." *CBQ* 72 (2010): 63–83.

Ashton, Josh. *Understanding the Fourth Gospel.* 2nd ed. Oxford: Oxford University Press, 2007.

Attridge, Harold W. "Genre Bending in the Fourth Gospel." *JBL* 121 (2002): 3–21.

Ball, D. M. *"I Am" in John's Gospel: Literary Function, Background and Theological Implications.* JSNTSup 124. Sheffield: Sheffield Academic, 1996.

Barrett, C. K. "The Old Testament in the Fourth Gospel." *JTS* 48 (1947): 155–69.

Bauckham, Richard. *The Testimony of the Beloved Disciple: Narrative, History, and Theology in the Gospel of John.* Grand Rapids: Baker Academic, 2007.

Bauckham, Richard, and Carl Mosser, eds. *The Gospel of John and Christian Theology.* Grand Rapids: Eerdmans, 2008.

Beck, D. R. *The Discipleship Paradigm: Readers and Anonymous Characters in the Fourth Gospel.* BIS 27. Leiden: Brill, 1997.

Bekken, Per Jarle. *The Lawsuit Motif in John's Gospel from New Perspectives: Jesus Christ, Crucified Criminal and Emperor of the World.* NovTSup 158. Leiden: Brill, 2015.

Bennema, Cornelis. *Encountering Jesus: Character Studies in the Gospel of John.* 2nd ed. Minneapolis: Fortress, 2014.

Bernier, Jonathan. *Aposynagōgos and the Historical Jesus in John: Rethinking the Historicity of the Johannine Expulsion Passages.* BIS 122. Leiden: Brill, 2013.

Blomberg, Craig L. *The Historical Reliability of John's Gospel.* Downers Grove, IL: InterVarsity, 2001.

Borgen, Peder. *Bread from Heaven: An Exegetical Study of the Concept of Manna in the Gospel of John and the Writings of Philo.* NovTSup 10. Leiden: Brill, 1965.

———. *The Gospel of John: More Light from Philo, Paul and Archaeology; The Scriptures, Tradition, Settings, Meaning.* NovTSup 154. Leiden: Brill, 2014.

Brant, Jo-Ann A. *Dialogue and Drama: Elements of Greek Tragedy in the Fourth Gospel.* Peabody, MA: Hendrickson, 2004.

Brown, Raymond E. *An Introduction to the Gospel of John.* Edited by Francis J. Moloney. New York: Doubleday, 2003.

Brown, Sherri, and Christopher W. Skinner, eds. *Johannine Ethics: The Moral World of the Gospel and Epistles of John.* Minneapolis: Fortress, 2017.

Bruce, F. F. *The Gospel of John: Introduction, Exposition, and Notes.* Grand Rapids: Eerdmans, 1983.

Brunson, A. C. *Psalm 118 in the Gospel of John: An Intertextual Study of the New Exodus Pattern in the Theology of John.* WUNT 2/158. Tübingen: Mohr Siebeck, 2003.

Carson, D. A. "John and the Johannine Epistles." In *It Is Written: Scripture Citing Scripture; Essays in Honour of Barnabas Lindars, SSF*, edited by D. A. Carson and H. G. M. Williamson, 245–64. Cambridge: Cambridge University Press, 1988.

Charlesworth, James H. *The Beloved Disciple: Whose Witness Validates the Gospel of John?* Valley Forge, PA: Trinity Press International, 1995.

Clark-Soles, Jaime. *Scripture Cannot Be Broken: The Social Function of the Use of Scripture in the Fourth Gospel*. 2nd ed. Leiden: Brill, 2003.

Coakley, J. F. "Jesus' Messianic Entry into Jerusalem (John 12:12–19 par.)." *JTS* 46 (1995): 461–82.

Coloe, Mary L. *God Dwells with Us: Temple Symbolism in the Fourth Gospel*. Collegeville, MN: Liturgical Press, 2001.

Coloe, Mary L., and Tom Thatcher, eds. *John, Qumran, and the Dead Sea Scrolls: Sixty Years of Discovery and Debate*. Early Judaism and Its Literature 32. Atlanta: Society of Biblical Literature, 2011.

Conway, C. M. *Men and Women in the Fourth Gospel: Gender and Johannine Characterization*. SBLDS 167. Atlanta: Scholars Press, 1999.

Culpepper, R. Alan. *Anatomy of the Fourth Gospel: A Study in Literary Design*. Philadelphia: Fortress, 1983.

Culpepper, R. Alan, and Paul N. Anderson, eds. *Communities in Dispute: Current Scholarship on the Johannine Epistles*. ECIL 13. Atlanta: SBL Press, 2014.

Culpepper, R. Alan, and C. C. Black, eds. *Exploring the Gospel of John: In Honor of D. Moody Smith*. Louisville: Westminster John Knox, 1996.

Daly-Denton, M. *David in the Fourth Gospel: The Johannine Reception of the Psalms*. AGJU 47. Leiden: Brill, 2000.

———. "The Psalms in John's Gospel." In *The Psalms in the New Testament*, edited by S. Moyise and M. J. J. Menken, 119–37. New Testament and the Scriptures of Israel. London: T&T Clark, 2004.

Dodd, C. H. *Historical Tradition in the Fourth Gospel*. Cambridge: Cambridge University Press, 1963.

———. *The Interpretation of the Fourth Gospel*. Cambridge: Cambridge University Press, 1953.

Duke, Paul D. *Irony in the Fourth Gospel*. Atlanta: John Knox, 1985.

Estes, Douglas, and Ruth Sheridan. *How John Works: Storytelling in the Fourth Gospel*. RBS 86. Atlanta: SBL Press, 2016.

Evans, Craig A. "The Function of Isaiah 6:9–10 in Mark and John." *NovT* 24 (1982): 124–38.

———. "The Voice from Heaven: A Note on John 12:28." *CBQ* 43 (1981): 405–8.

———. *Word and Glory: On the Exegetical and Theological Background of John's Prologue*. JSNTSup 89. Sheffield: Sheffield Academic, 1993.

Fortna, Robert T. *The Gospel of Signs: A Reconstruction of the Narrative Source Underlying the Fourth Gospel*. Cambridge: Cambridge University Press, 1970.

Fortna, Robert T., and Tom Thatcher, eds. *Jesus in Johannine Tradition*. Louisville: Westminster John Knox, 2001.

Glasson, T. F. *Moses in the Fourth Gospel*. SBT 40. London: SCM, 1963.

Grigsby, B. H. "'If Any Man Thirsts . . .': Observations on the Rabbinic Background of John 7,37–39." *Bib* 67 (1986): 101–8.

Gundry, Robert H. *Jesus the Word according to John the Sectarian: A Paleofundamentalist Manifesto for Contemporary Evangelicalism, Especially Its Elites, in North America*. Grand Rapids: Eerdmans, 2002.

Ham, C. "The Title 'Son of Man' in the Gospel of John." *Stone-Campbell Journal* 1 (1998): 67–84.

Hanson, A. T. "John's Interpretation of Psalm 82." *NTS* 11 (1964–65): 158–62.

———. "John's Interpretation of Psalm 82 Reconsidered." *NTS* 13 (1967): 363–67.

———. "John's Use of Scripture." In *The Gospels and the Scriptures of Israel*, edited by C. A. Evans and W. R. Stegner, 358–79. JSNTSup 104. Sheffield: Sheffield Academic, 1994.

Harstine, S. *Moses as a Character in the Fourth Gospel: A Study of Ancient Reading Techniques*. JSNTSup 229. Sheffield: Sheffield Academic, 2002.

Heil, John Paul. *Blood and Water: The Death and Resurrection of Jesus in John 18–21*. CBQMS 27. Washington, DC: Catholic Biblical Association of America, 1995.

Hengel, Martin. *The Johannine Question*. Translated by John Bowden. London: SCM; Philadelphia: Trinity Press International, 1989.

Horsley, Richard, and Tom Thatcher. *John, Jesus, and the Renewal of Israel*. Grand Rapids: Eerdmans, 2013.

Hultgren, A. J. "The Johannine Footwashing (13:1–11) as Symbol of Eschatological Hospitality." *NTS* 28 (1982): 539–46.

Hunt, Steven A., D. Francois Tolmie, and Ruben Zimmermann, eds. *Character Studies in the Fourth Gospel: Literary Approaches to Sixty Figures in John*. WUNT 314. Tübingen: Mohr Siebeck, 2013.

Hylen, Susan. *Imperfect Believers: Ambiguous Characters in the Gospel of John*. Louisville: Westminster John Knox, 2009.

Kerr, A. R. *The Temple of Jesus' Body: The Temple Theme in the Gospel of John*. JSNTSup 220. London: Sheffield Academic, 2002.

Klink, Edward W., III, ed. *The Audience of the Gospels: The Origin and Function of the Gospels in Early Christianity*. LNTS 353. London: T&T Clark, 2010.

———. "Light of the World: Cosmology and the Johannine Literature." In *Cosmology and New Testament Theology*, edited by Jonathan T. Pennington and Sean M. McDonough, 74–89. LNTS 355. London: T&T Clark, 2009.

———. *The Sheep of the Fold: The Audience and Origin of the Gospel of John*. Cambridge: Cambridge University Press, 2007.

Knapp, H. M. "The Messianic Water Which Gives Life to the World." *Horizons in Biblical Theology* 19 (1997): 109–21.

Koester, Craig R., and Reimund Bieringer, eds. *The Resurrection of Jesus in the Gospel of John*. WUNT 222. Tübingen: Mohr Siebeck, 2008.

Köstenberger, Andreas J. *A Theology of John's Gospel and Letters: The Word, the Christ, the Son of God*. BTNT. Grand Rapids: Zondervan, 2009.

Kysar, Robert. *John, the Maverick Gospel*. Rev. ed. Louisville: Westminster John Knox, 2007.

———. *Voyages with John: Charting the Fourth Gospel*. Waco: Baylor University Press, 2006.

Lamb, David A. *Text, Context, and the Johannine Community: A Sociolinguistic Analysis of the Johannine Writings*. LNTS 477. London: Bloomsbury T&T Clark, 2015.

Laney, J. C. "Abiding Is Believing: The Analogy of the Vine in John 15:1–6." *BSac* 146 (1989): 55–66.

Larsen, Kasper Bro, ed. *The Gospel of John as Genre Mosaic*. Studia Aarhusiana Neotestamentica 3. Göttingen: Vandenhoeck & Ruprecht, 2015.

Lee, D. A. *The Symbolic Narratives of the Fourth Gospel: The Interplay of Form and Meaning*. JSNTSup 95. Sheffield: JSOT Press, 1994.

Lierman, John, ed. *Challenging Perspectives on the Gospel of John*. Tübingen: Mohr Siebeck, 2006.

Lincoln, Andrew T. *Truth on Trial: The Lawsuit Motif in the Fourth Gospel*. Peabody, MA: Hendrickson, 2000.

Lozada, Francisco, Jr., and Tom Thatcher, eds. *New Currents through John: A Global Perspective*. Atlanta: Society of Biblical Literature, 2006.

Maccini, R. G. *Her Testimony Is True: Women as Witnesses according to John*. JSNTSup 125. Sheffield: Sheffield Academic, 1996.

Marcus, J. "Rivers of Living Water from Jesus' Belly (John 7:38)." *JBL* 117 (1998): 328–30.

Martyn, J. Louis. *History and Theology in the Fourth Gospel*. 3rd ed. Louisville: Westminster John Knox, 2003.

Meeks, W. A. *The Prophet-King: Moses Traditions and the Johannine Christology*. NovTSup 14. Leiden: Brill, 1967.

Menken, M. J. J. *Old Testament Quotations in the Fourth Gospel: Studies in Textual Form*. Contributions to Biblical Exegesis & Theology 15. Kampen, Netherlands: Kok, 1996.

———. "The Origin of the Old Testament Quotation in John 7:38." *NovT* 38 (1996): 160–75.

———. "The Provenance and Meaning of the Old Testament Quotation in John 6:31." *NovT* 30 (1988): 39–56.

———. "The Quotation from Isa 40,3 in John 1,23." *Bib* 66 (1985): 190–205.

———. "The Translation of Psalm 41:10 in John 13:18." *JSNT* 40 (1990): 61–79.

Moloney, Francis J. *Love in the Gospel of John: An Exegetical, Theological, and Literary Study*. Grand Rapids: Baker Academic, 2013.

———. "Reading John 2:13–22: The Purification of the Temple." *RB* 97 (1990): 432–51.

———. "Recent Johannine Studies, Part One: Commentaries," *ExpTim* 123, no. 7 (2012): 313–22.

———. "Recent Johannine Studies, Part Two: Monographs," *ExpTim* 123, no. 9 (2012): 417–28.

Motyer, Stephen. *Your Father the Devil? A New Approach to John and "the Jews."* Carlisle, UK: Paternoster, 1997.

Myers, Alicia D. *Characterizing Jesus: A Rhetorical Analysis on the Fourth Gospel's Use of Scripture in Its Presentation of Jesus.* LNTS 458. London: Bloomsbury T&T Clark, 2012.

Myers, Alicia D., and Bruce G. Schuchard, eds. *Abiding Words: Perspectives on the Use of the Old Testament in the Gospel of John.* RBS 81. Atlanta: SBL Press, 2015.

Neyrey, Jerome H. *The Gospel of John in Cultural and Rhetorical Perspective.* Grand Rapids: Eerdmans, 2009.

———. "The Jacob Allusions in John 1.51." *CBQ* 44 (1982): 586–605.

———. "Jacob Traditions and the Interpretation of John 4:10–26." *CBQ* 41 (1979): 419–37.

Ng, Wai-Yee. *Water Symbolism in John: An Eschatological Interpretation.* SBL 15. New York: Peter Lang, 2001.

Nicholson, G. C. *Death as Departure: The Johannine Descent-Ascent Schema.* SBLDS 63. Chico, CA: Scholars Press, 1983.

Nissen, J., and S. Pedersen, eds. *New Readings in John: Literary and Theological Perspectives.* JSNTSup 182. Sheffield: Sheffield Academic, 1999.

North, Wendy E. S. *A Journey round John: Tradition, Interpretation and Context in the Fourth Gospel.* LNTS 534. London: Bloomsbury T&T Clark, 2015.

O'Day, Gail R. *Revelation in the Fourth Gospel: Narrative Mode and Theological Claim.* Philadelphia: Fortress, 1986.

Parsenios, George L. *Departure and Consolation: The Johannine Farewell Discourses in Light of Greco-Roman Literature.* NovTSup 117. Leiden: Brill, 2005.

———. *Rhetoric and Drama in the Johannine Lawsuit Motif.* WUNT 258. Tübingen: Mohr Siebeck, 2010.

Pendrick, G. "Μονογενής." *NTS* 41 (1995): 587–600.

Porter, S. J. "Can Traditional Exegesis Enlighten Literary Analysis of the Fourth Gospel? An Examination of the Old Testament Fulfilment Motif and the Passover Theme." In *The Gospels and the Scriptures of Israel*, edited by C. A. Evans and W. R. Stegner, 396–428. JSNTSup 104. Sheffield: Sheffield Academic, 1994.

Pryor, J. W. "Covenant and Community in John's Gospel." *Reformed Theological Review* 47 (1988): 44–51.

———. "The Johannine Son of Man and Descent-Ascent Motif." *JETS* 34 (1991): 341–51.

———. *John, Evangelist of the Covenant People: The Narrative and Themes of the Fourth Gospel.* Downers Grove, IL: InterVarsity, 1992.

Reinhartz, Adele. *The Word in the World: The Cosmological Tale in the Fourth Gospel.* SBLMS 45. Atlanta: Scholars Press, 1992.

Richey, Lance B. *Roman Imperial Ideology and the Gospel of John.* Washington, DC: Catholic Biblical Association of America, 2007.

Robinson, John A. T. *The Priority of John.* London: SCM, 1985; Oak Park, IL: Meyer-Stone, 1987.

Rowland, C. "John 1.51, Jewish Apocalyptic and Targumic Tradition." *NTS* 30 (1984): 498–507.

Schuchard, B. G. *Scripture within Scripture: The Interrelationship of Form and Function in the Explicit Old Testament Citations in the Gospel of John.* SBLDS 133. Atlanta: Scholars Press, 1992.

Sheridan, Ruth. *Retelling Scripture: "The Jews" and the Scriptural Citations in John 1:19–12:15.* BIS 110. Leiden: Brill, 2012.

Skinner, Christopher W., ed. *Characters and Characterization in the Gospel of John.* LNTS 461. London: Bloomsbury T&T Clark, 2013.

Smalley, Stephen. *John: Evangelist and Interpreter.* Rev. ed. Downers Grove, IL: Inter-Varsity, 1998.

Smith, D. Moody. *The Theology of the Gospel of John.* Cambridge: Cambridge University Press, 1995.

Staley, Jeffrey Lloyd. *The Print's First Kiss: A Rhetorical Investigation of the Implied Reader in the Fourth Gospel.* SBLDS 82. Atlanta: Scholars Press, 1988.

Sturdevant, Jason S. *The Adaptable Jesus of the Fourth Gospel: The Pedagogy of the Logos.* NovTSup 162. Leiden: Brill, 2015.

Thatcher, Tom. *The Riddles of Jesus in John: A Study in Tradition and Folklore.* SBLMS 53. Atlanta: Society of Biblical Literature, 2000.

———, ed. *What We Have Heard from the Beginning: The Past, Present, and Future of Johannine Studies.* Waco: Baylor University Press, 2007.

———. *Why John Wrote a Gospel: Jesus-Memory-History.* Louisville: Westminster John Knox, 2006.

Thatcher, Tom, and Stephen D. Moore, eds. *Anatomies of Narrative Criticism: The Past, Present, and Futures of the Fourth Gospel as Literature.* RBS 55. Atlanta: Society of Biblical Literature, 2008.

Thatcher, Tom, and Catrin H. Williams, eds. *Engaging with C. H. Dodd: Sixty Years of Tradition and Interpretation on the Gospel of John.* Cambridge: Cambridge University Press, 2013.

Thomas, J. C. *Footwashing in John 13 and the Johannine Community.* JSNTSup 50. Sheffield: JSOT Press, 1991.

———. "'Stop Sinning Lest Something Worse Come upon You': The Man at the Pool in John 5." *JSNT* 59 (1995): 3–20.

Thompson, Marianne Meye. *The God of the Gospel of John.* Grand Rapids: Eerdmans, 2001.

Trozzo, Lindsey M. *Exploring Johannine Ethics: A Rhetorical Approach to Moral Efficacy in the Fourth Gospel Narrative.* WUNT 2/449. Tübingen: Mohr Siebeck, 2017.

van Belle, Gilbert, Michael Labahn, and Petrus Maritz, eds. *Repetitions and Variations in the Fourth Gospel: Style, Text, Interpretation.* BETL 223. Leuven: Peeters, 2009.

van Belle, Gilbert, J. G. van der Watt, and P. Maritz, eds. *Theology and Christology in the Fourth Gospel: Essays by Members of the SNTS Johannine Writings Seminar.* BETL 184. Leuven: Leuven University Press, 2005.

van der Watt, Jan G. *Family of the King: Dynamics of Metaphor in the Gospel according to John.* BIS 47. Leiden: Brill, 2000.

van der Watt, Jan G., and Ruben Zimmermann, eds. *Rethinking the Ethics of John: "Implicit Ethics" in the Johannine Writings*. WUNT 291. Tübingen: Mohr Siebeck, 2012.

Vawter, B. "Ezekiel and John." *CBQ* 26 (1964): 450–58.

Walker, W. O., Jr. "John 1.43–51 and 'the Son of Man' in the Fourth Gospel." *JSNT* 56 (1994): 31–42.

Williams, Catrin H., and Christopher Rowland, eds. *John's Gospel and Intimations of Apocalyptic*. London: Bloomsbury T&T Clark, 2014.

Witherington, Ben, III. *John's Wisdom*. Louisville: Westminster John Knox, 1995.

Young, F. W. "A Study of the Relation of Isaiah to the Fourth Gospel." *Zeitschrift für die neutestamentliche Wissenschaft und die Kunde der älteren Kirche* 46 (1955): 215–33.

Scripture and Ancient Writings Index

413

424

429

Subject Index